MANAGEMENT
& BUSINESS
RESEARCH

Sara Miller McCune founded SAGE Publishing in 1965 to support the dissemination of usable knowledge and educate a global community. SAGE publishes more than 1000 journals and over 800 new books each year, spanning a wide range of subject areas. Our growing selection of library products includes archives, data, case studies and video. SAGE remains majority owned by our founder and after her lifetime will become owned by a charitable trust that secures the company's continued independence.

Los Angeles | London | New Delhi | Singapore | Washington DC | Melbourne

MANAGEMENT & BUSINESS RESEARCH

6th Edition

Mark Easterby-Smith

Richard Thorpe

Paul R. Jackson

Lena J. Jaspersen

Los Angeles | London | New Delhi
Singapore | Washington DC | Melbourne

Los Angeles | London | New Delhi
Singapore | Washington DC | Melbourne

SAGE Publications Ltd
1 Oliver's Yard
55 City Road
London EC1Y 1SP

SAGE Publications Inc.
2455 Teller Road
Thousand Oaks, California 91320

SAGE Publications India Pvt Ltd
B 1/I 1 Mohan Cooperative Industrial Area
Mathura Road
New Delhi 110 044

SAGE Publications Asia-Pacific Pte Ltd
3 Church Street
#10-04 Samsung Hub
Singapore 049483

Editor: Kirsty Smy
Development editor: Lyndsay Aitken
Assistant editor, digital: Chloe Statham
Production editor: Sarah Cooke
Copyeditor: Gemma Marren
Proofreader: Sharon Cawood
Indexer: Silvia Benvenuto
Marketing manager: Alison Borg
Cover design: Shaun Mercier
Typeset by: C&M Digitals (P) Ltd, Chennai, India
Printed in the USA

Library of Congress Control Number: 2017958035

British Library Cataloguing in Publication data

A catalogue record for this book is available from the British Library

ISBN 978-1-5264-2479-2
ISBN 978-1-5264-2480-8 (pbk)
ISBN 978-1-5264-4695-4 (pbk & interactive ebk (IEB))

At SAGE we take sustainability seriously. Most of our products are printed in the UK using responsibly sourced papers and
boards. When we print overseas we ensure sustainable papers are used as measured by the PREPS grading system.
We undertake an annual audit to monitor our sustainability.

BRIEF CONTENTS

LECTURER SUPPORT MATERIALS

This book also comes with a range of instructor-only resources to support teaching. Visit https://edge.sagepub.com/easterbysmith6e to access the following:

- PowerPoint slides, including useful figures and diagrams from the book
- An instructor's manual
- Video presentation on 'Developing a convincing argument' by Professor Richard Thorpe

CONTENTS

Tree Metaphor Pull-out   end of book

LIST OF FIGURES

LIST OF TABLES

ABOUT THE AUTHORS

MARK EASTERBY-SMITH is an Emeritus Professor at the University of Lancaster. His field is organizational learning. He has a first degree in Engineering Science and a PhD in Organizational Behaviour from Durham University and has been an active researcher for over 30 years with primary interests in methodology and learning processes. He has carried out evaluation studies in many European companies, and has led research projects on management development, organizational learning, dynamic capabilities and knowledge transfer across international organizations in the UK, India and China.

He has published numerous academic papers and over ten books including: *Auditing Management Development* (Gower, 1980); *The Challenge to Western Management Development* (Routledge, 1989); *Evaluation of Management Education, Training and Development* (Gower, 1994); *Organizational Learning and the Learning Organization* (Sage, 1998); *The Handbook of Organizational Learning and Knowledge Management*, 2nd edn (Wiley, 2011).

At Lancaster he has been, variously, Director of the School's Doctoral Programme, Director of the Graduate Management School and Head of Department. Externally he spent several years as a visiting faculty member on the International Teachers' Programme, acting as Director when it was held at the London Business School in 1984. During the early 1990s he was national co-ordinator of the Management Teaching Fellowship Scheme funded by the UK's Economic and Social Research Council (ESRC), which was responsible for training 180 new faculty members across UK management schools. He is a former member of the ESRC Post-graduate Training Board and was President of the British Academy of Management in 2006 and Dean of Fellows in 2008.

RICHARD THORPE is an Emeritus Professor at the University of Leeds where he was latterly Professor of Management Development and Pro Dean for Research at Leeds University Business School. His early industrial experience informed the way his ethos has developed. Common themes are a strong commitment to process methodologies and a focus on action in all its forms; an interest in and commitment to the development of doctoral students and the development of capacity within the sector; and a commitment to collaborative working on projects of mutual interest. Following a number of years in industry, he joined Strathclyde University as a researcher studying incentive payment schemes. This led to collaboration on *Payment Schemes and Productivity* (Macmillan, 1986). In 1980 he joined Glasgow University where he widened his research interests to include small firm growth and development as well as making regular contributions to the Scottish Business School's doctoral programme. In 1983 he attended the International Teachers' Programme in Sweden where he met Mark and embarked on a PhD under Mark's supervision. Collaboration continued through the 1990s with the ESRC Teaching Fellowship Scheme. In 1996 he was instrumental in establishing the Graduate Business School at Manchester Metropolitan University and in 2003 joined the ESRC Training and Development Board. There, he was involved in establishing the training guidelines for both doctorate and professional doctorate provision and more recently in initiatives to address capacity building in management and business. In 2003 he contributed to the ESRC's Evolution of Business Knowledge programme. His research interests have included: performance, remuneration and entrepreneurship, management learning and development and leadership, and he has published (with others) a number of books including: *Remuneration Systems* (Financial Times/Prentice Hall, 2000); *Management and Language: The Manager as Practical Author* (Sage, 2003); *The SAGE Dictionary of Qualitative Management Research* (Sage, 2008); *Performance Management: Multidisciplinary Perspectives* (Palgrave, 2008); *Gower Handbook of Leadership and Management Development* (Gower, 2010) and, more recently, *Management Research* in the Sage 'A Very Short, Fairly Interesting and Reasonably Cheap Book About' series. He was President of the British Academy of Management in 2007, Dean of Fellows in 2012, and in 2009–2015 he was Chair of the Society for the Advancement of Management Studies.

PAUL R. JACKSON is Professor of Corporate Communications and member of the Business Economics and Strategy group at the Alliance Manchester Business School, University of Manchester. He has a first degree in Psychology from the University of Sheffield and an MSc in Applied Statistics from Sheffield Polytechnic (now Sheffield Hallam University). His first university post was as a research assistant in studies on impression formation, where he decided that it was worth learning how to write programs in Fortran so that the computer could do the tedious work of adding up and he could do the interesting bits. His research interests have included laboratory studies of impression formation, large-scale surveys of the impact of unemployment on psychological health, longitudinal field studies of the effects of empowerment and work design on employee health and performance, employee communication and team-working, CSR and innovations in business models.

He has published widely in journals such as the *Academy of Management Journal*, *Journal of Applied Psychology*, *British Medical Journal*, *Human Relations*, *Journal of Occupational Health Psychology* and *British Journal of Management*. His books include: *Developments in Work and Organisational Psychology: Implications for International Business* (Elsevier, 2006); *Psychosocial Risk Factors in Call Centres* (HSE Publications, 2003); *Change in Manufacturing: Managing Stress in Manufacturing* (HSE Publications, 2001); *Organisational Interventions to Reduce the Impact of Poor Work Design* (HSE Publications, 1998).

Over the years he has undertaken various roles, including Director of Doctoral Programmes at the University of Sheffield and, at UMIST, Head of the Division of Marketing, International Business and Strategy, as well as designing the doctoral training programme at MBS. He has been teaching research methods to undergraduate, Masters' and doctoral students since 1975 and has contributed to books on research methods teaching as well as workshops for students and teachers on behalf of the British Academy of Management.

LENA J. JASPERSEN is a University Academic Fellow in Innovation Management at the University of Leeds. As an early career researcher with a multidisciplinary background in international sociology and organization studies, her research interests have focused on the processes of technology innovation and diffusion. Part of her role as an Academic Fellow is to develop a portfolio of research projects; hers relate to the exploration of patterns of medical technology innovation, including investigations into the influence of regulation on innovation strategies in medical technology and strategies for managing innovation in complex innovation ecosystems.

Lena's background brings both an international and an interdisciplinary dimension to her research. She holds Masters' degrees from the University of Bielefeld (Germany) and Keele University (UK) and was awarded a PhD with Recommendation of Research Excellence from the University of Leeds. Her doctoral research focused on the role of cross-sector partnerships in creating low-carbon development pathways. The results provided a critical analysis of how partnerships can facilitate but also inhibit the adoption of off-grid renewable energy technologies in Central America. Lena has a strong interest in research methods, particularly working on participatory methods and visual tools that can enhance the collection of both qualitative and quantitative network data. Together with colleagues, she has conducted research on global development and published an interdisciplinary volume on conducting field research in development contexts (*Understanding Global Development Research*, Sage, 2017). She has also published an organizational ethnography of the work of the oldest UN human rights treaty monitoring body, the Committee on the Elimination of Racial Discrimination (*The UN-real World of Human Rights*, Nomos, 2012).

PREFACE TO THE SIXTH EDITION

Firstly, welcome to the sixth edition of *Management and Business Research*; we hope you find it both useful and enjoyable to read. It has always been our intention for students to read the whole book in order to gain as complete an overview as possible before they begin to make specific choices, but the book is also for individuals to gain some early insights into how various techniques and approaches might be used and the skills that might be needed for the methods and techniques described to yield the best results. Over its various iterations the book has gone from success to success in supporting students entering the magical realm of empirical research. Much of what we set out could not have been achieved without examples from both our own research and also examples from students' own research. This sixth edition is no exception and Lena Jaspersen brings both international and interdisciplinary research experience to this edition. We welcome suggestions and ideas from students and staff alike and invite anyone who would like to make suggestions for examples and improvements to email us. This will hopefully further improve the next edition.

The first edition of this book appeared in 1991, at a time when there were very few management research methods books on the market. It quickly became established as the leading text because it covered all of the essential ground, yet was not too long or intimidating for students to get an overview of the key issues in research and the nature of the research process – many commented that they could do this by reading the book in a weekend. Students and staff also commented that they liked it because it did not shrink from tackling difficult issues, but avoided either trivializing them, or making them unnecessarily complex. The success of the book was attested by the sales figures, and by the fact that it has become the most highly cited management methodology book in the world according to Google Scholar.

A second edition was published in 2002, which included a substantial updating of the material since methodology had by then become a hot topic. In addition, research methods had also begun to be taught at undergraduate level, resulting in a modest repositioning of the book.

The third edition maintained the continuity by continuing to provide a comprehensive treatment of philosophies and methods, with coverage of both qualitative and quantitative techniques; but it also introduced some radical departures both in terms of content and design. The most significant changes were the strengthening of the way in which quantitative methods were treated. The edition now covered not only basic techniques for collecting and analysing quantitative data but also multivariate analysis and structural equation modelling.

In keeping with our desire to avoid complications, we covered the principles and logic of analytic methods without introducing complicated algebra. We claimed in the third edition that this part of the book now provided advanced statistics without tears!

The fourth edition was the first edition that deployed full colour. There were additional boxed examples, usually drawn from our own experiences and from those of our students. We also rethought some of the material on philosophy and research design and extended the coverage of qualitative analysis, particularly with the use of computer-assisted methods. The exercises, based on our own extensive methodology teaching, were appropriately updated in response to student feedback. We retained the companion website, developing our guidance to teachers. Perhaps most striking of all to this edition was the addition of a system of icons based around the metaphor of research being like a tree that sucks up nutrients (data, ideas and experiences) from the ground and then converts them into leaves and fruits (reports, publications and theses). Without wanting to labour the metaphor exhaustively, we then went on to develop the icons to illustrate some of the points and as a general orientation tool.

The fifth edition built on changes made to the book's structure in the fourth edition. We changed the order of some of the chapters in order to improve the logic of our arguments and make the text flow better. As with other editions we increased the number of examples and exercises to help illustrate the points being made or the issues being discussed.

The sixth edition has made further use of extensive feedback made available through our publishers and aims to both update our material while ensuring that it includes relevant current practice. It is the first edition of the book to be published as an interactive e-book. This new format has enabled us to make use of a wide range of online resources and related exercises. The book also features a new series of interviews with academics, practitioners and students sharing experiences of conducting research.

ACKNOWLEDGEMENTS

This book is based on the personal research experience of the authors, but thanks should also go to a number of students and colleagues. Both have contributed to this edition in a number of ways, through their encouragement as well as their ideas. We have tried to reflect their suggestions as far as possible in the text.

Our students have taught us a great deal and we have included a number of their examples, both in this edition and in earlier editions. Those students and colleagues who have helped are now too numerous for all of them to be individually singled out, however all those who have contributed know who they are and are fully acknowledged in the previous editions of the book. Those who have made specific contributions to this sixth edition or have contributed material that remains in the book are mentioned in the section(s) where this occurs.

Various university colleagues have also assisted us by reading through the transcripts, making comments and suggesting ideas and to them we are extremely grateful. Again, this number grows with each edition but for this sixth edition we would especially like to thank those colleagues and students who have contributed to our new Research in Action textboxes:

Anne Kruckenberg

Catherine Cassell

Charlotte Coleman

Conor McDonald

David Mosse

Emmanuella Plakoyiannaki

Eva-Marie Muller-Stuler

Georgia Stavraki

Hakan Ozalp

José F. Molina-Azorin

Nicholas Loubere

Susanne Karstedt

Tony Morgan

William Ambler

Our editor at Sage for this sixth edition has been Lyndsay Aitken, who has always offered us encouragement and occasionally hectored us when progress has been slow; for this we are grateful. We also thank Kirsty Smy for her support during the revision process.

The authors are grateful to Sage for permission to include extracts from R. Thorpe and J. Cornelissen (2003) 'Visual media and the construction of meaning', Chapter 4 in D. Holman and R. Thorpe (eds), *Management and Language*, as well as a selection of online resources from the Sage Research Methods platform.

Finally, we would like to thank our families for their tolerance while this book was being written and rewritten – we hope they will consider the outcome to be worth the effort.

Publisher's Acknowledgements

Student Reviewers

We would like to extend our warmest thanks to the following students for providing invaluable feedback on the text:

Christian Bretter

Alan Chan

Eleanor Pownall-Gray

Sinead Shean

Andrew Wool

Andy Vicat

YOUR GUIDE TO USING THIS BOOK AND ITS ONLINE RESOURCES

This book comes with a wide range of useful learning features and online resources to help with your research.

Inside the book

Turn to the back of the book for your **'tree metaphor' pull out guide** to doing research and understanding the underlying philosophy. A great tool for visualizing the research process and working out your own stance!

'The "tree metaphor" has provided me with an excellent visual aid of how to approach my future research projects. Prior to seeing this metaphor I struggled with putting the wide range of features of research into perspective.'

Sinead Shean, postgraduate student MSC Human Resource Management

Research in Action – real-world research experiences from a range of academics, practitioners and students together with their own personal top tips

Examples – interdisciplinary research examples illustrate the application of key research steps in practice

Exercises – practical exercises on key aspects of carrying out research

Glossary terms – definitions in the margin enable you to understand key research terminology and concepts

Summaries – recap on the key topics that the chapter dealt with to help you consolidate what you have read

Further Reading – useful articles and books to help with specific aspects of the research process

'It's interesting to see how the decisions we're making during our research project are similarly faced by experienced researchers in the field.'
Andy Vicat, MBA student

Your digital resources

Don't forget to use the wealth of digital resources available with this book to help with your research. To access the resources just log into your interactive eBook and click on the icons or visit https://edge.sagepub.com/easterbysmith6e to access the book's website.

Icons throughout the book indicate when extra online resources are available:

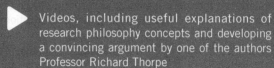 Videos, including useful explanations of research philosophy concepts and developing a convincing argument by one of the authors Professor Richard Thorpe

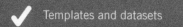 Articles, examples of research, podcasts and more

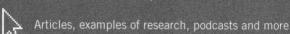 Templates and datasets

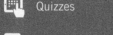 Quizzes

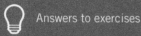 Glossary flashcards

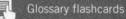 Answers to exercises

'I particularly like the individual login you receive to the eBook. As I student myself, I often use many difference devices.'
Eleanor Pownall-Gray, fourth year student BA Management

Learning objectives

To explain the characteristics of different forms of research.

To understand the key ingredients of research and how they differ in relation to the purpose of the study.

To consider the issues involved in preparing a research proposal.

To understand the interdependence of philosophy, design and methods in effectively addressing research questions.

To consider the importance of the impact and engagement agenda.

FINDING YOUR FEET IN MANAGEMENT AND BUSINESS RESEARCH

1

Chapter contents

Introduction

Welcome to the sixth edition of *Management and Business Research*. We hope you enjoy reading this book. When a book about research methods specifically focused on management and business research was first conceived there were no books on the market that covered this topic. This book became the first. Our intention at the outset was to write a book that helped students in this field to understand the research options available to them and to do so with enthusiasm. Unlike the natural sciences, the social sciences present the opportunity to study a topic in a variety of different ways and the research process can be a highly creative one. Our aim is to give students conducting research a comprehensive overview of what is needed to deliver a good project, dissertation or thesis; the choices and alternatives open to them; the skills required to design projects, collect and analyse data and to communicate the results. While this book has grown and developed through its various editions, our aim remains the same – not to provide definitive answers on every research issue but rather to instil in those new to research a sense of direction and enthusiasm for their own research.

This introductory chapter aims to offer insights into the wider landscape of management and business research and the different skills needed to navigate it successfully, and then to have a closer look at the function and content of the initial research proposal, concluding with the way the book is structured by way of pointing the reader to the various chapters.

The landscape of management and business research

Business and management research is a systematic inquiry that helps to solve business problems and contributes to management knowledge. Since the industrial revolution, management knowledge has become increasingly sought after and, since the mid-twentieth century, we have witnessed an exponential growth in business and management research. This is coupled with the growth of management and business as a subject taught within universities, the ingredients of which require students to conduct an extended, original piece of research.

Types of research

pure research research for which the primary objective/output is the development of theory

applied research studies that focus on tackling practical problems in organizations where the desired outcome will be knowledge about how to solve the problem

At the most fundamental level, we can differentiate three types of research based on their respective purpose. Basic research aims at the development, refinement and testing of general principles and theories that help us to explain social phenomena of relevance to the business and management disciplines. Its focus on 'pure' knowledge creation – it is indeed often called pure research – makes basic research the most prestigious type of research (at least within academia). However, much of basic research is not really concerned with achieving real-world impact. In contrast, applied research involves exploring the value of basic knowledge in an applied setting. Applied research aims at delivering outcomes that can be used by policy-makers and practitioners who seek to improve the conduct of business. Evaluation research takes this focus on application one step further by making the evaluation of a given policy or intervention the main purpose of the research. It is not really concerned with academic theory, but rather with helping practitioners measure and understand outcomes of particular practices. Table 1.1 provides an overview of the three types of research.

TABLE 1.1   Three types of research

	Basic Research	Applied Research	Evaluation Research
Nature of the Problem	Basic research seeks to derive new knowledge about social phenomena, hoping to establish general principles and theories with which to explain them.	Applied research seeks to understand how basic research can translate in order to help alleviate a particular organizational or policy-related problem, with well-grounded guidelines to remedial action.	Evaluation research assesses the outcomes of actions taken by organizations when based on either best practice or research applied to organizational problems or the outcomes of particular practices.
Goal	To produce new knowledge including the discovery of the nature of the relationships between variables, the development of frameworks or models (theory).	To explore the value of basic knowledge in an applied setting that can be used by policy-makers, practitioners or other organizational members who seek to improve the conduct of business.	To provide an accurate account of the outcome of a programme when applied to a business-related problem.
Theory	Theory creation and extension. Selection of an appropriate theory used to guide hypothesis testing.	Selection of a theory or theories to be used as a way of organizing an intervention, together with appropriate practitioner knowledge, in order to explore the dynamics of a business issue or problem.	Selection of an appropriate theory to fit the problem, programme or intervention under assessment.
Methods and Techniques	Theory formulation, hypothesis testing using experimental and quasi-experimental methods, sampling, data collection techniques, statistical treatment of data and validation or rejection of hypotheses.	Similar to basic research, only in a setting where the implications of the research are immediately obvious. Often, the applied nature of the investigation leads to more case-based qualitative approaches being adopted in order to understand the contextual issues related to solving specific organizational problems.	Use of conventional evaluation techniques appropriate to the question.

Source: adapted from Miller and Salkind, 2002: 3

scholarship
this is a term
given to the
development of
high levels of
knowledge about
a particular
issue or topic,
largely on
the basis of
secondary data

basic research
sometimes also
referred to as
fundamental
research;
its aim is to
develop theory
and greater
understanding
of an issue or
phenomenon
without there
necessarily
being any direct
impact on a
current problem

Some researchers (Ellwood et al., 2013) have suggested that the type of research that individuals undertake depends on what kind of academic the individual wishes to be, in particular what they want to be known for. Others have highlighted that the preferred type of research can change depending on the stage an individual has reached in either their career or in relation to the life cycle of their particular research. Thorpe et al. (2011) have argued that rather than see research as a selection of competing alternatives, knowledge should be seen more as translational flows where, at each stage of the knowledge translation process, different contributions can be made to scholarship. This diffusion process begins as practitioners use their own frames of reference and understanding, to both add to and interpret what the knowledge produced might mean and how it might be useful. Thinking of the translation process in this way enables students and researchers to make choices as to where their contribution might not only make the most impact but also show how different kinds of contributions can be made at different stages in their careers or working lives. The different stages of the knowledge translation value chain are set out below in Figure 1.1. Academic institutions prefer staff at the beginning of their research careers to focus on the first stage of the chain and to conduct pure basic research, but this might not always lead to the greatest impact. Where researchers undertake work at the second stage, the focus is on how theory can be brought into practice. The third stage places emphasis on collaboration with user groups or communities, which not only helps to define the new research questions but also assists in the dissemination of the research findings. The fourth stage focuses on designing appropriate vehicles and mechanisms to bring the research to the attention of the widest possible audience, whether this be with the active involvement of the knowledge producers, or not.

We believe that the depiction of knowledge as flows through a 'value chain' (and, in practice, through various feedback loops), where knowledge adapts and changes as a consequence of wider and wider engagement with users, offers a more realistic view of how research gets disseminated. This characterization helps researchers move their thinking beyond notions of production and implementation and onto the processes of knowledge diffusion.

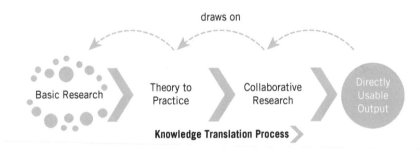

FIGURE 1.1   Knowledge value chain

Source: based on Thorpe et al., 2011

Assessing
impact

Levels of research

Different types of research tend to be linked to different levels of degree. Undergraduate research tends to be specific and bounded. Common projects assigned by tutors tend to include small market research studies, or interview-based studies of employee attitudes.

Research conducted as part of a postgraduate taught degree will normally have greater scope, and more time available – often several months over the summer. Postgraduate dissertations are required to produce contributions to knowledge and, as a consequence, an additional element is a having a certain degree of originality.

Funded projects are usually conducted by experienced researchers, but require many of the same decisions as projects conducted as part of university degrees.

Of course, research is not only undertaken by qualified and trained individuals. Research is something that managers do as a natural part of their everyday activity, collecting and analysing data, and drawing conclusions. Consultants also conduct research, and many management and business students go on to become consultants in later life.

Features of a research project

What differs is the level of sophistication in the methods used, the research methodology itself, and the speed with which answers are sought. Whoever undertakes the research, and at whatever level, certain conditions and requirements appertain. Table 1.2 summarizes the factors that are considered to be key aspects of academic work.

TABLE 1.2   The nature of academic scholarship

- Academic work
  - Recognised by others working in a similar area
- Original
  - Takes a different angle
  - Adopts a different methodology
  - Provides a different explanation
- Situated
  - Demonstrates knowledge of wider context, e.g. other literatures
- Critically reflective
  - Offers a critical evaluation of other literatures
  - Demonstrates critical understanding of its own limitations
  - Offers a critical evaluation of the theories generated
- Logically consistent
  - Is coherent, not internally contradictory
- Methodologically coherent
  - Methods and data collection and analysis support the aims and objectives
  - Offers a critically informed rationale for the selection of particular methods
- Synthesis
  - Combines theory and data into a cohesive argument
- Audience
  - Addresses primarily an academic as well as a practitioner audience

Source: adapted from Mauch and Birch, 2003. Reproduced by permission of Taylor and Francis Group, LLC, a division of Informa plc

Common to many of these factors is the importance of taking into account relevant previous literature. Students are expected to 'touch base' with key literature in the field in which they wish to be taken seriously. This is as true for research professionals as it is for undergraduates. For example, the UK's Research Assessment Exercise will only consider an *academic work* to be groundbreaking or 'world leading' if it is deemed to be of such noteworthiness that other scholars working in the field would need to reference it to demonstrate their rounded understanding of the topic. Academic writing should also include some dimension of *originality*.

For example, a research project might use a different methodology from previous research with the aim of yielding new insights into a problem, or may take a different perspective; in order to do this successfully, students need to know what approaches have gone before.

Another key aspect of research requires students to be self-aware of their own positions and biases but also the positions and biases that other researchers might have had before. All research is *situated* – both in terms of how it relates to previous research and theorizing and also in the way it is derived from or conducted in a particular empirical context. For some students this *critical reflectivity* can be written into the way the research is presented; others may choose to take this particular style of writing further by showing *how* they adopted a reflexive approach to the research process (for example, they might explain how their research changed as they became more conscious of challenges inherent in the topic as the research unfolded).

One of the most important aspects of research (if it is to be deemed of high quality) is its *logical consistency* and *methodological coherence*. That is to say, the research should be coherent and consistent both methodologically and in terms of its findings. It should *synthesize* by bringing into dialogue theory and data in a way that translates into a cohesive argument. This aspect of scholarship we will return to in the chapters on philosophy, design and analysis.

Aims of a research project

Finally in this introductory section, it is perhaps useful to consider the aims that a piece of scholarly research might contain. We believe that students conducting a dissertation project should be aiming to achieve *one or other* of the three elements illustrated in Table 1.3.

TABLE 1.3   What are the aims of a research project?

Contribution to knowledge

- Pattern recognition and theorizing
- Generalizability
- Realism of context/problem
- Replicability

Training and innovation in research methodolody

- Developing an appropriate methodology research design
- Being 'scientific' comes not from what you study but with the methodology

Impact and engagement: influencing policy and practice

- Dissemination of some kind, including also a recognition of the pathways required for impact
- Actually bringing about some kind of change or benefit
- Implications of findings and addressing how problems can be elevated and changes made as part of the overall conclusions

Let us have a closer look at each of these three elements.

Contribution to knowledge

Good research ought to produce some kind of contribution to knowledge. Of course, the level and sophistication of this knowledge will depend on the level of study and whether the research is being conducted by academics or practitioners.

One way academics sometimes think about knowledge is by using an ecclesiastical analogy. At the undergraduate level, students are given the knowledge to sit in the congregation of a church and understand the scriptures; at the postgraduate level, the student should have the knowledge and confidence to be able to choose from the scriptures and give the sermon; and at doctoral level, the student should be able and confident to go back and translate (and potentially reinterpret) the scriptures to offer new perspectives and understandings. These new understandings might relate to a whole range of things, from recognizing new patterns and associations between aspects of data that are new to these associations coming about as a consequence of interrogating a particular data set or making comparisons between a number of carefully chosen case studies. It might also come about from demonstrating that the insights gained are generalizable and relate to a population more generally. This is not to say that we are expecting students to develop theoretical contributions of universal applicability but rather that we expect them to understand how generalizable their findings are. New knowledge can also be manifest by explaining to the reader the nature of a particular issue in context. This might take the form of a detailed description or rich picture and interpretation of a particular situation or circumstance.

Training and innovation

In addition, we believe that research within an academic course should be about training in research. Derek Pugh, famous for leading the 'Aston Studies' into the nature of organizations and a person committed to capacity building, used to say that there are no examples of individuals getting a Nobel Prize directly from their undergraduate or graduate research. This is why we recommend that if the research is for a university audience, students should write their experience and learning into the final dissertation or thesis as opposed to sweeping all the problems they encountered under the carpet as though they never happened!

Of particular importance here is learning about methodology. It is very difficult if not impossible to really understand the topic of methodology in advance of doing some research, so reflecting on what was done, what might have been done, what went wrong and what might have been done better is essential – even if this is not written into the final account.

EXAMPLE 1.1

Developing a reflexive methodology

Being reflective and reflexive in methodology relates to the relationship between the production of knowledge and the context in which it is produced. This can include any effects from bias the researcher might bring into the process.

Alvesson and Sköldberg (2000) suggest that being reflective in research requires researchers to think carefully about how the cultural and political context and researcher interaction with respondents might affect the results and any interpretations that might be made.

The primary focus of reflexivity is interpretation. Having a reflexive standpoint involves accepting that even empirical facts or archival data are problematic: after all, all data is collected within particular cultural and historical contexts. Alvesson and Sköldberg (2000) also recommend that, in order to be reflexive, researchers should also focus inwards on such things as: the researcher themselves, the traditions of the research community, and language. Research therefore becomes increasingly about the interpretation of interpretation.

These issues and the main links between types and levels of research are discussed in more detail in later chapters; factors that require a particular emphasis in relation to management and business (for example, the political and the philosophical factors that can influence the way research is conducted in this field) are highlighted.

Perhaps the most important aspect of research for a higher degree is to demonstrate that you understand and can justify the methodological choices made and can ensure that these are manifest in the way the research has been designed and conducted, the data analysed and the results presented.

Impact and engagement

Researchers and students face conflicting demands when carrying out research projects. There is pressure to deliver parsimonious and abstract theory in order to contribute to academic debate, while at the same time there is an expectation to provide detailed solutions to practical problems. Closer linking of research to societal needs or challenges is becoming an irresistible pressure within management and business research – and within university research more generally – as increased emphasis is placed on relevance to the real world in all walks of life. This is a pressure that rarely exists for consultants – yet the evidence base for their conclusions is nevertheless still very important.

As a consequence of this pressure to consider relevance and make research impactful, it has been argued that undertaking research differently – by researching in teams, and focusing on problems that really matter to practitioners – could be a way in which management and business researchers can both write scholarly papers and at the same time create 'useful' knowledge. As we have shown above, basic research may not be as concerned with the impact agenda as are applied and evaluation research. Another way of looking at the role of impact in motivating and driving research is described by Gibbons et al. (1994) who identify two forms of research:

- mode 1 research concentrates on the production of knowledge, with academics working from the perspective of their own discipline and focusing on theoretical questions and problems
- mode 2 research generates knowledge through direct engagement with social practice and problems.

Practitioner Inquiry

In their SAGE Research Methods video Dr Elaine Hall and Dr Kate Wall discuss practitioner inquiry, which is a good example of mode 2 research.

Some scholars (e.g. Tranfield, 2002) argue that management research should focus on practical application. Others (e.g. Huff, 2000) suggest a compromise position where both theoretical and practical work is required: this is sometimes characterized as mode 1½ research.

Many institutions the world over are now committed to and being measured in terms of the relevance their research output has for practice and also the extent to which the school engages with business (which of course can also include research collaboration). As a consequence they now have in place performance measurement systems that address impact within research. Researchers therefore need to take the impact and engagement agenda seriously if they are to be successful within their careers. For example, in 2008 the UK government introduced an additional requirement within their periodic Research Assessment Exercise that required institutions to demonstrate the impact their research was

---

evaluation research research that has, as its focus, the systemic and rigorous assessment of an activity or object such that the information and insights gleaned can provide useful feedback

mode 1 research the generation of theoretical knowledge through detached scientific research

mode 2 research the generation of practical knowledge through direct engagement with practice

mode 1½ research the generation of useful knowledge through combining scientific research methods with practical engagement

having through case studies of the impact and outcomes of their research on third parties (other than students).

The article 'What is Management Research Actually Good For?' in *Harvard Business Review* (Davis, 2015) discusses the purpose of management research and the importance of business scholars knowing the constituency their research is serving.

What is management research for?

EXERCISE 1.1

Thinking about the role of research

1   **Individual**: Drawing on what you have learnt about the landscape of management research, create a diagram, picture or mind-map that illustrates the meaning and the scope of management research.

2   **Group**: In groups of four or five students, present your diagrams/pictures and explain what they illustrate. Who has created the most creative illustration?

3   **Group discussion**: In class, discuss the role of research in relation to the job of academics, compared to the role of research in relation to the job of practitioners.

4   **Individual**: Search the web for at least one example of management and business research that has achieved real impact. You can google or have a closer look at the REF website with impact studies.

5   **Group**: Present your example in class. What kind of evidence is provided for the research having achieved an impact?

REF: Impact case studies

Writing a research proposal

Following our concise introduction to the landscape of management and business research, how it presents itself to an outsider, and how impact can be achieved, we now shift the focus of our attention to an introduction to how to conduct management and business research, and hence to the perspective of an insider. As demonstrated in the previous section, it is important to know what kind of research one seeks to undertake and to be explicit when it comes to one's academic aspirations and desire for impact. It is no less important, however, to be clear about how to conduct a given piece of research. In the remainder of this chapter we focus on this question by examining what (student) researchers need to consider when writing research proposals.

A proposal can be defined as a suggested or intended plan – and not just as an offer of marriage. A research proposal is about proposing a research project, outlining what it involves, and convincing an audience (such as a supervisor or funder) of the value and soundness of the research and one's plan for carrying it out. All research, whether completed by a consultant practitioner, an academic or an undergraduate, a postgraduate or a doctoral student, begins with writing a research proposal. Research councils now

require very detailed (but concise) proposals before they will allocate money to applicants; there are similar requirements for those wishing to obtain a doctoral degree. Most
undergraduate and postgraduate students are asked to develop at least a short proposal
before embarking on their final year projects. Research proposals are no less important
when conducting research within businesses. The example in the Research in Action box
on page 11 offers an insight from a practising manager on the differences between academic and business proposals.

A research proposal is an opportunity for the researcher to carefully consider the
framing of the research to be undertaken, what has gone before, why this new study is
important, what new knowledge could potentially be revealed, resolved or explained, and
what methods or approaches would give the best results. The research proposal is, for many
students, the first opportunity to test out the logic and content of the research on which
they wish to embark.

Even when there is no formal requirement to produce a research proposal, the exercise of doing so is an extremely good discipline that can help students draw together
what they already know, their early ideas and what the literature says on the topic. There
is some truth in the saying that 'you don't know what you think until you see what you
say'! So, for many, writing a proposal offers the opportunity to begin to see how elements
of the research process come together, and to demonstrate for others the coherence of
what is being proposed.

Elements of a research proposal

To draw an analogy with cooking, a research proposal might be seen as a recipe, for which
ingredients are needed. Some of these ingredients are essential for good taste (i.e. quality),
while others are less important. Some chefs (researchers) will approach cooking the dish in
one way, and others in another. Bringing out certain textures or flavours while suppressing
others requires skill, and this both depends on preferences and requires practice, ideas and
a vision of what is being aimed for.

Thus, the purpose of proposals is to set out the ingredients required, and how the
food will be prepared and served. For example, what kind of dish is to be served? Is
it fast food of relatively poor quality or high-quality cuisine? What ingredients will be
used, and what cooking procedures and kitchen utensils will be required to prepare the
particular dish? This translates to the importance of students being both qualified and
capable of undertaking their study, and to supervisors being assured that the research
is feasible and likely to contribute to generating the knowledge claimed. Although the
requirements for research proposals differ from institution to institution, there are some
common elements. After a title and an introduction, all research proposals should identify clear research questions and objectives. They should provide a summary of the
background of the research (usually in the form of a literature review), and articulate
both the conceptual framework and the design of the research. A good research proposal
should further emphasize the significance of the proposed research without denying
its limitations and potential ethical issues. Finally, a research proposal should not only
convince the reader of the usefulness and desirability of the research but also of its fea-
sibility. A detailed work plan, often structured in the form of successive work packages
and milestones, accompanied by a research timeline, are part and parcel of any research
proposal. In this way, research proposals are not that dissimilar from business proposals,
as discussed by Tony Morgan in the box below.

RESEARCH IN ACTION

Writing proposals for business and academia

Tony Morgan is currently IBM UK's technical leader for the consumer industry. He has 30 years of experience in technology and is passionate about driving innovation. He is a Royal Academy of Engineering sponsored Visiting Professor in Innovation at the University of Leeds and author of *Collaborative Innovation: How Clients and Service Providers Can Work By Design to Achieve It* (Business Expert Press, 2017).

Tony Morgan

In your experience, what are the main differences between business and academic proposals?

Creating a well-written proposal is a key communication skill. The major differences between a business and an academic proposal are likely to include the objectives and the audience. However, many of the important factors will be the same, such as clarity of objectives, ensuring the paper meets these objectives and is written in a manner that is easy to read and consume.

The objective of a business proposal is often to 'sell' a compelling idea, solution or service to a client. The audience will usually consist of key client sponsors (decision-makers) and stakeholders (decision influencers) in the client and sometimes third-party organizations, for example advisory companies.

What makes a good business proposal?

A 'winning' proposal must demonstrate a clear understanding of the challenge or opportunity being addressed. It must show how and when the challenge will be addressed and articulate the net benefit and business value to the client.

The proposal must be easy to read, so key points can be quickly extracted by busy business executives and subject matter experts.

In competitive situations, a business proposal must also differentiate the submitting organization by communicating how the idea, solution or service is better than the competition's. Including a 'wow factor' can give the proposal greater impact and make it stand out from the crowd.

TOP TIP

Have empathy when writing a proposal. Put yourself in the reading glasses of the receiver. Verify what you'd wish to be included if you were that person.

Business proposal

Read Tony Morgan's example of a successful business proposal and what we can learn from this example for writing proposals with impact.

TABLE 1.4   Elements of proposals

Elements of a Research Proposal	Elements of a Business Proposal
• Title	• Title
• Abstract	• Summary
• Introduction	• Situation appraisal
• General research question and objective	• Objectives and deliverables
• Literature review	• Value of achieving objectives (benefits)
• Conceptual framework (theory and hypotheses)	• Process and timeline
• Specific research questions	• How to evaluate success
• Methods	• Timing
• Significance	• Resource commitments
• Limitations	• Credentials
• Ethical issues	• Appendix
• Work packages and timeline	
• References	
• Appendix	

Example of a good student proposal

EXERCISE 1.2

Proposal writing

1   **Group discussion**: What are the functions of each of the elements of an academic research proposal? (Why do we need an introduction? What is the literature review for? Why is it important to highlight limitations? etc.)

2   **Group**: In pairs, or on your own, draw up a list of the similarities and differences between writing proposals for business and research. Take notes and develop a visual illustration, table or figure that illustrates these differences.

3   **Individual**: Tony Morgan argues that good proposals are built on empathy. He highlights the importance of understanding your audience. In practice, this can sometimes be difficult to achieve. Have a look at the scenarios outlined below. Make a list of activities you can pursue to find out more about the respective audience of a proposal:

   • You are a new business consultant and you are asked to write a proposal for a consultancy for a small fast food chain you know relatively little about. They are interested in ways to enhance their online order and delivery service.

   • You plan a research project on women leadership in the IT industry. As part of your research you would like to observe team meetings but you need to establish field access.

   • You are asked to write a research proposal for a dissertation project on supply chain management in the apparel industry in China.

Research question and objectives

When developing a research proposal, clarity in relation to the focus of the research is usually achieved by setting out the main research questions to be investigated and describing the aims that will link to the outcomes of the research. Expressions such as 'to investigate' or 'to study' are not aims in themselves and should be avoided. We discuss clear research questions and objectives in the following Chapter 2. At this stage it is important to add that the aims of a given research project need to be consistent with the method or methodology adopted; in other words, they need to be capable of being achieved using the proposed methods. Overly general or ambitious aims can also be problematic. There have been many occasions when supervisors have been heard to remark that for this research to be completed six researchers would need to work on it for a lifetime!

Having a clear objective is extremely important as it helps us to understand and identify an interesting research project. It is important to know, for example, the relevant criteria for deciding that a research idea is worth pursuing and appropriate. There can be several purposes behind a particular research project and these need to be clearly articulated. They include the recognition of patterns in data or information; the development or refinement of a particular methodological approach; the ability to generalize to a wider population; and the ability to describe a problem in a sufficiently detailed way to show the realism of a particular context. We will consider all of these in later chapters of the book. At the same time it is important to bear in mind that all research projects are subject to weaknesses. A good research proposal therefore articulates the potential (and potential benefits) of a proposed study while also acknowledging its limitations.

Building on previous work

Understanding the literature in the area is an important prelude to a research project. Not only is it the means by which students see what work has been undertaken on the subject before, but it also provides a stimulus to the focus the study might have and how it might be undertaken. After all, when conducting research, most academics 'stand on the shoulders of giants' – a metaphor commonly used to refer to the fact that most research builds on previous research.

At every level – undergraduate, postgraduate and doctorate – there will generally be an expectation of evidence that the student has an understanding of what literature already exists on a particular subject. Although at the proposal stage students aren't expected to be definitive, sufficient evidence should be produced to indicate that there is a question to be answered. A simple test would be to reflect on whether the research proposal would convince someone with a good knowledge of the area that the individual has a sufficient grasp of the relevant current literature and the boundaries of that knowledge to claim that the topic warrants further research. While the literature review section should summarize existing knowledge, and identify gaps in that knowledge that are the focus for the research questions, the design and method sections then explain how the researcher intends to answer those questions.

Research design and methods

The third important element of a research proposal is a concise statement of the design to be adopted and the methods that will be used to meet the objectives. It is essential that the proposed design and methods of enquiry are appropriate to answering the research question(s). Figure 1.2 illustrates the balance that we believe should be struck between the

research design
a research design
may be defined
as a strategy
that lays out
the principles
of the research
methodology for
a given study.
It articulates
methods and
techniques for
all stages of the
research process
and justifies their
appropriateness
in relation to
both the research
question or
hypothesis and
the research
context

research design and the most appropriate methods to meet its requirements; the research questions asked within the field; the research it builds on; the setting or context in which it is conducted; and the skills and resources available to the researcher to carry out the research, undertake the analysis and communicate the results.

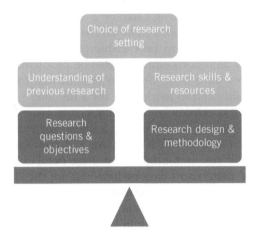

FIGURE 1.2   Finding the right balance

Proposal
development

The questions listed in this online extract 'Questions to Guide Proposal Development' in Punch (2006) can help you to develop excellent research proposals that drive relevant research with impact. Go through the list of questions and identify questions that are meaningful to you now as well as others that require further clarification. As you work through this book, pause occasionally to revisit these questions. You will find that they correspond to the material covered in each chapter.

Structure of the book

Richard
Thorpe's
video
presentation:
The research
context

The biggest section of this book is concerned with methods, and we follow conventional practice by looking separately at qualitative methods and quantitative methods.

A good research design is fundamental to achieving high quality research, and so we have brought together in Chapter 4 an analysis of design principles and applications in different areas of research. Before exploring design in detail, we think it is important for students to understand the different philosophical assumptions that underlie management and business research, and in particular to reflect on their own position, and we do this in Chapter 3. By developing an appreciation of the strengths and weaknesses of these different perspectives, students will be able to appreciate how different philosophical assumptions influence the criteria used when judging the quality of research, how the assumptions made about research philosophy directly impact on research design, and how the quality of the design proposed might also be judged.

Chapter 5 then focuses on the research process and some of the principal challenges faced by those conducting management and business research. The chapter provides guidance on how to achieve access to research settings and engage with research participants. It demonstrates the importance of being aware of the politics and power in research. The chapter also provides a comprehensive introduction to ethical issues and how they can be detected and addressed. It closes with a discussion of how the right attitude and mindset can help researchers to achieve their full potential.

Qualitative methods

Chapters 6 to 8 form the qualitative section of the book. Chapter 6 offers an overview of the nature of qualitative data and why data of this type are collected, focusing on textual data (both primary and secondary) and how data are created through language. We specifically examine the nature of the qualitative interview and how interviews might be appropriately conducted, as well as textual data (again primary and secondary) through such devices as diaries. A key characteristic of a skilled researcher is the ability to work with study participants to allow their opinions to surface. We conclude Chapter 6 with a reflection on how researchers might gain access to, and collect and store, data – including raising issues of data protection and the avoidance of bias.

Chapter 7 focuses on the creation of qualitative data through observation and interactions that take place between researchers and respondents and/or users. The techniques that we explain include participant observation and a variety of participatory tools that researchers might use in order to elicit understanding from the settings being studied. In studies like this, it is important to be aware of the ethical issues linked to these methods, as well as the risks and opportunities that occur through involvement and interaction in the field. It is particularly important in qualitative studies for the researcher to reflect on the ways in which they are influencing the individuals from whom information is being collected, the research process and the research outcomes. This kind of reflexivity is an important and valuable part of the qualitative research process, and we will examine later how adopting a reflexive approach helps us to conduct 'good' research.

Chapter 7 also introduces a range of computer-aided analysis tools and techniques, describing how these might be used, offering an overview of the main packages, and suggesting how students might find out more about them. Within the qualitative tradition, we highlight the importance of the interplay between theory, data and analysis through the process of research. The concluding part of the chapter discusses the criteria that might be used for assessing the quality of qualitative research.

Chapter 8 offers an overview of the different types of analysis of qualitative data, explaining how these map on and link to different philosophical traditions. Again, we stress the difference between pre-structured approaches (e.g. template analysis) and emergent approaches to analysis (grounded analysis), emphasizing the importance of adopting a systematic approach, while remaining flexible and creative in the analysis. The chapter covers data analysis techniques, focusing on how patterns within the data can be identified through the way the data are indexed and coded. More recent methods, such as the analysis of visual data, are also addressed.

Quantitative methods

Chapters 9, 10 and 11 detail the opportunities, expectations and methods that would be required if research students were to decide to undertake their research within a quantitative tradition. Chapter 9 builds on the foundations laid down in Chapters 3 and 4, and focuses on alternative sources of quantitative data and the craft of designing structured questionnaires with well-defined questions and appropriate measurement scales.

The next two chapters cover analysis of quantitative data. Here, we follow the same principle as everywhere else in the book, by focusing on understanding why particular methods are used rather than simply knowing what to do. Comments in a research proposal such as 'analysis will be undertaken using statistical methods' or 'the analysis will be undertaken using SPSS' will detract from the credibility of the research. SPSS is one of many software packages, and it almost never matters what software is used

participant observation a form of ethnography where there is close involvement in the organization in order to gain a detailed understanding of other people's realities

template analysis a method of qualitative data analysis that enables a systematic, thematic analysis of text

grounded analysis the linking of key variables (theoretical codes) into a more holistic theory that makes a contribution to knowledge in a particular field or domain

to achieve a result. What matters much more is the kind of analysis to be undertaken and how that analysis enables the research to answer the research questions specified in the proposal.

Chapter 10 discusses the principles behind summarizing quantitative data, and then considers the way in which significance tests can be used to make inferences from a researcher's sample data. Inference is a vital element in a research proposal, since it provides the link between summaries of sample data and answers to research questions, which will be expressed in terms of a more general population. Chapter 11 is more advanced in that it covers multivariate analysis, and we include it in the book because the methods we describe reflect more faithfully the reality of management and business research where many factors need to be considered at the same time.

The final Chapter 12 covers strategies and techniques for writing up management and business research. The chapter provides guidance on the requirements of different forms of output, most importantly a student dissertation. It examines how research outputs are evaluated, and also addresses the important issue of plagiarism and how it can be avoided.

inference
drawing conclusions about a population based on evidence from a sample

EXERCISE 1.3

Engaging with management and business research

1   **Group**: In her poignant autobiography, novelist and anthropologist Zora Neale Hurston writes that 'research is formalized curiosity. It is poking and prying with a purpose' (Hurston, 1942: 143). In groups of three or four, discuss this statement with a view to your understanding of management and business research. Why are we curious? What is the purpose? Why is it important that research is 'formalized'?

2   **Individual/group**: Develop a template with different headings and questions that will help you to develop a research proposal for a student project, for example a dissertation project. Draw on Table 1.4 and the 'Questions to Guide Proposal Development' (see online resource included above) for inspiration.

3   **Individual/group**: Print your template and bring it to the next class, where you swap your template with someone else in the group. Mark and comment upon each other's templates. Which template is the most elaborate one? Which one is easiest to use? Who has created the best template?

Conclusion

As you finish reading this first chapter, take some time to reflect on the emphasis you wish to give to your research. This book will help you in the choices you make and how you might go about conducting your research. Certainly, the next generation of management researchers will need to help in developing practices that enable new ways of integrating the demands of the modern-day research environment.

Further reading

A collection of chapters for readers who are exploring areas for critical research in business and management:

Alvesson, M. and Willmott, H. (eds) (2003) *Studying Management Critically*. London: Sage.

A useful guide for those undertaking a professional doctorate:

Anderson, L., Gold, J., Stewart, J. and Thorpe, R. (2015) *Professional Doctorates in Business and Management*. London: Sage.

This article discusses the role of relationships between practitioners and academics in generating and disseminating knowledge across 'the Great Divide':

Bartunek, J.M., Rynes, S.L. and Daft, R.L. (2001) 'Across the Great Divide: knowledge creation and transfer between practitioners and academics', *Academy of Management Journal*, 44: 340–55.

This is a step-by-step and very readable guide on how to conduct a research project:

Bell, J. and Waters, S. (2014) *Doing Your Research Project: A Guide for First-time Researchers*, 6th edn. Maidenhead: Open University Press.

As it says on the label, this book provides a succinct overview of theories of management and organization, and it is reasonably priced. It adopts a critical view in the sense that it has a slight preference for the perspectives of those who are managed, rather than the managers themselves:

Grey, C. (2016) *A Very Short, Fairly Interesting and Reasonably Cheap Book About Studying Organizations*, 4th edn. London: Sage.

A handy guidebook for readers embarking on doctoral study – and a good read:

Marshall, S. and Green, N. (2007) *Your PhD Companion: A Handy Mix of Practical Tips, Sound Advice and Helpful Commentary to See You Through Your PhD*, 2nd edn. Oxford: Cromwell Press.

A useful guide to developing research proposals:

Punch, K.F. (2016) *Developing Effective Research Proposals*, 3rd edn. Thousand Oaks, CA: Sage.

A comprehensive overview of skills required to conduct management research:

Thomas, A. (2004) *Research Skills for Management Studies*. New York: Routledge.

Check your understanding online

Visit the website **https://edge.sagepub.com/easterbysmith6e** for useful resources that will help reinforce what you've read in this chapter:

Take an interactive quiz to test your understanding of the key topics

Review suggested answers to Exercises 1.1 to 1.3 above

Use interactive flashcards to check your knowledge of essential concepts

Learning objectives

To appreciate what a literature review in management and business research entails, and why it is necessary.

To learn the practical skills needed to search, identify and record relevant literature.

To understand how to evaluate critically different sources of information, and know how to write literature reviews.

REVIEWING THE LITERATURE

2

Chapter contents

Introduction

This chapter considers how students at different levels can discover what is already known within a particular field, and identify gaps in the literature, for their own study. Whether it is for undergraduate dissertations, Masters' or doctoral level, a literature review is an essential part of any study. The main differences between levels of study are predominantly the time constraints in place, and the breadth and depth of the literature review required.

The literature review should provide students with a basic understanding of how the topic has developed over time and what remains to be investigated. Anyone starting a research project should be aware of the existing theories and research in their field. A good literature review not only deals with the traditional sources such as books and journal articles, but may also include knowledge gained from experts such as managers, consultants and official bodies. It is important for (management and business) researchers to be in touch with a range of perspectives and sources, whether these are held by the organization or in the public domain. Search engines and bibliographic databases make it easy to identify relevant books and articles, but there are also a range of other electronic resources, such as topic-related websites, podcasts and news items. The first part of this chapter defines what a literature review is and details its purposes. It then gives an overview of the literature review process and of different sources of information. The second part outlines how to prepare a literature review, beginning with a section on how to identify relevant keywords, followed by sections on undertaking bibliographical searches, and accessing and recording relevant material. The third part explains how to classify, read and evaluate literature throughout the review process. This leads to the fourth part, which discusses how to align a literature review with the context and approach of a given study. The chapter concludes with some final reflections on the role of the literature review in qualitative and quantitative research.

search engine
a program that will find text relating to the keyword(s) entered

What is a literature review and what are its main purposes?

A literature review is an analytical summary of an existing body of research in the light of a particular research issue. In a literature review, researchers describe, evaluate and clarify what is already known about a subject area. There are different types of literature reviews. Stand-alone reviews are published as individual review articles, and provide an overview and synthesis of a particular research topic or field of study. More often, however, literature reviews are a part of a wider research output such as research proposals, reports, papers, dissertations or monographs.

Given that the ability to advance current understanding depends on prior knowledge of the subject under study, literature reviews are fundamental to any research endeavour. Literature reviews help researchers to *learn from previous research* but they also serve a number of additional purposes. A well-written literature review *provides a context* for a research project and helps to *refine its topic*. It can help highlight flaws in previous research and outline gaps in the knowledge about a certain topic. In this way, a literature review indicates *what a research project is adding* to the understanding of a field. It justifies why the research is being undertaken and ensures that the research undertaken *fits in* with the existing wider research within the subject area.

The literature review in the research process

It is important to note that when researchers talk about their literature reviews, they often mean the process of reviewing the literature as much as the selection of literature they work with, and the actual output of this process (i.e. the literature review as a specific type of text). Most literature reviews are continued throughout all stages of the research process. When planning a research project, researchers prepare literature reviews to explore a subject area and to develop ideas about how they can conduct research in this area. By reviewing the literature around their research topic, they improve their understanding of the key issues, concepts, theories and methodologies that define their field of study. They identify leading scholars and research organizations, and develop a sense of how past and ongoing debates have shaped the development of their fields. Once a gap has been identified in the area of knowledge that they wish to research, researchers continue to work on their literature reviews as they re-evaluate their position in ongoing debates, revise their research questions, and figure out how to frame their research. As their research progresses, they expand the catalogue of keywords they use for their literature searches, check for new research findings, and venture into related fields. Most reviews require further modifications as the research progresses. This is due in part to empirical findings that might lead the research in a new direction, or the emergence of new findings that have to be taken into account in order to be as up to date as possible. Finally, in the process of writing up a report, thesis or dissertation, most literature reviews have to be revised in the context of the research findings and their contribution to the subject area. The completed review provides the context and justifies the research for which it has been prepared.

Sources of information

What is considered to be an appropriate source for a literature review depends on the aim and topic of the review, and also on the traditions of the discipline. In most academic disciplines, *peer-reviewed journal articles* are considered to be the most important source of information because it is through the peer-review process that the quality and relevance of the research can be judged. *Academic books* and *reference works* are another important source of established knowledge; *working papers* and *theses* provide access to the latest research, as do some *academic websites*, *research blogs* and *podcasts*. Many supervisors advise their students to stick only to peer-reviewed academic literature. Some ask them to focus exclusively on articles published in journals included in the so-called 'ABS List'.

For more information on the ABS list, visit the CABS website, where you can register to download the list.

 ABS list

Published by the Association of Business Schools, the ABS list or 'Academic Journal Guide' ranks business and management journals based on citation scores and the judgements of leading scholars. In the most recent list, only 33 journals were awarded the status of 4* ('journal of distinction'). For example, in the field of management, the *Academy of Management Journal*, *Academy of Management Review* and *Administrative Science Quarterly* are all ranked 4*. Below that is a ranking of 4, achieved by 85 journals, which according to the guide still indicates the 'most original and best executed research'. Grades 3, 2 and 1 are defined as 'original and well executed research', 'original research of an acceptable standard', and 'recognised, but more modest standard' respectively. It is true that journals ranked 4* to 3 tend to publish leading research. Many of the top-tier journals have rejection rates of 90% and higher so the assumption is that the publication of an article in one of these journals is in itself an indication of distinction. However, we also agree with the editors of the Guide that 'exceptional scholarly work may be found in many places'. For example, newly established or specialized journals are often more open to novel approaches and innovative methods. The ABS list has been criticized in recent years for preventing rather than encouraging interdisciplinary research. This said, we encourage our students to read widely but also to ensure that their literature reviews cover the most prominent papers on their topic published in the top journals (3–4*).

Many topics require researchers to consider academic as well as non-academic sources; these sources are known as 'grey' literature. Examples of these are *publications and websites by governmental and non-governmental bodies*, including firms and media outlets. Professional associations and expert groups often run their own *websites*, *email lists*, *newsletters* and *online forums*; and they organize conferences and workshops that facilitate networking and the exchange of information. Last but not least, there is the *Internet*, which allows access to information on all sorts of topics.

A literature review can and should be based on a wide range of information, but it should also aim to give a truthful and balanced account of the research and knowledge that exist on a certain topic. It is evident that some sources of information are more appropriate and more reliable than others: a peer-reviewed article has been reviewed and accepted by several international experts in the field; and a book has been published by a publisher who considers it worthwhile, often after seeking the support of external reviewers. A blog or website, however, might reflect the ideas of just one person – perhaps even an individual with very little understanding of the topic. Data made available through governmental websites, for example, may be much more reliable than data posted by someone from a lobby group. This, of course, does not imply that state-sponsored websites are somehow value-free or neutral; they should still be considered critically.

In our information age, researchers should embrace the opportunities that arise from the Internet, while at the same time remaining cautious about the credibility and appropriateness of the information they access. Given the absence of quality controls, many researchers see the Internet as both a blessing and a curse (Lee, 2000; Fink, 2005). It appears to offer them immediate access to 'everything' – but ultimately can be a very time-consuming resource to work with, as it also requires them to assess the quality of each piece of information they wish to include in their review (Fink, 2005). Table 2.1 lists four areas that require thorough consideration before web-based information can be included in a literature review.

> **grey literature**
> literature that is not formally published in journals. As a consequence it is usually considered to be not widely accessible or available, e.g. reports or working papers; however, with the Internet, this is increasingly less the case

TABLE 2.1   Criteria for evaluating sources of information

1   *Purpose*: What is the purpose of this source? What are the motivations or interests that led to its creation?

2   *Authorship*: Who is responsible for the source? Are the authors/producers authoritative in this subject?

3   *Credibility and accuracy*: Why should this be credible information? Do the authors give enough information so that their claims and methods can be evaluated? Has this information been taken up or mentioned in peer-reviewed sources? If not, what might be the reason? Is the information it contains objective or biased? How accurate is the information?

4   *Timeliness*: When was the source created? When was it last updated?

Source: based on a similar set of more specific questions developed by Fink, 2005

Types of literature reviews

As can already be seen from these introductory paragraphs, conducting a literature review is a research activity in itself, requiring a wide range of research skills and analytical capabilities. Before moving on to the next sections, which detail what skills are needed to conduct a literature review, it is worth pausing to consider the different types of literature review:

A *traditional literature review* summarizes a body of literature and draws conclusions about the topic in question (Jesson et al., 2011). This review should aim to be 'systematic, explicit, comprehensive and reproducible' (Fink, 2005: 17). However, some reviewers adhere to stricter criteria than others. Traditional literature reviews are defined by what the reviewer considers to be the most interesting or most relevant sources. While they discuss a bounded area of research, traditional reviews might leave out debates or issues that the reviewer considers less relevant. For most traditional reviews, the criteria for the selection and evaluation of literature remain implicit; that is, they structure the review but are not openly stated.

In contrast, *systematic literature reviews* strive to 'comprehensively identify, appraise and synthesize *all* relevant studies on a given topic' (Petticrew and Roberts, 2006: 19, emphasis added). They require reviewers to provide explicit and rigorous criteria for identifying, including, evaluating and synthesizing their material. Typically, systematic reviews consider peer-reviewed academic articles only. Through searches of the main bibliographic databases, topic-related peer-reviewed articles are identified that correspond to the search criteria stated in the literature review. Each filtering decision is noted down in order to ensure that articles are not selected on the basis of personal preference. The selected articles are then evaluated against a previously defined set of criteria, using rigorous methods.

systematic review a means of synthesizing research on a topic or within a field in such a way that is both transparent and reproducible

Systematic reviews have become increasingly common, but they have their advantages and disadvantages (see Table 2.2 and Exercise 2.1 below; and see Example 2.2, in the last section of this chapter, for a description of a systematic review). Many academics value systematic reviews as the more objective and 'scientific' type of review, given that they are replicable and more transparent. However, if they cover a wider field, systematic reviews can be time-consuming. They also tend to favour journal articles over other sources such as book chapters or reports; and many reviewers rely heavily on the assessment of abstracts rather than full-text articles, which can lead to misconceptions and oversights. As noted by Jesson et al. (2011: 15), traditional reviews can provide 'insights that can be neglected or passed over in the steps towards inclusion and quality control that are required in the systematic review model'. The formalized structure of systematic reviews can make it difficult to justify innovative approaches or to start new discourses that break with the predominant understanding of a topic.

TABLE 2.2   Pros and cons of systematic reviews

Pros	Cons
• Involving collection from a broad range of sources that might cross over into other disciplinary areas related to management and business	• Limiting creativity and intuition
	• Overlooking important 'grey' literature, e.g. reports
• Aiding interdisciplinarity through highlighting cross-disciplinary themes	• Being restricted by the accessibility of sources
• Increasing transparency of the review	• Requiring keyword search strings to be identifiable
• Increasing replicability of the review	
• Being 'systematic' and so offering a sense of rigour	• Failing to reach older 'scanned' texts
• Aiding the process of synthesis through the increased scope possible	• Relying on databases that support 'keyword' search
	• Relying on the quality of the abstract (often limited to 100 words)

Source: Thorpe et al., 2005. Reproduced by permission of John Wiley and Sons, Inc.

However, a high-quality systematic review can make an important contribution to the understanding of its field. Although literature reviews remain a secondary methodology (i.e. they do not report any new research findings), they can synthesize a research topic or problem in a novel or particularly illuminating way.

Systemic
review

EXERCISE 2.1

Systematic reviews

Download and read the following article:

Kolk, A., Rivera-Santos, M. and Rufín, C. (2013) 'Reviewing a decade of research on the "Base/Bottom of the Pyramid" (BOP) concept', *Business & Society*, 53 (3): S. 338–77.

Examine how the review has been conducted.

1 **Group**: In pairs, write down a detailed list of all the stages of the review process. Pay attention to the various checks they used to ensure that they had done a thorough job.

2 **Group**: In groups, have a closer look at the coding procedure outlined in the paper. In your view, did they cover all important points? What sections are fairly generic (could be used for any systematic review) and which ones are more topic-specific?

3 **Individual**: Pick one article listed in the appendix and search for it. If you cannot get access to it, try another one. Once you have downloaded one of the articles reviewed for this paper, apply the coding framework used by the authors. Prepare a brief summary to share in class.

The review process

Conducting literature reviews requires, but also enhances, a broad range of academic skills. First, researchers need to develop appropriate skills in information-seeking, which allow them to identify and access relevant sources of information. Second, researchers enhance their critical appraisal skills by evaluating existing research in writing.

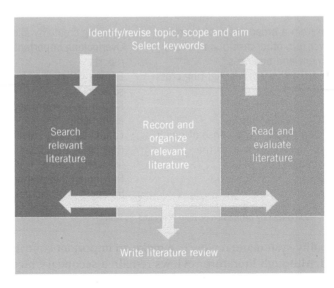

FIGURE 2.1   The review process

It can be useful to structure the review process into a number of general stages or steps involving different skills and techniques. Figure 2.1 gives an overview of the review process in three different stages. First, the topic, scope and aim of the literature review need to be established, so that keywords and search terms can be identified (top row). Second, literature needs to be found, recorded and evaluated – three tasks that require a transparent and systematic approach, consistent and orderly 'housekeeping', and critical thinking and analytic rigour (middle row). Third, the reviewed literature needs to be summarized and organized around different themes. Once these have been aligned with the wider research project, writing a literature review can be the easiest step of the entire process (bottom row). The arrows between the different tasks indicate that most literature reviews evolve not in a linear process but rather in several loops. For example, it might become necessary to revise the topic or research question throughout the review process and, as a result, to repeat and modify certain literature searches.

Choosing a topic

Research is about both a creative and a disciplined sense of curiosity. Coming up with interesting research ideas is the creative part. Tracy (2013) gives some useful advice on this first step in choosing a topic, suggesting that there are a number of ways for students to generate their research ideas. For example, ideas may stem from:

- personal life – such as family, work, political beliefs and travel
- current societal problems or organizational dilemmas – such as the cost of food waste, or issues relating to ethnicity and employment
- current events – such as societal needs or policy debates
- topics one has studied or read about and developed an interest in.

Having developed some research ideas, it is important to evaluate their relative merit. Is the topic one that is of relevance and interest to the audience the researcher wants to address (including their examiners)? Why would anyone agree that the proposed topic requires further research? It is at this stage when a more disciplined sense is required and the hard work begins. In order to understand the value of a given research idea, we need to examine it in the light of existing research on the same (or similar) topics. This requires us to engage with the literature. So whenever we start with a new line of research, we face a chicken and egg problem: in order to write a literature review one has to select a topic; but it is rather unlikely that one selects a good research topic without knowing the literature. In management and business research, students at the earlier stages of their dissertation projects are usually encouraged to identify a research or knowledge gap they wish to address. Research gaps can be defined in at least four ways:

- to take a well-understood problem within a particular discipline that has been explored in a particular way, and to investigate the same phenomenon using a different approach
- to identify contradictory results and try, through the research, to reconcile them or produce new findings
- to identify a novel social phenomenon that cannot be explained by existing research and theorizing
- to take well-understood methods from one area of the social sciences and use them (perhaps for the first time) in another.

The task of research students is then to show how their research serves to fill the gap and, in so doing, to offer explanations that are new and original, producing knowledge that extends understanding of the problem or the field. But how do we identify a research gap in the first place? A good way to start is to read literature that offers a summary of research in a given field. Published reviews of literature can be seen in specialist review journals such as *International Journal of Management Reviews, Academy of Management Review, Annual Review of Organizational Psychology and Organizational Behavior* and *Psychological Review.* These journals act as invaluable resources for those wishing to gain an overview of existing studies in a particular field – and hence are an important source of information when starting a new literature review. Another great starting point is current research debates – as expressed, for example, in the Point Counterpoint papers in the *Journal of Management Studies.*

It is important to be precise about the *topic,* the *scope* and the *aim of a literature review* from the beginning, as the review might otherwise cover too broad a field or not stay sufficiently focused. The topic of a review arises from the main theme or research question of a given research project. At the early stages of a review, the researcher may search for more research gaps. As a result, the focus and scope of the research topic and the literature review may shift. For example, if the selected topic is one that has already attracted a lot of research, it often makes sense to narrow it down further, in order to avoid becoming overwhelmed by too much information. If the topic is very narrow or innovative, it might be necessary to broaden it out in order to find enough related material.

However, in order to avoid getting lost in the literature (and all the interesting opportunities that present themselves while reading), it is essential to be clear about the more specific research topic. When reading and conducting literature searches, it can be useful to have a visual reminder of the current research topic and research question, which remains always in sight (such as a Post-it note with the main research question right next to the screen).

Preparing a literature review: finding and recording relevant literature

Once the topic is clear, there are numerous ways in which a literature search can be done – but it should always follow the aim of the research. It can be very helpful to start a literature review with a brief written research statement covering the following questions:

- What is the topic of my research?
- Why is this topic relevant, important or interesting?
- How does this project relate to past research in this field?
- What are the main concepts and theories that could be relevant?
- What is the aim of the literature review, and how does it relate to the aim of my research?
- What could be an appropriate working title for this review?

A written research statement marks the official starting point of the review process. While none of the responses has to be perfect, it is helpful to write these down in order to make research questions, expectations and knowledge gaps more explicit.

EXERCISE 2.2

Defining your topic

1   **Individual**: Decide on a working title for your literature review and write a short research statement that addresses the six questions listed above (about 500 to 1,000 words in total). The statement should help you to articulate your ideas and assumptions. It does not have to be perfect and should be considered work in progress.

2   **Interactive**: Give your research statement to one or two students in your group and ask them to comment on it. Do they understand the topic and intention of your research? What aspects do they find most/least interesting? Why?

Identifying keywords

Once the topic and aim of a literature review are decided, keywords are much easier to identify. This second step can be facilitated by some initial reading of scholarly publications on the topic, noting down important terms and concepts. It can also be helpful to consult a wider range of sources, such as the *Financial Times*, or the *World Investment Reports* (WIR), published annually by the United Nations Conference on Trade and Development (UNCTAD). Most articles carry keywords beneath the abstract that identify themes addressed in the study. These can be invaluable filters when looking to focus one's literature review. The most useful source, however, is usually the research statement, which already identifies a number of relevant concepts. By noting down such concepts and their relationships (e.g. when creating a mind-map or a Venn diagram of overlapping circles), researchers can further explore their ideas and identify additional keywords. Figure 2.2 gives an example of a simple Venn diagram for a literature review on the roles played by creativity and innovation in science and engineering.

As the Venn diagram becomes more detailed and includes more keywords, it might begin to look more like a daisy with several overlapping petals (Luker, 2008). In the process of revising the diagram, it is useful to start an accompanying list of keywords, taking into account synonyms and alternative terminologies, and variations in word endings. Library classification systems provide for alternative 'labels' to identify each category. Researchers should try to become aware of the most likely alternatives. An alternative term might be as straightforward as changing the word slightly; for example, when using 'organizational innovation' as keywords, it would also be useful to try 'organizational innovating'. Most databases allow the researcher to truncate when a term can have several endings; for example, 'innovat*' would search for 'innovation' and 'innovative' in some databases. Similarly, 'wildcards' are symbols that can be used to look for variant spellings; for example, in some databases, 'organi?ational' covers 'organizational' and 'organisational'. The symbols used for truncations and wildcards can vary between different databases, catalogues and search engines, so researchers are advised to consult the help pages before they start their searches.

A literature review often starts from a broad strategy, becoming more focused, with a narrow research scope. Conceptualizing a broad field can be difficult, and bringing together literature from a vast range of traditions and disciplines can be a gargantuan task. Mind-maps can be helpful for identifying linkages between different fields of study, and for establishing the scope and structure of a literature review. Figure 2.3 shows a mind-map created for the same systematic review of the roles played by creativity and innovation in science and engineering. When compared with the Venn diagram, this mind-map gives a clear indication of the amount of work required to develop such an advanced systematic review. It also shows the way in which literature reviews contribute to the understanding of how a certain research area has developed over time, and how current research trends and debates may shape a given topic.

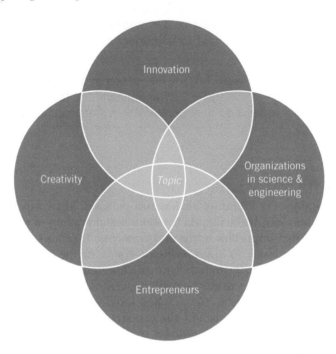

FIGURE 2.2   Venn diagram of keywords

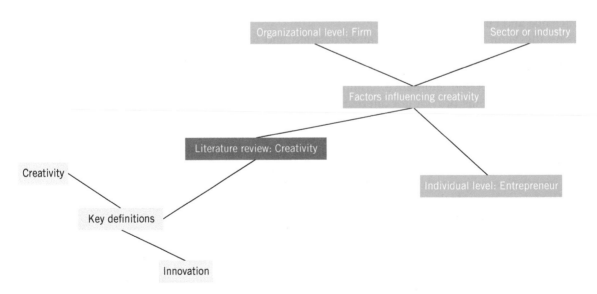

FIGURE 2.3   Mind-map of a literature review

EXERCISE 2.3

Mapping your topic

1 **Individual**: After re-reading your initial summary once or twice, draw a simple Venn diagram or mind-map for your own research project, adding all the items you think your study should cover. Think about how the different items relate to one another and what keywords could be used to describe them. Prepare a list of keywords, adding alternative expressions and synonyms. Decide what kinds of truncations or wildcards could be useful. For example, the term 'orga*' might turn out too many results but, combined with 'innovat*' and 'manag*', could form part of a useful search.

2 **Group**: Share your Venn diagram with two or three members of your group. Can you use it to explain your research project? What words do you use? Show them your initial list of keywords and ask them to revise this list with you. Do they have any useful suggestions?

Finding relevant literature

For hundreds of years, the most obvious place to begin a literature search was the library. Today, this seems to be an outdated approach, given the vast amount of information that can be accessed via the Internet. However, the information age leaves many researchers struggling with 'information overload'. A visit to the local university library can help to prevent or overcome such problems. After all, the library remains an important gateway to information – and these days not only to books and journals, but also to online resources. Librarians have an overview of the information that is available, and they know how to navigate the various systems by which it can be accessed. As noted by Luker (2008: 85), researchers could hardly afford to ignore their librarian in the past, but today such ignorance can be 'downright suicidal'. Most researchers benefit hugely from getting to know their library early in the research project. Many libraries offer guided tours, handouts and online courses – in addition to the usual support by librarians.

While browsing through stacks of books is still a great way to start a literature search, it is of course not the only way. When searching for literature, different search strategies and search tools (e.g. search engines or databases) will yield complementary results. According to Selvin and Stuart (1966), there are two main ways of tackling a literature search. First, there is 'trawling', which involves a wide sweep to see what information can be brought in to get an overview of a field, and then there is 'fishing', which involves a more targeted search for more specific information. Trawling and fishing should not be seen as opposites, more as different starting points, independent of the extent of the researcher's prior knowledge and focus. Before setting out on a trawl (i.e. sweeping up whatever information exists on a topic), researchers can save time by deciding and being selective in what they are after. When starting a literature search, researchers must be clear about *what* they look for (topic and type of information), *where* they look for it (sources), and *how* they look for it (search queries and search skills).

This means it is necessary for them to consider how the review will develop and benefit their studies and understanding. Systematic reviews can provide a more objective or comprehensive overview, and they can help to identify where gaps in the current research exist.

However, they may also unintentionally reduce researchers' ability to use their creativity for opening up new perspectives and fields of research. Whatever the motivations, the decision to conduct a certain type of review has to be taken at the first stage of the review process. This is because systematic reviews require explicit review protocols and clear criteria for accessing, retrieving and judging the quality and relevance of studies in the research area.

Searching literature in libraries

Most libraries classify books in subject themes according to one of the major published classification schemes. A library's online catalogue is an index used to search and locate all electronic and print material held in the library. There are two limitations to library catalogues. First, library catalogues tend to list publications such as books or journals, but they do not allow searching of their content (i.e. individual chapters or journal articles). In order to access this information, other databases and search engines have to be used; these will be introduced below. The second limitation arises from the speed at which research accumulates: today, it seems unlikely that any library, however large, will be able to meet all a researcher's needs from its own resources.

Once the stock of books available in the university library has been reviewed, appropriate catalogues should be consulted to see what else has been written. A comprehensive list of links to major libraries is usually available on most university websites. Very large libraries such as the British Library or the Library of Congress (USA) contain almost all publications in the English language, along with many foreign-language publications. In addition, there are national/international online catalogues such as Copac (a merged online catalogue of many major university research libraries in the UK and Ireland), Bibliothèque Nationale (France), Deutsche Nationalbibliothek (Germany) and Biblioteca Nacional (Spain). Specimens of more specific catalogues can be supplied by, for example, the Institute of Chartered Accountants (current accounting literature) and the Baker Library at Harvard Business School. Books, journal articles, maps, recordings and other resources can be ordered from other libraries through the inter-library loan system. This service, offered by most college and university libraries, usually takes a few weeks and is often accompanied by nominal fees.

EXERCISE 2.4

Getting to know your library

1 **Individual**: Look up the webpages of your library and browse through its online support pages. Can you answer the following questions?

- Are there any online courses or workshops that could help you to improve your skills?

- Who is the subject librarian responsible for your topic or discipline?

- On the website, what information can you find on literature searches in your field, such as a list of relevant databases?

- What kind of classification system does your library use?

- What kind of materials can you find using the library's online catalogue (e.g. books, journals, journal articles, videos, book chapters and research reports)? Is there any guidance on how to use the library's online catalogue?

- Is it possible to use truncations or wildcards? What are the relevant symbols?

2   **Individual**: A 'classmark' is a set of letters and numbers assigned to a library item, allowing the item to be shelved with other items on the same topic. Classmarks are used to locate individual items but they can also help to explore a topical area. With this in mind, conduct a search with your keywords using your library's catalogue. Go to the sections labelled with the classmarks you have identified as being relevant and browse through the books that have been placed there. Have you found anything useful? If not, ask your local librarian for help. Note down or save the references of all sources that appear particularly useful.

3   **Individual**: Consult encyclopedias, guides, handbooks and dictionaries available in the library under the classmarks for management and business, such as *The International Encyclopedia of Business and Management*. Look up your key concepts and note down definitions, additional keywords and key references that may help you with your literature search.

British Library: Business and management reports

4   **Individual**: Some libraries offer specialized web portals and guidance for researchers in management and business research. Have a look at the British Library business and management portal, the Walden University business and management research database and the Baker Library research guides online then answer the questions that follow:

- How can the resources offered on these web pages help you to develop your literature review?

- What resources might be particularly useful for your topic?

- Can you access all the resources? If not, are some of the resources available at your library?

Walden University: Business and management research: databases: articles & more

5   **Group discussion**: Discuss what you have learned from the websites listed above. What resources did you find more/less useful? Why?

Baker Library (Harvard Business School): Guides

Designing literature searches

It is one thing to know where to look for a certain type of literature; it is another to develop the skills to conduct an advanced literature search. The majority of online catalogues and literature databases have a basic search interface in which researchers can enter strings of keywords. Advanced search interfaces allow researchers to define where to search for certain keywords (e.g. in the title, author names, abstract or full text), and to use result limiters to restrict the output to a specified range of dates (e.g. 2012 to 2017) or publication type (e.g. electronic sources). Some search engines allow for the use of quotes to search for exact phrases such as 'organizational innovation'.

A good search query requires careful consideration. What are the most relevant terms, and how can they be combined to retrieve what the researcher is looking for and nothing else? In most search operations, Boolean operators should be used to carefully delineate the scope and depth of search results. For example, the operator 'AND' narrows down the scope and leads to more specific results (e.g. articles that contain both 'innovation AND creativity'); 'OR' can be used to cover similar concepts (e.g. 'organization OR firms'); and 'NOT' allows for the exclusion of irrelevant results (e.g. 'creativity NOT art'), but can also create a filter, inadvertently removing relevant results. Figure 2.4 illustrates the use of Boolean operators and below is an example of a keyword search.

EXAMPLE 2.1

Keyword search

An example of too broad a keyword might be 'management' or 'innovation'; there will be literally hundreds of thousands of articles using this term, in many different disciplines, with different meanings and linked to different concepts. It may refer to different aspects of management or innovation. Too narrow a keyword might be 'crucial'; sometimes this can be achieved by choosing a verb rather than a noun, for example 'innovate' rather than 'innovation'. In the example below, we illustrate how the use of different keywords and combinations of them give different results. The title of this search example is: 'How is management of innovation and new technology dealt with in the corporate social responsibility literature?' The searches are limited to the years 1995 to 2010 in the database ABI (ProQuest). The numbers of hits returned are shown in Table 2.3 below.

TABLE 2.3   Search strings and numbers of hits

Search string	Number of hits
Manage* AND innovat* AND tech*	71,269
(Corporate responsibility OR environment) AND innovate*	41,904
(Corporate responsibility OR environment) AND innovate* AND tech*	23,051
Corporate responsibility AND tech*	691
Corporate responsibility AND innovate*	374
Corporate responsibility AND environment AND innovate*	140

A well-defined search can save hours of browsing. All searches should always be noted down in a *search record* for future reference (Jesson et al., 2011). This is not only considered to be 'good practice' and a requirement for conducting systematic reviews, it is also very useful as follow-up searches take less time and existing searches can be modified. See Table 2.4 for an example of a simple search record. Some reference-management software packages offer tailored solutions to save search records and tasks.

Search record template

The point behind systematic reviews is that each search and filtering decision is noted as completed, making it easy for others to see what has been done, and to judge the relevance and substantive nature of a given review. Articles that are returned are not seen to have been selected on the basis of personal preference.

TABLE 2.4 Example of a search record

Source	Date	Search/query	Output	Comments
Google Scholar	10/09/2017	Innov* AND creative* AND organi* OR entrepren* NOT art; since 2010	~ 17,000 results, examined 100	Revise query, try bibliographic database
PhD Seminar	11/09/2017	Recommendation: review by M.A. Runco	1 reference	Look up/assess review
Literature review: Shalley and Gilson, 2004	12/09/2017	Examined references	4 key references	Look up highlighted references; citation search

Source: based on Jesson et al., 2011

How to use Boolean operators

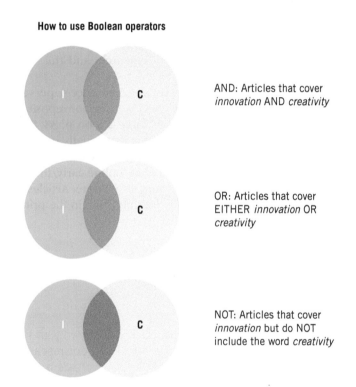

AND: Articles that cover *innovation* AND *creativity*

OR: Articles that cover EITHER *innovation* OR *creativity*

NOT: Articles that cover *innovation* but do NOT include the word *creativity*

FIGURE 2.4 Boolean operators

Finding articles and papers using literature databases

Today, most researchers conduct their literature searches using multiple databases. The selection of the 'right' databases depends on the topic and the type of review; for example, systematic reviews require databases of peer-reviewed articles. It is recognized that there are a limited number of searchable databases for book chapters and reports, though currently there are a number of national and university libraries working to increase the number of books available online. Research institutions usually subscribe to some but not all of the databases. With regard to journal articles, there are two types of scholarly databases. Bibliographic databases (e.g. Web of Science) simply list search results and often offer a broad range of content. Full-text databases, meanwhile, provide direct access to articles but often are more limited in scope (e.g. Business Source Premier).

Journal articles can often be accessed through several search paths, but not all sources provide access to full-text articles. Therefore, one might need to consult different databases or access the journal directly through the university library. Some articles will be available only via an inter-library loan; others can be purchased online, albeit often at a significant cost. Some databases allow researchers to save searches or to receive the results of a saved search on a regular basis (through a 'saved search alert'). Others allow for the setting up of subject-related or journal-related alerts. For example, Zetoc Alert is a service that automatically emails the tables of contents of journals and articles that match searches for authors' names or keywords from article titles.

Different databases produce complementary but also redundant results. It can be rather time-consuming to integrate several lists with results. This is one of the reasons why Google Scholar has become such a popular search option in the past decade. A quick search in Google Scholar can identify seminal texts across the academic disciplines. The main drawback of this is that it quickly widens the field of research, and this can work against the need for research focus.

Many researchers publish their most recent work in conference papers and working papers, which can be accessed online via their own university websites or repositories, such as that of the Social Science Research Network (SRRN) – see Table 2.5 on p. 38. Some of these papers are later published in peer-reviewed journals, a process that usually involves several rounds of revisions. Electronic resources have now been extended to include articles approved for publication in future editions, a service that is referred to as 'online early/first' or 'published ahead of print'; this service is usually available via the journal's website. Articles published online in this way are identical to those that will eventually be published in the printed journal.

Zetoc

Zetoc a current awareness service for higher education institutions in the UK; the service gives access to the British Library's table of contents database and a Zetoc alert can provide users with information on the contents of new journals as soon as they are issued

EXERCISE 2.5

Performing literature searches

1   **Individual**: Make it a habit to think about and write down your literature searches before you open a search engine. Have a look at your research statement, list of keywords, and Venn diagram or mind-map, and create a search record. What combinations of keywords could be found in the texts you want to read? What keywords could be too wide or ambivalent in their meaning? Construct a minimum of five searches using Boolean operators (AND, OR, NOT), limiters (such as date of publication), truncations (*) and/or wildcards (?). Next to the searches, note down the reasoning behind the search. What do you hope to find with this combination of keywords?

2   **Individual**: Test your searches on one specialized database (such as Web of Science, ABI ProQuest, Business Source Premier or JSTOR), on SRRN and on Google Scholar. Have you found what you expected? What were the problems? How do the results of the scholarly database compare with those listed by SRRN and Google Scholar?

3 **Individual**: Which journal is the most prominent journal in your field? Find the website of the journal and look through the table of contents of the past two volumes/years. Note down the details of three articles you found most interesting. Check whether the journal publishes ahead of print/online first. Set up a 'table of contents' (TOC) alert using the journal's website or Zetoc.

4 **Group discussion**: Decide one common research question/topic and let each member use different software to collect the literature. Compare and analyse the outcome. If the outcome differs, discuss why it differs and how you used different search terms.

5 **Group**: Give a short presentation on your chosen journal to a group of peers, covering:

   • name, publisher, editor and history of the journal

   • subject areas covered by this journal

   • two to three topics or debates that were particularly prominent in this journal in the past two years

   • why this journal is an important resource for your research.

6 **Group**: In pairs, discuss the advantages and disadvantages of using systematic searches compared to a more personally directed approach to the identification of appropriate sources.

Snowballing and tracing citations

When searching for a wider body of literature, most researchers deploy multiple search strategies. They search online databases and library catalogues, but they also consult review articles and trace citations listed in relevant publications. Just as Hansel and Gretel followed breadcrumbs, they can reconstruct the development of an academic discourse or entire field by tracing citations back in time (Luker, 2008). They can identify the key scholars of their fields and, by looking up their CVs and lists of publications, learn more about past and current debates around their topic of interest. The objective is to find a number of key studies; exactly how many will depend on the focus and scope of the review.

Some bibliographic databases also allow access to the details of all publications that have subsequently referred to a given journal article. This is the only indexing method that enables a researcher to search forwards (rather than backwards) in the literature. Citation searching is available within many databases including Web of Science, ScienceDirect and Google Scholar. Citation searches can be complemented by 'citation alerts' that send out emails whenever a new publication comes out that cites a particular piece.

Citation searches in both directions are a productive technique for identifying the seminal works of a given research area, particularly those that offer an overview of the approaches to an extant literature upon a particular topic. For example, Easterby-Smith (1997) has published a review of organizational learning from the perspective of six different disciplines. A systematic review of knowledge in small and medium enterprises (SMEs) can be seen in Thorpe et al. (2005). Both reviews could be used as starting points for researchers investigating these particular areas.

Another way of getting started is to begin with studies written on the topic over the years. Some journals give a systematic précis of the articles published in issues of that year. For example, the *Journal of Marketing* includes several pages covering all types of significant articles and publications on all aspects of marketing (e.g. distribution, publicity, sales and strategy) for that volume.

One of the problems with comprehensive reviews is that they often encourage the use of secondary sources at the expense of primary sources. Some academics have made cutting remarks about researchers who are happy to quote material that they have not actually read (instead assimilating concepts and ideas from the original articles). One must be clear and point it out if the material is a quotation from a secondary source; it is advisable to rely on primary sources whenever possible.

EXERCISE 2.6

Using citation searches and alerts

1   **Individual**: Pick an article that appears to be particularly useful for your review. Go through the reference section of this article and look up five references that could be relevant to your literature review. Note them down in a search record. Assess titles, keywords and abstracts (if available). Then, have a look at the reference sections of at least three papers. Can you identify citations that appear in more than one paper? Which citations seem to connect these papers and why are they important?

2   **Individual**: What is the most relevant journal article you have found so far? Set up a citation alert for this article on Google Scholar.

3   **Individual**: Go to the homepage of Zetoc (see online resources included above). You should be able to log in by selecting your research institution and using your institutional username and password. If you have problems, your librarian should be able to help you. Once logged in, follow the instructions on the site. More detailed information about setting up a Zetoc alert can be found at http://zetoc.mimas.ac.uk/alertguide.html.

4   **Individual**: Identify a key scholar in your field and Google their profile. Can you access their full list of publications or CV? Evaluate the list and see if they have published more relevant articles or books on your topic.

Alternative sources and networking

When starting a new research project, it is also an excellent strategy to join subject-specific research communities. This can be a very fruitful way of getting to know like-minded colleagues who are working on a similar topic all over the world. The British Academy of Management (BAM) and USA-based Academy of Management (AoM) both have special interest groups or divisions; these cover a range of disciplines and cross-disciplinary topics, hold regular seminars and workshops, and are very welcoming to new researchers. Many useful leads and references can come from participating in email discussion groups. Contacts for such groups are often found at conferences or similar academic associations. For doctoral candidates, this kind of networking is perhaps even more important than for those simply engaged on an individual research topic. Doctoral streams and colloquia are organized at most of the big international conferences; for example, those of BAM, the European Group for Organizational Studies (EGOS), AoM, the European Academy of Management (EURAM), the European Doctoral Education Network (EDEN) and the European Institute for Advanced Studies in Management (EIASM). All these groups enable researchers to submit their current research for discussion and debate.

The Economic and Social Research Council's *Society Now* magazine brings the latest and most topical social science research to key opinion formers in business, government and the voluntary sector. Other possible sources of information include the registers of current research published by several leading business schools.

Society Now

Social networking sites such as ResearchGate LinkedIn and Twitter offer a newer means to share research ideas and literature review tips in real time. People who are reading an interesting article or book can update their status to share this article or to have an online discussion about the content or concepts.

EXERCISE 2.7

Finding your research community

Group discussion: Discuss in small groups of three to six students what research groups and professional organizations could be relevant for your research. Conduct a search online and identify at least one academic and one non-academic institution for each member of the group. Sign up to their research newsletters or email lists if possible.

Dissertations and theses

For those undertaking research, it is often important to know what theses have already been completed, if only to identify the individuals with whom to make contact. In Britain, many theses are available through EThOS (Electronic Theses Online Service), a service provided by the British Library. At the European level, DART-Europe is a useful portal for finding electronic theses and dissertations. The Networked Digital Library of Theses and Dissertations (NDLTD) attempts to build a wider international database. The commercial service ProQuest Dissertations and Theses claims to be the world's most comprehensive international collection. It can take quite a while to look through these different databases. However, it is an important task since it is helping to ensure that there is no duplication of research. As the cost (in time) of duplication of research is high, searches of this kind can be a very worthwhile exercise – even if no similar theses are found in the end.

Table 2.5 gives an overview of the advantages and disadvantages of using the different sources of information presented above. Figure 2.5 illustrates the different pathways of a systematic search for literature.

Recording and organizing selected literature

It can take some time to develop the skills necessary for searching academic literature in a focused and efficient way, but for many researchers it takes even longer to adopt a consistent system of recording the results of searches. Good housekeeping and consistency in record-keeping in the early stages of the review process can save a lot of

TABLE 2.5 Overview of sources

Source	Description	Advantages (+) and disadvantages (−)	More information
Library	Libraries collect and organize information, and provide access to printed and digital material; the literature available varies, depending on the kind of library and the main topic areas it covers	+ Gateway to library resources but also to other libraries (inter-library loans) and bibliographic databases + Information available that is difficult to access elsewhere (in particular, printed material) + Access to selected electronic resources and bibliographic databases + Assistance available − Visits can be time-consuming − Hardcopies rarely cover the latest research in the field	Most libraries have online catalogues and webpages with further information on literature searches Look out for dedicated sections for management and business research: www.bl.uk/collection-guides/business-and-management-studies Some libraries have created merged catalogues such as www.worldcat.org and http://copac.ac.uk
Google Scholar	Freely accessible search engine that searches full text, and covers most books and online journals of the largest academic publishers, along with working papers and other types of scholarly texts	+ Quick and easily accessible + Easy to get an overview − Tends to broaden the scope of the review − Relative coverage varies by discipline and topic − Does not contain an easy method to sort results	There are special manuals available with tips on how to use Google Scholar, e.g. www.otago.ac.nz/library/pdf/Google_Scholar_Tips.pdf
Scholarly databases such as Web of Science, ZETOC, ABI (ProQuest), Business Source Premier and JSTOR	Databases contain journal articles (in the case of Web of Science, Business Source Premier and JSTOR), business news (e.g. Nexis) and reports on market and business research, industries and company profiles	+ Mostly high-quality, peer-reviewed articles + Usually easy to use; lists of results can be saved and exported − Duplicates when using several different services − Fee-based online research service (access via libraries) − Embargo on the current issues of some journals − May not include earlier print issues (with the exception of JSTOR)	There are different databases and subscription services available; some academic publishers have also developed useful search interfaces For further information, contact the librarian. An annotated list of relevant databases can be found here: https://library.leeds.ac.uk/databases_explained/162/business and www.library.hbs.edu/Find/Databases?limit=&offset=&sort=&query=&spellcheck=&search_within=

Source	Description	Advantages (+) and disadvantages (−)	More information
SRRN	Website aiming at the rapid dissemination of research across the social sciences, featuring specialized research networks	+ The latest research + Circulates papers at an early stage, permitting authors to incorporate comments + Over 360,000 authors − Mixed quality	See www.ssrn.com/en
Literature reviews	Existing reviews around the subject area give an overview of what is already known	+ Good general overview and starting point + Identify seminal studies − Secondary literature often based on abstracts and summaries − Widen the field of research − Lack depth	For literature reviews in management and business research, search main journals such as *Journal of Management Research* (review issues), *Academy of Management Review*, *International Journal of Management Reviews* and *Journal of Marketing*
Special interest groups and academic networks	Associations and professional organizations aiming at the professional development of their members and the advancement of management and business research	+ Insights into ongoing research + Email lists and conferences + Internal journals and working paper series − Mixed quality of outputs − Usually membership fees	See American, British and European academies of management: http://aom.org www.bam.ac.uk www.euram-online.org Or see EGOS: www.egosnet.org
Theses and dissertations	Can give important insights into recent research and research trends	+ Detailed accounts of recent research + Can help to anticipate new developments (as most PhD students publish after completing their PhD) − Theses and dissertations can be tedious to find and access	See http://ethos.bl.uk/Home.do http://search.proquest.com/pqdtft www.dart-europe.eu/basic-search.php www.ndltd.org

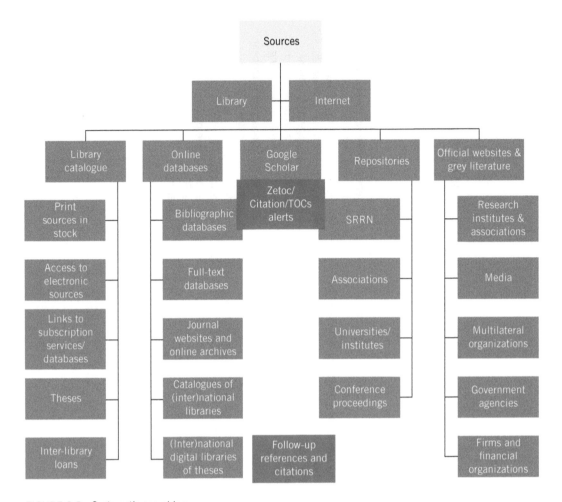

FIGURE 2.5   Systematic searching

time down the line, when patchy notes require endless repeat searches. Once books have been read and returned to the library shelves, it is extremely difficult and very time-consuming to find references unless the researcher has developed some kind of systematic cataloguing system.

We recommend devising a system of storing results – either an electronic database or something much simpler, such as hand-written record cards in subject and alphabetical order. For up to a certain number of references, this can be a useful strategy. Reviews based on more than 50 references – or for a project that is likely to lead to follow-up projects – make this strategy less viable in the long term. In this case we would recommend the use of reference-management software or 'reference organizers', which allow for fast and easy processing of large amounts of bibliographic data.

Universities and colleges often subscribe to specific packages that help students keep track of their references. Researchers and students can create their own personal databases or libraries into which they can import references from a bibliographic database or Google Scholar. In addition, many packages enable users to insert citations into documents when writing reviews or other academic texts, while at the same time creating a list of references in whatever style required (see, for example, Figure 2.6). More elaborate packages (such as Citavi; see Figure 2.7 for an example) facilitate knowledge management more generally; they feature

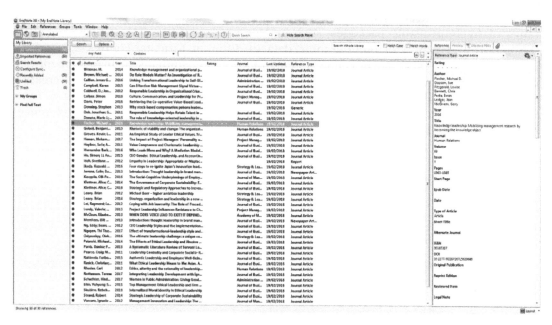

FIGURE 2.6   EndNote reference list. Reproduced by permission of Clarivate Analytics

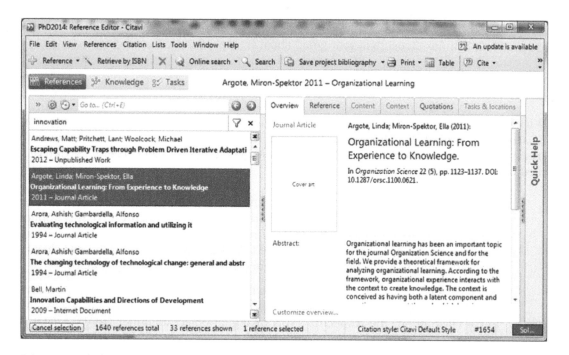

FIGURE 2.7   Main interface of Citavi. © Swiss Academic Software, reproduced by permission.

different types of indexing and coding systems that can be linked to individual quotations, comments and ideas. In this way, they turn what used to be seen as 'virtual filing cabinets' into knowledge-management tools, assisting analysis.

Most universities acquire licences to a number of reference-management packages such as EndNote, RefWorks, ProCite and Reference Manager, but there are also a wide range of freely available packages, such as Mendeley or Zotero. Most packages allow the import and export of bibliographic data in different formats. Figures 2.6 and 2.7 illustrate the reference-management systems of two PhD students in management and business. However, researchers are advised to compare packages before they create a digital library for their own research. There are multiple reviews and comparative overviews available on the Internet that can help with the selection process (see references listed in Exercise 2.8 below).

EXERCISE 2.8

Choosing reference-management software

Wikipedia comparison

UCSF Guide

1   **Individual or group**: Go online and access these two lists of reference organizers:

 - Comparison of reference-management software (Wikipedia)

 - EndNote, RefWorks and other reference managers (UCSF Library)

2   **Individual or group**: Then search the name of the package you are most interested in on YouTube. See if you can find a video review and tutorial. Look at the website for further information. Review the package for the group.

3   **Group**: Ask students in your group about their experiences with reference organizers. Establish a list of criteria for choosing a suitable reference organizer.

Whatever system or software is used, there is a need to build bibliographies from the start of a research project. It is important that users make it a habit to store all references to research literature in their 'library' as soon as they come across them. There are different methods of doing this:

 - Most references can be transferred directly from bibliographic databases just by clicking on 'download reference' or 'export reference' (see Figure 2.8); this applies to individual references as well as lists of references. References can also be downloaded from Google Scholar (as illustrated in Figure 2.9) and from the websites of most academic journals (as shown in Figure 2.10).

 - Some packages are connected to public databases, which can make it easy to download the bibliographic information for books and journal articles just by typing in (or clicking on) the respective ISBN or digital object identifier (DOI). A DOI is a character string used as a unique identifier of an electronic document (see, for example, highlighted DOI number in Figure 2.10); hence, it allows for persistent citations in scholarly materials, such as journal articles and book chapters.

- Some references have to be registered manually, for example for older material not available online and for 'grey' literature.

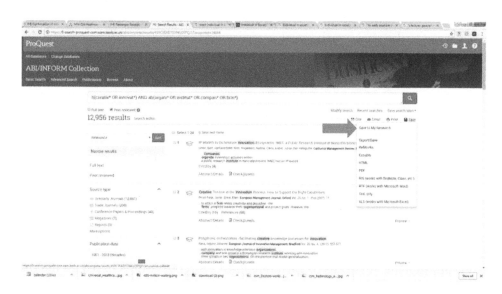

FIGURE 2.8   Importing references from ABI (ProQuest). The screenshots and their contents are published with permission of ProQuest LLC. Further reproduction is prohibited without permission.

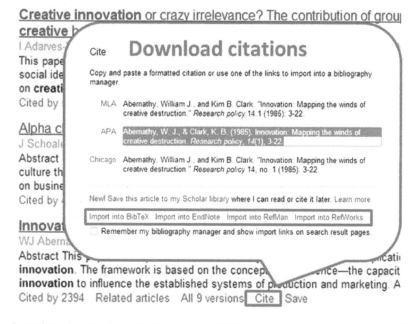

FIGURE 2.9   Importing references from Google Scholar. © 2015 Google Inc, used with permission. Google and the Google logo are registered trademarks of Google Inc.

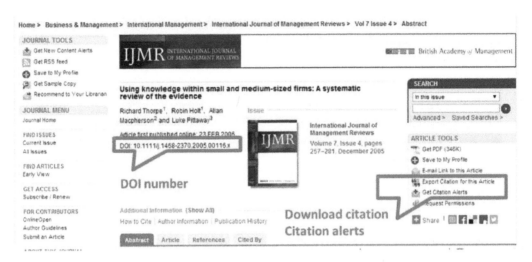

FIGURE 2.10   Importing references from a journal's website. Copyright © 1999–2018 John Wiley & Sons, Inc. All Rights Reserved.

It is essential to double-check downloaded references to make sure that they are complete, and to add appropriate keywords to each reference. Using keywords based on the research statement means that efficient access to the relevant literature is less likely to become a problem once the library has grown beyond a certain size. Keywords should reflect the topic and substantial content of the reference. Additional keywords might relate to individual themes or sections of the literature review.

Evaluating literature

After establishing a first overview of the research area, a more thorough examination of the literature is required. A literature review does not merely summarize an existing body of research; it also analyses and synthesizes this body of literature with a view to a specific problem, issue or question. The process of searching and recording literature should therefore always be accompanied by 'a critical evaluation of the literature according to argument, logic and/or epistemological or ontological traditions of the review subject' (Petticrew and Roberts, 2006: 19). The critical reflection of the literature should start as early as possible, as this helps to identify weaknesses in published research and to pinpoint research gaps.

The art of reading and analysing scholarly text is perhaps one of the key skills of a researcher – a skill that is usually acquired over the course of years, if not decades. Not all relevant aspects of this art can be covered in this section. More elaborate and in-depth guidance on how to critically evaluate literature for a literature review can be found in Hart (2018).

Reading techniques

Many students and newer researchers feel overwhelmed by the amount of literature they are expected to read – which is often beyond what they can manage. This can lead to two problems. Some students read less and less; others develop a rather passive approach (Jesson et al., 2011), reading and memorizing material for exams but failing to question this. However, *reflection and critical analysis are essential* when it comes to reviewing literature.

The amount of literature to read for a decent review can be difficult to reconcile with the time available for its production. For many, the prospect of reading dozens – if not hundreds – of articles and books is not particularly tempting. Against this background, it is essential to develop *different reading techniques* and to learn when to use them. Most important, however, is never to forget that *reviewing is reading with a purpose*, a purpose that arises from the topic and questions of the reviewer – and not the authors of the reviewed literature.

Selection of a piece of literature is usually based on limited bibliographic information about the author, title, keywords and/or context of publication (e.g. edited volume or special issue). Hence, the first evaluative step is to review whether the initial selection is justified. Does a particular book, article, report or newspaper clipping really merit further examination? For this first assessment, it is usually sufficient just to skim through the text, noting its structure and topic.

Systematic reviews require transparent and consistent criteria for judging which studies should be included. With some studies, there may be wholly inadequate abstracts and this may mean that the introduction and/or conclusions of the article need to be examined; this is sometimes referred to as 'examining in detail'. The chosen studies in the literature review need to be discussed and contrasted to justify the use of each, based on explicit criteria.

After the initial decision to include the material, it should be established which parts of the text could be useful for the review. A quick read through the abstract, table of contents, introduction and conclusion usually allows the reader to identify relevant sections that should be perused in more detail. Often, it is not necessary to read the entire book or report, as just a couple of sections address the topic under review.

These sections, however, should be read more carefully. By circling important concepts and marking definitions, claims, arguments and conclusions as such, the reader starts delving into the text. At this stage, it is important to identify the main argument of the text and the authors' position, which becomes visible in their methodologies, theories and questions. If, after this first read, the resource still appears to be useful – that is, topical and non-redundant – a summary record should be created.

Summary records

A summary record allows the reviewer to identify and record the contribution of a piece of literature to the topic under review. Summary records make it easier for the reviewer to compare, analyse and synthesize different studies without losing themselves in the details of each one. They also make it easier to track what has been read over months and years, so that the acquired knowledge can be sourced and reassessed long after the source has been returned to the library. Table 2.6 presents a simple template for a summary record that can be kept either on paper or as a digital spreadsheet. Some reference organizers also include special tools for creating summary records.

Summary record template

TABLE 2.6   Principal sections of a summary record

Author and year	Research question/ topic/ problem and main findings	Argument	Design: theory, concepts and method	Key references	Why relevant/ problematic	Comments

Source: adapted from Hart, 2018

The following questions can help to create a useful summary record:

- What is the main topic of the study?
- What are the key findings?
- How is the research justified?
- Why is this important for my literature review?
- What is the main unit of analysis (individual, firm, etc.)?
- What is the analytical approach of the author(s)?
- How was the topic researched (methodology, data, sampling, etc.)?
- What main concepts and theories were used?
- What is the scope of the study?
- What are the strengths and limitations of this research?
- How did this piece impact on subsequent research (citations, responses, etc.)?

Critical assessment

A summary record forces the reader to determine the main message or key contribution of a text. It includes a summary of the main argument, and identifies important features of the theoretical framework and research design (if appropriate). In the first few columns, it invites the reviewer to assess a piece of literature in its own right; this assessment may be supportive or critical. The last columns then draw the attention of the reviewer away from the recorded piece of literature to the literature review. Here, the assessment of the reviewed literature follows the criteria and (emerging) themes of the review. Both steps require critical assessment: an evaluation of strengths and weaknesses, and of appropriateness and interest.

Key sources often merit a deeper analysis of the ways in which they construct an argument. Arguments involve a claim (a statement such as 'heterogeneous teams are more creative'), followed by some evidence to support or refute the claim (e.g. a comparative case study of work teams in the film industry). A critical assessment enquires how the claim and backing are related, and whether this relationship is sufficiently accurate and appropriate.

It is important to note that there are different types of claims. *Claims of fact* – such as 'heterogeneous teams are more creative' – require appropriate backing in order to be accepted; this backing can be based on facts but also on inferences, illustrations, scenarios and analogies (Hart, 2018). Many authors also make *claims of value*, such as 'the more profitable a business is, the better it can serve its customers and community'. While this judgement is widely shared, it remains a judgement in the sense that a business could also be better because it makes an important social contribution to the life of its employees. Claims of value can also relate to *claims of policy* (e.g. 'free childcare has to be expanded in order to achieve gender equality in the workplace'). Some claims arise from the use of certain *concepts and interpretations*; for example, claims regarding tax avoidance and tax fraud could arise from the same case. Finally, there are claims that ultimately rest on *authority* (e.g. 'because a Nobel laureate said it, it is true' or 'because this fact was published in a peer-reviewed article, it is true'). The first challenge for the reviewer lies in identifying what kinds of claims are used, on what assumptions these claims are based, and whether claims and assumptions can be verified. The second challenge arises from the need to then assess the implications of claims, arguments and assumptions for the topic under review.

Finally, it is also important to be able to adopt a critical stance towards the authors' claims. This does not mean being negative or dismissive. It is rather about developing an attitude of scepticism and open-mindedness that helps you to scrutinise arguments in a constructive way. Common questions that can put you in the right mindset are:

- Do I find what I read convincing? Why?

- Is an alternative argument or evidence being presented?

- What evidence do I have for agreeing or disagreeing with the author?

Argumentation analysis

Another technique for evaluating the literature is argumentation analysis. One well-known method of argumentation analysis was set out by Stephen Toulmin (1979) who broke up arguments into several different elements. We simplify his model of argumentation somewhat by focusing on three key elements: claim, evidence and warrant. A *claim* is an arguable statement of belief or truth. For example, the following statement is a claim: 'firms do not do enough to address gender inequality in the workplace'. *Evidence* is then provided to support the claim, usually in the form of *data*. For example, the author may add that 'according to a recent survey, only 34% of Americans say that their current workplace puts a high priority on having women in leadership positions'. The *warrant* is then the expectation or principle that connects the evidence to the claim. In our example, the warrant rests on the assumption that the survey data reported above are of relevance to the claim. (i.e. that the responses recorded in this survey show that firms are failing to address gender inequality in the workplace). Arguably, there may or may not be better sources of evidence for this claim. What is important here is to examine whether or not the presented evidence and warrant are appropriate. Figure 2.11 below provides a simple illustration of the framework. It shows how a claim cannot be supported by evidence if the warrant is missing or inappropriate. Dissecting arguments into claims, evidence and warrants can be a very useful strategy for critical assessment.

FIGURE 2.11   Simple argument analysis

Source: based on Toulmin, 1979

EXERCISE 2.9

Evaluating two articles

1   **Individual exercise**: Select two journal articles that are particularly relevant to your research – one that has been published within the last two years, and another published before 1990. Answer the 14 questions in the two bullet lists above (pp. 46–7).

2   **Group**: In pairs, select three arguments that you dissect using argument analysis. What is the claim? What is the evidence? What is the warrant? How do the three relate to one another?

3   **Group**: In pairs, select, read and discuss a journal article. What are the key findings presented in this article? Underline all conclusions. What argument leads to these findings? By circling all inference indicators such as 'therefore', 'thus' and 'hence', you can identify arguments more easily. Highlight or mark reasons and evidence. Discuss what kinds of claims and evidence are used to support the argument. Are there any underlying assumptions that remain unmentioned? What are the strengths and weaknesses of this article?

Identifying problems and themes

Throughout the review processes, researchers examine and revise their own research questions as they learn more about the field they wish to study. While, on one hand, it is pivotal for a researcher not to forget about their own questions when reading the work of others, on the other hand their reading can and should influence the way their research evolves. The aim of the literature review can change as a result of critically reviewing more literature, which is a part of flexible research design.

By revising the research statement, and related Venn diagrams and mind-maps, this process becomes more transparent and so easier to control. Initial jottings that stated merely the links between some concepts evolve into more elaborate mind-maps identifying more complex webs or relationships between different concepts, discourses and fields of study. Figure 2.12 shows how the review process that followed Figures 2.2 and 2.3 led to the creation of a much more detailed mind-map that details the scope and structure of the review.

In this example, the identification of common themes and factors affecting creativity (leadership, hierarchy, creative environments and climates, and individual characteristics) gave a focus and structure to the entire review project. Common themes can be identified by comparing summary records or by indexing or coding different resources with keywords (a technique that will be introduced in more detail in Chapter 8). The analysis of the reviewed material may aim to establish different categories that facilitate comparison between different studies, such as types of methodology used, titles of journals in which they were published, types of organizations studied, and conclusions reached; each of these can be further classified, and so common themes discovered. The resultant categorization then forms the basis of the structure for writing up the literature review.

The creation of overview tables and evaluation sheets can aid the process of comparing the features of different studies and synthesizing their results. Table 2.7 shows an example of an evaluation sheet with four columns that was designed for the review process depicted

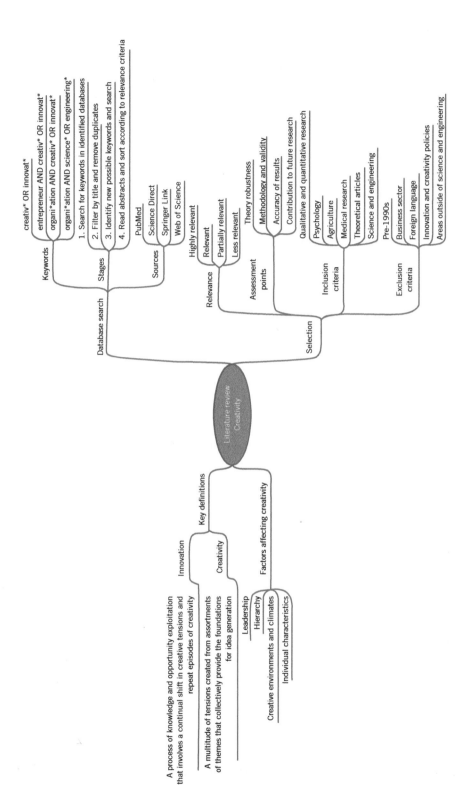

FIGURE 2.12 Elaborate mind-map of a literature review

in Figure 2.12. Please note how, in the case of this evaluation sheet, the headings are already well aligned with the focus of the review.

TABLE 2.7   Example of an evaluation sheet

Template

Author/ year	Definitions of creativity and innovation	Factors affecting creativity identified	Main findings

A review of the literature may be in a single disciplinary area or in several areas, depending on the nature of the research and its subject area. Studies concentrating on a narrow subject domain will require a critique of the literature in that specific area. However, multidisciplinary and practice-based studies might require a review that spans different literatures and synthesizes them.

Whether study focuses on one discipline or takes a more multidisciplinary approach, the literature review will need to be consistent with the study as a whole. This means that the study's epistemology, strategy, literature review, design, methods and empirical sections should all be linked and should demonstrate an internal coherence (see Chapter 4). At the same time, as we have indicated, a simple description of previous research is not sufficient. Rather, the review needs to incorporate interpretation and analysis, as well as being critical, so as to underpin the research questions identified.

RESEARCH IN ACTION

Reflections on a literature review journey

Georgia Stavraki

Georgia Stavraki is Teaching Fellow in Marketing at Surrey Business School, University of Surrey. She holds a PhD in Consumer Behaviour from the Aristotle University of Thessaloniki, Greece. Georgia's research interests include visual research methods for consumer behaviour topics.

What gave you the idea for your research on 'consumer's multiple identity positions and identity narrative creation'?

Researching a well-established topic with a rich literature can be rewarding but also a challenging task, as it can be difficult to come up with a novel perspective or question. Through my literature review, I 'discovered' the puzzling concept of multiple and dialogical selves. This topic fascinated me because it approaches a well-established concept (i.e. self-identity) from a fresh perspective.

How did you approach the literature review?

I started my literature review by studying seminal articles on the relationship between identity, identity narrative creation and consumption, which I identified by reading about this topic from consumer behaviour textbooks and from literature review journal articles. I then moved on to the most recent publications on this topic published in academic journals. Both approaches can be very helpful for learning about the milestones of the development of a theory or concept, identifying dominant approaches, defining key constructs and understanding the main theoretical assumptions behind the relevant theories. During this process, note-taking, the creation of mind-maps and figures depicting (inter) relationships, and the compilation of tables listing underlying assumptions, key findings and research purposes are all very helpful to better understand and organize the literature review data. Visualizations in particular can be very helpful for tracing and synthesizing ideas, arguments and approaches (for example, see Stavraki, 2016).

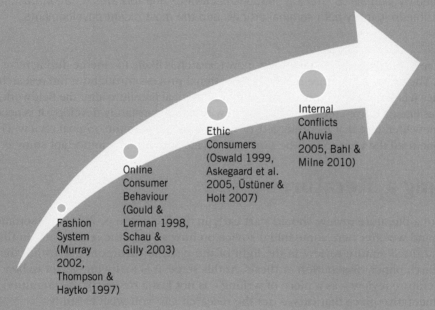

Internal
Conflicts
(Ahuvia
2005, Bahl &
Milne 2010)

Ethic
Consumers
(Oswald 1999,
Askegaard et al.
2005, Üstüner &
Holt 2007)

Online
Consumer
Behaviour
(Gould &
Lerman 1998,
Schau &
Gilly 2003)

Fashion
System
(Murray
2002,
Thompson &
Haytko 1997)

FIGURE 2.13   Ways of visualizing and organizing literature review data

The figure above constitutes an example of how I visualized and organized my literature review data for my PhD. Specifically, it shows a visual classification of consumer behaviour studies on consumers' multiple identity positions and the context of these studies (e.g. multiple identity positions in the context of fashion system or in the context of online consumer behaviour).

Was it difficult for you to determine the scope of the review? How did you go about that?

Often, we are exposed to so much research on 'our' topic that it can be difficult to narrow down. In my literature review journey, the first step was to expose myself to the wider literature

(Continued)

I considered relevant at the time and through this to create the research objective and questions. This strategy rarely translates into a linear process. For example, once I had determined my research questions, I could narrow down my review of literature on identity, identity narrative creation and consumption, but I also embarked on a much more interdisciplinary review of literature on the multiplicity of selves.

TOP TIP

In my experience, the 'traditional' online keyword search is not very efficient and it can also be confusing, in particular when researching a well-established topic. I prefer browsing through the reference lists of the most relevant journal articles published in high-quality journals. By tracing citations backwards and forwards (citation tracking), it is possible to identify both seminal articles and the most recent developments.

Because research projects can take years, new research is likely to emerge during most research projects. Therefore, a literature review is a continual process throughout the research project. Sometimes it is necessary to consult and review additional literature after the fieldwork, if a new aspect has emerged from the data. Because new research constantly develops, it is necessary to consult new literature that has emerged, or was not included in the original review. This needs to be done until the very end of the project, to make sure no new important study is omitted.

Writing a literature review

Writing of a literature review should start early in the life of the project or dissertation. With that in mind we offer here some initial advice on how to craft the review, and in Chapter 12 we revisit the literature review in the light of the need to incorporate it within the context of a research paper, dissertation or thesis. At this stage, it is really important to bear in mind that a literature review – as a piece of writing – is not just a review of the literature; it is also an argumentative piece that carves out the research gap you wish to study.

Zina
O'Leary

Watch our colleague Zina O'Leary explaining why this makes a literature review such a difficult text to write – and how one can overcome some of the challenges associated with writing a good literature review.

We suggest that the literature review be written in a discursive style that allows the writer freedom to develop their own arguments and flow, building progressively towards the focal research topic. They should not present just a series of summary records but should start with a rigorous explanation of what is being reviewed, followed by a critical evaluation of the existing knowledge, identifying how the research by the reviewer will relate to, complement and/or challenge this knowledge. When engaging with and critiquing previous studies, researchers need to strike a balance that simultaneously displays criticality with regard to the assumptions, theories and methods of previous studies, while at the same time acknowledging the insights and strengths of these studies.

Literature reviews vary significantly in length and depth, and in how they are presented, in articles, reports, books and theses. Some literature reviews are organized around a topic structure of different themes (like the one indicated in the mind-map above) or around a series of research questions or problems; others identify what is known about a phenomenon before exploring what remains unknown. Then, there are reviews that follow a method-oriented order, identifying different types of studies and how they have contributed to a certain field of knowledge.

Ultimately, it is not so relevant which organizational scheme is chosen – as long as it is followed consistently and *corresponds to the aim of the literature review*. For example, a *critical review* assesses the value of existing research in a critical light; a *theoretical review* evaluates and synthesizes a corpus of theory that has accumulated around a concept, theory or phenomenon; and a *scoping review* maps the territory for future research and develops a new research agenda (see Jesson et al., 2011, for more detail and examples).

Usually, it makes sense to develop a plan for the written review based on the research statement, diagrams and mind-maps, summary records and evaluation sheets. The plan should state the topic and purpose of the review, followed by an abstract summarizing the main points and conclusions of the review. It should then indicate what information should be covered in the introduction, main body and conclusion. Drafting an appropriate structure might take some time, but will enable the reviewer to build up a full draft step by step.

EXERCISE 2.10

Structuring a review

1   **Individual**: Select two review articles related to your research topic and evaluate their structure. What are the aims of the two articles? What organizational themes have been used to structure these articles? How do aims and structure correspond? Think about alternative ways in which the reviews could have been organized.

2   **Individual**: Draft out a plan for your own literature review.

3   **Individual**: Assess your review using the criteria listed in Table 2.8.

4   **Group**: Exchange and discuss your plan or draft with someone else in your group. Have you chosen a different/similar approach? Why?

TABLE 2.8   Checklist for literature reviews

☐   Topic, aim and scope are clearly identified
☐   Relevance or significance of the topic are indicated
☐   Context of the topic is established
☐   A clear understanding of the relevant terms and concepts is shown
☐   The review includes appropriate material and states why the material was selected
☐   Key resources and landmark studies are covered
☐   The review includes up-to-date material
☐   Existing research is summarized and critically evaluated
☐   The relationship between theory and empirical research is addressed; main methodologies are identified
☐   Existing research is synthesized in a way that opens up a new perspective
☐   The reviewer shows a reflexive approach when detailing the analysis undertaken for the review
☐   Appropriate quotations and examples are used to justify the main arguments
☐   The review meets expected standards of academic writing (references, spelling, etc.)

Lit review
checklist

Once the review is complete, the reviewer should assess the quality of the review, bearing in mind its more specific aim as well as the overall purpose of literature reviews. Table 2.8 lists some general criteria for evaluating literature reviews that can be used as a checklist for most traditional types of reviews.

Systematic reviews – with their standardized and protocol-driven methodology – have to meet additional criteria, as they aim at a comprehensive and exhaustive coverage of all relevant literature (see the list of further reading, at the end of the chapter, for recommended literature on systematic reviews). PRISMA (Preferred Reporting Items for Systematic Reviews and Meta-Analyses) is a set of standards that aims to help researchers improve the reporting of systematic reviews and meta-analyses. PRISMA was developed for systematic reviews of health-care interventions, but its checklist can also be applied to other disciplines and fields of research, such as management and business research.

PRISMA
checklist

Literature reviews involve a lot of referencing. While it can be tedious to work through a huge amount of bibliographic data, it is essential that references are included for all materials covered in a review, in order to avoid (unintended) plagiarism. Depending on the context of a literature review, the use of different reference styles might be required. Reference management software allows the selection of citation templates, so that all references appear in the right style and in the right place. We will be returning to such issues in Chapter 12 of the book when we consider the writing up of management and business research.

EXAMPLE 2.2

Key stages of the study by Thorpe et al. (2005)

The example presented below gives an overview of the review process of Thorpe et al. (2005), who conducted a systematic review of how SMEs create and use knowledge.

Background preparation

A review panel was first formed, consisting of the study's authors. The panel considered prospective sources of information and decided to use peer-reviewed journals – both practitioner and academic. Books, reports and book chapters were excluded on the grounds that they did not provide the opportunity for searchable bibliographical databases. The team then used terms relevant to the study as keywords to determine the most appropriate databases, given the peculiarities of the research. Thus, words such as 'know*' and 'learn*' were employed. The asterisk helps retrieve variations on, and words related to, the ones entered in the search. For example, searching for the word 'know*' encapsulates 'knowledge' and its derivatives, including 'knowing'. The returns were analysed and used as guides in narrowing down the type of databases. In this case, the databases with the highest number of returns were chosen: ABI (ProQuest), Business Source Premier and Ingenta (incorporating ScienceDirect). Up to this point, the process involved identifying relevant databases. The next step was to do detailed keyword searches.

Keyword search

Since the topic was knowledge and learning within SMEs, the team's principal keywords and search strings included 'know*', 'learn*', 'SME OR small firms' and 'entrepreneur*'.

When keywords were deemed to complement one another, the word 'AND' was used to enable the retrieval of a comprehensive result (e.g. 'know* AND learn*'). When keywords were seen to be substitutes, 'OR' was used instead (an example here is 'SMEs OR small firms'). Of course, 'know*' and 'learn*' may also be viewed as substitutes, and this was reflected in searches, with keyword searches alternating between the formats 'know* AND learn*' and 'learn* OR know*'.

Exporting results

The results were downloaded into a citation software program (ProCite). This gave each article's keywords and abstracts. In the first instance, the team sifted through the abstracts, determining each article's relevance to the subject of study. Those articles considered irrelevant were excluded, as were those from other fields (such as education and engineering). The key guiding idea at this stage was relevance, rather than the depth of the articles.

Further exclusions

With the articles put together, the next step was to interrogate them based on a number of criteria: theory robustness, implications for practice, coherence between data and arguments put forward, theory, relevance to SME knowledge (on account of findings, methods and theories) and contributions made. The result of this exercise was the identification of articles that dealt with SME knowledge while meeting the set criteria.

Themes and conceptualizations

The study portrayed a landscape of studies into SME knowledge, and produced broad themes as well as sub-themes about the subject. These findings were eventually published as an academic paper. (For further information and the published review article, see Thorpe et al., 2005.)

Conclusion

You should now have a clear grasp of what a literature review is – and what it is not; that is, it is not a mere list of sources, a series of summary records or an annotated bibliography. In this chapter, we have aimed to provide insights into where to find relevant literature and other sources for a research project, and what aspects are important when actually writing a literature review. The key points of this chapter are:

- A literature review is a continuous process, requiring writing and refocusing throughout the research project. It should be used as a tool to learn about existing research. It should inform the creative development of research and strengthen the arguments for such research, rather than blindly repeating what has been said before.

- As with research in general, a literature review is about crafting. Conducting a literature review is a research activity all in itself that requires a wide range of research skills and analytical capabilities. It takes time and effort to develop these skills.

- The quality of literature reviews also depends on good 'housekeeping'. It pays to learn the various techniques that enable researchers to search, select, record and evaluate literature in a systematic and efficient way.

We would like to close this chapter with a brief note on the role of literature reviews in different research designs. Literature reviews are defined by their aim, topic and scope. All three aspects are in turn influenced by the research strategy and the underlying philosophical assumptions of the reviewer. Depending on whether the researchers follow a more positivist (theory-testing) research strategy or a more constructionist (theory-generating) research strategy, a literature review plays a different role in their overall research process and is likely to reflect a different style of writing. Theory-testing studies derive their hypothesis from a review of existing research; they value a systematic approach that aims at representativeness. In contrast, theory-generating studies often treat the literature review as a more open exploration of their field of study: an exploration that can help to inform the development of more appropriate questions about the phenomenon under study. Here, the aim of the review is not to come to a generalizable synthesis of existing research but rather to critically assess what has been done, and to identify what has previously been left out of sight. The main differences between these approaches and their underlying philosophical assumptions will be discussed in the next chapter.

Further reading

We recommend in particular the following literature:

Easterby-Smith, M. (1997) 'Disciplines of organizational learning: contributions and critiques', *Human Relations*, 51 (9): 1085–116.

Fink, A. (2005) *Conducting Research Literature Reviews: From the Internet to Paper*. Thousand Oaks, CA: Sage.

Excellent introduction on how to plan a literature review, which also offers important guidance on how to read and critically evaluate research publications (with a focus on traditional literature reviews). The book includes an excellent chapter on argument analysis:

Hart, C. (2018) *Doing a Literature Review: Releasing the Social Science Research Imagination*. London: Sage.

An extremely helpful textbook that covers both traditional and systematic reviews:

Jesson, J., Matheson, L. and Lacey, F.M. (2011) *Doing Your Literature Review: Traditional and Systematic Techniques*. London: Sage.

The following book focuses more specifically on systematic reviews:

Petticrew, M. and Roberts, H. (2006) *Systematic Reviews in the Social Sciences: A Practical Guide*. Malden, MA: Blackwell.

Published reviews of literature can be seen in specialist review journals such as *International Journal of Management Reviews*, *Academy of Management Review*, *Annual Review of Organizational Psychology and Organizational Behavior* and *Psychological Review*. The following four articles were chosen to illustrate different kinds of literature reviews:

Easterby-Smith, M. (1997) 'Disciplines of organizational learning: contributions and critiques', *Human Relations*, 51 (9): 1085–116.

Shalley, C.E. and Gilson, L.L. (2004) 'What leaders need to know: a review of social and contextual factors that can foster or hinder creativity', *The Leadership Quarterly*, 15 (1): 33–53.

Thorpe, R., Holt, R., Macpherson, A. and Pittaway, L. (2005) 'Knowledge within small and medium-sized firms: a review of the evidence', *International Journal of Management Reviews*, 7 (4): 257–81.

Tranfield, D., Denyer, D. and Smart, P. (2003) 'Towards a methodology for developing evidence-informed management knowledge by means of systematic review', *British Journal of Management*, 14 (3): 207–22.

Check your understanding online

Visit the website **https://edge.sagepub.com/easterbysmith6e** for useful resources that will help reinforce what you've read in this chapter:

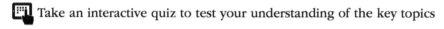 Take an interactive quiz to test your understanding of the key topics

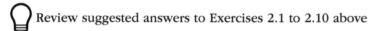 Review suggested answers to Exercises 2.1 to 2.10 above

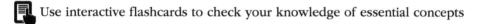 Use interactive flashcards to check your knowledge of essential concepts

Learning objectives

To understand the different philosophical assumptions 'hidden' beneath management research, and to appreciate the strengths and weaknesses of each.

To appreciate how different philosophical assumptions influence criteria for judging research quality.

To develop the ability to recognize and identify latent philosophical assumptions.

THE PHILOSOPHY OF MANAGEMENT AND BUSINESS RESEARCH

3

Chapter contents

Introduction

> It is a capital mistake to theorise before one has data. Insensibly one begins to collect facts to suit theories, rather than theories to suit facts. (Arthur Conan Doyle, 1891: 63)

The relationship between data and theory has been hotly debated by philosophers for many centuries. Failure to think through such philosophical issues can adversely affect the quality of management and business research. They are therefore of central concern in its design and evaluation. The aim of this chapter is to consider the main philosophical positions that underlie the designs of research – in other words, how do philosophical factors affect the delivery of satisfactory outcomes from the research activity?

There are at least four reasons why an understanding of philosophical issues is very useful. First, researchers have an obligation to understand the philosophical underpinnings of their research in order to have a clear sense of their reflexive role in research methods. After all, how do we think about what we know and what we study? For example, when we study leadership in organizations, to what extent is our research shaped by our own experiences with authority? How can we know whether an observed action amounts to leadership? We believe that researchers have to be able to answer these and similar questions if they are to make a creative contribution to their field.

Second, understanding the philosophical foundations of one's research is essential for clarifying research designs (see Chapter 4). This involves considering not only what kind of evidence is required and how it is to be gathered and interpreted, but also how this will provide good answers to the basic questions being investigated in the research. Third, knowledge of philosophy can help researchers to recognize which designs will work and which will not. It should enable them to avoid going up too many blind alleys and should indicate the limitations of particular approaches. Fourth, it can help researchers to identify, and even create, designs that may be outside their past experience. It may also suggest how to adapt research designs according to the constraints of different subject or knowledge structures.

Arguments, criticisms and debates are central to the progress of philosophy. We believe that it is important to understand both sides of an argument because research problems often require eclectic designs that draw from more than one tradition. In this chapter, we try to provide a balanced view of the different philosophical positions underlying research methods and designs. Therefore, the chapter starts by reviewing some key debates among philosophers of the natural sciences and the social sciences. Then, we explore these philosophies further, and review a number of alternative positions.

The tree as a metaphor for the research process

This chapter uses the metaphor of a tree to represent how the research process unfolds. It is intended to help students understand key concepts such as ontology, epistemology, methodology, and methods and techniques, and make the links between them and how they are related. These are concepts that students have traditionally found difficult to grasp – yet they are so important to coherent and robust research. We encourage our readers to engage with this metaphor and to revisit the pages explaining its elements.

The tree metaphor

We use the metaphor of a tree to represent how the research process unfolds. The key elements of the tree are the *roots*, the *trunk* and *branches*, the *leaves*, and the *fruit* – and each of these parallels an aspect of conducting research.

Richard Thorpe explains the tree metaphor

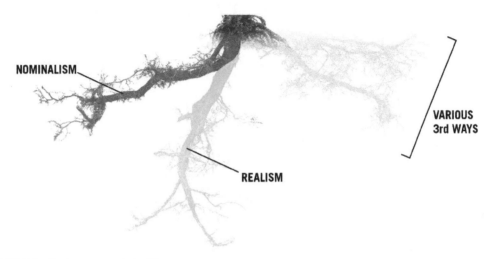

FIGURE 3.1   Roots as research traditions

The *roots* of the tree represent the research traditions. In the same way as *roots* draw nutrition from the soil, the research traditions are drawn up and form the basis of the researcher's ideas in relation to aspects of the research such as design, methods and forms of analysis.

The roots of the tree (see Figure 3.1) show three different possible research traditions that we will return to later in the chapter – a realist perspective, a nominalist perspective and one that we have identified as 'various other third ways'. The various third way approaches are invariably a mixture of the realist and nominalist traditions.

The *trunk* transports the nutrients from the roots through the branches to the leaves and fruit; it also provides strength and shape to the tree. The simplified cross-section of the tree trunk shown above represents the four main features of a research design: ontology, epistemology, methodology, and methods and techniques. Each of these concepts relates to the others. The inner ring of the trunk (heartwood) is the densest part of the trunk, and represents ontology, the basic assumptions that the researcher makes about the nature of reality.

The second ring of the trunk represents epistemology, the assumptions about the best ways of inquiring into the nature of the world.

The third ring from the centre represents the methodology, the way research techniques and methods are grouped together to provide a coherent picture.

The outer fourth ring of the trunk – the bark – represents the individual methods and techniques that are used for data collection and analysis, such as interviews and questionnaires. These are the most observable but their use depends on the underlying assumptions and decisions made about methodology, epistemology and ontology.

The four rings are named and ordered in this way because the most visible parts of research projects are, as we have said, the methods and techniques yet, although they are increasingly hidden from the external observer, for them to be both used and chosen a

ontology
views about the nature of reality

epistemology
views about the most appropriate ways of enquiring into the nature of the world

methodology
a combination of methods used to enquire into a specific situation

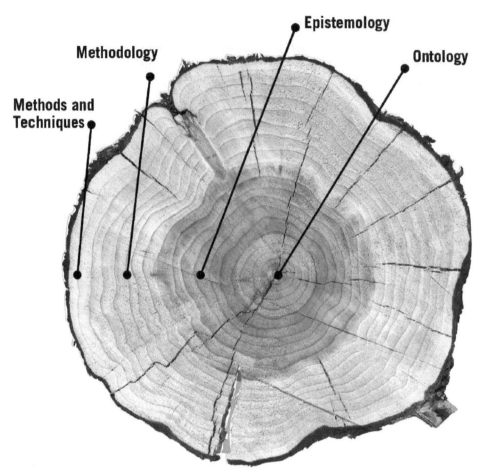

Epistemology

Methodology

Ontology

Methods and
Techniques

FIGURE 3.2   The trunk of the tree: ontology, epistemology, methodology, and methods and techniques

considerable amount of thinking and consideration will be necessary. The three inner rings then can be said to each make a critical contribution to the strength, vitality and coherence of the research project. Without a strong and healthy trunk, a tree can easily be blown over. Similarly, a piece of research that lacks a clear ontology, epistemology or methodology cannot withstand critical review.

The essence of ontology, epistemology, methodology, and methods and techniques is summarized in Table 3.1 below.

Moving up and along the branches, the *leaves* form the tree's canopy. They collect energy from sunlight, and so represent the *collection and analysis of data* within a research project. It is the collection of research data that stimulates new ideas and enables the evaluation of existing theories. We distinguish between three main kinds of data based on the underlying *epistemology* (second ring in the trunk), according to whether they are essentially positivist, constructionist or hybrid approaches. We explain the meanings of these concepts below.

The *fruit* of the tree represents the writing up and dissemination of the research. Here again we show the relationship between the research output, and the ontology, epistemology, methodology, and methods and techniques that all underpin the research.

A realist ontology is usually linked to a positivist epistemology, which in turn tends to produce a quantitative study design (methodology) and some numerical data collection and

methods and
techniques
the instruments
and processes
for gathering
research data,
analysing it
and drawing
conclusions
from it

TABLE 3.1   Ontology, epistemology, methodology, and methods and techniques

	What it is about?	**Questions we ask**
Ontology	Philosophical assumptions about the nature of reality	What is reality? What types of beings are there? How is it that different 'types' of beings exist? What is a 'type'?
Epistemology	A general set of assumptions about ways of inquiring into the nature of the world	What is knowledge? How do we know what we know? How is knowledge acquired?
Methodology	A combination of methods used to enquire into a specific situation	What question am I asking and what kind of conclusion do I hope to come to? How can I best research this question? What data is available?
Methods and techniques	Individual techniques for data collection, analysis, etc.	How can I collect and analyse this data? How does this method or technique help me to answer my research question? Is this method or technique appropriate to the context and research question I am investigating?

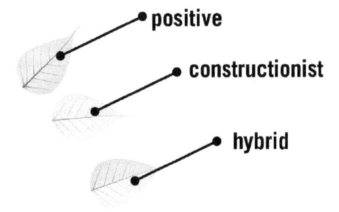

FIGURE 3.3   Leaves representing positivist, constructionist or hybrid approaches

FIGURE 3.4   Relationship between the research output, and the ontology, epistemology, methodology, and methods and techniques

analysis (methods and techniques). The fruits of this labour will see the output characterized as 'hard' (in the sense that they emulate the outcomes of 'hard' or natural sciences) – hence are depicted as an acorn or a walnut.

A nominalist ontology connects with a constructionist epistemology, which in turn will suggest a qualitative approach to data collection and analysis being adopted and perhaps multiple perspectives being taken on a particular phenomenon. The fruits (outputs) from research conducted in this way might be 'softer' (i.e. akin to soft skills) and we can characterise them as a fig or a bunch of grapes.

One of our various third way positions, for example a critical realist perspective to be discussed later in the chapter, might result in a mixed methods design involving the use of both quantitative and qualitative data collection and analysis. In this case the output might be both 'hard' and 'soft' and involve both words and numbers. Such output may be illustrated by fruit such as an apricot or a plum – a soft outside and a large, hard stone at its centre. In this way, the views and values adopted by the researcher from the early stages of the framing of the research, the design of the research project and the collection of the data are coherently connected and linked.

The philosophical debates

Most of the central debates among philosophers concern matters of ontology and epistemology. Ontology is about the nature of reality and existence; epistemology is about the theory of knowledge and helps researchers understand best ways of enquiring into the nature of the world. At this point it is important to note that natural and social scientists generally draw from different ontological and epistemological assumptions when developing their methodologies for conducting research. Sometimes, they do this consciously and deliberately; more often, they simply follow the traditions passed on by those who trained them.

We think this is a shame. Awareness of philosophical assumptions can both increase the quality of research and contribute to the creativity of the researcher.

Ontology: from realism to nominalism

Ontology is the starting point for most of the debates among philosophers. Although there are strong parallels between the ontological debates within the natural sciences and the social sciences, there are also differences. Since the scientific community has been debating methodological issues for much longer than social scientists, we still start with a summary of the methodological debates among scientists before coming back to discuss social sciences specific to this form of research. We introduce four ontological positions, which are situated on a continuum.

Realism   Internal realism   Relativism   Nominalism

FIGURE 3.5   Continuum of ontological positions

Ontologies and natural science

Among philosophers of *natural science*, the main debate has been between realism and relativism. There are several varieties of realism. A long-standing position emphasizes that the world is concrete and external, and that science can progress only through observations that have a direct correspondence to the phenomena being investigated. This position has been modified by philosophers of science in recent decades, who point out the difference between the laws of physics and those of nature, and the knowledge or theories that scientists have about these laws.

The next position along the continuum is internal realism. This position holds that there is a single reality, but that it is never possible for scientists to access that reality directly. It is only possible to gather indirect evidence of what is going on in fundamental physical processes (Putnam, 1987). A nice illustration of this is the 'bubble chamber', which was developed in the 1950s to track the paths of sub-atomic particles during experiments. The bubble chamber is a tank filled with an unstable transparent liquid, such as superheated hydrogen; as these high-energy particles pass through the chamber, they make the liquid boil, leaving a track of tiny bubbles that can be photographed. Thus, the bubbles provide a visible record of the activity of sub-atomic particles, which cannot otherwise be 'seen' directly.

Internal realism does accept, however, that scientific laws, once discovered, are absolute and independent of further observations. The position of *relativism* goes a stage further in suggesting that scientific laws are not simply out there to be discovered, but that they are created by people. It has been strongly influenced by the work of Latour and Woolgar (1979), who have studied the way scientific ideas evolve within research laboratories, and noted the amount of debate and discussion that take place about how to explain observed patterns and phenomena. People hold different views, and their ability to gain acceptance from others may depend on their status and past reputation. Thus, the 'truth' of a particular idea or theory is reached through discussion and agreement between the main protagonists. Furthermore, Knorr-Cetina (1983) points out that the acceptance of a particular theory, and hence the 'closure' of a scientific debate, may be highly influenced by the politics of business and commercial resources.

The international debate about climate change is a good example of the difficulties in reaching agreement about the significance of 'scientific' evidence. Although the same evidence is potentially available to all protagonists, no single piece of evidence is accepted as definitive by all, and both supporters and sceptics of the climate-change hypothesis tend to select evidence that specifically supports their own views. This links closely to the quotation at the start of this chapter. In addition, there are bodies with very strong, entrenched interests – oil companies, environmentalists and national governments – which see their political and economic concerns as bound up with a particular outcome from the debate. The relativist position assumes that there may never be a definitive answer to the climate-change debate, just different accommodations as the interests of different groups interact with the gradual accumulation and acceptance of scientific evidence. We shall return to some of these political and ethical issues in Chapter 5.

Realist scientists have responded to the relativist challenge by arguing that even if scientists work through social and political networks, the truth of scientific laws is quite independent of the process of discovery. Richard Dawkins, the biologist, has famously said that even the most dedicated relativist does not believe, when flying at 40,000 feet in a Boeing 747, that the laws of physics that hold the jet in the air are mere constructs of the imagination (Irwin, 1994).

realism
an ontological position which assumes that the physical and social worlds exist independently of any observations made about them

relativism
an ontological view that phenomena depend on the perspectives from which we observe them; also an epistemological position that observations will be more accurate/credible if made from several different perspectives

internal realism
a philosophical position which assumes that reality is independent of the observer, but that scientists can only access that reality indirectly

TABLE 3.2   Ontological positions

Realism	The world is real and exists independently of perception. Science is based on observations of real phenomena, observable behaviour and facts that are considered to be 'hard facts'.
Internal Realism	The world is real and causally independent of the human mind but it is impossible to observe it directly as our understanding of its structure (types, kinds, categories, etc.) is a function of the human mind. Scientific laws, once discovered, are absolute.
Relativism	Scientific laws are created by people who are embedded in a context (so it's in the eye of the beholder).
Nominalism	Reality is created by us and as such does not exist independently of our perception.

Ontology and the social sciences

There have been similar debates within the *social sciences*. Here, we are interested in the behaviour of people rather than inanimate objects; and this raises an important question about whether the assumptions and methods of the natural sciences are appropriate to be used in the social sciences (Blaikie, 2007). In our view, the answer depends both on the topic of enquiry and the preferences of the individual researcher. Therefore, concepts such as social class and racial discrimination, for example, can be treated as real phenomena, which exist independently of the researcher, and which have real consequences for the life chances and career success of people of different classes or races.

Debates within the social sciences have primarily been between the three positions towards the right of the continuum (Figure 3.5): internal realism, relativism and nominalism. When researching race or class, internal realists argue that it can be difficult to agree what these concepts mean or how to measure them, but that such disagreements do not alter the reality of their consequences.

Relativists argue that social class and racial discrimination are defined and experienced differently by different people, and this will depend greatly on the class or race to which they belong, and the contexts or countries in which they live. This means, for example, that when studying a concept such as motivation, how someone (or a group) might be motivated might be highly dependent on their cultural historical context – their background, age and interests. Thus, there is no single reality that can somehow be discovered, but there are many perspectives on the issue. The relativist position assumes that different observers may have different viewpoints and, as Collins (1983: 88) says, 'what counts for the truth can vary from place to place and from time to time'.

The nominalist position goes further by suggesting that the labels and names we attach to experiences and events are crucial. Postmodern authors, such as Cooper and Burrell (1988), view social life as paradoxical and indeterminate, and argue that social reality is no more than the creation of people through language and discourse (Cunliffe, 2001). According to this position, there is no truth; and the interesting questions concern how people attempt to establish different versions of truth. An example of this is the current trend in politics where seemingly irrefutable 'facts' reported in the media are being regularly challenged with 'fake truths' by other parties offering alternative perspectives. Here, we witness truths being created, claimed and negotiated that at times may appear as 'out of touch with reality'. It is often the rhetoric and language used that connects with certain constituencies, as well as the way an argument is put together that wins the day (makes the most persuasive case).

nominalism
an ontological view that objects in the world are 'formed' by the language we use and the names we attach to phenomena

EXERCISE 3.1

Social media and fake news

Individual: Go online and read the article 'Social media and fake news in the 2016 election' by Allcott and Gentzkow (2017). What can you learn from this article about the social construction of truths?

Fake news

Applied to issues of class, the idea of 'social class' is not a 'truth' but a social construction that offers an explanation of why some people (and families) are systematically more successful than others. For some, it provides a critique of the way privilege is maintained through educational and employment institutions; for others, it may provide a justification of the superiority of some classes over others. Similarly, in the context of race, the label 'institutional racism' provided a sharp critique of the internal practices of the Metropolitan Police following their botched investigation into the murder in London of the black teenager Stephen Lawrence in 1993.

These four ontological positions are summarized in Table 3.3.

TABLE 3.3   Four different ontologies

	Realism	**Internal realism**	**Relativism**	**Nominalism**
Truth	Single truth	Truth exists, but is obscure	There are many 'truths'	There is no truth
Facts	Facts exist and can be revealed	Facts are concrete, but cannot be accessed directly	Facts depend on viewpoint of observer	Facts are all human creations

It is important to note that the adoption of a distinct ontology has implications for the kind of questions we ask. We can illustrate this with two examples, one physical and the other social. First, consider investigating winners in the game of tennis as played on the professional circuits. A *realist* view of tennis would concentrate on aspects of performance that can be measured – the speed of service, the number of 'break points' won or lost within a game, the duration of a match, whether they do better on grass or clay courts, and other past statistics for each player.

The *internal realist* would also be concerned with measurement, but with an emphasis on accuracy, and the tension between human judgements made by line judges and referees, and the technological data provided by technology such as the Hawk-Eye equipment used to determine whether a tennis ball falls within the lines of the court. This perspective would place emphasis on identifying any distinctive physical characteristics of successful players. These features can be monitored and enhanced through fitness training, physiotherapy and practice.

From a *relativist* position, the focus would be less on the physical characteristics of the players and more on their mental capabilities. How do they develop their strategies in advance to deal with different types of opponent, and how might these strategies be adapted in 'real time' while playing? Another important aspect from this perspective is the relation between the players and the crowd: how can they get the crowd to support them rather than the opposition?

From a *nominalist* perspective, the focus could be on the way players make sense of particular successes and defeats in post-match interviews, and then what happens in the discussion with the trainer afterwards. Given the impact that partisan crowds can have on the performance of players, the development of media-friendly personas could be very important. And then, there are other less visible aspects such as who controls the finances of the professional game, the way careers are forged, and the stories of the vast majority of hopeful young people who never make it onto the professional circuit.

The second example, which is more relevant to conventional business, is the notion of corporate profit. Again, the adoption of different ontologies lets us examine different aspects – a bit like wearing different sets of glasses. A *realist* view will assume that there is a single figure that represents the difference between income and expenditure, and that the accounts posted by companies at the year-end are an accurate account of their corporate profit that is how much money came in and went out over the financial year.

The *internal realist* will see a more complex position: the boundaries may be permeable, with acquisitions and divestments taking place during the year; highly diverse activities may be woven into single threads; and decisions will be taken about how to divide ongoing activities between one year and the next. Thus, the profit figure posted will appear more like an approximation of the 'true' profit of the company.

From a *relativist* position, it would be recognized that profit is just one indicator of corporate health, and other indicators (such as sales growth, innovation rates and stock market valuations) may be equally relevant – with no one view taking precedence.

The *nominalist* perspective will draw attention to the way profit figures are constructed from many operational decisions about what to show or hide, and at corporate levels may well be manipulated so that tax liabilities are minimized, or so that directors can maximize their annual bonus payments.

EXERCISE 3.2

Applying the tree metaphor

The following quiz takes us back to the metaphor of a research tree. Based on the examples discussed in the previous section, can you answer the following questions?

1   If the research is based on a nominalist position (i.e. the roots draw their sustenance from soil infused with nominalist principles) what kind of research output might be most appropriate and expected in terms of the kind of fruit the tree produces?

2   If the research is based on a realist position (i.e. the ontology infused in the heartwood – centre ring of the tree) what epistemological position (i.e. the adjacent ring in the tree) might be most appropriate and expected in terms of the kind of data that would be collected?

3   If the research is based on one of a number of 'third way' positions (i.e. the roots draw their sustenance from soil infused with a mixture of both nominalist and realist principles) how might this reflect the data collected and the type of fruit produced on our fictional tree?

Epistemology: positivism versus social constructionism

As indicated above, epistemology is the study of the nature of knowledge and ways of enquiring into the physical and social world: how do we know what we know? It has formed the basis for a sustained debate among social scientists as to how social science research should be conducted. There are two contrasting views: positivism and social constructionism. Each of these positions has to some extent been elevated into a stereotype, often by the opposing side. Although we can draw up comprehensive lists of philosophical assumptions and methodological implications associated with each position, there is no single philosopher who subscribes to all aspects of one particular view.

Indeed, when we look at the actual practice of research, even self-confessed extremists do not adhere consistently to one position or the other, as we shall see below. And although there has been a gradual trend from positivism towards constructionism since the early 1980s, there are many research studies – both in management and the wider social sciences – that deliberately combine methods from both traditions. These so-called mixed methods have great potential for finding deeper insights into management and organizational research, but researchers sometimes come unstuck when using them because they are not aware of the pitfalls of combining worldviews that are fundamentally different from each other. It follows that we need to understand these differences at an early stage in the research process.

Positivism

The key idea of positivism is that the social world exists externally, and that its properties can be measured through objective methods, rather than being inferred subjectively through sensation, reflection or intuition. The nineteenth-century French philosopher Auguste Comte (1853: 3) was the first person to encapsulate this view, saying: 'All good intellects have repeated, since Bacon's time, that there can be no real knowledge but that which is based on observed facts'. This statement contains two assumptions: first, an ontological assumption that reality is external and objective; and second, an epistemological assumption that knowledge is of significance only if it is based on observations of this external reality; it is the result of empirical verification. It isn't simply related to the consideration of a method of inquiry. It also relates to where the judgement resides in respect to evidence. This has a number of implications, although not all of them were proposed by Comte (see Table 3.4).

positivism the key idea of positivism is that the social world exists externally, and that its properties should be measured through objective methods

social constructionism the idea that 'reality' is determined by people rather than by objective and external factors, and hence it is most important to appreciate the way people make sense of their experience

TABLE 3.4 Philosophical assumptions of positivism

- **Independence**: the observer must be independent of what is being observed.
- **Value-freedom**: the choice of what to study, and how to study it, can be determined by objective criteria rather than by human beliefs and interests.
- **Causality**: the aim of the social sciences should be to identify causal explanations and fundamental laws that explain regularities in human social behaviour.
- **Hypothesis and deduction**: science proceeds through a process of hypothesizing fundamental laws and then deducing what kinds of observations will demonstrate the truth or falsity of these hypotheses.
- **Operationalization**: concepts need to be defined in ways that enable facts to be measured quantitatively.
- **Reductionism**: problems as a whole are better understood if they are reduced to the simplest possible elements.
- **Generalization**: in order to move from the specific to the general, it is necessary to select random samples of sufficient size, from which inferences may be drawn about the wider population.
- **Cross-sectional analysis**: such regularities can most easily be identified by making comparisons of variations across samples.

It is worth repeating that these assumptions are not simply the view of any single philosopher; they are a collection of points that have come to be associated with the positivist viewpoint. Some 'positivists' would disagree with some of these statements. Comte, for example, did not agree with the principle of reductionism.

The view that positivism provides the best way of investigating human and social behaviour has developed into a distinctive paradigm over the last 150 years. The term paradigm came into vogue among social scientists, particularly through the work of Thomas Kuhn (1962). Most of the time, according to Kuhn, science progresses in tiny steps, which refine and extend what is already 'known'. But occasionally, experiments start to produce results that do not fit into existing theories and patterns. Then, perhaps many years later, a Galileo or an Einstein proposes a new way of looking at things, which can account for both the old and the new observations. It is evident from these examples that major scientific advances are not produced by a logical and incremental application of scientific method. Rather, they also and significantly result from independent and creative thinking that goes beyond the boundaries of existing ideas. The result of this is a 'scientific revolution', which not only provides new theories, but also may alter radically the way people see the world, and the kind of questions that scientists consider as important to investigate. The combination of new theories and questions is referred to as a new paradigm.

paradigm
a consensual pattern in the way scientists understand, and inquire into, the world

Social constructionism[1]

A new paradigm has been developed by philosophers during the last half-century, largely in reaction to the limited success that has been achieved from applying the principles of positivism to the social sciences. This stems from the view that 'reality' is not objective and exterior, but is socially constructed and is given meaning by people in their daily interactions with others. The idea of social constructionism, as developed by authors such as Berger and Luckman (1966), Watzlawick (1984) and Shotter (1993), focuses on the ways that people make sense of the world – especially through sharing their experiences with others via the medium of language. Social constructionism is one of a group of approaches that Habermas (1970) has referred to as interpretive methods. We will touch on these, and a number of other approaches, in the course of this and the following chapter.

What, then, is the essence of social constructionism? First, it is the idea, as mentioned above, that many aspects of 'societal reality' are determined by people rather than by objective and external factors. As formulated in 1928 by William Isaac Thomas and Dorothy Swaine Thomas: 'If men define situations as real, they are real in their consequences' (Thomas theorem). According to this view, we should therefore try to understand and appreciate the different experiences that people have, rather than search for external causes and fundamental laws to explain behaviour. This is because human action arises from the sense that people make of different situations, rather than as a direct response to external stimuli. Hence, the task of the social scientist should not only be to gather facts and measure the frequency of patterns of social behaviour, but also to appreciate the different constructions and meanings that people place upon their experience (for example, what people, individually and collectively, are thinking and feeling, and the ways they communicate with each other, whether verbally or non-verbally).

Constructivist project

---

[1]There are a number of terms equivalent to 'social construction', notably constructivism and interpretivism, which we will encounter again in later chapters.

Comparing the two approaches

The methods of social constructionist research can be contrasted directly with those characteristic of positivist research, as summarized in Table 3.5. Again, it should be emphasized that these represent a composite picture rather than the viewpoint of any single author or project.

TABLE 3.5   Contrasting implications of positivism and social constructionism

	Positivism	**Social constructionism**
Researchers	must be independent	is part of what is being observed
Human interests	should be irrelevant	are the main drivers of science
Explanations	must demonstrate causality	aim to increase general understanding of the situation
Research progresses through	hypotheses and deductions	gathering rich data from which ideas are induced
Concepts	need to be defined so that they can be measured	should incorporate stakeholder perspectives
Units of analysis	should be reduced to the simplest terms	may include the complexity of 'whole' situations
Generalization through	statistical probability	theoretical abstraction
Sampling requires	large numbers selected randomly	small numbers of cases chosen for specific reasons

EXAMPLE 3.1

Study of managerial stress

The implications of holding these different views may be seen, for example, in the way researchers study managerial stress. The positivist would start with the assumption that occupational stress exists, and would then formulate measures of stress experienced by a large number of employees in order to relate them to external causes (such as organizational changes, interpersonal conflicts and critical performance reviews). Measures of stress could be based on standardized verbal reports from the managers or on physiological factors, such as blood pressure.

Social constructionists would be interested in the aspects of work that managers consider 'stressful', and perhaps in the strategies that they develop for managing these aspects. They would therefore arrange to talk with a few managers about their jobs, and about the aspects they find more (or less) difficult, and would attempt to gather stories about incidents that the managers had experienced as stressful.

It should be clear by now that there is a link between epistemology and ontology, with positivism fitting with realist ontologies, and social constructionism fitting with nominalism.

The links between epistemologies and ontologies are summarized in Table 3.6, where positivism and social constructionism are linked to internal realist and relativist ontologies, while strong positivism and strong social constructionism are linked to the realist and nominalist ontologies. We take the argument a step further by suggesting that, with the weaker versions of both epistemologies, there are overlaps in these positions, and the methodologies that follow from them combine different features of each. However, as already indicated in Figure 3.5, the different ontologies can be seen as being situated on a continuum. It is therefore easier, and indeed more appropriate, to mix neighbouring approaches (and related methodologies) rather than those located on opposite ends of the spectrum.

TABLE 3.6   Methodological implications of different epistemologies

Ontology	Realism	Internal realism	Relativism	Nominalism
Epistemology	Strong positivism	Positivism	Constructionism	Strong constructionism
Methodology Quantitative ←				→ Qualitative
Aims	Discovery	Exposure	Convergence	Invention
Starting points	Hypotheses	Propositions	Questions	Critiques
Designs	Experiments	Large surveys; multi-cases	Cases and surveys	Engagement and reflexivity
Methods and techniques **Data types**	Numbers and facts	Mainly numbers with some words	Mainly words with some numbers	Discourse and experiences
Analysis/ interpretation	Verification/ falsification	Correlation and regression	Triangulation and comparison	Sense-making; understanding
Outcomes	Confirmation of theories	Theory-testing and generation	Theory generation	New insights and actions

In the *strong positivist* position, it is assumed that there is a reality that exists independently of the observer, and hence the job of the researcher is to discover the laws and theories that explain this reality. This is most readily achieved through the design of experiments that eliminate alternative explanations and allow key factors to be measured precisely in order to verify or falsify predetermined hypotheses.

Less strong versions of positivism accept that reality cannot be accessed directly. The research therefore needs to infer the nature of this reality indirectly through conducting surveys of large samples of individuals, activities or organizations. Data will normally be expressed in quantitative form, but this may be supplemented by qualitative data. This should enable patterns and regularities in behaviour to be identified, thus allowing propositions to be tested and new ideas to be developed. Even so, it is only a matter of probability that the views collected will provide an accurate indication of the underlying situation.

triangulation using different kinds of measures or perspectives in order to increase confidence in the accuracy of observations

From the *constructionist* position, the assumption is that there may be many different realities, and hence the researcher needs to gather multiple perspectives through a mixture of qualitative and quantitative methods, and to collect the views and experiences of diverse individuals and observers. This is sometimes described as triangulation.

The idea behind triangulation is that it can be useful to combine research methods when investigating social phenomena. So the term is mostly used to indicate a triangulation of methods of a similar type (such as different qualitative methods). This said, some also use the concept of triangulation when referring to sources of data. For example, researchers investigating incentive schemes – such as performance-related bonuses – have used questionnaires and interviews (Bowey et al., 1986). In order to gain a more complete understanding of the motives of managers and employees in relation to these new schemes, the research team then undertook a number of ethnographic studies where they observed what was happening. These studies revealed important new insights into aspects of motivation and the whole nature of what constituted a 'reward' to those working under the scheme. By triangulating the data (survey data, interview transcripts, records of observations), it was therefore possible to come to a more complete picture of the incentive schemes operated and the effects they had on performance.

This idea of connecting different elements to come to a more accurate understanding of the whole is what the notion of triangulation ultimately is about. Have a look at Example 3.2 below to find out more about the origin of the term.

EXAMPLE 3.2

Triangulation

Triangulation is based on the idea that seafarers, wishing to avoid rocks hidden just below the surface in coastal waters, need to identify their position with reasonable accuracy. In the days before the invention of radar and GPS, this could be done only by taking compass bearings on three different landmarks, and then drawing lines on the chart from these points, thus producing a small triangle that would indicate the position of the vessel. The degree of accuracy is indicated by the size of the triangle (small triangles generally being better than larger ones). The course of the ship can then be plotted on the chart by joining up the series of triangles created by such sightings, and the navigator can then see whether or not they are in danger of hitting the rocks.

Triangulation

The *strong social constructionist* perspective is different again because it assumes there is no pre-existing reality, and the aim of the researcher should be to understand how people invent structures to help them make sense of, and influence, what is going on around them. Consequently, much attention is given to the language and discourse that can be used both to create meanings and to influence – or 'enact' – the environment. Researchers following this path are encouraged to be critical of the way meanings can be imposed by the more powerful on the less powerful. Furthermore, the recognition that the observer can never be separated from the sense-making process means that researchers acknowledge that theories which apply to the subjects of their work must also be relevant to *themselves*. Such reflexive approaches to methodology are recognized as being particularly relevant when studies are considering power and cultural differences (Anderson, 1993; Easterby-Smith and Malina, 1999; Cunliffe, 2003, 2011).

Epistemological
challenges –
The New Yorker

EXERCISE 3.3

Spotting the epistemology

Group discussion: Researchers normally betray their epistemology in the language they use. Have a look at the examples below. What epistemologies are likely to be associated with the following statements?

1. 'We advance research on absorptive capacity by extending and empirically validating the conceptual distinction between potential and realized absorptive capacity' (Jansen et al., 2005: 1000).

2. 'This paper develops a holistic model of the overall process, by integrating knowledge oriented, routine oriented, and social/context of perspectives' (Hong et al., 2006: 1027).

3. 'This article contributes to the study of managerial agency in the absorption of new knowledge and skills ... Empirical data are drawn from a longitudinal study of a ...' (Jones, 2006: 355).

4. 'We (also) examine the influence of tacit and explicit knowledge on IJV performance. We find that relational embeddedness has a stronger influence on the transfer of tacit knowledge than it has on the transfer of explicit knowledge' (Dhanaraj et al., 2004).

5. 'These findings can be explained by elements of JCT and social exchange theory. As expected, when both LMX quality and empowerment were low the most negative outcomes resulted, and in general, when both variables were high the most positive outcomes resulted' (Harris et al., 2009: 397).

6. 'Organizational routines are ubiquitous, yet their contribution to organizing has been under-appreciated. Our longitudinal, inductive study traces the relationship between organizational routines and organizational schemata in a new research institution' (Rerup and Feldman, 2011: 577).

7. 'This brings me to a discussion of the credibility performance of agency–client relations. In some respects the very structure of a corporation can be seen in how it arranges performances ... Like an individual, a corporation may be seen as a performer ...' (Moeran, 2005: 917).

Epistemological
foundations

Strengths and weaknesses of the main traditions

Here, we summarize some of the strengths and weaknesses of each position (see Table 3.7). This should help the researcher to choose which methods are most likely to be of help in a given situation.

We start with quantitative methods, which are based on the stronger version of the positivist paradigm. In this case, the main strengths are that they can provide wide coverage of the range of situations; they can be fast and economical; and, with statistical analysis of data from large samples, their outcomes may be of considerable relevance to policy decisions.

On the debit side, these methods tend to be rather inflexible and artificial; they are not very effective in understanding processes, or the significance that people attach to actions; they are not very helpful in generating theories; and, because they focus on what is (or what has been recently), they make it hard for the policy-maker to infer what changes and actions should take place in the future. In addition, much of the data gathered may not be relevant to real decisions, even though they can still be used to support the covert goals of decision-makers.

The strengths and weaknesses of stronger forms of the *social constructionist* paradigm and associated interpretative methods are fairly complementary. Thus, they have strengths in their ability to look at change processes over time, to understand people's meanings, to adjust to new issues and ideas as they emerge, and to contribute to the evolution of new theories. They also provide a way of gathering data, which is seen as natural rather than artificial.

There are, of course, weaknesses. Data collection can take up a great deal of time and resources; and the analysis and interpretation of data may be very difficult, and depend on the intimate, tacit knowledge of the researchers. Qualitative studies often feel very untidy because it is harder to control their pace, progress and end points. There is also the problem that many people, especially policy-makers, may give low credibility to studies based on apparently 'subjective' opinions.

TABLE 3.7   Strengths and weaknesses of different epistemologies

	Strong positivism	**Positivism**	**Constructionism**	**Strong constructionism**
Strengths	If it works, it can provide highly compelling conclusions	Can provide wide coverage; potentially fast and economical; easier to provide justification of policies	Accepts value of multiple data sources; enables generalizations beyond present sample; greater efficiency, including outsourcing potential	Good for processes, and meanings; flexible and good for theory generation; data collection less artificial
Weaknesses	Hard to implement social experiments and to control for alternative explanations of results; focus may be very narrow	Inflexible and artificial; not good for process, meanings or theory generation; implications for action not obvious	Access can be difficult; cannot accommodate institutional and cultural differences; problems reconciling discrepant information	Can be very time-consuming; analysis and interpretations are difficult; may not have credibility with policy-makers

Mixing approaches and methods

The overwhelming amount of research in business and management is underpinned by the weaker forms of positivism and social constructionism. Given this, it is tempting for researchers to seek out, or see advantage in, compromise positions that serve to combine the strengths, and avoid the limitations, of each of the more extreme positions. This is a trend we have identified recently, particularly among PhD students. However, mixing approaches can be a very challenging endeavour and, as we will explain in the following chapter, you can't really mix everything! Is it methods within one family (qualitative or quantitative), or is it methods between families (qualitative and quantitative data), or is it the mixing between epistemologies?

Richard Thorpe presentation: Disciplines and paradigms

Finally, students might ask themselves whether their approach really reflects what they want to achieve. We often see, for example, a qualitative study where an inordinate amount of counting has been done and is then relied upon as the basis of understanding to the exclusion of rich qualitative data and insights, which were originally going to form the basis of new theory and understanding. Conversely smallish surveys, which aren't in any way random or checked for their bias, are nevertheless used to conduct some statistical analysis and draw inferences.

While it is possible – at times even rewarding – to conduct research situated at the boundary between the four approaches illustrated above, we usually advise our students to limit such experimentation to neighbouring columns as otherwise they are likely to encounter internal contractions that can be difficult to dissolve. We will return to this point in the section on mixed methods in Chapter 4.

RESEARCH IN ACTION

Philosophy in action

Emmanuella Plakoyiannaki

Emmanuella Plakoyiannaki is Professor of International Business at Leeds University Business School, UK. She holds a PhD in Marketing from the University of Strathclyde and has published in various academic journals, including the *Academy of Management Review, Journal of International Business Studies, Journal of World Business* and *Journal of Management Studies*, among others.

Can you tell us why it is so important to know about the philosophy of business research?

It is important to know about the philosophy of business research in order to understand our own research journeys but also the wider social system in which we work. Let me explain. Our assumptions about the world shape the way we see, understand and investigate phenomena. Leonardo Da Vinci used to say that all knowledge is ultimately grounded on perceptions. Therefore, the production of knowledge is not value-free but stems from our assumptions about the nature of reality. Paradigms serve as lenses that bring together such assumptions and tools for knowledge creation (Welch et al., 2011): our assumptions about ontology (nature of reality) shape our perceived relationship with the knowledge we are uncovering (epistemology) and the tools we use to examine reality (methodology). They have substantial impact on our definition of rigour and producing 'reliable' science.

The philosophy of business research also allows us to understand and position ourselves in society. It helps us to pick up the dynamics and transformations taking place in the (business) world (e.g. social networks), problematize contemporary phenomena and address grand challenges such as poverty, inequality or immigration.

Most problems can be approached from different perspectives. Using as an example the context of higher education, student satisfaction with a degree programme can be investigated from a positivist perspective using a questionnaire survey that fractionates and reduces the phenomenon into a set of variables (e.g. satisfaction with the content, teaching standards, support and resources, etc.). While greater precision and broader understanding can be derived from this simplification, it fails to capture some of the deeper social or emotional aspects. Moreover, a survey approach makes it harder to tap into dynamic, individualized, student-specific understandings of programme satisfaction. A phenomenological study based on biographical interviews could capture student experiences through language and discourse, emphasizing the simple presence and use of words denoting positive or negative cues.

How do you determine your ontological and epistemological stance when you conduct your own research?

My personal starting point is always my understanding of the phenomenon through experience. This experience is generated by (academic) reading (trying to understand qualities and dimensions of the phenomenon) and reality (trying to understand manifestations of the phenomenon). It is then my research question that guides my ontological and epistemological assumptions. Finally, it is my own identity as a researcher and the research identity of my co-authors that play a crucial role in thinking about my/our paradigmatic positioning. I have to say that this process is often implicit, tacit and comes with experience.

Can you give us an example?

Together with Pavlos Dimitratos, Jeffrey Johnson and Stephen Young, I have investigated how behavioural differences in the way firms internationalize (time, market presence, entry mode) can be attributed to their International Entrepreneurial Culture (IEC). Given the tacit nature of our focal phenomenon, we adopted a qualitative, multiple case study design. We opted for a qualitative positivist approach to *case study research* (see Welch et al., 2011) with an emphasis on theory building through the development of testable propositions across settings (Eisenhardt, 1989). We chose this paradigmatic positioning (the theory-building view of Eisenhardt) as it emphasizes comparison and replication logic through the identification of patterns. This resonated with our research question that sought to investigate behavioural differences across dyads of internationalized SMEs. We examined 18 knowledge-intensive companies, using the firm-level process of opportunity exploitation as the principal unit of analysis. We sought to address the questions 'whether and how, if at all, there were differences in terms of IEC attitudinal characteristics linked to the pursuit of international opportunities (Dimitratos et al., 2016: 1214). We obtained evidence from a variety of data sources including company archives, in-depth interviews with managers and structured observation in different company settings in the USA, the UK and Greece. We found that firms within each of these dyads manifest dissimilar IEC features and hence dissimilar behaviour in international markets. Our findings were enriched by contextual nuances associated with industry sector, nationality, internationalization experience and size of the investigated companies.

How would it have mattered if you had adopted a different stance?

Our research question and our emphasis on theory building through replication and pattern matching inspired the ontological and epistemological positioning of the study. Adopting a different paradigmatic perspective would have changed the focus of the study and most likely generated different findings altogether. For example, a focus on managerial cognition and sense-making processes of opportunity exploitation would point to a constructivist approach, which allows bringing to the forefront the individual voices of our interviewees and shared meanings of the phenomenon contributing different nuances to IEC and internationalization debates.

TOP TIP

It is important to develop an understanding of philosophy of business research so as to select methodological authorities and sources that echo our own research questions, focus and philosophical assumptions. In doing so, we enhance the coherence of our work and avoid confusion.

Paradigms and research approaches

Richard
Thorpe
discusses
paradigms
and
research
approches

In this section, we review the philosophical positions and assumptions that underpin some of the more popular approaches and methodologies that you'll encounter when doing research into business and management.

In the context of academic research, some of the current approaches might be considered as *paradigms* because they contain distinct sets of assumptions about ontology and epistemology that are shared by supporters and that largely exclude adherence to other points of view. Others, perhaps less grand than paradigms, might be regarded as schools of thought, or meta-methodologies.

Epistemology and researcher engagement

Up to this point, we have reviewed the fundamental philosophical positions that underlie the practice of management and business research, with an emphasis on the epistemological dimension. In this section, we introduce a second dimension that is particularly relevant to both the status and the future potential of such research: the engagement of the researcher with the research context.

This second dimension contrasts two views on the relationship between researchers and the objects of their research: first, that researchers should strive to be independent of, and 'detached' from, the people and processes that they are studying; and second,

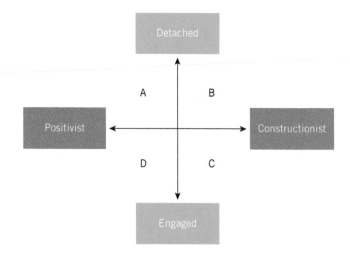

FIGURE 3.6   Epistemology and research style

that – when studying social systems like complex organizations – there is positive value in getting close to the things they are studying, and this is increasingly known as an 'engaged' style of research.

Thus, we can take the epistemological dimension of positivist–constructionist, and add this new dimension of detached–engaged. We will treat these as being orthogonal to each other, and this produces a two-by-two matrix, which is illustrated in Figure 3.6.

engaged research involves close collaboration between academics and practitioners in determining the research aims, its implementation, and the practical implications

EXAMPLE 3.3

The analogy of the detective

In order to make sense of this matrix, consider the analogy of the business researcher and the fictional detective. Both are seeking answers to questions, albeit different kinds, and their careers and reputations depend on their ability to solve problems. In the case of the detective, to identify the murderer (normally within one or two hours if on TV); and for the researcher, to identify (for example) how the advent of social media is affecting public perceptions of organizations (within four months if an undergraduate project, or three years if a doctorate).

The point is that there are a number of distinct ways in which fictional detectives operate, and these are similar to the choices that researchers have when they conduct their investigations. Using the horizontal dimension of Figure 3.4, which represents two contrasting epistemologies, we can compare the scientific approach of Sherlock Holmes with the more intuitive style of the Agatha Christie character, Miss Marple. Whereas Holmes relies on detailed observation of physical evidence, and the process of logical deduction about the circumstances of the crime, Marple acts as an insider to the scene of the crime and makes use of her intuitive feel about the characters involved. Sherlock Holmes therefore represents the positivist side, and Miss Marple represents the constructionist side.

We can also identify characters who personify the vertical dimension in Figure 3.4. Thus, the other famous Agatha Christie character, Hercule Poirot, is a classic example of the detective who is totally *detached* and unruffled by the number of homicides that surround him as he travels around with his high-society friends. His only concern is his apparent inability to solve the crime immediately, although it is his superior intellect – those 'little grey cells' – that always enable him to get there in the end (and well before Superintendent Japp).

Poirot stands in sharp contrast to many of the Hollywood detectives, who become actively *engaged* in the world of the criminals they hunt, and who regularly provoke violent exchanges with their quarries. Clint Eastwood's portrayal of Dirty Harry provides an example of a cop who acts first and thinks later – in contrast to the effete, intellectual style of Hercule Poirot, who is all brain and no action.

Of course, the poles in Figure 3.6 represent extreme positions and, in many respects, it is interesting to explore the spaces between the axes, shown in the matrix as the four quadrants A, B, C and D. Continuing with the detective analogy briefly, in quadrant A, we could envisage Dr Temperance Brennan, the straight-laced scientist in the American forensic science drama *Bones*, or Amanda Burton who plays Professor Sam Ryan in *Silent Witness*. Both characters have high intellectual ability and demonstrate strong belief in the primacy of scientific technique. In quadrant B, we might find Inspector Morse, also

(Continued)

with a combination of his high intellect and his intuitive feel for the community in and around Oxford University. There would be many contenders for quadrant C, but perhaps our favourite would be lead detective Sarah Lund, who wears the same Nordic sweater throughout ten episodes of *The Killing*; highly intuitive, she is always getting herself into dangerous situations. Finally, for quadrant D, our favourite representative would be Lisbeth Salander, heroine of *The Girl with the Dragon Tattoo*, who combines extraordinary technical ability with devastating martial arts performance.

We have organized the research paradigms into a matrix of four quadrants, since they rarely fit precisely into any single category, and the quadrants provide greater flexibility. In developing this model, we were influenced by *Sociological Paradigms and Organisational Analysis* (Burrell and Morgan, 1979). Although the paradigms themselves are conceptually distinct, this does not necessarily mean that all research approaches fall neatly into one paradigm or another. Some fit neatly into one quadrant; others may spread over two or more.

In the sections that follow, we will review a number of different research approaches associated with each quadrant defined in Figure 3.6. We present them by the quadrant from which their primary inspiration comes.

Quadrant A: detached positivism

The scientific method

Scientific method is closely associated with positivism and therefore shares many of the same assumptions, including the need for independence of the observer from the subject of observation; specifying in advance the expected findings; and defining terms in ways that enable them to be measured. There is also a preference for large samples that can enable statistical analysis, in order to establish how far the results can be generalized.

Scientific method is used widely in most disciplines: it underpins most 'hard' sciences (such as physics, chemistry and biology) and medical research, but is also extensively used in business and management research, including in the areas of strategy, human resource management, market research, financial modelling and simulation.

One of the problems in management research is that the top journals are dominated by studies that use this scientific method. Roughly 80 per cent of papers published in the leading US-based journals are positivist, against around 25 per cent in the leading Europe-based journals (Easterby-Smith et al., 2009). The lack of balance here has several consequences. First, it discourages ambitious researchers from getting involved in more qualitative/ constructionist approaches. Second, it means that research projects may try to follow positivist methods, when other methods would be both cheaper and more insightful. Third, there is a lack of understanding, and occasional intolerance, from researchers operating out of the scientific model when evaluating non-positivist work. This is because they unconsciously use the criteria for assessing positivist research to judge work that is based on another, sometimes incompatible paradigm.

critical realism
an approach to social research with an explicit ontological position, which combines features of both positivism and constructionism

Critical realism

Critical realism is sometimes portrayed as a compromise position between the stronger versions of positivism and constructionism, but with more emphasis on the former. Over the last three decades, it has been adopted by a number of management and organizational researchers because it provides a structured way of thinking about social and organizational problems.

It starts with a realist ontology, which recognizes social conditions (such as class or wealth) as having real consequences, whether or not they are observed. It then incorporates a relativist thread, which recognizes that social life is both generated by the actions of individuals and has an external impact on them (Ackroyd and Fleetwood, 2000).

A key feature of critical realism is the idea of a 'structured ontology', which differentiates between three levels:

- the *empirical* domain, which comprises the experiences and perceptions that people have

- the *actual* domain, which comprises events and actions that take place, whether or not they are observed or detected

- the *real* domain, which comprises causal powers and mechanisms that cannot be detected directly, but that have real consequences for people and society (Bhaskar, 1978: 13).

These three domains correspond roughly to three of our ontological positions, respectively relativism, internal realism and realism.

Two other features are important in critical realism. First is the idea that causality exists as the potential – rather than the automatic – correlation of events (the latter is normally associated with strong positivism). Second is the idea drawn partly from critical theory (which we return to when discussing quadrant C) that many of these underlying mechanisms do not work in the interests of ordinary people and employees. So there is a more or less explicit focus on power and powerlessness – and an underlying assumption that greater awareness of underlying causes among those without power (ordinary people and employees) will provide potential for their emancipation from their effects. For example, a critical realist studying incentive systems may focus on how employees experience the effects of such schemes and their reaction to them. In many studies into pay, what is found is that managers tend to think that employees will behave in entirely rational ways: whenever additional pay is made available, employees will work harder to earn it, leading to higher pay for the employee and increased performance for the organization. Research has shown, however, that employees can operate in very different ways (Thorpe, 2000). Employees may use *whatever resources they have* in order to gain additional pay, and this does not necessarily lead to higher performance of the organization. For example, it can make sense for an employee to slow down midweek so that the firm schedules overtime.

We have located critical realism as being only just in the detached positivism quadrant because its proponents are explicit about its realist ontology; also, there is more emphasis on theory-building than on direct engagement with the world through empirical research. Still, there are implications for management and business research, suggesting an agenda that may be critical of the status quo.

Quadrant B: detached constructionism

Hermeneutics

Although hermeneutics were originally developed by Protestant groups in seventeenth-century Germany as a means of interpreting the Bible, the theory still has some relevance to management research. Essentially, it provides a way of interpreting textual material, which can comprise both formal written texts and spoken words that can be recorded. Two of the best-known proponents of hermeneutics are Ricoeur (1981) and Gadamer (1989).

hermeneutics
a philosophy and methodology about the interpretation of texts; stresses that textual materials should be understood in the context within which they are written

Gadamer is particularly concerned about the context within which texts are written. He points out that contemporary interpretations of earlier texts are influenced by the culture in which the interpreter is located; so, in order to understand a particular text, one must try to understand what was going on in the world of the writer at the time that the text was written. When interpreting textual material, we therefore have to be aware that there may be no single correct interpretation of a particular text because both the writing and the reading will be context-dependent.

In the context of management research, some of the insights from hermeneutics have obvious relevance if the researcher wishes to analyse corporate documents such as annual reports. In this case, instead of (for example) conducting a content analysis of statements about the environment in annual reports for 1980, 1990 and 2000, one would need to analyse references in each report separately in relation to the social, economic and political context at each point of time. Thus, the analysis would be between context-based observations, rather than simple additions and enumerations of mentions.

Postmodernism

postmodernism
a collection of philosophies that are opposed to realism, and are generally critical of scientific progress

Postmodernism first came to wide academic attention with the English publication of Jean-François Lyotard's (1984) book, *The Postmodern Condition*, although the term had been used intermittently in relation to literary criticism since 1926 (Chia, 2008). A loose cluster of other (mainly French) philosophers have been associated with the development of ideas around postmodernity, including Derrida (1978) and Foucault (1979).

There are two key ideas to postmodernism. First, it provides a critique of scientific progress, suggesting that it is not necessarily a good thing. Lyotard, for example, examines the impacts of computerization on the control of knowledge, and demonstrates how technology enables many large corporations to become more powerful than states. Thus, scientific progress is discontinuous and contested, rather than linear and continuous. Second, postmodernism contains an ontological position, which is opposed to realism, in that it negates the possibility of a single truth and objective reality. As a consequence, it is associated with adopting a relativist stance and sometimes dismissed as supporting extreme relativism and even nihilism.

There are several implications for management research. First, the opposition to systematic control and regularity leads to an emphasis on flux and flexibility. Thus, postmodernists do not see organizations as static and monolithic, and this makes their perspective particularly appropriate for studying organizational dynamics and change. Second, the opposition to realism places an emphasis on the invisible elements and processes of organizations, including tacit knowledge and the informal processes of decision-making. Finally, postmodernism retains a critical edge and is sceptical about the role and motivation of large

Postmodernism

industrial organizations, and questions whether they are of lasting value to society.

Quadrant C: engaged constructionism

Pragmatism

pragmatism
a philosophical position that argues that knowledge and understanding should be derived from direct experience

Pragmatism originated in the writings of early twentieth-century American philosophers, particularly William James ([1907] 1979) and John Dewey (1916). It is often seen as a compromise position between internal realism and relativism: it does not accept that there are predetermined theories or frameworks that shape knowledge and truth; nor does it accept that people can construct their own truths out of nothing. The key point is that any meaning or structures must come from the lived experience of individuals. Dewey, in particular, talks about the need to balance concrete and abstract on one hand, and reflection and observation on the other.

Pragmatism is a valuable perspective in management research because it focuses on processes that are particularly relevant to studies of knowledge and learning. Its impact on methods can be seen in the tradition and methods of grounded theory, which we discuss in some detail in the next chapter.

Critical theory

Critical theory started as an intellectual movement, also known as the Frankfurt School, which sought to critique the effects of society and technology on human development. The key figure in this movement is Habermas (1970), who argues that society leads to inequalities and alienation, yet this is invisible to people who do not realize what is taking place. He therefore argues that there is a degree of irrationality in capitalist society, which creates a false consciousness regarding wants and needs. Thus, people are, for example, seduced into wanting consumer products that they do not really need.

Habermas (1970) also identifies clear differences between the natural and social sciences, the former being based on sense-related experiences, and the latter on communicative experiences. This means that although understanding in the natural sciences is one-way (monologic), with scientists observing inanimate objects, communication in the social sciences should be two-way (dialogic), with both researchers and the researched trying to make sense of the situation. Hence, Habermas suggests that it is only through dialogue that social scientists will be able to work effectively. He also introduced the important idea that knowledge is determined by interests, and that very often it is the more powerful people in society who determine what is regarded as 'true'.

Critical theory has several implications for management and organizational research. It casts a sceptical eye on the motives and impact of powerful groups and individuals, which – in an emancipatory way – shows a concern for the interests of the least powerful members. Of course, awareness of the way in which knowledge is determined by political processes is of increasing relevance – especially within knowledge-intensive organizations.

We have found it difficult to pin critical theory to a single location on the map in Figure 3.6. Perhaps this is because scholars working in this area are more concerned with theory than with empirical research. But the distinction made by Habermas (1970) between the natural and the social sciences suggests that research informed by critical theory should be located away from the scientific end of the map, and the importance given to dialogue as a potential basis for change means that it fits best in quadrant C.

critical theory a philosophy that critiques the structures and outcomes of capitalist society, and examines how powerful members of society maintain their dominance over the less powerful members

Feminism

Feminism is critical of the status quo, but from a specific angle: that women's experiences have been undervalued by society and by scientific enquiry. From a philosophical viewpoint, it contains a strong critique of science on the grounds that women's perspectives have been ignored by most scientific enquiry, in at least five respects (Blaikie, 2007): there are very few women employed within science; there is gender bias in the definition of research problems; there is bias in the design and interpretation of research; there are too many rigid dualisms in male-dominated science; and science is not as rational and objective as it claims to be. Furthermore, feminist theory identifies similar processes operating in the social sciences, especially with structured interviews, which create a status difference between the interviewer and respondent, even when the interviewer is a woman (Cotterill, 1992). As such, feminist theory argues that external knowledge is impossible and that we must therefore understand human behaviour from within, through understanding the experiences of women themselves.

feminism a philosophy that argues that women's experiences and contributions are undervalued by society and by science; also an emancipatory movement to rectify these inequalities

There is also an emancipatory agenda to feminism, although in relation to social sciences, there is a split between epistemologies known as 'feminist empiricism' and those known as 'feminist standpoint'. The former assumes that the problem is not with science itself, but with the way it is conducted; therefore, there is a need to rectify the norms and procedures of the natural and the social sciences so that they incorporate a gendered perspective. The feminist standpoint, on the other hand, is more radical. It suggests that social science and its methods are fundamentally flawed, and need to be completely rethought. In particular, social science needs to include issues of power dynamics and gender differences, and should make far greater use of subjective experiences and the procedures of reflexivity.

The relevance of feminism to management research is that it provides not only a spotlight on the historical and continuing inequalities of women working in most organizations, but also sensitivity to other areas of discrimination within organizational life, which may be caused by other factors, such as race and age.

Structuration theory

structuration theory
an epistemology that assumes that social structure and individual behaviour are interlinked, and that each is produced and reproduced by the other

Structuration theory is most associated with the work of Anthony Giddens (1984), who developed the idea of 'duality of structure': that structure and agency should not be regarded as pre-ordained. Instead, he suggested that social structures are created and recreated through social action and the agency of individuals – but that this structure then guides and constrains individual agency. Hence, there is a continual interaction between social structure and social action. We all interact in a context that is already structured but by interacting we (re)create and sometimes change the structure. From the perspective of structuration theory, agency and structure may therefore be seen as two sides of the same coin.

Philosophically, he is at pains to point out that the laws of the natural and the social sciences are fundamentally different, because the former are potentially universal, while the latter depend upon the context (including both structure and action) within which things are taking place.

He is also concerned about the use of language, pointing out that words are not precisely 'representational', and that their use depends on agreement about their meaning, which may be the product of debates and reinterpretations. Because language is essentially problematic, he therefore advocates that social scientists should try to avoid specialist language, because it potentially obscures and creates confusion for outsiders. In order to communicate insights from social science, he suggests that social scientists should attempt to use common-sense language in the normal course of their work.

In the context of management research, structuration theory has relevance to understanding the relationships between employees and the organizations within which they work, or between communications and the information systems that are supposed to facilitate them. In other words, it can throw light on aspects of organizations where there is some kind of structural duality.

Quadrant D: engaged positivism

Systems theory

Systems theory was first developed in the 1950s as an interdisciplinary methodology for studying systems, both living and inanimate. The key figure at the start was Ludwig von Bertalanffy, a biologist who developed systems theory from observations of systematic processes within biology.

Systems theory has a number of basic assumptions. First of all, there is the assumption that complex systems should be studied as wholes, rather than through breaking them down into their constituent parts. Second is the idea that when studying systems, human or otherwise, it is the relationships between parts that provide the most important information. Third is the belief that there are common properties in all systems, which therefore provide the potential for methodological unification across the social sciences.

Two variants of the basic systems theories are soft systems methodology and critical systems theory. The former is distinguished from traditional systems methods by its focus on learning (Checkland, 1989: 278). It has been successful as a framework for students doing projects within companies, because it is designed to be used collaboratively when looking for unstructured problems within organizations. The second variant is critical systems theory, which adds elements of critical theory, such as the need to develop critical social awareness, accept pluralism in organizations, and have a concern for emancipation. This can be most useful when investigating situations that contain conflict or sharp differences in the power of participants.

Within business schools, the proponents of systems theory are most likely to be found in management science departments, project-management groups or IT units. Since the methodology associated with many systems approaches encourages engagement and active collaboration with companies and other organizations, this approach fits well with the wider agenda (in the UK, at least) of encouraging collaboration between universities and companies.

Mapping philosophies and approaches

In Figure 3.7, we provide a sketch of how these nine philosophies relate to each other against the basic epistemological dimension introduced earlier in this chapter. The positions are intended to be indicative rather than precise mappings.

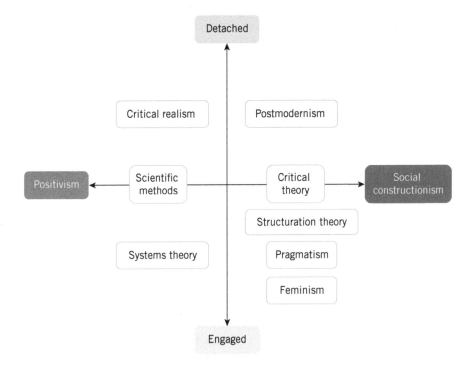

FIGURE 3.7   Mapping philosophies and approaches against epistemologies

Some helpful examples of research on payment that cover all four quadrants are available on the book's website.

Payment
research

EXERCISE 3.4

Identifying philosophical positions

1 **Individual**: Write down a very brief description of some research that you are planning to do, or might do, including a title, the main question and how you would do it (one sentence for each). Consider:

- what ontology you are adopting (i.e. realist, internal realist, relativist or nominalist)

- what epistemology you are likely to adopt (strong/weak positivist or strong/weak constructionist).

Share your answers with two others and try to challenge the analysis that each provides.

2 **Group**: The idea of a 'balloon debate' is that contestants imagine that they are travelling in a hot-air balloon that is running out of fuel and is about to crash into a mountain. In order to save the lives of the majority, it is decided that one person must be tipped out of the basket. Each person in the basket must argue why they would represent the greatest loss to society if they were sacrificed. In groups of four or five people, argue the case for one of the philosophical positions outlined above. Each group should:

- pick one general philosophical position described in the penultimate section (i.e. critical theory, feminism, hermeneutics, etc.)

- summarize its main features

- draw out the methodological implications for researching a question or issue

- make the case to the rest of the class for why this is a valuable philosophy/ method and why it should not be thrown out of the balloon.

After each group has presented, groups must identify one of two philosophies that should remain in the balloon. (There must be no self-nominations or tactical voting!)

It is worth watching the YouTube video 'How to get clear about method, methodology, epistemology and ontology, once and for all' in which David James explains how to get a clear understanding of these – once and for all.

Philosophy
explained

Conclusion

The way we think the world is (ontology) influences: what we think can be known about it (epistemology); how we think it can be investigated (methodology and research techniques); the kinds of theories we think can be constructed about it; and the political and policy stances we are prepared to take. (Fleetwood, 2005: 197)

In this chapter, we have concentrated on philosophies that underlie management research. Our main aim has been to help readers to identify philosophical assumptions underlying other people's work, and to understand how these might influence and assist their own research endeavours. At this point, we can emphasize the following key points:

- All researchers hold philosophical assumptions, although these are often tacit rather than explicit positions.

- Researchers need to be aware of their own philosophical assumptions.

- The strongest philosophical contrast is between realist and nominalist ontologies.

- There is usually correspondence between ontologies, epistemologies and methodologies.

In Chapter 5 we will start to work on how these philosophical positions influence specific research methods, and will provide a number of illustrations and practical exercises to assist in developing research plans and designs. But first, in the following Chapter 4, we examine research as an experience and examine how to engage with those involved in our research (research participants as well as supervisors and colleagues) and consider the ethics of management and business research.

Further reading

One of the few books that articulates what 'critical' management research looks like, and how it can be conducted , for example through increasing sensitivity to the aspects of organizations that normally lie hidden. Also provides a much deeper review of critical theory and why it is important:

Alvesson, M. and Deetz, S. (2000) *Doing Critical Management Research*. London: Sage.

A useful collection of readings that cover both the theoretical assumptions of critical realism and their applications to organizational research in different contexts, such as medicine and high-technology companies. The authors emphasize different features of critical realism and do not follow a single party line:

Ackroyd, S. and Fleetwood, S. (eds) (2000) *Realist Perspectives on Management and Organizations*. London: Routledge.

This book provides an excellent overview of different philosophical approaches to social research, with particular attention to the question of whether the research methods in the natural sciences are appropriate for the social sciences. It is quite comprehensive and very useful, provided you are prepared to put in the effort!

Blaikie, N. (2007) *Approaches to Social Enquiry*, 2nd edn. Cambridge: Polity Press.

A useful introduction to the principal epistemological debates in management research:

Johnson, P. and Duberley, J. (2000) *Understanding Management Research: An Introduction to Epistemology*. London: Sage.

Since postmodernism is such a wide and disparate field, it is probably best to start with edited collections. This book is one of a number of edited works on postmodernism, but has the advantage that it focuses on the relevance and application of postmodernism to organization and management theory. Contributors include many of the leading European management scholars with expertise in postmodernism.

Hassard, J. and Parker, M. (eds) (1993) *Postmodernism and Organizations*. London: Sage.

For those interested in understanding organization as process, the following book provides a useful discussion of process philosophy and process studies drawing on some of the most influential thinkers on process theory:

Hernes, T. (2009) *Understanding Organization as Process: Theory for a Tangled World*. London: Routledge.

Check your understanding online

Visit the website **https://edge.sagepub.com/easterbysmith6e** for useful resources that will help reinforce what you've read in this chapter:

 Take an interactive quiz to test your understanding of the key topics

 Review suggested answers to Exercises 3.1 to 3.4 above

 Use interactive flashcards to check your knowledge of essential concepts

Learning objectives

To appreciate how research philosophies impact research designs.

To understand what is regarded as good theory within each tradition.

To be able to critique research designs.

To be able to develop and justify research designs.

DESIGNING MANAGEMENT AND BUSINESS RESEARCH

4

Introduction

Research designs are about organizing research activity, including the collection of data, in ways that are most likely to achieve the research aims. Let us start with an example.

In 1985, the US businessman Kenneth Lay founded Enron after merging Houston Natural Gas and InterNorth. The company expanded very rapidly, first as an energy company and then through diversification, so that by mid-2000 its stock was valued at over $60 billion. But on 2 December 2001, it filed for bankruptcy following the failure of a rescue bid from a rival company. It quickly emerged that the company had systematically developed accounting practices that had inflated revenue while keeping debts and liabilities off the books. Not only had these practices been fostered by Lay and his colleagues at the top, but also the global consultancy firm Arthur Anderson, which had regularly audited Enron, had failed to report any problems. This raised major implications about the efficacy of accepted practices for auditing corporate accounts. Imagine that you wish to conduct empirical research into the changes in corporate accounting practices following this scandal. In the previous chapter we outlined an ontological dimension containing the positions of realism, internal realism, relativism and nominalism. Following each of these positions in order, your research design might involve approaches and decisions outlined in Table 4.1:

TABLE 4.1   Research and decision-making

Approach	Decision
Review new legislation and accountancy practices published over the period 2002–2005	To focus on two categories of written documents published over a specific period of time
Send out a postal questionnaire to 200 members of the Chartered Institute of Management Accountants	To design a questionnaire, which will be mailed to a specific number of people who belong to one professional association
Arrange to interview one accountant from each of 20 different organizations including companies and consultancies	To focus on gathering views from a medium sample of people likely to have different perspectives and experiences
Get a job for a year in the accounting department of a US energy company	To invest personal time in observing accountancy practices in a US company within a specific industry

This is the essence of designing research: it is about making choices about *what* will be researched, and *how*. Initially, it may appear rather straightforward to make such choices but the development of a research design usually gives rise to a long list of follow-up questions.

This chapter aims to provide an initial overview of some of the main options and choices open to researchers wishing to conduct business and management research. As such, the chapter works a bit like an introduction to a cook book. It shows you what types of dishes are on offer and gives you some first insight into what may be involved in preparing them and what fundamental tools, ingredients and skills the remainder of the book may draw on. We hope that this chapter will inspire your interest and creativity as well as drawing your attention to critical decisions associated with the development of a research design. The subsequent Chapters 5 to 11 will then provide you with more detailed insights and guidance on conducting the actual research.

We start this chapter with positivist research designs. We then turn to constructionist research designs before we examine designs that bridge across quadrants, or combine elements of constructionism and positivism. We refer to these as *mixed methods*. We conclude the chapter with a discussion of common design dilemmas and the role of theory in the development of research designs. At the end of the chapter we provide a downloadable research design template to assist you in the development of the research design for your own study.

Types of research design

A research design is a statement written, often before any data is collected, which explains and justifies what data is to be gathered, how and where from. It also needs to explain how the data will be analysed and how this will provide answers to the central questions of the research.

Research designs differ depending on the underlying orientation of the researcher. For example, returning to Table 1.1 (page 3), it is easy to see that the research designs of basic research, applied research and evaluation research are likely to differ, as these three orientations translate into distinct research problems and objectives, which are likely to require different strategies and principles. Research designs also differ according to the philosophical stance adopted by the researcher. A detached positivist and an engaged constructionist are likely to adopt different methods for data collection and particular data analysis. As these underlying philosophical principles can sometimes be difficult to grasp, we have designed this chapter around the matrix we introduced in Chapter 3 (page 78).

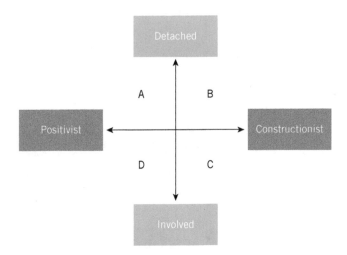

FIGURE 4.1   Epistemology and research style

Remember that the poles in the matrix represent extreme positions, and because it is relatively rare for research designs to be purely one or another we will now focus on the space between them (quadrants, A, B, C and D). It's also important to remember that the horizontal dimension is a continuum between strong positivism on the left-hand side, and strong constructionism on the right-hand side. In the next two sections we give examples of typical methodologies that fit into each of these quadrants, although we have grouped them as primarily positivist or constructionist methodologies. There are also some methods and designs that bridge across quadrants, or combine elements of constructionism and positivism. We refer to these as mixed methods, and we will cover these in the third section.

Positivist research designs

As we noted in Chapter 3, positivist methods (quadrants A and D) usually incorporate the assumption that there are true answers, and the job of the researcher is either to start with a hypothesis about the nature of the world, and then seek data to confirm or disconfirm it, or the researcher poses several hypotheses and seeks data that will allow selection of the correct one. The ideal methodologies for doing this are experimental and quasi-experimental methods, and we will describe the key principles of each below. We then look at survey methodologies, which are generally associated with positivism in the sense that they are looking for patterns and causal relations that are not directly accessible.

Experimental methods

random assignment where the objects of the experiment (e.g. people) are assigned at random to either the experimental treatment or to the control (non-treatment) groups

Classic experimental method involves random assignment of study participants to either an experimental or a control group. Conditions for the experimental group are then manipulated by the researcher in order to assess their effect in comparison with members of the control group who are receiving no unusual conditions.

Possibly the most famous experimental studies in the field of management were the Hawthorne experiments conducted by Elton Mayo at the General Electric Hawthorne Plant in Illinois between 1927 and 1932. One experiment involved the relocation of six women (the experimenters selected the first two, who were each asked to select two more) into a room separate from the rest of the employees who assembled telephone relays. Their working conditions were modified systematically in order to establish whether there was any link between

FIGURE 4.2   Women workers who took part in the Hawthorne study

Source: Woman in the Relay Assembly test Room, ca. 1930. Western Electric Company Hawthorne Studies Collection, Baker Library, Harvard Business School. Reproduced by permission.

physical conditions and productivity. An observer was located in this room, making notes of what was happening and also keeping them informed about progress of the experiment and listening to their ideas and complaints. Over a period of many months, changes were made, including shortening the working day, introducing increasing amounts of breaks into the day, and eventually providing a hot meal in the middle of the morning shift. With each change, productivity increased, which would suggest a correlation between productivity and the easing of working conditions. However, at the end of the experiment they returned conditions to the situation at the outset, expecting productivity to decrease to the initial level – but it increased once more. This observation led to the development of human relations theory, which stressed that positive relationships between employees and their supervisors were more significant than the physical circumstances of their work as predictors of productivity.

human relations theory assumes that performance of both individuals and organizations is dependent on the commitment and involvement of all employees, and hence managers need to foster positive relationships with, and between, employees

EXERCISE 4.1

The Hawthorne experiment

Group discussion: As a class, discuss the following questions:

- What is the primary question/hypothesis of the researchers?
- What are the key features of the research design?
- In what ways does the Hawthorne experiment diverge from classical experimental design?

There are three important implications from the Hawthorne experiment. First, the study showed that the most significant findings emerged because the experiment went *wrong*, in the sense that the expected results were not obtained. Second, the design was very systematic, including the return to the original condition. The third implication is that it has raised awareness of the experimenter effect whereby human behaviour can be affected, and potentially 'distorted', by the presence of an observer. Most people behave differently if they think they are being watched.

Hawthorne

Go online and find out more about the Hawthorne study by visiting the website.

The main *advantages* of experimental research designs are that they encourage clarity about what is to be investigated, and should eliminate many alternative explanations because the random assignment ensures that the experimental and control groups are identical in all respects, except for the focal variable. It is also easier for another researcher to replicate the study, and hence any claims arising from the research can be subjected to public scrutiny. The *disadvantages* are practical and ethical. With medical research, for example, there is always the danger that volunteers will be harmed by drug tests; hence stringent ethical guidelines have been developed, which are now filtering into social science and management research (see Chapter 5). Also, when dealing with people and business situations it is rarely possible to conduct true experiments with randomization. For example, if a company wants to assess the value of an elite highflier career development scheme, it cannot simply assign managers at random to the scheme because the managers themselves will be aware of what is happening, and there will also be strong ethical, performance-related and employment law objections to this arbitrary assignment. For this reason, quasi-experimental methods have been developed in order to circumvent the problem of random assignment.

experimenter effect the idea that the act of observing or measuring any social process actually changes that process

Quasi-experimental designs

A key feature of many a quasi-experimental design is the use of multiple measures over time in order to reduce the effects of control and experimental groups not being fully matched (Shadish et al., 2002). Individuals are not allocated randomly to the experimental group and the control group, but rather allocation takes place on some other criterion, usually by using intact groups (such as different teams of employees). As a result, the validity of inferences from this type of design depends critically on how equivalent the two groups actually are. Since equivalence cannot be guaranteed in this type of design, some purists insist that they be called non-experimental designs; although in practice many forms of quasi-experimental design can allow relatively strong inferences in settings where true experiments would be impossible to achieve.

Grant and Wall (2009) reviewed the business and management literature on quasi-experiments and propose that there are five benefits of quasi-experimental designs:

1. They strengthen causal inference when random assignment and controlled manipulation are not possible for practical or ethical reasons.

2. They help the researcher to build better theories of time and temporal progression.

3. They can minimize or avoid ethical dilemmas of harm, inequity, paternalism and deception.

4. They facilitate collaboration between researchers and practitioners.

5. They can use context to explain conflicting findings.

Scholars often face a trade-off between relevance and elegance in designing research. We believe that quasi-experiments can minimise this trade-off by allowing researchers to conduct studies that are both relevant and elegant. (Grant and Wall, 2009: 672)

Quasi-experimental methods share some of the advantages of full experimental methods such as clarity, transparency and repeatability. However, as we have indicated, they have problems accommodating the politics and agency of human beings in work settings. And there are also other subtle problems with pre-test and post-test designs because changes over time may be a consequence of measurement itself (a testing effect). For example, the first measurement (e.g. survey) may get respondents to reflect on their initial answers, and this can lead to them answering differently the next time – not because of the intervention itself, but because they have been measured before. Thus, the process of measurement itself becomes a kind of intervention, but one that cannot easily be directly assessed.

EXAMPLE 4.1

How a CEO survey can lead to change in a board of director network

In 2004, Marc-David L. Seidel and James D. Westphal published a study that examined the effect of researchers conducting a network survey on board of director networks. They showed how conducting a social network survey where randomly assigned CEOs respond to different types of network questionnaires affected the respondents' subsequent decisions regarding the selection of board members. In this way the study provided novel insights into how the formation and maintenance of board network ties can be influenced, but also into unintended effects in social network research.

Returning to Figure 4.1, the aspiration of quasi-experimental methods is to conduct research without affecting the people under study, which would locate it in quadrant A. But as we have seen, the necessary level of detachment is often difficult to sustain. Figure 4.3 shows four common forms of research design, in increasing order of sophistication.

The cross-sectional comparison

The first form of design (Figure 4.3a) is the commonest in business and management research, but also the weakest. It involves selecting a group of people who have experienced something that you are interested in (attended a training course, graduated from a prestigious university,

a) Cross-sectional comparison: the post-test only design

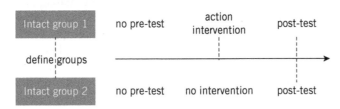

b) Longitudinal design

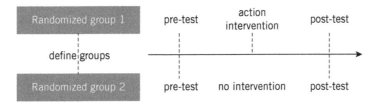

c) Randomized control group design

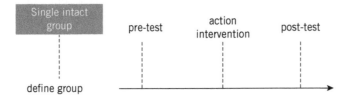

d) Non-equivalent control group design

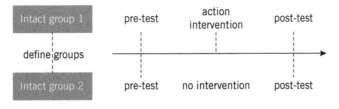

FIGURE 4.3 Common forms of quasi-experimental design

worked with a charismatic mentor, etc.), and then comparing that group with others who have not had the same experience. If we find a difference between the two groups on some variable that is theoretically interesting, it is tempting to jump to conclusions about causality. Although a great deal of the empirical literature relies on cross-sectional comparisons of this kind, it is obvious that no firm conclusion can be reached about cause-and-effect relationships unless groups being compared differ only on those variables (such that no other factor could be responsible for the observed difference in group means). Since this can never be guaranteed outside of the research laboratory, cross-sectional studies have only limited potential for advancing knowledge in a convincing way.

The pre-test/post-test design

It is a commonplace principle that when something changes, you have to measure before and after the change. Figure 4.3b shows a simple form of design with a single group measured twice, with an intervention of some kind taking place between the two measurements. The intervention might be the introduction of group exercises in a classroom, or a new form of recording product defects on an assembly line. In another example, the effects of a leadership course on a group of managers might be evaluated by measuring the managers' attitudes and behaviour before and after the course.

What interpretation could be placed on a change in means from pre- to post-test? The most obvious question to ask is whether the same change would have been observed if the intervention had never taken place. Change could reflect the influence of the *history effect* (due to some other event that took place between pre- and post-test), or the *maturation effect* (due to respondents growing older, wiser, stronger or more disillusioned) in ways that have nothing to do with the intervention. Both history and maturation effects are those that would have happened anyway, with or without the researcher's presence.

More subtly, changes over time may be a *testing effect* (a consequence of measurement itself). If there is a danger that the properties of a measuring instrument change if it has been answered before, it may make sense to change the instrument from pre- to post-test. However, this brings new problems unless it can be guaranteed that the instrument, though different, measures the same thing in the same way (the *instrumentation effect*).

The randomized control group design

The classical way to deal with history and maturation as threats to the internal validity of a design is by using a control group of individuals who are the same as the treatment group in every way except that they do not receive the intervention (Figure 4.3c). The way in which this is achieved is by randomization in allocation to groups. The consequence of randomization is that the whole of the prior history of individuals is detached from the intervention itself: individuals either receive the intervention or not based on a criterion (tossing a coin, or the equivalent) that is quite separate from any characteristics on which they differ. Any change in the treatment group that is not paralleled by an equivalent change in the control group is thus attributed to the intervention, on the basis that the control group shows what the treatment group would have been like but for the intervention. History effects and maturation effects will show in changes in the control group, and the effect of the intervention can be seen by comparing changes in the two groups. However, sometimes it can be difficult to avoid a *selection bias* introduced at the initial sampling stage. For example, if you want to evaluate the performance of an evening maths club you may find that those who agree to take part in the study in the first place may stand out of the larger group of university students. Maybe they are more motivated or have higher marks and are therefore likely to benefit from the club more than others. It is therefore important to pay attention to the first stage of the sampling as well as to the randomized allocation or assignment that follows.

The non-equivalent control group design

Another form of research design, which captures some of the strengths of the randomized control group design, is the non-equivalent control group design (Figure 4.3d). Although the formal specification of this design looks similar to design (c), the crucial difference is that individuals are not allocated randomly to the treatment group and the control group, but rather allocation takes place on some other criterion, usually by working with intact groups. As a result, the validity of inferences from this type of design depends critically on how equivalent the two groups actually are.

The non-equivalent control group design is the simplest of a family of research designs, which are termed quasi-experimental designs. Since equivalence cannot be guaranteed in this type of design, some statisticians insist that they be called non-experimental designs; though the reality is that many forms of quasi-experimental design can allow relatively strong inference in settings where true experiments would be impossible to achieve.

There are substantial problems when using this form of design in real organizations. For example, the design assumes that 'nothing' happens to the control group during the period that the treatment (for example, course attendance) is being given to the experimental group. This is a naive assumption, as Easterby-Smith and Ashton (1975) found, when attempting to evaluate a project-based management development programme held at Durham University Business School. While the 'chosen few' were away on the course, several members of the control group seized the opportunity to improve relationships with their bosses and strengthen their political standing in the company, thus harming the career prospects of a number of managers who had attended the course.

> **validity**
> the extent to which measures and research findings provide accurate representation of the things they are supposed to be describing

EXERCISE 4.2

Designing a call centre

Call centres are important for many companies for lots of reasons. First, they are often the primary point of contact between the company and its customers, and so the call centre staff *are* the company as far as customers are concerned. The company's reputation is in the hands of those people. Second, call centres have to be accessible 24 hours a day for global companies operating in many time zones and in many languages. Finally, the turnover of staff in call centres is very high, and can be over 90 per cent per year.

People who run call centres therefore have to pay attention to recruiting the best people and treating them well so that they stay with the company. There is some truth in the saying that a happy worker is a productive worker (not always, but often); and it is not a coincidence that First Direct (the online banking arm of HSBC) has year after year won awards for the quality of its customer service and also for how it treats its employees.

> **Individual/group**: You have been contacted by a company seeking to set up its own call centre, and your task in this exercise is to design a study to identify which factors are

(Continued)

important for the company to consider in the design of its call centre. Consultants have identified the following general factors as being important:

- density of workstations

- layout of the space

- ergonomics of the workstation (the chair, the desk, lighting, etc.)

- colour of the walls

- the view – is there a view out of the windows?

Answer the following questions:

1   What primary questions/hypotheses would you investigate?

2   Based on the list of factors identified by the consultants, how would you go about designing a study for the most effective call centre using one of the positivist experimental methods you outline above?

Validity of positivist experimental designs

Experimental methods are particularly concerned to ensure that results provide accurate reflections of reality. They distinguish between internal and external validity, with the former relating to *systematic* factors of bias and the latter being concerned with how far the conclusion can be generalized across other types of person, settings and times.

internal validity assurance that results are true and conclusions are correct through elimination of systematic sources of potential bias

The aim of experimental designs is to maximize internal validity, and this requires the elimination of plausible alternative explanations for any differences observed between groups. That is why full experiments require random assignment to control and experimental groups, and efforts are then made to ensure that the subsequent experiences of the two groups are identical in all respects, except for the focal variable. But there are many threats to internal validity, including history (experiences of the two groups diverge in some unexpected way), maturation (group members get older or other life changes take place) or mortality. The latter can be a problem in medical research where people literally die before the experiment is completed, and in organizational studies people may vanish from the research because they move jobs, leave the company or lose interest. Threats to internal validity are systematic rather than random, and they tend to focus on factors that cloud the interpretation of differences between groups in change over time.

external validity whether the results of the research can be generalized to other settings or contexts

External validity is about generalizability of results beyond the focal study. In order to demonstrate external validity, management research designs need to demonstrate a number of features. First, they need to demonstrate that the results observed are not just a product of the selection of individuals or organizations. Sometimes the people who volunteer to take part in research are open-minded and keen to help; sometimes they will put themselves forward because they have strong opinions or 'axes to grind'. Managers will often 'volunteer' employees to take part in research because they believe they will show the organization in a positive light, and will not offer individuals who are likely to be critical; or they will allow access to the organization because they hope research will add legitimacy to a new innovation or policy that they wish to promote. These issues of access and sampling are discussed further in later chapters (Chapters 5 and 9), but the key point to remember is that selection should avoid sources of bias as far as possible.

Other threats to external validity come from the setting and history. In the first case, the results of a piece of research in the health service may be difficult to generalize to an automobile manufacturer. Similarly, research conducted in large organizations may not apply to small organizations; and research conducted in one national setting may not apply to other national settings. For example, a study on reward systems conducted in one country where the supply of skilled labour is plentiful might not be relevant in another country where there is a marked shortage of skilled labour. With regard to history, it is important to note that patterns and relationships observed in one era may not apply in another era. For example, at the present time, with the emergence of new economies such as China and India as global economic forces, the theories about the behaviour of financial markets that were developed during the era of US dominance are now having to be rewritten.

Survey research

The dominant epistemology underlying survey research methods is positivism. As explained in the previous chapter, this assumes that there are regular, verifiable patterns in human and organizational behaviour, although they are often difficult to detect and extremely difficult to explain due to the number of factors and variables that might produce the observed result. Consequently, survey research tends to use cross-sectional designs with large samples, which enable multiple factors to be measured simultaneously and hence potential underlying relationships to be examined.

There are three main types of survey that seek to take a detached viewpoint: factual, inferential and exploratory studies. Factual surveys can also be used in an engaged way, where they are established as survey feedback processes. The three main types generally fit with quadrant A of Figure 4.1, whereas engaged factual surveys fit into quadrant D. We will briefly describe and illustrate each type here. More detailed information on the technical design of surveys can be found in Chapter 9.

Factual surveys are most often associated with opinion polls and market research, and involve collecting and collating relatively 'factual' data from different groups of people. Thus, in order to assess market share or loyalty we might be seeking to identify what percentage of the population of Manchester entered either an Aldi or a Tesco supermarket at least once in the previous week. This is reasonably factual data, which could be gathered by a postal questionnaire or structured interviews; however, it could be affected by people's ability to recall what they did in the previous week, and possibly by social desirability factors where they claim loyalty to one supermarket over another in order to project a particular image of themselves to the researcher.

A common use of factual surveys within companies is survey feedback. This involves distributing a questionnaire to all employees asking for their views on the management of the organization, the quality of communications, their job satisfaction, feelings of security, and so on. Data is then aggregated by department, level or job category and results are discussed in public. This puts pressure on management to change systems, procedures and their own behaviour in order to get 'better' results next year.

Inferential surveys predominate in academic management research, particularly in the fields of strategy, marketing and organizational psychology. They are aimed at establishing relationships between variables and concepts, whether there are prior assumptions and hypotheses regarding the nature of these relationships. Inferential surveys generally assume an internal realist ontology, although epistemologically they involve a weaker form of positivism than experiments. The usual starting point for inferential surveys is to isolate the factors that appear to be involved, and to decide what appears to be causing what.

factual surveys involve collecting and collating relatively 'factual' data from different groups of people

social desirability where people adjust their answers to a survey in order to project a positive image of themselves to the interviewer

survey feedback the collection of opinions about the management of an organization, which is then fed back to all employees to stimulate change and improvements

inferential surveys surveys that are aimed at establishing relationships between variables and concepts

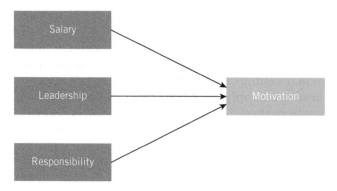

FIGURE 4.4   Possible predictors of motivation at work

dependent
variables
the factors
that research
is trying to
predict (see
independent
variables)

predictor
variables
the factors that
are believed
to cause the
effects that are
to be observed;
also called
independent
variables (see
dependent
variables)

cross-sectional
surveys
these usually
involve selecting
different
organizations,
or units, in
different
contexts, and
investigating the
relationships
between a
number of
variables across
these units

independent
variables
the factors that
are believed
to cause the
effects that
are to be
observed; also
called predictor
variables (see
dependent
variables)

This means that researchers have to identify the main dependent variables and predictor variables:[1] it is the latter that are assumed to be causing the former.

In Figure 4.4, we are suggesting (hypothesizing) that the predictor variables of salary, leadership and responsibility have an impact on the dependent variable, motivation at work. In order to test this hypothesis it would be necessary to define ways of measuring each of these variables, generally through a small number of items in a questionnaire, and this would need to be completed by a sample of employees in one or more places of work. Naturally, this requires that the measures of the four variables are accurate, and that the sample is appropriate in terms of size and constitution in order to test the hypothesis; we discuss how to do this in more detail in Chapter 9. Moreover, the four factors identified in Figure 4.4 could be examined in more detail. For example, one might be interested in the interactions between some of the variables, such as whether some forms of leadership result in greater responsibility being distributed around the workforce; or one might be interested in whether some of the arrows might work in other directions, so that a highly motivated workforce would lead to particular styles and strategies of leadership. These are some of the relationships that can be analysed, particularly with more complex models, through the use of structural equation modelling (see Chapter 10). Studies of this kind are often known as cross-sectional surveys because they involve selecting different organizations, or units, in different contexts, and investigating how other factors, measured at the same time, vary across these units.

EXAMPLE 4.2

Which variable is which?

Chen's (2008) doctoral thesis examined how workers in virtual teams doing different tasks used instant messaging to support their work. Her respondents were all Chinese-language speakers in China or Taiwan. Some of them worked with people in the same location (building or city), while others worked with colleagues in other countries (such as Canada, the USA, Germany).

---

[1]The term independent variable is often used instead of 'predictor variable'. We prefer the latter term because in practice, even independent variables tend to be related to each other, and therefore use of the former term is misleading.

The focus of the study was on what led people to switch communication media or languages, and this therefore was the *dependent* variable. The *predictor* variables were task characteristics, indices of relationship quality (how well people knew each other), and whether they worked in the same or different locations.

Instant messaging is not a variable because everyone in the study used it; but other communication technologies (such as email, videoconferencing and face-to-face meetings) are variables because some people use them while others do not. Similarly, dual-language use (Chinese and English) is not a variable because the whole sample spoke both languages.

Similarly, Lyles and Salk (1996) were interested in the conditions that led to greater transfer of knowledge from foreign parent companies to international joint ventures. So they selected a sample of 201 joint ventures that were regarded as small or medium-sized across four manufacturing industries in Hungary. Through comparing indicators of performance across the whole sample, they were able to conclude first that there was a strong link between knowledge transfer and performance, and second that this transfer was most likely to take place when the foreign and domestic parents had equal (50/50) equity stakes in the new venture. The sample size of 201 was sufficient for them to demonstrate that the results were statistically significant, but one of the key problems for researchers using cross-sectional designs is to know how large the sample needs to be.

Geert Hofstede's (1980) study of national cultural differences provides an example of an exploratory survey. He attempted to develop a universal set of principles against which any culture can be measured, in the hope that this would provide a basis for predicting the behaviour of individuals and organizations in almost any country. However, he did not start with an explicit set of hypotheses; rather, he had a large number (about 216,000) of questionnaires completed by employees of IBM with regard to their views and values, and he was looking for patterns in the data. His four dimensions – power distance, individualism/collectivism, uncertainty avoidance and masculinity – emerged from his data, and by demonstrating that they fitted reasonably well with prior research into this topic, he was able to substantiate his claim to the importance of these four dimensions.

Principles in judging the quality of a sample design

When decisions are made that can have significant consequences for people, it is important that those decisions are based on evidence. The trustworthiness of the evidence base for decisions depends on many factors. We begin with the difference between a population and a sample drawn from that population. The term 'population' refers to the whole set of entities that decisions relate to, while the term 'sample' refers to a subset of those entities from which evidence is gathered. The inference task then is to use evidence from a sample to draw conclusions about the population. Samples are very commonly used, both for research and for policy-making.

Companies estimate morale among employees from quantitative surveys of samples of employees (either by deliberately picking names from the payroll, or by letting employees choose whether or not to respond). Here, the *population* is the whole set of employees within the organization, and management want to gain a picture of their staff by summarizing the results from a *sample* of those who respond to the survey. Companies such as Gallup and Towers Watson are leaders in carrying out such opinion surveys, and one of the benefits that they claim is that they can compare the profile of a company (and sub-units within it)

exploratory surveys
these are similar to cross-sectional surveys, but tend to focus on identifying patterns within the data through the use of factor analysis or principal components analysis

population
the set of entities about which a researcher wishes to draw conclusions

sample
a subset of the population from which inferences are drawn based on evidence

inference
drawing conclusions about a population based on evidence from a sample

with that of other companies where the same survey questions have been used. This gives a method of benchmarking, which senior management often find very informative and powerful in shaping their strategy.

Many companies also use small-scale surveys repeated frequently (perhaps once a month) as a kind of barometer of how employees or customers are feeling. Companies may set up a panel to represent the entire body of employees, and their responses are used to monitor the state of the organization at that time. This can be very valuable during the course of a period of major change. During the UK general election in 2017, for example, opinion polls appeared every day monitoring the state of the electorate and their response to the offerings of the political parties.

The UK government also uses sample surveys of companies on their annual pay negotiations in order to get an estimate of wage inflation in the economy. In most countries, estimates of activity in the labour market (whether people are unemployed, self-employed, economically inactive, etc.) are derived from samples and not from complete counts.

sampling strategy sets out the criteria to be adopted by a researcher when selecting a subset (or sample) from a wider population of individuals, organizations, industries (or whatever unit of analysis that is being investigated)

Sometimes, a research project involves collecting evidence from every member of an organization (or every member of a project group), but more often this is not the case and the researcher needs to decide on a sampling strategy. A sample might be a proportion of employees in an organization, a selection of companies operating in a specific market, a number of specific periods of time for assessing the quality of customer responses in a call centre, or a selection of transactions for audit purposes. For each of these examples, the researcher has to make a decision about what the sampling unit is (the person, the company, the transaction, etc.), how many sampling units to take, and on what basis sampling is to be undertaken.

representativeness in sampling design, this refers to how much the characteristics of a sample are the same as the characteristics of the population from which the sample is drawn

Generally speaking, the purpose of collecting data from a sample is to enable the researcher to make statements about a larger group that the sample is drawn from. Many people say that they only want to talk about their sample data, but we almost never believe them. Even if there is no formal generalization beyond the sample, both the writer and the reader are interested in what this study's findings tell us that would be useful when thinking about other settings. This places a responsibility on researchers, whether we like it or not, to say where our findings might be relevant.

precision the level of confidence that the researcher has in estimating characteristics of the population from evidence drawn from a sample; it depends on sample size but not on the sampling proportion

The claims that can legitimately be made from sample data depend absolutely on the relationship between the sample and the population (the larger group that the researcher wants to make claims about). Get the sampling wrong, and accuracy in calculating the results is of no consequence. The opposite is also true: get the sampling right, and even rough-and-ready calculations or 'eyeballing' of the data can be immensely valuable. There are two basic principles that underlie decisions about sampling design: representativeness and precision.

Representativeness in sampling

sampling frame the list of all of those eligible to be included in a sample

The accuracy of conclusions drawn from a sample depends on whether it has the same characteristics as the population from which it is drawn. If the sample is systematically different in some way, then the sample is biased. A simple definition of bias in sampling is that it occurs when some members of the population have a higher chance of being included in the sample than others. There are two steps involved in defining a sampling design: first, to draw up a sampling frame, a list of all who are eligible to be included in the study; second, to achieve a valid response from all those included in the sampling frame. Bias can be introduced into a sampling strategy in many ways, through choices made in the design of the study itself and also through features of the process of collecting research data. The following are quite common examples of bias in a business setting:

- *Excluding groups of people*: leave out home-workers, casual staff, new recruits, part-timers. If your study involves selecting people to interview, it is tempting to prefer people who are articulate and have 'interesting' stories to tell, or people who have already taken part in previous studies within the organization and therefore are more familiar with academic research.

- *Distribution method*: send out a questionnaire survey using an out-of-date list of mailing addresses to exclude those who have recently moved; distribute an invitation to interviews or a focus group by email to exclude those without a PC on their desks.

- *Language used*: use English to exclude those who don't speak English, and introduce biasing factors for those who do because of differences in how well people can use the language.

One of the key ways of judging the representativeness of a sample is to compare the characteristics of the sample to those of the population; this kind of information is commonly reported in published papers that are based on quantitative surveys but less so in interview studies. Even if the sampling frame accurately represents the population, non-response is a major source of problems in getting outsiders to believe the results. In itself though, non-response is not a problem, as long as those who do take part in the study have similar characteristics to those who do not. Of course, there is usually a big problem in assessing whether this is true, because (obviously) you do not have data from those who did not take part. It is sometimes possible to get some idea about potential bias due to systematic non-response by comparing those who respond quickly with slow responders. If the slow responders have similar characteristics to rapid responders, then the researcher can have greater confidence that non-responders would also have been similar, and can help to build credibility in a study.

bias in sampling design, a biased sample is one that does not represent the features of the population from which it is drawn (see representativeness)

Precision in sampling: sampling proportion and sample size

Precision is about how credible a sample is. How confident is it possible to be about predicting election outcomes from opinion poll samples? Does the precision of the estimate depend on how big the sample is? It seems plausible that it should. Does it also depend on what proportion of the population the pollsters talk to? If the number of electors is 10,000 then a sample of 1,000 (i.e. 10 per cent) might be OK. However, many people would be less happy with a sample of 1,000 if the number of electors was one million instead (0.1 per cent). Intuitively, this proportion seems too small. However, the first intuition is correct, but the second is not.

Nguyen (2005) provides a clear and graphic example of cooking chicken soup to show why the size of a sample matters but how big a proportion the sample is of the population (the sampling proportion) does not. Consider three scenarios: cooking at home for four people using a small pot; cooking for a dinner party with 12 guests using a medium-sized pot; and cooking a banquet for 200 wedding guests using a huge pot. Regardless of the number of guests, the only way to tell if there is enough salt in the soup is to taste it. The way to find this out is: first, stir the soup so it is well mixed and is the same all the way through, and second, use a tablespoon to draw off some soup. A tablespoon will do because there is no point taking more than that: taste it all and there is no soup left for the guests; taste more spoonfuls and each will taste just the same, so nothing is learned. It is not necessary to use a large ladle to sample from the large pot simply because the pot is bigger, or a tiny spoon to sample from the small pot because the pot is smaller: the same sized tablespoon

sampling proportion the size of a sample relative to the size of a population

is enough to judge the adequacy of the seasoning regardless of how big the batch of soup is, as long as the pot is stirred first.

The soup in the pot is the *population*; the spoonful to taste is the *sample*. The size of the spoon is the sample size, and that is what matters. The cook needs to taste enough soup to be able to make a judgement about the pot as a whole. Now apply these principles to the task of making judgements about attitudes in a society towards an issue of concern. Consider the question of whether organizations should aim to maximize their profit or should consider their social responsibilities. The precision of the answer to this question has nothing to do with the size of the population but rather depends on the size of the sample. Small samples will always be less precise than large samples.

sample size
the number of entities included in a sample

Combining precision and representativeness to achieve a credible sample

We have looked at the two design principles of bias and precision, and clearly both are important in achieving a credible sampling design for a quantitative research project. Low bias means that conclusions from a specific sample can reasonably be applied to a larger population, and high precision means that the margin of error in the claims that are made will be low – the researcher can expect to be precisely right (see Table 4.2). However, high precision is no way of saving a study where the sample is biased (the claims the researcher makes are precisely wrong).

Most projects carried out by students (at whatever level) are a compromise in some way, simply because resources are limited. As a result, there will always be trade-offs when it comes to decisions about design. Is it better to have a large sample (giving higher precision) if the cost of achieving it is to introduce bias into the sample achieved? Put more simply, which is better: to be imprecisely right or to be precisely wrong? In our opinion, the answer is straightforward. Imprecisely right is better: it is preferable to have a sample that properly represents the population even if the precision is lower because of a small sample.

TABLE 4.2   Principles in designing a sample

		Bias	
		High	**Low**
Precision	**High**	Precisely wrong	Precisely right
	Low	Imprecisely wrong	Imprecisely right

simple random sampling
a form of sampling where every entity in the population has an equal chance of being included in the sample

proportional stratified random sampling
a form of sampling where the population is divided into subsets (called strata) and within strata the same sampling proportion is used for selecting a sample

Probability sampling designs

This section describes forms of sampling design where the probability of each entity being part of the sample is known. Some sampling methods have the same probability for every entity in the sample, while others have the same probability within segments of the design but differing probabilities across segments.

Simple random sampling

With simple random sampling, every sample entity (company, employee, customer, etc.) has an equal chance of being part of the sample. In the past, this was done using printed random number tables. Now computers are used for this, and it is easy to draw up a list of random numbers as a basis for selecting a sample.

Stratified random sampling

One drawback of simple random sampling is that it can mean that small but important parts of a population are missed altogether or sampled so little that the researcher cannot make confident statements about them. For instance, customer surveys of a healthcare facility would be badly served by a simple random sample. Most users of a healthcare facility have relatively minor ailments and perhaps visit only once or twice in a year. There will, however, be a small number of patients with major health problems whose treatment is perhaps extensive. It is quite reasonable to expect that a sample should be informative about the chronically ill minority as well as the occasionally ill majority. The way to achieve this is to divide the population up into homogeneous groups called *strata*, and then take a simple random sample within each stratum. Proportional stratified random sampling has the same sampling proportion within all strata; but this has the disadvantage that rare groups within the population would be badly represented. The way to deal with this problem is to take a larger proportion of sample units in small strata, and a smaller proportion in the larger strata. This is called non-proportional stratified random sampling.

non-proportional stratified random sampling a form of sampling where the population is divided into subsets (called strata) and different sampling proportions are used for each stratum for selecting a sample

Systematic random sampling

Systematic random sampling relies on there being a list in some form or other of the units in the population that the researcher is interested in. This might be a customer database, or a list of employees of a company or students registered at a university. Suppose that a researcher wants to achieve a sample of 500 students in order to assess their satisfaction with the virtual learning environment (VLE) system that a university has just introduced. If there are 20,000 students, then 500 represents a sample of 2.5 per cent, corresponding to selecting 1 in 40 students from the population. This proportion could be achieved by choosing a number at random between 1 and 40. If that number were 27, then the researcher would go down the list taking every 27th student in order to derive a sample list of 500 names. What this process relies on is that the population list is essentially organized randomly, so that picking in this systematic way does not introduce bias. There could be a problem if the list is ordered alphabetically by individuals' last name, since all those students with the same name will be listed together and individuals with the same name will have less chance of being selected than if the list were randomly ordered.

systematic random sampling a process of random sampling where every *n*th entity from the population is selected

cluster sampling a modification of random sampling where the population is first divided into convenient units, called clusters, and then all entities within a cluster are selected

Cluster sampling

Any method that involves random sampling can lead to practical problems where the population units are spread very widely, such that the cost of approaching them can be very high. Cluster sampling deals with this by first dividing up the population into what are called 'clusters', and then by sampling all the units within the selected clusters. A study of company success in emerging economies might first identify all the countries where the company operates, select randomly a number of those countries to study in detail (the clusters), and then approach all the relevant contacts in those countries. This would allow the study to use local research staff who are familiar with the language and culture of each country.

multi-stage sampling a process of dividing up a population into hierarchical units, such as countries, regions, organizations, work groups, and applying random sampling at each level

Multi-stage sampling

Multi-stage sampling combines together the methods described above in order to achieve higher operational and technical efficiency. For example, stratified random sampling divides the population into strata and then samples from within all of them. Instead, a study might use a sampling approach at each level, and this is very common in large-scale social research. Suppose there was a national change in the organization of schools to give greater management autonomy to head teachers, and researchers wanted to know whether this change had any effect on the performance of students in schools. It would be very inefficient to select students at random, even if the research team actually had a national database of all school students. It makes more sense to divide the country up into regions, select some regions for detailed attention, identify all the schools in the targeted regions, and then select a sample of schools. Having defined a sample of schools within selected regions, the same process could be used to sample classes within the selected schools, or perhaps take a sample of students from all of the classes in a selected school. In this example, the criterion of randomness applies at each of several stages in the design of the study; hence the name 'multi-stage sampling'. The aim is to balance the need for representativeness of the sample with the highest possible cost-effectiveness.

As we will discuss in the following Chapter 5, there are also practical issues to consider such as how to gain access, time constraints and ethical considerations. For example, it can be very difficult to obtain ethical clearance for a study that involves children.

Probability samples

EXERCISE 4.3

Knowing about probability samples

Individual: Download the activity 'knowing about Probability Samples' from this book's website and follow the instructions.

Source: Dawson, 2016

Why are probability sampling designs valuable?

It is only with probability sampling that it is possible to be precise about the relationship between a sample and the population from which the sample is drawn. Knowing what this relationship is allows the researcher to make a firm judgement about the relationship between characteristics of a sample and characteristics of the population from which the sample was drawn. All forms of probability sampling design have this feature in common: it is always possible to state the probability of each individual respondent being selected for inclusion in the research study. The statistical theory behind the inference process (often called 'significance testing' – we discuss this in Chapter 10) relies fundamentally on sampling based on probabilities. There is always uncertainty about any claim made from data, but using probability sampling designs can allow the researcher to quantify that uncertainty. Thus, sample data can tell us whether the risk associated with using a mobile phone while driving is higher, but only a properly constructed sample design can allow us to decide how worried we should be about that extra risk.

Non-probability sampling designs

Non-probability sampling designs all share the same characteristic: that it is not possible to state the probability of any member of the population being sampled. As a result, it is harder for the researcher to be confident that claims made about the sample can apply to the larger group that the sample is taken from. For example, these days many students conduct research using self-selected online surveys that are open for anyone to participate in. Such surveys are promoted in various ways (including social media and leaflets put up in student toilets!) but, of course, by having no restrictions on who can participate potential self-selection bias is difficult, if not impossible, to avoid.

Convenience sampling

Convenience sampling involves selecting sample units on the basis of how easily accessible they are, hence the term 'convenience sampling'. A student who uses a list of friends on Facebook for their dissertation is taking a convenience sample. Such a sample may well reflect the individual's own social network, but is clearly not representative of students as a whole or of the population of the UK. Convenience samples are very common in research because they are – well – convenient! It is impossible to guarantee that any sample achieved in this way represents a specific population that may be of interest. However, they can still have a value. It rather depends on what the *purpose* is for collecting data. For a very long time, people thought that all swans were white because no one had ever seen one of any other colour. It only takes an Australian researcher with a convenience sample of one black swan to prove the old generalization to be wrong.

Quota sampling

Quota sampling divides the relevant population up into categories (perhaps male/female, or country of origin for students) and then selection continues until a sample of a specific size is achieved within each category. The aim is to make sure that each of the categories is represented according to the quota proportions. For example, in doctoral research on whether the Internet empowers consumers, quota sampling enabled the researcher to ensure that she had users of a variety of ages, whereas a convenience sample would be more likely to result in a preponderance of people similar to the researcher and her friends.

Purposive sampling

In purposive sampling, the researcher has a clear idea of what sample units are needed according to the purposes of the study, and then approaches potential sample members to check whether they meet the eligibility criteria. Those that do are used, while those that do not are rejected. The guiding principle for sampling might be theory and theory development (theoretical sampling), and the basis of sampling could therefore change as a study is carried out if an analysis of the initial data is used to guide theory development. For example, a research student may wish to conduct research on the learning choices of students who study abroad. She may decide to conduct and analyse a series of initial interviews to identify emerging themes and explore these further in the light of the extant literature. Later in the study she may then purposefully select interviewees who are more likely to allow her to further develop her themes until they are fully explained.

Snowball sampling

Snowball sampling starts with someone who meets the criteria for inclusion in a study, who is then asked to name others who would also be eligible. This method works well for samples where individuals are very rare and it is hard to identify who belongs to the population. Dissertation students often do this by starting out with people they or their supervisor know personally, and then ask those people to pass them on to others who would also be suitable. It works well too for individuals, groups or companies that are part of networks whose membership is confidential (LinkedIn is a useful resource here, and its owners actively promote the professional network as a useful way of finding interesting people to get in touch with). Students who conduct research on illegal activities and other topics that require a high level of trust and confidentiality also tend to use snowball sampling.

quota sampling a form of non-probability sampling design where the population is divided into units and a target sample size (quota) is defined for each unit; entities that meet the criteria for a specific unit are added to the sample until the target sample size for the unit is achieved

purposive sampling a form of non-probability sampling design where the criteria for inclusion in a sample are defined, and entities are first screened to see whether they meet the criteria for inclusion; those entities that meet the criteria are included in the sample

snowball sampling a form of non-probability sampling design where the criteria for inclusion in a sample are defined; entities that meet the criteria are included in the sample and then asked whether they know others who also meet the criteria

Why are non-probability sampling designs valuable?

The sampling approaches described in this section are answers to a variety of practical problems that researchers have encountered in carrying out their work. But how do these sampling methods stack up against the key quality criteria of bias and precision that we started this section with? *Precision* is most straightforward, since its main focus is the size of the sample achieved. A convenience sample can meet the first requirement of a big-enough sample most easily; quota sampling and purposive sampling both aim to ensure that every sector in a sampling design is filled; while snowball sampling addresses the problem of ensuring an adequate sample of hard-to-find people.

However, the principle of *bias* is where non-probability sampling methods can most easily fall down, especially for convenience sampling. Many management researchers have been seduced by the lure of large samples for quantitative studies (perhaps feeling themselves under pressure from journal editors to report large samples) and achieved them simply through collecting respondents by any means (MBA classes, lists of Facebook friends, etc.). There is no guarantee that the findings reported are credible, since the credibility of findings relies in large measure on the character of the sample. It is not surprising, then, that reviews of research often highlight contradictions in findings between different studies, given that researchers often take little care in defining their sampling design. Qualitative researchers are not immune to issues of bias either, and can be seduced by the richness of data from small samples. Rich data can be powerful persuaders in that they give researchers the feeling that whatever they observed in a small sample of firms applies to all similar firms or instances. However, every research study involves a sample, and it is vitally important to the credibility of results that the researcher considers how the sample used sits within the larger group from which the sample is drawn.

Validity in survey research

reliability
the consistency of measurement in a composite variable formed by combining scores on a set of items; can be measured by Cronbach's alpha coefficient

There is a concern about whether the instruments and questionnaire items used to measure variables are sufficiently accurate and stable. Most of this is ascertained through pre-testing instruments before the actual research is carried out, and hence measures of reliability are important because they assesses whether an instrument will produce the same score on each occasion that it is used. There is also the question of external validity: whether the patterns observed from the sample data will also hold true in other contexts and settings. And again, the technicalities of assessing reliability and validity with survey data will be discussed further in Chapter 9.

EXERCISE 4.4

Non-probability sampling

1   **Individual**: Conduct a literature search online and identify three studies in which the following sampling techniques were used: a) quota sampling, b) snowball sampling and c) purposive sampling.

2   **Group**: In groups of three, present the examples you have chosen. Who has identified the most interesting example?

3   **Group discussion**: Discuss the reasons underlying the decision to adopt a sampling strategy based on a) quota sampling, b) snowball sampling and c) purposive sampling. How do the authors of the studies you selected justify their choice?

Constructionist research designs

Constructionist research designs (quadrants B and C) are linked to the relativist and nominalist ontologies. They start from the assumptions that verifiable observations are potentially subject to very different interpretations, and that the job of the researcher should be to illuminate different truths and to establish how various claims for truth and reality become constructed in everyday life. Hence it is not surprising that there is a wide range of methodologies which fit within the constructionist paradigm. Here we cover some of the main methodologies – action research and cooperative inquiry, archival research, ethnography and narrative methods – which are primarily based on constructionist designs. In the subsequent section we will look at methods that often bridge the epistemological divide, notably case method, grounded theory and so-called mixed methods.

Action research and cooperative inquiry

One of the key assumptions of positivism, and of natural scientific methods, is that the researcher should be objective, maintaining complete independence from the object of study. In the social sciences, where claims of the researcher's independence are harder to sustain, many people have tried to turn this apparent problem into a virtue. This is the tradition of action research, which assumes that social phenomena are continually changing rather than static. With action research, the researchers are often part of this change process itself. The following two beliefs are normally associated with action research designs:

> **action research** an approach to research that seeks understanding through attempting to change the situation under investigation

1. The best way of learning about an organization or social system is through attempting to change it, and this therefore should be an objective of the action researcher.

2. The people most likely to be affected by, or involved in implementing, these changes should as far as possible become involved in the research process itself.

Some forms of action research appear to follow the principles of positivism, for example by attempting to change the organization from the outside and then measuring the results. Kurt Lewin (1948), who originated the action research tradition, used experimental designs when investigating the efficacy of different ways of getting housewives to change their nutritional habits during the Second World War (see Example 4.3).

EXAMPLE 4.3

An early example of action research

During the Second World War, Kurt Lewin and his associates experimented with groups of American housewives to see if they could be persuaded to serve unpopular types of meat, such as beef hearts, sweetbreads and kidneys, to their families. They used two methods to try to persuade them to change their habits. In the first case, a lecturer gave an attractive talk to members of the group on the dietary and economic value of using

(Continued)

these meats, and offered some good recipes. In the second case, the same information was provided to the housewives, but they were invited to discuss the information and at the end to indicate by a show of hands whether they intended to serve the new meats. In a follow-up study it was found that only 3 per cent of the members of the lecture groups served one of the meats, compared with 32 per cent for the discussion/decision groups.

Similar results were obtained when persuading mothers to give orange juice and cod liver oil to their infants, although in these cases the discussion/decision method was only found to be twice as effective as the lecture method.

Source: Krech et al., 1962: 229–30

Kurt Lewin's studies were, however, different from traditional experimental research because there was an emphasis on changes in behaviour, and his housewives were active participants in deciding whether or not to change. The weakness with his initial experimental design was that it did not allow him to discover *why* the changes took place. This required subsequent experiments and qualitative studies in order to build up deeper understanding of why behaviour changed under these different circumstances. Given the strong emphasis on intervention as part of the research process, and the focus on debate and discussion, these later studies fit within quadrant C in Figure 4.1.

Involvement in the research process is taken a stage further in what has come to be known as cooperative inquiry (Reason, 1988; Heron, 1996). This has been developed for researching human action mainly at individual and community, rather than at organizational levels. It starts with the idea that all people have, at least latently, the ability to be self-directing, to choose how they will act and to give meaning to their own experiences. It fits with stronger versions of constructionism, and rejects traditional positivist methods where people are studied as if they were objects under the influence of external forces. Cooperative inquiry not only focuses on the experiences and explanations of the individuals concerned, it also involves them in deciding in the first place what questions and issues are worth researching. Thus the 'subjects' become partners in the research process.

A study of the development of Afro-Caribbean entrepreneurs in the West Midlands adds a further dimension. Ram and Trehan (2010) have worked for five years with a group of eight entrepreneurs. The group meets on a monthly basis and determines its own agenda, and more importantly controls its own membership. The primary goal for the entrepreneurs is to gather ideas and develop strategies from their interaction with other owners, which will enable them to grow their businesses (none of the businesses are in competition with each other). The academics are present at these meetings in the roles of process consultant, facilitator and researcher; they are also given access to company documents and conduct interviews with group members. This approach, known as critical action learning, is driven largely by group members and takes place within a social and political context. The academics thus become partners in the problem solving of the group, and contribute particularly through surfacing the feelings and emotions of members.

In his action research video David Coghlan, Professor Emeritus at Trinity College Dublin, discusses what kind of approach and research questions lend themselves to action research.

cooperative inquiry
a form of action research where the research 'subjects' not only play a part in sense-making, but also are encouraged to determine the main questions to be researched

critical action learning
a group-based inquiry that takes account of the viewpoint and feelings of members within a social and political context. The agenda and process are determined largely by members, rather than by academics

Action research

Archival research

It is not always necessary to gather new data when conducting research. An enormous amount of data already exists in the public domain as corporate and government reports, and statistical and financial databases that can be accessed online. Our focus here is mainly on textual information and its analysis, which we call archival research. Given the focus on words and on existing texts, this type of research fits with quadrant B in Figure 4.1 (page 93).

Favoured sources of archival data in management and business research are the annual reports from companies where statements from chief executives review achievements from the past year and outline plans and priorities for the next year. Analysis of the language used over time can demonstrate, for example, the emerging concern among large companies about sustainability issues, or increasing emphasis being placed on employee engagement. By analysing policy statements produced by central and local government in the UK between 1997 and 2008, O'Reilly and Reed (2010) were able to follow the changing rhetoric about the desirable behaviour of public sector managers over this period (see Example 4.4).

financial databases archives of records about companies or other entities, which contain financial data, such as income data, cash flow, profit and loss, share prices

archival research collection and analysis of public documents relating mainly to organizational or governmental strategies

EXAMPLE 4.4

An archival study

O'Reilly and Reed (2010) analysed 29 'high-level' government documents published between 1997 and 2008, which focused on management of the public sector. They searched these documents for strings of text containing <profession>, <manag> and <leader>. By looking at the frequency of usage they were able to show how the discourse of leadership, which emphasizes change and reform, has started to take over from the older 'new public management' discourse of managerialism, which emphasized efficiency and performance.

Today, there is a tremendous amount of textual data available online and it seems that we are only beginning to discover the opportunities for new kinds of archival research. We distinguish here between *reactive data* where the data are created because the researcher has provided some sort of stimulus (e.g. sent out a questionnaire) and *non-reactive data* that have not been created in the context of the research but are still of relevance, for example for an archival study. Textual data created for websites (including blogs or online job sites) are non-reactive data, which in many ways resemble archival data.

Ethnography

The key principle of ethnography is that the researcher should 'immerse' him- or herself in a setting, and become part of the group under study in order to understand the meanings and significances that people give to their behaviour and that of others. It is thus a strong form of constructionism. Most outsiders who are new to an organization or group will encounter things that they do not understand. These are what Agar (1986) calls 'breakdowns': events or situations where the researcher's past experience gives no help in understanding what is going on. This breakdown therefore represents something unique about that organization, and which was previously unknown to the researcher. For example, most groups have 'in-jokes', based on experiences shared only by members of the group. In order for an outsider to make sense of the breakdown provided by an in-joke, it will be necessary to track

ethnography approaches to research and data collection that emphasize gaining access to the perspectives and experiences of organizational members

back to the original experiences (Roy, 1952; Collinson, 2002). The breakdown provides a kind of window into exploring aspects of the experiences and meaning systems of groups and organizations. It will only be possible to resolve the breakdown when the researcher has understood these meaning systems.

emic
insights into communities, societies or organizations as seen from the perspective of insiders

Another important distinction is between what are known as emic and etic perspectives. These two terms were first coined by the American linguist Kenneth Pike (1954): *emic* refers to the sounds within a language which can only be distinguished by speakers of that language; and *etic* refers to features of a language that are easily identified by outsiders, but are largely inaudible to people who speak that language. For example, there are four tones in Chinese; these are *emic* because they cannot easily be distinguished by a non-Chinese speaker, yet are absolutely critical to understanding the language. On the other hand, most native English speakers are unaware that their speech is seen (from an *etic* perspective) as tight-lipped and monotonic by French and Italian speakers.

etic
insights into communities, societies or organizations as seen from the perspective of outsiders

The distinction has led to a view that better insights can be gained into management and organizations through participant observation, where insider and outsider perspectives are combined. Thus, Bartunek and Louis (1996) advocate methods which involve research teams that combine people working inside the organization with people working from the outside. Using methods like this, the ethnographer has the opportunity to challenge and extend conventional wisdom, and to generate new insights into human behaviour. However, in many organizations it can be difficult to conduct full ethnographic research because of access restrictions, although it is often possible to combine observation of meetings with interviews of participants. The emphasis of involvement of the researcher in the research setting, combined with the strong constructionist element, locates ethnography within quadrant C in Figure 4.1 (page 93). In Chapters 6 and 7 we develop the idea of participant observation further.

The growing scope and diversity of social interaction that takes place online has opened up new opportunities for ethnographic research. Virtual ethnographies of social media or online communities can provide useful insights into the experiences of those who contribute or take part in them. There is no one method for conducting ethnographic research online but in Chapter 7 we will provide an introduction to the creation of qualitative data using observational methods in a virtual environment.

Narrative methods

narrative methods
ways of conducting research that concentrate on collecting the stories told among organizational members

Another group of constructionist research designs has been given the general label of narrative methods (Boje, 1995; Czarniawska, 1998; Boje, 2001; Daiute and Lightfoot, 2004). These contain both ontological and epistemological elements. The ontological view suggests that stories and myths form a central element of organizational reality, and therefore research on organizations, which ignores stories, can be seen as incomplete. The epistemological position is that by collecting organizational stories, the researcher will gain insights into organizational life that could not be reached by more conventional means. Narrative methods may involve participant observation, where the researcher can become part of the process of constructing and transmitting stories, or they may be collected through interviews by asking people for the stories that they have heard about particular events (see Example 4.5). In essence, narrative methods rely on literary theory (Hatch, 1996), and hence both the position of the narrator and the role of the analyst are very important.

EXAMPLE 4.5

A narrative-based study

Humphreys and Brown (2008) investigated the way corporate social responsibility (CSR) was introduced as an important function within a financial services company. The authors, consistent with our definition above, saw stories and narratives as central to the way managers and employees make sense of what was going on in the company. Their research design involved the collection of stories from key actors involved in the establishment of corporate social responsibility within the company. From the analysis of semi-structured interviews with 64 employees, they identified three major themes/narratives associated with CSR – idealism and altruism; economics and expedience; and ignorance and cynicism – which summarized the conflicting perspectives on CSR in that company.

One of the criticisms of narrative methods is that they do not offer much that is distinctive or additional to 'normal' qualitative research. Nevertheless, they do have a number of strengths: they provide a holistic perspective on organizational behaviour; they are particularly useful in developing social histories of identity and development; they are useful in helping to examine relationships between individuals and the wider organization; and they introduce values into the research process. Returning to the matrix in Figure 4.1 (page 93), narrative research may be seen as more detached (quadrant B) if the collection of existing stories is emphasized, or more involved (quadrant C) if the researcher plays a role in encouraging people to invent new stories that illustrate their feelings. An example of research that adopted such an 'involved' stance is presented in Chapter 8 (pages 238–9) where Catherine Cassell tells us about a study of taxi drivers' experiences of dignity and abuse.

Validity of constructionist designs

There is much debate about how to assure and demonstrate the quality of constructionist designs, although authors rarely use the term 'validity'. In a classic paper, Golden-Biddle and Locke (1993) identify three key criteria:

1. authenticity
2. plausibility
3. criticality.

Authenticity involves convincing the reader that the researcher has a deep understanding of what is taking place in the organization; *plausibility* requires the research to link into some ongoing concern/interest among other researchers; and *criticality* encourages readers to question their taken-for-granted assumptions, and thus offer something genuinely novel. More recently, Amis and Silk (2008) suggest that good research within the constructionist tradition should be partisan, taking the side of the less powerful members of society and organizations, and supporting a 'moral-sacred' philosophy. Thus, quality would be indicated by the presence of the audience in the text, the sharing of emotional experience, stressing political action, taking sides, moving people to reflect and act, and providing collaborative, reciprocal, trusting and friendly relations with those studied.

Another perspective is provided by Silverman (2013), who argues for a more objective stance (and hence a weaker form of social constructionism) because there are few safeguards to prevent researchers from picking evidence out of the mass of data to support their particular prejudices. In order to defend themselves against charges of 'anecdotalism' he suggests several principles, including refutability, constant comparison, comprehensive data treatment and tabulations. *Refutability* involves looking for examples that might disconfirm current beliefs; *constant comparison* follows the principles of grounded theory (see next section) in looking for new cases and settings, which will stretch the current theory; *comprehensive data treatment* involves carrying out an initial analysis of all of the data available before coming up with conclusions; and *tabulations* imply greater rigour in organizing data, and accepting that it can also be useful to add up the occurrence of phenomena sometimes.

Our own view is that the results of constructionist research should be believable, and they should be reached through methods that are transparent. Thus, it is very important for the researcher to explain how he or she gained access to the particular organization, what processes led to the selection of informants, how data was created and recorded, what processes were used to summarize or collate it, how the data became transformed into tentative ideas and explanations, and how he or she felt about the research.

Case method and grounded theory

There are several methods that, despite having a single label, can be used in quite different ways by different proponents. This is particularly true with case method and grounded theory. Although the dominant texts about case method come from the positivist end, the method can also be designed in ways consistent with relativist and constructionist perspectives. On the other hand, grounded theory was designed as a constructionist alternative to positivist methods, yet some respected versions now contain positivist elements.

Case method

Essentially the case study looks in depth at one, or a small number of, organizations, events or individuals, generally over time. There is a very extensive literature on the design, use and purposes of case studies. In the management field, authors tend to coalesce around those who advocate single cases and those who advocate multiple cases. Advocates of single cases generally come from a constructionist epistemology; those who advocate multiple cases usually fit with a more positivist epistemology.

Robert Yin is one of the best-known exponents of case method in the social sciences. According to Yin (2013), case studies are vulnerable to a number of criticisms from more *positivist* researchers. In particular, it is suggested that they do not have the rigour of natural scientific designs; they rarely allow generalizations to be made from specific cases to the general population; and they produce huge piles of data, which allow researchers to make any interpretations they want. In response to these criticisms, Yin suggests that all case studies should have clear designs produced before any data is collected, and these designs should cover: the main questions or propositions, the unit of analysis, links between data and propositions, and procedures for the interpretation of data. He is anxious to demonstrate that case studies may contain the same degree of validity as more positivist studies, and therefore his exposition of the method contains both rigour and the application of careful logic about comparisons.

---

case method
a research design that focuses in depth on one, or a small number of, organizations, events or individuals, generally over time

grounded theory
an open (and inductive) approach to analysis where there are no a priori definitional codes but where the structure is derived from the data and the constructs and categories derived emerge from the respondents under study

unit of analysis
the main level at which data is aggregated: can be individuals, groups, events, organizations, etc.; within relativist studies researchers look for relationships between attributes that vary across different units of analysis

In contrast, the alternative approach to case method, which is informed by a *constructionist* epistemology, is much less concerned with issues of validity, and more concerned with providing a rich picture of life and behaviour in organizations or groups. Robert Stake (2006) writes about qualitative case studies, and distinguishes between *instrumental* and *expressive* studies. The former involves looking at specific cases in order to develop general principles; the latter involves investigating cases because of their unique features, which may or may not be generalizable to other contexts. An example would be Andrew Pettigrew's research into organization development within the chemical company ICI during the 1970s and early 1980s. In those days ICI was the most powerful manufacturing company in Britain, so there was naturally a lot of interest in understanding how they were managing and developing themselves. In that respect the study was expressive, but there was also an instrumental element since Pettigrew was interested in understanding the phenomenon of organization development, and ICI was regarded as one of its leading proponents. His research involved numerous interviews with key actors in the company over several years, and this provided a longitudinal element to his research, which enabled him better to understand both the contextual and historical settings of the company (Pettigrew, 1985).

From a similar perspective, Nikkolaj Siggelkow (2007) provides a spirited defence of case studies, arguing that they are particularly valuable for demonstrating the importance of particular research questions, for inspiring new ideas and for illustrating abstract concepts. He also points out that even single cases can provide very convincing tests of theory by quoting the famous 'talking pig' example. Thus, we only need to produce a single talking pig to demonstrate the error of the popular idea that pigs are incapable of intelligent speech. The logic being that we only need one example of an anomaly to destroy a dominant theory – as in the case of Einstein's refutation of Newton's theory. And although we are unlikely to identify a 'talking pig' organization, there are many examples where single cases can be uniquely interesting; for example, the company that does significantly better (or worse) than all others in the same industry, or the entrepreneur who builds a fortune from small beginnings.

EXERCISE 4.5

A longitudinal case study

A study conducted by Prieto and Easterby-Smith (2006) explored the links between dynamic capabilities and knowledge management through a case study of the evolution of a single company over several years. Because the researchers were interested in dynamic capabilities – which are by definition about continuous change – it made sense to observe processes over time so they could examine how, for example, the introduction of knowledge-sharing routines led to greater strategic flexibility. Accordingly, the researchers spent time observing management meetings, talking with participants at meetings, and interviewing other managers. They also followed information exchanges with partner organizations by conducting visits to their sites, repeating interviews with key informants, and feeding back emerging insights to senior managers to 'validate' their interpretations and to stimulate further insights.

1   How would you justify that this research was 'valid'?

2   What possibilities are there for generalizing the findings from this research?

3   Do questions about validity and generalizability make any sense in this instance?

There are a few important points to note about constructionist studies. First, they are based on direct observation and personal contacts, generally through interviews. Second, they take place within single organizations, but then involve sampling from numbers of individuals. Third, the collection of data takes place over a period of time and may include both live observations and retrospective accounts of what has happened.

There is also an intermediate position, which has been developed particularly through the work of Kathy Eisenhardt (Eisenhardt, 1989; Eisenhardt and Graebner, 2007). This view draws inspiration from both the positivist and constructionist positions, and has been adopted widely by researchers using case methods, particularly in North America. She is eclectic in her advice about methodology: using designs that are established at the outset, but then being flexible about their adaptation; recommending data collection through using multiple methods; and conducting both within-case and across-case analysis.

Above all, Eisenhardt is concerned about building theory from case-based research, and this takes the form of developing hypotheses. She recommends that hypotheses can be formed, or shaped, through three main stages. The first stage involves sharpening up the basic constructs, and this is essentially an iterative process of moving back and forth between the constructs and the data. The second stage involves verifying that emergent relationships between constructs fit with the evidence from each case. In this respect she comments that 'Each case is analogous to an experiment, and multiple cases are analogous to multiple experiments' (Eisenhardt, 1989: 542). The third stage involves comparing the emergent theory/concepts/hypotheses with the existing literature. In particular, she suggests paying attention to literature that is contradicted by the evidence, both because any evidence of having ignored contradictory findings is likely to reduce confidence in the final conclusions, and because the highlighting of contradictory conclusions is likely to make the original contribution from the research most explicit.

EXAMPLE 4.6

Comparative case study design

In a comparative study of investment decisions in Chinese and UK companies (Lu and Heard, 1995), case studies of 16 decisions in 8 companies were compared and contrasted in order to establish the cultural and institutional variations in business decision-making between China and the UK. The study involved collecting both qualitative and quantitative data, including extensive site visits to companies in both China and the UK. Each UK company was matched, in terms of size and industry, with the equivalent Chinese company. This allowed for a number of comparisons, between different industries, and between China and the UK, which led to new insights. For example, in the latter case the researchers noticed that the mean time between the inception and the implementation of a major investment decision (approximately £100 million) was virtually identical in both China and the UK (approximately 3.4 years). This significantly contradicted existing theory about the speed of decision-making, which had suggested that decision-making in China was far slower than in the UK. Of course, with the benefit of hindsight it is now possible to see how fast Chinese companies have been developing over the last two decades, but this study was one of the first to demonstrate the speed of economic development in China.

Although the variations in case study design and application are complex and sometimes blend into each other, we summarize in Table 4.3 some of the main distinctions in the use and application of case method at three points along the epistemological continuum.

TABLE 4.3   Key features of case method informed by different epistemologies

	Positivist (Yin)	Positivist and constructionist (Eisenhardt)	Constructionist (Stake)
Design	Prior	Flexible	Emergent
Sample	Up to 30	4–10	1 or more
Analysis	Cross-case	Both	Within case
Theory	Testing	Generation	Action

Grounded theory

Grounded theory was first formulated by Glaser and Strauss (1967). They saw the key task of the researcher as being to develop theory through 'comparative method', which means looking at the same event or process in different settings or situations. For example, the researcher might be interested in the workings of performance appraisal interviews and would therefore study a number of interviews handled by different managers, in different departments or in different organizations. As a result of the studies, it might be noticed that most appraisal interviews either focus on reviewing performance in relation to last year's objectives, or on future goals and how the subordinate may be helped to achieve these. They might then be labelled as 'judgemental' or 'developmental' interviews, and the distinction would represent a *substantive theory* about appraisal interviews.

However, the theorizing could be taken further. For example, it might be observed that neither form of interview has much effect on individual performance, nor on the relationships between the managers and their subordinates. Then we could conclude that both forms of interview are simply organizational rituals, which have the function of demonstrating and reinforcing hierarchical power relations. This would be the beginning of a more generalized *formal theory* about power and organizational rituals. Glaser and Strauss consider both substantive and formal theory to be valuable, and they propose two main criteria for evaluating the quality of a theory. First, it should be sufficiently *analytic* to enable some generalization to take place; at the same time it should be possible for people to relate the theory to their own experiences, thus *sensitizing* their own perceptions.

It is important to note that 'I'm doing grounded theory!' should not be used as a justification for doing some vaguely qualitative research without any clear view of where it is supposed to lead. Grounded theory contains precisely articulated methods and presuppositions. The problem is, as Locke (1997) explains, that methods have evolved and developed since their initial exposition, and at the heart of this was a rather acrimonious debate between Barney Glaser and Anselm Strauss.[2] In essence, Glaser believes that researchers should start with no presuppositions, and should allow ideas to 'emerge' from the data (Glaser, 1978, 1992), whereas Strauss recommends familiarizing oneself with prior research and using structured, and somewhat mechanistic, processes to make sense of the data (Strauss, 1987; Corbin and Strauss, 2015). Either way, the researcher should be aware that

---

[2] We understand that Glaser and Strauss did meet up and resolve their differences shortly before the untimely death of Anselm Strauss (personal communication).

there are different versions of grounded theory, and will need to articulate his or her own position when writing up the research. Agreed features are shown in Table 4.4, and differences between Glaser and Strauss are summarized in Table 4.5.

TABLE 4.4   Agreed features of grounded theory

Grounded theory

Must:	fit the substantive area
	be understandable and useable by actors
	be sufficiently complex to account for variation
Key analytical operations are:	cycle of theoretical sampling
	constant comparisons
	evolving theory, *leading to* ...
	theoretical saturation

The debate is extended further by Kathy Charmaz (2000), who characterizes the methods of both Glaser and Strauss as 'objectivist'. She argues that both authors separate the researcher from the experiences of the subjects of the study. She also feels that the recommendations of Strauss and Corbin (1998) about detailed analysis of transcripts, including line-by-line analysis and 'fracturing of data', reduce the ability to represent the whole experience of the individuals involved. In her view, a constructionist should recognize 'that the viewer creates the data and ensuing analysis through interaction with the viewed' (Charmaz, 2000: 523). As such she is located a little further in the constructionist direction than Strauss because she emphasizes the interaction between the researcher and the researched, rather than between the researcher and the data.

TABLE 4.5   Grounded theory: points of disagreement between Glaser and Strauss

	Glaser	Strauss (and Corbin)
Researcher roles	Maintain distance and independence	Active interrogation of data
Theory	Emerges from data itself	Arises from theorist/data interaction
Ontology	World is 'out there'	Reality and experience are constructed
Pre-understanding	Avoid literature from immediate area	Flexible approach; insights from many sources

In order to make sense of these differences, we need to look both at the ontology and epistemology of the authors. Ontologically, Glaser comes across as a realist, or possibly an internal realist, whereas both Strauss and Charmaz have a more nominalist ontology because they assume that the social world is created through the interaction of actors. Epistemologically, Strauss adopts a weak positivist position, which emphasizes systematic and reductionist approaches to the analysis of data. Glaser, on the other hand, promotes a more relaxed epistemology, insisting that the data should be analysed. Charmaz adopts a constructionist stance.

EXAMPLE 4.7

Grounded theory

With her study 'Thick as Thieves', Tammy MacLean (2001) generated new insight into rule-breaking in organizations by investigating deceptive sales practices in a major life insurance company in the USA. Using grounded theory techniques, she developed a theoretical model illustrating the persistence and proliferation of rule-breaking in organizations. Her research question evolved through an iterative cycle of informal preliminary interviewing, reading accounts of a scandal, and surveying the literature relevant to rule-breaking. She used a snowball technique to create a sample of 20 former employees of the insurer who had been subjects of a regulatory investigation of its sales practices. She interviewed the former employees and started analysing the first interview transcripts while still conducting interviews in the field. Her findings identified important mechanisms of diffusion and facilitation of rule-breaking that are embedded in relationships between managers and employees.

Before completing this section, it is important to note that the methods of grounded theory have been developed mainly within educational and health settings where the researcher can have relatively easy and flexible access to data and cases. But access is far more difficult within commercial organizations, and researchers are rarely given the freedom to select their samples on theoretical grounds – hence some of the assumptions of grounded theory have to be amended further to deal with this kind of situation (Locke, 2001). Organizational researchers have to accept the interviewees assigned to them by powerful organizational members who act as gatekeepers (see the discussion on strategies for gaining research access in Chapter 5); there are also limits imposed in terms of timing, topics and the use of data. This often requires a number of compromises to be made in terms of research design, as can be seen from the reflections of Suzanne Gagnon in Exercise 4.6 about her study of identity formation among highflying managers in two different international organizations.

Grounded theory, in its different guises, is one of the most popular qualitative methods in business and management research. Suddaby (2006) gives much helpful advice for researchers seeking to use grounded theory methods and publish their work. He lists some common misconceptions:

- Grounded theory is not an excuse to ignore the literature.

- Grounded theory is not presentation of raw data.

- Grounded theory is not theory testing, content analysis or word counts.

- Grounded theory is not simply routine application of formulaic technique to data.

- Grounded theory is not perfect.

- Grounded theory is not easy.

- Grounded theory is not an excuse for the absence of methodology.

EXERCISE 4.6

How grounded is this? A letter from a doctoral student

Hi Mark

I started with a general area for study – the interplay of personal and organizational identities in multi-nationality, multicultural organizations (how important is organizational culture in such settings, and why? What identities do people see themselves as having in these settings, and why?).

Once having been in the sites for some time and gathered some data through interviews, I found that *identity regulation* was a term (perhaps even a central category, in Strauss' and Corbin's words) that had explanatory power; I got this term from the literature, having continued to iteratively study the literature and the data, while continuing to gather data.

My 'sample' was more or less set from the beginning (all participants on two management development programmes), so in this sense I did not use theoretical sampling. However, I did add questions and change emphases in the interviews as I proceeded.

Whether I reached theoretical saturation, I am not fully sure. In a sense it was more a question of talking to everyone, and then sampling the data (with some follow-up and changes to subsequent questioning and focus, as above).

I see this as a kind of 'theory elaboration' rather than deduction per se. But there is definitely a deductive side to it. It may also be the case that I come up with my own theory (hope so), especially, perhaps, in comparing results across the two cases.

That's as far as I can go at the moment. What do you think? How grounded is this?

Suzanne

Individual/group discussion:

1   How grounded is this?

2   Should she be sticking more closely to grounded theory principles, and if not, why not?

Mixed methods

In recent years there has been growing interest in the use of research methods that draw from both positivist and constructionist epistemologies, and which combine both qualitative and quantitative methods in the same study. This has been stimulated by several influential books (Creswell, 2003; Teddlie and Tashakkori, 2009; Tashakkori and Teddlie, 2010) and by the founding of the specialist *Journal of Mixed Methods Research* in 2007. It is important to distinguish between mixed methods and multi-method. The first refers to the use of both quantitative and qualitative methods, whereas the second implies the use of multiple methods of the same type (either qualitative or quantitative).

There has also been a debate between proponents of mixed methods and those who are sceptical about their value. Those in favour argue that by using a range of different methods within the same study the researcher will increase the validity and generalizability of results and the potential theoretical contribution; the sceptics point to practical limitations such as the competence of researchers in conducting different methods, and to possible contradictions between the paradigms underlying different methods.

There are many variants of mixed methods in social research, but the key idea is that they involve combinations of qualitative and quantitative methods for data collection and analysis. We will therefore start by discussing the choices with regard to data collection, then consider different strategies for analysis, and finally consider some of the arguments for and against the use of mixed methods.

Designs for data collection

There are two main considerations in the design of studies that use both qualitative and quantitative methods to conduct research: sequencing and dominance. Sequencing refers to whether one method goes before the other, and if so which goes first. Dominance is a matter of whether one method uses significantly more time and resources than the other, or whether they are roughly balanced in importance. These considerations are summarized in Table 4.6.

By combining these choices we can identify three distinct designs, which incorporate both quantitative and qualitative methods. We call these master–servant, partnership and compensatory designs.

With *master–servant* designs the key point is that one method serves the needs of the other. There is usually a definite sequence in the use of methods, and naturally one method dominates the other. The most common format is the qualitative pilot study based on interviews or direct observation, which is used to develop, and maybe test, the items for the main study, which involves a (quantitative) questionnaire survey. Here the questionnaire survey is dominant, and the pilot study serves no function in the final result of the work, other than helping the researchers to design a questionnaire that is likely to yield accurate and reliable data.

sequencing in the context of mixed methods research this refers to whether or not the methods are used in a discernible order

dominance in the context of mixed methods research this refers to whether, or not, one method uses significantly more time and resource than the other

TABLE 4.6   Choices in designing mixed methods research

Design features	Alternatives to consider
Sequencing of methods	Qualitative first, or quantitative first, or both at the same time
Dominance of methods	Predominantly qualitative, or quantitative, or balanced

There are also examples of the reverse process, where a quantitative survey is used to identify a small number of 'interesting' cases for in-depth investigation, and then the survey results are largely ignored in the final results. For example, Macpherson et al. (2010) conducted a survey based on single interviews with 92 entrepreneurs. From this sample they identified three critical cases where they conducted repeated interviews over a year in order to establish how various tools (such as knowledge-management software, benchmarking and problem-solving forums) contributed to the learning processes of the SME. In this case it is the qualitative study that dominates the published paper, with the survey merely in the background.

Partnership designs typically involve combining more than one method, such as a questionnaire survey and interviews, where both assume similar importance in the study.

For example, entrepreneurial behaviour can be investigated by interviewing a small sample of entrepreneurs about their origins, motives, strategies, successes and failures, supplemented by a questionnaire containing similar questions sent out to a larger sample. When combined, the interview data will contain greater detail, clarifications and added explanations; the questionnaire data will contain shorter answers, possibly more focused, but will be able to cover responses from a wider range of entrepreneurs who could be divided into sub-groups to explore possible differences according to family history, levels of funding, types of technology, and so on.

Compensatory designs combine qualitative and quantitative studies where each is used to make up for the weaknesses of the other. Typically qualitative studies are seen as weak on generalization, and quantitative studies are weak at explaining why the observed results have been obtained. Thus, there is a growing trend in leading US publications such as the *Academy of Management Journal* for quantitative studies that establish statistical relationships between variables to be supplemented by quotations from substantial numbers of interviews focusing on the mechanisms and processes, which may provide explanations for the observed results.

RESEARCH IN ACTION

Mixed methods research

José F. Molina-Azorin is a Senior Lecturer in the Department of Management, at the University of Alicante, Spain. His research focuses on strategic management, environmental management, organizational design, quality management, competitiveness of the tourism industry and research methods. He is co-editor of the *Journal of Mixed Methods Research*.

José F. Molina-Azorin

What makes mixed methods a distinct methodological approach?

The central premise of mixed methods is that the integrating of quantitative and qualitative approaches can provide a better understanding of research problems than either approach alone (Creswell and Plano Clark, 2011; Fetters and Freshwater, 2015). This better understanding can be achieved through triangulating one set of results with another, with the aim of enhancing the validity of inferences. Other rationales for integrating qualitative and quantitative methods are: complementarity, for example when the results obtained from using one method elaborate or clarify findings derived from the other; development, when the researcher uses the results from one method to help develop the use of the other method; and expansion, when using different methods extends the breadth and depth of an enquiry.

Mixed methods research has been championed by methodologists from several fields, including education, health sciences, psychology and sociology. Although management and business scholars have combined quantitative and qualitative methods, the attention devoted to mixed methods has been relatively low in comparison to other disciplines (Molina-Azorin and Cameron, 2015). However, over the past decade, several reviews about mixed methods in business and management research have been published, such as

Hurmerinta-Peltomaki and Nummela (2006), Molina-Azorin (2012) and Molina-Azorin et al. (2012). Together with Donald D. Bergh, Kevin G. Corley and David J. Ketchen, I published the first special issue on mixed methods in a management journal (*Organizational Research Methods*) in 2017.

How do you approach designing a mixed methods study?

First, mixed methods research is not a panacea. Different methods (quantitative, qualitative or mixed methods) are appropriate for different situations. Specifically, the research question(s) and contexts should dictate the choice of the appropriate research method. Second, when a mixed methods approach is adequate, then we try to determine a specific mixed methods design, taking into account two main dimensions: sequencing of methods and dominance of methods. Again, the choice will depend on our objectives, research question(s) and context.

Can you provide us with an example?

In our mixed methods study in the hotel industry (Molina-Azorin et al., 2015), a sequential study was designed, where first a qualitative research is performed, followed by a quantitative stage. Both the qualitative and quantitative stages had the same importance. In this work, it was appropriate to develop an initial qualitative stage due to the inconclusive and even contradictory results found in the literature, and also due to the need to contextualize this study in the hotel industry. The purpose of this exploratory qualitative stage was to establish a number of propositions, which were then tested in the second quantitative stage.

Can mixed methods research be conducted by research students or early career researchers?

Yes, of course. In fact, there are many PhD dissertations that implement a mixed methods approach. A key point is that a mixed methods study must be competently designed and conducted, and as a consequence, researchers must have the skills and training to carry out both quantitative and qualitative studies and the ability to properly integrate these methods. Therefore, research students who want to design and conduct a mixed methods study must have knowledge about quantitative, qualitative and mixed methods approaches. Mixed methods studies may also require more time, work and financial resources than mono-method studies.

TOP TIP

My main tip for research students is: try to widen and extend your methodological skills and your repertoire of methods, and try to learn about mixed methods earlier in your career. After we graduate, we usually continue to rely on the methods we initially learned. When we develop expertise in using some methods where we feel

(Continued)

comfortable, it is hard to break from that. My point here is that there is a reciprocal influence between research questions and methods. Research questions determine appropriate methods. But methods may also influence the research questions we ask. So, by extending our methodological skills, we can increase the rigour of our conceptual thinking, see new ways to answer research questions, and even identify questions that would not have occurred to us otherwise (Edwards, 2008). Mixed methods research can play a key role here as this methodological approach combines and integrates quantitative and qualitative methods. By conducting mixed methods studies, the research student is motivated to develop a broader set of research skills.

Analysis

Another form of mixed methodology can be introduced at the analysis stage. Although qualitative and quantitative data are normally analysed within their respective traditions, there is also the possibility of cross-over designs. Thus, quantitative data can be analysed in qualitative ways and qualitative data can be analysed in quantitative ways. The most common form of the latter is when frequency counts are made of the use of particular words, phrases or themes from a sample of interview transcripts. The study by O'Reilly and Reed (2010) (see Example 4.4) provides an example of qualitative archival data in the form of government policy documents being analysed quantitatively for the occurrence of particular words and expressions. Slightly less common is when quantitative data are analysed by techniques such as factor analysis and principal components analysis, which look for patterns that are largely hidden. Techniques such as the repertory grid technique (see Chapter 6) involve starting with qualitative data, which then become quantified and analysed statistically, and the result is then interpreted qualitatively.

principal components analysis a mathematical procedure that assists in reducing data and by so doing indicates possible relationships between a number of uncorrelated variables: the first principal component accounts for as much of the variability in the data as possible, successive components (of which there may be two, three or four) account for as much of the remaining variability as possible

semi-detached design a mixed methods design where there are no direct linkages between the two parts of the study

Arguments for and against mixed methods

There are many reasons why mixed methods are regarded as a good thing: they have the potential to throw new perspectives on research questions, to increase the credibility of results, to demonstrate generalizability, and to provide deeper insights that explain why things take place. But there are also plenty of reasons for being cautious about their wholesale adoption. We summarize some of these pros and cons in Table 4.7.

There is, however, a more fundamental critique of the use of mixed methods, which hangs on the notion of paradigm incommensurability (Burrell and Morgan, 1979; Morgan and Smircich, 1980). The argument is that it is unwise to combine different paradigms within the same study because the different underlying assumptions mean that it will not be possible to join the two parts of the study together. At the extreme this can produce a semi-detached design, because like two semi-detached houses, they are physically linked together, yet there is no adjoining doorway between the two parts of the house.

The weakness of the incommensurability argument is that it assumes that paradigms are always distinct and that there can be no overlaps. Recent thinking about paradigms suggests that boundaries are more fluid than originally portrayed (Cunliffe, 2011), and hence it may be acceptable to combine paradigms up to a point. In our view the limits can be defined by the matrix presented in Figure 4.1, so that it is possible to combine adjacent ontologies and epistemologies within a mixed methods study, but this becomes increasingly problematic when combining more distant positions. For example, a positivist study might demonstrate that 80 per cent of corporate performance could be predicted by three variables: size, market share and growth rate. But when combined with an ethnographic study exploring the micro-politics of constructions of corporate performance, this would not contribute in any way to identifying the remaining 20 per cent in the predictive formula. It would be more likely to undermine the credibility of the main study by arguing that the concept of 'performance' is a sham.

The use of mixed methods can also lead to contradictory results. If the ontologies are very different there will be no way of resolving the confusion. However, if they are close enough then resolution may be possible, as illustrated in Example 4.8.

TABLE 4.7   Pros and cons of mixed methods

Arguments for mixed methods	Arguments against mixed methods
• They increase confidence and credibility of results	• Replication is difficult
• They can increase validity	• They take up more resources and often more time than single method studies
• They stimulate creative and inventive methods	
• They can uncover deviant dimensions	• Their use requires a competent overall design
• They can help synthesis and integration of theories	• The researcher needs to be skilled in the use of both methods
• They may serve as a critical test of competing theories	
• They can combine confirmatory and exploratory research at the same time	• It is not helpful if one method simply provides window dressing for the other
• They can present greater diversity of views	
• They can provide better (stronger) inferences	

Sources: Jick, 1979; Bryman and Bell, 2007; Tashakkori and Teddlie, 2010

EXAMPLE 4.8

Problems with mixed methods

Morgan Tanton and Mark Easterby-Smith carried out a comparative evaluation study of two executive management programmes (Courses A and B), held in two different business schools (respectively, Institutions A and B). Observations during the course, and qualitative data obtained from follow-up interviews, showed quite clearly that Course A was superior to Course B, but the quantitative data in the form of student ratings about the two courses showed clearly that Course B was preferred to Course A. Was this discrepancy caused by the methods used, or could it highlight some unusual features of the two courses being examined?

To resolve this dilemma we showed the survey results to participants and asked for their explanations. First, participants commented that they were cautious when filling in multiple choice rating forms, because they could never be sure what the data would be used for; therefore, they usually avoided unduly negative responses. Second, the course designs and institutional settings affected the criteria that participants used for evaluating the two courses. In Institution A the emphasis was on the longer-term application of what had been learnt; in Institution B the emphasis was on the immediate quality of sessions conducted within the classroom. Thus, it was not surprising that the rating forms that were completed at the end of the course showed one pattern, whereas follow-up interviews conducted some months later showed another pattern. In this case, it was possible to combine the two sets of data because the survey and interviews were respectively backed by internal realist and relativist perspectives, and both parts shared a common research question.

Finally, we can note that much of the interest in mixed methods comes from those on the positivist side of the spectrum, who hold at least an internal realist view of the world, on the grounds that added data and more perspectives will enable them to get closer to the intangible objects of their enquiries. Cynics might say that positivists need to incorporate more constructionist methods to make up for the shallowness of their traditional methods!

Guidelines for designing mixed methods research

mixed methods research involves utilizing and integrating methods from different research traditions

Mixed methods

Mixed methods research has advanced management and business research in important ways, but it needs to be planned with care. Molina-Azorin and colleagues (2017), in the introduction to their special issue of *Organizational Research Methods*, testify to the diversity and potential of contemporary mixed methods research in management and business research. When designing a mixed methods study, it is important to work out in advance a clear rationale for each method, and take care to ensure that they are reasonably compatible. There is always a danger in using mixed methods of trying to achieve too much with one study, or avoiding making some fundamental decisions about research objectives and research design. An ad hoc combination of different kinds of methods may lead to a situation where none is done properly.

Table 4.8 provides a list of guidelines for designing mixed methods research, which our colleague and expert Molina-Azorin has put together for you.

TABLE 4.8 Guidelines for designing mixed methods research

- Identify the core reasons for collecting both forms of data (quantitative and qualitative).
- Understand the relationships between the quantitative and qualitative phases in data collection (sequential or simultaneous).
- Make informed decisions about the weight or attention given to quantitative and qualitative parts of the research (balanced status or a part is dominant).
- Take into account the 'opportunistic nature' of mixed methods research: a mixed methods study may have a predetermined/planned research design, but new components may evolve as data are collected and analysed.
- Be creative and do not be limited by the existing mixed methods designs. Create designs that effectively answer your research question(s).
- Read mixed methods works published in your research topic. A good approach to learning about how to conduct a mixed methods study is to analyse mixed methods works published and examine the features that characterize them as mixed methods research.

EXERCISE 4.7

Mixed methods

1 **Individual**: Conduct a literature search to identify two articles that report mixed methods research in management research (the review articles mentioned by José F. Molina-Azorin on page 125 may be a good starting point). Examine the methods section of each of the two articles and make a list of the different steps of the research process. What did the researcher(s) do first? What steps followed?

2   **Group discussion**: Compare your notes with Molina-Azorin's guidelines for designing mixed methods studies. Do you think the authors followed the guidelines? Discuss in class.

3   **Group discussion**: Discuss in groups of two to four students: What did the authors of the two articles gain from adopting a mixed methods approach? What were the challenges? Take notes so that you can summarize your discussion in a plenary session at the end of the class.

4   **Individual**: Think about your own research project or a research idea you may wish to pursue. Do you think mixed methods research would be an appropriate approach? Write a short essay (600–1000 words) on the reasons why a mixed methods approach would (or would not) be appropriate. Make sure to highlight both potential benefits and opportunities as well as limitations or reasons to reject a mixed methods approach.

Common design dilemmas

In this section we identify five areas that require decisions when formulating research designs, irrespective of the ontology or epistemology that informs the study. These are:

- identifying the unit of analysis
- universal theory or local knowledge
- theory or data first
- cross-sectional or longitudinal
- verification or falsification.

Identifying the unit of analysis

The *unit of analysis* is the entity that forms the basis of any sample. Samples may be formed from one or more of the following: countries, cultures, races, industrial sectors, organizations, departments, families, groups, individuals, incidents, stories, accidents, innovations, and so on. In positivist forms of research, including multiple case studies informed by an internal realist perspective, it is important to be clear about the unit of analysis in advance, because this is the basis for collating data that will subsequently be analysed. It is not essential in constructionist forms of research, but with highly unstructured data it can help to provide an initial guidance for analysis. In the above example from our research, which compared decision-making between China and the UK (Example 4.6), the unit of analysis was the company, but there was a subsidiary unit of analysis (what is sometimes referred to as an embedded case), which was the investment decision. Hence it is possible to have more than one unit of analysis, provided the theoretical aims of the research justify this, but it is not advisable to have too many.

embedded case a case within a larger case, for example, the A&E department within a hospital that was the primary case

Universal theory or local knowledge?

One of the key principles of scientific methods and positivist knowledge is that theories and observations made in one context should be applicable to other defined contexts.

generalizability
the extent
to which
observations
or theories
derived in one
context can be
applicable to
other contexts

universal theories
theories that
may be derived
in one social
organizational
setting, and
which are
applicable in
any other setting
or context

local knowledge
ideas and
principles that
are relevant
to the setting
of a particular
organization or
social setting,
but which may
not apply in
other contexts

As we have discussed above, being able to provide assurances of generalizability, or external validity, are critical features both of experimental designs and the statistical procedures that are employed to interpret realist research data. In these cases, as with Kathy Eisenhardt's intermediate position on case method, the objective is to produce universal theories.

On the other hand, a number of scholars argue that local knowledge is more significant. For example, according to post-colonial theory, many theories of race, economic development and culture are constructs of scholars in Western countries, which typically cast non-Western culture and institutions as being somehow inferior to their own (Said, 1978). Similarly, from feminist theory there is a strong view that many of the dominant theories of social behaviour are blind to the effects of gender and patriarchy (Ahmed, 1998). In both cases the argument is that any generalized statement about the social world is likely to contain within it assumptions that mask the relations of power between those who formulate theories and those to whom they are applied. As such, there is a strong view that significant social theory should be understood in relation to the context whence it is derived.

Local knowledge is also important for management and organizational research. First, practical knowledge used by managers is essentially contextually bound, and is learnt through engaging in practice (Cook and Brown, 1999; Rouleau, 2005). If this is the case then it follows that for research to have theoretical value it should focus on these local practices – which may well be unique to that situation. Second, some people argue that managerial behaviour is culturally relative, including both national and organizational cultures (Boyacigiller and Adler, 1991). Hence researchers should formulate their ideas separately within each cultural context, and should not try to generalize across cultures.

For example, it has been accepted for some time that some models derived from Western management research are unlikely to be relevant in Asian contexts. Over the last decade there has been much interest in the development of entrepreneurial capabilities in Asian countries such as China, Vietnam, Malaysia and India. It is increasingly accepted that the cultural and institutional differences between these countries are such that local theories to explain entrepreneurial behaviour are necessary in each country (Taylor, 1999; Hobday and Rush, 2007).

Theory or data first?

The third choice is about which should come first: the theory or the data? Many academic researchers start their research with a gap in the literature that they seek to close, others conduct more phenomenon-driven research (they want to find out more about a particular and often novel phenomenon of interest) and a third group is predominantly problem-driven (e.g. researchers conducting action research). The question of whether a study starts with theory or with data again represents the split between the positivist and constructionist paradigms in relation to how the researcher should go about his or her work. The Straussian view of grounded theory assumes that preconceptions are inevitable. After all, it is common sense to assume that someone will not be interested in a research topic or setting without knowing something in advance about it. Hence he argues that the researcher should make him- or herself aware of previous work conducted in the general field of research before starting to generate his or her own theory. However, it is important to avoid imposing theory on data where it is misplaced, as such research easily 'misses the point'! Therefore, it can sometimes be advisable to make an attempt to distance oneself from what one already knows. By keeping one's mind open to new perspectives and views, new discoveries can be made, which can still be brought into dialogue and extend pre-existing theory.

The intermediate position suggests that the relationship between theory and data needs to be an interactive process. When researchers observe something that seems surprising or novel in a company, it is important to go back to the literature in order to see whether anybody else has remarked on it. This ongoing dialogue between existing knowledge and what the data have to say that is novel is one reason why initial literature reviews are almost always modified before the final write-up of a research project. Similarly, when a new paper gets published it may have a direct impact on the ongoing collection and interpretation of data.

Cross-sectional or longitudinal?

Cross-sectional designs, particularly those that include questionnaires and survey techniques, generally belong to positivist traditions. As we have noted earlier, they have undoubted strengths in their ability economically to describe features of large numbers of people or organizations. But a major limitation is that they find it hard to describe processes over time and to explain *why* the observed patterns are there. Thus, although Lyles and Salk (1996) were confident that balanced equity stakes led to the highest chance of knowledge transfer, their study itself could not explain what mechanisms or processes led to knowledge being transferred.

In order to understand processes of change over time, it is necessary to adopt longitudinal designs. From the positivist side these include quasi-experimental methods and diary methods because repeated measurements are taken over time, but it is more often associated with constructionist research, where repeated visits are made to the same individual or companies over months or years, or when the researcher conducts an ethnographic study working continuously in the same location.

Verification or falsification

This final decision is slightly different from the four preceding ones since it is not linked to resolving the broader debate between positivist and constructionist views. However, it is very important both for researchers and for managers, as we will explain below. The distinction between verification and falsification was made by Karl Popper (1959) as a way of dealing with what has become known as Hume's 'problem of induction'. This is the philosophical problem that, however much data one obtains in support of a scientific theory, it is not possible to reach a conclusive proof of the truth of that law. Popper's way out of this problem is to suggest that instead of looking for confirmatory evidence one should always look for evidence that will *disconfirm* one's hypothesis or existing view (as in the 'talking pig' example on page 117). This means that theories should be formulated in a way that will make them most easily exposed to possible refutation. The advantage then is that one only needs one instance of refutation to falsify a theory, whereas irrespective of the number of confirmations of the theory, it will never be conclusively proven.

The example often given to illustrate this approach takes as a start the assertion that 'all swans are white'. If one takes the verification route, the (non-Australian) researcher would start travelling around the country accumulating sightings of swans, and provided that he or she did not go near a zoo, a very high number of white sightings would eventually be obtained, and presumably no black sightings. This gives a lot of confidence to the assertion that all swans are white, but still does not conclusively prove the statement. If, on the other hand, one takes a falsification view, one would start to search for swans that are *not* white, deliberately looking for contexts and locations where one might encounter non-white swans. Thus, our intrepid researcher might head straight for a zoo, or perhaps book a flight to Western Australia where most swans happen to be black. On making this discovery, the initial hypothesis would be falsified, and it might then have to be modified to include the idea that 'all swans have either white or black feathers'. This statement still has

verification a research design that seeks evidence to demonstrate that the current assumptions or hypotheses are correct

falsification a research design that seeks evidence to demonstrate that the current assumptions or hypotheses are incorrect

what Popper calls high 'informative' content because it is expressed in a way that can easily be disproved, whereas a statement like 'all swans are large birds' would not be sufficiently precise to allow for easy refutation.

Much of the debate about verification and falsification fits within the positivist view because ideas of 'truth' and 'proof' are associated mainly with that paradigm. But there are also important lessons that the constructionist might take from this discussion. If the idea of falsification is to be applied more fully to constructionist research, then one should look for evidence that might confirm or contradict what one currently believes to be true, by applying 'critical sensitivity' (Alvesson and Deetz, 2000) or 'critical subjectivity' (Reason, 1988). A falsification strategy is also an important element of abductive research (Dubois and Gadde, 2002), which emphasizes ways in which data can generate new theory rather than either confirm or disconfirm existing theory.

This advice not only applies to researchers but also to managers who are concerned to investigate and understand what is taking place within their own organizations. Most managers are strongly tempted to look for evidence that supports the currently held views of the world. This is not surprising if they are responsible for formulating strategies and policies within a context that is very uncertain, and hence they will be looking for evidence that demonstrates that their strategies were correct. The logical position that follows from the above argument is that, even if *disconfirmatory* evidence is unpopular, it is certainly both more efficient and more informative than confirmatory evidence. Moreover, if managers adopt the falsification strategy and fail to come up with evidence that disconfirms their current views, then they will be able to have far more confidence in their present positions.

Contributing to theory

Good research designs need to have some link to theory. In the case of student projects and dissertations it is generally necessary to *use* theory, whereas for doctoral theses and papers in academic journals it is necessary to demonstrate a *contribution* to theory. This is not as daunting as it might seem, and in this section we elaborate on the types and purposes of theory, and explain how they can be incorporated into research designs.

The term 'theory' often has negative connotations. Someone might report back on a lecture saying, 'It was all a lot of theory!', meaning that it was either difficult to understand or just plain boring. Or someone might react to a new idea saying, 'Well that's all right in *theory*, but ...', meaning that although the idea sounds plausible, it would not work in practice. So, in this case theory is seen as the opposite of practice. On the other hand, there is the well-known saying, 'There is nothing so practical as a good theory' (Lewin, 1943: 118, cited in Weick, 2003: 460). In order to unscramble this confusion, we offer distinctions between everyday and academic theory, the latter subdividing further into middle-range and grand theories.

everyday theory
the ideas and assumptions we carry round in our heads in order to make sense of everyday observations

Everyday theory refers to the ideas and assumptions we carry round in our heads in order to make sense of everyday observations. For example, if you observe an old man walking down the street arm in arm with a young woman, you might conclude that they were grandfather and granddaughter. In order to reach this conclusion you might hold two assumptions about family relations: that grandparents often live close to their family members, and that grandparents often have very close relations with their grandchildren. If the man is leaning slightly on the woman, then it would strengthen the grandfather–daughter hypothesis; but if the man's walk was very unsteady this might suggest a new theory, that they are patient and nurse. On the other hand, if the man is well dressed and the woman is conspicuously glamorous, an alternative hypothesis might suggest itself: that the man is a wealthy philanderer and the woman is a mistress or 'trophy' wife.

Although everyday theories enable people to make sense out of specific events or situations, academic theories tend to look for higher levels of generalization. Following the above example for just a moment, in order to explain what was going on, a sociologist might draw on theories about the power of male patriarchy, palliative care for the elderly, or the evolution of the institution of marriage. The distinction between middle-range theories and grand theories is a matter of scale and formality. An example of the former would be the key idea of absorptive capacity: that the ability of an organization to absorb new external knowledge depends on whether it already possesses related knowledge (Cohen and Levinthal, 1990). It is middle-range because it is a generalizable proposition that can potentially be tested empirically.

On the other hand, grand theories tend to be more abstract and contain whole edifices of assumptions that are often not testable. The theory of psychoanalysis is one example because it provides a self-contained set of ideas to explain human behaviour. A number of the integrated philosophies summarized at the end of Chapter 3, such as critical theory or structuration theory, are grand theories in the way we have described them here.

Where researchers are seeking to build theory, this is normally at the level of middle-range theory, and is an incremental process. For example, work by Todorova and Durisin (2007) has argued that Cohen and Levinthal's (1990) model of absorptive capacity is too rational and unduly focused around R&D, and consequently more attention needs to be paid to political and systemic processes. But how we can evaluate the quality of theories, or theoretical contributions, and how can we distinguish a good contribution from one that is less good? Some criteria are fairly obvious: good theories need to be simple, have good explanatory power and be relevant to issues that need explaining. But, beyond this, the evaluation of contribution is largely a matter of judgement among people who already know the field quite well, which is why peer review is normally used to evaluate the theoretical contributions of research proposals and academic papers. We will be returning to these issues at various points later in the book, especially in Chapter 12.

academic theory explicit ideas developed through exchanges between researchers to explain and interpret scientific and social phenomena

middle-range theory a set of ideas and concepts relevant to explaining social or physical phenomena within relatively specific contexts, normally empirically testable

grand theory a coherent set of assumptions intended to explain social or physical phenomena; may or may not be empirically testable

Contrasting views on validity and reliability

There is an underlying anxiety among researchers of all persuasions that their work will not stand up to outside scrutiny. This is very understandable since research papers and theses are most likely to be attacked on methodological grounds, and one of the key justifications for doing 'research' is that it yields results that are more accurate and believable than common everyday observations.

The technical language for examining this problem includes terms such as 'validity', 'reliability' and 'generalizability'. But as we have indicated above, these mean different things within different research traditions. In Table 4.9 we therefore summarize how these terms are discussed from the philosophical viewpoints of positivism, relativism and constructionism.

The implication of Table 4.9 is fairly obvious: that depending upon where people stand on the epistemological continuum, they are likely to use different criteria for judging the quality of research. This will affect how they design and conduct their own studies and how they assess the quality of others' work, particularly when they are acting as examiners, reviewers or just colleagues.

TABLE 4.9 Four perspectives on validity, reliability and generalizability

	Strong positivist	Positivist	Constructionist	Strong constructionist
Validity	Has the design excluded all rival hypotheses?	Does the design make it possible to eliminate plausible alternative explanations?	Have a sufficient number of perspectives been included?	Does the study clearly gain access to the experiences of those in the research setting?
Reliability	Do the measures correspond closely to reality?	Do the measures used provide a good approximation to the underlying concepts of interest?	Will similar observations be reached by other observers?	Is there transparency about data collection and interpretation?
Generalizability	Does the study confirm or contradict existing findings in the same field?	Are the patterns observed in the sample data consistent with findings from other studies?	Is the sample sufficiently diverse to allow inferences to other contexts?	Do the concepts and constructs derived from this study have any relevance to other settings?

Research design template

Research design template

We have argued throughout this chapter that research designs should take account of epistemology, and hence formal research designs need to focus on different issues. In Table 4.10 we list some of the main headings that need to be covered within each epistemology. To use this template, decide which epistemology is most appropriate to your research study and then follow the questions down the relevant column.

EXERCISE 4.8

Research design template

1 **Individual**: Download the research design template from this book's website. Think of a research project you would like to conduct (for example for your dissertation) and use the template to make a first attempt at developing a research design for the study. Which questions are particularly difficult to answer? Why do you find them challenging? Write up an outline of the research design and try to address all 14 points listed in the table.

2 **Group**: In pairs, present and discuss your draft research designs. Provide feedback on whether you find the respective other's choices convincing and if not, why not. Take notes of comments and suggestions for later use.

3 **Group**: Discuss your experience of working with the template in class. How many of you have adopted a strong positivist, positivist, constructionist or strong constructionist approach? Whose research design appeared to be particularly well developed? What research design was particularly difficult to develop and give feedback on? Discuss the reasons as to why some projects are more difficult to develop than others.

4 **Group**: Consider the case of researchers conducting applied research or evaluation research. In order for them to use the template, would you add or omit any questions? If yes, which ones? Can you explain why?

TABLE 4.10 Research design template for an academic study

		Strong positivist	Positivist	Epistemology Constructionist	Strong constructionist
1	Background	What is the theoretical problem and what studies have been conducted to date?	What is the theoretical problem and what studies have been conducted to date?	What are the ongoing discussions among researchers and practitioners?	What are the ongoing discussions among researchers and practitioners?
2	Rationale	What is the main gap in existing knowledge?	What are the main variables, and how are they related to one another?	What perspectives have been covered and what are missing?	What are the limitations in the discussions so far?
3	Research aims	Specify testable hypotheses.	List the main propositions or questions.	Identify the focal issue or question.	Explain how the research will add to the existing discussion.
4	Setting	Determine the wider population from which you will draw your sample.	Determine the research setting and the population from which you will draw your sample.	Identify an appropriate research setting and justify your choice.	Describe your research setting and justify that the methods you intend to use are appropriate to the setting.
5	Data (see Chapters 6, 7 and 9)	Define variables and determine measures.	Define the dependent and independent variables and determine measures.	Explain and justify a range of data collection methods.	Identify main sources of data. How will interviews be recorded/transcribed, etc.?
6	Sampling (see Chapters 4 and 9)	Explain how group selection and comparison will eliminate alternative explanations.	Justify sample size and explain how it reflects the wider population.	How will the sample enable different perspectives to be included?	Explain sampling strategy. Will it be opportunistic, emergent, comparative, etc.?
7	Access (see Chapter 5)	How are experimental subjects to be recruited?	How can responses to questionnaires etc. be assured?	What is the strategy for gaining access to individuals, organizations?	How will insights from co-researchers be combined?

(Continued)

TABLE 4.10 (Continued)

		Epistemology		
	Strong positivist	**Positivist**	**Constructionist**	**Strong constructionist**
8 *Ethics (see Chapter 5)*	Is participation voluntary?	Could results be used to harm any participants?	Will the interests of individuals and organizations be protected?	How 'open' is the research? Will there be any deception?
9 *Unit of Analysis*	Differentiate between control, experimental groups, etc.	Specify whether individuals, groups, events or organizations.	How will units/cases be compared with each other?	What are the entities that are to be compared with each other?
10 *Analysis (see Chapters 8, 10 and 11)*	Statistical procedures for examining differences between groups.	Statistical procedures for examining relationships between variables.	Arrangements for coding, interpreting and making sense of data.	How will co-researchers be involved in sense-making?
11 *Process*	Explain stages in the research process.	Explain stages in the research process.	Explain what can be pre-planned and what can be open-ended.	Provide realistic timing including adequate provision for contingencies.
12 *Practicalities (see Chapter 5)*	How will groups be recruited? Where will experiments take place?	Who will gather data? How will it be recorded/stored? Who will analyse it?	How will researchers share observations? Who will do transcriptions etc.?	How will co-researchers be engaged?
13 *Theory*	How will hypotheses be tested?	In what ways will the results add to existing theories?	Will the research build on existing theory or develop new concepts?	Will the research build on existing theory or develop new concepts?
14 *Outputs (see Chapter 12)*	Where will the research results be published?	What is the dissemination strategy?	What is the dissemination strategy?	How will insights be shared with colleagues and collaborators?

EXERCISE 4.9

Classification exercise worksheet

Classification

Individual/group: Using Table 4.11, classify the following according to whether you consider them to be ontologies, epistemologies, methodologies or methods: grounded theory; unobtrusive measures; narrative; case method; ethnography; critical realism; participant observation; experimental design; falsification; theoretical saturation. If it is a weak association put * into the corresponding box, ** for a moderate association, and *** for a strong association. Explain your reasoning. (Note: many of them could be more than one thing.)

TABLE 4.11   Classification exercise

	Ontology	Epistemology	Methodology	Method
Grounded theory				
Unobtrusive measures				
Narrative				
Case method				
Ethnography				
Critical realism				
Participant observation				
Experimental design				
Falsification				
Theoretical saturation				

Conclusion

In this chapter we have discussed some of the key philosophical debates underlying research methods in the social sciences, and we have looked at the implications these have for the design of management research. Some key points are:

- A research design is a strategy that lays out the principles of the research methodology for a given study. It articulates methods and techniques for all stages of the research process and justifies their appropriateness in relation to both the research question or hypothesis and the research context.

- Researchers differ in their research orientation. These differences shape decision-making in the research design process.

- There is a clear dichotomy between the positivist and social constructionist worldviews, but the practice of research involves a lot of compromises.

- Each position has its own language and criteria for evaluating research designs.

- Methodologies such as case studies can populate different quadrants in the matrix.

- There is considerable diversity of methods and designs, especially within the constructionist research tradition.

- Differences in opinion about research methods are often underpinned by ontological differences.

The worldview held by an individual researcher or institute is an important factor, which affects the choice of research methods. But there are other factors, too. Senior academics can exert pressure on junior colleagues and students to adopt methods that they favour. Governments, companies and funding organizations can exert pressure on institutions to ensure that the aims and forms of research meet with their interests. The politics of research are complex, and researchers neglect them at their peril. That is why we have chosen to devote the next chapter on the research experience to a discussion of these issues.

Further reading

A good textbook that introduces how to design and conduct a grounded theory study. Charmaz is a prominent advocate for constructionist approaches to grounded theory, distancing herself from the more positivist leanings of the founders of grounded theory:

Charmaz, K. (2014) *Constructing Grounded Theory: A Practical Guide Through Qualitative Analysis*, 2nd edn. London: Sage.

A great beginner's overview of the three different paradigms:

Creswell, J.W. (2003) *Research Design: Qualitative, Quantitative and Mixed Methods Approaches*, 2nd edn. Thousand Oaks, CA: Sage.

An accessible introduction to conducting case studies for management and business research:

Farquhar, J. (2012) *Case Study Research for Business*. London: Sage.

This is an excellent overview of the origins of grounded theory including the differences of opinion between Glaser and Strauss, the key methods and approaches as currently practised, and the specific adaptations that may be required when conducting organizational or management research:

Locke, K. (2001) *Grounded Theory in Management Research*. London: Sage.

A very useful, albeit slightly dated, handbook for further reference with excellent chapters on how to develop a research design, formulate a research problem and compose a research proposal. It also includes a section on applied and evaluation research.

Miller, D.C. and Salkind, N.J. (2002) *Handbook of Research Design & Social Measurement*, 6th edn. Thousand Oaks, CA: Sage.

A practical guide to the field of mixed methods research:

Plano Clark, V. and Ivankova, N. (2016) *Mixed Methods Research: A Guide to the Field*. Thousand Oaks, CA: Sage.

An updated version of the classic book on experimental forms of social research:

Shadish, W.R., Cook, T.D. and Campbell, D.T. (2002) *Experimental and Quasi-Experimental Designs for Generalized Causal Inference*. Boston, MA: Houghton Mifflin.

Chapter 7 of this authoritative text on mixed methods research considers research designs for studies that combine quantitative and qualitative methods:

Teddlie, C. and Tashakkori, A. (2009) *Foundations of Mixed Methods Research: Integrating Quantitative and Qualitative Approaches in the Social and Behavioral Sciences.* London: Sage.

Check your understanding online

Visit the website **https://edge.sagepub.com/easterbysmith6e** for useful resources that will help reinforce what you've read in this chapter:

 Take an interactive quiz to test your understanding of the key topics

 Review suggested answers to Exercises 4.1 to 4.9 above

 Use interactive flashcards to check your knowledge of essential concepts

Learning objectives

To become aware of politics and power in research.

To be able to identify stakeholders, evaluate their role and interests in the research process and recognize those potentially at risk.

To develop awareness of personal and organizational ethics and develop judgement in dealing with 'grey' ethical issues.

To learn how to engage with research participants and supervisors.

THE RESEARCH EXPERIENCE

5

Chapter contents

Introduction

Conducting research involves a lot more than the development of a good research question and an appropriate research design. It is also an experience of continuously being challenged – personally, academically, socially and in many other ways. If you follow your curiosity, it is likely to take you to unknown places. Such places may delight but they can also be well beyond your comfort zone! In this chapter we examine some of the practicalities associated with conducting research on business and management. We start by discussing the importance of being aware of politics and power in research, and of the ways in which our environment shapes our research. We then discuss one of the biggest challenges faced by most social scientists, the problem of gaining access, before we turn to the most important section of this chapter, which discusses ethics in business and management research. In the last three sections, we examine the academic context in which many of us conduct our research and then address the supervisory relationship and the importance of having the right attitude and mindset when embarking on a research project. We have entitled this chapter 'The research experience' and our focus is on the wider sense of this experience, and of becoming a researcher, along with some useful guidance for making the most of this experience.

Research process

Before starting on this chapter, why not take a look behind the scenes by watching the video 'Sharlene Hesse-Biber reflects on the research process' by our colleague Sharlene Hesse-Biber, Professor of Sociology at Boston College, on the research process and how we experience it and try the exercise below.

EXERCISE 5.1

A behind the scenes view

Individual: Take some notes while listening to Hesse-Biber's account of 'unintended consequences'.

1   What does she mean by front stage/back stage?

2   What unintended consequences is she referring to?

3   What kind of unintended consequences could arise from your research?

Politics and power in research

A common view about research is that it is essentially an 'ivory tower' activity, which is carried out by independent scholars, dedicated selflessly to the pursuit of knowledge. Although this characterization may be an aspiration for some of our colleagues, it is rarely possible for researchers to divorce themselves from the realities of everyday life. For a start, scholars have regularly got themselves into trouble for following beliefs that were politically unpopular. The Greek philosopher Socrates was condemned to drink a cup of hemlock because he did not seem sufficiently respectful of current Athenian divinities; and Galileo was forced to recant his belief, which was based on careful observation of sunspots and planetary orbits, that the Earth moved around the Sun.

Although many academics have tried in the past to maintain their independence, it has never been altogether possible to separate scholarship from politics. But what do we mean by 'politics'? Our basic premise is that it concerns the power relationships between the individuals and institutions involved in the research enterprise, plus the strategies adopted by different actors and the consequences of their actions on others. Crucial relationships may be between: students and supervisors/tutors, funders and grant holders, authors and journal editors, companies and research institutes, managers and their bosses, and so on. Influence within these relationships may be exerted over: what is to be researched, when, by whom; how information is to be gathered and used; and how the products of research are to be evaluated.

For those doing management and business research, there is an important difference compared to other forms of social and psychological research: that it usually needs to be carried out in the context of organizations. Access to organizations usually has to be negotiated through managers, who are responsible for controlling, influencing and structuring the awareness and actions of others. It is the central process whereby organizations achieve the semblance of coherence and direction. This process is political, and various authors have commented on the same point (Hardy, 1996; Buchanan and Badham, 2008). It is very hard to think of an organization which is not political in some way!

This highlights a comparison with the wider social sciences, where research is often carried out on members of society who are often less powerful than the researchers. When conducting research into management and business, however, the subjects of research tend to be more powerful than the researchers themselves. Furthermore, most organizations are both tightly structured and controlled, so that gaining access to the corporate boardroom, for example, is exceedingly difficult. Managers are usually in a position where they can easily decline to provide information for researchers; they are also adept at handling face-to-face interviews and at managing interactions with strangers. So, in the case of research into management and business, the boot is firmly on the other foot.

Before discussing strategies for dealing with this situation, we offer a simple model, which we have found useful in making sense of the politics of research. This is based on the classic study by Boissevain (1974) of social networks, especially in the Sicilian Mafia.

EXAMPLE 5.1

Study of Sicilian Mafia

In the early 1970s, the anthropologist Jeremy Boissevain conducted a study in Sicily of the roles and relationships between members of the Mafia. He identified two distinct roles played by participants: brokers and patrons. *Brokers* are social 'fixers' who use their secondary resources, such as information and a wide range of contacts, in order to achieve their ambitions. *Patrons* have direct control over primary resources, such as people and money. But when they need information or the resolution of a problem the patrons turn to brokers who have the contacts and a past record of solving problems. A skilful broker will also specify a tariff that is only part of the real cost – so that when the transaction is made he will have built up further goodwill with the patron. This will in turn increase the broker's overall credit for future problem solving.

While we would not wish to suggest a direct correspondence between the worlds of Mafiosi and business researchers, there are a number of parallels. In the research world, senior academics and tutors can act as brokers because they know their way round the system, and are known by others. They may be able to arrange for access to a particular organization, to clarify and negotiate assessment criteria, to advise on how to obtain funds from research councils, to identify appropriate external examiners, or to make links with journal editors who are most likely to be interested in a particular paper. Successful researchers can also develop brokerage skills. Within companies, training and human resource managers can often act as brokers because, although they have little formal power, they usually have a wide range of contacts at all levels of the organization. Thus, corporate 'gatekeepers' (e.g. HR managers) are more likely to help provide access to their company if they think the researcher may be able to provide them with something in return – whether it be expertise, credibility or other contacts.

It should be clear from this that there are at least as many sources of (political) influence on our research as there are stakeholders involved. Figure 5.1 summarizes some of the most common factors influencing the questions we ask and ways we research them. We do not regard this as a mechanistic model; instead, we see research ideas evolving in an incremental way through a continual process of negotiation with stakeholders. In the following section we discuss these factors in turn. We start with the corporate stakeholders and the wider context of the research before moving to academic stakeholders and, finally, the researcher him- or herself.

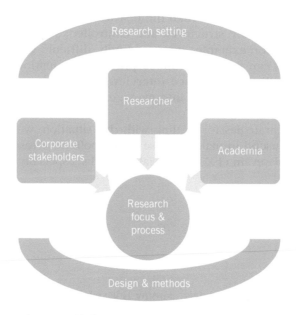

FIGURE 5.1 Stakeholders and sources of influence

Corporate stakeholders

We use the term 'corporate' loosely here, to include companies, public organizations and others generally within the user community. These stakeholders are becoming very significant because they participate in but also sponsor and make use of management research. Many companies invest heavily in executive education, sponsoring managers to attend MBAs and other programmes, and most of these involve projects conducted within the sponsoring organization. There is also growing interaction between companies and universities through enterprise development networks, knowledge transfer partnerships and the sponsorship of research.

In the case of student projects, there are several potential sets of expectations. A production manager attending a part-time programme might, for example, want to set up a three-month project in the marketing department. This means that the main stakeholders will include: the project sponsor in the marketing department; the academic supervisor; the training department that has organized sponsorship in the first place; and the manager. There is often tension between the sponsor who wants a solution to a problem, and the academic supervisor who will be looking for a well-argued case that uses recent literature and is supported by tangible evidence. Sometimes it is necessary to write two separate reports. Occasionally the two sets of expectations can be met with one seamless report that blends academic theory with practical action. Alternatively, there is the 'sandwich' model where the client report is prefaced by an academic introduction and literature review, and then followed by a methodological and substantive critique.

One key consideration is whether research that is conducted for corporate clients will become 'contaminated' because of the funding relationship. There are two ways in which this might happen. For example, corporate funders are likely to exert some influence on the direction of research and the kinds of questions that are considered to be significant. But this is likely to be the case with all forms of funded research, whether following a positivist or constructionist approach, and we think that the differences due to the presence or absence of corporate funding are merely a matter of degree. The other form of contamination may come from people within the organization deliberately feeding information into the project, which is likely to support their political agendas.

Given that contamination inevitably arises from political factors, the question is how best to deal with it? Our view is that these political factors and their consequences should not be kept hidden, rather they should be incorporated explicitly into the reports of the research process. The researcher's own interests, the process of gaining access or funds from organizations, or discussions about the dissemination of results may all be relevant. Thus, we would advise researchers not only to keep regular records of formal research data, but also to chronicle their own views and moods, and the processes of organizing and conducting the research. Further, we think it important that researchers are prepared to reflect critically on all of these influences on their research, and to make these thoughts available to others. This requires an element of reflexivity – which should increase, rather than decrease, the credibility of the results.

EXAMPLE 5.2

Collaborative research project with engineering companies

The Knowledge and Information Management (KIM) project was funded by the Engineering and Physical Science Research Council (EPSRC) between 2006 and 2009. It involved teams from 11 universities looking at the social and technical problems of information management within engineering companies that were seeking to add a significant service

(Continued)

element to the products that they sell. The project had a steering committee comprising representatives of 16 companies, which provided general guidance on the direction and potential outputs of the project.

There were many forms of collaboration here: between universities; between engineers and social scientists; between companies and universities; and between companies (some of which are normally in direct competition with each other). Sponsoring companies were able to exert influence by allowing research access only to those projects that had potential to contribute to the business, but they also contributed significantly to the quality of the academic debates by making presentations at the universities, and organizing workshops and seminars on their own sites.

Thus, there is no particular reason why academic and practical goals should not be achieved simultaneously; indeed, as in Example 5.2, we have found that many practitioners will become enthusiastically involved in theoretical debates created from the academic perspective. Such managers may not only be familiar with academic debates about culture and values but may also wish to contribute substantially to these debates. This increasingly leads to the possibility of managers, sponsors and gatekeepers being seen as collaborators in the research process itself.

RESEARCH IN ACTION

Industry-based dissertation projects

Anne Kruckenberg

Anne Kruckenberg is a business development manager in the packaging industry, where she develops complex logistics solutions with pharmaceutical and biotech companies as well as with governmental and non-governmental organizations. In this interview, Anne reflects on industry-based dissertation projects from the perspective of the industry partner.

As an experienced business development manager, you have recently advertised a dissertation project on risk management. What were your expectations?

A novel approach or outsider perspective can lend itself to the generation of the kind of insights needed to enhance business structures, marketing concepts or even strategy. Day-to-day business often keeps us so busy that it can be difficult if not impossible to make time to attend to underlying problems. Often we stick with familiar procedures that we know are not ideal just because we don't have the headspace to conduct a thorough analysis of a complex problem.

When we work with students on dissertation projects, we hope that both sides commit the time and energy required to produce a rigorous piece of research. Usually, we suggest a broader topic or problem of particular relevance to us. Once a student has agreed to work with us, and following an initial meeting, we expect the student to present a short proposal along with a timeline that identifies the student's demands in terms of access and support. We need this information well in advance so that we can allocate the time and resources needed to complete the project. Sometimes, it can also be helpful if the student's supervisor takes part in the first meeting to ensure that we are all on the same page. Ideally, we also expect a document from the university that lays out the terms and conditions of our project partnership. At the end of the project, we'd typically expect a presentation of the main results and a brief project report.

What advice can you give to students wishing to conduct an industry-based research project? If you were approached by a student, what would you look out for?

I would look for a somewhat structured and professional approach, creative thinking, social skills, and the ability to summarize and come to conclusions. While we do our best to enable students to deliver a great dissertation, we also need them to bear in mind that cooperation with external partners (including students) has to be communicated and 'sold' within the business – and not just to their supervisors! So when planning an industry-based project, it makes sense to start early so that there is enough time for internal and external communication and approval procedures. Other guidance may include:

- Do some research on the industry partner you want to work with.

- Think about what the industry partner can gain from working with you.

- Make an effort to sell your project – without raising unrealistic expectations.

- Define your demands in terms of information, resources and access to contacts clearly and well in advance.

- Try not to send any proposals or information sheets of more than two pages in length.

- When you arrange a meeting, send an agenda and questions three to five days in advance.

TOP TIP

Make sure to discuss changes in your approach, research question or schedule with your industry partner as they may have communicated project details internally. Email regular updates – just two or three lines are fine!

Access and engagement

In this section we consider the politics that are involved in gaining access to research sites. We distinguish between *formal* access, which involves gaining permission from senior management to gather data from within the organization, and the *informal* process of gaining access to people and documents. Similar to Buchanan et al. (1988), we would argue for an opportunistic approach.

Most researchers seriously underestimate the amount of time and patience that can be required to gain this initial access. The good news is that there seems to be a growing acceptance of the value of in-company projects – possibly because a growing number of middle managers have now been through business schools themselves.

It is can be extremely difficult to gain access to companies out of the blue (sometimes called 'cold calling'). In our experience it is essential to start with some kind of personal contact, however tenuous. If one's supervisor or institution does not have the right links, then it is often worth trying the relevant trade or professional associations, or using contacts in related organizations. We have found associations to be very helpful here, and they rarely object to being mentioned as the source of the contact – because, of course, brokerage is the lifeblood of most trade and professional associations (see Example 5.3).

Once the initial contact has been made by phone, letter or email, the gatekeeper is likely to consider two questions: (1) is this individual, and his or her project, worth supporting? and (2) will it be possible to 'sell' to others whose cooperation is being requested? The latter question hangs on a consideration of whether the potential benefits will outweigh the likely costs, or potential risks, of the project. Given that information about costs and benefits will be very imprecise, it usually helps at this stage if:

- the project has potential relevance and benefit to the organization
- the time and resources requested are minimal
- the project appears not to be politically sensitive
- the individuals concerned and their institution have a good reputation.

EXAMPLE 5.3

Trade associations and access

Selen Kars wanted to explore dynamic capabilities in medium-sized Turkish companies. She decided to focus on three different sectors – olive oil, motor components and tourism – which represented increasing degrees of dynamism. Within each sector she needed matched pairs where two companies should be as similar to each other in all respects, except that one would have a reputation within the industry for being particularly innovative, and the other would be well known for sticking with 'traditional' methods. Accordingly, she visited the national industry association for each sector, and they helped her to identify companies that fitted her criteria and then provided introductions to the chief executives.

However, projects can still go wrong. In a recent ESRC-funded project on the evolution of business knowledge, the research design required us to gain access to four distinct companies. Within the first six months of the project we obtained access to, and had commenced fieldwork in, the first three companies – and these all yielded valuable data and stories. We also gained an official letter of invitation from the fourth company, but before we were able to arrange the first meeting our sponsor, who had written the letter, abruptly left the company. Three months later at a dinner, Mark mentioned the problem to a senior manager from the company, and she agreed to provide another introduction. We attended a meeting and presented our proposals to a new group of managers, but were informed a few weeks later that the company had taken a policy decision to engage in research links with a very small list of universities, and ours was not on that list.

A few months later, Mark discovered that a Lancaster alumnus was working as PA to the UK managing director of the company. She offered to organize a meeting with the top man, which meant that we might be able to outflank the earlier policy decision. Unfortunately, a week before the meeting the company announced an international structural reorganization, which threatened the role of the UK managing director, and hence the meeting was cancelled. By this time we were three months from the end of the project and it was too late to replace that company with another company. The moral of this story is that it is always important to plan for contingencies: don't count your chickens, and keep something in reserve!

The principle of reciprocity is important: the more the company gives, in time or money, the more it expects in exchange. Another feature that is common to the above examples is that the initiative usually comes from the researcher, and organizational brokers may then be used to reach the patrons. However, there are occasions when patrons themselves may wish to initiate some research. At least six reasons for sponsoring research are common, and these are summarized in Table 5.1.

TABLE 5.1   Six reasons why companies may fund or sponsor research

1	To gain support for a new idea
2	To demonstrate the success of a recent project
3	To help the individual or unit defend against attack
4	To act as a sounding board
5	To support research for its own sake
6	As a means of enhancing legitimacy and reputation

Access proposal

Preparing for a first contact with the field requires a significant amount of background research in order to get a clearer picture of whom to contact and how. At this stage, researchers are advised to consider whether access to their chosen field is actually a realistic option – and whether they have a direct or indirect personal link to the field (e.g. a friend, neighbour, family member or colleague) who could help with getting a first contact.

Once this first contact or potential *gatekeeper* is identified, the best way of contacting this individual or institution needs to be established; this may be by letter, email, appearing in person, or a phone call. While preparing for the first attempt to secure access, it is important to think about the research project from the perspective of the potential participant. Why should this person be interested in this project? How can such interest be sparked in the best way? Lengthy academic proposals, unrealistic promises and sloppy template letters are unlikely to be successful. A contact request or access proposal should be polite, personal and appropriate in style and language. It should include:

- a short introduction to the study and its purpose, written in clear language

- an overview of what kind of data collection the study will involve

- a (flattering) statement about why the contact person is particularly qualified to contribute to the study
- a summary of the experience or background of the researcher (if it is thought it will help)
- a section addressing issues surrounding confidentiality and data collection.

Credibility can be enhanced by using the headed notepaper of an independent body, such as a university, institute or college. The language used in the access proposal merits particular attention. Certain presentations or framings of a research project can make it appear overwhelming, inappropriate, threatening or simply too inconvenient. Such considerations point towards the importance of a patient and incremental approach. While negotiations should not be rushed, continuous follow-up and initiative are likely to be required in order to get the first appointment, telephone call or email, which will decide whether or not access can be established. Whatever choices researchers make about how to approach the field, they should be guided not only by their own research interests but also by considerations about how their behaviour or appearance might be received in the field. One way to obtain trust is to make sure that one is well clued-up about the company. A scan through the company's website will give a quick impression of the issues that are currently considered significant. Another way to obtain the trust of the company one wishes to research is to present the research in a professional and enthusiastic way so that the company sees a benefit. We believe there to be two kinds of benefit which might be offered:

1. Outcomes from the research itself.
2. Contributions to issues within the company, which the researcher can offer as a side-benefit of the research. This might be through adding extra topics or themes into interviews or surveys, or carrying out extra work on analysing company data which does not directly benefit the research but adds value to the company.

These can both serve to build a stronger relationship with key people in the company, and can also build up 'credit' where the research itself is of more value to you than it is to the company.

EXERCISE 5.2

Preparing an access proposal

Individual: Prepare a sample access proposal for a planned or hypothetical research project. Reflect on how the access proposal might have to be amended when used for different audiences. Ask friends or colleagues to comment on your proposal. Would they be willing to get involved? What elements of the proposal would convince them to do so, and what elements could have the opposite effect?

Internal blockages to access

Barbara Czarniawska (1998) provides a fascinating account of her experiences in Warsaw, where she had obtained agreement to conduct a ten-day observational study of the director of finance of the city council. Most of this period seemed to be taken up with the director finding excuses not to talk to her, or to exclude her from meetings. Even when the director, in a moment of helpfulness, tried to arrange for Barbara to meet the deputy mayor, she only managed a passing contact and never managed to schedule an actual interview. Barbara Czarniawska is a senior professor with an international reputation, so perhaps it was hard for the director to resist her openly. With younger researchers, more direct 'put downs' may be used. One 'put down' technique is for the interviewee to cross-examine the interviewer at the outset in order to establish that she has very little relevant experience of the organization or context that she is apparently studying, and is very naive about the realities of anything outside the academic environment. Having established who is really in control of the interaction, the senior manager may then be prepared to sit back for 40 or 50 minutes and respond honestly to questions.

Even experienced researchers occasionally get caught out by this tactic. Beynon (1988) provides a nice example of a senior National Coal Board manager attacking the credibility of an expert academic witness involved in a colliery enquiry by asking such direct questions as: 'Are you qualified to manage a coalfield?', 'What practical management experience have you had in operating?', 'Have you any personal knowledge of selling to commercial buyers?'. This form of discrediting the external expert provides a very effective form of corporate defence, and perhaps the minor 'put downs' given to researchers by senior employees may be an anticipatory form of defence just in case the 'wrong' results are produced by the study.

Sometimes it is a *macro-political* problem (i.e. to do with wider organizational politics, as opposed to *micro-political* issues, which are about relationships between individual employees), for example when the researcher becomes trapped between two major groups or factions. When Mark Easterby-Smith was researching for his PhD, he had been asked by the works manager of a large chemical company to conduct a study into the consequences of a large plant closure. This exercise had apparently been handled very successfully and had led to the voluntary redundancy of over 1,000 workers, without any overt industrial relations strife occurring. This was exceptional at a time when industrial relations were riven with conflict.

About a week after starting the study he noticed that people were beginning to become less available for interview, especially those with access to personnel records. He was, however, very much reassured to be invited to lunch one day by a director of the wider company. Discussion ranged over the research project that had recently started, and the manager showed much interest in some initial observations. It was later the same day that Mark met one of the personnel managers from the site who informed him regretfully that a meeting had been held that same morning to discuss the research project, and that one person who had been very insistent about stopping it was the director with whom Mark had just dined.

This was unexpected, since nothing had been mentioned at lunchtime. It was even more surprising that the personnel manager thought there was nothing unusual about the director's behaviour. It later emerged that the decision to ban the project was the focal point in a major battle between the works manager and the director with regard to the appropriate management style on the site. The former was backing a rather paternalistic line of management, and the results of the study would no doubt have helped him in his argument. The director was arguing for a much harder form of managerialism, and unfortunately for the research project it was an argument that the latter won. Mark was simply 'collateral damage' in this wider dispute. The lesson from these political examples is that we often only see the 'tip of the iceberg' as many aspects of organizations are hidden from our view. Informal day-to-day practices and attitudes often lie below the surface. Researchers need to be aware of conflicts that may be far deeper and more complex than will be evident to a relative newcomer in the organization.

We can offer three pieces of advice on how to deal with such politics. First, try to identify one or two 'key informants' who may be prepared to help in a disinterested way. They need to be generally well informed but not directly concerned with the issues under investigation. Key informants may be able to advise on whom to talk to, and they should be able to explain why things are, or are not, happening. Second, deliberately look for people who have different perspectives on key issues. Talk further to them and others in order to understand *why* they hold different views. Third, always assume that there is more than meets the eye. People may withhold information because they think it is not important, or is irrelevant, or they may genuinely have forgotten things. In organizations that have a policy of moving people around every two years, the collective memory may be very short. The departmental secretary may be the only person who knows that your topic has already been researched and written up twice in the last five years!

Interviews
in China

It is also important to bear in mind that depending on the research setting, different strategies for gaining access may be deemed more or less appropriate. In the blog entry '"Renqing" in conducting interviews with Chinese business people: Insights from a returning researcher', Yue Wang tells us about the importance of paying attention to how different strategies for gaining access can play out differently when conducting elite interviews in China.

EXERCISE 5.3

Role-play about access

Group: Your group has the possibility of being given access to a local Internet company, which sells broadband and associated services to small and medium-sized businesses across the country. The task is to conduct fieldwork into 'leadership', and you need to complete a number of interviews in a real organization in order to complete your assignment. The initial contact with the company is through the training manager, and she has arranged for a meeting with the chief executive to discuss the possible research. The meeting will take place on site, and the chief executive has a busy schedule. He has also indicated that he would like to see just two members of the team in this first instance.

- Roles:

  o *Student 1, student 2*: Their aim is to gain access on behalf of their colleagues for a project that both fits their academic needs and is also ethically acceptable.

  o *Chief executive*: He is prepared to give access providing the project uses minimal resources/time, offers some potential benefit to the company, and carries absolutely no risks for the company or individuals within it.

  o *Training manager*: She is a former employee of the university at which the students are studying, but her own position in the company is slightly insecure.

  o *Other group members*: They should act as observers during the role-play and as facilitators of the debrief afterwards.

- Role-playing process:
  - The chief executive is in control of the meeting throughout. He has given himself 15 minutes in which to make a decision about whether or not to let the students in.
- Timescale:
  - 15 minutes: preparation. Student representatives; CEO and training manager; observers to discuss in separate groups their agendas and how they will handle/monitor the role-play.
  - 15 minutes: role-play.
  - 20 minutes: debrief. To be chaired/facilitated by the observers. Try to cover: pre-meeting strategies of different parties; degree of satisfaction with the outcome; what was unexpected; general lessons learnt about the process of access.

The role of the researcher

Another issue that researchers have to consider before entering the field is the role they will assume when conducting their data collection. Some factors that may be kept in consideration when making this choice are:

- *The purpose of the research* may provide a researcher with an indication of which role is most appropriate. Does the research require the continued and active involvement of a participant observer, or will a series of in-depth interviews give the kind of insights required?

- *The cost of the research* is another factor that needs to be kept in mind. To what extent can the researcher afford to be committed for extended periods of time, and are there any additional costs involved, such as training or housing costs?

- *The extent to which access can be gained* may seem a simple issue, but is an important one to be aware of when choosing a researcher's role. Gaining access where the role of the researcher is either explicit or covert can be difficult and may take time.

- *The extent to which the researcher is comfortable in the role* is of course vital to the choice. For example, with covert, or insider research, if the researcher is uncomfortable about taking on a false identity, will it be possible to develop the kind of trusting relationships that are important? Even when permitted, covert research is particularly stressful for the researcher, and not necessarily suitable for inexperienced researchers (Goodall, 1989).

- *The amount of time available* can also be influential. Some methods involve a considerable commitment of time.

Whichever role is chosen, each provides the means to obtain a detailed understanding of values, motives and practices. As Fairhurst (1983: 321) comments, 'The crucial personal skill is to be seen as someone who can be trusted no matter what role is adopted – this will enable much to become possible'.

In a recent example, a PhD student was able to gain access to conduct a three-company case comparison of the effect of performance-related pay on the behaviour of school teachers by taking a job as a lunchtime assistant in one school, a playground supervisor in another and a classroom assistant in another. Although the lunchtime assistant role was not ideal as the student would have preferred to be more closely involved in the practice of teaching, it served its purpose in enabling the researcher to get close to teachers, and in helping the early formulation of ideas. As we have indicated above, research of this kind invariably raises ethical dilemmas, and gaining access can be extremely difficult. However, students who require part-time work to undertake their studies can be sitting on very rich research material without realizing it.

Formal access usually has to be granted by decision-makers or authorities that bear some responsibility for the setting that the researcher wants to study. However, this does not generally imply that all potential participants are equally happy to engage with the researcher. Eileen Fairhurst (1983) chose for her research a geriatric ward, and this is where she met her first problem. It took a considerable amount of time to obtain agreement to conduct her research in a particular unit, for two reasons, which illustrate a number of problems involved in this type of research. The first was that consultants in the hospital viewed 'research' in two distinct ways: some saw it as something in which they must become personally involved and that they must 'vet'; others saw it as a self-indulgent activity in which they wanted no part. Even after she had gained agreement for the location of the research, there were additional problems associated with the sensitive focus of the study. Old people are especially vulnerable, and there was real concern that researching them might be viewed as a form of exploitation. To experience delay in the setting up of this kind of study is not in any way unusual. In the case of Thorpe's researcher-as-employee study (see Example 7.5 in Chapter 7), establishing access took a number of months!

Researchers, as we have discussed in relation to interviewing, must find strategies that will allay people's fears, and offer the organization (or the managers and employees who control access) either reassurance or something in return. This might involve many meetings, and even presentations to the employees, about the aims and potential value of the research. Once accepted, Fairhurst explained how a principal task was to move from a position of stranger to that of friend – someone who could be trusted. When she had achieved this, she found individuals were very willing to tell her about the organization – whether they were nurses, cleaners or ward clerks. While on the wards, she felt it appropriate to help make beds and assist generally; for example, with distributing food and drink at meal times, and collecting bed linen and clothes for patients. At such times, she was not only participating but also strengthening relationships. She recalls that there were times when she simply had to observe, for example when patients were spending time with occupational therapists or physiotherapists (and on other occasions when she did not possess the technical qualifications to take on any role in the work). People understood this and accepted it.

With most informants the relationship begins when you try to negotiate an appointment. As employees work under increasing pressure, they are becoming very protective over their time, and will make assessments of the likely costs and benefits of cooperating. Far too often, researchers are perceived to be 'all cost and no benefit' (Luker, 2008: 147), when there are in fact opportunities for them to give something back in a way that enhances their relationships with research participants. At the very least, researchers should never forget to thank research participants in an individual way that reflects their appreciation of the contribution they have made – whether or not this contribution is likely to be helpful.

RESEARCH IN ACTION

The politics of field exit

David Mosse

David Mosse is Professor of Social Anthropology in the School of Oriental and African Studies (SOAS) at the University of London. His research interests connect the anthropology of Christianity, South Asian society and popular religion with that of development and activism, environmental history and natural resources management. In his book *Cultivating Development: An Ethnography of Aid Policy and Practice* (2005), David examines this tension through an in-depth investigation of a development project, which he was involved in as a consultant practitioner for more than a decade. Here we present an extract of an interview in which he discussed his experience of conducting 'insider research' (Mosse and Kruckenberg, 2017).

What was your experience of becoming an inside researcher?

In my experience there are tensions associated with shifting from the position of an insider and colleague to that of an outsider and researcher. In the case of field-based research, you usually have to negotiate your position at the beginning and at the end (and often in between). At the beginning, because people will ask questions such as 'what are you doing here? How is this going to help us? What is this going to contribute?' And at the end, it's about how people have been represented and whether they feel happy about it.

Conducting research from within a development organization can appear to be the easier choice. You already have established access – and your presence is taken for granted. But in the case of insider research, problems are more likely to arise at the end, when one seeks to negotiate the 'exit'. When I went back to turn my experiences of over ten years into a research project – into an independent and ethnographic whole – I went through several rounds of discussions. I had to negotiate my right to an independent academic analysis. Unlike previous outputs, this was not a collective project, and in the end my analysis differed from the outputs I had generated as a member of the team. My findings became a source of misunderstanding, tension and ultimately conflict.

Looking back, do you think that there might have been a better way?

Paradoxically, in the case of insider research, 'field entry' occurs when you negotiate your exit from the sets of relationships that previously had made you an insider – so that you can reflect, generate data and analyse. The problem is that once you have done that, you will be thinking and researching from within a set of epistemological assumptions that are, in some ways, fundamentally different from those that you had been tied up in when you were an insider. As an independent analyst, you are likely to generate and analyse data that, from within the organization, would simply not be construed as data: for example, observation of informal activities and relationships, which become hugely important for your ethnographic understanding as an outsider. From an insider perspective, such

(Continued)

data may be dismissed as gossip – as being irrelevant, trivial, unprofessional, disrespect-ful or other critical terms – which is another way of saying 'we do not accept this as data'.

The very basis of your analysis might be impossible to justify within the framework of that organization. And it only becomes possible through a change in positionality, which, from the point of view of those who remain in the organization, can be perceived as ille-gitimate. As the basis of these relationships changes, some differences and difficulties may be inevitable. At the end, after a process of analysis and writing, one can even reach a point where it becomes impossible to renegotiate those relationships anymore. This doesn't mean one should not do this kind of research. But one has to be very attentive to the possible implications for those who have taken part.

So in a way, this problem is also about consent?

Yes, but I think there are different types and levels of consent. Informed consent relating to the participation in a study is part of the normal process of social science research. It becomes difficult, however, when there's an expectation that such consent should be extended to the results of the research. And that isn't necessarily part of informed consent unless you're premising your research on some sort of collaborative expectation. This was the core of the problem that I got into with my book. Colleagues of mine who, in the end, objected to its publication did so on various grounds, but one of the principal ones was that the analysis ought to be consensual. Anything written about the project should be collectively agreed on. And we disagreed because I said that this would make it impossible to analyse the whole process – and that I wasn't willing to abandon the entire project. This is something that researchers in this field continue to have problems with. Whether we like it or not, there is always an in-built tension around participation, which can be difficult to handle but is a necessary part of the research process.

Ethics

There are ethical issues bubbling under the surface of several of the examples we have given above. In this section we focus on the ethical issues that can arise when doing research into management and business and provide an overview of measures that can be taken to ensure that staff and student behaviour is ethical when conducting research.

Ethical codes and principles in business and management research

Although management and business researchers generally do not undertake studies that could put at risk the lives of those who take part – in a way doctors may do, say, when undertaking surgery – many ethical principles still apply, the first of which states that researchers are expected to ensure that they 'do no harm'. Certainly, research could lead to economic harm through plant closures or changes in work patterns or payment systems. A student breaking rules of confidentially may also trigger the dismissal of an employee. Informed consent and the right of confidentiality are therefore also just as important for management and business research as they are in medical research.

While researchers should normally protect the interests of the organizations they are investigating, there may be times when they come across illegal or unethical behaviour within the organizations themselves – and some people would argue that this should be published in a way that will expose the organization. An extreme example of this would be the case of Julian Assange who, between 2006 and 2010, took on the might of the US military and State Department by publishing over a million secret documents on his website, WikiLeaks. The debate about whether or not Assange was morally justified in what he did has been highly divisive. So, even though most organizational research is on a far more modest scale, it becomes difficult to establish hard-and-fast ethical principles, and good practice requires considerable judgement from the researcher.

Up until the turn of the century, management researchers, and their professional associations such as the British Academy of Management and the (US-American) Academy of Management, were relatively relaxed about the provision of ethical codes. But there is growing pressure from other academic disciplines, such as medicine and psychology, for all universities to adopt definite ethical codes and practices, and there is growing coherence, especially in the social sciences, around a common set of principles. Bell and Bryman (2007) conducted a content analysis of the ethical principles of nine professional associations in the social sciences. They identified ten principles of ethical practice, which were defined by at least half of the associations. These principles are summarized in Table 5.2.

TABLE 5.2   Key principles in research ethics

1	Ensuring that **no harm** comes to participants	*Protection of research participants*
2	Respecting the **dignity** of research participants	
3	Ensuring a fully **informed** consent of research participants	
4	Protecting the **privacy** of research participants	
5	Ensuring the **confidentiality** of research data	
6	Protecting the **anonymity** of individuals or organizations	
7	**Avoiding** deception about the nature or aims of the research	*Protection of integrity of research community*
8	Declaration of affiliations, funding sources and **conflicts** of interest	
9	Honesty and **transparency** in communicating about the research	
10	Avoidance of any **misleading** or false reporting of research findings	

Source: adapted from Bell and Bryman, 2007

Essentially, the first six of these principles are about protecting the interests of the research subjects or informants; the last four are intended to protect the integrity of the research community, through ensuring accuracy and lack of bias in research results.

The circumstances of management and business research are largely similar to the social sciences in general, but are distinct in one important respect, which we have already mentioned. Although the interests of informants still need to be protected, it can no longer be assumed that the researcher is in the all-powerful position held by clinical and social researchers. Indeed, when research is conducted into companies, it is the researcher who is often the least powerful party to the transaction. This situation poses its own challenges for conducting ethical research.

There are three main areas where management researchers are likely to get into trouble. The first refers to the use of participant observation research methods, which, as Ditton (1977) says, are essentially deceitful. That is, if you are participating in a situation, and at the same time observing and recording (perhaps later) what has taken place, you cannot avoid some deception about your real purposes. Although, as will be seen in Chapter 7, observations do not have to involve deception. Our preference is to be as open as possible when people ask challenging questions about the purpose of the research, for two main reasons: first, because they may well be interested in the nature of the research and might have valuable insights into what you are investigating; and second, because if they suspect that you are withholding information they are most unlikely to be cooperative if you ask for their help. Trust is important.

The second is about trade-offs when conducting fieldwork. Within organizations there is always the possibility of betraying the confidence of employees if one comes under pressure from senior managers. Informants who are politically adept can often read a great deal into the questions that the interviewer is asking. For example, on one occasion, one of the authors happened to be interviewing the head of a national investigatory organization about the longer-term effects of a particular management development programme. He asked a carefully focused question about how the reward system was working, to which the director immediately came back with: 'I take it you have been talking to John about that ... Well in that case ...'. Even though most managers are not professionally trained as investigators, they will often be able to work out the nature and sources of information already collected by researchers who are sufficiently unfamiliar with the detailed political context of the organization to be aware of the significance of the questions that they are asking.

The third ethical issue is around the control and use of data obtained by the researcher. In most cases he or she has control and ownership of the data, and therefore must exercise due ethical responsibility by not publicizing or circulating any information that is likely to harm the interests of individual informants, particularly the less powerful ones. There is an interesting story, however, where this particular assumption was neatly turned upon its head. A senior British professor happened to be interviewing a royal duke, and at the end of the interview he offered to have the tape transcribed and to send a transcript to the interviewee who could then strike out any passages to which he objected, whereupon the Duke stretched out a hand, saying 'No. I shall retain the tape and will let you have the portions that I am prepared to have published'.

Finally, there is an ongoing debate about the value, or otherwise, of ethical codes in relation to research. It is argued that at least some codes need to be made explicit in order to ensure that people are alerted to some of the likely ethical dilemmas that they may face. Such codes should also provide some kind of sanction in cases of blatant abuse and exploitation. But there is a problem here. As Snell (1993) points out, ethical issues are extremely complex. They involve not only the dynamics of power but also the competing claims of different ideologies. The danger is that ethical guidelines will not only be too rigid and simplistic to deal with real cases, they will also contain the biases that are inherent in one or another ideological position.

Mason (1996) and Bell and Bryman (2007) make similar points about ethical codes being generally written in abstract terms, aimed at preventing serious and unambiguous cases of abuse. The problem is that most of the ethical issues faced by the researcher are small-scale, incremental and ambiguous. Mason argues that researchers should operate as thinking, reflective practitioners who are prepared to ask difficult questions about the ethics and politics of their own research practice on a regular basis.

Although ethical review procedures have been criticized for being overly bureaucratic, they can help students and researchers to reflect on critical issues.

Ethical review procedures

At most universities in the UK, research students (and staff) who are involved in research that collects data from human 'subjects' are required to take part in a formal ethical review of the research they are undertaking. The chief value of these procedures is that they provide formal encouragement for researchers to start thinking of possible ethical issues before they arise.

There are some problems associated with the ethical review procedures implemented in most universities that relate to the fact that such procedures were built around a model of scientific research where the full research design must be specified *before* the research is conducted. In the case of management and business research, this is not always the case as many researchers work with emergent designs which evolve, sometimes in an opportunistic way, as the project progresses. However, it is certainly important to carefully consider the implications of our activities *before* we embark on any fieldwork or data collection. The list of key principles (see Table 5.2) can be used to stimulate reflection on how different activities and data can create ethical issues.

The difficulty in getting ethical approval for some projects is something that shouldn't be underestimated. This is particularly the case when projects are more action-oriented with emergent designs. In our experience many ethics committees are far more used to positivistic projects where the aims, methods and instruments to be employed can be specified in advance. It is harder to persuade ethics committees to approve of projects where the type and level of intervention might well change or where the interactions with members of the organization might change over the period of the research.

It is in the process of writing the proposal (at the very latest) that researchers should start thinking about how they can conduct their research in the most ethical way. The exact rules for the structure of such proposals vary, but they generally include:

- a brief *description of the project*, its guiding research questions, objectives, duration and scope

- an *overview of the methods used for data collection*, and how data will be stored and safeguarded

- an outline of *how participants will be recruited* (with a sample contact letter, information sheet and consent form, if required)

- a *reflection on potential issues* and how they can be addressed.

Some review processes also evaluate potential risks to the researchers, and therefore require a statement of how the lead researcher can protect the health and safety of all individuals involved in the research (including participants and assistants). Depending on the kind of research planned, researchers may be required to develop appropriate critical management plans. More generally, it is the responsibility of all researchers to ensure that they use a safe method of work when working off campus. For example, we ask all our students conducting field research (including interviews) to ensure that at least one contact is informed about their whereabouts at all times and is prepared to raise the alarm if they do not get back to them at a pre-set time. Buddy systems, as well as doubling up for first visits, can also increase safety during fieldwork.

The ethical review templates used by the Trinity Business School are available online. The template is meant to facilitate the drafting of a comprehensive project proposal for an ethical review procedure. While the wording and structure of such templates may vary from university to university, this template can give you some initial understanding of what is likely to be required. Depending on the university, undergraduate and postgraduate taught students may be exempt from having to complete a full review though not from the obligation to conduct ethical research. They are usually asked to discuss potential ethical issues with their supervisor or tutor and may be required to complete a shorter form.

Trinity Business School research ethics templates

Social
media
research

In recent years, a growing number of research students have started to use social media platforms in their research. While social media enable us to address new research questions and data, they also raise some important ethical issues. For example, it is important to consider whether social media data are private or public – and when we need to obtain informed consent. Leanne Townsend discusses these and related issues in the video 'Social media research & ethics'.

EXERCISE 5.4

Considering ethical review procedures

1 **Group**: Go online and download the standard application from template used by the Trinity Business School. Browse through the document. In pairs, make a list of what information is required to complete the form. What are the reviewer's criteria? What sections would you consider as most challenging?

2 **Individual**: Find out about whether your institution has established a review process or review mechanism. What are the requirements for postgraduate students? What are the requirements for research staff? Think about how you would approach the preparation of a review proposal. In your view, what issues should be addressed?

3 **Group discussion**: In the past, researchers could conduct research without the need for approval by some review panel. Discuss whether or not you find the introduction of ethical review procedures useful. What are the strengths and weaknesses of such procedures? Why is it so important to ensure the ethical conduct of research?

4 **Individual**: Make a list of key ethical concerns relating to social media research.

Academia

Returning to our initial overview of stakeholders and influence factors, we have now turned to academia. Ethical review procedures constitute one of many institutional and cultural factors shaping our research that are associated with researching and working in an academic environment. Research councils exert influence on the direction of research through control of funds; disciplinary associations determine quality criteria in their own fields; journal editors, referees and conference organizers act as final arbiters of academic quality; and senior academics control career rewards. In almost all circumstances, members of the academic community operate with a high degree of probity and professionalism; nevertheless, given the amount of competition for relatively few prizes, there are bound to be criteria and processes that are not totally transparent. Our aim in this section is to make these relationships and criteria more visible.

The research subject

It is not the least the subject or topic of study that may exert considerable influence on the nature and direction of a research project. Each academic discipline, whether it be engineering, sociology or organizational theory, tends to have a number of key debates and issues at any one time. There is also a tendency among researchers to follow fads and fashions with regard to both method and focus (Calhoun et al., 2011). For example, in the early 1990s when the first edition of this book was published, some of the fashionable debates stimulated by academic management researchers in Europe were postmodernism, ethics and critiques of the enterprise culture. A decade later, some of the hottest areas were the knowledge economy, globalization and e-commerce. Now there is particular interest in the rising economies of India and China, dynamic capabilities and innovation. There are clear advantages to situating one's work close to the mainstream: others will be interested in the subject, debates will be lively, and there will be conferences and special issues of journals being commissioned on the topic. On the other hand, there will be a lot of competition. And the fashion may also turn, so that unless the research topic is defined in a flexible way there is a danger of being stranded with good ideas and materials that excite no further interest.

A 'strategic' approach may be to try to spot issues that are currently regarded as mundane, in the hope that they will suddenly pick up interest. This is another reason for working the conference circuit to find out what the 'industry leaders' think will be important issues for the future. At a wider level, though, the focus on fashion may result in other important or 'ordinary' issues being overlooked. Finally, there are of course topics that are of particular interest to practitioners in the context of applied or evaluative research. More generally, it appears that from the side of research funders there is a growing expectation to demonstrate the relevance and impact of our research (the 'impact agenda' was discussed in Chapter 1).

Funding bodies

Academic funding bodies, such as research councils, have to respond to political pressures from the governments that fund them. A common response is to target resources at specific initiatives such as entrepreneurship or competitiveness. At the present time, political pressures in the UK are demanding that government-funded research should demonstrate usefulness, which means that user engagement is very much on the agenda. But there is also a danger if funding becomes *too* responsive to political priorities and pressures, because research results may be used by one group directly to harm another group, and it is very easy for researchers to become compromised in the process. The personal and social consequences of losing a power struggle, or a job, can be very profound indeed. Researchers should therefore be very wary of the ends that they may be serving, and this is why increasing attention must be given to ethical issues, as discussed earlier in this chapter.

Funding bodies always receive more proposals than they can accommodate. Proposals in the UK are given an *alpha* rating if the independent referees consider them to be technically worthy of funding, but the ESRC only has funds for around 20 per cent of the alpha-rated proposals, and so it has to take into account other criteria such as the track record of applicants. This is an advantage for established professors, but a major obstacle for the newcomer. Hence we offer some advice to newcomers wishing to get their feet on the ladder:

- Start with modest-sized proposals.[1]

- Make the best use of your own experience through highlighting any related work or publications you may have.

- Get known by key people in the field by going to conferences and submitting papers for publication.

- Take the opportunity to attend workshops that provide guidance on crafting proposals.[2]

- Make use of networks, possibly by submitting proposals jointly with people who are already established, and by sending drafts to potential referees. In both of these cases, senior colleagues may be able to act as brokers by establishing initial contacts, or they may be willing to collaborate directly.

House style

Academic departments usually have their own house styles, which support and encourage particular kinds of work, whether quantitative or qualitative, and there is also much pressure on departments to prioritize their research interests. This can make it hard to find the right supervisors and examiners. The ideal examiner not only needs to share the same research philosophy as the candidate, but also needs to know a lot about the subject of investigation. In the case of doctoral research in particular, it is advisable in most cases to start looking for potential external examiners at a fairly early stage in a research degree.

Conferences

Conferences provide a valuable form of contact within the academic community, and it is essential for anyone doing a doctorate to get onto the right conference circuits. Attending a conference in a field of interest can also be a great networking opportunity for taught students thinking of developing a career in research, whether inside or outside academia. Some conferences are not too competitive, and will accept papers on the basis of 1,000-word abstracts; those that are more competitive, such as the US or British Academies of Management, often run a separate conference for doctoral researchers who may not have succeeded in getting papers accepted for the main conference. The British Academy of Management also offers some very attractive funding schemes for a limited number of doctoral students.

The benefits of conference participation should be obvious, but here is a list of points:

- they provide visibility for you and your ideas

- at an early stage, they can provide you with an opportunity to find out about ongoing research and to identify a suitable adviser or supervisor

---

[1]Most research councils have schemes that fund relatively small grants (say, up to £100,000), which are available exclusively to younger researchers who have never received grants before. Individual universities often have much smaller 'starter grants' of £3,000 to £10,000.

[2]The British Academy of Management runs excellent workshops on grant applications every year.

- they enable you to get feedback on papers that you will subsequently submit to journals

- they enable you to identify others working in your own field

- they give access to early copies of publications that may not appear in journals within two or three years

- they help research students to spot potential external examiners.

In addition, conferences act as recruitment fairs, explicitly in the USA and implicitly in the UK.

Supervision

Whether at undergraduate or postgraduate level, most students will be assigned an academic supervisor or adviser when they embark on research projects for their theses and dissertations. The exact role of the supervisor may differ depending on the institution – but also varies with the level of studies. For example, undergraduate students often receive hands-on supervision in a rather structured setting, sometimes complemented by addition support sessions or tutoring. In contrast, the relationship between academic advisers and PhD students is more long-term and often a changing one. Some doctoral students develop a life-long affiliation with the work of the supervisor – and see themselves as her or his 'student' for their entire academic career. Others establish more superficial relationships, in particular if their research interests do not align very well with those of their supervisors. On the most general level, however, all supervisors fulfil the same role: they provide guidance to students so that they may carry out a given research project and present their results to the best advantage. This role comes with a number of responsibilities, including:

- assisting the student with the selection and planning of a suitable research topic

- discussing the appropriateness of theory and methodology

- being available for meetings (within set limitations) for consultation and discussion of the student's academic progress and research

- providing (again within a set limitation) comments on written work in a timely manner

- assisting the student in gaining access to facilities or research materials

- helping the student to ensure that the research will be conducted safely and ethically.

In our view the dissertation supervisor is not (or at least not primarily) a consultant giving advice but rather, by questions and discussion, a kind of mentor who helps the student to define problems and conduct research, which allows them to formulate solutions. These days, universities produce handbooks that outline the responsibility of both supervisors and supervisees. The latter are usually expected to show a degree of independence and demonstrate initiative. They are asked to develop a plan and timetable for completion of all stages of their thesis project, adhere to a schedule, meet appropriate deadlines and keep the supervisor updated without imposing unduly on their time.

As with all relationships, some expectation management is required. When starting a new project it is always helpful to clarify expectations – and to be honest about them. When something goes wrong it can be easy to blame the supervisor (or the student) when often both could have done a better job of working together. As a student, it is also important to bear in mind that many academics have an incredibly busy schedule and therefore have to insist on a professional approach to supervision that makes good use of their time.

Given the inherent ambiguity of the supervisory relationship, we advise all research students to study their respective research degree handbook, with the aim of making themselves aware of the responsibilities of both students and supervisors set out by their institution. The use of a Supervisory Expectations Questionnaire – like the one created by the Oxford Learning Institute – can also help to ensure that supervisor and research student are both (quite literally) on the same page. We strongly encourage their use.

Supervisory
Expectations
Questionnaire

Team dynamics

A large portion of management and business research is carried out by students and academics working on their own. But increasingly teams are being used, both as student project groups and as teams of funded researchers. A team that balances perspectives, backgrounds and skills may be much more effective than individuals at conducting research.

Although teams can have the advantage of efficiency, and positive educational outcomes, there are always tensions that arise at some stage. These usually come down to disagreements over the right direction to take, or whether everybody is pulling their weight to the same extent (sometimes called the 'free-rider' problem). Various solutions can be applied to problems in group dynamics, including: doing team-building exercises at the beginning of the project; agreeing roles that fit with people's skills/interests; formally allocating regular time to review how the team is working; and, if all else fails, going to and see the tutor!

Mindset and attitude

Research work can be tremendously rewarding – but at times it can also be very demanding. At some point or another, most researchers encounter uncertainties, doubts and crises. Many describe their experience of conducting a dissertation project as an emotional roller-coaster. While it is important to consider the support, both emotional and technical, that can be obtained, it also helpful to reflect on (and sometimes question) one's own mindset and attitude. For example, we have often observed students and colleagues developing a bitter or cynical view on their field following a failed attempt at gaining field access. Such an attitude is understandable but rather unhelpful. A research diary can be helpful in articulating and dealing with one's thoughts, expectations and emotional responses. They can also make for a great source at the data analysis and write-up stages, in particular when conducting qualitative research.

We cannot emphasize enough the importance of seeking a positive attitude towards one's research and those who are involved in it. Researchers planning to conduct fieldwork involving interviews or participant observation in particular have to avoid putting themselves into a position where they no longer can engage with research participants in a constructive way. Example 5.4 is one – albeit extreme – case in point.

EXAMPLE 5.4

The importance of respect

As an early career researcher, Jean Grugel, Professor of Politics at the University of York, conducted research on right-wing political thought in Chile. She was asked to interview members of the political and military elite who had been responsible for gross violations of human rights. She recalls the experience in the following way:

> in Argentina, [...], I found myself interviewing one of the ex-Junta and I felt physically contaminated. I never again wanted to go into a place where I would have to sit and talk to somebody who I did not have the desire to recognise as a fellow human being. I did not want the possibility that my relationship, my view of that person would change as a result of sitting and talking with them. I did not want to see them as rounded human beings. I wanted to recognise above all the terrible things that they had done. As I said earlier, in order to conduct a good interview, it is necessary to open up a rounded and nuanced view of your respondent – I did not want to do that with these people. I did not feel equipped as a person to deal with that kind of research. I think that people involved in repression often come to see the interview as an opportunity for justification and that was not what I wanted to deal with. (Grugel and Morgan, 2017: 128)

In the end, Jean Grugel decided not to continue with this research. Few of us will ever find themselves in the position of interviewing powerful elites, criminals and human rights abusers of the kind Jean Grugel encountered in her interviews in Argentina. Nevertheless, there is a lot to learn from her account about the importance of personal and mental preparation and about the importance of being able to respect those we intend to work with. It is impossible to interview someone you are not prepared to listen to, whatever the reasons may be for you to feel this way.

Encountering challenges

Most research projects involve moments in which researchers face unexpected challenges – whether an interview has fallen through, a dataset is lost or a new discovery questions emerging findings that had been perceived to be of great potential. The question is not really whether such situations arise, but rather how we deal with them. It is also important to be clear (and realistic) about the objectives of one's research and that these should always include some personal learning objectives as well as the substantial, theoretical and/or methodological contributions usually sought after. By welcoming the fact that such research is first of all an *opportunity to learn*, one is more likely to develop a positive approach to challenges and failures. It is also very important when encountering challenges to respond ethically and maintain integrity.

Table 5.3 showcases some of the more common problems encountered by researchers and identifies some potential responses. We hope that after reading this chapter you are able to add a few more.

TABLE 5.3 Encountering challenges

	Potential problems	Ethical responses	Grey areas/issues that might raise concern
Stage 1: Determining the direction	Undue pressure from tutor or sponsor to fit with their ideas.	Write the proposal and present for ethical clearance.	Clarify stakeholders' interests. Negotiate between what you and they want.
Stage 2: Gaining access	Try to avoid deception when proposing your research. It can be difficult to define privacy and confidentiality for individuals and the host organization.	Frame the relationship with the company in non-judgemental terms. Introduce the principle of informed consent for all individuals. Prepare an access proposal.	Quid pro quo: what does the organization want in exchange for access?
Stage 3: Gathering and interpreting data	Organizational politics and conflicts can inhibit access and lead to biased accounts. Interviewees may withhold information or they may try to mislead you. Certain questions can reveal the identity of informants.	Be sensitive to the context of your research, including organizational politics and potential conflicts of interest. Look out for areas of agreement and disagreement. If everyone tells the same story, be suspicious.	Try to cultivate someone (maybe your gatekeeper) who can interpret information you are receiving if it doesn't 'add up'.
Stage 4: Writing up and dissemination	You might publish information that could harm both the company and/or individuals within it.	Stick to all confidentiality/anonymization requirements, especially for individuals. Consider carefully the key principles listed in Table 5.2 before disseminating any results.	Check through data to ensure that it doesn't reveal the identity of respondents. Send drafts of reports and publications to the company and ask them to let you know if there are any problems (within 2–4 weeks if possible).

EXERCISE 5.5

Political dilemmas in conducting student project

Group discussion: You are required to do an in-company project as part of the assessment for your degree. Your tutor has arranged access to a local supermarket to investigate the quality of customer relations, and the contact, who is deputy manager, has suggested that you talk to members of two departments: one appears to be very successful, and the other is regarded as problematic. Here are some possible scenarios. What would you do? Discuss in groups.

1   When you arrive for the initial meeting with the deputy manager you are informed that she has been called on urgent business to the regional head office and cannot see you.

2   When you meet the deputy manager she asks you to sign a non-disclosure agreement.

3   During a one-to-one interview with a checkout assistant she comments that there have been incidents of sexual harassment in her department. What do you do with this information, if anything?

4   After conducting a number of interviews in both departments the deputy manager asks you for your opinion of the qualities of both supervisors.

5   During the project, one team member persistently fails to pull his weight. How do you deal with this?

Conclusion

At this point we can identify some general implications for the researcher:

- It is important to recognize that power and political issues will be significant even when they are not obviously present.

- There are no easy answers, nor solutions, to the political web. It exists in the form of ideologies, of personal interests, of power differences and of ethical dilemmas.

- The researcher needs both clarity of purpose and much flexibility in tackling problems.

- Clarity of purpose can come from self-awareness of one's own interests and assumptions about the world, and these can be incorporated into reflexive accounts.

We have discussed the issues of ontology, epistemology, research design, politics and ethics in the last four chapters. In the next part of the book we consider the range of methods and techniques that are at the disposal of the researcher. We stress consistently that these should not be seen as entirely free-standing: they should be subordinated to the considerations of purpose and philosophy, which have been outlined above.

Further reading

The authors suggest that management researchers face ethical issues that are distinct from those encountered by other social science researchers. They provide a review of ethics codes formulated by nine social scientific associations, and argue that reciprocity is a central principle for management research:

Bell, E. and Bryman, A. (2007) 'The ethics of management research: an exploratory content analysis', *British Journal of Management*, 18 (1): 63–77.

This edition, which focuses on how managers can act as internal change agents, emphasizes the contexts in which they initiate and achieve change. It provides an accessible overview of organizational politics, which is useful for the researcher both in conducting and implementing research:

Buchanan, D. and Badham, R. (2008) *Power, Politics and Organizational Change: Winning the Turf Game*, 2nd edn. London: Sage.

This textbook provides an extensive discussion of ethics and access in Chapter 6:

Saunders, M., Lewis, P. and Thornhill, A. (2012) *Research Methods for Business Students*, 6th edn. Harlow: Pearson.

Renowned sociologist William Foote Whyte passes on his experience and knowledge with a look at problems he encountered when conducting fieldwork, and how he was able to overcome them:

Whyte, W.F. (1997) *Creative Problem Solving in the Field: Reflections on a Career*. Walnut Creek: AltaMira Press.

Check your understanding online

Visit the website **https://edge.sagepub.com/easterbysmith6e** for useful resources that will help reinforce what you've read in this chapter:

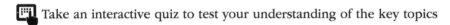 Take an interactive quiz to test your understanding of the key topics

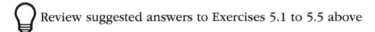 Review suggested answers to Exercises 5.1 to 5.5 above

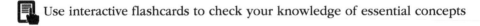 Use interactive flashcards to check your knowledge of essential concepts

Learning objectives

To gain an overview and general understanding of different approaches
and methods for collecting qualitative data through language and text,
and to appreciate their advantages and disadvantages.

To get practical insights into how to prepare for the collection of
qualitative data using language and text.

To learn about how to plan qualitative interviews and focus groups,
and to become aware of the skills needed to conduct them.

CRAFTING QUALITATIVE DATA THROUGH LANGUAGE AND TEXT

6

Chapter contents

Introduction

Many of the approaches that are included in this chapter are quite loosely specified. This offers researchers considerable opportunity to use their creative abilities. Qualitative research is often compared to singing or dancing, implying that everyone can do it, but that it requires training and practice to do it well (Luker, 2008). At some point or another, everyone has heard someone singing out of tune – or has seen a video of a dancer performing a ridiculous dance routine. In both cases, a mismatch between action, context and purpose becomes painfully obvious. In this book, we aim to show our readers how to avoid such problems when conducting qualitative research. We introduce fundamental principles of conducting qualitative research in an incremental way and, to stay within our metaphor, we also showcase different types of music and dance. Most importantly, we highlight the importance of listening to the music that surrounds you before taking the first step.

Like singing and dancing, qualitative research requires a certain degree of creativity. Indeed, good qualitative research cannot be done 'by numbers'. For example, depending on the research setting, interviews may be designed in different ways: interviewing cab drivers in England about their experiences of customer abuse (as discussed by Catherine Cassell in Chapter 8) requires a different approach from interviewing rural elites about microfinance programmes in China (as discussed by Nicholas Loubere in this chapter). There are also many more methods to consider, including diary methods or participant observation, with the latter involving the researcher talking part in the activities of research participants. Each method provides different insights – and it is important to consider carefully whether or not these insights are likely to be useful for answering a given research question. Depending on their philosophical stance and methodology, researchers also process and analyse their data in different ways. In short, there are a lot of decisions to be made (and justified) when conducting qualitative research!

qualitative data the authors of this book see the logic or framing that defines the research questions of social scientists as little different, whether structural equation models are used or methods of discourse analysis. Qualitative data requires relevance to be identified, categories and concepts defined, and theories developed, as well as particular truths. In addition, data is usually (but not always) gathered through the engagement of the researcher

The openness of many qualitative methods can pose a challenge to students and early career researchers who often ask us for the one correct method for conducting interviews and demand recipe-style instructions that can be used in whatever research context. However, as we will show in the next three chapters, more often than not, there are different ways of collecting and analysing certain types of data and, depending on the research context and research topic, some may be more appropriate than others. This is not to say that 'anything goes'! In fact, quite the opposite is true. The variety and flexibility of qualitative methods come with the responsibility to select an appropriate one and to use it wisely (that is reflexively). There are often a few methods that will allow a researcher to answer a particular research question. In this book, we have therefore attempted to move away from presenting a simple list of methods and have instead grouped them into headings that depict the most basic approaches that are available (like different styles of music, to use the same metaphor). We examine a wide range of methods and techniques for creating qualitative data with the aim of giving you an overview of what is out there – and what method could work for your particular project. In this way we encourage you to reflect on the advantages and disadvantages of different methods, taking into account the research setting, the aims of your research as well as your own experience, skills and resources.

Following a general introduction to qualitative data collection in this chapter (the first of three chapters on qualitative research), we present a more in-depth discussion of approaches that create information (data) through language and text. Most methods for the collection of qualitative data involve the use of language and text, including some of the methods we introduce in the next chapter on observational and participatory methods.

However, in this chapter we want to focus on methods where the spoken or written word takes centre stage. Natural language data can be collected from individuals and groups of individuals whether they are managers or employees. In management research, language data are used to gain insights into social and organizational realities. This takes place through discovering the views, perceptions and opinions of both individuals and groups through the language they use in conversation as well as in writing. The main methods to achieve this are the qualitative interview and participatory methods based on interviews, such as mapping and repertory grid techniques. Valuable information can also be gained from diaries and the examination of a range of textual data, such as company reports and written correspondence.

In the following chapter, we explore a different range of approaches for creating qualitative data through observation and interaction, such as observational, ethnographic and participatory techniques. Here, the ways in which data are collected are rather different; they include the examination and understanding of symbols, settings and observations in a context. Both chapters (and indeed Chapter 8) contain sections that look at some general issues that surround qualitative methods of data collection: in this chapter, we discuss practical issues surrounding the preparation of interviews.

Crafting qualitative data

Qualitative data are pieces of information gathered in a non-numeric form. The most common types of qualitative data are accounts of what research participants have said or done; for example, interview recordings and transcripts, written notes of observations, and images, videos and documents (e.g. company reports and meeting minutes). Qualitative data can be defined by their form (non-numeric) and by the interactive and interpretative process in which they are created. Contrary to what the term 'data collection' suggests, data rarely are discovered and collected like mushrooms. More often than not, qualitative data have to be developed by the researcher: interviews must be prepared for, conducted and transcribed; pictures must be taken; and field notes must be written. It is the process of creating qualitative data that will be explored here and in the following chapter. (The creation and analysis of quantitative data will be covered in Chapters 9, 10 and 11.)

While there is some overlap between some of the techniques used by qualitative and quantitative researchers, it should be noted that the strategy of data creation, and its degree of standardization and structuration, vary in significant ways. Qualitative research tends to be of a more explorative nature and involves open-ended rather than pre-coded questions and responses. This makes it important to record the entire interaction between researcher and research participant. The lack of standardization of many techniques for creating qualitative data restricts the numbers of individuals or organizations that an individual researcher can work with; it also limits the aggregation of data and the use of statistical comparisons.

We begin the next section of this chapter by starting with more passive forms of collecting existing secondary data, such as company reports, websites and letters. We then move towards more interactive forms of creating primary data, such as field diaries.

Secondary textual data

Secondary textual data are written sources of information produced for a purpose other than research but with some relevance to a given research project. They are therefore often

natural language data the term is used in this book to signify data that are presented in the form of words (spoken) or text (written). These data can be analysed and interpreted in a variety of different ways in order to make inferences in relation to such things as content, meaning and practice

qualitative interviews offer ways by which rich and detailed information can be gathered from respondents to reveal aspects of their lives, understandings or experience.

secondary data research information that already exists in the form of publications or other electronic media, which is collected by the researcher

primary data new information that is collected directly by the researcher

called non-responsive data because they were not created by research participants respond-ing to a researcher. Secondary data sources include company and government reports, websites, archival data, advertisements, newspaper articles, books and blogs. They can provide information related to a specific company, market, customer, product or supplier. Internet search engines can facilitate the quest for secondary sources. Secondary data are often used to complement primary data (such as interviews), and sometimes data consist only of secondary sources.

The advantages of secondary data are, first, savings in time and effort for the researcher. Second, the data sources often appear to be of high quality, especially when published by firms and governments. However, notwithstanding an excellent first impression, one should always critically evaluate the sources of secondary data and assess their credibility. Secondary data are created because they serve a purpose and it is essential to keep this purpose in mind when collecting and analysing them. For example, the main purpose of a company's (published) sustainability report may not be a critical reflection on its envi-ronmental impact. Third, secondary data can open up a historical perspective to a given project, which might not be feasible through the collection of primary data. The main dis-advantage of secondary sources is that the data do not necessarily fit into the research we want to investigate. Therefore, it is essential to let the research questions guide and frame the data – and not the other way round (Ghauri and Grønhaug, 2010). Sometimes it is also important to accept that a particular research question cannot be answered by relying on the secondary data available to the researcher. In this case, it is important to either consider opportunities for the collection of primary data – or to change the research question to a more appropriate one.

Even in the digital age, the collection of some secondary textual data, such as inter-nal reports or written correspondence, can be difficult and requires the development of a strong and trusted relationship between the researcher and the research participant who has access to these texts. Such a relationship might be developed during interviews, participant observation and action research. Whatever method is chosen, the processes of data creation through language and text require a fair amount of strategic thinking and planning that go beyond the development of an appropriate research design (see Chapter 4).

EXERCISE 6.1

Gathering secondary data

1 **Group**: When thinking of secondary data, most of us think about company reports, but individuals and organizations produce all kinds of written docu-ments that are rarely analysed. For example, complaint letters can tell us a lot about stakeholder relations, and seasonal greetings can reflect a firm's values, as can its guidelines and manuals for employees. In pairs, prepare a list of unusual secondary sources that could be analysed for a management research project. Who came up with the most innovative ideas? Whose suggestions are the most practical?

2   **Individual/Group**: Conduct a search for corporate sustainability reports online (many firms post such reports or reviews on their websites) and select and download three of them. Examine their content, make a list of the issues covered, and identify who has authored them. In class, discuss what we could learn from an analysis of these reports. How important is it to consider authorship when analysing secondary data?

Primary textual data

In contrast to research aiming at the collection and analysis of secondary data, primary research aims at the creation of original (primary) data.

Diary methods

A useful – but rather unusual – technique for creating *primary textual data* is the use of diaries. By diaries we do not mean historical diaries (which we would classify as secondary data) but rather diaries that result from researchers asking research participants to keep a diary for a given period of time and on a given topic (such as certain types of experiences, routines, emotions or reflections).

Diaries can be either quantitative or qualitative, depending on the kind of information that is recorded. They can be useful in management and organizational research on a number of levels. At one level, diary-keeping by organizational members can provide a simple journal or record of events. A *quantitative* analysis might take the form of activity sampling, from which patterns may be identified statistically. This approach is sometimes used by management services practitioners who wish to measure the frequency of certain activities so that they can reorganize or 'improve' the work. At other times, it is used by managers to reflect on aspects of their own work, as in time-management analysis (see, for example, Stewart, 1967, 1982). At another level, diaries might take the form of a personal journal of the research process, and include emergent ideas and results, reflections on personal learning, and an examination of personal attitudes and values, which may be important at the data analysis and writing-up stages. At yet another level, diaries can provide a rich *qualitative* picture of motives and perspectives, allowing the researcher to gain considerable insight into situations being examined. It is this latter use of a diary that we wish to explore in a little more detail here.

There are a number of advantages to using diaries. First, they provide a useful method for collecting data from the perspective of the research participant. In participant observation, researchers cannot help to some extent imposing their own reference frame as the data are collected, but in a diary study, the data are collected and presented largely within the reference frame of the diary-writer. Second, and in contrast to face-to-face interviews, diary methods are asynchronous methods, meaning that the research participants can choose when to write a given entry (within certain limitations). This gives both the researcher and the research participants a degree of flexibility. Third, a diary approach allows the perspectives of several different writers to be compared and contrasted simultaneously, and it allows the researcher greater freedom to move from one situation or organization to another. Fourth, diaries allow the researcher to collect other relevant data while the study is in progress. Finally, although diary studies do not allow for the same interaction and questioning, they can sometimes be an alternative to participant observation when, for example, it is impractical for a researcher to invest the time in an extended longitudinal study as observer or when it is impossible for the researcher to be present.

A number of important lessons were learnt from a multiple diary study conducted by Bowey et al. (1986) in an English coal mine during a national study into incentive schemes. These lessons are described in Example 6.1.

EXAMPLE 6.1

Diary study of incentive schemes

First, it was found to be important to select participants who were able to express themselves well in writing. In cases where a group of associates had been asked to keep a diary and where there was doubt about one member's writing ability, a judgement had to be made as to the likely consequences of the individual taking offence if excluded. Second, some structure was found necessary to give the diarists focus. To assist this, a list of general headings developed from an earlier pilot study was provided to participants in the scheme:

Please write about the following:

- Your relationships with other people, including your supervisor, your workmates, anyone you supervise, and other people you come into contact with.

- Any particular difficulties you encountered during the day with machinery, raw materials or people.

- Whether the incentive bonus scheme affected you at work, and if so in what way.

- Anything that you were especially pleased about or that made you feel angry.

- Anything else you feel is important, especially if it has something to do with the incentive bonus scheme.

A third lesson highlighted was the need for continued encouragement and reassurance during the study. An earlier pilot study had left diarists very much to their own devices, and they had continued to write for only four to six weeks. In the main study, where regular contact was maintained and feedback given in the form of additional questions or clarifications, almost two-thirds of the sample kept writing into the third month, and more than one-quarter completed the full three-month period. (An improvement we might have made would have been to supplement the diaries with interviews. This would have enhanced the effect of maintaining interest, as well as providing the opportunity to probe areas of interest further.)

Fourth, the importance of the need for confidentiality was confirmed. In a pilot study, jotters had been issued to record instances that occurred during the day, and this had led to problems. One particularly uncomplimentary entry in a respondent's jotter had been left in an accessible place and was read by the person described. This caused the relationships between the two people to be soured, even though thoughts entered 'in the heat of the moment' did not generally reflect the opinions of the individual. It was therefore decided that, even at the cost of a loss of spontaneity, it was preferable for diaries to be written up away from the workplace.

Finally, the study confirmed individuals' willingness to cooperate at every level, and their enthusiasm for doing so. There was no evidence to justify the view that individuals might be nervous of participating in this kind of research. In fact, there was more nervousness among the researchers themselves who felt that asking people to maintain a diary for up to three months would be unacceptable to those under study.

Source: Bowey et al., 1986

All diarists in the study described above (including those who stopped writing before the end of the three-month period) maintained that they had welcomed the opportunity to express their feelings, observations and opinions about their life and work to somebody who was interested. All maintained that they enjoyed writing the diary, and some confided that they were flattered that outsiders were taking an interest in them as individuals. No payment or other inducements were made, although pens and folders were regularly provided. This was sufficient reward for many, and it shows how important it is to find out what individuals wish to gain from participating in the research. The practicalities of undertaking diary research are fully discussed in Bowey et al. (1986).

EXERCISE 6.2

Diary methods

1   **Individual:** Think about what kind of research questions lend themselves to the use of diary methods. Write a paragraph on a project that could involve diary methods and a second paragraph justifying your choice of method. If you cannot think of any project, conduct a literature search.

2   **Group:** In groups of four to six, present and discuss the examples you have chosen. Who has come up with (or identified) the most interesting study?

Written correspondence

Postcards, *e-postcards* and *emails* can also be used to create and gather primary textual data; they can also provide a means of overcoming some of the recognized difficulties of organizational research, such as problems of access (Thorpe and Holt, 2008).

Diaries, letters and postcards used to be 'hard copy' ways of creating a wide range of primary textual data. More recently, e-postcards, blogs, emails, Twitter, Instagram and WhatsApp offer new opportunities for data collection. They give evidence to the rapidly changing ways in which we communicate, and illustrate how new information technologies enable innovative research strategies and methods for data collection (Fielding et al., 2017). Today, we have more tools than ever that allow us to engage with research participants through the spoken or written word: we can use video conferencing for synchronous interviewing, engage in asynchronous interviewing via email or chat but also access an unprecedented variety of textual data. We are still in the process of developing and adapting methods that allow us to take full advantage of this situation.

Images of Britain: Stonehenge – Just a bunch of old stones or a pinnacle of human achievement in astronomy, engineering and spiritual insight?

Please answer the four questions below by clicking on and typing in the spaces and return as an email attachment to Professor Richard Thorpe at rt@lubs.leeds.ac.uk. **Many thanks**

What do you regard as your ultimate goal in business?	To be well known as excellent in my ability to challenge thinking and develop the true potential of others, in a variety of ways, while enhancing my own life situation.
Why is this your goal?	Because I have realized that this is what I have always wanted to do from being a small child, and because it gives me great 'job' satisfaction.
Who/what helps or hinders you in reaching your goal?	*Who/what helps?* Having time allocated separately from family life helps me to focus on what needs doing My new found ability to strike up relationships and make opportunities by just ringing people up Persistence and determination Listening to what others say and then if necessary ignoring it Belief that I am doing the right thing for me at this time Finding a network of like-minded people *Who/what hinders?* Organizing house and family Working alone
If you could picture your goal, what image or object would best symbolize it?	It would be a purple, shiny runner bean seed – which embodies the development and growth which I support in every area of my life, from my garden to my business to my family and in my artwork.

FIGURE 6.1 Postcards

Source: Gold, 2008: 159

Qualitative interviews

Qualitative interviews are directed conversations evolving around questions and answers about a certain topic (Lofland and Lofland, 1984). Interviews differ from everyday conversations in that they are based on series of questions that follow a particular purpose, usually the in-depth exploration of a particular topic or experience (Charmaz, 2014). An interview is always contextual and negotiated, and – in contrast to an interrogation – its purpose has to be negotiated between the interviewee and the interviewer. As noted by Tracy (2013: 132), 'interviews provide opportunities for mutual discovery, understanding, reflection, and explanation [...] and elucidate subjectively lived experiences and viewpoints'. Interviews therefore enable researchers to access information in context, and to learn about phenomena that are otherwise difficult or impossible to observe.

The label 'qualitative interview' has been used to describe a broad range of different interviewing techniques, from those that are supposedly totally non-directive, or open, to those where the interviewers have prepared a list of questions, which they are determined to ask, come what may. While, as Jones (1985) outlines, there is a range of practices – and therefore theory – between these two extremes of interviewing technique, the main aim of qualitative interviewing is generally seen as attempting to gain an understanding from the respondent's perspective, which includes not only what their viewpoint is but also why they hold this particular viewpoint (King, 2004). As Kvale and Brinkmann (2009) note, the aim of qualitative interviews should be to collect information that captures the meaning and interpretation of phenomena in relation to the interviewees' worldviews. Researchers must therefore be able to conduct interviews so that the opportunity is present for these insights to be gained. Failure to achieve this might well result in a superficial exchange of information, which might have been better achieved via a semi-structured questionnaire.

In order to be able to achieve these insights, the researcher will need to be sensitive enough and skilled enough to understand the other person's views, but also, at times, to assist individuals to explore their own beliefs. Charmaz (2014) offers a useful approach as to how researchers might do this to advantage, and a number of techniques are discussed later in the chapter. Interviews, both semi-structured and unstructured, are therefore appropriate methods when the following apply:

- The aim of the interview is to develop an understanding of the respondent's 'world' so that the researcher might influence it, either independently or collaboratively – as in the case with action research.

- It is necessary to understand the constructs that the respondents use as a basis for their opinions and beliefs about a particular matter or situation.

- The step-by-step logic of a situation is not clear; the subject matter is highly confidential or commercially sensitive; or there are issues about which the interviewee may be reluctant to be truthful, other than confidentially in a one-to-one situation.

Remote interviewing

Managers sometimes prefer mediated interviews (interviews that are conducted via telephone, email or chat), as opposed to more traditional face-to-face interviewing.

Remote interviewing offers more flexibility, and managers feel less committed, because they do not have an obligation to host the researcher or to meet them at a certain time. However, exactly because of these reasons, remote interviewing does not always benefit the researcher. Mediated interviews lack the immediate contextualization, depth and non-verbal communication of a face-to-face interview. Therefore, it is important to consider carefully whether mediated interviews are an appropriate choice for a given research project.

Synchronous mediated interviews – such as telephone conversations and Internet-based chats – resemble face-to-face interviews in the sense that interviewer and respondent converse at the same time (O'Connor et al., 2008). They may, for example, prove very effective in the context of real-time and process-based research. In such research projects, researchers are interested in understanding the detail of a situation and an exact 'real-time' chronology of events or unfolding processes. In order to establish this, it is perfectly reasonable for the researcher to have frequent telephone conversations centred around current activities and decisions rather than retrospective developments.

Other remote interviews, for example interviews conducted via emails or in Internet forums, are asynchronous in that they allow individuals to participate at different times, giving them greater flexibility. Asynchronous interviews give interviewees more time to think about their responses and so increase their ability to control their representations. Depending on the topic of the research, this can be a problem or an advantage. Asynchronous interviews can also be more affected by distraction and sudden drop-out (Tracy, 2013).

Interviews conducted in writing save the researcher the time and costs of transcription, but by having the participants 'transcribe' their own responses, the likelihood of short responses and drop-out increases. Some topics lend themselves more to remote interviewing than do others. A biographic interview about a manager's professional career requires a stronger relationship between the interviewer and the respondent than does an expert interview with a government official that aims to collect data on a particular policy framework. Once a good relationship of trust has been established between the researcher and the research participant, remote interviewing can also be a useful approach for conducting follow-up interviews.

EXERCISE 6.3

Exploring the potential of qualitative interviews

1   **Individual**: There are various types of qualitative interviews, not all of which are discussed in this chapter. Conduct a literature search for more information on different types of qualitative interviews, using the resources and search strategies introduced in Chapter 2 on literature reviews. Identify at least five types of qualitative interview. Prepare a short briefing (800–1,000 words) on the more specific features, advantages and disadvantages of expert interviews, narrative interviews and ethnographic interviews.

2   **Group**: In pairs, discuss the advantages of qualitative interviews for different research projects. What kind of interviews could be useful for your own research project or assignment? Would you prefer face-to-face interviews or remote interviewing? Why?

Group interviews and focus groups

Interviews need not take place on a one-to-one basis, and for some types of investigation, group interviews and focus groups can be very useful. Group interviews and focus groups are similar but distinct methods. If the group is occurring naturally within a certain setting, such as, for example, a project team, we usually speak of 'group interviews' (Steyaert and Bouwen, 2004). In contrast, the term 'focus groups' is predominantly used to indicate group interviews where the group has been put together by the researcher, for example when a researcher invites project managers from different organizations. Furthermore, the term 'interview' may be seen as somewhat misleading as group interviews, and particular focus groups, usually take the form of loosely structured, guided conversations among a group of individuals.

Both group interviews and focus interviews can provide useful insights into how certain groups of individuals react to an issue or shared experience; they are therefore used extensively in market research and politics. The quality of focus groups depends on their composition; if the participants of a group do not share an experience or point of reference, it can be difficult to moderate their discussion (Tracy, 2013). When planning a focus group study, it is therefore very important to carefully consider the criteria that guide the selection of participants and the social dynamics they are likely to experience. For example, when conducting focus groups with employees of the same company, the dynamics are likely to differ depending on whether participants are of a similar or different status in the organizational hierarchy.

In any interview, the skill of the interviewer both as initiator and facilitator is of vital importance. In group interviews, this role is called 'moderator', and the added complexity of the situation means that the skills of initiating and facilitating are of particular relevance. As Walker (1985) outlines, a group interviewer should attempt not to conduct numerous interviews simultaneously, but rather to create a situation where all participants feel comfortable expressing their views and responding to the ideas of those around them. Although the focus interview is loosely structured, it should never be entirely without structure (Stokes and Bergin, 2006). As with individual interviews, the format of the interview should be organized using a topic guide (see page 186).

However, regardless of how group interviews are structured, the problems of group interviews can sometimes outweigh the advantages. Social pressures can condition the responses gained, and it may well be that people are not willing to air their views publicly or are too shy to do so. This effect might be less pronounced in some mediated forms of focus groups, such as Internet forums. However, group interviews are often used because researchers are interested in finding out more about the social dynamics within a given group. For example, a researcher interested in leadership may be just as interested in the way decision-making is negotiated among members of a team than in the arguments that are put forward. Similarly, it can be very revealing to moderate a focus group of experts with very different views on a certain topic; again, participants are likely to respond to each other's points of view but the way in which they respond can tell us a lot about the wider discourse, and about how they seek to validate or legitimize their perspective. Arguably, there is always a chance that research participants change their view because they participated in a focus group. Depending on the philosophical stance, research question and objective, such an outcome can be very welcome, if not the objective of the exercise, for instance in the case of action research, but it can be considered problematic. Our own view is that one has to be very careful in the selection of criteria for assessing methods for data collection.

In recent years, a growing number of researchers have started to use online tools, and in particular video conferencing, for conducting focus groups. Some have also tested the potential use of avatar-based focus groups in three-dimensional virtual worlds such as Second Life (Gadalla et al., 2016). While we acknowledge the potential of such methods, it is important to bear in mind the practicalities. Not everyone is familiar with

Second Life or willing to engage with researchers in this way. Little is known about the medium effects of virtual realities. For example, are interviewees more or less inclined to tell the truth? Do they feel more or less comfortable? Overall, we still advise most of our students to conduct face-to-face interviews because in many contexts they are able to provide a more authentic opportunity for engagement and are less prone to technical difficulties. However, online group interviews can enable researchers short of time and resources to conduct focus interviews with participants based at multiple locations and in this way can also open up new opportunities for involving research participants who live in remote locations.

Living in the digital age, we have more tools than ever that allow us to engage with research participants through the spoken or written word: we can use video conferencing for remote interviewing, engage in asynchronous interviewing via email or chat but also access an unprecedented variety of textual data. Many methods that initially can appear slightly outdated (such as the use of postcards or diaries) can easily be adapted and sometimes enriched by the use of digital communication technologies. We therefore live at a time of opportunity but also at a time of uncertainty as methods that aim to make best use of electronic communication are still evolving.

EXERCISE 6.4

Conducting individual and group interviews

1 **Group:** In groups of two to four, discuss the advantages and disadvantages of individual interviews and focus groups. For what kind of research would you choose to conduct individual interviews? What kinds of projects would benefit from the use of focus groups? Prepare a list of three projects (comprising a title and a short abstract) that could be undertaken using just one of these two approaches (individual interviews or group interviews) without stating the approaches you have chosen on your list. Exchange the list with another group. Can you guess whether the list suggests projects for individual interviews or focus groups? Which group did a better job in identifying suitable projects? Why?

2 **Individual:** Conduct a search online for online tools and platforms that could be used for online focus groups. Identify what appears to you the best option and compare your solution to those that were identified by others on your course.

3 **Group:** Watch the video 'Janet Salmons defines qualitative e-research'. How does Janet Salmon define qualitative e-research? What examples does she give?

Janet
Salmons
defines
qualitative
e-Research

critical incident technique
a method of teasing out information often employed within interviews, which goes to the heart of an issue about which information is sought

Critical incident technique

One method of teasing out information is the critical incident technique (CIT). Proposed by Flanagan (1954), the technique offers an opportunity to go straight to the heart of an issue and to collect information about what is really being investigated, rather than gathering large quantities of data that may or may not be directly relevant to this. CIT is often used to identify behaviours that contribute to the success or failure of an individual or organization in a particular situation, based on the analysis of retrospective data on events or 'past incidents' gathered through an interview or a questionnaire.

The technique has been used by qualitative researchers to great effect, particularly in conjunction with in-depth interviews. Respondents might, for example, be asked to track back to particular instances in their work lives, and to explain their actions and motives with specific regard to those instances. In his PhD research, Thorpe used the technique to ask owner-managers of small companies what their particular barriers to growth had been. At a given point in the interview, he would ask if there had been any particular problems in the development of the company. He would then encourage the manager to explain that problem in some detail and to illustrate how the problem was eventually surmounted.

in-depth interview an opportunity, usually within an interview, to probe deeply and open up new dimensions and insights

EXAMPLE 6.2

Social face concerns and conflict avoidance

In a study on behavioural strategies in conflict avoidance and how they are related to social face concerns, Ann Chunyan Peng and Dean Tjosvold (2011) used critical incident technique with 132 Chinese employees working for Chinese and Western managers in Beijing and Hong Kong. Participants were asked to describe a recent incident where they avoided conflict with their superior. Once they provided a detailed description of the incident, participants were asked to rate a number of items in a short questionnaire. Confirmatory factor analysis supported that avoidance is multi-faceted and includes approaches such as yielding, outflanking, delay and passive aggression. The study showed that Chinese employees were more influenced by social face concerns when they avoided conflict with Chinese managers than with Western ones.

Source: Chunyan Peng and Tjosvold, 2011

Preparing for interviews

The first step in the preparation for data collection is the development of a sampling strategy that informs the selection of potential research participants and methods for data collection. For quantitative studies aiming at representativeness, sampling strategies aim to generate samples that are *representative of a larger population*; they adhere to a number of rigorous rules (see Chapter 4). Different qualitative research traditions also have established distinct strategies of how to select and compare pertinent data to develop an emerging theory (see, for example, Charmaz, 2014, on theoretical sampling in constructivist grounded theory). On the most general level, qualitative sampling strategies aim to identify reasonable *instances of the (larger) phenomenon under research* (Luker, 2008). Such a non-probabilistic strategy is guided by considerations of a more or less theoretical nature; it seeks to select a purposeful sample, while at the same time reducing the likelihood that the way a sample is chosen influences the outcome of the research. Whether or not this is the case depends to a large extent on the research design of a study, how it frames the population and phenomenon to be researched, and what kind of comparisons it uses to develop or enhance theory.

Table 6.1 gives an overview of some of the most prominent non-probabilistic sampling strategies used in qualitative research. Most researchers aiming to collect qualitative data through language and text design a sampling plan based on one or more sampling strategies when they start data collection; such a plan helps them to identify and contact research participants.

TABLE 6.1   Sampling strategies

Sampling strategy	Procedure and purpose
Random sampling	Probabilistic selection of cases or interviewees such that the sample is likely to reflect the target population (see Chapter 9 on creating quantitative data)
Ad-hoc sampling	Cases are selected based on availability and ease of access; this strategy is most appropriate in situations where the priority is speed of data collection and low cost
Snowball sampling	Selected participants recruit or recommend other participants from among their acquaintances; useful strategies in settings with limited/difficult access
Maximum-variation sampling	Selection aims to include a wide range of incidents of a given phenomenon, including extreme cases
Typical-case sampling	Selection aims at identifying the most typical instances
Theory-guided sampling	Selection of cases depending on whether they meet certain theoretical characteristics/embody specific theoretical constructs
Negative-/deviant-case sampling	Selection of cases or interviewees that are likely to contradict a theory or explanation

Source: adapted from Tracy, 2013, and Miles et al., 2014

The size of the sample and the amount of data to be collected depend on the study and its objectives. Ideally, the selection of cases, the collection/creation of data, and the analysis of these data should evolve in a circular process until the further collection and analysis of data on additional instances appear less and less likely to reveal new or relevant information.

Interview preparations

Before adopting any method of data collection, it always helps to be clear about the overall objectives of the research. This applies to the choice of the in-depth interview or focus group as a method, as well as to the wide range of ways in which interviews may be conducted. Jones (1985) highlights a number of issues that researchers need to consider in order for interviews to be successful. The first is the problem that all researchers must resolve: how much structure to put into the interview.

Jones argues that no research exists without presupposition, by which she means that prior to the interview all researchers have some level of understanding of the research surrounding the interview topic. Moreover, researchers often enter the interview situation with some key questions; however, these are likely to change as new and interesting areas are uncovered, and researchers may want to tailor their questions depending on the participants' positions or responses.

Interviews can be highly formalized and structured; for example, in market research, where interviews follow a detailed interview schedule listing all questions that are asked in a predefined order, sometimes with a selection of predefined responses (*highly structured interviews*). Other interviews are based on a list of questions that can be addressed in a more flexible manner (*semi-structured interviews*). Finally, there are interviews where questions are used to stimulate a conversation rather than to guide responses. In the context of ethnographic research, such 'conversations' are often of a rather spontaneous nature and, as such, difficult or impossible to prepare for (*unstructured interview*). Table 6.2 gives an overview of different types of interviews, according to their degree of structuration.

Although interviewing is often claimed to be the best method of gathering information, its complexity can sometimes be underestimated. It is time-consuming to undertake interviews properly, and they are sometimes used when other methods might be more

TABLE 6.2   Types of interview

Level of structure	Type of interview	Guidance and preparation
Highly structured	Market-research interview	Detailed interview schedule: questions in a predefined order, some of them with a narrow selection of predefined answers
Semi-structured	Guided open interview	Topic guide: selection of topics or issues to be covered
Unstructured	Ethnographic interview	Individual questions stimulate an informal conversation; no interview schedule or guide

appropriate. If researchers wish to obtain answers to a number of fairly simple questions, then a questionnaire might well be more appropriate. Highly structured interviews are based on carefully prepared sets of questions piloted and refined until the researcher is convinced of their 'validity'. The assumption is made that the interviewer will ask each interviewee the same questions in the same way. The simplest form of such interviews is where there are short answers to questions, the interviewer simply ticks boxes, and no deep thought is required by either party. Large numbers (hundreds or thousands) will be required in order to have confidence that the responses obtained can be generalized to the population at large; this is very much the territory of the professional political pollster, for example.

Particularly in the case of using less-structured interviews, we would encourage researchers, as they collect their data, to make choices as to which lines of questioning to explore further, and which to discard. Certainly, researchers need frameworks from which to plot out the developing themes, but – as Jones (1985) reminds us – although they are to some extent tied to their frameworks, researchers should not be 'tied up' by them. One way in which this can be achieved is to prepare a topic guide, which can be used as a loose structure for the questions (see the next section on crafting a topic guide). Although there may be some deviation from the sequence in order to follow interesting lines of inquiry and to facilitate an unbroken discussion, the interviewer should attempt to cover all the issues mentioned.

Finally, on the subject of structure, the researcher should be warned against assuming that a 'non-directive' interview, where the interviewee talks freely without interruption or intervention, is the best way to achieve a clear picture of the interviewee's perspective. This is far from true. It is more likely to produce no clear picture in the mind of the interviewee of what questions or issues the interviewer is interested in, and no clear picture in the mind of the interviewer of what questions the interviewee is answering! Too many assumptions of this kind lead to poor data, which are difficult to interpret. Researchers are therefore likely to be more successful if they are clear at the outset about the exact areas of their interest. In the section on avoiding bias, this issue is dealt with in more detail (see page 198).

It is important to be aware of the advantages and disadvantages of the different ways of conducting interviews. Whereas structured interviews allow for a high degree of standardization of questions and answers, more open (or semi-structured and unstructured) interview questions often give a higher degree of confidentiality, as the replies of the interviewees tend to be more personal in nature. In addition, the interviewer has the opportunity to identify non-verbal clues (e.g. in the inflection of the voice, facial expressions or clothes that the interviewee is wearing), which can be used to develop secondary questions. Sometimes, these verbal clues may offer important reasons for misinformation (Sims, 1993).

This chapter deals primarily with in-depth qualitative interviews, where the main purpose is to understand the meanings that interviewees attach to issues and situations in contexts that are not structured in advance by the researcher. For more detail on the use and application of highly structured questionnaires, readers should refer to Chapters 9 and 10.

structured interview where the interviewer follows a prescribed list of questions each of which may have predetermined response categories

topic guide a prepared list of areas (rather than specific questions) that need to be covered during the course of an interview

standardization the process of transforming a variable in order to express it on a scale with a mean of zero and a standard deviation of one; often carried out for variables measured on interval scales (with no true zero point) so that regression weights can be compared between predictor variables

Crafting a topic guide

As noted above, interview schedules involve scripts of questions that follow a predefined order. In contrast, topic guides refer to more informal lists of topics and questions that can be addressed in no particular order. When preparing a topic guide or interview schedule, researchers first revisit their research questions, research design and sampling strategy. This helps them to clarify the purpose of the interviews that they would like to conduct. There is often a tendency to approach interviews as an exercise of 'data extraction' as opposed to 'meaningful conversation'. This can create problems not only for the respondent but also for the interviewer. Respondents who face difficult, unsuitable or inappropriate questions tend to disengage, and the outcome of such interviews is likely to be unsatisfactory for both parties. Therefore, when designing a topic guide or preparing individual questions, it is important to reflect on how potential respondents might understand and feel about certain questions, in order to ensure that questions relate to the world and identity of the respondent as well as to the research interests of the interviewer.

In contrast to research questions, interview questions should avoid abstract theoretical concepts, jargon and scholarly talk. Instead, they should be clear and easy to understand. Good questions promote open-ended answers and allow respondents to report or reflect on an experience and certain pieces of information; they are followed up by appropriate 'probes' or other questions (e.g. 'Please tell me more about this'). Research questions should not be too leading. A question such as 'Don't you admire your managers for their excellent track records?' is likely to produce a predictable response. It is important to bear in mind that natural conversations tend to be organized around stories, and so organizing research interviews in a similar way can be useful. There are interview situations in which challenging questions are required and appropriate, but great care should be taken that such questions are worded in the right way. If abstract concepts such as 'innovation' or 'collaboration' cannot be avoided altogether, respondents should be asked to clarify their understanding of these concepts, and they should be provided with some examples that can help to develop a shared definition. When developing a particular question, ask yourself first if your research participants can actually respond to your question in a spontaneous way. If not, the question is either too difficult or is likely to require a series of introductory questions that help the interviewee to understand what you are asking them to do and put their mind in the right place.

Topic guides may be more flexible than interview schedules, but they should nonetheless be organized into at least three sections: opening questions, questions around a number of key topics, and closing questions. Topic guides should remind the interviewer to ask for the consent of the respondent to be interviewed, and they should include 'icebreaker' questions that build rapport, as well as closing questions or comments that make the respondents feel appreciated. Towards the end of the interview it can be useful to ask respondents whether they have anything to add. Depending on the sampling strategy, closing questions should also include a question about follow-up contacts and recommendations.

probe a device used as an intervention technique to improve and sharpen the interviewees' response

Strategies for qualitative interviews

EXERCISE 6.5

Strategies for qualitative interviews

1   **Group**: In groups of three to four, make lists of the main rules that researchers should follow when developing interview questions.

Managing
conflict

2   **Individual**: Download and read the online resource 'Strategies for qualitative interviews' cited above. Based on the document and everything you have learnt so far, develop a checklist that will help you to develop a topic guide for a current or future project.

3   **Individual**: Go online, download and read the article 'Managing Conflict Between Departments to Serve Customers' (Tjosvold, Dann & Wong 1992). What kinds of interviews were conducted for this research?

4   **Group**: Examine the interview schedule included in the Appendix of the article (i.e. Tjosvold, Dann and Wong 1992). In pairs, discuss how each item helped the researchers to explore the role of power in the dynamics and outcomes of conflict.

Informed consent

The planning of data collection, including interviews, involves a couple of formal steps to address issues arising from data protection, confidentiality and informed consent. As we have discussed in Chapter 5, permission to conduct research must first be granted by the university before the research can be conducted; the interview process also requires the preparation of a consent form to be signed by each research participant. Consent forms should be understandable by the target population and they are usually complemented by an information sheet or at least an interview preamble. They should confirm that research participants were informed about the research and its expected benefits ahead of the data collection, and that they have a right to withdraw voluntarily from the research at any time. Consent forms also detail how the confidentiality of the respondents is protected. If appropriate, they include a statement about risks that could arise from participation.

Conducting interviews

Various skills are required for interviewing; these can take quite a while to learn. Understanding issues from an interviewee's point of view can be extremely difficult, especially when the respondent may not have a clearly articulated view of the answers to the questions posed, or may not wish to divulge sensitive information. It is here that the skills of the interviewer come to the fore.

McClelland (1965) conducted careful studies about common-sense notions of 'motivation'. He concluded that people cannot be trusted to say exactly what their own motives are, as they often get ideas about these from commonly accepted half-truths. For example, a person may claim to be interested in achievement because of having made money. But a careful check using different probing methods may reveal quite a different picture. Often, people simply are not aware of their own motives. Mangham (1986), in his studies of managerial competence, met this problem. From survey work conducted quantitatively, he found that many managers sought subordinates who could better motivate staff and act in leadership roles within their organizations. In follow-up interviews, he was able to ask managers exactly what they meant by 'leadership'. Some gave ambiguous answers and became confused, offering examples of leadership that ranged from highly autocratic styles to highly democratic forms.

From a positivistic standpoint, the fact that there is ambiguity about the meaning of 'leadership' invalidates the research, but for the in-depth interviewer who probes, questions and checks, these are important data. The fact that people are confused and cannot agree on what they mean by leadership, or the way they construct particular situations, is the essence of the research.

The skills of an interviewer, then, centre on the ability to recognize what is relevant and remember it, or tape it, so that afterwards detailed notes can be made. This requires the ability to be perceptive and sensitive to events, so that lines of inquiry can be changed and adapted as one progresses. Above all, interviewers need to be able to listen, and to refrain from projecting their own opinions or feelings onto the situation. This is more difficult than it sounds, since one of the ways of obtaining trust is to empathize with the respondent. The interviewer needs to *listen to what the person wants and does not want to say*, without helping (Charmaz, 2014). In recognizing these situations, non-verbal data might be crucial in providing clues, for example the loss of eye contact or a changed facial expression. From time to time during the interview, as patterns or uncertainties arise, it is useful to check that one understands by summarizing what has been said. This should be presented as a way of seeking clarification. The process of 'testing out' is a way of safeguarding against assuming too quickly that understanding has been achieved.

Laddering

As questions are asked, the researcher might like to think about how to get more from a question.

laddering up
a method of questioning that can be employed within interviewing, which can elicit the values that underpin statements or actions made by respondents

Employing the technique of laddering up will help the respondent move upwards from statements of fact or descriptive accounts about the questions posed so as to begin to reveal the individual's value base (Wansink, 2003; Bourne and Jenkins, 2005).The best way to achieve this is to ask 'why' questions. An instance of this process can be seen in Example 6.3. The technique is very valuable for qualitative researchers; however, sensitivity and common sense do need to be applied, as persistent use of 'why' type questions can spoil an interview since the respondent will eventually run out of things to say. Varying the way in which the question 'why' is asked is one strategy, as Susan Baker does in Example 6.3, to make the exchange more varied and interesting as she explored the reasons why individuals purchased a particular make and style of running shoe.

laddering down
a method of questioning that can be employed within interviewing, which can elicit examples that evidence general statements, views or values expressed in interview responses

Laddering down (also called 'pyramiding') is where the researcher seeks to obtain illustrations and examples or occurrences of events. For example, the researcher might say 'Could you give me an example of that?' or 'When was the last time that happened to you?' Through such a process it is possible to explore a person's understanding of a particular construct. A process of laddering up and down using five or six questions (the number of themes contained in a topic guide) will quite easily fill out the whole of an interview, while gaining significant insights into the topic under investigation.

EXAMPLE 6.3

Laddering

Question: Anything else about the design?

Answer: I think the weight of the shoe is important. The shoes shouldn't be too heavy.

Question: Why is this?

Answer: Because a lighter shoe is more comfortable.

Question: Why is this important to you?

Answer: It means I can move around quickly at tennis …

Question: Tennis is important to you?

Answer: Yes … I like it … It means I can get some fresh air … It's good for the heart, the nerves and your cholesterol … It makes me feel better. I feel good when I play tennis.

Source: Baker and Knox, 1995: 85

EXERCISE 6.6

Laddering up and down

Group: In pairs, ask each other a simple question that relates to a personal view or preference the person might have. Then try to ladder up from this question to see if you can learn something about the person's values (normally this can be done by asking 'why' questions). Then ladder down to see if you can learn something about the detail that surrounds these preferences. (This is normally done by asking about specific instances.)

Avoiding becoming biased

Readers will see in Chapter 9, on quantitative research methods, that interview bias – where the process of conducting an interview might influence the responses given – is regarded as crucial. With in-depth interviewing, the issue is a slightly different one. Since the aim of in-depth interviews is to uncover the meanings and interpretations that people attach to events, it follows that there is no one 'objective' view to be discovered that the process of interviewing may bias. However, there is a very real concern about interviewers imposing their own reference frames on the interviewees, both when the questions are asked and when the answers are interpreted. The researcher is in something of a dilemma, because – as has been suggested in an earlier section – open questions may avoid bias, but they are not always the best way of putting an interviewee at ease. Moreover, they are not always the best way of obtaining the desired information. There will be some occasions when researchers will want to focus on discovering responses to specific alternatives, and in this case probes can be useful as an intervention technique to improve, or sharpen up, the interviewee's response to open questions. A number of probes are listed in Example 6.4.

interview bias occurs when the process of questioning influences the interviewee's response

EXAMPLE 6.4

Probes in data collection

The basic probe involves simply repeating the initial question, and is useful when the interviewee seems to be wandering off the point.

Explanatory probes involve building onto incomplete or vague statements made by the respondent. Ask questions such as, 'What did you mean by that?' and 'What makes you say that?'

Focused probes are used to obtain specific information. Typically, one would ask the respondent, 'What sort of ...?'

The silent probe is one of the most effective techniques to use when respondents are either reluctant or very slow to answer the question posed. Simply pause and let them break the silence.

The technique of drawing out can be used when interviewees have halted or dried up. Repeat the last few words they said, and then look at them expectantly or say, 'Tell me more about that' or 'What happened then?'

Giving ideas or suggestions involves offering the interviewee an idea to think about, for example, 'Have you thought about ...?', 'Have you tried ...?', 'Did you know that ...?' and 'Perhaps you should ask Y ...'.

Mirroring or reflecting involves expressing in your own words what the respondent has just said, for example, 'What you seem to be saying/feeling is ...'. This is very effective because it may force the respondent to rethink the answer and reconstruct another reply, which will amplify the previous answer.

To avoid bias, probes should never lead. An example of a leading probe might be: 'So you would say that you were really satisfied?' Instead of this, the interviewer should say, 'Can you explain a little more?' or 'How do you mean?'

General interview concerns

Using interviews as the main method of obtaining qualitative data in a successful way, however, does not depend only on researchers' personal interview skills, capacity to organize and structure interviews, and ability to avoid bias. Researchers should be aware of six important practical issues involved in conducting interviews; these may affect the outcome of an interview. These are: obtaining trust; being aware of social interaction; using the appropriate attitude and language; getting access (as discussed already in Chapter 5); choosing the location for the interviews; and recording interviews.

Obtaining trust is an important element in ensuring that interviews will provide the researcher with the information sought. Obtaining trust can be difficult, especially in one-off interviews where the people involved have not met before. Failure to develop trust may well result in interviewees simply resorting to telling the researcher what they think is expected. But an open and trusting relationship may not be possible or sufficient when dealing with particular elites or individuals in positions of power, as we have discussed in Chapter 5. One way to obtain trust is to make sure that one is well informed about the company. A scan through the company's website will give a quick impression of the issues that are currently considered significant. Another way to obtain the trust of the company one wishes to research is to present the research in a professional and enthusiastic way so that the company sees a benefit, as managers will be weighing up the likely costs and benefits of the potential intrusion.

Social interaction between the interviewer and the interviewee is another important factor that may influence the interview process. Jones (1985) suggests that people will attribute meaning and significance to the particular research situations in which they find themselves. The questions that an interviewer may ask and the answers that an interviewee gives will often depend on how their situations are defined. Similarly, Jones (1985) points out that interviewees will 'suss out' what researchers are like, and make judgements – from their first impressions – about whether they can trust the researchers with their data, or whether they might be damaged in some way by sharing information. Such suspicions do not necessarily mean that interviewees will refuse to be interviewed, but it might mean, as Jones indicates, that they just 'seek to get the interview over as quickly as possible, with enough detail and enough feigned interest to satisfy the researcher that he or she is getting something of value but without saying anything that touches the core of what is actually believed and cared about in the research' (1985: 50). It is, furthermore, important to be able to recognize when an interviewer is being misinformed (Sims, 1993). Individuals will often select answers that they think will be easily understood by interviewers, rather than providing the 'whole truth', simply because it would take too long to give all the nuances.

Appropriate attitude and language should also be kept in mind when preparing for and conducting one's research. Interviewers should appear knowledgeable, competent, humble and sensitive. They should be attentive and avoid judgements. It is not a good strategy to baffle a potential gatekeeper by mentioning too many theoretical concepts, but clarity also needs to be ascertained with respect to the interviewee's use of language, as what is said may not always be what is meant. Clarifying probes can help to reveal the latent interpretations and understandings of the interviewee. In Table 6.3, we provide a few examples of the way words may be interpreted. Towards the end of the interview, interviewers should leave time for respondents to reflect on the interview and to volunteer additional information they consider relevant. Whether or not an interview has turned out to be helpful, interviewers should never forget to thank respondents for their time in a specific and appreciative way.

TABLE 6.3   Use of words and the different impressions they can give

Words	Impression given
Student	Implies an unskilled 'amateurish' inquiry, which may be a waste of time, although unthreatening
Researcher	Implies a more professional relationship, although questions of access might need to be managed more carefully
Interview	Implies a formal structured interrogation, which is under the control of the researcher
Discussion	May make managers feel more relaxed and less threatened, with the potential for genuine exchange

In addition to issues of *getting access* (see Chapter 5), the *location of the interview* and the setting in which the interview takes place can also be important. Good locations are those which are easy for both parties to access, are comfortable (e.g. the furniture and temperature), and are characterized by low levels of noise and distractions (without lots of people coming and going, and with no loud music or TV in the background). One should also be careful to understand the impact of spaces on people's understanding of the interview situation. A manager's office, for example, might not always be perceived as a neutral space by other employees. One strategy used by a PhD student, Neil, was to conduct interviews well away from the workplace. When researching aspects of management development, he undertook this fieldwork by sitting in the first-class compartments of trains. He would sit next to executive-looking individuals, armed only with a folder marked 'Management Development' in the hope that managers would talk to him. This they usually did, and – without prompts – he was able to elicit their views on a range of management-development issues. What struck Neil was the extent to which the views and opinions expressed by managers, off-guard and to a person they were unlikely ever to meet again, contradicted the 'reality' contained in much contemporary management literature. Had the interviews taken place in the managers' offices, the results might well have been quite different. This example not only illustrates how a researcher managed to obtain data that the manager may have found hard to articulate in the office, it also shows how a method can be undertaken in a 'natural setting', where each person views the other as having equal status. This kind of research would normally be extremely costly, yet it does illustrate the lengths that might have to be gone to in order to obtain data.

Recording interviews is a sixth aspect that may affect the outcome of an interview. The decision of whether or not to use a voice recorder lies with the interviewee. Some interviewees harbour concerns about confidentiality and the use to which any information divulged can be put (see Chapter 5). Therefore, the question of whether or not a meeting can be recorded should be approached with tact. Concerns can be addressed, for example, by handing over the responsibility for switching the voice recorder on and off to the interviewee, so that the latter has control over which parts are recorded. The main reasons in favour of using a voice recorder are that it aids the listening process and gives the opportunity of an unbiased record of the conversation. Good audio recordings are essential for accurate transcripts and also enable the researcher to listen again to the interview, possibly hearing things that were missed at the time. It is important to test the chosen recording technology ahead of the interview, if possible in the proposed location. If interviewees oppose the recording of interviews, researchers should depend on their own ability to take accurate notes and write down everything they are able to remember as soon as possible after the interview has ended. Even if allowed to record conversations, interviewers are advised to take notes during the interviews. This makes the interviewees feel more appreciated, can aid the researchers in developing probes and follow-up questions, and reduces the amount of direct eye contact (which many interviewees find uncomfortable). What is particularly important is for researchers to create a verbatim account as soon as possible after the interview is completed.

Finally, group interviews and in particular focus group interviews can present some particular challenges, some of these organizational and others more personal. First, it can be difficult to convince potential participants to attend. Many research participants seek to minimize the time they spend with researchers and having to travel to a different location can be a barrier to participation. The logistics of a group interview are therefore very important. Moreover, when contacting potential participants, it is essential to communicate the purpose of a group interview in an effective way but also to highlight why the participation of a prospective participant is of great importance to the researcher. Once research participants have agreed to take part, it is important to follow up immediately, thank them and schedule a polite reminder. During the group interview, challenges arise from facilitating and guiding the group interview. Sometimes it can be quite hard or even impossible to get everyone involved. Working in pairs can help, as can probes such as asking for examples and further elaboration (Kandola, 2012).

EXERCISE 6.7

Interviewing

Demo
interview 1

Demo
interview 2

1 **Individual or group**: Watch the YouTube video 'Demo interview 1' and make a list of the mistakes made by the interviewer.

2 **Group discussion**: Watch the YouTube video 'Demo interview 2'. Can you see the difference? Discuss what the interviewer does better this time around. Why does it matter?

3 **Individual**: Qualitative researchers need to have good personal engagement to gain trust so that 'good' data can be obtained. Think about a time when you have been interviewed, either as a research respondent or at a recruitment interview. Did the interviewer do anything to gain or lose your trust?

4 **Group discussion**: Think about which of your own characteristics and traits could affect your relationship with research participants. In pairs, discuss these traits and write them down. What characteristics or traits are likely to have a positive or negative impact on your data collection?

5 **Individual**: Pick a general topic that relates to an experience that most students in your group are likely to have had (such as recount how you felt when you arrived at your first school, completed your first application for a job, or had your first job interview) or to attitudes and expectations (such as career expectations, environmental protection or growth of local business). Prepare an interview topic guide of at least ten questions, including an opening question and a closing question. Write down what you expect to find in your interview (500 words). Conduct the interviews in pairs, so that everybody plays the part of the interviewer and that of the respondent at least once each. Each interview should last a minimum of 20 to 40 minutes. Discuss how you have experienced the interview as interviewer and as respondent. What would you do differently next time you conduct an interview?

6 **Individual/group**: Read the Research in Action box below and discuss the advantages and disadvantages of the Systematic and Reflexive Interviewing and Reporting (SRIR) method. What are the underling philosophical assumptions of this method? In what 'quadrant' (as defined in Chapter 3) would you position it?

RESEARCH IN ACTION

Reflexive interviewing

Nicholas Loubere

Nicholas Loubere is an Associate Senior Lecturer in the Study of Modern China at Lund University in Sweden. His research examines socioeconomic development and government-run microcredit programmes in contemporary China. Nicholas has also published on the methodological challenges of fieldwork.

Can you tell us about the role of fieldwork in your research?

My research on microcredit programmes in China aims to understand the impact of development programmes on rural communities. In order to analyse how development interventions – such as microcredit – are constituted on the ground, it is necessary to conduct in-depth fieldwork in rural areas. For this reason, my research involves extended periods of fieldwork in Chinese townships and villages where I conduct semi-structured interviews with a wide range of local inhabitants, including government officials, farmers, managers of financial institutions, and proprietors of small and medium-sized enterprises.

(Continued)

Have you found it difficult to conduct your interviews in a different language?

Conducting interviews in a second language is always a challenge – after all, even interviewing in one's native language is no easy task! However, the difficulties with language can be magnified when working in areas where interviewees speak with a strong accent or even communicate in local dialects. For example, when I work in rural areas, I often find myself relying on research assistants or collaborators from the local area as my Mandarin Chinese only takes me so far. Initially, I found it quite difficult to be in a situation where I was relying on translations of conversations with interviewees who I wanted to be able to speak with myself. Translation always creates an additional layer of interpretation. It is particularly important to be aware of this when your research is about how people articulate their thoughts.

Compounding these linguistic challenges is the equally important – but often overlooked – issue of cultural fluency (Veeck, 2001). When we conduct interviews it is of crucial importance that we understand the context. China is a very large and diverse country. For this reason, simply spending a few years living and studying in coastal Chinese cities – as I did prior to beginning my research on rural microcredit – does not provide the level of cultural fluency necessary to conduct interviews in a rural village in central China. It takes time and patience to gain insight into local history and culture, social norms and the ways in which people are connected, and to get a sense of how people express themselves. I guess that if a Chinese management student would decide to conduct research on family businesses in Lund they would face similar difficulties. I always advise my students to familiarize themselves as much as possible with the context in which they conduct their research. Sometimes it is also a matter of organizational culture. For example, a government official is likely to adopt a different view on a microfinance programme than, let's say, a farmer.

Instead of transcribing your interviews, you used an approach you have termed the Systematic and Reflexive Interviewing and Reporting (SRIR) method. Can you tell us more about this method?

Responding to challenges relating to linguistic and cultural fluency, I developed the Systematic and Reflexive Interviewing and Reporting (SRIR) method during my PhD fieldwork. The SRIR method is based on semi-structured interviews conducted by small teams of two or more researchers. During the interviews, researchers (or researcher and local translator) take turns asking questions and everyone takes notes. Interviews are recorded if possible, but this is not necessary, as verbatim (word for word) transcription is not required. Instead, the researchers engage in reflexive dialogue after the interview. This dialogue provides a forum for researchers to explain how they understood the information presented during the interview, and to discuss divergent perspectives. Researchers then jointly write systematic interview reports (SIRs), which summarize each interview, as well as the preliminary analysis that emerged from the reflexive dialogue. The reports are then analysed in the place of verbatim transcripts (Loubere, 2017).

The SRIR method is designed to make the most of the work with local research assistants/collaborators. It can also be very useful to begin the process of analysis during fieldwork rather than afterwards. When engaging in a reflexive dialogue, we combine insider and outsider perspectives. Some would call the epistemological position adopted for such research 'transactional', as it implies the assumption that knowledge is constructed 'in and out of interaction between human beings and their world, and developed and transmitted within an essentially social context' (Crotty, 1998: 42).

TOP TIP

If I could give one piece of advice to students conducting interviews for the first time, it would be to remain open and flexible. Of course, it is necessary to be well prepared for an interview. However, there is such a thing as over-preparation. Long lists of questions can blind researchers to important information that does not fit into their preconceived notions. I would always suggest treating an interview like a meaningful conversation, and allowing it to develop naturally.

Interview-based mapping techniques

After having discussed qualitative interviews as an interactive way of creating qualitative data on a more general level, we now introduce two interactive mapping methods that combine interviewing techniques with participatory methods: *repertory grid technique* and *cognitive mapping*. Both techniques help researchers to identify an individual's or a group's view of the world, and enable the simple and relatively immediate presentation of complex information. To this end, both techniques integrate processes of data collection with those of data analysis.

Repertory grid technique

Based on personal-construct theory (Kelly, 1955), a repertory grid is a special interviewing technique that is used to identify the ways in which respondents interpret their experience, draw conclusions about patterns of cause and effect, and behave according to those conclusions. The technique is useful for investigating areas that the respondent might not have thought much about, or that they find hard to articulate. It has been used extensively in areas such as career guidance, and for the development of job descriptions. In Example 6.5, a housing manager within a large metropolitan council used the approach to assist in identifying what householders valued in terms of bathroom and kitchen design.

repertory grid a tool for uncovering an individual's (or group's) view of the world based on the constructs they develop and hold

EXAMPLE 6.5

Repertory grid

Mackinlay (1986) used the repertory grid technique to elicit the values and perceptions that householders in a particular housing district held of different types of bathroom and kitchen colour schemes and layouts, as elements to be compared and contrasted. He showed photographs to householders, and asked them to compare and contrast the different photographs; in so doing, he elicited the 'constructs' they used to differentiate between the photographs, and to reveal their likes and dislikes. The method proved extremely useful, with the photographs helping to resolve differences and deal with the complex issues involved in the notion of what people valued and preferred. This demonstrates that grids can elucidate what might not be immediately observable, so that new insights or perspectives can be gained.

Repertory grids help individuals to look not only at the words people use, but also at the wider constructs employed when making decisions and taking action. Often, these may not be known even to the individuals themselves, so representation in the visual form of a grid can be the beginning of a process whereby individuals learn more about the ideas they have, how they might have been formed and how they might be changed.

Grids can also be used in group situations as a basis for discussion about how different people view the world; they enable complex relationships to be represented with the objective of building up shared understandings (Easterby-Smith et al., 2010). The technique is used to understand individuals' perceptions and the constructs they use to understand and manage their worlds. A repertory grid shows how constructs and elements are related to each other; the space can be shown geometrically through principle components analysis. The principal components analysis gives a mathematical relationship between the underlying dimensions and the constructs and elements. Repertory grids can also be used with people who have low verbal ability and can be used with either dyads or triads.

The standard procedure for generating a repertory grid is as follows:

1. Decide on the *focus* of the grid. This should be quite specific, and the interviewee should be reminded of it at regular intervals. The focus might be on the qualities required of a manager in a particular function.

2. Select with the interviewee a group of *elements* (between five and ten) that are relevant to the chosen focus, and that are also likely to provide a good range. If, for example, the focus of the grid was on the skills required of a manager, it would be appropriate to choose individuals who were familiar to the interviewee, and who have different leadership styles.

3. *Constructs* are elicited, usually by asking the respondent to compare and contrast elements in groups of three, known as 'triads'. Each element is written onto a card and then three cards are selected at random. The interviewee is asked to decide which pair of cards is similar in a way that also makes them distinct from the third. They are asked to provide a word or phrase that describes the pair, and a contrasting word or phrase to describe the remaining card. For example, in the case of a grid with the focus on the competencies required of a manager, someone might choose two cards of named people as similar because they see them both as *dynamic*, and the third as *staid*. In this case, the construct elicited is a continuum on which *dynamic* is at one end and *staid* is at the other. This process is repeated with different triads of elements until a reasonable number of constructs (perhaps six to ten) has been produced.

4. Each of the elements needs to be *linked* to, or rated against, each of the constructs. This can be done in several different ways: by deciding which of the two 'poles' of the construct provides the best description of the element; by determining the position of the element on a rating scale (often with seven points), constructed between the poles of each construct; or by rank-ordering each of the elements along the dimension indicated by each of the constructs. The results of these ratings or rankings are recorded as ticks and crosses, or as numbers in a matrix.

Small grids can be analysed manually (i.e. by eye), by looking for patterns of relationships and differences between constructs and elements. This can form the basis of an interesting collaborative discussion between interviewer and interviewee. With larger grids (say, five-by-five or more), it is more common to use computer analysis packages.

In terms of analysis, there are two very different kinds of output in terms of visual representation: a map and a dendrogram. The map plots the elements within dimensions and axes, defined by the constructs. The dendrogram shows how close the constructs are to one another in terms of how they have been scored.

Grids have both advantages and disadvantages, as shown in Table 6.4, which indicates the main advantages and disadvantages of using repertory grids, identified by Stewart et al. (1981). Our view is that grids not only offer assistance in seeing patterns and associations – and, as a consequence, new insights – but they also provide a medium of communication that can spur new understandings and new acts of sense-making (Easterby-Smith et al., 2010). So, they are not simply a graphical representation of an individual manager's concerns and beliefs, but operate in a reflexive manner (see Harper, 1989), helping managers respond to the map or picture that is produced.

TABLE 6.4   Pros and cons of using repertory grids

Advantages	Disadvantages
They involve verbalizing constructs that otherwise would remain hidden	Grids are hard work to complete and can take considerable periods of time: a 20 x 10 matrix can take up to 1.5 hours
They are based on the individual's own framework, not that of the expert	They require a high degree of skill from the interviewer if the interviewee's construct framework is to be fully explored
They provide insights for both the researcher and the researched	They can be difficult to analyse and interpret, and there is some danger that individuals will rely on the structure of the technique to produce packaged (rather than meaningful) results
	The technique has become 'popular' and, as a consequence, is sometimes used mechanistically, forgetting the underlying theory of personal constructs

For those interested in learning more about the repertory grid technique, there is an example of a repertory grid study with some exercises available on this book's website. Further reading is provided at the end of this chapter, and Easterby-Smith et al. (2010) illustrate a number of applications in the field of management.

Repertory grids

Cognitive mapping

This method of data collection is based on the same personal-construct theory as repertory grid technique. Cognitive mapping is a modelling technique that aims to portray managers' ideas, beliefs, values and attitudes – and to show how they interrelate. A cognitive map represents the relationships between the constructs of a number of individual managers regarding a managerial issue or problem (Eden et al., 1983; Huff and Jenkins, 2002). A cognitive map is not supposed to be a scientific model of an objective reality in the way that some influence diagrams are, but instead should be a presentation of part of the world as a particular person sees it – it can never be shown to be right or wrong, in an 'objective' sense (Eden et al., 1983: 44). Cognitive maps therefore capture managers' professed theories-in-use, and their conceptual and symbolic uses of language.

cognitive mapping a method of spatially displaying data in order to detect patterns and by so doing better understand their relationship and significance

Cognitive maps can work at either an individual or group level, and can be used *statically* as a method of simple data collection (instead of field notes) or *dynamically* with groups of managers. As with repertory grids, various *tools* have been produced that help mediate the intervention; many are computer-based and offer added promise to enhance strategic thinking. We begin with suggesting individual approaches and then give some examples of the collective uses of cognitive mapping.

Individual cognitive maps

Figure 6.2 shows a typical individual map produced by a PhD student (Baker, 1996) undertaking a comparative study of consumer perceptions. In this example, we provide a map about running shoes.

The map is produced through questioning and laddering. The lines running between the numbers (content codes) represent the linkages. Readers will notice that there are fewer *values* (those constructs at the top of the map) than *attributes* (those constructs at the bottom), with consequences tending to come towards the middle. This map might be interpreted in the following way. The main value (primary value 26 at the top of the map) is *well-being*. Below this, there are three further elements, each of which has a large number of elements leading into it. These are: *design* (value 2), *weight/shape* (value 3) and *enhanced performance* (value 14). Baker and Knox's (1995) interpretation is that it is the design of the shoes that enhances what they call 'the performance and well-being chain', and that this is illustrated by the high number of relations among its respective elements, which implies that the product was purchased for the perceived benefits it might deliver in terms of performance.

In order to gain understanding and to interpret the map, the interviewer again needs to go through a process of laddering, in order to explore the person's understanding in more depth. As the constructs deployed in this map are presumed to have a hierarchical relationship, the process of laddering employed in the interviews helps to gain a better understanding of a person's construct system (remember, *laddering down* is where the interviewer explores a person's understanding of a particular construct; *laddering up* is where the interviewer explores why a particular construct is important to the person and helps to explore the latter's value system).

Dominoes

A less systematic way of developing constructs – and one that might be preferred, particularly where there are issues of power and control (e.g. when working with senior managers) – is to use a process called 'dominoes'. This method allows the manager more control over the process and can save considerable time. The process involves the researcher simply identifying elements (whether these are people or objects) and placing them in front of the manager all at the same time. The managers are then asked to place the elements into groups. Elements that come together are then given a name or phrase (labelled) based on what it is that all the elements have in common. Managers are then encouraged to explain the relation between these groups and this is done by encouraging them to explain aloud how the different groups of elements relate together to form a pattern. Their comments are then recorded by the researcher and questions can be asked to obtain clarification as necessary. Using this approach, the managers often find the exercise 'fun' to complete, and differences between elements that produce the constructs can be drawn out.

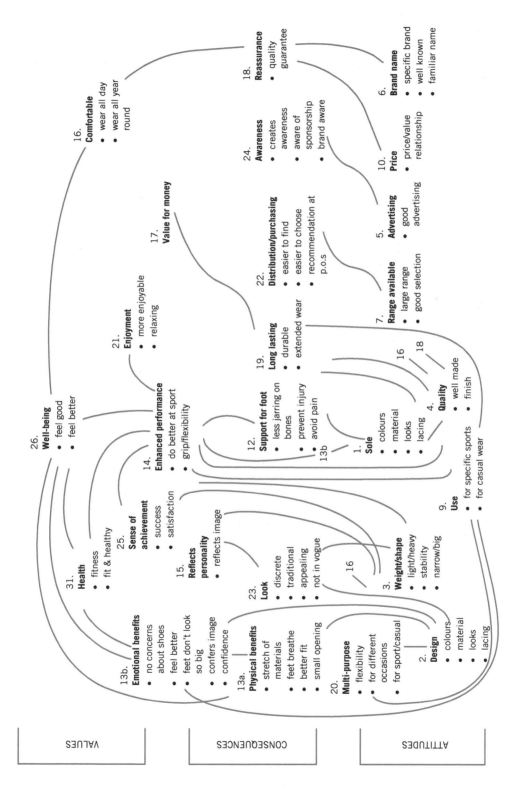

FIGURE 6.2 Hierarchical value map: combined trainers

EXERCISE 6.8

Using the dominoes technique

Group: Ask a colleague to:

- identify seven people – a mixture of people the person likes and dislikes
- write the people's names down on cards and place them on the desk in front of you
- find a feature that differentiates some of these individuals from the others
- place the names of those with similar features adjacent to each other
- supply a word or phrase that best describes the common attributes held – this is one construct.

Now repeat the process and see how many different constructs can be found.

Group maps

Cognitive maps are now being used by researchers in a whole variety of contexts, from helping managers clarify and design strategy to providing tools of mediation. Used interactively, they can help groups think around issues as well as formulate plans. Such approaches have spawned an industry known as 'strategic support', and the improvement in computers and software has enabled a large number of software products to be designed; these can sit within a group of managers or employees to help them map out their perspectives on problems or issues within an organization and, from this collective set of views, clarify next steps. Used in this way, the research clearly takes on an action research flavour, where change is decidedly part of the process of data collection, making the approach an attractive proposition for those undertaking consultancy.

As a consequence, cognitive-mapping methodologies have been increasingly used in action research, where groups of individuals, managers or employees collaborate to model the complexity of their organizational problems as *they* see them so that they can subsequently be analysed and solved. Here the focus is not just on collecting and presenting large amounts of data, but on stimulating new learning that will lead to change – hence its use in strategy development. Originally a manual system, the computer packages now available (e.g. Decision Explorer) provide powerful support both to assist the analysis process and to explore an organization's strategic options (Eden, 1990).

Eden is critical of the traditional view that the formulation of strategy can be conducted quite independently from its implementation. One of the advantages of cognitive mapping is that the process enables those taking part to challenge the views and perspectives of others, and it is often the realization of differences between individual managers – together with the following discussion – that proves most useful, by giving prominence to distinctions and making connections that might otherwise be overlooked (Ackermann and Eden, 2011). A final beneficial outcome of the cognitive-mapping process is that it helps managers reach a collective judgement about issues that are ambiguous, complex and often contested.

In practice, members of an organization are brought together in a room facing a blank wall or large projector screen. The focus of the session or problem on which they are to work is presented to them by a researcher or facilitator. In comfortable surroundings and with a continuous supply of coffee, the individuals then begin to consider aspects of the situation.

Decision Explorer a software program for collecting, conveying and managing ideas and other kinds of qualitative information that surround complex and uncertain situations; available from Banxia software (www.banxia. com)

Each contribution made is either written down on sticky notes (called 'ovals') or stored by computer, and the unfolding cognitive map, which represents the individuals' view of the issue, is projected onto the screen or posted on the wall for participants to alter and refine.

The approach not only allows individual managers to offer their perceptions of a problem, but also gives those responsible for strategy formulation the opportunity to understand the perspectives of others. In this context, interaction among participants – and collaboration between researcher and researched – is a decidedly good thing. An example of using a cognitive-mapping approach is described below and represented in Figure 6.3.

This example involved the use of a cognitive-mapping approach in the strategy- development process when working to surface issues and produce an agenda for change in a hospital merger. Both hospitals were 'hot' sites and, as such, had the prestige of dealing with accident-and-emergency patients. As a consequence, both hospitals had maternity wings (for which accident-and-emergency on site was a necessity), each location was represented by a different Member of Parliament who represented their local catchment, and each hospital had historically been part of a different regional health authority (and, as a consequence, developed a very different culture, organizational structure and set of uniforms). Following pressure to merge from both the government (for reasons of efficiency) and the Royal Colleges (for reasons of improved clinical practice), researchers undertook an action-learning approach to change. At one stage in the change process, they introduced the concept of cognitive mapping as a tool to surface the views of the senior management team, and to engender debate. Working with the management team (all managers and all clinical directors) from both hospitals, the researchers created maps to depict both collective and individual perspectives of the issues faced by the hospital in the context of the impending merger. By first interviewing managers and clinicians individually, they created a number of maps, which were then discussed and debated within a larger group. The trigger questions for discussion were:

- What is your vision for what needs to be done for the merger to be a success?
- What actions need to be taken for this to be realized?

The maps were then modified, with the views expressed captured, grouped and structured into a causal map offering a synthesis of each participant's view on the two questions. Simultaneously, managers were asked to discuss the suggested clustering of concepts, and the content and priorities of the strategic issues. One of the early observations was the speed with which it helped the group to surface the strategic issues facing the hospital.

An initial review of the map, part of which is shown in Figure 6.4, indicated the complexity of the problem. There was a multiplicity and a diversity of social, economic and governmental issues facing the hospital, as well as conflicting views about the current state of the organization and the likely challenges it faced. Despite these differences, we observed that during the cognitive-mapping process, we faced few difficulties achieving interaction between team members as they negotiated their way through the dynamics of reaching consensus on the key strategic issues presented. As Churchill (1990) has observed, this kind of process can be seen to indicate a collective form of organizational learning. The main issues, broken down by cluster, related to politics, performance, staff development, communications and reputation. We found that using this technique enabled all those involved to experience the difficulties of other departments and, with this insight, to begin to understand how the hospital as a whole functioned. The resultant map reduced the messiness and ambiguity that characterized the situation, and enabled the different groups to:

- manage the resultant complexity by identifying emergent themes
- prioritize these themes so that they could subsequently be developed.

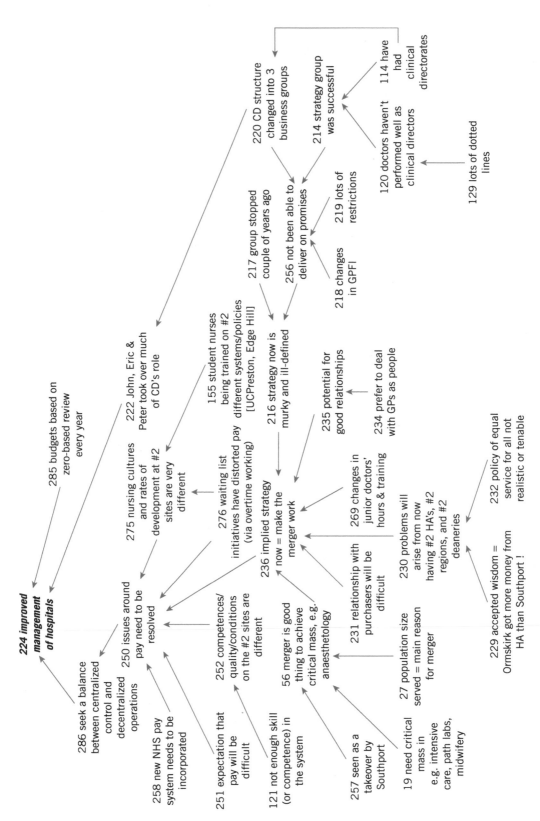

FIGURE 6.3 Cognitive mapping 1

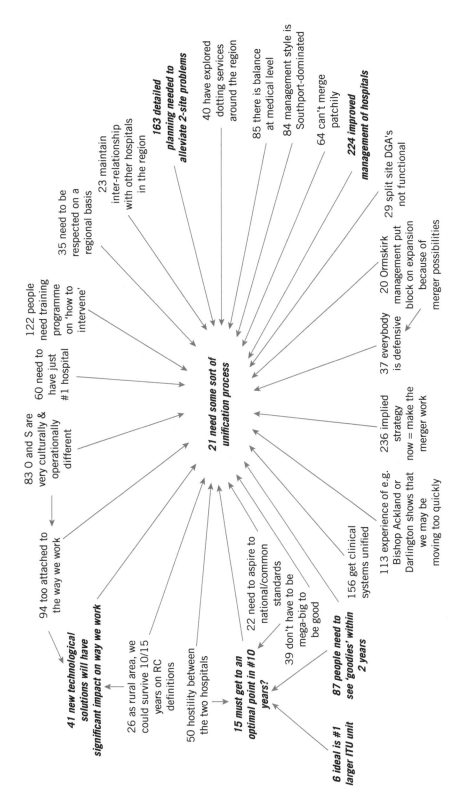

FIGURE 6.4 Cognitive mapping 2

As a consequence, group discussion of the cognitive map not only enabled the transmission of information and of the implications of the issues raised for the management of the local authority, but it also helped to overcome disagreement about goals, the interpretation of issues, and subsequent courses of action.

Conclusion

In this chapter we have provided an overview of some of the main methods for 'crafting' qualitative data through the modalities of language and text. The key points of this chapter that we would like to emphasize are:

- Qualitative research is a creative process, which aims to understand the sense that respondents make of their world. If done well, processes of data collection can be beneficial for everybody involved.

- There are many techniques for crafting qualitative data in a spoken or written form. Although we can give guidelines, each piece of research is unique, and the decision must be taken on which of these alternative and often-competing approaches is most appropriate.

- The flexibility of qualitative research does not mean that anything goes. Processes of data creation require a fair amount of planning and strategic thinking, and the time and skills needed to create useful data should never be underestimated.

In Chapter 7, we explore a different set of approaches for crafting qualitative data, namely those based on *observation and interaction*, such as observational, ethnographic and participatory methods. This next chapter also addresses some overarching issues around the role of the researcher, and the necessity of reflexivity of the researcher's involvement. In Chapter 8, we then complete the section on qualitative methods by presenting strategies for data management, along with different approaches for framing and analysing qualitative data.

Further reading

Three useful articles on conducting interview-based research in management and business studies:

Alvesson, M. (2003) 'Beyond neopositivists, romantics, and localists: a reflexive approach to interviews in organisation research', *Academy of Management Review*, 28 (1): 13–33.

Bourne, H. and Jenkins, M. (2005) 'Eliciting managers' personal values: an adaptation of the laddering interview method', *Organizational Research Method*, 8 (4): 410–28.

Butterfield, L.D., Borgen, W.A., Amundson, N.E. and Maglio, A.T. (2005) 'Fifty years of the critical incident technique: 1954–2004 and beyond', *Qualitative Research*, 5 (4): 475–97.

A practical and thoughtful introduction for (research) students on how to design and conduct research interviews:

Cassell, C. (2015) *Conducting Research Interviews for Business and Management Students* (Mastering Business Research Methods). Thousand Oaks, CA: Sage.

A useful guide with chapters on how to use different methods and techniques in organizational research (including interviews, critical incident technique, repertory grids, cognitive mapping and other methods):

Cassell, C. and Symon, G. (2004) *Essential Guide to Qualitative Methods in Organizational Research*. London: Sage.

An introduction to cognitive mapping in management and business research:

Eden, C. (1992) 'On the nature of cognitive maps', *Journal of Management Studies*, 29 (3): 261–65.

A useful collection of chapters on how to conduct research using the Internet, including a chapter on Internet-based interviewing:

Fielding, N., Lee, R.M. and Blank, G. (2017) *The SAGE Handbook of Online Research Methods*, 2nd edn. London: Sage.

An excellent resource with chapters on all aspects of interviewing:

Gubrium, J.F., Holstein, J., Marvasti, A.B. and McKinney, K.D. (2012) *The SAGE Handbook of Interview Research: The Complexity of the Craft*, 2nd edn. Thousand Oaks, CA: Sage.

This explains in detail how to plan and moderate focus groups:

Krueger, R.A. and Casey, M.A. (2009) *Focus Groups: A Practical Guide for Applied Research*, 4th edn. Thousand Oaks, CA: Sage.

A useful overview of different interview methods:

Kvale, S. and Brinkmann, S. (2009) *InterViews: Learning the Craft of Qualitative Research Interviewing*, 2nd edn. Thousand Oaks, CA: Sage.

The following article provides a useful starting point for those interested in critical incident technique, repertory grids and cognitive maps:

Rogers, B. and Ryals, L. (2007) 'Using the repertory grid to access the underlying realities in key account relationships', *International Journal of Market Research*, 49 (5): 595–612.

A useful volume of chapters presenting core methods, such as interviews and focus groups but also visual methods and action research among many others:

Symon, G. and Cassell, C. (eds) (2012) *Qualitative Organizational Research: Core Methods and Current Challenges*. London: Sage.

An excellent textbook for students planning to conduct a qualitative study; Chapters 7 and 8 cover many practical aspects of interview planning and interview practice:

Tracy, S.J. (2013) *Qualitative Research Methods: Collecting Evidence, Crafting Analysis, Communicating Impact*. Chichester: Wiley-Blackwell.

Check your understanding online

Visit the website **https://edge.sagepub.com/easterbysmith6e** for useful resources that will help reinforce what you've read in this chapter:

 Take an interactive quiz to test your understanding of the key topics

 Review suggested answers to Exercises 6.1 to 6.8 above

 Use interactive flashcards to check your knowledge of essential concepts

Learning objectives

To find out about a range of different methods for crafting qualitative data through observation and interaction with research participants.

To understand the potential and limitations of these methods.

To reflect on the role of researchers in the field, and the importance of reflexivity in the research process.

CRAFTING QUALITATIVE DATA THROUGH OBSERVATION AND PARTICIPATORY RESEARCH

7

Chapter contents

Introduction

In the previous chapter, we introduced a range of text-based and interview-based methods. We now consider a number of approaches for creating qualitative data through observation and interaction, including visual methods, participant observation and participatory methods. We address these methods along a continuum: from the relatively passive collection of existing secondary data to intrinsically interactive methods aiming at the co-creation of qualitative data with research participants. We then discuss a number of general issues that surround qualitative data collection, such as the necessity of researchers taking a reflexive approach to their own involvement in the research process. Together with Chapter 6, this chapter gives an overview of the manifold approaches and techniques that facilitate and structure the crafting of qualitative data. It is intended to inspire a creative and reflexive attitude towards data collection, acknowledging that it often requires some effort to identify the most appropriate methods for a given research project, since this decision depends on the research question as much as on the field under study.

Visual data

Despite the pervasive nature of the visual in our everyday lives, management research has continued to privilege verbal over visual forms of communication. Historically, visual methods of data collection have been viewed as being highly subjective, difficult to interpret and prone to researcher bias. Consequently, most qualitative management research has been limited to textual data-gathering techniques. Yet, as Secrist et al. (2002) note, despite writers' eloquent verbal descriptions of their research experiences, words alone cannot always communicate the complex and intricate situations they encounter. Consequently, there has been an increasing interest in what visual methods can offer management researchers.

Following Knoblauch and colleagues (2008: 3), we define visual data as 'any kind of visual material, either produced by actors (such as lay photographs) or social scientists (such as video records of social interactions) that depend in their meaning and significance on [...] visualized records, be it diagrams, photographical reproductions or video-taped records'.

Visual data offer the opportunity for a situation to be held captive or frozen in time. Whether we look at organizational charts or pictures accompanying news reports, or watch videos on YouTube, visual data provide us with a sense of the situation and reveal meaningful insights into all kinds of human experience. Researchers can investigate the meaning of visual data as well as the ways in which they are created and interpreted.

Secondary visual data

secondary visual data relates to the analysis of verbal accounts that respondents give in response to visual images

A growing number of qualitative studies involve the analysis of secondary visual data, such as videos from the Internet or photographs taken for purposes other than research. The range of potentially relevant visual data is as broad as the capacity of humans to express themselves in a visual way. Buildings, cartoons and complex academic diagrams: in one way or another, these all reflect human experience. The proliferation of information technologies has led to an unprecedented increase in the use of visual forms of communication. Through the growth of digital media, researchers can get access to contemporary records made by research participants (e.g. pictures taken with mobile phone cameras), in this way blurring the distinction between the researcher and the researched (Back, 2006).

FIGURE 7.1   Historical photographs of market traders

Credits: Three Lions/Hulton Archive/Getty Images and Jim Wilson/Archive Photos/Getty Images

Photographs taken from archives can open up a historical dimension to research projects. For example, Figure 7.1 shows photographs of market traders' gestures in 1869, 1987 and 1925. Such pictures could be used to explore how communication between traders has changed over time. Images, however, would not need to be the main focus of attention; they could be complemented with written accounts, video material, interviews and the observation of traders engaging in increasingly decentralized practices of trading. Indeed, as Pink (2001) highlights, the relation of images to other sensory, material and linguistic details of the study will result in the images being of interest to most researchers. It is important to remember, however, that secondary data are produced for purposes other than research – and, for that reason, they might not fit into a given research project. If we cannot understand or if we misinterpret the background or purpose of a data fragment, this can compromise the quality of our research. Students are also reminded to consider any copyright implications when collecting visual material. If this is not taken into consideration at the outset they may find their research difficult to publish later down the line.

EXERCISE 7.1

Collecting secondary visual data

Group discussion: Pick a picture, video, organizational chart or other visual data fragment that could be analysed for a study in your field. Present your data fragment to the group and explain why you have chosen it, where you have found it and the context of the fragment (who produced it, when and where, and for what purpose). Who has identified the most fascinating data fragment? Who has come up with the most innovative idea for a research project? Who has outlined the most practical research project?

Primary visual data

In contrast to secondary visual data, primary visual data such as photographs or videos are responsive data: they have been specifically created for a research project or study. A body of research known collectively as 'workplace studies' has made extensive use of video recordings to examine the effects of the material environment and technologies on action and interaction in a variety of organizational settings (Luff et al., 2000; Heath and Hindmarsh, 2002). Example 7.1 gives an account of a study by Clarke (2011), who employs a visual ethnographic approach. Although visual ethnographic approaches, which involve video-taping individuals in contexts of natural interactions, have a long-standing tradition in the fields of visual sociology and anthropology, this was the first attempt to employ such an approach in the management domain.

EXAMPLE 7.1

Using visual tools in a research study

Clarke (2011) incorporated visual tools into her research in order to explore how entrepreneurs use visual symbols to create legitimacy for their ventures. Her study is based on material collected during visual ethnographies of three entrepreneurs, during which she captured videos of entrepreneurs in a range of different interactions with investors, employees and customers over a three-month period. She was aware of the influence that the video camera could have on the unfolding interactions, and attempted as much as possible to reduce the 'reactivity' of participants. Over time, participants became accustomed to the camera and reacted less to its presence. Also, the camera used was small, compact and portable, making it as unobtrusive as possible. Approximately 60 hours of raw video-taped interactions were digitized and captured for audio and video analysis.

She found that entrepreneurs use a range of visual symbols during performances to stakeholders, namely settings, props, dress and expressiveness. Entrepreneurs used these visual symbols in order to present an appropriate scene to stakeholders, to create professional identity and emphasize control, and to regulate emotions. When used systematically, visual symbols helped entrepreneurs access much-needed resources through addressing the low levels of legitimacy that typically exist when novel ventures are launched. More experienced or serial entrepreneurs are likely to be more effective at employing a wider range of visual symbols systematically during interactions with stakeholders. By studying in detail how entrepreneurs use their visual surroundings during performances with stakeholders, this study showed that language is only one of the symbolic tools used by entrepreneurs.

Observational research

Video recordings such as those undertaken by Clarke stand in the tradition of observational research; that is, research based on researchers observing research participants in particular settings. Table 7.1 gives an overview of the different stances that researchers may take when conducting observational research. First, there are *complete observers*, who maintain a detached distance when observing research participants in the field. Second, there are *observers-as-*

participants, who participate in activities in the field but seek to reduce the impact of their presence as much as possible. The third stance, *participant-as-observer*, implies more direct interaction with the field. Participant observers of this kind are more active in their engagement with the field they study. Finally, there are *complete participants*, whose primary role is that of participant (e.g. employee or consultant). Some complete participants conceal their intention to conduct research; this can facilitate access but also gives rise to critical ethical issues.

TABLE 7.1   Four types of observational research

---

1   Complete observer: Researcher maintains distance to the object and context, and avoids all direct engagement.

2   Observer-as-participant: Researcher engages with the field in a relatively passive way, e.g. by asking questions, while trying not to influence the field under study.

3   Participant-as-observer: Researcher does not conceal the intention of observation and participates in the context as researcher and participant. This is the most common type of participant observation in management and business studies.

4   Complete participant: Researcher conceals the intention to study and adopts more fully the role of a participant when observing the field.

Source: Anderson, 2008a

As this overview shows, different types of observational research differ in their understanding of the *role of the researcher*. Depending on their role, researchers employ different methods of data creation. Researchers conducting complete observation usually create observational records (such as written records, audio recordings and videos) and collect secondary data. Adopting the role of a participant as well as an observer opens up additional avenues for the creation of qualitative data (such as conversations and field interviews) and the (co)creation of visual data (e.g. by drawing an organizational chart with a group of employees). Such methods allow researchers not only to observe certain activities or interactions but also to explore *why* they are pursued. In the following sections, we explore the four types of observational research in more detail.

All observational methods usually require researchers to record their observations. In some cases, this can be done using video or audio recordings, but the most common technique is to

TABLE 7.2   Tips for writing field notes

---

1   *Discreetness*: Be careful not to irritate or annoy research participants when taking notes.

2   *Write-up*: Write up your full accounts/field notes as soon as you can, and before speaking to anyone about what you have observed

3   *Headings*: Never forget time, date, place and a list of the participants involved.

4   *Detail*: Be as detailed as possible. Things that appear unimportant at first can turn out to be very important later down the line. Don't forget to describe characters and settings.

5   *Openness*: Just write and do not worry about style or grammar. Your field notes are *your* material.

6   *Perspective*: Ask yourself why you chose a certain perspective on an event or episode – and whether some participants could have experienced this episode in a different way.

7   *No analysis*: Avoid evaluative or judgemental language. Field notes should record facts – analysis comes later.

8   *Quotations*: Indicate direct quotations as such.

9   *Emotions*: If you are tired or emotional, it can be useful to write in the research diary (mentioned in the previous chapter) first.

10   *To-do list*: Note down follow-up questions at the end.

---

make some preliminary scribblings in a notebook, and to return to the notebook later in the day in order to transform the notes into comprehensive written accounts. Writing detailed field notes requires method, skill and practice – and involves an active process of interpretation. In Table 7.2 we include a list of some tips for writing field notes. Readers who wish to conduct an observational study are advised to obtain more in-depth guidance on how to write field notes (see, for example, Emerson et al., 2011).

EXERCISE 7.2

Exploring the role of the researcher in observational research

1   **Group discussion**: Burawoy (2009: 204) notes that as participant observers, 'we don't have access to some Archimedean standpoint' (a hypothetical vantage point from which an observer can objectively perceive the subject of inquiry): instead we are always located somewhere 'in the site, which has grave consequences to what we say'. In groups or pairs, discuss how this statement relates to the four types of observational research presented above. What are the implications of the different standpoints for researchers and research participants? What kind of observational research is the most useful/the most problematic?

2   **Individual**: Reflect on what kind of observational research could be useful for your own project, and what standpoint could be most appropriate when taking into account the objectives of your research and the nature of the field you wish to study.

Complete observation

By *complete observation*, we refer to observations conducted by researchers who avoid any interaction with the field. As a research method, complete observation is of limited use to those interested in a social constructionist view. It is most commonly used in the field of management services where, for job design and specification purposes, requests are made for 'objective' accounts of the content of work. Practitioners conducting complete observation usually do not ask people for accounts of their own actions because of the requirement for detachment. This limits the depth of the data obtained in significant ways.

Complete observers are often disliked by those whom they observe, since detached observation can appear like snooping, and prevents the development of trust and rapport between researchers and research participants (which, as we have noted before, is fundamental for the creation of qualitative data). However, for trained practitioners, complete observations can give accurate pictures of specific activities in the workplace, and inform assessments of how long they take, even if they fall short of giving a full account of why things are happening in a certain way. While, in the past, detached accounts of non-participant observers were valued as more 'neutral' and so more scientific than participant observations, the artificial character of such observations has sometimes undermined the apparent 'neutrality' of this as a research method, as in Example 7.2.

EXAMPLE 7.2

The challenges of complete observation

In *Kitchen Stories*, a film by the Norwegian director Bent Hamer (2003), scientific observers placed on tall chairs attempt to survey the kitchen habits of elderly single men in an attempt to optimize their kitchens. The observers are instructed not to communicate with the 'objects' of their research, as a result of which the observed men avoid their kitchens and engage in a similarly detached observation of the unusual behaviour of the scientific 'intruders' until both sides cannot avoid direct engagement. This and similar films and anecdotes show how the artificiality of complete observation can have as strong an impact on the field as open interaction and engagement. This raises questions about the kind of settings that allow for *complete* (i.e. *non*-participant) observations.

Participant observation and ethnography

Methods of *participant observation* are defined by a continuum, running from very limited observations to answer specific questions (such as where to place the sink in kitchens for single retired men) to rather open and general observations of an entire social system or culture (such as the life of elderly single men in rural Norway). Looking at participant observation from this perspective helps us to determine the difference between *participant observation* as a method and *ethnography* as a research strategy, two concepts many consider as synonymous.

Participant observation can be used as a method for just a couple of hours to answer very specific research questions. The observer can be present sporadically over a period of time: moving, for example, in and out of an organization to deal with other work or to conduct interviews with, or observations of, different people across a number of different organizations. In contrast to such interrupted involvement, *ethnography* usually refers to the long-term and in-depth use of participant observation, often in conjunction with other methods (such as interviews or the collection of demographic data), to understand an entire social system or culture (Macdonald, 2010). Ethnography requires a systematic and sustained engagement with a field, where the researcher becomes immersed in a new context that poses unexpected challenges and puzzles to solve. Ethnographic research can be an overwhelming experience. Many researchers find it challenging to remain aware of themselves as observers. Hence, ethnographers not only observe research participants, they also observe themselves and how they engage with their environment.

EXAMPLE 7.3

The Illegality industry

For his ethnography *Illegality, Inc.*, published in 2014, Ruben Andersson travelled along a migration trail from Senegal and Mali to the Spanish North African enclaves of Ceuta and Melilla. He conducted several hundred interviews with migrants, border guards, charity

(Continued)

workers, international officials, activists and smugglers. His study traces the subterranean migration flow from Africa to Europe, and shifts the focus from the illegal immigrants themselves to the vast industry built around their movements. Andersson argues that as more and more money is spent in an attempt to regulate movement, more illegal behaviour is created by industries set up to control migration. In 2015, Andersson's ethnography won the prestigious 'Thinking Allowed Award for Ethnography' awarded by the British Sociological Association and the radio programme 'Thinking Allowed'. Further information on the study and the ethnographic fieldwork it involved is available on the book's website.

Ruben Andersson

Podcast: Discussion of Ruben Andersson's Illegality Inc.

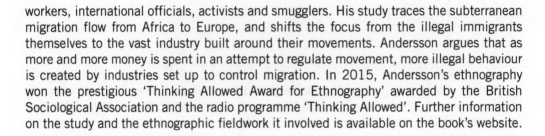

EXERCISE 7.3

Ethnography

1   **Individual**: Based on Example 7.3 and the associated online material above, write a 1,000-word essay on Ruben Andersson's ethnographic research and why it won the award. What made this ethnography stand out?

2   **Group discussion**: In his online article 'Ethnography – what is it and why do we need it?', Ruben Andersson argues that we need ethnographic research more than ever. Can you explain the reasoning behind his statement? Do you agree?

Example 7.3 presents a multi-sited ethnography that aimed to understand an entire field or 'industry' and the (re-)production and valorization of 'illegality' through this industry. While Andersson's study testifies to the fact that analytical depth and accessibility are not mutually exclusive, it also points to the enormous efforts required to conduct this kind of research. In business and management research, and in particular in research conducted by research students of these disciplines, ethnographic research is often concerned with one or a small number of organizations. Example 7.4 illustrates such an approach and the 'insider–outsider' challenges that studies of this kind can produce, as well as the importance trust plays in getting data and making the most of opportunities that present themselves.

EXAMPLE 7.4

A social constructionist perspective on conducting a rural ethnography

In conducting this research, a PhD student aimed to understand how different communities construct, maintain and change their self-identities. The research took place within the particular context of workers on a tea plantation in Sri Lanka (see Figure 7.2). During the fieldwork phase, the student became far more aware of her own identity as a researcher than had hitherto been the case, and she was able to see and understand her identity both as an academic and as a Sri Lankan national. The latter enabled her to understand the social and cultural values, and her Buddhist background allowed her to live with the community and adapt to the prevailing social norms. At times, she saw herself as an outsider, while at others she became an insider within the research site. Living both outside and inside different tea plantations, developing close relationships with local people, she was able to make sense of the practices and rituals she was able to observe. At times, some of the elders became protective and supportive of her as a young female researcher. When inside the plantation, she seized the opportunity to spend as much time as possible with those on the plantation, talking and observing. Due to the size of the plantation, when 'on site' she was often accompanied by a representative from management; although this was meant to be helpful, it made it difficult for her to get close to people and to establish the kind of trusting relationship she would have liked. She later learnt that part of the difficulty experienced was due to the fact that workers had been warned by the police not to talk to strangers inside the plantation. This made them hesitant to approach her, although, as she got to know them, she developed sufficient trust to win their confidence. The PhD student summarizes her experiences of an ethnographic approach as being a complex process. The process is not a logical step-by-step approach, and skills of sensitivity are required, as well as a flexibility and willingness to change the plan and to be open to where the research might lead.

FIGURE 7.2   Tea-leaf picking

Source: Geetha Karunanayake

TABLE 7.3 Examples of observational research in business and management studies

Articles

Knox, H., O'Doherty, D., Vurdubakis, T. and Westrup, C. (2008) 'Enacting airports: space, movement and modes of ordering', *Organization*, 15 (6): 869–88.

Lok, J. and Rond, M. de (2013) 'On the plasticity of institutions: containing and restoring practice breakdowns at the Cambridge University Boat Club', *Academy of Management Journal*, 56 (1): 185–207.

McCann, L., Granter, E., Hyde, P. and Hassard, J. (2013) 'Still blue-collar after all these years? An ethnography of the professionalization of emergency ambulance work', *Journal of Management Studies*, 50 (5): 750–76.

Roy, D. (1952) 'Quota restriction and goldbricking in a machine shop', *American Journal of Sociology*, 57 (5): 427–42.

Roy, D. (1954) 'Efficiency and "The Fix": informal intergroup relations in a piecework machine shop', *American Journal of Sociology*, 60 (3): 255–66.

Books and Chapters

Dalton, M. (1959) *Men Who Manage: Fusions of Feeling and Theory in Administration*. New York: Wiley.

Kunda, G. (1993) *Engineering Culture: Control and Commitment in a High-tech Corporation*. Philadelphia, PA: Temple University Press.

Van Maanen, J. (1991) 'The smile factory: work at Disneyland', in P.J. Frost, L.F. Moore, M.R. Louis, C.C. Lundberg and J. Martin (eds), *Reframing Organizational Culture*. Newbury Park, CA: Sage.

There is extensive literature on participant observation and ethnography, particularly in sociology and anthropology (Bernard, 2011). Since organizations can easily be viewed as 'tribes', with their own strange customs and practices, it is by no means surprising that participant observation has also been used in organizational and management research – where it usually implies some kind of close involvement in an organization, with the purpose of uncovering accounts that may not have been accessed by other methods, such as interviews (Watson, 1994; Anderson, 2008a). The object is to gain an insider perspective that enhances a researcher's understanding of other people's realities. In Table 7.3, we list some examples of research involving participant observation in business and management studies.

EXERCISE 7.4

Exploring ethnographic studies in management

Individual: Conduct a brief literature search to identify a recent article or book on an ethnographic study in management research, or pick one of the publications listed in Table 7.3. Read and evaluate the publication to answer the following questions in writing:

- How do the authors describe their methodology? How do they describe their role in the field? Do they detail the length/depth of their engagement with the field? What was their role in the field? Are there any important details missing?

- How does the methodology of the study relate to its outcome?

- Do you think it would have been possible to conduct the study with other methods? If yes, what would have been the advantages and disadvantages of using different methods?

Complete participation and covert research

In contrast to complete observation and participant observation, *complete participation* implies that the role of the researcher in the field is defined by their role as participant (e.g. as colleague, employee or consultant). Donald Roy (1952) used the method to great effect when working as an employee in the machine shop of a large company. He was able both to show how workers manipulated the piecework incentive scheme and to understand the motives behind this. For anyone wishing to learn about the craft of participant observation and how the methodology might be written up, they would do well to read one or two of the original articles that Roy produced from his research (see Table 7.3).

Complete participation often implies that researcher participants either are unaware of the fact that a particular co-worker, manager or employee conducts research (i.e. in covert observation) or do not consider this fact relevant. Researchers who are creating data as complete participants and members of organizations may find themselves negotiating a minefield of ethical issues. *Covert research* is generally difficult to reconcile with the key principles of research ethics (stated in Chapter 5). When reflecting upon this dilemma, it can be helpful to consider whether the potential benefits of the research can really outweigh the ethical issues created through covert observation.

Semi-concealed research

Semi-concealed research is not the same as covert research, in that researchers are more open about their rationale for studying the company. The aspect of concealment relates to the way the focus of the research is defined, and the view the researcher takes on the practices under observation. An example of this would be the research of Collinson (1992), who conducted his study into the recruitment and selection practices of large companies without emphasizing that his particular focus was on how the mainly white, male, middle-aged managers controlled entry into the companies in ways that had the effect of excluding women. In this way, he could negotiate access into organizations that otherwise could have inhibited his access for fear of being presented in an unflattering or critical light.

In another study conducted by Thorpe (1980), the researcher was able to gain an understanding of how management's failure to address the motivational needs of the workforce led to disillusionment and apathy. Not all individuals involved were aware of the research taking place. However, the company chairperson and the works convener had agreed to the research being conducted, as they considered it useful. In Chapter 5, David Mosse describes his experience of transitioning from the role of a colleague and consultant to that of a researcher (see page 155–6). He highlights some of the challenges associated with such transition. In his view, researchers who conduct insider research may not worry about access – but about 'exit'!

semi-concealed research a form of ethnography where there is negotiated access with research agendas that the researchers are not always willing to reveal to all those they meet

EXAMPLE 7.5

Researcher as employee

Poor planning of work meant that workers were often bored: by experiencing this boredom himself, Thorpe was better able to understand its causes and the ways in which the employees attempted to alleviate it. His team developed a pattern of activity where they worked for the first hour or so, and then took a break, and had a wash and a walk outside. On certain days, they changed their overalls in the laundry, which involved a walk of about 600 yards and a break of about half an hour. After mid-morning, the pace became much slower; and after lunchtime, very little work was done at all.

On one occasion (a Wednesday afternoon), the researcher saw that the conveyor belt was beginning to back up for no apparent reason. On questioning his colleagues about it, he learnt that they saw this as a good strategy to put pressure on management and guarantee themselves overtime at the weekend (at time-and-a-half pay). Since overtime working had to be notified to the employees three days in advance, it was important to slow things down on Wednesday. By Friday, the backlog had all but been cleared but the promise of the overtime remained, making for a fairly easy Saturday morning's work!

Naturally, Thorpe's questioning did not stop at this observation, for it then became of interest to know why the extra pay was required, and why this strategy was used in preference to others.

Auto-ethnography

Participant observation requires researchers to reflect on their own role. If researchers give up the awareness of their own position as participant *and* researcher, they risk becoming assimilated into the field in a way that limits their analytic ability. Practices with which researchers are well acquainted go unnoticed or remain unchallenged more easily than those that appear unfamiliar. Most classical anthropological ethnographies were undertaken in fields that were alien to the researcher, as the incremental reduction in the distance between the researcher as an 'outsider' and a field of 'insiders' was seen as aiding the observational process. While there is certainly some truth in this argument, it can also be difficult for an 'outsider' to understand the motivations and interpretations of 'insiders': something that complete participants have less trouble with.

Being an 'insider' can (literally) 'open doors' that an external observer would not even be aware of; it reduces resource requirements and facilitates the establishment of trust and rapport (Karra and Phillips, 2007). At the same time, it can also imply role conflict and a lack of critical distance, and begs the question of to what extent the focus of the observation is on *other insiders* or on the experiences, practices and identity of the *researcher as an insider*. Ethnographic studies that shift the focus from the field to the observer are usually referred to as auto-ethnographies (or self-ethnographies). An interesting example of an auto-ethnography with a strong autobiographical dimension is a study by Goodall (2007) entitled *A Need to Know*, in which he explores how his father's work for the CIA during the Cold War shaped the history of his family, and his own biography.

auto-ethnography
a form of insider research often conducted by those studying in the organization in which they work

EXAMPLE 7.6

Auto-ethnographies in management research

Historically, (auto-)ethnographies in international management research were accounts of becoming familiar with the unfamiliar. These days a growing number of management researchers choose to investigate social phenomena in their own cultural and professional context. In an article published in 2007, Neri Karra and Nelson Phillips discuss the strengths and challenges of researching 'back home', arguing that autoethnographic approaches have important strengths. They usually require fewer resources, there are fewer problems when it comes to access and translation and it is much easier to establish trust and rapport. However, at the same time it can be difficult to maintain critical distance and role conflicts are not uncommon. Moreover, autoethnographers generally study organizations with which they already have existing relationships of some sort, which are a matter of existing conditions over which the researcher has little control. The authors conclude that 'autoethnographic methods are therefore a two-edged sword. The more autoethnographic a study becomes, the more benefit the researcher will experience in terms of the strengths of the method. At the same time, the more autoethnographic the method becomes, the more he or she will need to manage the challenges' (Karra and Phillips, 2007: 556).

Virtual ethnography

There is not one but many ways of conducting observational research in virtual (online) fields. Methods for conducting observational research online differ in the online and social media platforms they use and the ways in which the researcher engages with research participants (Hine, 2017). They involve distinct design decisions that relate to the boundaries of the phenomenon and the media through which it is studied. For example, a researcher may choose to study multiple sites that are similar in character as well as multiple modes of communication. Some researchers adopt a networked approach by tracing the flow of information between a given set of people (Hine, 2017). In this chapter, we do not have the space to discuss these particularities in more detail but we provide below some guidance for those who are considering conducting observational research online.

Ethical concerns have been raised about online research, and in particular about issues relating to consent. While the public nature of large parts of the Internet may suggest that consent forms are not a necessity, it should be obvious that adherence to principles of ethical research is a must and by no means dependent on the context under investigation. Questions have also been raised about the authenticity of online encounters. Here, the underlying philosophical assumptions of the research are again important. Some may argue that online interactions may open up opportunities to create alternative realities – but that these realities nevertheless have real impacts on society today. For example, a team of economists recently published a study that examined how innovations in gaming and recreational computing may have led to a decline in working hours among younger men in the US (Aguiar et al., 2017).

Netnography
defined

Interactive and participatory methods

We now turn to interactive and participatory methods for the creation of qualitative data. Many of these methods combine techniques of methods we have introduced earlier, such as qualitative interviews, participant observation and the creation of primary visual data. What makes interactive and participatory methods stand out is that they aim at the *interactive (co)creation of qualitative data* in a process that encourages researchers and respondents to develop a joint understanding of what is taking place. Used in this way, interactive and participatory methods become 'tools for thinking' that can help to stimulate reflection and discussion among research participants upon complex management issues. In this way, these methods can be beneficial for the research participants as well as the researcher, as in many cases both parties learn from their application.

In Chapter 6, we discussed some interview-based and text-based techniques that involve the co-creation of data (repertory grid and mapping techniques). Here, we introduce a number of additional approaches that employ a visual media component, such as participatory methods that involve videos, photographs and pictures.

Video recordings, photographs and pictures

One example of applying a visually based methodology is Cunliffe's (2001) postmodern perspective on management practice, where she video-taped interviews she conducted with a number of managers. She subsequently played these video-taped interviews back to the managers to explore with them how they had co-created meaning through the course of the interview. In this way, the meaning of the interviews was discussed and deciphered in collaboration with the participant, as a form of co-inquiry – rather than just by the researcher.

Photographs can be a useful way of gathering information when there is only a small amount of data on an issue to begin with, when getting information is proving difficult, or when the matter under discussion is seen as contentious or problematic. Researchers can ask the general public, employees of an organization, or other research participants to take photographs of specific events that are of interest. This can serve to complement other sources – say, interviews, diaries and postcards. Assessing the role that photography has played in organizational research, Buchanan (1999) stated that while it has enjoyed a rich tradition in disciplines such as sociology and anthropology (Collier and Collier, 1986; Harper, 1994; Banks, 1995), it has been used far less within the field of management. His research involved the use of photographs to stimulate discussion and debate between members of staff at a hospital as part of a programme to re-engineer the patient's experience. He collected photographs in order to record complex scenes and processes. The use of photographs triggered informants to talk much more about the ideas they had around the images, and this helped to develop a more complex, joint understanding of the chains of activity that occurred. Photographs of the process also contributed to a more accurate sequencing of this, as well as to a more detailed written analysis of the process.

RESEARCH IN ACTION

Talking about pictures of football stadiums: A photo-elicitation project

William Ambler is a final-year BA Management student at the University of Leeds. After a summer internship at a former UK Premier League football club, Will decided to conduct research on the management of football clubs.

Can you tell us what your research was about?

William Ambler

In my dissertation project, I investigated the impact of football stadium infrastructure on the management of the club–supporter relationship. During my operations internship the year before, I had noticed that some football clubs have little understanding of the club–supporter relationship and how to manage it. My dissertation project identified varying opinions on the management of this relationship at a time when football is no longer just a game played on a pitch but has developed into an entertainment industry.

How did you go about this research? Did you just ask fans to take pictures?

After I told my tutor about my research idea, she suggested photo-elicitation as a method for my research. I consulted the literature and decided to use Venkatraman and Nelson's (2008) photo-elicitation methodology as a model for my project. I conducted my research in the following way:

- Initially, I set up introduction meetings in which I outlined the research procedure to each participant and asked them to 'take photos of a supporter's experience' at 'their' football stadium. This meeting helped to engage the participants and answer any questions they had. I also explained ethical guidelines and my consent form. I worked with members of staff and supporters of two football clubs.

- Once the participants had taken the photographs, they sent them to me via email and we arranged dates and times for the interviews.

(Continued)

- These interviews were photo-elicited, which meant that I had no set list of questions but instead asked participants to describe the photo and to explain why they had taken it. I recorded the interviews using a voice recorder. Interviews lasted well over an hour and yielded rich data.

- Finally, I transcribed the interviews and analysed them using thematic analysis. This involved coding the data using different colour highlighting pens.

Can you give us an example of how that worked out?

Although a cliché, it is true that a picture can 'tell a thousand words'. During one interview, a participant explained to me that he took two photos because he wanted to compare his club's old stand with its newly built stand. The comparison allowed the participant to discuss his views, not just on stadium infrastructure but also on other themes. For example, he said he 'can appreciate that modern stadiums cost a lot of money' but he also felt that 'the club should reduce the cost of tickets as a compensation' when they could not offer the same standard to all supporters. This statement, as well as many others similar in kind, aided the development of the theme of 'business in football' and helped me to explore how business-related thinking on both sides impacts the club–supporter relationship.

Do you think that you would have come to the same results if you had just conducted interviews? What was the benefit of using photo-elicitation?

I believe that if I had conducted just regular interviews then the interviewees would not have been 'caught in the moment' in the same way, and their responses would not have been as detailed. My friends who conducted conventional interviews for their own dissertation projects reported that they struggled to get their participants to develop their responses; however, I never encountered such problems.

In my view, this was the main benefit of the photo-elicitation method: participants appeared to be more engaged as they felt that the research process was more personal. As a result it elicited rich and unexpected responses from participants.

TOP TIP

If you consider an unorthodox method for your dissertation project, it's helpful to familiarize yourself with the relevant literature early on. In the beginning, I had no idea what photo-elicitation was about but because it was different I became more engaged with it. Consequently, the research process became much more enjoyable, which is vital since a dissertation process is long and can seem daunting at times.

EXERCISE 7.6

Photo-elicitation

1 **Individual**: Conduct a literature search and identify a research article that reports a study that involved photo-elicitation. (If you cannot find one, you may try to access the one William cites above.) Download and read the article. Make a list of *all* steps of the research process and write a critical discussion (500 words) of what the use of photographs added to this research.

2 **Individual**: For three days, take pictures of all advertisements you come across that catch your attention in a positive or in a negative way. Select four pictures for a photo-elicitation exercise in class.

3 **Group**: In pairs, conduct brief photo-elicitation interviews. Each 'interviewer' selects one of the interviewee's pictures and asks the interviewee to describe why they have taken it. Using laddering techniques, the interviewer tries to obtain as much information from the interviewee as possible. During the interview the interviewer takes notes. After 10–15 minutes stop and swap roles. Discuss your experiences in class. What was it like to be the interviewer/interviewee? What worked and what did not work? How important were the pictures in the interview process?

Pictures and drawings are another form of visual data that can be used to elicit the views of individuals or groups. Individuals, for example, might be asked to represent the issues that concern them in the form of pictures or drawings. Birgit Schyns et al. (2011) have used

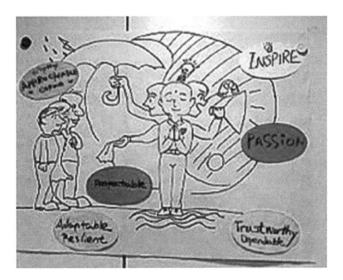

FIGURE 7.3   Drawing depicting an effective East Asian leader

Source: Schyns et al., 2011: 403

this approach to great effect in their studies of how leaders are perceived by followers in different cultures. In her and her colleagues' research, people from different nationality groups were asked to draw pictures of leaders; from these, understandings were gained into the dimensions and perspectives of very different national groups in relation to leadership. Figure 7.3 shows one of the outputs from this study, illustrating the wider societal purpose of leadership in relation to followers, as seen by students from East Asia. In this example, it can be seen how effective leaders are expected to take responsibility for employees' and their families' well-being.

Visual metaphors

visual metaphors an approach to eliciting the views of individuals or groups with the notion of metaphors in order to get individuals (or groups) to draw and describe issues or events as they currently see them or would like to see them in the future

The use of visual metaphors can be a powerful way of developing a common understanding of an issue – and for groups to move forward with a vision for the future. An example of a group of managers being asked to draw a picture of the organization as if it were a person is shown in Example 7.7.

EXAMPLE 7.7

A visual metaphor

In research conducted in a large multinational organization, a visual metaphor approach was used to explore how the senior staff viewed their organization (Simpson, 1995). The research was conducted using a series of focus-group interviews. At each session, the groups were asked the following questions:

1   If the organization were a parent, how do you think it would relate to its children?

2   If you were asked to write an honest character reference for the organization, what would it say?

3   Try to imagine the company as an old friend whom you have not seen for the last ten years. How would you judge whether the friend's personality had changed?

4   Finally, individuals were asked to draw a picture of the company as the 'person' is today.

The questions produced very rich data indeed, which was taped and analysed, but perhaps the most interesting aspect of this metaphor approach was the drawings that the individuals produced and their interpretation. An example is shown below.

The way the group discussed the drawings was as follows:

Jean: He's a man again, is he?

Mirjam: Yes.

David: Yes, I think he is a man.

Mohamed: It's impossible to get away from that, I think.

Jean: Tell us about your picture; what does your picture show for us?

FIGURE 7.4   Example drawing. Credit: Brian Simpson

Mohamed: Shall I defend this? Since I drew it, I got the short straw! Well, I was thinking of the bumbling-uncle-type person: perhaps not the sharpest person in the world, but at least you might get your pocket money off him. Next time you meet him, he's got 30 years younger; he's got a flat top, a nice suit and a BMW. What was I trying to show [indicating hand on the drawing]? I'm not much of an artist as you can see – was basically just 'No!'. It looks like 'On yer bike!', which is just as appropriate.

Lisa: What's this in his other hand?

Mohamed: It's a mobile phone; it's trying to show he's a yuppie, flat-top hair, double-breasted suit, trendy glasses, small chin.

(Continued)

Lisa:	It's interesting about the other hand because we thought there would be a lot of gesticulation rather than the sort of verbal interaction; it's sort of hi over there …
Liam:	We were going to put him with a bag of money in one hand …
Lisa:	But the portable phone gets that across.
Jean:	So he's gone from being a friendly uncle to a yuppie?
Mohamed:	Yes.
Clare:	And younger instead of older?
Mohamed:	Yes, yes.
Jean:	Perhaps we should all find out what he is on then!
Lisa:	Didn't that also happen to the bloke who sold his soul to the devil?
Jean:	I don't know.
Mohamed:	What's the film called? It's a baseball film, basically about an old guy who sold his soul to the devil – it's the Faust legend – and became a young baseball player. I don't know what happened to Faust, whether he got younger.

The above interpretations of the changes that had occurred revolved around the symbolism of a more business-like future – the more conservative style of dress (double-breasted suit) and a more frantic (even harassed) appearance – and symbolized the increasing pace of organizational change and activity. An overall theme of the pictures from all the groups was the recognition of the change there had been from a friendly, caring, calm demeanour to an aggressive, impersonal characterization of the organization. This example illustrates how, by making comparisons – in this case with something invented – a metaphor picture can help people to articulate their hopes and fears in a relatively non-threatening, non-confrontational and even humorous manner. Drawing pictures and drawing metaphors in groups may also enable employees to work to create a shared landscape, to which they all have contributed and in which they can all see their contribution and role.

EXERCISE 7.7

Exploring the creative use of visual data

Group discussion: Discuss the potential use of visual data for different kinds of management research. Think about some research projects that you know about or are planning to do. What participatory methods could be useful for these projects? Try to be creative when considering how different participatory methods could help to engage with research participants. What are the opportunities and challenges that are presented by different kinds of tools? For example, some research participants might not be inclined to draw pictures, instead preferring the use of digital tools, such as the creation of an interactive photo story or a digital memory game on a tablet. Others might lack the experience of working with such technologies.

Action research

As we have discussed in Chapter 4, action research is a particular method that is about change and intervention, where researchers work with practitioners on matters of shared interest (Eden and Huxham, 1995; Saunders et al., 2012). Eden and Huxham (1996) suggest that as the interventions will naturally be 'one-offs', they can be criticized for their lack of replicability and lay themselves open to a claim of lack of rigour. In addition, action research transcends descriptive and explanatory accounts of organizations. According to Gummesson ([1988] 1991), a researcher comes with a theoretical trajectory or a 'pre-understanding' of a research topic and setting. While it is common for other research approaches to be explicit about the assumptions a researcher might be making at the outset of a research project, it is important for action research to resist making too many assumptions before the project, because alternative interpretations are likely to emerge if pre-understanding is suppressed (Eden and Huxham, 1995). Although Eden and Huxham recognize that this might be difficult to achieve in practice, at least it should be pushed into the background as far as possible. By avoiding these pitfalls, the analysis of the research may be enriched, which in turn may facilitate finding new insights and concepts.

Action research

Researchers who want to use the action research method should be aware that the skills required are not entirely the same as those needed for other research methods. Eden and Huxham (2007: 539) identify 15 characteristics of action research which they think need to be considered, even though they recognize that some might be hard to achieve (see Table 7.4).

TABLE 7.4   Characteristics of action research

1   Action research demands an integral involvement by the researcher with an intent to change the organization. This intent may not succeed – no change may take place as a result of the intervention – and the change may not be as intended.

2   Action research must have some implications beyond those required for action or generation of knowledge in the domain of the project. It must be possible to envisage talking about theories developed in relation to other situations. Thus, it must be clear that the results could inform other contexts, at least in the sense of suggesting areas for consideration.

3   As well as being usable in everyday life, action research demands valuing theory, with theory elaboration and development as an explicit concern of the research process.

4   If the generality drawn out of the action research is to be expressed through the design tools, techniques, models and methods, then this alone is not enough. The basis for their design must be explicit and shown to be related to the theories that inform the design and that, in turn, are supported or developed through action research.

5   Action research will be concerned with a system of emergent theory, in which the theory develops from a synthesis of that which emerges from the data and that which emerges from the use in practice of the body of theory that informed the intervention and research intent.

6   Theory-building, as a result of action research, will be incremental, moving through a cycle of developing theory, to action, to reflection and to developing theory, from the particular to the general in small steps.

7   What is important for action research is not a (false) dichotomy between prescription and description, but a recognition that description will be prescription, even if implicitly so. Thus, presenters of action research should be clear about what they expect the consumer to take from it, and present it with a form and style appropriate to this aim.

8   For high-quality action research, a high degree of systematic method and orderliness is required in reflecting about, and holding on to, the research data and the emergent theoretical outcomes of each episode or cycle of involvement in the organization.

(Continued)

TABLE 7.4 (Continued)

9   For action research, the process of exploration – rather than collection – of the data in detecting emergent theories and developing existing theories must be either replicable or at least capable of being explained to others.

10 The full process of action research involves a series of interconnected cycles, where writing about research outcomes at the latter stages of an action research project is an important aspect of theory exploration and development, combining the process of explicating pre-understanding and methodical reflection to explore and develop theory formally.

11 Adhering to characteristics 1 to 10 is a necessary but insufficient condition for the validity of action research.

12 It is difficult to justify the use of action research when the same aims can be satisfied using approaches that can demonstrate the link between data and outcomes more transparently (such as controlled experimentation or surveys). Thus, in action research, the reflection and data-collection process – and hence the emergent theories – are most valuably focused on the aspects that cannot be captured by other approaches.

13 In action research, the opportunities for triangulation that do not offer themselves with other methods should be exploited fully and reported. They should be used as a dialectical device, which powerfully facilitates the incremental development of theory.

14 The history and context for the intervention must be taken as critical to the interpretation of the likely range of validity and applicability of the results of action research.

15 Action research requires that the theory development, which is of general value, is disseminated in such a way as to be of interest to an audience wider than those integrally involved with the action and/or with the research.

Of course, the researcher needs to be skilled in techniques for probing and eliciting information from respondents. But the researcher is also required to have good facilitation skills, and the ability and flexibility to alternate between the roles of co-interventionist with practitioners and academic researcher who steps back and derives abstractions about the immediate experience.

Participatory AR

EXERCISE 7.8

Conducting action research

Download 'Participatory Action Research: Improving Professional Practices and Local Situations' by Mary M. Somerville.

1   **Individual**: Read the case study by Mary M. Somerville and make a list of the main features of Participatory Action Research (PAR).

2   **Group discussion**: Discuss in class ways of determining how to gather, organize and manage data within a PAR framework.

Reflexivity

When collecting data, researchers need to think about their role and the way they affect the research process. A research diary or reflective journal is a way of being reflective and using a critical mindset about the research in progress. As discussed earlier in this chapter, qualitative research attempts to capture subjective understandings of the external world from the perspective of participants, and abandons the task of representing an 'objective' unchanging external reality. Rather, qualitative research aims to develop knowledge on how participants' understandings are created through patterns of social interaction. In this way, communication is seen as a 'formative' process in which individuals' worldviews are created through interaction with the social world around them. In relation to this, qualitative researchers suggest that meanings are continuously negotiated and renegotiated. However, failing to take account of the place of the researcher in the construction of these meanings enables researchers to remove themselves from the processes that are occurring and allows them to make pronouncements on the role of others. This unfortunately brings a static understanding to meanings that are inherently fluid in nature (Alvesson and Sköldberg, 2000).

For this reason, the notion of reflexivity has become central to any discussion of the collection and representation of qualitative data. That said, though a range of diverse definitions from all corners of the social sciences have been put forward, it is difficult to find a commonly agreed definition of reflexivity. What they all share is a deep underlying scepticism for the truth claims put forward in social science research. One commonly used definition is that outlined by Alvesson and Sköldberg (2000: 5), who define reflexivity as continuous awareness and attention to 'the way different kinds of linguistic, social, political and theoretical elements are woven together in the process of knowledge development, during which empirical material is constructed, interpreted and written'.

Anderson (2008b) defines reflexivity as that quality that enables the researcher to be aware of their effect on the process and outcomes of research based on the premise that 'knowledge cannot be separated from the knower' (Steedman, 1991). Denzin (1994) takes this further still, arguing that there is *only* interpretation, as nothing speaks for itself and, as a consequence of carrying out qualitative research, it is impossible to remain 'outside' the subject matter as the presence of the researcher will have an effect of some kind.

Reflexive approaches then, as Anderson argues, take into account researcher involvement. Aiming to incorporate reflexivity into their research practice, many qualitative researchers aim to be aware throughout the research process of how the various elements of their identities become significant, and write this into the research presentations (e.g. Brewer, 2000; Pink, 2001). This often involves paying tribute to social characteristics such as race, gender and class, and writing these attributes into the research process. This strategy, it is proposed, allows the researcher to understand how their personal characteristics may have in some way influenced the research process and affected their understanding of the results. However, there has been increasing criticism of such approaches to reflexivity. As Cunliffe outlines (2003: 990), 'critics of reflexivity argue it has little to offer […] questioning what is real, what is knowledge, and who (or what) is self, leads only to intellectual chaos, self-indulgent navel-gazing aporia […] and politically motivated subjectivism'. Therefore, some qualitative researchers argue that reflexivity involves too much introspection on the part of the researcher, which may both problematize the research process and paralyse the researcher.

While reflexivity has been discussed in this chapter in the context of data collection, these issues are no less relevant in the representation of this data; therefore, readers should keep these ideas in mind when reading the next chapter on qualitative data analysis.

Conclusion

In this chapter we have aimed to provide an overview of some of the main methods for collecting qualitative data through observation and interaction. The key points of this chapter that we would like to emphasize are:

- Qualitative research requires researchers to engage with the field they wish to study.

- Observational, participatory and interactive methods are particularly useful for conducting research on social practices as they allow researchers to explore how intention and action come together.

- Observational and interactive methods of data creation can give rise to serious ethical issues. This is no reason not to use these methods, but rather an opportunity to be more reflexive about our research and its benefits.

- Whatever the method, qualitative data collection should not be unnecessarily burdensome to research participants, but should instead seek to stimulate their interest and involvement.

Together with Chapter 6, this chapter has provided a broad overview of different methods for creating qualitative data, and has discussed a number of key issues concerning the practical use of these. It has built on – and extended – insights into the practical and ethical concerns outlined in Chapter 5. In Chapter 8, we shift our attention from data creation to how the created data may be stored, managed and, most importantly, analysed.

Further reading

A helpful overview of visual methods:

Banks, M. (2008) *Using Visual Data in Qualitative Research*. London: Sage.

A practical manual on how to prepare for action research in your own organization:

Coghlan, D. and Brannick, T. (2014) *Doing Action Research in Your Own Organization*, 4th edn. London: Sage.

A useful discussion of questions around how to carry out reflexive research:

Cunliffe, A.L. (2003) 'Reflexive inquiry in organizational research: questions and possibilities', *Human Relations*, 56 (8): 983–1003.

An overview of the history of organizational ethnography:

Cunliffe, A.L. (2010) 'Retelling tales of the field: in search of organizational ethnography 20 years on', *Organizational Research Methods*, 13 (2): 224–39.

A helpful introduction to action research for management and business:

Eden, C. and Huxham, C. (1996) 'Action research for management research', *British Journal of Management*, 7 (1): 75–86.

A very helpful guide on how to write – and work with – field notes:

Emerson, R.M., Fretz, R. and Shaw, L.L. (2011) *Writing Ethnographic Fieldnotes*, 2nd edn. Chicago, IL: University of Chicago Press.

An exquisite and comprehensive handbook, which provides a helpful first point of call for those considering conducting research online whether in the form of surveys, interviews or observational methods:

Fielding, N.G., Lee, R.M. and Blank, G. (eds) (2017) *The SAGE Handbook of Online Research Methods*, 2nd edn. London: Sage.

An entertaining (cartoon) introduction to ethnography for novice researchers:

Galman, S.C. (2007) *Shane, the Lone Ethnographer. A Beginner's Guide to Ethnography.* Lanham, MD: AltaMira.

A helpful article on autoethnography:

Karra, N. and Phillips, N. (2007) 'Researching "back home": international management research as autoethnography', *Organizational Research Methods*, 11 (3): 541–61.

An excellent collection of chapters on a broad variety of methods and techniques for creating (and analysing) visual data, including participatory approaches and photo-elicitation:

Margolis, E. and Pauwels, L. (2011) *The SAGE Handbook of Visual Research Methods.* Thousand Oaks, CA: Sage.

A practical example of how a research diary can be used to aid reflexivity:

Nadin, S. and Cassell, C. (2006) 'The use of a research diary as a tool for reflexive practice: some reflections from management research', *Qualitative Research in Accounting & Management*, 3 (3): 208–17.

A concise student version (400 pages) of the most comprehensive compendium on action research:

Reason, P. and Bradbury, H. (2006) *Handbook of Action Research: The Concise Paperback Edition.* Thousand Oaks, CA: Sage.

Van Maanen's excellent discussion of ethnographic research as involving fieldwork, head-work and textwork:

van Maanen, J. (2011) 'Ethnography as work: some rules of engagement', *Journal of Management Studies*, 48 (1): 218–34.

A collection of chapters in which authors explore the particular challenges faced by scholars and students conducting ethnographic research in and with organizations:

Ybema, S., Yanow, D., Kamsteeg, F.H. and Wels, H. (eds) (2009) *Organizational Ethnography: Studying the Complexity of Everyday Life.* London: Sage.

Check your understanding online

Visit the website **https://edge.sagepub.com/easterbysmith6e** for useful resources that will help reinforce what you've read in this chapter:

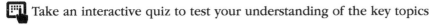 Take an interactive quiz to test your understanding of the key topics

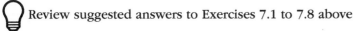 Review suggested answers to Exercises 7.1 to 7.8 above

Use interactive flashcards to check your knowledge of essential concepts

Learning objectives

To get an overview of different approaches to qualitative data analysis, and to understand how they frame qualitative data in different ways.

To learn about different methods and techniques for analysing qualitative data.

To understand how different software packages can assist with the preparation, management and analysis of qualitative data.

To gain insights into how the quality of qualitative research is assessed.

FRAMING AND INTERPRETING QUALITATIVE DATA

8

Introduction

One of the most common issues that qualitative researchers face is how to condense highly complex and context-bound information into a format that tells a story in a way that is fully convincing to others. In management research, this goes beyond the requirements of 'good journalism' (where sources are well referenced and interpretations are 'balanced'); it requires both a clear explanation of how the analysis was undertaken and how the conclusions were reached.

Chapter 4 has outlined how to design management research; Chapters 6 and 7 have given the reader some ideas of how qualitative data might be collected; and Chapter 12 discusses how findings could be written up in the project or thesis. This chapter, then, indicates a number of ways in which we might make sense of qualitative data, and how systems can be developed that will make explicit the links between the data collected, the analysis undertaken and the inferences drawn.

framing
the theoretical lens or device that guides and shapes the way research is conducted; framing can apply equally well to research design, data collection and analysis

In this chapter, we use the term framing to refer to a range of ways in which information or data can be made sense of. The analogy is akin to a window that limits and frames what is observed. There are many ways in which data can be 'framed' and looked at, and these ways shape our analysis and our understanding of these data. Hence, the way in which we approach data analysis does not depend merely on our research design and the type of data we have collected, but also on our research questions and how we frame our data.

Going reflective

EXERCISE 8.1

Reflections on conducting an interpretative study

In Chapter 2, Georgia Stavraki discussed the literature review she conducted for her PhD (see also her extended case study online). Georgia's research methodology was a dynamic process, which used interviews, diaries and a visual method. While each of these methods yielded rich data, they required different analytical techniques.

1   **Individual**: Read the methods case study 'Going Reflective' online. Are there any elements you cannot understand or find surprising? Write 400–500 words reflecting on what you have learnt from the author's experience about developing and conducting a qualitative study.

2   **Group**: In pairs, swap and read your reflective accounts. Have you learnt the same or picked up on different aspects? Can you explain the similarities and differences?

3   **Group**: Discuss the advantages and disadvantages of each of the three types of data created for this research.

Before data can be analysed, they have to be *organized*. While this appears to be common sense, many researchers still waste significant amounts of time and energy on poor data management. With this in mind, we have started this chapter with a brief summary of how to prepare and organize data for qualitative data analysis. We then proceed with an overview of seven different approaches for analysing qualitative data, beginning with approaches that frame qualitative data as proxies for human experience, then moving towards approaches that treat the data themselves as the main object of analysis (Ryan and Bernard, 2003). After this, we show how specialist software packages can facilitate data analysis, and advise readers on how to identify tools that are appropriate for their own research. We conclude this series of three chapters on qualitative methodologies and methods with a discussion on how the quality of qualitative research can be assessed.

Preparing and managing qualitative data

Before starting the analysis, *all* relevant data that have been collected should be filed *systematically* and *in an appropriate format*; digital data should be *formatted* and *labelled in a consistent way* so that individual data fragments can easily be identified and retrieved. Lists of contacts and pseudonyms, and an *overview of all data*, should also be prepared and regularly updated.

It is important to ensure that all data are stored in a way that *prevents unauthorized access*, for example in a locked filing cabinet or as password-protected files on a computer. In the digital age, data protection has become more of an issue; this is because digital databases have important implications for the ownership of data and raise complex issues around confidentiality, anonymity and consent (Parry and Mauthner, 2004). These issues should be covered in the research proposal submitted for ethical or institutional review (see Chapter 5 for details). The principles stated in the reviewed proposal should be adhered to at all times. All data should be *backed up and archived* in a place that meets the same standards of data protection. Depending on the study, data might be archived for the duration of the study or for long periods of time. Again, this is an issue to be covered in the review proposal and consent form.

Data preparation also involves writing up and organizing field notes. Qualitative data collected as audio or video recordings are usually transcribed into written text, a process often experienced as a tedious chore, albeit one that can be facilitated by the use of specialist software. It can be argued that the process of preparing data for analysis is a first analytical step in itself (Bailey, 2008). Researchers sift through their data and get an overview of what they have got; they identify fragments of particular interest, and look at some of their material for the very first time. For example, when transcribing their data, many researchers already frame these in a certain way. Some just type what they hear word by word; others also note other verbal utterances, silences and hesitations; and then there are some who also cover certain non-verbal dimensions of interaction, such as gestures. The level of detail required for a transcript depends on the aims and methodological approach of a study; that is, whether it is important to note a prickly undertone in the discussion between two managers (e.g. when analysing their decision-making) or not (e.g. when it is merely the decision or outcome of the meeting that is relevant).

Depending on the research design and analytic approach, contact-summary records may also be used instead of full written transcripts. Figure 8.1 provides an example of such a contact form; this was used to document observations in a study of a new school curriculum (Miles and Huberman, 1994: 53). A contact-summary form of this kind implies a significant reduction in the richness of the data at a relatively early stage, as information that does not relate to the questions listed in the form will not be further considered. Detailed field notes would also reduce the richness of the initial observations, but in a less rigorous and less structured way.

EXERCISE 8.2

Preparing your data

1 **Group**: In pairs, prepare a list of issues you need to consider when preparing qualitative data for analysis. Discuss how you would organize your data (chronologically, thematically, by type of data, etc.) and how you would label them.

2 **Individual/group**: Compare the use of a contact-summary form to the Systematic and Reflexive Interviewing and Reporting (SRIR) method introduced by Nicholas Loubere in Chapter 6. What are the similarities and what are the differences?

3 **Group**: Do an online search to find out more about guidelines and tools for preparing interview transcripts such as https://transcribe.wreally.com. Pick a method or (freely available) transcribing tool of your choice and learn how it works. Transcribe an audio file of five minutes' length, such as a conversation with a friend, a podcast or a scene in a film, using your method. Present the outcome in class. Who has identified the most practical tool? Who has prepared the most accurate transcript?

Framing and interpreting qualitative data: eight approaches

In many ways, approaches to qualitative data analysis are closely linked to the different research philosophies discussed in Chapter 3. For example, when conducting a social constructionist study, researchers assume a relativist ontology (multiple realities) and a subjectivist epistemology (knowledge is co-created). These assumptions suggest a research process that evolves in a cyclical rather than linear manner: where knowledge is created by researchers interacting with research participants. In such a research process, it makes little sense to draw a distinction between data creation and data analysis. In contrast, researchers conducting a study with a more positivist research design usually assume a realist ontology and an objective epistemology. As a result, they will see a sharper distinction between data and the process of analysis, to the extent that the data collection and analysis may well be performed by different people. They will also be more concerned with examining frequencies within qualitative data, which will enable them to turn their data into numbers. Such an approach can be persuasive since, for many managers or for funders, the political need for numbers wins against attempts to provide rich descriptions.

Most approaches to qualitative data analysis frame data in a way that allows for a systematic reduction of their complexity and facilitates the incremental development of theories about the phenomenon under research. However, the ways in which *complexity is reduced* (i.e. which window or frame is chosen) and how *theories are developed* (i.e. how data are organized and interpreted to achieve meaningful conclusions) vary between different approaches. In this section, we will examine eight different approaches to qualitative data analysis: content analysis, grounded analysis, template analysis, visual analysis, discourse analysis, conversation analysis, argument analysis and narrative analysis. Each of these approaches frames data in a certain way, and involves a number of methods and techniques for exploring, interpreting and comparing data. As will be seen, some of these methods and techniques are closely related to a particular approach, while others are employed across a wide range of different approaches. In this section, we present approaches that frame qualitative data as windows into human experience as well as approaches that focus more explicitly on the structure of language and text, treating the data themselves as the main object of analysis.

Contact Summary Form: Illustration (Excerpts)

Contact type:			Site:	Tindale
Visit	X_____		Contact date:	11/28–
Phone	_____	29/79		
	(with whom)		Today's date:	12/28/79
			Written by:	BLT

1. What were the main issues or themes that struck you in this contact?
    Interplay between highly prescriptive, 'teacher-proof' curriculum that is top-down imposed and the actual writing of the curriculum by the teachers themselves.
    Split between the 'watchdogs' (administrators) and the 'house masters' (dept. chairs & teachers) vis a vis job foci.
    District curriculum coordinator as decision maker are school's acceptance of research relationship.

2. Summarize the information you got (or failed to get) on each of the target questions you had for this contact.

Question	Information
History of dev. of innov'n	Conceptualized by Curric. Coord'r, English Chairman & Assoc. Chairman; written by teachers in summer; revised by teachers following summer with field testing data
School's org'l structure	Principal & admin'rs responsible for discipline; dept chairs are educ'l leaders
Demographics	Racial conflicts in late 60 × 2 's; 60 × 2 % black stud. pop.; heavy emphasis on discipline & on keeping out non-district students slipping in from Chicago
Teacher response to innov'n	Rigid, structured, etc. at first; now, they say they like it/NEEDS EXPLORATION
Research access	Very good; only restriction: teachers not required to cooperate

3. Anything else that struck you as salient, interesting, illuminating or important in this contact?

    Thoroughness of the innv'n's development and training.

    Its embeddedness in the district's curriculum as planned and executed by the district curriculum coordinator.

    The initial resistance to its high prescriptiveness (as reported by users) as contrasted with their current acceptance and approval of it (again, as reported by users).

4. What new (or remaining) target questions do you have in considering the next contact with this site?

    How do users really perceive the innov'n? If they do indeed embrace it, what accounts for the change from early resistance?

    Nature and amount of networking among users of innov'n.

    Information on '/' stubborn '/' math teachers whose ideas weren't heard initially–who are they? Situation particulars? Resolution?

    Follow-up on English teacher Reilly's 'fall from the chairmanship.'

    Follow a team through a day of rotation, planning, etc.
    CONCERN: The consequences of eating school cafeteria food two days per week for the next four or five months . . .

FIGURE 8.1   Contact-summary form

Source: Miles and Huberman, 1994: 53

RESEARCH IN ACTION

Unsung heroes or predators? Taxi drivers at work

Catherine Cassell

Professor Catherine Cassell has a longstanding interest in the use of qualitative methods in management and organizational research. She is Dean of Birmingham Business School at the University of Birmingham, UK.

Tell us about your research into dignity at work

We interviewed taxi drivers because we were interested in their experiences of dignity and customer service. Most research on this topic had been on feminized occupations, so our study with taxi drivers opened up a new theoretical angle. However, the new research setting presented us with unexpected challenges. What have you got to offer to taxi drivers so that they can take part in your study? The answer is simple – somewhere to park! So we organized a dedicated parking space outside the Business School and came up with a procedure where they could call us when they were free, and we would get them a cup of tea while they parked. We also provided shopping vouchers to compensate them for the business they missed out on. We conducted the interviews in the taxis. Many taxi drivers cherished the opportunity to tell us about their work. Some found it unusual, as it is often the passengers who tell them about their lives, not the other way around. Later in the study we conducted the research at taxi ranks – sometimes while they were moving up the ranks!

How did you go about analysing the interviews?

We analysed the data using three different methods: template analysis, story analysis and metaphor analysis. In our semi-structured interview schedule we included questions on stories and metaphors, such as 'Can you tell me a story about a difficult customer?' and 'If you were to choose a metaphor for what it is like to be a taxi driver, what would you choose?' We followed up using a critical incident technique, which worked really well. The focus on stories and metaphors really offered a way in – and there were a lot of emotions around the stories. I don't think we would have obtained similarly rich data if we had just asked them 'How do you feel about taxi driving?'

Why did you conduct a study with three different analytic methods?

We were interested in the distinct opportunities for theorizing enabled by the three methods. We particularly sought to demonstrate how a more diverse analytic toolkit allows researchers to achieve a better fit between research question, data and analysis.

What was the outcome?

Each analytic approach indeed opened up a different view on the data. For example, by integrating relevant sections from different interviews, template analysis helped us to identify theoretical linkages across the whole dataset.

In contrast, story analysis opened our eyes to the episodic nature of the individual stories the taxi drivers had shared with us about customer abuse. The analysis revealed important emotional aspects of the work of taxi drivers, which we otherwise might have missed.

Metaphor analysis allowed us to dig even deeper. Many metaphors are used in the customer service literature – the most obvious being 'the customer is king'. We were interested in what metaphors taxi drivers used to make sense of their work, and, as it turned out, they had quite a few different ones, ranging from the rat or vulture to the unsung hero or even the barmaid or hairdresser (in the sense that their customers talk to them a lot about private matters). Metaphor analysis revealed that drivers experience dignity (or the lack thereof) in different ways. Moreover, their interpretation of dignity is closely related to their relationship with customers, which can change from encounter to encounter.

We concluded that the use of the three methods had enriched our study. Whether or not this would necessarily make sense for other studies depends on the research question and objective as well as the data and the analytic methods themselves. After all, the three methods we used can all be aligned within an interpretivist framework. It is much more challenging to mix methods of distant paradigmatic stances (these would be positioned at opposite ends of Figure 3.7).

TOP TIP

Be prepared for ambiguity. Often there is no one right answer – and that is absolutely fine because that is what qualitative research is about. There are different interpretations and it is important to accept and work with them.

Content analysis

Content analysis is an approach that aims to *draw systematic inferences from qualitative data that have been structured by a set of ideas or concepts*. Researchers interrogate their data for the presence, meanings and relationships of these ideas or concepts, which are derived from a pre-existing theory or hypothesis, from the research questions or from the data themselves (Hsieh and Shannon, 2005; Flick, 2009). In this way, content analysis can be used for hypothesis testing as well as for theory building. The major differences between types of content analysis arise from:

content analysis a relatively deductive method of analysis where codes (or constructs) are almost all predetermined and where they are systematically searched for within the data collected

- how organizing ideas or concepts are determined
- the ideas and concepts themselves and how they frame the data
- the methods and techniques used for organizing and evaluating data.

Although content analysis is an interpretative, qualitative method, its underlying positivist framework makes it possible to introduce some element of quantification into the process. For example, some researchers count the occurrence of certain words, phrases or ideas as part of their analysis. Content analysis can be used with all kinds of data, although researchers tend to stick to textual data, including (but not limited to) company reports, observational records, interview transcripts and diaries. Content analysis is also used for conducting systematic literature reviews. For example, Duriau and colleagues (2007) have used content analysis itself to examine how content analysis has been used in organization studies. After drawing a sample of 98 journal articles, they used an indexing (or 'coding') technique to examine what research themes, theories, frames and methods were used in the management literature, based on content analysis. In this case, the indexing scheme they used was organized around nine themes. More formal methods of content analysis have also been used successfully in the examination of historical artefacts; for example, to determine the authorship of anonymous plays (by analysing the use and recurrent patterns of words and phrases) and, more recently, to determine whether criminals' statements have been added to, or amended, by others at a later date!

The procedure for conducting content analysis is quite straightforward. The first step is usually to *determine a number of criteria for the selection of relevant material* based on the main research question(s) of the study. The selected material is then analysed with a view to what emerging factors or concepts appear relevant for answering the research question(s). These factors can be determined by a pre-existing theory or by the research question, or they can be identified and refined in the process of analysing the selected material. Once the factors are established, a table, matrix or network diagram can be used to identify variations within and between these factors. With the matrix format, for example, the researcher creates an 'intersection' between two different lists that are set up as rows and columns (Miles et al., 2014). In these matrices, ideas or concepts are on one side, and the respondents or instances on the other. Like checklists, matrices of this kind can be used to facilitate the display and analysis of factors and their relationships.

Table 8.1 shows an example of a matrix that Miles and Huberman (1994) used to assess the presence (or absence) of supporting conditions for the uptake of a new reading programme in a school. It shows widespread support for the programme among teachers and key administrators, but also reveals a lack of understanding about the implementation of the programme.

TABLE 8.1 Checklist matrix: conditions for supporting preparedness at Smithson School for the uptake of a new reading programme

Condition	For Users (Teachers and Aides)	For Administrators
Commitment	*Strong* ('wanted to make it work')	*Weak* at building level; prime movers in central office committed; others not
Understanding	*Basic* for teacher ('felt I could do it, but I just wasn't sure how') *Absent* for aide ('didn't understand how we were going to get all this')	*Absent* at building level and among staff *Basic* for two prime movers ('got all the help we needed from developer') *Absent* for other central-office staff
Materials	*Inadequate*: ordered late, puzzling ('different from anything I ever used'); discharged	Not applicable
Front-end training	*Sketchy* for teacher ('it all happened so quickly'); no demo class *None* for aide ('totally unprepared. I had to learn along with the children')	Prime movers in central office had training at developer site; none for others
Skills	*Weak-adequate* for teacher *None* for aide	One prime mover (Robeson) skilled in substance; others unskilled

Source: adapted and abridged from Miles and Huberman, 1994: 107

Matrices are particularly useful when a new area is explored. The matrix can develop during the analysis, so one starts with a few easily identifiable components. Matrices can also facilitate data collection, making it more systematic, and encourage comparison. However, it is important to justify the selection of quotes and how rankings are made. Table 8.1 illustrates only one type of matrix design, constructed for one particular purpose. Yet there is a wide degree of flexibility. Matrix designs can range from simply counting the occurrence of various phenomena to complex matrices that order variables against the dimension of time (for an example of this, see Miles and Huberman, 1994: 201). Matrices can also be complemented by network diagrams or 'mind-maps' that help researchers to reflect on and illustrate the relationships among a larger number of factors.

EXAMPLE 8.1

Content analysis with a research team

In a study of payment systems (see Bowey et al., 1986: Chapter 6), data was collected from a large number of companies in relation to the introduction of payment systems. Content analysis was used to analyse the results. This approach was taken so that a number of researchers would be able to read the transcripts and apply a comment framework, dramatically speeding up the process of analysis. A number of problems became apparent at the outset of the data analysis process: given the large number of people involved, control over the data collection process had been poor. Not all the core questions had been asked of each respondent and, due to a shortage of tape recorders, field notes had been taken but transcripts were not available for all the interviews, which made comparability difficult. This was far from satisfactory. However, to solve this difficulty, all the material was read by each member of the research team. Subsequently, three substantial interviews were chosen and read in detail and coded by three researchers. Issues that appeared to require elaboration in further interviews were identified. Then, the coding frame that had been developed was discussed with all the researchers and modified in the light of inconsistencies. At the same time, definitions were agreed in relation to the three pilot interviews and detailed notes were made of how answers might be interpreted. Finally, all the interviews were distributed to all the researchers and the same analysis framework used to interpret them. Regular checks were made to reduce the number of inconsistencies between coders. Once all interviews had been coded, they were transferred into SPSS (computer software used for the analysis of quantitative datasets) to sit alongside data derived from a large-scale survey of over 1,000 employees. In this example, all the information had derived from interviews, although many of the themes had been identified as relevant in advance. However, new unexpected themes could be accommodated and added into the framework. At a later date, using this method, it was possible to compare answers derived from interviews with those derived from questionnaires – and, moreover, to separate these into definite and probable responses.

In this example, more than one hypothesis was tested, and multiple interviewers and coders were used. Moreover, the separation between the collection and the analysis stages is clear. The study also shows the difficulties associated with arriving at a common understanding of data creation and analysis processes in team-based research. The study also offers an example of how qualitative data were coded, and then imported into a quantitative dataset and analysed together. This was an example of qualitative data being used to offer behavioural explanations for data collected through a survey instrument.

EXERCISE 8.3

Exploring content analysis

1   **Individual**: Think back to Chapter 2 on how to write a literature review. What concepts or ideas could you use to structure your literature review? Would you derive this scheme from an existing theory, from your research question, or from what you have already read? Make a mind-map of the concepts/ideas that you have thought of, and consider how they relate to one another. How could what you have now learned about content analysis improve your literature review?

2   **Group discussion**: In pairs, discuss what ideas or concepts could be used in a study about the advantages and disadvantages of doing an MBA earlier or later in life. Create a checklist matrix that could be used to analyse interviews with current MBA students and alumni.

3   **Group discussion**: It has been argued that content analysis can be a qualitative, theory-building – as well as quantitative, theory-testing – approach. Why is this so? Discuss the criteria that determine whether content analysis is used in a qualitative or quantitative way.

Grounded analysis

grounded analysis
the linking of key variables (theoretical codes) into a more holistic theory that makes a contribution to knowledge in a particular field or domain

Grounded analysis is a more intuitive and 'open' approach to qualitative data analysis than content analysis. While both types of analysis share some techniques, they use them in rather different ways. Researchers who conduct grounded analysis do not start by imposing external structure on their data in the form of concepts or predefined ideas. Instead of testing and elaborating existing theories, grounded analysts aim at building theory from categories that are 'grounded' in the data, meaning that they are identified by a systematic analysis of the data themselves (Charmaz, 2014). Hence, grounded analysis tends to be more holistic than content analysis as it aims to *derive structure (i.e. theory) from data in a process of comparing different data fragments with one another*, rather than framing data according to a pre-existing structure. This is what makes grounded analysis 'open' to new discoveries. Grounded analysts also try to *understand the meaning of data fragments in the specific context in which they were created*. This approach implies a stronger commitment to the voices and views of research participants, and requires researchers to engage with the cultural and historical dimension of their data. Although we characterize content analysis and grounded analysis as competing alternatives, between them there is a raft of practice, and in many ways the choices that researchers face lie on a continuum (see Table 8.2).

Grounded analysis as an analytic approach is closely linked to grounded theory, which is a more comprehensive research strategy comprising methods for sampling, data collection and data analysis. Readers who plan to conduct a study using grounded analysis are encouraged to engage with a well-developed body of literature on grounded theory, which will offer them deeper insights into the manifold methods and techniques that constitute grounded theory today (Charmaz, 2014). Researchers conducting studies using grounded theory usually engage in a research cycle, alternating between phases of data collection and data analysis. Originally conceived by Glaser and Strauss (1967), grounded theory has a long tradition and

TABLE 8.2   Qualitative data analysis: content versus grounded methods

Content analysis	Grounded analysis
Searching for content	Content derives from an understanding of context and time
Causally linked concepts and ideas structure analysis	Holistic associations guide analysis
Objective/subjective	Faithful to views of respondents
More deductive	More inductive
Aims for clarity and unity	Preserves ambiguity and illustrates contradiction

prominent standing across the social sciences. However, what is considered to be grounded theory has also changed significantly over the course of two (and soon three) generations of researchers working with it. This history has been marked by grounded theorists who encouraged researchers to be more creative when developing theory while, at the same time, forwarding rather rigorous, 'recipe-like' sets of methods for conducting such research.

In this section, we outline grounded analysis as a practical approach to sifting through volumes of qualitative data with the aim of teasing out themes, patterns and categories that can be developed into theory. Broadly speaking, there are seven steps to grounded analysis:

1. *Familiarization*: First, it is important to sift through all available data, drawing on unrecorded as well as recorded information. This is where any additional field notes and a personal research diary can be important to the process of analysis. Glaser (1978) suggests that, at this initial stage, researchers should remind themselves just what the focus of the study is, what the data suggest and whose point of view is being expressed. The relationship between the researcher and the people interviewed should also be accounted for.

2. *Reflection*: At this stage, desperation may begin to set in. There is usually so much rich data that trying to make sense of them seems an impossible task. Evaluation and critique become more evident as data are evaluated in the light of previous research, academic texts and common-sense explanations. The kind of questions researchers might ask themselves are:

    *   What are these data about?

    *   Do they support existing knowledge?

    *   Do they challenge it?

    *   Do they answer previously unanswered questions?

    *   Are they different?

    *   What is different?

3. *Open coding*: A code is a word or a short phrase that summarizes the meaning of a chunk of data. Codes create a link between messy and overwhelming data and more systematic categories, which are developed from sets of codes that appear similar or related. Open coding is guided by open questions such as:

    *   What are these data about?

    *   Whose point of view is reflected in the data?

    *   How is this view expressed?

    See Table 8.3 for additional information on open or first-cycle coding.

open or first-cycle coding techniques used by researchers as a first analytical step; such codes are often *descriptive* or aid the *organization of the data* (e.g. coding of actors and attributes)

4. *Conceptualization*: At this stage, the researcher seeks to discover patterns among the codes that are characterized by *similarity, difference, frequency, sequence, correspondence* or *causation* (Saldaña, 2009). By comparing codes and organizing them into different categories, the researcher identifies concepts and themes that seem to be important for understanding what is going on. For example, in an examination of performance, these might include: management style, technology, absence rates, demographic qualities of the labour force, and locus of power. Charmaz (2014) suggests that codes should be simple and that the researcher should try to stay close to the data when identifying relevant codes and categories. Writing a short description for each code and an analytic note (or 'memo') on each emerging category helps the processes of identifying and cataloguing concepts.

5. *Focused re-coding*: Once the most significant codes and categories have been established, the researcher codes and re-codes large amounts of data with a limited number of more focused codes. This process of focused or second-cycle coding is usually highly iterative; it can require the researcher to go back to check against the original data, comparing incidents in order to identify particular properties. It may well be that individuals in the same organization were interpreting what appear to be similar concepts in very different ways. While the first coding cycle aims at the development of a framework, the second coding cycle frames data in a way that allows for a more in-depth analysis of what is deemed important.

6. *Linking*: At this stage, the analytical framework and explanations should be becoming clearer, with patterns emerging between concepts. This is achieved by conceptualizing how key categories and concepts relate to one another, and how emerging hypotheses can be integrated into a theory (Charmaz, 2014). Based on analytic memos, diagrams of concepts and lists of quotations, a first draft can be produced, which can then be tried out on others (both colleagues and respondents), so that the argument and supporting data can be exposed to wider scrutiny and some degree of verification. It is important that all data that form the basis of research conclusions remain available for scrutiny.

7. *Re-evaluation*: In the light of the comments of others, the researcher may feel that more work is needed in some areas. For example, the analysis may have omitted some factors or have over-emphasized others. This stage takes some time; as with the other stages, it may have to be undertaken more than once.

focused codes
codes that are directed, conceptual and analytical

focused or second-cycle coding
techniques that build on the previous coding cycle and aim at developing a sense of the categorical and conceptual order arising from the open codes; based on a thorough examination of all codes created in the first cycle, researchers organize and synthesize them into more analytic secondary codes

Figure 8.2 illustrates a 'codes-to-theory model' for grounded analysis that is implied in the seven stages listed above (Saldaña, 2009: 12).

The researcher may well feel that, for much of the time, the analysis of qualitative data is chaotic and extremely messy. Since grounded analysis reduces the complexity inherent in qualitative data in a slow, incremental process, it often feels overwhelming at the initial stages. This can be seen as an advantage and disadvantage of grounded analysis. On the one hand, grounded analysis opens up a way of developing new insights, because it keeps the researcher open and close to the data until relatively late into the research process. This can make research explorative and exciting. On the other hand, maintaining such openness can be difficult and time-consuming, and researchers can easily get lost in the confusing complexity of their data. By using systematic coding and memo-writing techniques, they can avoid some of these problems. Table 8.3 gives a general introduction into techniques for coding qualitative data. For a more comprehensive overview, see Saldaña (2009).

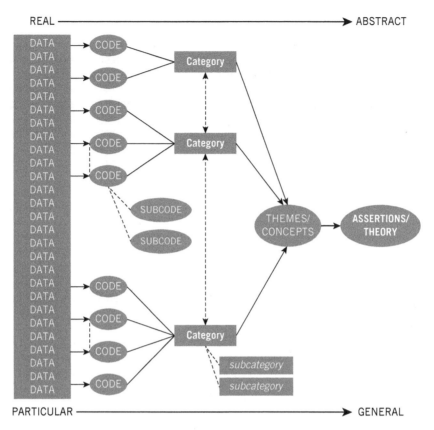

REAL ──────────────────────────────────────▶ ABSTRACT

PARTICULAR ──────────────────────────────────────▶ GENERAL

FIGURE 8.2   'Codes-to-theory model' for grounded analysis

Source: Saldaña, 2015: 14

code
a word or a
short phrase
that summarizes
the meaning
of a chunk of
data, such as
a statement, a
sentence or an
element in a
picture

TABLE 8.3   Coding qualitative data

A code is a word or a short phrase that summarizes the meaning of a chunk of data, such as a statement, a sentence or an element in a picture (Saldaña, 2015; Charmaz, 2014). However, as Miles and colleagues (2014: 93) note, 'a code is more than a filing system'. Coding is an interpretative exercise. Many approaches to analysing qualitative data involve some kind of coding method. In content analysis, codes are often used to frame data according to a predefined coding scheme (deductive coding); in grounded analysis, they are usually the first step in the development of categories and concepts (inductive coding). As the research progresses, researchers compile an annotated list of codes, and later a more systematic codebook that includes definitions and examples of all codes.

Coding can be undertaken on paper – e.g. by highlighting lines of texts and writing on the margins. For such manual coding, three copies of all data (transcripts, observational records, documents, etc.) are required. The first one is the reference copy, the second one is used for the first coding cycle, and a copy of this one is then used in the second cycle (Luker, 2008). Some researchers cut out particularly important quotations and paste them on index cards, which can then be arranged in network diagrams to reflect on how they relate to one another. Computer-assisted qualitative data analysis software (CAQDAS) has become increasingly popular in the past few decades, as CAQDAS software packages facilitate the management of larger data sets, and support an impressive range of analytic methods and techniques – including coding, memo-writing and diagramming. Most of these packages not only assist in the coding of data and development of codebooks; they also feature search tools that operate with Boolean operators to retrieve data that have been assigned with several codes. For more information, see the section on computer-aided analysis below. In grounded analysis, there are two different types of coding procedures: open or first-cycle coding, and focused or second-cycle coding.

(Continued)

TABLE 8.3 (Continued)

Open or first-cycle coding techniques are used by researchers as a first analytical step. Such codes are often *descriptive* or aid the *organization of the data* (e.g. coding of actors and attributes). For example, a line of an interview stating 'now that they have sent us these new machines, we spend less money on electricity and produce twice as much' could be labelled with 'new technology', 'cheaper' or 'production increase'. Open codes are used to break up long texts and complex pictures into manageable chunks, for example by assigning a code to every single line of a text (line-by-line coding). If appropriate, several codes can be assigned to the same section or visual element. First-cycle codes reflect the 'what, who, where and when' of a social phenomenon, the 'how' and 'why' usually being addressed at the second stage (Tracy, 2013). Codes slowly become more systematic as the coding progresses, and similarities and differences are noted when comparing data with other data (Charmaz, 2014). While each analysis is unique in its material and topic, and hence will generate different codes, the coding strategy as such varies with the analytical approach chosen. For example, a researcher conducting a grounded analysis will ask different questions and create different codes from a researcher embarking on a narrative analysis. Saldaña (2009) presents an impressive range of coding first-cycle techniques – such as process coding (using gerunds to code action in the data), values coding (a framework for examining attitudes, values and beliefs expressed by participants) and evaluation coding (assigning judgements about the value or impact of a programme or activity).

Focused or second-cycle coding techniques build on the previous coding cycle and aim at developing a sense of the categorical and conceptual order arising from the open codes. Based on a thorough examination of all codes created in the first cycle, researchers organize and synthesize them into more analytic secondary codes (Saldaña, 2009). For example, the codes above could become part of a group of codes on 'energy efficiency'. Focused codes are usually more abstract, because they are based on a preliminary analysis of more descriptive first-cycle codes. They should be accompanied by an analytical note explaining how the code was generated, how it is defined, and how it relates to other codes and emerging categories. Second-cycle coding techniques aim at comparing codes to other codes and categories in order to advance theory-building. They help the researcher to develop a more elaborated 'cognitive map' of their research (Miles et al., 2014).

Memo-writing is a method of crucial importance for grounded analysis (Charmaz, 2014). Memos are written notes that allow researchers to document and reflect on codes, categories and concepts, as well as research questions and emerging ideas (Saldaña, 2009). When coding and re-coding, researchers make many important decisions about where they take their analysis, and how they frame their data. Analytic memos serve to document and justify these decisions. Successive memo-writing also aids theorizing by enabling researchers to slowly increase the degree of abstraction in their thinking. Memos are usually written in an informal way as they are notes to the researchers themselves and not intended to be shared with a wider audience. However, as the quality of memos improves over the course of a study, they can develop into important building blocks for a research report or thesis.

memo-writing
written notes that allow researchers to document and reflect on codes, categories and concepts, as well as research questions and emerging ideas; a method of crucial importance for grounded analysis

EXAMPLE 8.2

A study of a northern park

Thorpe and Danielli (1996) conducted a study into the use of a local park, and information was collected from ten different groups of park users. These included a parent-and-toddler group; representatives from two schools who used the park as a consequence of changes in the requirements of the national curriculum; an Asian women's group; a disabled group (who used the uncongested pathways to exercise in their wheelchairs); and a young Asian youth team (who used the bowling green to play football). Interviews were transcribed and analysed using the grounded theory approach described. It was striking that, from the data collected from each group, fear emerged as a central category. Further analysis showed that the manifestation of fear was quite different in each group. For the parent-and-toddler group, it was fear of large groups of Asian boys playing football on the bowling green. For the Asian boys, it was fear of being intimidated by white youths if they went to the sports hall in the town centre. For the Asian women's group, it was a fear of spirits, which they believed to inhabit parts of the park, particularly those that were poorly lit where the trees hung over the walkways. Through focused coding, it was possible to connect the category of 'fear' to other categories, such as 'absence'. Over the years, for a variety of reasons, there had been a gradual withdrawal of park staff, which created a situation in which antisocial behaviour had become more widespread.

Understanding the interrelationships between categories in this way is central for all qualitative research. It is also important, however, to relate such findings to the wider context of the phenomenon under study. So, for example, when explaining and presenting the results of the above park study, Thorpe and Danielli placed the concept of a northern town park in the context of its role in civic society in late nineteenth- and early twentieth-century Britain, when transport was limited and expensive, and parks were seen as places where local people could meet and promenade in 'Sunday best' clothes. The increase in affluence, changes in the population of the neighbourhood, changing hours of work, and advent of Sunday shopping have all contributed to the decline of town parks. Problems that emerged around 'fear' and 'absence' have to be understood in this context.

One final instructive anecdote from this particular study relates to what happened when the findings were presented to the council. The leader of the council sub-committee thanked Richard Thorpe for his presentation but questioned him as to the validity of the study as there were no large samples or statistics. Later, during the coffee break, park-warden staff approached him to say that the report revealed something very close to their experiences on a day-to-day basis.

EXERCISE 8.4

Coding and memo-writing

1   **Individual**: Take two pages of an observational record or interview transcript produced in one of the previous exercises. (If no such material is at hand, copy a random email, news report or entry from an online forum into a text document with a wider margin.) Read these two pages carefully and then try to assign codes that summarize the meaning of each line – just the line, not the entire sentence or paragraph. After you have finished with the whole text, go slowly through the codes and think about whether they tell you something new about the text. What have you coded: people, actions, locations? Have you considered any implicit views, assumptions or actions when you have coded? Are there any codes that relate to one another? How? Write a memo about the relationship between the two codes that appear most interesting to you.

2   **Group discussion**: As a class, discuss what kind of information should be included in a codebook and how it should be organized.

Template analysis

Template analysis is a method located at the interface between quantitative content analysis (predetermined codes) and grounded theory (where codes emerge during the analysis). The key component of template analysis is the design of a template that assists with the categorization of qualitative data. By coding data in a thematic way, a structure or template is produced that guides the analytical process. Template analysis usually combines deductive and inductive reasoning in the incremental development of a template of codes to reveal patterns in data (King, 2014). It can be used for all kinds of textual data including interviews and field notes. Figure 8.3 below provides an example of the template used by Catherine Cassell and her colleague when they conducted their study of how taxi drivers experience customer abuse (see Research in Action box, pages 238–9).

Customer abuse

2.1 Location and time of abuse

        2.1.1   Frequency

2.2 Responses to abuse

        2.2.1   Changes in behaviour

        2.2.2   Dealing with it at the time

        2.2.3   Family

        2.2.4   Other taxi drivers

        2.2.5   Police

        2.2.6   Switching off

2.3 Suggestions for combating abuse

2.4 Types of abuse

        2.4.1   Attacking the cab

        2.4.2   Direction disputes

        2.4.3   Not paying/doing a runner, aka bilking

        2.4.4   Other customer anti-social behaviour

        2.4.5   Racism

        2.4.6   Robbery

        2.4.7   Rudeness and stroppiness

        2.4.8   Swearing, verbal and general abuse

        2.4.9   Unexpected behaviour

        2.4.10 Violence and physical abuse

FIGURE 8.3   Example of a template

Source: Cassell, 2015

In contrast to other methods for qualitative data analysis, template analysis is quite flexible when it comes to how a template is created. However, most researchers adhere to a sequence of seven stages summarized in Figure 8.4 below. This process starts with a relatively open coding procedure and ends in the application of a template in a more theory-testing way, so in a way it follows the notion of theory generation (or theory extension) and saturation.

While the techniques used for the initial coding are similar to those used by those conducting grounded and content analysis, many researchers use spreadsheets when working with the finalized template. This said, CAQDAS software can facilitate the transition from a more open coding procedure to the application of a template.

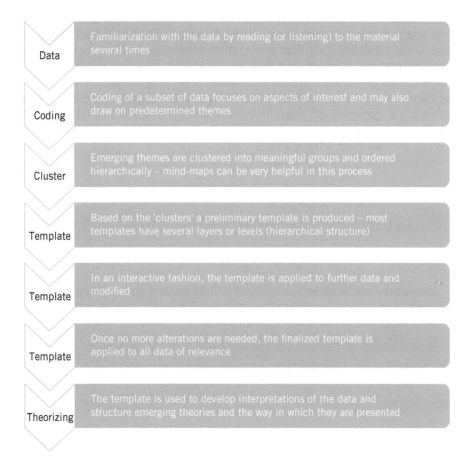

FIGURE 8.4   Template analysis procedure

Source: based on King and Brooks, 2017: 3–4

EXAMPLE 8.3

Reflections on career journeys

Madeleine Wyatt and Jo Silvester (2015) used template analysis in a study of leadership journeys. They interviewed 20 black and minority ethnic (BME) and 20 white senior managers from a UK government department. Interviewees were asked to complete a career 'timeline' recording incidents considered to have had a significant positive or negative

(Continued)

impact on their career. These career incidents were explored during interviews using the critical incident technique (which we discuss in Chapter 6). Template analysis was then used to analyse passages that contained causal attributions about career incidents. The initial template was developed based on an analysis of transcripts of the interviews with the BME managers. A second template was then created by amending the BME template during an analysis of the interviews with white managers. The two researchers found that BME and white managers identified four common themes (visibility, networks, development and line manager support), but that they differed in how they made sense of formal and informal organizational processes to achieve career progression: 'While BME managers may have to rely on explicit knowledge about formalized paths to reach their goal, it seems that white managers are more likely to be passed a "golden thread" to help guide them through informal channels, allowing them to progress more quickly to leadership roles' (Wyatt and Silvester, 2015: 1263).

BME leader
career
experiences

EXERCISE 8.5

Exploring template analysis

1   **Individual**: Download and read Wyatt and Silvester's article. Make a list of all the steps of the research process (however small or banal) they mention. Why do they emphasize the importance of reflexivity?

2   **Group discussion:** Discuss the following questions as a class:

   •   What kind of themes did Wyatt and Silvester use? Were they all derived from the data?

We have now discussed three of the most prominent approaches for analysing textual qualitative data as a proxy for human experiences. Along the way, we have introduced a number of methods and techniques for qualitative data analysis, such as coding, memo-writing and analytic matrices. While these are important methods that can be used for a wide range of data, there are many more that can be helpful. For example, there are *ethnographic decision models*, which combine many of the techniques employed in content analysis and grounded analysis for the creation of decision trees or yes/no flow charts from ethnographic data (Ryan and Bernard, 2003). Such decision trees are used to document and predict decisions under specific circumstances, for example how fishermen decide where to fish (Gatewood, 1983), or how people decide whether to recycle cans (Ryan and Bernard, 2006).

As is the case with qualitative data collection, the art of conducting qualitative research lies in identifying and refining the approaches, methods and techniques that are most appropriate for a given study. This depends on the research design as much as on the research questions, the field under research, the kind of data collected, and the researcher's experience, skills and creativity. We encourage all our readers to learn more about *how* qualitative data analysis is undertaken by different researchers in their particular fields of interest.

Visual analysis

Visual data can be analysed using existing approaches such as content analysis or grounded analysis or discourse analysis. The problem is that most of the methods and techniques developed for these approaches were developed for textual data. True, visual data can be regarded as text: 'Photos tell a story' (Flick, 2009: 246). In many cases, however, visual analysis is conducted via transcripts, descriptions and summaries of visual material, which are then studied using methods for the analysis of text, with the visual data merely illustrating what is ultimately a textual analysis. Methods and techniques that are tailored for the analysis of visual data still appear underdeveloped (Flick, 2009). In this section, we therefore discuss some of the issues that should be considered when analysing visual data. We have positioned this section between approaches for analysing data as proxies for human experience and approaches that look more into the structure and internal organization of the data themselves. This is because the analysis of visual data can entail both.

Figure 8.5 (adapted from a diagram by Gillian Rose (2001: 30) in her textbook on visual methodologies) illustrates the different dimensions of visual analysis. It shows how the analysis of visual data can focus on the context of their *production*, on the *imagery and its effect*, or on their *reception by an audience*. The three sites are represented in the form of three different segments of a circle. Analytical approaches, such as content analysis or different variants of discourse analysis, frame data in a way that anchors the analysis in one of these sites. Figure 8.5 also illustrates the different modalities used in analysing visual data: the technical modality of how visual data are created or transmitted (inner circle); the composition modality of how the data are embedded in a genre or relate to other visual data (second circle); and the all-encompassing social modality that refers to the wider social context (outer circle).

What this figure suggests is that visual imagery is constructed through various practices and interpretations. Consequently, when researchers analyse visual data, they need to be clear what sites and modalities they are looking at – and what aspects they are ignoring.

The process of conducting a visual analysis can be described in six steps (Rose, 2001; Flick, 2009):

1. *Familiarization*: Getting a sense of an image or film as a whole, while noting down first impressions and questions.

2. *Exploration*: Reflection on how the meaning of the image or film is created on the three sites (site of production, the image itself and the audience: see Figure 8.6 for guiding questions).

3. *Framing*: First attempt to interpret the meaning of the data with a view to the research question, noting down key observations, elements or scenes.

4. *Micro-analysis*: Examination of details or sequences (film) that appear particularly relevant. How do these details contribute to the overall meaning? What patterns emerge?

5. *Re-contextualization*: Critical examination of the 'agency' of the image or film (what does it do with the producer and different audiences?). This should be informed by complementary information on the background of the data and their reception by different audiences.

6. *Interpretation*: All notes prepared in steps 2 to 5 should be reviewed, with a view to the research question.

visual analysis a combination of research traditions that come together to analyse various forms of visual data, typically characterized by its volume, homogeneity and dynamic nature

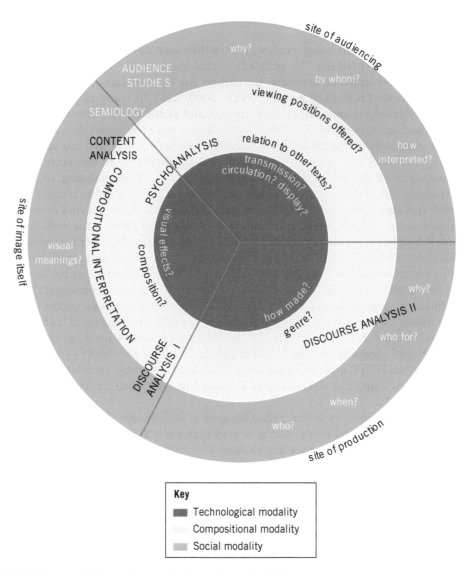

FIGURE 8.5   Sites, modalities and approaches to analysing visual data

Source: adapted from Rose, 2001: 30

Coding and memo-writing can assist in the analysis of visual data, as they do when working with textual data. Depending on the chosen approach, codes may be derived from an external theory or framework, or they can be developed throughout the analytic process. However, it is important to decide *which of the three sites is most relevant for a study before choosing an approach for analysing data*. For example, content analysis of visual data is usually limited to the site of an image itself and does not cover its production or reception. Grounded analysis can combine an interpretation of a picture itself with an analysis of other types of data that reveal more information about its context. Some variants of discourse analysis treat visual data themselves as the main object of analysis (see *Discourse Analysis I* in Figure 8.5), whereas others frame visual data as reflecting the practices and institutions that enabled their production (see *Discourse Analysis II* in Figure 8.5).

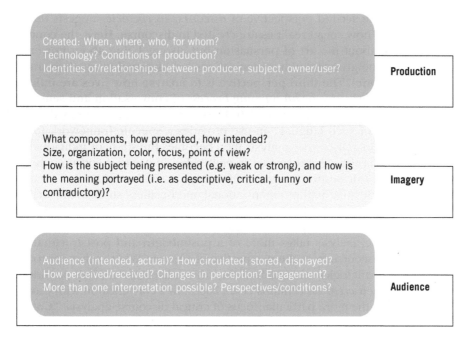

Created: When, where, who, for whom?
Technology? Conditions of production?
Identities of/relationships between producer, subject, owner/user?

Production

What components, how presented, how intended?
Size, organization, color, focus, point of view?
How is the subject being presented (e.g. weak or strong), and how is
the meaning portrayed (i.e. as descriptive, critical, funny or
contradictory)?

Imagery

Audience (intended, actual)? How circulated, stored, displayed?
How perceived/received? Changes in perception? Engagement?
More than one interpretation possible? Perspectives/conditions?

Audience

FIGURE 8.6   Analytic questions for the interpretation of visual data

Source: based on Rose, 2001: 188–90

Discourse analysis

According to Ann Cunliffe (2008), discourse analysis covers a range of approaches that focus on language itself or the much wider relationship of how language is used in a particular context.

Discourse analysis has become a more prominent approach since the 'linguistic turn' of the social sciences, by which we mean the wider recognition that language not only reflects our social world but also creates it. Since then, more research has been undertaken into *how* language is used for achieving inter-subjective understanding. In this context, a number of analytic approaches have been developed that combine methods used in the social sciences with those coming from linguistics and psychology, including both discourse analysis and conversation analysis.

As we have seen in Figure 8.5, different types of discourse analysis exist, which have developed from different backgrounds, in particular linguistics, psychology and sociology. In this section, we consider discourse analysis as an approach for analysing the *content of 'talk' in its wider social context* (Cunliffe, 2008). Discourse analysis of this type (type II in Figure 8.5) goes beyond the detailed micro-analysis of conversations (an approach we will discuss in the next subsection) and aims at wider discourses that can be traced in conversations, writing, visual data, observation of social practices, symbolic artefacts and media items. In management research, discourse analysis has been used in a number of studies (Phillips et al., 2008). Examples include Munir and Phillips' (2005) study, 'The birth of the "Kodak moment"', in which they showed how the meanings and uses of new technologies are discursively constructed.

There are three main ways of viewing discourse: as structure, rhetoric or process (Gergen, 1999). Gergen suggests that to view *discourse as a structure* is to see it as a set of recurring conventions (such as metaphors or narratives) that are woven throughout both our speech

discourse analysis covers a range of analysis approaches that focus on data in the form of language. This could be the language used or the context in which the form of language is used. Researchers focus on the development of and contribution to aspects of social theory and social action and ways of living. The second perspective of *discourse as rhetoric* suggests that there is a hierarchical aspect to how social realities are created in discourse. Here, the concept is seen not simply as being about the art of persuasion but also as being about power (consider, for example, why some groups within organizations are favoured over others and how this is manifested in rhetoric). The third perspective is to analyse how lives are influenced and 'constituted' through *discourse as an ongoing process* of conversation and sense-making.

As noted by Alvesson and Kärreman (2011), organizations are settings defined by talk and text. An analysis of such language-in-use provides a specific framework for exploring how organizations work. Discourse analysis then becomes the study of individual fragments of discourse, which form a discourse that is embedded in a wider social context (Phillips et al., 2008). Figure 8.7 illustrates this way of framing qualitative data.

Cunliffe (2008) notes that within organizational and business studies, the analysis of discourse has essentially been divided into two main streams: discourse analysis and critical discourse analysis. Discourse analysis, she argues, takes a social constructionist perspective, while critical discourse analysis takes more of a postmodern and poststructuralist point of view, and examines discourse from the perspective of *rhetoric*. Where other approaches focus on the *effects* of dominant logics on organizations, critical discourse analysis provides us with a frame for exploring their *creation* (Phillips et al., 2008). In a conversation with Gavin Kendall, Ruth Wodak describes the more particular focus of critical discourse analysis: '"Critical" means not taking things for granted, opening up complexity, challenging reductionism, dogmatism and dichotomies, being self-reflective in my research, and through these processes, making opaque structures of power relations and ideologies manifest' (Kendall, 2007).

Critical discourse analysis has been a useful approach for both social scientists in general and management-studies scholars in particular, as it facilitates an examination of aspects of power and persuasion within organizations. Critical discourse analysis places an emphasis on aspects of where power lies within relationships (Chouliaraki and Fairclough, 2010) as well as 'ideologies that are created by and represented in language' (Fairclough and

critical discourse analysis
the analysis of natural language data, which emphasizes the power relations and ideologies that are both created and conveyed

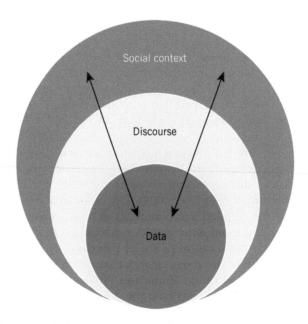

FIGURE 8.7   Critical discourse analysis: analytical framework

Source: based on Phillips et al., 2008: 774

Hardy, 1997; Cunliffe, 2008). An example of this is Prasad and Elmes' (2005) study of the language of practicality in environmental management. For Cunliffe, it is the *emphasis that is placed on context* that distinguishes critical discourse analysis from traditional linguistics. The context, she argues, is influenced by factors such as space, time, practice, change and frame (Chouliaraki and Fairclough, 2010; Leitch and Palmer, 2010).

According to Fairclough (1992), discourse analysis should integrate an analysis of the levels of discourse:

- *Textual level*: by involving techniques used in critical linguistics.

- *Discourse level*: by investigating how the text is produced and interpreted, and what kinds of 'preferred' reading it suggests.

- *Social practice level*: by scrutinizing the institutional practices a text may imply, and then exploring whether it reproduces or upholds dominant discourses or social practices characterized by asymmetric power relations.

Due to the wide range of approaches for conducting discourse analysis, it is difficult to give an overview of the various methods and techniques that are used. Some argue that discourse analysis works better as a frame or 'scholarly orientation' (Locke, 2004: 2) than as a methodological approach. Researchers who plan to conduct a study of discourse are advised to think carefully about their research questions, their framing and the scope of their study before engaging with the exuberant literature on discourse analysis for identifying the methods and techniques best suited to assist them in their study.

Sally Wiggins explains critical discourse analysis

EXERCISE 8.6

Using discourse analysis

Group discussion: Discuss the use of discourse analysis for research in management and business. What kind of research questions could be answered using critical discourse analysis? Come up with two or three topics and discuss what framing and what methods could be appropriate to research them.

Conversation analysis

An *approach* closely related to discourse analysis is conversation analysis, which was developed to facilitate the formal analysis of the *structure* of everyday 'interaction as a continuous process of producing and securing meaningful social order' (Bergmann, 2004: 296). The term 'conversation analysis' is actually somewhat misleading, as the data of interest are not limited to everyday casual conversation, but encompass any naturally occurring interaction between two or more people (e.g. telephone calls, talk at the dinner table, job interviews). For this reason, conversation analysts often describe their interest as being in 'talk-in-interaction' rather than 'conversation'. However, even this can be confusing as, in addition to 'talk', the non-verbal aspects of interaction, such as eye gaze and gesture, are also significant (Psathas, 1995: 2).

There are three fundamental assumptions to conversation analysis:

conversation analysis
an analysis of natural language data used with naturally occurring conversations to establish linguistic patterns through the detailed examination of utterances

1.   That all interaction exhibits stable, organized patterns irrespective of who is talking, and that people orient to and produce that order themselves when they interact with each other.

2.   That interaction is organized sequentially, and that it is possible to make sense of a statement only in relation to an ongoing sequence of utterances.

3.   That analysis should be grounded in a detailed empirical examination of the data.

The job of the analyst is to discover and describe the order of the interaction, and its underlying rules and practices. In order to do this, the analyst will examine audio or video recordings of interactions and, using detailed transcripts based on the recordings, look for the practices that people use in interaction, and the interactional significance of these and of where they occur. A key question that conversation analysts keep in mind when looking at something of interest in a piece of interactional data is: 'Why that now?' (Schegloff and Sacks, 1973: 299).

Sally Wiggins explains conversation analysis

There are four main areas of technical findings in conversation analytic research: sequence organization (the order in which utterances are produced in talk); turn-taking (how speakers manage the taking of turns); repair (how speakers deal with problems in hearing or understanding); and word selection (the words chosen by speakers). The level of detail looked at when doing conversation analysis ranges from how whole utterances are constructed, through what individual word choices speakers make, to where silences occur and how long they last (with even a pause of a tenth of a second potentially being interactionally significant). This emphasis on detailed empirical analysis has resulted in very precise conventions for transcribing recordings of interactions. We give some examples in Table 8.4. (For the full list of transcription conventions and an accompanying discussion of their benefit, see Jefferson, 2004.)

When approaching a piece of data from a conversational analysis perspective, there are several things to take into consideration:

●   How is the taking of turns managed by the speakers? Does one speaker select another, or do speakers select themselves? Is there a predetermined order to the turn-taking, such as in particular institutional settings (e.g. in a news interview the interviewer asks a question, followed by the interviewee providing the answer, similarly in a courtroom interaction)?

●   What actions are done by speakers' turns, for example are they requesting, complaining, inviting, assessing, etc.?

●   How are the speakers' turns constructed? The basic unit of talk is the turn constructional unit (TCU), which can range in length from a sentence to a phrase or just one word, and that is audibly complete grammatically, intonally and in terms of the action it is doing. Are the turns made of one or more TCUs?

●   How do these actions fit together to form a sequence? Actions generally come in pairs known as 'adjacency pairs' made up of a first pair part (FPP) and a second pair part (SPP); for example, a question is followed by an answer, an invitation by an acceptance or a declining, a greeting by a return greeting. Are there any turns that do actions prior to the main 'base' first pair part, for example a pre-request ('Are you busy this afternoon?') before the request is produced? Are there any that come between the 'base' first pair part and the 'base' second pair part, for example a request for clarification?

When you notice something of interest in the data, such as choice of words or instances of silence, think about where they occur in the interaction: what action is being done by the utterance, where is it in the sequence, was there any problem with its production or understanding? When you find a phenomenon of interest, think about why it occurs in the sequence where it does.

TABLE 8.4   Simplified transcription symbols

Symbol	Example	Explanation
[	A: for quite a [while B: [yes, but	Left bracket indicates the point at which the current speaker's talk begins to be overlapped by another's talk
=	A: that I'm aware of = B: = Yes. Would you confirm that?	Equal signs, one at the end of a line and one at the beginning, indicate no gap between the two lines
.hhhh	I feel that.hh	A row of h's prefixed by a dot indicates an in-breath; without a dot, an out-breath; the number indicates the length of breath
( )	future risks and ( ) and life ( )	Empty parentheses indicate an undecipherable word
_____	What's up? _____	Underscoring indicates some stress through pitch of amplitude

Source: Silverman, 1993: 118

Conversation analysis has been used extensively to examine workplace interactions, including in classrooms (e.g. Macbeth, 2004), in doctor–patient consultations (e.g. Heritage and Maynard, 2006), on calls to emergency services (e.g. Zimmerman, 1992) and helplines (e.g. Baker et al., 2005), in job interviews (e.g. Glenn and LeBaron, 2011) and even in airport operation rooms (e.g. Goodwin and Goodwin, 1996). The findings from these institutional settings can be used to change practice in the workplace.

EXAMPLE 8.4

What a difference a word makes

An example of the significance of one word can be seen in research carried out with family doctors and their patients in the USA. Patients frequently have more concerns than those that they give as their primary reason for making their appointment with a doctor. Family-practice doctors are encouraged to ask patients whether they have concerns – typically with a question such as 'Is there anything else that we need to take care of today?' – but patients still frequently come away from their appointment with unmet concerns. Heritage et al. (2007) wanted to see whether altering the recommended question might have an effect on patients raising more concerns in their appointments. They instructed 20 doctors to pose one of two questions during appointments with patients, just after the patient had stated their main reason for seeing the doctor: 'Is there anything else you want to address in the visit today?' or 'Is there something else you want to address in the visit today?'. The researchers found that patients were more likely to have their extra concerns met when 'some' was used in the question, and suggest that the problem of patients not raising concerns can be reduced just by substituting one word when asking whether they have other concerns.

EXERCISE 8.7

Looking at conversation analysis

Individual: Conduct a literature search on studies that have used conversation analysis. Pick one article you find interesting and examine how the authors of this article have used conversation analysis. What kind of data did they use? How did they frame their data? What methods and techniques did they use in their analysis? If you cannot find any relevant articles, pick one of those listed in the further reading at the end of this chapter.

Argument analysis

argument
analysis
an approach
to the analysis
of natural
language data
that identifies
the data used in
making claims,
the premises
made and the
conclusions
drawn by
individuals
about issues of
relevance

Another approach for analysing discourse is to frame it as a series of *arguments* that reflect people's negotiations of the social world and their role in it. Gold et al. (2002, 2007) employed argument analysis as part of a management-development intervention, using arguments to interpret research participants' understanding of their role in the management process as well as in a developmental way (see Example 8.5).

This subsection explains how argument analysis can be used in an interactive research design in which both data creation and data analysis require the active involvement of research participants. Two approaches are illustrated: the first one employs the ideas of Toulmin (2001); the second is based on the work of the philosopher Gadamer (1989). Both examples should encourage our readers to reflect on how applied management research can help to develop critical thinking in research participants, and how this may enhance the impact of management research.

EXAMPLE 8.5

Helping managers become more reflective

In their study of Barclays Bank managers, Gold, Holman and Thorpe (2002) asked eight managers to write accounts in which they reflected on their interactions at work. Managers were asked to write stories of events at work and then to reflect critically on what they had produced. The exercise aimed at making them more aware of their views and arguments; of how these views and arguments were formed and justified; and of how they could be changed. The research process was part of a programme for career development. The participating managers were asked to address the following issues:

- *Story*: They were encouraged to write about significant incidents or 'stories' at work that involved themselves and others.

- *Statement*: They were asked to explain why they cared about the particular issues described and what they believed was the explanation for events as they emerged in the story. *This part of the task was completed in small groups.*

- *Claims*: They were then asked to identify the claims that they had made in the stories, and provide an explanation for these claims.

- *Evidence*: Having returned to their organizations, managers were requested to identify and substantiate evidence for their claims (e.g. the data on which these claims were based).

What became apparent was that some managers lacked sufficient evidence to support the claims they made, while others found that the evidence that they had offered was at best spurious, and at worst wrong. For example, one manager had misread someone else's opinion as a fact. For many participants, the impact of the programme was profound, as they had gained an insight into how to understand and analyse arguments, a skill they considered even more useful after the study had revealed how much they had just taken for granted without ever checking properly.

The study reported above was based on the work of Toulmin (2001), one of the most prominent exponents of argument analysis. His approach frames arguments as having three components:

1. *Claims*: Arguable statements.

2. *Evidence*: Data that are drawn on to support the claims.

3. *Warrant*: Explanation why claims and data are connected.

When this framework was used in the management-development context outlined in Example 8.5, the text of the story was seen as the 'data' from which underlying claims and the warrants could be derived.

Toulmin's (2001) framework can also be applied when evaluating literature for a literature review (see Chapter 2). Identifying the main claim (or hypothesis) of an article, evaluating the evidence that is provided to support this claim (e.g. data and analysis), and interrogating the warrant that connects the evidence to the claim, comprise one of the principal methods to evaluate academic publications (Hart, 2018).

Our second example is based on Gadamer (1989) and his work on the importance of the 'practice of understanding'. This approach frames *thinking and doing as being part of the same process*, and not separate to managers immersed in the flux of everyday life. Gold et al. (2007) used this approach in a critical study of difficult situations experienced by managers, in which they hoped to enhance the managers' critical faculties by developing new perspectives on their problems.

EXAMPLE 8.6

Argument analysis to enhance reflexivity

In Gold, Thorpe and Holt's study (2007), managers were asked to reflect on their experiences at work by drawing a diagram in the shape of a circle with three segments (see

(Continued)

Figure 8.8). In the first segment, managers were asked to write about a difficult situation they had encountered; in the second segment, they were asked to read and interpret what they had written in a reflexive way; and in the third segment, they were encouraged to 'reason authoritatively': taking into account the interpretations they had drawn, they were asked to consider possibilities that might lead to some solutions, and articulate the solution they saw as having the most potential. Each manager agreed to keep a record of the use of the diagrams over a period of ten weeks in the form of a small log or memo. A review took place after four weeks and again after ten weeks, when the findings were discussed. All the managers who conducted the exercise demonstrated a considerable willingness to embrace the approach. As they worked through the process, it was clear that they acquired new understandings and gained in experience by engaging critically with their own ideas and assumptions. The researchers gained valuable insights into the perspectives of the management team.

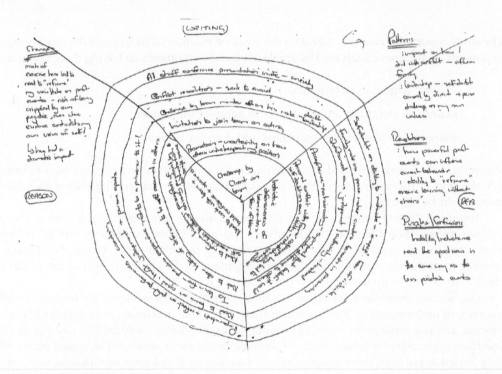

FIGURE 8.8   From the three 'Rs': writing, reading and reason

Source: Gold et al., 2007

The two examples presented in this subsection are examples of an analytic approach to analysing discourse that does not focus on the structure of discourse (as in conversation analysis) or on the context in which it is produced (as in critical discourse analysis), but rather aims to improve our *understanding of how discourse is used in management as a process* (applied management research). However, argument analysis can be a useful approach for a wide range of research projects. As the example of the literature review has shown (Chapter 2), it can be used for a formal analysis of a written text, as well as for an informal discussion of management decisions. The methods and techniques used for argument analysis ultimately depend on the research question, on the data and on *how they are framed* by the research question.

EXERCISE 8.8

Applying argument analysis

Individual: Pick one journal article that is relevant to your studies or research and conduct a thorough argument analysis based on Toulmin's (2001) framework introduced above. What claims are made? What kind of evidence is provided? Is the warrant connecting claims and evidence convincing? After conducting the argument analysis, what do you think about the article? What are the strengths and weaknesses of the arguments it presents?

An alternative but related way of framing arguments can be found in Charles Tilly's (2006) book *Why?*, in which he describes four varieties of *reasons*: conventions, stories, codes and technical accounts. The first type, the *convention*, is a widely accepted reason for why something works out a lot better or worse than anticipated (e.g. 'She managed to catch the train because it was late' or 'because she is a lucky girl'). The second type of reason, the *story*, is defined as a narrative that explains an unfamiliar phenomenon or exceptional event in terms of cause and effect. Stories are used when a simple statement is not enough and when some kind of justification is required (e.g. 'She had to take the train because the day before, her car had been stolen'). The third type of reason, the *code*, does not have to bear the same explanatory power as the story because it refers to widely accepted rules, whether these are religious or legal (e.g. 'Without a ticket, she was not allowed on the train'). The fourth reason is a *technical account* (e.g. of how a faulty power line delayed the arrival of a train). As can be seen from Table 8.5, reasons can be based on common popular knowledge (in the case of conventions and stories) as well as on more specialized knowledge (in the case of codes and technical accounts); they can be based not only on accepted rules and formulas (conventions and codes), but also on cause–effect accounts (stories and technical accounts).

TABLE 8.5   Tilly's four varieties of reason

	Popular	**Specialized**
Formulas	Conventions	Codes
Cause–effect accounts	Stories	Technical accounts

Tilly argues that each way of offering reasons contains distinctive properties, and that these properties can be used in strategic ways. Bankers who have to account for a major loss need to consider whether their technical accounts are likely to be understood by the general public, or whether they would be better off with a story or an explanation based on conventions. What kind of reasoning is appropriate depends on the situation and on who is involved. If we frame argument analysis in this way, we can see how this opens up another approach to analysing discourse, an approach that may help us to better understand *exactly how* the formal configuration of an argument relates to both its content and its context.

Narrative analysis

narrative analysis focuses on stories or accounts of individuals (or groups)

Unlike conversation analysis (which focuses on the formal structure of interactions) and argument analysis (which examines the patterns of reasoning), narrative analysis is concerned with the ways in which people create and use stories to make sense of the world. Narrative analysis is based on collecting people's stories and then analysing them through a narrative methodology. These stories are usually not treated as sets of facts but as 'devices through which people represent themselves [and their worlds] to themselves and to others' (Lawler, 2002: 242). We all have numerous experiences every day, but we pay particular attention to those we perceive to be part of our 'story' (see Table 8.6 for examples). As we have seen in the section on Tilly's types of reasons, stories help us to explain the unfamiliar, unexpected or exceptional; they infuse with meaning what could otherwise be a confusing sequence of random events.

TABLE 8.6 Elements of stories

Stories:

- are concerned with the temporal ordering of ideas
- usually tend to focus on the sequential patterning of events and the role of various actors within them
- enable a researcher to build a complex picture of social situations in order to examine the actions of the various actors in a story, and explore their values, ideas and beliefs.

Narrative analysis can reveal valuable insights into how organizations shape social life. Storytelling is a common way of communicating within and about organizations, and it can occur among individuals or collectively. Organizations can be seen as 'collective storytelling system[s] in which the performance of stories is a key part of members' sense-making' (Boje, 2003: 43). Managers, entrepreneurs and employees tell stories as a way to describe and accomplish their everyday work. Stories can be used to evaluate the past, but they also lend themselves to expressing visions and goals, exchanging information (and knowledge), communicating emotions and instructing others how to act. Managers are taught and socialized to evaluate stories in complex and ambiguous circumstances.

Narrative analysis can be applied to all kinds of data that communicate stories, whether these are in-depth interviews, corporate texts, videos, blogs or autobiographical accounts. Researchers have studied organizational narratives such as founding myths about how a company came to embody certain values; see, for example, Boje's (1995) study on Disney. Others have researched individual narratives of organizational life and identity, such as Sims' (2003) research into the 'vulnerability of middle managers' storying'. Narratives of change and resistance have also been examined (e.g. Humphreys and Brown, 2002). In doing so, researchers have identified plots, characters, tropes and different types of narratives that offer insights into issues such as organizational culture, strategy, change, identity and the nature of management. Narrative analysis invites researchers to recognize the producers of a story, the context of its production, and how it is performed, shared and controlled.

Boje (2003) suggests there are four main streams of storytelling in organization and business studies: bureaucratic, quest, chaos and postmodern. In *bureaucratic storytelling*, stories are linear and rationalized, and attempt to make controlling the employees and the organization more predictable. The *quest* is the second form of storytelling, in which the mission is to have the most compelling story. This often begins with a call, a journey and return; often, it is the voice of the CEO of the company that gets the most attention here. The third type of storytelling is *chaos*, where the stories are lived and not told. Therefore, it is anti-narrative, without coherence, and inherently non-linear – here, no one is in control. The fourth type of storytelling has been referred to as *postmodern*, which (like chaos) lacks coherence; but (unlike in chaos) the postmodern storyteller works in a conscious, self-reflexive manner (Boje, 2003: 43).

Within these streams, there are a number of trends that can be discerned. The first is where stories are investigated out of context, for example interview text. A second is where stories are produced within a particular context, for example from a functionalist stand-point. Yet another trend is where a managerialist perspective is taken. Here, storytelling is used as a tool; these stories are often positive, with a happy ending. One might suggest, for example, how a complex organizational change might turn out to be ignoring all the possible problems that might result. The fourth and final trend is a story that takes a functionalist or managerialist perspective, and includes research within critical theory, postmodernism and poststructuralism. The main focus of this approach is for the researcher to highlight the multiple approaches to interpretation of the story, and to attempt to uncover hidden stories and perspectives (in contrast to reporting only the storyline of one spokesperson). Here, pluralism is celebrated so that there might be perspectives that pick up themes in relation to gender or race. Boje (2008) argues that the critical issue is how knowledge becomes transferred from individuals to the organization. Managerialist and functionalist researchers set about transferring 'knowledge' and ideas, whereas critical theorists see their role as liberating individuals through the plurality of the perspectives set out, while those undertaking storytelling from a postmodern perspective examine a variety of storytelling forms. Again, the main message here is that the researcher's approach to the story will differ, depending on its purpose and focus (Boje, 2008: 214).

We have now identified different ideal types of stories commonly encountered in organizations, and we have discussed some of the more recent trends in how stories are used and researched. We have shown how narrative analysis is yet another approach to frame qualitative data in a way that sheds light on the structure and process of discourse – and, in some cases, on its rhetoric. But what methods and techniques are used to conduct narrative analysis? In general, narrative analysis follows a few simple steps that are similar to the ones we have identified for discourse analysis, visual analysis and argument analysis:

- *Selection*: Stories or storytellers are selected based on the research question. There are various kinds of data that lend themselves to narrative analysis, including in-depth interviews, field diaries and correspondence. It is important to accompany the collection of stories with information on the background and context of these stories.

- *Analysis of the narrative*: This usually involves a detailed examination of the plot of the story; the main actors, activities and places that appear in the story; and any problems that the story addresses. As stories are not always presented in a chronological order, it can be useful to reorganize or rewrite the story in order to evaluate causal links. The rewritten story can be compared with the original to trace patterns of storytelling. It can be useful to identify formal elements such as beginning, middle and end, and then to divide the story into episodes and sequences. These sequences can then be analysed one by one, with a special emphasis on how they relate to each other and how transitions are made. Key elements such as conflict, surprise and predicament can be identified. Postmodern narrative approaches deconstruct stories further, looking for dichotomies, contradictions, subtle hints and disruptions.

- *Re-contextualization*: At this stage, stories are re-examined with a special view to the context in which they were told, for example the social, cultural and political background of the story; the position of the storyteller; the relationship between the storyteller and the audience (in some cases, the researcher); and the historical context (including, for example, the history and current situation of an organization of which the storyteller is a member). The timeline of a story can be contrasted with a more general timeline of its context, in writing or using a diagram. Finally, the researcher should also enquire into underlying assumptions that might have gone unnoticed without a detailed understanding of the context. Sometimes, it can be useful to involve participants in this step.

- *Interpretation and evaluation*: Against this background, the meaning and the function of a story can be assessed. What were the reasons for a story to be told? What made it interesting to the storyteller or the audience? Why was it told in a certain way (of all the possible ways in which it could have been told)? How does the story relate to other stories in its content, structure and context? Coding, diagramming and the preparation of matrices can help to identify different types of narratives. Finally, the researcher should reflect on the contribution of the story to the research endeavour as a whole: what makes the story relevant to this research?

While this process appears relatively straightforward, albeit time-consuming, it is important to note that different models of narrative analysis exist that emphasize different steps of this process (Riessman, 2003). For example, the emphasis can lie on the second step – the examination of the content of stories with the aim of developing common themes, like those created in grounded analysis. Such *thematic analysis* focuses on *what is being said* as opposed to how it is said, and the context in which it is said. This decontextualization can be problematic because it ignores the fact that different people can attach very different meanings to their stories, or have different reasons to tell them (Riessman, 2003). Whether this translates into a weakness of a study depends on its research questions and objectives.

Narrative analysis

Other studies on narratives emphasize structure. *Structural analysis* still requires an examination of the content of a story, but its main focus is on *how the story is told*. Here, language is not ignored but becomes an 'object for close investigation – over and beyond its referential content' (Riessman, 2003: 706). *Interaction analysis* shifts the attention of the researcher to the *context* and to the *effect* of a story, and hence to the third and fourth steps outlined above. It acknowledges the fact that stories evolve in a dialogue between the storyteller and an audience situated in a certain context (Riessman, 2003). For the study of direct interaction, such analysis tends to involve techniques akin to those used in conversation analysis. Studies of mediated and indirect interactions may employ methods we have presented in the section on discourse analysis. Interaction analysis becomes *performance analysis* when the analysis focuses on non-verbal interaction as well as verbal interaction. This type of narrative analysis can be useful for studies of communication and identity construction. An example could be a study of how Steve Jobs performed the introduction of new products in a way that affirmed his position and the 'story' of Apple as a company.

EXERCISE 8.9

Narrative analysis

1 **Individual**: Download a transcript of a biographic interview with a Bay Area venture capitalist from the website of the Venture Capitalists Oral History Project at the Bancroft Library:

   Browse through the document and identify the section in the beginning in which the interviewee's *background, upbringing, schooling* and *early work experience* are described. Read this section carefully and think about a research question that could require the analysis of this section. Write down the research question and analyse the section as if it were the first document to be examined for this study. Think carefully about how you want to frame your data, what model of analysis would be appropriate, and the elements you will need to emphasize. You may wish to use the Internet to collect additional information on the context of the biography. Apply at least two of the following methods in your analysis: coding; creation of a timeline or diagram; reorganization/rewriting of the story in chronological order.

2 **Group**: Give a short presentation about your experience in class. Explain the choice of your research question, how you have framed the data, and the methods you have used. What has been the main result?

3 **Group**: Based on a number of presentations, discuss differences and similarities between the different approaches that were chosen. Would it be possible to link some of the presentations into a group project because they focused on similar themes, used similar frames or employed similar methods?

Venture Capitalists Oral History Project

Computer-aided analysis

CAQDAS is the general term describing the software packages that can be used to aid the analysis of qualitative data, such as text, audio, video and graphics. In the past two decades, such packages have become an essential tool for many researchers working with qualitative data who value the wide array of tools offered by CAQDAS packages for the management and analysis of large volumes of data. However, concerns have been raised that the use of such packages can divert the attention of less experienced researchers away from the actual analysis to the software (Gibbs, 2014). This is indeed a problem, as CAQDAS packages do not analyse data; they merely *facilitate the application* of methods and techniques by the researcher, who (in most cases) could just as well work with paper and pencil. There is certainly an argument to be made that basic techniques such as coding should be practised on hard copies of data before moving to software packages – an approach we have taken with the exercises in this book. However, once the researcher attempts a bigger research project, which requires the analysis of larger amounts of data, CAQDAS packages can become an indispensable tool (Saldaña, 2009). Moreover, as research becomes more collaborative, some CAQDAS packages become even more attractive because they enable researchers to share and analyse their data in research teams.

CAQDAS computer-assisted qualitative data analysis software

ATLAS.ti a software package that assists in the building and testing of theories through the creative assembly of qualitative analysis of textual, graphical and audio/visual data; available from www. atlasti.com

There are many CAQDAS packages available, with the most prominent being ATLAS.ti, NVivo and MAXQDA. These and other CAQDAS packages provide some common functions for project management, data management, searching and mapping data, data analysis (in particular coding and the development of categories and themes) and visualization (see Table 8.7).

TABLE 8.7 Core features of CAQDAS packages

Task	Features
Project management	Assistance in organizing and managing a larger research project using memos, a project diary and other features.
Data management	Organization and management of large volumes and different kinds of data; creation of an 'audit trail' that assists in documenting the analysis and developing ideas. Hyperlinking allows data to be linked to other data files.
Searching and mapping data	All CAQDAS packages have an array of search capabilities – from simple word searches through to complicated multiple-attribute searches – that can interrogate datasets and retrieve coded data. Additionally, most packages include tools to map data and codes in diagrams.
Analysis	Coding functions facilitate the analysis of data. Further, the capability to re-code data, to organize and change codes, and to link themes to developing ideas in memos aids continuity and can increase the overall transparency of the analysis process.
Visualization and outputs	Most CAQDAS packages have the ability to generate outputs such as reports, models and charts, which can help to visualize data that are being conceptualized and relationships that are being made. Further, this enables data and analysis to be easily shared among the research team.

NVivo a software package that assists in the building and testing of theories by classifying, sorting and arranging information; available from QSR International (www. qsrinternational. com)

Choosing the right package

Setting aside the tools that most of the packages have in common (such as basic search capabilities), different software packages come with various additional features. Whether or not these are relevant to a certain study depends on the design of the study and the kind of analysis the researcher wants to conduct. There are a number of general factors to consider when choosing a CAQDAS package, which can be summarized in the following key points:

- *Availability*: Most universities and research institutes acquire licences for only one or two of the major packages. As a result, research students or researchers employed in bigger projects usually work with the package they were trained on and have access to. There are also a number of free/open-source packages available. Some of these feature a graphical user interface, but others do not. The price for commercial packages varies; for students, licences can usually be obtained at a reduced price. Before purchasing such a licence, it is important to check that the program can be installed (i.e. that the operating system and capacity of the computer are suitable).

- *Requirements*: Researchers should be clear about what *kind of data* they will be analysing (text files, PDF documents, audio or video files, images, etc.), what *kind of analysis* they wish to undertake, and the *methods and techniques* they will be using before they set out to choose a particular software. For example, a content analysis of interview transcripts that is part of a mixed methods study will require different features (such as word-crunching tools) from a grounded analysis of company reports (which might require more advanced diagramming tools, and the facility to process formatted PDF files).

- *Skills and training*: Many CAQDAS packages have advanced significantly over the past decade and already offer features of which many of their users are not fully aware. In some cases, the selection of the program should also be guided by consideration about how much time the researcher wants to spend on learning how to use the software. At least for the bigger packages, plenty of manuals and tutorials can be found online (e.g. on YouTube and university websites). More advanced packages or specialized techniques might require more extensive training, using courses that may not be available free of charge.

- *Teamwork*: Not all packages support teamwork. If a project requires several researchers to work on the same dataset, this will limit the choice of suitable packages to some degree.

Once these points have been considered, websites like that of the CAQDAS Networking Project of the University of Surrey can be consulted for guidance on choosing the right package (see the list of further reading at the end of this chapter). Such sites provide up-to-date information on the features and limitations of all major packages, along with detailed reviews and further guidance on where to look for training and support. On the companion website accompanying this book, readers will find an introduction to the main features of Atlas.ti, NVivo and WordSmith (a linguistic analysis software). Given the rapid development of these platforms, such information quickly goes out of date. For this reason, we have decided not to include this material in the print version of this book and instead to advise readers to consult the webpage of the CAQDAS Networking Project and the homepages of CAQDAS packages. Useful tutorials can also be found on YouTube.

CAQDAS package

Finally, we would like to consider three important points regarding the use of computers for analysing qualitative data. First, the success and the strength of the analysis always depend on the judgement of the researcher; computers cannot substitute for this.

This brings us to the second point, which is about the importance of developing the right skills. Before undertaking work with any CAQDAS package, it is essential to undertake sufficient training and allow for a period of familiarization. Learning about a software package is not the same as using it. In combination with the software developers' guides and any training courses they may offer, another excellent source of reference is *Using Software in Qualitative Research* (Silver and Lewins, 2014), which offers a step-by-step guide, including detailed sections on NVivo and ATLAS.ti. For Atlas.ti, we would also recommend Friese's (2012) excellent introduction.

Third, we would like to add a word of caution. Even if a suitable package has been found and sufficient training has been undertaken, researchers should be aware of the fact that CAQDAS packages affect how researchers relate to their data, and how they process and frame them. For example, Luker (2008) observes that she tends to generate many more subcodes when coding on the computer, and that this changes the way she creates and reflects upon her categories. Code-based programs facilitate the retrieval of coded segments or quotations, making it easier to compare fragments of text sourced from different data. However, in contrast to piles of coded hard copies, it also makes it a lot easier to decontextualize what has been coded. This can be very problematic when individual sentences taken from different sources (e.g. an internal report, an interview, a legal statement and a field note) are treated as if they were derived from the same document or context. When coding diverse material, it is therefore essential always to remind oneself that words are used in different ways by different people situated in different contexts. Even if an analysis aims 'merely' to identify themes, it should aim also to be accurate – which brings us to the more general issue of how we can assess the quality of qualitative research.

Quality in qualitative research

If we want our research to be useful, we need to consider how to make it relevant, credible and attractive to others. But how can we assess whether the findings that emerge from our analysis are any good? In this section, we explore some answers to this question. We start by arguing that the quality of qualitative research ultimately depends on how researchers approach their research – from the development of the proposal to the publication of their work. Researchers who aim to conduct their research in a reflexive and transparent way rarely produce bad research. To illustrate this point, we discuss some of the main problems around the quality of the data, the analytical process, the documentation of this process and the evaluation of outcomes. We will then conclude this discussion with an overview of relevant criteria for the assessment of qualitative research.

Just as good and well-prepared ingredients are vital for a chef, so too are good and well-prepared data vital for a researcher. A chef who, without much thought, just uses whatever can be found in the kitchen is unlikely to produce a great meal. One cannot over-emphasize the importance of closely examining the quality of data before embarking on the analysis. This starts with a reflection on what kind of data were collected – and what kind of data were *not* collected, i.e. are missing. For example, a study finding that the damage caused by a fire is greater when more firefighters were involved in extinguishing it would suggest that an important mediating factor has been overlooked. While this might be a rather simplistic example, it should be considered that the complexity of phenomena examined in management research can easily give rise to problems, which may be much less obvious.

Sampling strategies, and the potential bias they can introduce, should be examined carefully to assess what kind of inference can be drawn. Qualitative research aims at transcending anecdotal evidence. If relevant material is ignored or omitted from the analysis, this kind of 'cherry-picking' can limit severely the inferences and generalizations that can be made (Barbour, 2014). Researcher effects should also be considered. Interviews are based on a short period of interaction between an interviewer and an interviewee, and they usually do not give the interviewer much opportunity to fully assess the background of the interviewee, or the motivations of the interviewee to respond in a certain way. Interviewees might wish to impress interviewers or try to enlist them in their own cause (Maxwell and Chmiel, 2014). The triangulation of different data sources, different methods of data collection, and different kinds of data can reduce such problems (Miles et al., 2014) – but triangulation can make the analysis more complicated too. Whenever possible, evidence should be carefully weighed and checked against 'hard facts'.

A good qualitative study is systematic and thorough. Superficial thematic analysis based on anecdotal evidence rarely advances our thinking. Themes should be developed, and the relationships between them explored, with the aim of contrasting, evaluating and integrating findings. Many studies are simply not useful because researchers stopped their analysis somewhere in the middle (Barbour, 2014). Negative evidence that can inform alternative interpretations is essential for good theory-building, as it can inform rival explanations that are needed to assess the robustness and scope of a theory. Such alternative interpretations are part and parcel of the process of constant comparison on which qualitative research builds; as such, they should not be fought against, but should be welcomed as an opportunity to improve the analysis. Alternative interpretations can be developed by researchers who critically examine their analysis in a reflexive way, but they can also be put forward by research participants, colleagues and supervisors. Seminars that allow researchers to present work-in-progress, including ambiguous fragments of data, in order to obtain alternative interpretations, provide an invaluable opportunity to enhance the quality of a study. Table 8.8 presents questions that can help in the preparation of such seminars, and in the development and documentation of a *good* study.

TABLE 8.8   Questions enhancing self-reflexivity and transparency

Data

- What information is included in my data? What information is missing?
- What sampling strategy was used to collect these data?
- What status do I attach to my data (e.g. facts, opinions, views and stories)?
- To what extent do my data include 'outliers', or negative or deviant cases?
- Do I like some data fragments more than others? Why?
- How do my data help me to address my research topic?
- What other data might be needed to answer my research question?
- To what extent is the quality or scope of my data limited by practical issues (e.g. time, funding and access)?

Analysis

- How do I frame my data?
- Are my framework and perspective appropriate to my data and to my research question?
- On what grounds have I chosen my methods and techniques?
- Am I clear what I am doing?
- Have I included all my data in my analysis? If not, why not?
- What are/were the most important decisions I have/had to make in this analysis?
- Does my analysis go beyond a simple list of descriptions and themes?
- What is my theoretical contribution (however small)?
- Am I making too large claims about my research?

Good feedback and honest evaluations can only be given to those who disclose what they are doing. Detailed documentation and 'reflexive accounting' (Barbour, 2014: 505) of the research process (e.g. by answering questions like those listed in Table 8.8) enhance the quality of the study. Transparency is also essential when it comes to convincing others of the quality of the research undertaken. Audiences have to gain some insights into how a study was done in order to consider it credible. Moreover, few audiences are interested in research that does not relate to their own interests or that simply replicates what has already been done. Only through continuous engagement with debates among practitioners and academics can practitioners ensure that their research can be understood in the context of what has already been done. A good literature review is therefore the foundation of a good study.

It is important to be honest about what a project can – and cannot – achieve. Qualitative researchers tend to acknowledge subjectivity where quantitative researchers claim objectivity; qualitative research usually aims at *internal generalizability* (the capacity to explain what has been researched within a given setting) and not *statistical generalizability* (inferences beyond those that have been studied), which is the gold standard of quantitative research. More often than not, qualitative studies cannot be replicated as they have been conducted by individuals engaging with a particular setting at a particular point in time. The contribution of qualitative research often lies in its *uniqueness* – and not in whether it can be replicated (Janesick, 2003). As a result, qualitative research may fail some of the standards used for quantitative research (e.g. objectivity, statistical generalizability and replicability). This does not mean, however, that it is not *good* research.

As we noted earlier in the book, qualitative research aims at theory-building. While qualitative researchers often cannot know whether their theories can be transferred to settings beyond the one they have studied, they can identify factors that are likely to determine the *transferability* of certain theories, thereby giving readers room for informed speculation about the settings in which their theories can be applied. As noted by Barbour (2014: 507), 'unlike claims to "statistical generalizability", which purport to provide a universal answer, the invoking of "theoretical generalizability" can simply involve posing a general (but clearly articulated) *question* or tentative hypothesis'. A clearly articulated question can go a long way towards addressing some of the complex phenomena with which management research is concerned.

TABLE 8.9   Checklist of eight criteria for assessing the quality of qualitative research

Criterion	Questions to consider
Worthy topic	Is the research topic relevant, original, timely, significant and/or interesting?
Rigour	Does the study use appropriate data, concepts and methods?
Sincerity	Is the study characterized by (self-)reflexivity and transparency? Does it provide me with the information I need to evaluate the study?
Credibility	Is the study marked by detailed descriptions, the explication of tacit knowledge, and triangulation?
Resonance	Does the research affect readers/audiences through evocative representations, appropriate generalizations and transferable findings?
Contribution	Does the research make a significant contribution in one or more of the following areas: theory/concepts, methodology/methods and practical impact?
Ethics	Does the research consider ethical issues?
Meaningful coherence	Does the study fulfil its aims? Do the methods and techniques used fit with the stated aims? Does the research meaningfully connect literature, research questions and findings?

Source: based on Tracy, 2010: 840

Finally, this leaves us with the question of whether there are any formal criteria for the quality of qualitative research, given that some of those developed for quantitative research seem not to be suitable. In Chapter 3, we showed how different epistemological stances translate into different views on validity, reliability and generalizability – so these 'traditional' criteria can be used if they are re-interpreted in order to better accommodate research conducted within the qualitative paradigm (Miles et al., 2014: 311). However, several attempts have been made to develop lists of criteria that qualitative researchers would acknowledge to be genuine. Given the impressive range of methods that are considered to be 'qualitative', mainly because they are 'not quantitative', this has not been an easy exercise (Flick, 2007). In Table 8.9, we present an abridged version of a checklist that was developed by Tracy (2010) to facilitate the assessment of the quality of qualitative research. While we believe that such a checklist can only complement a previous and in-depth consideration of the issues raised above, we consider it a useful tool for assessing the quality of one's own research and the research of others.

Conclusion

In this chapter we have attempted to provide an overview of some of the main approaches for framing and interpreting qualitative data. We have then advised readers on how they can identify CAQDAS packages that can assist them in their research. Finally, we have discussed how the quality of qualitative research can be assessed.

The main points raised are:

- The methodology of each qualitative study is unique as it has to be appropriate to the research question, and to the setting or phenomenon under research.

- Different analytical approaches frame qualitative data in different ways and prescribe different methods for their analysis and interpretation. Researchers may wish to adapt and combine different approaches as long as they can be integrated in a coherent research design.

- Good qualitative research builds on the creativity, focus and reflexivity of the researchers, and on their willingness to account for the research process in a transparent way.

While there remains a continual tension between those who aim at building theory and those who aim at assessing its generalizability and exploratory value, a growing number of mixed methods studies suggest that the long-assumed abyss separating the qualitative and quantitative paradigms is shrinking, and indeed easy enough to bridge. In the next two chapters, we cross this bridge, discussing the merits and methods of quantitative research.

Further reading

This volume discusses a wide range of visual data produced by researchers and research participants:

Banks, M. (2008) *Using Visual Data in Qualitative Research*. London: Sage.

A useful guide for analysing qualitative data using the package NVivo:

Bazeley, P. (2013) *Qualitative Data Analysis with NVivo*, 2nd edn. London: Sage.

An excellent introduction to conversation analysis:

Bergmann, J.R. (2004) 'Conversation analysis', in U. Flick, E. Kardorff and I. Steinke (eds), *A Companion to Qualitative Research*. London: Sage, pp. 296–302.

A seminal textbook on how to conduct data creation and data analysis using grounded theory:

Charmaz, K. (2014) *Constructing Grounded Theory: A Practical Guide Through Qualitative Analysis*, 2nd edn. London: Sage.

This article details steps on how to create a codebook for coding interview data:

DeCuir-Gunby, J.T., Marshall, P.L. and McCulloch, A.W. (2011) 'Developing and using a codebook for the analysis of interview data: an example from a professional development research project', *Field Methods*, 23 (2): 136–55.

A great example for applied content analysis and a useful overview of how it has been used in organization studies:

Duriau, V.J., Reger, R.K. and Pfarrer, M.D. (2007) 'A content analysis of the content analysis literature in organization studies: research themes, data sources, and methodological refinements', *Organizational Research Methods*, 10 (1): 5–34.

In this slim volume, Flick goes a long way in explaining how to distinguish good from bad qualitative research:

Flick, U. (2007) *Managing Quality in Qualitative Research*. London: Sage.

A comprehensive collection of chapters on a wide range of approaches, methods and techniques for analysing qualitative data. We recommend in particular the chapters by Barbour (on analysing focus groups) and by Maxwell and Chmielin (on generalization):

Flick, U. (2014) *SAGE Handbook of Qualitative Data Analysis*. London: Sage.

A useful guide to analysing qualitative data using Atlas.ti:

Friese, S. (2012) *Qualitative Data Analysis with ATLAS.ti*. London: Sage.

A comic-style textbook for novices to qualitative analysis:

Galman, S.C. (2013) *The Good, the Bad, and the Data: Shane the Lone Ethnographer's Basic Guide to Qualitative Data Analysis*. Walnut Creek, CA: Left Coast Press.

A useful introduction to template analysis for (research) students:

King, N. and Brooks, J.M. (2017) *Template Analysis for Business and Management Students* (Mastering Business Research Methods). Thousand Oaks, CA: Sage.

This offers a comprehensive overview of the debates and possibilities available to researchers when considering grounded approaches to data collection and analysis:

Locke, K. (2001) *Grounded Theory in Management Research*. London: Sage.

One of the leading introductory textbooks on qualitative data analysis in the social sciences. Miles, Huberman and Saldaña cover a wide range of methods for exploring, describing, analysing and explaining qualitative data as well as drawing and verifying conclusions:

Miles, M.B., Huberman, A.M. and Saldaña, J. (2014) *Qualitative Data Analysis*, 3rd edn. Thousand Oaks, CA: Sage.

A practical introduction to coding, which also provides an excellent overview of different frameworks for coding qualitative data:

Saldaña, J. (2015) *The Coding Manual for Qualitative Researchers*, 3rd edn. Thousand Oaks, CA: Sage.

A comprehensive introduction to how to use CAQDAS packages with text, video and mixed data:

Silver, C. and Lewins, A. (2014) *Using Software in Qualitative Research: A Step-by-Step Guide*, 2nd edn. Thousand Oaks, CA: Sage.

A more recent compilation of quality criteria for qualitative research:

Tracy, S.J. (2010) 'Qualitative quality: eight "big-tent" criteria for excellent qualitative research', *Qualitative Inquiry*, 16 (10): 837–51.

Check your understanding online

Visit the website **https://edge.sagepub.com/easterbysmith6e** for useful resources that will help reinforce what you've read in this chapter:

 Take an interactive quiz to test your understanding of the key topics

 Review suggested answers to Exercises 8.1 to 8.9 above

 Use interactive flashcards to check your knowledge of essential concepts

Learning objectives

To be able to select an appropriate form of sampling design for the objectives of the research.

To be able to select among alternative sources of quantitative data according to the purpose of the research, taking into account the benefits and drawbacks of each.

To be able to design structured questionnaires using well-defined questions and appropriate forms of measurement scale.

CRAFTING QUANTITATIVE DATA

9

Introduction

This chapter is divided into three main parts. The first part covers three sources of quantitative data: collecting data through surveys, collecting data through observation and using secondary data sources. Each has benefits and drawbacks, and we consider how to make choices between them. The second section looks at the process of measurement in two parts: how to design structured questions for surveys and interviews, and alternative forms of measurement scale for recording responses. The third section examines the conceptual basis of measurement models.

Sources of quantitative data

In thinking about where to get data that could be analysed using quantitative methods, there are broadly two ways of going about it: researchers can collect their own primary data, or they can use secondary data already collected and stored within archival databases. Each approach has advantages and disadvantages. Broadly, collecting one's own research data gives control over both the structure of the sample and the data obtained from each respondent. This gives greater confidence that the data will match the study objectives. However, that benefit comes at a price since it can be much more expensive (in time and effort) to collect one's own data, compared with using secondary data from an existing archive.

Collecting data through surveys

Surveys can be good ways of collecting data about the opinions and behaviour of large numbers of people, as long as they are done well. The choice between them will depend on many factors, so that there is no single best way. Survey data can be collected either through self-completion questionnaires where respondents record their own answers, or can be administered by interviewers face-to-face or over the telephone. While these two methods still have an important place, advances in communications technology have brought a variety of new options within the scope of the researcher in business and management. The new methods offer many advantages, yet also pose challenges.

Self-completion questionnaires

postal questionnaire survey
a form of survey distribution that involves postal distribution, and relies on respondents to complete a survey themselves and return it to the researcher

Postal questionnaire surveys have the advantage that the cost per respondent is low for large samples compared with any method that requires face-to-face contact with individuals, especially when the sample members are widely dispersed. However, response rates can be very low (for many researchers, a 20 per cent response rate would be regarded as good) because there is no personal contact with the respondent that can encourage cooperation. Financial or other inducements are sometimes effective, but the normal guarantee of anonymity makes it difficult to reward people for responding because the researcher has no way of knowing who has replied and who has not. The researcher has little control over whether the person targeted is the one who answers the questions (CEOs are reputed to hand survey questionnaires over to their PAs to fill in on their behalf), and also over how they answer them. As a result, checking the quality of data from postal surveys, both completeness and accuracy, is particularly important.

Another application of modern communications technology is the web-based survey. As the Internet has become a taken-for-granted part of business and domestic life, carrying out web-based surveys (Callegaro et al., 2015) is now fairly commonplace. Respondents can be invited to take part in the survey in a number of different ways: by email including a link to the survey, by embedding the survey questions within a website, by a link through social media such as Twitter or Facebook, or by including a clickable link for visitors to a site. Whichever method is used, the survey is then completed online, and responses are stored directly in an online database for statistical processing later.

Web Surveys

Survey Example

Tools such as Qualtrics, SurveyMonkey and Verint have dramatically reduced the cost of web-based surveys by making each step in the process easy for those without technical training. Web-based surveys offer a number of advantages. They can be customized for individual respondents much more easily than postal surveys. Moreover, web technologies allow for a degree of interactivity with respondents: pop-up instructions and drop-down boxes can explain parts of the survey that are more difficult to understand; questions at different points in a survey can be personalized using responses to earlier questions; and skip-logic and conditional branching make it easy to skip over topics that are not relevant based on answers to earlier questions. It is also possible to build in dynamic error-checking of answers to ensure that people respond consistently throughout. Finally, data can be downloaded directly into analysis programs such as Excel or SPSS, avoiding the cost of data entry and transcription errors. Woo et al. (2015) provide a good example of a web-based survey.

Web-based surveys are attractive to researchers but they do have some drawbacks. The most obvious is that they rely on access to the Internet. There are many parts of the world where there is no Internet access, as well as places where access is poor or intermittent. Employees of organizations do not always have access to the Internet in their place of work, and so web-based surveys would automatically exclude some staff.

web-based survey a form of survey where a website link is sent to each potential participant, and respondents complete the survey by recording their answers online; answers may be checked for consistency and then stored on a database for analysis

Interviewer–administered questionnaires

Structured interview surveys are much more expensive per head because an interviewer has to be present while each respondent's answers are recorded. The cost of interviews includes the time of the interviewer, which has to cover initial training, time spent in setting up each interview, travel to where respondents are located and an allowance for broken appointments. They are most often used when accurate data are the main priority, and where there are complicated instructions for how to answer survey questions or where different questions need to be asked depending on individual circumstances. Many people are understandably reluctant to divulge confidential or sensitive personal information in a postal questionnaire, and a skilled interviewer can build a relationship of trust with respondents that can reassure them about why the data are needed and how they will be kept secure. An interview method may be the most effective way to collect survey data for groups such as customers in a shop or a service facility, where postal addresses or other contact details are not available.

Telephone interview surveys are now commonplace in many research projects, since they combine the low cost of the postal survey with the interactivity of the face-to-face interview. Collecting data by telephone is of most value where the design of the research project requires contact with respondents who are widely dispersed (so that travelling to them would be time-consuming and expensive) or where the researcher is located in a different part of the world (e.g. many Asian students studying in the UK want to conduct their research in their own country, but cannot afford to travel there to collect data).

structured interview survey a form of survey where an interviewer locates each participant, and completes the survey face-to-face by asking structured questions

telephone interview survey a form of survey where an interviewer locates each participant, and completes the survey by telephone by asking structured questions

EXERCISE 9.1

Advantages and disadvantages of alternative survey strategies

Individual: Table 9.1 below outlines three different research projects where survey methodology might be appropriate. Taking into account the topic, the resources available to you and the target group, make a list of the advantages and disadvantages of the four methods of administering your survey. Which method will you use and why?

TABLE 9.1 Alternative survey strategies

	Postal survey	Web-based survey	Face-to-face interview survey	Telephone interview survey
A project in a small business to assess views on introducing charging employees for car parking				
Advantages				
Disadvantages				
A worldwide survey in a multinational company of staff attitudes to HRM practices				
Advantages				
Disadvantages				
An investigation to understand the nature of bullying within the Social Services Department of a local authority				
Advantages				
Disadvantages				

Improving the quality of data from surveys

A high response rate in a survey is clearly important: it gives a larger body of data, which the researcher can use to address research questions, and it makes it much more likely that the sample is representative of the population of interest. This section draws on advice by Dillman (Dillman et al., 2014), and gives a number of steps that the researcher can take to increase response rates as well as the quality of the information that respondents give. Underlying these steps is a simple principle derived from social exchange theory. Providing data is a cost to each respondent, you should increase the perceived benefit as much as possible (see Table 9.2) and reduce the effort involved as much as possible (see Table 9.3).

Ways of establishing trust

A survey is a request for people to do something (in this case, answer questions and return the survey) based on the expectation that something will follow. As with many things in life, willingness to act depends on trust that the other person will fulfil what they promise.

So, when you contact people to ask them to take part in your survey, it makes sense to increase as much as possible their trust in the promises you make. This can be difficult, since you will almost certainly not know your respondents personally, and so they do not know if they can trust you.

The first way to increase trust is to obtain sponsorship by a legitimate authority. Compliance is higher if the request comes from a source that is regarded as legitimate. If you are a student, it may be better to describe your survey as part of the research being carried out by your supervisor (who of course is wise and experienced). Throughout many years of carrying out employee opinion surveys, we have also found that it makes a big difference that we are academics working in a university rather than paid consultants (we are not being paid to carry out the survey). We work *with* the company (which gives us the legitimate right to be there), but we are not working *for* the company (which would mean that the company controls what we are allowed to ask, and how the answers will be used). We often insist that replies come directly to us rather than to a company HR department, in order to avoid the possibility that employees' answers might be seen by management.

The second way to increase trust is to make the current task appear important. You can increase trust in a survey by showing how the findings from previous surveys have been used to make significant changes. Of course, such claims need to be credible, and you should think about how your own study will be used to make a difference. Doing nothing with your results makes the study less important in the eyes of your participants, and it can be very harmful. There is nothing more likely to damage credibility than asking people's opinions and then doing nothing with their answers.

The third way to increase trust is by ensuring confidentiality and security of information. Many people are completely unaware of the ways in which social media sites and search engines use information about them to customize advertising and search options (the terms under which they do this are buried deep within the terms and conditions fine print). Such big data offer the potential to collate fragmented health information in order to identify (for example) rare combinations of treatments that would be effective for devastating diseases. But there continues to be debate in the UK about how to use data for these purposes in a way that protects privacy, for example whether individuals should opt in or opt out of having their data used for other purposes. In your research project, you should make sure

big data extremely large datasets arising from the everyday processes of businesses, which may be structured or unstructured

TABLE 9.2   Ways of increasing the rewards for participation

- *Show respect for participants*: for example, explain why the survey is being done, offer a point of contact for questions, address people by name where possible.
- *Say thank you for taking part*: through a follow-up letter or email.
- *Frame the survey as a request for their help or advice*: an example request to patients in a GP practice could be: 'I am writing to you because the only way that we know whether we are doing a good job is by asking people who use our service'.
- *Appeal to the values of a group*: explain the survey in terms of what matters to the group of people involved.
- *Give token rewards*: offering a small reward can increase the sense of obligation to give a completed survey in return.
- *Make the questions interesting*: better responses are obtained for topics that matter to the people taking part.
- *Social validation*: you can increase participation by showing that people similar to them have completed it already.
- *Opportunities to respond are limited*: telling people that they only have a limited time to respond can increase participation rates.

that data are kept confidential and anonymous (unless there is a really good reason otherwise), and telling your participants that this is so will make it easier for them to trust you and to give their informed consent to take part in your study.

TABLE 9.3   Ways of decreasing the costs of participation

- *Make it as convenient as possible to respond*: for a web survey, include a link in an email; for a postal survey, include a reply-paid envelope.
- *Don't talk down to people*: consider the difference between the following requests to take part in a survey of student satisfaction:
  - 'as a student, you are required to respond to this survey of school administration'
  - 'as a student, you are the best person to help us to improve the service that the school gives you'.

  The first is likely to lead to resistance, since most of us don't like being told what to do, while the second puts the respondent in charge.
- *Make the survey short and easy to complete*: surveys with fewer questions achieve higher response rates. Don't try to cram as many questions as possible onto a page just to make it look shorter. Sometimes going to the other extreme is actually beneficial. If your target sample consists of older people, then using a bigger font and spreading the text out to make it easier to read is almost certainly more important than skimping on the number of pages used.
- *Minimize requests for personal or sensitive information*: many people are reluctant to divulge information about their income, and health, so only ask questions about such topics if they are essential. If you absolutely need to know these things, then explain why this is important and show how you will respect the person's confidentiality. In workplace surveys, we have also found that personal information is better placed at the end of a survey after questions on neutral and less sensitive topics, rather than at the beginning.

RESEARCH IN ACTION

Survey design

Susanne Karstedt

Susanne Karstedt is a Professor of Criminology at Griffith University, Queensland, Australia. Susanne has conducted a number of surveys on crime and justice with different social groups.

How do you approach the development of a new questionnaire?

I often compare designing a questionnaire to engineering an airplane: you need a perfect blueprint for building it as it has to fly after take-off. After fieldwork has started a survey cannot be changed; therefore it has to be as perfect as possible. The first and foremost requirement is a robust conceptual framework on which the design of questions can build. Without such a framework your questions will go nowhere, but unfortunately you will only find out when analysing your data. It is here where every good questionnaire starts.

When developing a new questionnaire it is essential to research existing surveys and questions on the respective topic. Previous surveys are treasure troves for good question design, as most of the questions that we want to ask have been addressed before in one way or the other, and can serve as models when we develop our own questions. Moreover, when designing questions, items and answer categories it is essential to consider the prospective respondents. How they interpret the questions, how they understand the answer categories, and how this relates to their experience and thinking are most important for the robustness and validity of their responses. Do not ask people about things that are remote from their own lives, but stay close to their experience, their beliefs and activities.

Finally, just like a plane should carry as little weight as possible, a survey should not be burdened with endless questions and items that the researcher of course deems all equally important. A survey needs to be neat and lean; it should not exceed a maximum of 35–45 minutes; beyond that the researcher will receive random answers. Researchers need to be ruthless with themselves in weeding out questions and items until the bare minimum of questions is achieved. Less is more here!

A few years ago you conducted a survey on middle-class crime. Can you tell us a bit more about this?

The idea for the survey started – as ever so often – from observation and real-life experience. I had seen colleagues talking openly about how to evade taxes and cheat on insurance claims, and was wondering what else the respectable middle classes, comfortably situated in the centre of contemporary societies, were capable of doing. Was it need or greed, lure or moral decay in consumer society? Or did we have to look at economic trends such as deregulation of markets? The concept of the 'moral economy' (first developed by historian E.P. Thompson) provided a perfect framework for our research on how citizens and consumers committed crimes, or engaged in shady practices or immoral behaviour.

It is, however, difficult to ask adults and those who think of themselves as respectable people about their deviant behaviour, and consequently this has rarely been done. We therefore combined it with a victimization survey, i.e. we asked respondents whether they had been a victim of fraudulent, damaging and negligent behaviour by banks and insurers, tradespeople or fellow citizens. We presented them with several vignettes to probe their intentions to engage in insurance fraud and tax evasion. These core questions were supplemented by a number of attitude scales that were designed to gauge perceptions of the moral economy in their country.

TOP TIPS

- Do not underestimate the time it takes to develop a good questionnaire that 'can take off' in the field. Depending on the length, it can take up to six months.

- Avoid long lists of items for which the answer is always 'agree' etc. This is boring!

- Make your questionnaire interesting! However, bear in mind that what interests you does not always interest your respondents …

Collecting data through observational methods

Observational methods are used in order to code and analyse behaviour, which may include visual data as well as behavioural data (Banks, 2008). Observational data are less common in business and management research, but could be very useful in areas such as the study

observational methods ways of collecting data that involve direct sampling of aspects of behaviour

of team-working, managerial decision-making and negotiation. Observing what people do during a task gives a directness and richness that cannot be achieved by asking people to describe what they did. Behaviour may either be coded live or be recorded (e.g. using audio or video or by capturing key presses and screen displays on a PC) for later coding. The most common way in which observational methods are used is with the observer as a non-participant, although participant observation can also be used, as we discussed in Chapter 7.

Types of observational data

There is no single way of classifying observational data, because behaviour is very complicated and the purposes of studies vary enormously. The most obvious distinction is between verbal and non-verbal aspects of behaviour. The researcher may be interested in *verbal* behaviour – the words that people use to express meanings through the content of messages, complexity of syntax, formal versus informal language – in order to explore different ways of explaining how to perform a task. *Non-verbal* behaviour is divided into vocal aspects to do with tone of voice (angry, apologetic, loving, calm, etc.), pitch (high or low) and the pacing of speech (talking quickly or slowly), and also visual aspects to do with facial expressions, gestures, body posture and so on. A detailed analysis of the success or failure of a negotiation exercise would need to include an analysis of these aspects of non-verbal behaviour since they carry a substantial proportion of information. For example, Mehrabian's (1981) experimental studies of communications of feelings and attitudes led him to the following formula:

Total Liking = 7% Verbal Liking + 38% Vocal Liking + 55% Facial Liking

In other words, most of the information about whether one person likes who they are talking to comes not from what is said (only 7 per cent) but from how it is said and from their facial expressions (93 per cent). We can conclude that relying for data only on a written transcript of what was said during a conversation or a meeting will miss much of the most important information about what is going on, particularly regarding relationships between people.

Factors affecting observational data

There are a number of things that need to be kept in mind when designing studies that will use observational data. First, observer effects are common, which refers to the fact that most of us behave differently when we know (or think) that we are being observed. Often, initiatives within local communities rely on exactly these effects to influence the behaviour of members of the public: those boxes on poles at the side of the road often do not contain speed cameras (but they might, so we slow down). From the perspective of positivistic research, observer effects are bad news since they alter the very thing that the researcher is interested in learning about. Consider how difficult it is for many people to pose naturally for a photograph: it is easy to tell the difference between a natural smile and a posed smile since the muscle groups used are different. In practice though, people whose behaviour is being recorded quickly get used to being observed and forget about the cameras. One way to avoid observer effects is to act covertly so that no one knows that they are being watched, but this violates one of the basic principles of ethical research (see Chapter 5), that research participants give their informed consent to take part in a study. Indeed, recording of telephone calls without consent is illegal in the UK, and that is why calls to companies often start with a message saying that calls may be recorded or monitored for security and quality control purposes.

observer effects influences on behaviour that result from study participants knowing that they are being observed

The second factor to bear in mind in using observational data relates to how decisions are made about *what behaviour is sampled*. Some kind of selectivity is inevitable, simply because human behaviour is so rich and complex. One approach is to try to obtain a complete record, and then sample from within it later. A popular TV show in many countries is *Big Brother*, where individuals live in the 'Big Brother House' and a large number of cameras record what they say and do. Even if the output from every camera and every microphone is available for analysis, some kind of selectivity is essential. The editors broadcast a tiny proportion of all that material, and their editing judgements can be a source of complaint and comment. For example, 'inmates' of the house often complain that *Big Brother* did not show the 'real me' when features of their behaviour that show them in a particular way are selected and others neglected. A second approach is to record only a sample of behaviour: either by *time* sampling (e.g. take a photo every two seconds, or record for five minutes every hour through the day) or by *activity* sampling (e.g. record every phone call that is a customer complaint, or select company orders for a specific range of products).

Coding observational data

One of the most widely used systems for coding behaviour in small groups is *interaction process analysis* (IPA), originally developed by Bales (1950, 1970) and later modified. The original system grouped behaviour into 12 categories according to a focus either on social-emotional aspects of the relationship (e.g. liking vs disliking) or on aspects of the task (e.g. giving answers vs asking questions). The categories form six pairs; for example, seems friendly vs unfriendly; gives vs asks for information. Using the IPA requires substantial training for observers to break behaviour down into discrete units and then classify each unit into one of the categories. A more detailed elaboration of the IPA is the *system of multiple level observation of groups* (SYMLOG) (Bales et al., 1979; Bales, 1988). The two forms of the system code either values or behaviour into 26 categories, which can then be combined to give a position in a three-dimensional interpersonal space: dominance, friendliness and task orientation.

EXAMPLE 9.1

Using observational data

A Masters' student sat in as an observer on selection interviews for engineering apprentices and coded some aspects of the verbal and non-verbal behaviour of each candidate during the interview. Interviews were classified according to the outcome (accept or reject) and were then examined for differences in the behaviour of the candidates. All the candidates treated the interview as a formal situation and were nervous: they sat upright in the chair with their legs together in front of them and their hands together on their knees. The candidates who were *accepted* showed that they were interested in the interviewer by lots of eye contact, and smiling. They reinforced their replies to the interviewer's questions by moving their head – nodding or shaking. By contrast, the *rejected* candidates avoided eye contact with the interviewer, and showed their apparent lack of interest by wandering eyes when the interviewer was talking, and they were much less expressive in their non-verbal behaviour.

EXERCISE 9.2

Types of questions that observational data can answer

Group: In groups, consider the research questions in Table 9.4 below. Each group selects one of the research questions below. The task is in two parts:

1 Draw up a coding scheme for the types of behaviour that the group is interested in.

2 Design a sampling strategy for collecting the data.

Then bring the groups together to present their coding schemes, and compare them. What factors influence the content of the coding scheme and the choice of sampling strategy?

TABLE 9.4 Research questions

Research question	What data to collect	How to sample
Do people buy more cold drinks in hot weather, and more soup in cold weather?		
Does the presence and type of background music in a store alter customers' buying behaviour?		
How do people use online help sources?		
When do people who work in different places (virtual teams) switch between media (instant messaging, email, video-conferencing and phone) in order to manage a project?		
How does the conversational style adopted by a call handler influence the effectiveness of telephone helplines?		
In negotiations, how do same-sex and mixed-sex groups differ?		

Using secondary data sources

The final method of getting quantitative data that we consider in this chapter is using archival sources of secondary data. Most research areas in business and management have data collected by other people. Organizations and individuals keep many different kinds of data for a variety of reasons: regulatory reasons (e.g. personal tax records), for monitoring past and present performance, and as a protection in the event of requests for information about the basis for past decisions. Although much of this data is confidential, a research study may gain access to data provided they meet confidentiality conditions. It is also the case that data of many kinds have to be deposited in archives, which can then be accessed for research purposes. Some of that data is in the public domain, though access to other material may depend on licence agreements of some kind, which the researcher's host institution may have negotiated.

Sources of big data

In a digital world, we are all users of technology and we leave traces of our activities wherever we go, in the form of active clicks on web pages, user-generated content, social media, online business transactions, as well as passive forms of data such as tracking of mobile phones via Bluetooth or GPS. All of these types of information are actively used by companies such as Facebook, Amazon and Google to target advertising, and are increasingly being used for other purposes too such as predicting energy use, traffic flows, as well as in healthcare, finance and operations management.

Some types of data are public or private data deliberately held by firms and individuals to support their activities (George et al., 2014). These include energy use, healthcare, website browsing histories, mobile phone usage, and such data will usually be very difficult for researchers to access since those who hold it will be very keen to protect the privacy of individuals as well as their own commercial interests. Other types of community data are unstructured data in the form of consumer reviews (on sites such as Amazon and TripAdvisor), comments on news sites, voting buttons ('I find this review useful') and social media news feeds. Data like this is proving to be very useful to management and business researchers. It gives them access to data on a variety of concepts that would be very difficult to study by other methods. For example, Twitter and Facebook feeds can give rich insights into consumer behaviour, such as the responses of consumers to different kinds of advertising appeals. For small amounts of data, manually copying data such as text comments may be feasible, but for larger studies this becomes impractical. The key to accessing large-scale unstructured data from social media is the Application Programming Interface (API), which is the basic resource for getting data out of and into sites like Facebook and Twitter. There are many tools now available (often based on the Python programming language) to enable researchers to scrape data from websites and store it in a format that can then be used for further analysis.

Secondary datasets

The UK Data Service (www.data-archive.ac.uk) is a comprehensive resource for some kinds of research and it contains datasets that are accessible to registered users free of charge. These data collections are immensely valuable for social scientists, though of much more limited use to business and management researchers. You can search through the UK Data Service archive using the Discover interface; other tools include ReShare (http://reshare. ukdataservice.ac.uk), Relu (http://relu.data-archive.ac.uk) and the European CESSDA catalogue (www.cessda.org).

Data
Service

Much more useful for business and management researchers are databases that include different kinds of company data. Examples of financial databases include:

Compustat

- Compustat (https://marketintelligence.spglobal.com/client-solutions) provides annual and quarterly income statements, balance sheets, cash flow and supplemental data items for North American companies.

Datastream

- Datastream (www.datastream.com) is one the largest financial statistical databases, and holds current/historical financial data for international companies/indices and bond data.

SDC
Platinum

- SDC Platinum (https://financial.thomsonreuters.com/en/products/data-analytics/ market-data/sdc-platinum-financial-securities.html) is an international mergers and acquisitions (M&A) database.

WRDS

- The Wharton Research Data Service (WRDS; www.whartonwrds.com) provides access to databases in the fields of finance, accounting, banking, economics, management, marketing and public policy.

CRSP

● The Center for Research in Security Prices (CRSP; www.crsp.com) holds a variety of databases including: monthly/annual security prices, returns, and volume data for the NYSE, AMEX and NASDAQ stock markets.

The following example is of a study by a Masters' student, Isabelle, which uses archival data.

EXAMPLE 9.2

Event study of impact of CSR index on share prices

Isabelle studied 21 firms in Brazil and Colombia and the effect (if any) on market stock returns of the firm entering the Dow Jones Sustainability Emerging Markets Index (DJSEMI). Although there are specific CSR indexes for individual countries, she chose to look at the DJSEMI because it is available in four Latin American countries (Brazil, Chile, Colombia and Mexico), and this would allow her to generalize her findings across more than one country. The original intention was to examine several Latin American countries, but only Brazil and Colombia had multiple companies that were included in the Index.

The design of an event study includes two elements:

1 Event window: the time period over which the impact of an event will be measured. Isabelle chose a window of three days before and three days after the announcement of DJSEMI inclusion.

2 Estimation window: the time period before the event, which is recent but long enough to allow for estimation of normal market behaviour for the company. She chose to look at a year of trading days (n = 252).

The impact of the event is the difference between (1) and (2).

Isabelle obtained her data on stock prices from FactSet and Datastream, and from local and regional market indexes. Bloomberg Professional provided the market-trading calendar to identify active trading days in both markets. Prices were collected in both local currencies and in US dollars for securities traded in the NYSE market. She supplemented her quantitative data with qualitative information from Factiva and ThomsonOne databases, which she used to identify confounding events that might play a role in abnormal returns (such as publication of annual reports, resignations of CEOs).

RESEARCH IN ACTION

Secondary data

Hakan Ozalp is a Lecturer in Strategy at the Leeds University Business School. He holds a PhD in Business Administration and Management from Bocconi University. His research focuses on the impact of industrial and technological change.

Hakan Ozalp

What are the advantages of using secondary data?

In management and business research, we often use data collected for archival reasons to undertake deductive research, often focusing on macro-level analysis. The biggest advantage of such data is its scale – there are hundreds, thousands, or even millions of observations we can use to test our hypotheses. Secondary data can be cross-sectional, meaning that we have data on observations made at one point in time, but it can also be longitudinal and be based on repeated observations of the same variables over long periods of time. In contemporary business research, the latter is almost always preferred because it allows for comparisons over time and enables research into dynamics such as the evolution of an industry.

Where can you obtain secondary data of relevance to business and management research?

We are living in the age of digitalization and so it is easy to think that there are numerous sources of data. However, it can actually be quite difficult to identify and access the right data for a particular research question. One way of identifying potential sources of data is to read publications on similar topics and evaluate what sources of data the authors have used.

Another good starting point would be to have a look at some of the most commonly used databases. In management research these are, for example, COMPUSTAT, which is a database of financial and market information on global companies throughout the world that goes back a few decades; and the US Patent & Trademark Office (USPTO) database, which provides information on patent and trademark related information (in the US; there is an equivalent EPO database that covers Europe), generally used to measure innovation within firms.

More often than not, individual data sources are matched or combined to create one large dataset. For example, you may take some firm-level information from COMPUSTAT and then match it with USPTO data to measure the patent and trademark portfolio of each firm. Most datasets in management research are combined datasets of this kind – and it is a big 'plus' to have access to a unique part of a dataset which allows you to answer a question that could not be addressed by relying on the publicly available data only.

How can you evaluate the quality of secondary data?

Although often the most pressing concern for secondary data is availability (and access), there are also multiple criteria to evaluate its quality. One can start with the completeness of the data. Ideally, researchers want data capturing the whole population (of an industry, for example) to avoid sampling bias or censoring. Both these issues can still be handled with the right econometric approaches, however. Then there is the accuracy of the data. If a dataset has too many entries that are above or below the correct values, this gives rise to what we call 'noise' – a term that we use for unexplained variation or randomness. Too much noise means that you cannot 'hear' the music of your model. Finally, and maybe most importantly, there is the question of appropriateness or relevance. A researcher may have access to a very comprehensive and accurate dataset, but without it being relevant to the research question at hand, it will be a fruitless effort. And of course there are also research questions that cannot really be addressed using secondary data, either because they are not accessible or because they are simply not available (for example, where the researcher is interested in phenomena that are rare or hidden).

TOP TIP

If your question and your data do not make for a great match, you have to change one or the other or both (I wish someone had told me this when I started my PhD ...).

It can be very valuable to work with data collected for another purpose, but it is most unwise to plunge straight into a data archive without thinking carefully. The most important factor affecting the quality of what can be done with secondary data is the design of the database. Generally speaking, archival data will have been collected according to a specific design, which means that the researcher's first task in assessing the value of secondary sources is how close the study objectives are to those that influenced the original collection of the data. For example, someone who is interested in how small and medium-sized enterprises (SMEs) are using the Internet to internationalize their businesses is unlikely to find an archive of publicly quoted companies of much use, since SMEs are much smaller than a typical publicly quoted company.

An essential accompaniment to a secondary data archive is the documentation that goes with it. MacInnes (2017) lists 12 questions to ask about data, and answers to all of these should be found in the data documentation:

1.   *When was the survey fieldwork carried out?* Survey data will obviously reflect the circumstances of the time, and so can become outdated, especially during periods of rapid change. For example, some studies of organizational life from only a few years ago will have very little relevance today given the impact of mobile technology and social media on how work is organized.

2.   *Is the survey one of a repeated series?* Many surveys are repeated and so can be used to look at trends over time. But just as circumstances change, so too do the features of a target population. Most large-scale surveys adjust their sampling to account for changes in the structure of the population.

3.   *Is there a panel element to the survey?* Most surveys are cross-sectional, and even when they are repeated they use a new sample drawn from the same population. Some repeated surveys are based on a panel where the same respondents are contacted at regular intervals. This kind of study design is particularly useful for observing change over time within the same respondents, and a longitudinal design like this is essential for studying causal change processes (Example 9.2 shows some of the issues involved in designing a study on the impact of a regulatory change).

4.   *What was the target population?* The target population defines who it is that the survey is intended to give information about. Surveys that target individual people will need to specify who is or is not included (for example, do organizational surveys include contractors who provide vital services but are not employed by the company?). Surveys that target households or organizations will need to take great care in defining the intended target unit (for example, is a sole trader with no employees an organization?).

5.   *What was the sampling method?* Most surveys use complex sampling strategies (see Chapter 4) in order to ensure that they can allow precise inferences about different parts of the target population.

6. *What was the response rate?* Not everyone who is included in a target population will agree to take part in a survey, and the quality of a secondary data survey will depend greatly on how high the response rate was and (more important) whether non-respondents are similar to respondents.

7. *Who answered the questions?* Surveys of organizations can ask about different aspects of the organization, and sometimes a single respondent may not have access to all of the information required. Some respondents may be more trust-worthy than others.

8. *Does the survey contain modules administered only to subsets of respondents?* Complicated survey designs may divide samples into subsets of respondents for different aspects of information, and so it could be that only parts of a survey archive are relevant for your own purpose.

9. *What data did the survey collect?* Large-scale surveys will generally have been designed with great care, and so you can learn from the variables in a dataset and the wording of questions used to assess them.

10. *What use have others made of the data?* Secondary data archives generally include publications that are based on datasets within the archive, and these can be useful for helping you to understand issues that are important in using and interpreting the data.

11. *How can I access the data?* You can usually download data over the Internet after first registering. Pay attention to the terms and conditions for using the dataset, since you have an ethical responsibility to the original respondents as well as to those who deposited the data.

12. *How do I cite the data I use?* Citing the source of the data that you use is obviously important, and the data documentation will tell you how you can format your citation of the dataset.

EXAMPLE 9.3

Using databases

A doctoral student in her PhD work looked at cross-border mergers involving a British company taken over by a non-UK company. She started her search using the Thomson Financial M&A database to identify mergers that met her criteria. Here is her story:

> In my thesis, I needed to draw up a list of acquisitions with particular characteristics, which I would later contact. I needed only majority acquisitions, and it allowed me to search for above 50 per cent acquisitions. I also needed only UK companies that were bought by foreign companies – the database allowed me to 'include' or 'exclude' acquirers and targets from particular countries from my search. For example, by 'excluding' UK acquirers I was able to search only for foreign acquisitions. It also allowed me to search for deals of a certain age,

(Continued)

completed as opposed to only announced deals, deals of a certain value, deals in a specific industry, and so on. The database also contained very small as well as very large M&As. Overall, I found it an incredibly versatile tool. I was able to get the list of M&As with the precise specifications that I wanted in a matter of minutes. Thomson Financial, however, did not provide me with addresses or websites of the companies, so I had to search for these myself.

Many archives contain company records for each year (things like profit figures etc.). Databases differ in their coverage of companies: some are more comprehensive for US companies, others for European companies, while yet other databases only contain data for companies above a minimum size. A researcher interested in other regions, for example the growth of Latin American companies, may find it difficult to locate sources of data. Another challenge is that of linking data over time for organizations in a world where companies are formed, they grow, they merge with others and they die. Thus, profits data for a company will only be available for those periods where it is independent, so that a takeover will mean that it becomes part of a larger organization, while re-structuring may leave the name intact but changes the sub-units that make it up. It may thus prove impossible to compare like for like over a lengthy period of time. The practical consequences of dealing with such changes are outlined in Example 9.4.

EXAMPLE 9.4

Designing a study to assess the impact of the Sarbanes-Oxley Act 2002

Consider the research question of assessing the impact on companies of the Sarbanes-Oxley Act of 2002, which changed the governance regulation and reporting obligations of US public companies after the Enron scandal. The obvious way to assess its impact is to use data for companies before and after the Act came into force. The first task is to decide on a sampling frame (whether to select companies within specific sectors, or companies of a specific size) and the second is to decide what time points to look at (e.g. three years before and after the Act came into force). The research could end up with four kinds of sample, and there are issues with all of the sampling strategies:

1   The first approach is to select only companies with complete data throughout the study period. This makes the most sense on the face of it, since it gives a complete picture for the whole of the study period. It gives good answers to the question of how key variables change for companies whose ownership structure stays the same throughout. However, it misses out: companies that went out of business at any time during the study period; start-ups during the study period; and companies that were involved in M&A activity.

2   The second approach is to select all relevant companies at the start of the sampling period regardless of whether they still exist. This strategy would ensure

that the researcher has a sound sample at the start of the study period, but then the study design suffers from the same problem of incomplete data for companies that went out of existence or changed their structure through M&A activity. This would make it impossible to compare data before and after, but it could still be possible to assess a slightly different question: the likelihood of a company surviving intact until the end of the study period (this is called 'survival analysis' in statistics).

3   The third approach is to select all relevant companies at the end of the sampling period regardless of when they came into existence. This ensures a sound sample at the end of the study period, but suffers from incomplete data at the start for companies that are newly formed or re-formed from M&A activity.

4   The fourth approach is to select a representative sample of companies at each sampling point, with varying amounts of data for each. This would give a representative picture of companies at each point, but the analysis of change over time would be greatly complicated by different patterns of incomplete data.

Given that there is no ideal solution, a researcher will need to weigh up the relative merits of each alternative and the risks involved. Much will depend on how much change there has been in organizational structures during the study period, and the precise nature of the research questions under consideration.

Similarly, where companies are required by regulation to report particular kinds of information, then that is what they will do. When regulations change, there will be an associated change in what is recorded. As a result, great care needs to be taken by the researcher to make sure that the data have a consistent meaning throughout the study period. For example, Wall et al. (1992) were interested in whether empowering shop-floor workers by allowing them to manage machine breakdowns had an effect on productivity. Each machine had a tachograph (similar to those used in vehicles to record driving performance), which automatically logged when the machine was working and when it was not. Production managers also kept their own records of production within each of the departments for which they were responsible. However, the research team had to design their own productivity measures, once they found that company managers had made several changes during the study period to how they recorded productivity. Line managers had designed productivity indices that helped them to achieve the objectives set for them by the company's senior management, but there were frequent changes to corporate priorities during the study period and managers responded to shifting priorities by adjusting what they measured and how they measured it.

The task of the researcher is to interpret the data recorded in a secondary data archive in terms of particular study objectives. This might mean forming *derived* measures by aggregating variables together to form an index, or by creating rates rather than absolute amounts. For example, comparing absolute change rarely makes sense, while percentage change relative to a starting point is generally more informative. Other examples are: measures of earnings per share, which take into account differences in company capitalization; productivity indicators (such as those used in the study in the previous paragraph), which relate outputs to the resources needed to deliver them; and sickness rates for companies, which adjust number of days of recorded sickness absence according to the number of employees.

Question design

In this section of the chapter, we look at how to structure the wording of questions in interviews and surveys and how to record the responses that people give to them.

Principles in designing structured questions

There are five principles of good design when thinking about how to word questions. The first principle is that *each item should express only one idea*. If a question asks more than one thing at the same time, then it is not possible to know which one people are thinking of when they give an answer; for example, 'Do you subscribe to or read magazines or periodicals related to your profession?'

The second principle is to *avoid jargon and colloquialisms*. Jargon is insider knowledge in the form of expressions that some people (but not others) know. So using it only makes sense where it is possible to be confident that respondents are all 'in the know'. Colloquialisms are informal expressions in a language that may not be familiar to people who are not native to that country, or do not belong to a specific group. Mobile phone textspeak is becoming that, where 'cu l8r' is simple for some ('see you later') but impenetrable to others. The message is clear: play safe and use plain language.

The third principle is to *use simple expressions*. Using the active rather than the passive tense is generally better ('I did it' is better than 'It was done by me'). Dividing up complicated statements into a series of simple steps is better than expressing it all in one long sentence. Consider the question 'How many times did you eat together as a family last week?' At first glance, this seems to be unproblematic, but the following questions arise: 'Where did you eat – at home, in the car, in a restaurant?', 'What does "eat" mean – main meal, snack, take-out pizza?', 'What does "as a family" mean?'

The fourth principle is to *avoid the use of negatives*. In English, this is often done by adding 'no' or 'not' to a verb in order to give the opposite meaning, but two problems can arise. The first is that a quick read of a sentence may miss the negative, so that the respondent answers a question the wrong way around. There is research by Schmitt and Stults (1985) which suggests that around 10 per cent of respondents in large-scale studies may make this kind of mistake; and it obviously disturbs the clarity of data analysis. The second problem is that response scales such as the Likert scale are bipolar – they go from negative (*disagree*) through neutral (*not sure*) to positive (*agree*). People who feel good about something would have to show it by disagreeing with a statement worded negatively. This means it can get difficult to work out how to report what they feel.

The fifth principle is to *provide appropriate time referents* – memories fade and so asking people to think back over a long period may not give accurate responses. In general, we prefer to ask people to think about the last week or month rather than the last year when they are asked about regular day-to-day activities, because more recent events are more accessible in memory (and so asking about the last year will result in responses weighted in favour of recent events anyway). However, some events have a specific pattern, which should be reflected in question wording. For example, asking about the setting of exam papers would appropriately be phrased in terms of the 'last academic year' since such activities only occur at specific times.

The final principle is to *avoid leading questions*. The concept of a leading question comes from legal settings, where the way that a question is phrased gives a strong lead on what answer is expected. All research has an element of 'leadingness' about it – the researcher chooses what to ask about, and this focuses attention on some areas and not on others.

However, leading questions do more than this: they make it easier for the respondent to give the answer that the researcher wants, instead of the answer that the respondent thinks is right.

Exercise 9.3 gives some examples of poorly worded questions that might be asked in a questionnaire survey or an interview. Some have been taken from real research, while others have been invented to make a point. The exercise invites the reader to think through the design principles, work out what is wrong with each example question and then devise a better form of words. Like many things in life, asking clear questions seems remarkably easy until we set out to do it ourselves.

EXERCISE 9.3

Examples of poor question wording

Individual/group: For each question below:

1 What is the problem?

2 Which of the principles is violated?

3 Rewrite the question, and explain why your version works better than the original. (Clue: this might involve replacing it with more than one question.)

How strongly do you agree that smoking is harmful to health?

☐ Not at all   ☐ Slightly   ☐ Quite strongly   ☐ Very strongly

How good is your voting record in local elections?

☐ Not at all   ☐ Quite good   ☐ Very good   ☐ Excellent

If you wanted to express your opinion about genetically modified foods would you consider taking part in a boycott of your local supermarket?

☐ Not at all   ☐ Probably not   ☐ Not sure   ☐ Probably   ☐ Definitely

How much do you agree or disagree with the following: Politicians never keep the promises they make before an election, once they are in office.

☐ Strongly disagree   ☐ Disagree   ☐ Not sure   ☐ Agree   ☐ Strongly agree

How much do you agree with the following: My training supervisor is dynamic and well organized.

☐ Strongly disagree   ☐ Disagree   ☐ Not sure   ☐ Agree   ☐ Strongly agree

How much do you agree with the following: I am not satisfied with the progress of my research.

☐ Strongly disagree   ☐ Disagree   ☐ Not sure   ☐ Agree   ☐ Strongly agree

How much do you agree with the following: The presence of humorous literary allusions is conducive to an accessible presentation mode in academic pedagogy.

☐ Strongly disagree   ☐ Disagree   ☐ Not sure   ☐ Agree   ☐ Strongly agree

Guidelines for ordering questions within a survey

First, group together related questions that cover similar topics. This will allow respondents to think through different aspects of a topic and give more thoughtful answers. In employee opinion surveys, we often introduce each group of questions like this: 'The next group of questions are about how you feel about working conditions where you work'.

Second, ask about facts before opinions. In employee opinion surveys, it is better to ask factual questions first so that respondents are guided to think through what they do in their job, features of the work environment, technology, and so on. This primes people by 'walking through' their work before asking them questions about their emotional responses to work features. Starting with questions on job satisfaction runs the risk of giving ill-considered responses, which may then colour everything that comes later in the survey.

Third, place sensitive or objectionable questions near the end. Once people have answered several questions and thought through interesting issues, they are less likely to stop if they encounter something more objectionable. Well-designed surveys lead respondents to think about issues on which they may not have already worked out opinions, and so giving them time to reflect on less contentious issues may reduce their objections to 'difficult' topics.

Fourth, it is usually better to ask questions about events in the order that they occurred. In asking about different periods of employment, start from now and work backwards or start from the past and work forwards.

Measurement scales for recording responses

There are two kinds of measurement scales that quantitative researchers commonly use, and they differ according to the number of distinctions between alternative points on the measurement scale. Category scales consist of few distinctions, while continuous scales consist of many distinctions.

Category scales

Category scales may be either unordered (these are called nominal scales) or ordered (these are called ordinal scales). The difference between nominal and ordinal category scales lies in whether shuffling the assignment of numbers to categories makes any difference to the meaning of the variable. Nominal scales have no natural ordering. A study by Goldacre et al. (2004) considered the ethnic origin of UK medical consultants, recorded as White, Black, Asian, Chinese and Other. It makes no sense to treat a concept such as ethnic origin as anything other than a nominal scale since the five ethnic groups could equally well be written in any order. Similarly, studies of branded consumer products coding countries of origin could list them in any order. By contrast, ordinal scales have a natural ordering. An example of an ordinal scale is socioeconomic status, such as the classification scheme used by the UK government (the Registrar General's classification: I Professional, II Intermediate, IIIa Skilled non-manual, IIIb Skilled manual, IV Semi-skilled, V Unskilled), which is based on such criteria as educational qualifications and occupation. Similarly, honours degrees awarded to UK undergraduates are graded as first class, upper second class (2:1), lower second class (2:2) and third class. The higher the aggregate mark in assessed work, the higher the degree classification.

Sometimes, however, the status of a variable in a research study is less clear. For the purpose of recording trade flows, country of origin would be recorded on a nominal scale. However, a project on boycotts within Arab countries of consumer products might well rank

---

category scale
a form of measurement scale where responses are recorded in a small number of discrete units, for example makes of car purchased (cf. continuous scale)

continuous scale
a form of measurement scale where responses are recorded in a large number of discrete units, for example age recorded in months (cf. category scale)

nominal scale
a form of category scale where the scale units have no natural ordering, for example makes of car purchased (cf. ordinal scale)

ordinal scale
a form of category scale where the scale units have a natural ordering, for example social class (cf. nominal scale)

countries according to how closely they are associated with the USA, thus giving an ordinal scale. This illustrates an important point: that concepts or variables do not carry around with them a measurement scale that is intrinsic to them. Rather, the properties of scales are just that: properties that apply when we measure something.

The measurement of attitudes and opinions

Psychologists are not alone in being interested in what people think about things: the effect of the Lisbon Treaty on political relationships within Europe, the reputation of the company that supplies electricity, and so on. Everyone has opinions, and there is a lot of money to be made out of knowing what those opinions are. It is no surprise then that a lot of attention has gone into understanding effective ways of measuring attitudes and opinions.

Consider the statement 'My organization is a friendly place to work' (see Example 9.5). The most obvious approach would be to ask people whether or not they agree with the statement. However, this approach misses out on a lot of useful information because strength of opinion varies. To capture some of this subtlety, Rensis Likert developed a five-point response scale that still bears his name, the *Likert scale*. The scale has a neutral mid-point to allow for the possibility that an individual may have no opinion on an issue. Then, on each side of the mid-point there are two alternative response options to record moderate and extreme views for or against. Both types of attitude response scale are ordinal scales in that *agreeing* reflects a more positive attitude towards the issue raised than does *disagreeing*.

EXAMPLE 9.5

The Likert scale

My organization is a friendly place to work. How much do you agree or disagree with this statement?

☐ Strongly disagree   ☐ Disagree   ☐ Not sure   ☐ Agree   ☐ Strongly agree

Continuous scales

Continuous scales are types of ordered scale where it is possible to speak in terms of 'more' or 'less' about whatever is being measured according to the value on the scale. The difference between the two types of continuous scale, interval and ratio, lies in whether there is a true zero point. If there is a true zero point on a scale, then that gives a ratio scale; it is possible to speak meaningfully of a data point of 20 being twice as high as another data point with a value of 10 (for example). Height is measured on a true ratio scale, and we can meaningfully speak of an adult being twice as tall as a child. Time is also measured on a ratio scale, for example how long it takes for MBA graduates to get a job after their programme finishes. A graduate's income compared to what it was before joining the MBA programme is also measured on a ratio scale.

If there is no true zero point (as, for example, temperature comparison where we have Celsius and Fahrenheit scales), then we typically have an interval scale. On an interval scale, differences between alternative values can be described meaningfully, but ratios cannot. Suppose we have four data points with values of 1, 2, 9 and 10 measured on an interval scale.

ratio scale
a form of continuous scale that has a true zero point, so that ratio calculations are meaningful, for example height (cf. interval scale)

interval scale
a form of continuous scale that has no true zero point, so that ratio calculations are not meaningful, for example temperature (cf. ratio scale)

We may say that the difference between the first two data points is the same as the difference between the last two, but not that the last data point is ten times bigger than the first. Travelling from England with a temperature of 15° to Hong Kong with a temperature of 30° is a doubling of temperature when we measure in degrees Celsius but not in degrees Fahrenheit (15° Celsius is 59° Fahrenheit, while 30° Celsius is 86° Fahrenheit). Many continuous measurement scales in social science are truly interval scales rather than ratio scales. The difference is captured succinctly by asking the question: is the data still meaningful if a fixed value (say 50) were subtracted from each score? For much data on attitudes or preferences, scales are arbitrary and such an adjustment would not matter.

Measurement models

Rationale for measurement models

It is often not possible to measure directly the characteristic that a researcher is interested in, and it may be necessary to rely on indirect indicators of it. This is very common in studies using secondary data sources where variables that are present in a dataset are often used as *proxies* for constructs that are the main focus of interest but are not themselves available directly. For example, Berrone et al. (2013) used the ratio of working capital to sales as a proxy for the concept of 'organizational slack'.

Where a construct cannot be observed directly, it is common practice to select a set of items that are assumed to reflect the construct. A measurement model is the relationship between a set of observed variables and the construct that they are intended to measure. Then answers are combined together to form a composite variable to represent the construct (Spector, 1992; DeVellis, 2012).

The rationale behind this approach is that many of the characteristics that management researchers are interested in are complex (particularly in marketing and work psychology), being made up of different elements. A simplistic approach to measurement would take the following view: if we want to measure how people see the reputation of an organization, then just ask them 'Does company X have a good reputation?' While this approach has some appeal on grounds of simplicity, it scarcely does justice to the complexity of the concept of corporate reputation (Davies et al., 2002). Individuals' attitudes, motivation and commitment are all impossible to observe directly, but understanding them is key to explaining why consumers buy what they do, and why workers stay in a job or leave it. In such circumstances, the researcher is faced with the choice of whether to select a single variable for analysis or to combine several variables together into a single index. The latter approach has many advantages: it allows greater richness in measurement, capturing nuances of a construct, and it also allows the researcher to assess how reliably the construct has been measured.

The structure of measurement models

observed variables
a class of variables in a multivariate model that are directly measured; they can be used to estimate latent variables

latent variables
a class of variables within a multivariate model, which are not measured directly but are inferred from observed variables

The basic logic here is that items that reflect features of an underlying construct will show common patterns of answering. For example, a manager who feels good about his or her job will tend to respond in a consistently favourable way to questions about different aspects of that job. Consistency in responses from study participants will produce correlations among items, and these correlations are the starting point for identifying patterns that reflect underlying constructs. In a measurement model, the observed variables are those that are measured directly by the researcher, and the latent variables are the constructs that the researcher assumes are causal factors influencing how sample members respond to the observed variables.

EXAMPLE 9.6

Identifying measurement models

A hot topic among HR professionals is that of employee engagement and its possible link to business success. Investigating this relationship requires great care, and involves a number of steps:

1. The first step identifies the variables involved. The sentence above proposes a causal relationship between two variables (let us call them EE for employee engagement, and BS for business success), where EE → BS.

2. In the second step we consider both variables in turn, and it quickly becomes pretty clear that we cannot measure either of them in a direct way. The success of a business could be assessed in a variety of ways, and the same applies to employee engagement. So both EE and BS are really latent variables, and for each one we need to specify a number of observed variables, which can be used to indicate the value of the latent variable. For example, the kinds of behaviours we might associate with an engaged employee are: putting effort into work over and above what is required; staying in the organization despite offers of better pay elsewhere; taking the initiative to solve work-related problems; praising the organization as a good place to work.

common factors a class of latent variables in a measurement model, which are assumed to account for the covariances among a set of observed variables (see also specific factors)

factor loading the weight allocated to the path between a latent variable and an observed variable in a measurement model

specific factors a class of latent variables in a measurement model, which is assumed to account for idiosyncratic aspects of an observed variable (see also common factors)

Figure 9.1 shows a measurement model for six measured (observed) variables and two unmeasured latent variables. The model distinguishes between two influences on how respondents answer for each observed variable:

- Those that reflect common features of the constructs being assessed, indicated by the two common factors. The first common factor is what respondents are assumed to have in mind when they respond to variables 1–3, while the second common factor is assumed to influence answers for variables 4–6. The stronger the influence of the common factors (this is the value attached to each of the paths in Figure 9.1, and is called a factor loading), the higher will be the correlations among the observed variables.

- Those that are idiosyncratic to the wording of each variable, indicated by the specific factors, one for each observed variable. These are unique to that question and will not influence answers to other questions.

exploratory factor analysis (EFA) a multivariate method for fitting measurement models, which describes the covariances among a set of observed variables in terms of a set of latent variables (see also confirmatory factor analysis)

confirmatory factor analysis (CFA) a multivariate method for testing measurement models of the relationship between a set of observed variables and a hypothesized set of latent variables (see also exploratory factor analysis)

Analysis methods for measurement models: CFA and EFA

Sometimes, the researcher has a set of questionnaire items with no clear idea of what constructs might underlie them, and here the method of choice for analysing the measurement model is exploratory factor analysis (EFA). More commonly, though, researchers know what constructs they are trying to measure and design their questionnaires to do just that. In that case, the aim is not to explore what constructs there might be but rather to confirm (or otherwise) a structure that has been designed into a study. This leads to confirmatory factor analysis (CFA) as the method of choice. Both types of model share a distinction between common factors and specific factors. Where the methods differ is in the prior specification of a measurement model. EFA analyses can be carried out by many general purpose statistical packages, such as SPSS (Bryman and Cramer, 2004; Blunch, 2008; Field, 2017); while CFA requires one of the specialist structural equation model programs, which we consider in Chapter 11.

In the EFA method, there may be as many common factors as there are observed variables, and all the observed variables have loadings on all the common factors. Two methods in use are common factor analysis and principal components analysis, and both methods derive estimates for the factor loadings of each of the common factors and the specific factors, and give summary indices (called eigenvalues) of the importance of each of the common factors, shown by how much of the covariation among the observed variables each one accounts for. The researcher uses these estimates to select a subset of common factors, usually retaining only the largest. The size of the loadings for the common factors determines the correlations among the observed variables. The size of the loadings for the specific factors determines the reliability of the common factors.

In the CFA method, the researcher defines in advance how many common factors are expected and the pattern of predicted loadings for observed variables. The common factors represent the latent variables that the researcher is interested in measuring: one factor for each latent variable. Observed variables are selected specifically to measure each of the latent variables, and so these observed variables are usually assumed to load on only one factor. The method derives estimates for each of the factor loadings for common factors and for specific factors, and gives an overall test statistic for how well the measurement model fits the data. Ullman (2006) gives a readable introduction to CFA with particular reference to personality assessment, and shows how measurement models can be fitted and tested using structural equation modelling (SEM) software.

eigenvalues
the term used in exploratory factor analysis for the summary measure of the amount of variance in the observed variables accounted for by a factor

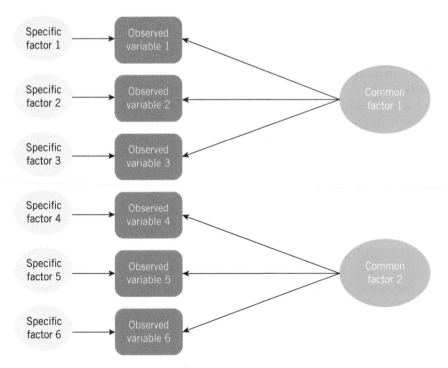

FIGURE 9.1   Measurement model for six observed variables and two latent variables

EXAMPLE 9.7

Measurement models for measures of work design characteristics: EFA and CFA results

This example takes six variables from the dataset used by Sprigg and Jackson (2006) in their study of the impact of work design on the health of call handlers in UK call centres. The variables fall into two groups: three items measuring timing control (TC), the extent to which call handlers had control over work timing; and skill utilization (SU), how much their work enabled them to use the skills they had. The sample was large, over 1,000 people drawn from a large number of call centres throughout the UK.

The matrix of correlations is shown in Table 9.5(a), and the high correlations are emboldened. It is clear that they form two groups reflecting the constructs that the items were designed to measure. The factor loadings from exploratory factor analysis are shown in Table 9.5(b). The first thing to note is that there are two factors, as would be expected, and that all six variables have loadings on both factors. The second thing to note is that the loadings of the three timing control items are very high on the first factor, but very low on the second factor, while the reverse is true for the skill utilization items (again, the high values are emboldened). It would be reasonable to label the two factors according to the content of the times that load on them, and that is what we have done in Table 9.5. However, this is an inference on our part; the statistical analysis is agnostic about what these latent variables are called.

Table 9.5(c) gives the factor loadings for confirmatory factor analysis, and the major difference is that each item is constrained to load onto one factor. The values of zero are called *fixed values* because they were constrained as part of the input specification for CFA. The reason is that we hypothesized that the first three items would measure a timing control construct and the second three items would measure a skill utilization construct. The factor loadings from CFA are not identical to those given by the EFA analysis because the models that were fitted to the data are different, but the conclusion is broadly the same. Finally, the measurement model from CFA is shown diagrammatically in Figure 9.2.

TABLE 9.5   Measurement model for measures of work design characteristics: EFA and CFA results

(a) Matrix of correlations among variables

	TC1	TC2	TC3	SU1	SU2	SU3
TC1	–					
TC2	**.40**	–				
TC3	**.48**	**.45**	–			
SU1	.16	.16	.14	–		
SU2	.16	.18	.15	**.52**	–	
SU3	.16	.15	.13	**.55**	**.56**	–

(Continued)

(b) Factor loadings from exploratory factor analysis

	Timing control	Skill utilization
TC1	**.78**	.10
TC2	**.76**	.11
TC3	**.82**	.06
SU1	.09	**.82**
SU2	.12	**.82**
SU3	.09	**.84**

(c) Factor loadings from confirmatory factor analysis

	Timing control	Skill utilization
TC1	.61	0
TC2	.67	0
TC3	.63	0
SU1	0	.78
SU2	0	.73
SU3	0	.71

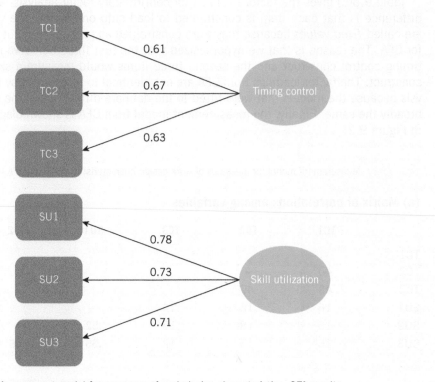

FIGURE 9.2   Measurement model for measures of work design characteristics: CFA results

Conclusion

The assumption that underlies the methods described in this chapter is that the researcher uses quantitative data derived from a sample in order to draw conclusions about a defined population. The material we have covered in this chapter includes:

- Types of sampling design and the criteria that the researcher can use to select a form of design that is appropriate for a specific purpose.

- Sources of both primary and secondary data, emphasizing the issues involved in using each source, which can affect the quality of data that are available for analysis.

- The process of measurement.

At each stage of the data collection process, decisions made by the researcher can influence the quality of data that can be obtained and the inferences that can be made from that data about the character of the population of interest. The next two chapters describe methods for analysing quantitative data. In Chapter 10, we first consider ways of summarizing key features of data and then examine the principles and practice of hypothesis testing that allow the researcher to make inferences about populations based on evidence from samples. Chapter 10 considers univariate tests, taking one variable at a time, and Chapter 11 extends this treatment to cover the multivariate case where many variables are dealt with simultaneously.

Further reading

The following two texts describe the System of Multiple Level Observation of Groups (SYMLOG), which is a more detailed elaboration of the IPA:

Bales, R.F., Cohen, S.P. and Williamson, S.A. (1979) *SYMLOG: A System for the Multiple Level Observation of Groups*. New York: The Free Press.

Bales, R.F. (1988) 'A new overview of the SYMLOG system: measuring and changing behavior in groups', in R.B. Polley, A.P. Hare and P.J. Stone (eds), *The SYMLOG Practitioner*. New York: Praeger, pp. 319–44.

This is a useful source for web-based surveys:

Callegaro, M., Manfreda, K.L. and Vehovar, V. (2015) *Web Survey Methodology*. Thousand Oaks, CA: Sage.

Covers the foundations of scale construction and measurement in an accessible manner:

DeVellis, R.F. (2012) *Scale Development: Theory and Applications*, 3rd edn. Thousand Oaks, CA: Sage.

Another useful source for web-based surveys:

Dillman, D.A., Smyth, J.D. and Christian, L.M. (2014) *Internet, Mail, and Mixed-Mode Surveys: The Tailored Design Method*, 4th edn. New York: John Wiley.

A discussion of emerging trends around big data in business and management research:

George, G., Haas, M.R. and Pentland, A. (2014) 'Big data and management', *Academy of Management Journal*, 57: 321–6.

A comprehensive and easy-to-follow guide to using secondary data sources, with special relevance to social surveys:

MacInnes, J. (2017) *An Introduction to Secondary Data Analysis with IBM SPSS Statistics*. Thousand Oaks, CA: Sage.

A comprehensive handbook with a useful introduction to assessing social variables, scales and indexes:

Miller, D.C. and Salkind, N.J. (2002) *Handbook of Research Design & Social Measurement*, 6th edn. Thousand Oaks, CA: Sage.

A comprehensive introduction to the principles of survey research:

Sapsford, R. (2006) *Survey Research*, 2nd edn. London: Sage.

A practical introduction to quantitative methods for beginners with a helpful part on data collection:

Waters, C.D.J. (2011) *Quantitative Methods for Business*, 5th edn. Harlow: Financial Times/Prentice Hall.

Check your understanding online

Visit the website **https://edge.sagepub.com/easterbysmith6e** for useful resources that will help reinforce what you've read in this chapter:

Take an interactive quiz to test your understanding of the key topics

Review suggested answers to Exercises 9.1 to 9.3 above

Use interactive flashcards to check your knowledge of essential concepts

Learning objectives

To be able to choose effective ways of summarizing key features of data.

To know which summary measures to use for location and spread of data.

To understand which statistical tests to use when comparing groups and testing association between variables.

SUMMARIZING AND MAKING INFERENCES FROM QUANTITATIVE DATA

10

Introduction

Big data
skills

The most obvious feature of quantitative data – evidence expressed in the form of numbers – is their sheer quantity, especially in the age of big data. It is generally expensive in time and money to accumulate good quality data, and so researchers make the most of each study participant by collecting as much data as possible from each person, and quantitative research designs also often involve large samples. The big challenge then is seeing the wood for the trees – identifying patterns in numerical data and making sense of those patterns. In this chapter, we address this in two parts. First, we consider the key features of numerical data, focusing on both the common statistical indices that are used to assess those features, and on the graphical methods for visualizing numerical data (Kirk, 2016). The second part of the chapter introduces the logic of statistical inference as a tool for 'going beyond the data' and introduces a variety of statistical tests for looking at data one variable at a time.

summarizing
describing a
characteristic of
a dataset such
as location or
spread based
on aggregating
data from all
respondents

Quantitative methods are an important part of the research process in management and business. Table 10.1 gives some examples from two of the leading journals in strategy and marketing of research questions addressed using quantitative data. Behind the most sophisticated research question and the most complex datasets is a simple basic principle. All quantitative researchers do the same two things: they identify what features tell the best story about the data (we call this summarizing the data); and then they look for patterns in the data that can be used to draw conclusions about the study's research questions (we call this making inferences about populations based on sample data).

TABLE 10.1 Examples of studies using quantitative methods from *Strategic Management Journal* and *Journal of Marketing*

State-owned enterprises (SOEs) in China (Ralston et al., 2006). They compared the organizational cultures of state-owned enterprises with private-owned enterprises and foreign-owned businesses in order to decide whether SOEs are dinosaurs or dynamos for China's economic future.

Should multinational enterprises (MNEs) adapt their marketing strategy to each market or standardize across markets? (Katsikeas et al., 2006). They looked at the international marketing strategies of US, Japanese and German MNEs operating in the UK. They found that standardization only makes sense when there is a good fit to the market environment.

Knowledge transfer in business-to-business relationships (Dyer and Hatch, 2006). They found that Toyota were much better than US car companies (GM, Ford and Chrysler) in getting better quality out of their suppliers. They concluded that there can be specific capabilities within relationships between customers and suppliers that are not easily transferable to other relationships.

How to influence a company on environmental issues (Eesley and Lenox, 2006). They used a database of secondary stakeholder actions to check out what it takes to get positive responses out of companies.

Home or away? Where to put your HQ (Birkinshaw et al., 2006). They found that MNEs put their business unit headquarters overseas when it made sense for *internal* reasons; while the location of their corporate HQ was influenced most strongly by the demands of *external* stakeholders – global financial markets and shareholders.

Is corporate social responsibility (CSR) smart as well as good? (Luo and Bhattacharya, 2006). They used secondary data archives to test the link between CSR activities such as cash donations and employee volunteerism, customer satisfaction and the market value of the firm. They found that CSR can be smart – good for the company – but there is a dark side too.

What do website visitors value on a manufacturer's site? (Steenkamp and Geyskens, 2006). The authors found that the answer depends on the country where the consumers live. They looked at over 8,000 consumers from 23 countries, visiting the sites of 16 consumer packaged goods companies.

The idea behind summarizing and making inferences is a simple one, which can be illustrated quite easily. The year 2010 was a bad one for BP, following the explosion on the Deepwater Horizon drilling rig, which killed 11 people and led to a massive leak of oil into the Gulf of Mexico. The company's share price showed a high of 655 and a low of 302 for the year, reflecting the impact of the explosion on the investment community's view of BP's reputation and its future viability. Behind the bald figures of share price movements is also an inference process – one might say a kind of guesswork or betting – that predicts the future profits of BP, based on its past performance. The judgements of investment analysts are based on an inference process (not formal statistical inference, but rather informed guesswork) about future data on the performance of BP. Management researchers follow the same kinds of inference processes when they make judgements about the world based on their data.

Example datasets for the chapter

This chapter uses datasets from a variety of sources. Table 10.2 shows the midday temperature for selected world locations on Thursday 2 December 2010. The lowest temperature recorded in the table is a distinctly cold –15°C in Moscow; while the highest temperature is a very pleasant (but perhaps rather humid) 33°C in Bangkok. The table itself is presented in alphabetical order according to the name of the location, and so it is not easy to gain much of an impression of what this body of data looks like.

TABLE 10.2   Maximum midday temperatures for 94 world locations, Thursday 2 December 2010

Alicante	N	13	Madeira	N	18
Amsterdam	N	–6	Madrid	N	5
Athens	N	23	Majorca	N	14
Auckland	S	19	Malaga	N	15
Bahrain	N	24	Malta	N	20
Bangkok	T	33	Melbourne	S	23
Barbados	T	29	Mexico City	T	15
Barcelona	N	9	Miami	N	28
Beijing	N	4	Milan	N	1
Beirut	N	25	Mombasa	T	31
Belgrade	N	8	Moscow	N	–15
Berlin	N	–8	Mumbai	T	32
Bermuda	N	20	Munich	N	–4
Bordeaux	N	2	Nairobi	T	25
Brussels	N	–5	Naples	N	15
Bucharest	N	0	New Orleans	N	12
Budapest	N	1	New York	N	15
Buenos Aires	S	30	Nice	N	10
Cairo	N	22	Nicosia	N	24
Calcutta	T	26	Oslo	N	–14
Canberra	S	24	Paris	N	–2
Cape Town	S	26	Perth	S	24

(Continued)

TABLE 10.2 (Continued)

Chicago	N	−4	Prague	N	−10
Copenhagen	N	−2	Reykjavik	N	−2
Corfu	N	0	Riga	N	−8
Delhi	N	22	Rio de Janeiro	T	29
Dubai	N	28	Riyadh	N	22
Dublin	N	−1	Rome	N	14
Faro	N	14	San Francisco	N	9
Florence	N	12	Santiago	S	21
Frankfurt	N	−7	Sao Paulo	S	26
Geneva	N	−1	Seoul	N	12
Gibraltar	N	13	Seychelles	T	25
Harare	T	18	Singapore	T	31
Helsinki	N	−3	St Petersburg	N	−9
Hong Kong	T	23	Stockholm	N	−12
Honolulu	T	28	Sydney	S	25
Istanbul	N	21	Tel Aviv	N	28
Jerusalem	N	28	Tenerife	N	21
Johannesburg	S	26	Tokyo	N	21
Kuala Lumpur	T	30	Toronto	N	16
Lanzarote	N	20	Vancouver	N	7
Las Palmas	N	21	Venice	N	4
Lima	T	21	Vienna	N	0
Lisbon	N	11	Warsaw	N	−8
Los Angeles	N	19	Washington	N	6
Luxor	N	27	Zurich	N	−3

Source: The Times, 3 December 2010

Note: N indicates north of the Tropic of Cancer, S indicates south of the Tropic of Capricorn, and T indicates a city in the tropics

Stem and leaf plot

Figure 10.1 uses a stem and leaf plot to organize the data in a rather more helpful way. This form of display groups the data into a number of categories (called 'stems'), and then shows the number of data points within each category (each data point is called a 'leaf'). The stems are labelled according to the second digit of each data value. At the bottom of the plot, the temperatures of 30°C and higher are grouped under the stem labelled as '3', the temperatures of 20–29°C are grouped under the stem labelled '2', and so on. The lowest temperatures of −10°C and below are grouped together at the top of the plot under the stem labelled '−1'. In this plot, there are six stems, and the column to the left shows how many leaves there are attached to each stem. There are four locations in the coldest category (stem value −1), and the leaf shows the second digit of the temperature for each one: Prague (−10°C), Stockholm (−12°C), Oslo (−14°C) and Moscow (−15°C). The next stem is labelled '−0' and holds the leaves showing locations with temperatures between −1°C and −9°C. The frequency column shows that there are 16 of these locations, and with the exception of Chicago and Reykjavik they are all in Europe. As some UK readers may remember,

December 2010 was a period of record low temperatures. At the other end of the distribution, the plot shows six locations with temperatures of 30°C or more: Bangkok, Mumbai, Buenos Aires, Kuala Lumpur, Singapore and Mombasa.

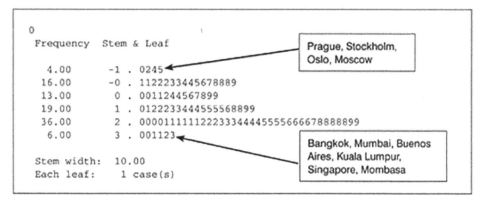

FIGURE 10.1   Stem and leaf plot for world temperature data

Having introduced the dataset, we now turn to describe different ways of summarizing key features of the data.

Summarizing and describing data

world temperatures

There are three sections to this part of the chapter. The first looks at ways of showing the shape of data distributions, and it capitalizes on the highly developed capabilities that humans have for seeing visual patterns. The second section considers a variety of measures that summarize data in terms of different attributes. The third section draws out two formal characteristics of summary measures that we can use to help us understand why alternative measures work the way that they do. These formal characteristics give the criteria for making smart choices about which summary measures to use in practical situations.

bar chart a form of graphical summary for category scales, with bars whose length indicates the frequency of responses for each category

Showing the shape of data distributions

Although Table 10.2 reports the temperature scores, the general shape of this set of data is difficult to visualize from a table of numbers. Many of the characteristics of data distributions that have important consequences for analysis and interpretation can be seen very easily provided that data can be displayed informatively. Kirk (2016) gives a handy summary of different chart type options for representing data graphically. Two obvious forms of data display are provided by most statistical packages, including SPSS, R and Excel: bar charts and histograms. A bar chart summarizes the distribution of a category variable: bars are drawn to represent each category and the length of the bar reflects the number of cases in the category – the more people, the longer the bar. If variables are measured on an ordinal scale, then it would be strange to do other than order the bars in the chart accordingly. For variables on a nominal scale, where the categories are not ordered, it makes sense to apply some thought to how to order the bars on the chart. A histogram is a bar chart drawn for a continuous variable, after grouping adjacent scale points together.

histogram a form of bar chart for continuous scales, where scale points are first grouped together and the length of bars indicates the frequency of responses for each category

Bar charts

Figure 10.2 shows a bar chart for the temperature data from Table 10.2. Along the bottom of the chart is the measurement scale for the variable, the temperature in Celsius, and it runs from –15°, the lowest value recorded in this dataset, through to +33°, the highest value recorded for these data. Essentially, the bar chart is a visual representation of the frequency table. Each figure in the frequency distribution is translated into the height of a bar in Figure 10.2. The height of each bar is marked by the vertical axis of the figure, labelled 'frequency', and this shows how many respondents gave each alternative response. The higher the bar, the more respondents recorded this answer.

frequency distribution
a summary representation of a sample of data containing the number of responses obtained for each alternative on the measurement scale

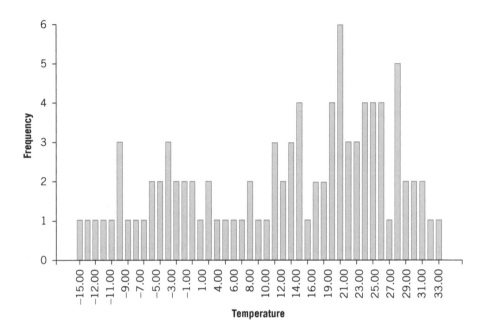

FIGURE 10.2   Bar chart for the world temperature data from Table 10.2

EXERCISE 10.1

Bar chart for separate groups

Individual: Table 10.2 groups the 94 cities according to latitude: N indicates north of the Tropic of Cancer, S indicates south of the Tropic of Capricorn, and T indicates a city in the tropics. Since there are very few southern cities in this dataset, it makes sense to combine the southern and the tropical cities together. Repeat the analysis in Figure 10.2 separately for the northern region and for the combined southern and tropical regions. You could either show them as two separate charts, or combine them in a back-to-back bar chart. What do the charts show?

Histograms

A histogram is a special form of bar chart, with the points on the scale grouped into a smaller and more manageable number of categories. The histogram in Figure 10.3 shows the temperature data with the 94 different scores grouped together into 15 categories instead of 45. The labels on the horizontal axis are the mid-points of the categories shown by each bar. Histograms have immediate visual appeal and show gross features of data very easily. The peak in the data around 20°C is more obvious, and the 'holes' in the data have been hidden by combining categories together. The shape is thus smoother to the eye. We can also see that there are more values at the top end of the scale than there are at the bottom. These data are not completely symmetrical.

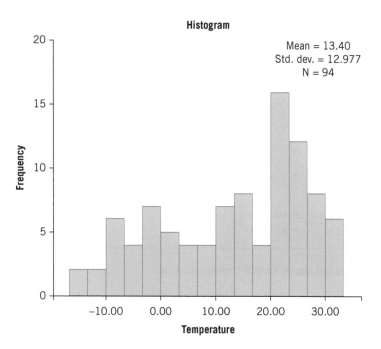

FIGURE 10.3   Histogram for temperature data from Table 10.2

This chapter started with Table 10.2 showing 94 temperature values, but it is obviously impossible to carry all that information around in one's head. Instead, it is much more efficient to capture some key features of the data in convenient summary form. This section covers three features of data that are most informative and most useful: location, spread and symmetry. We will describe summary measures of some of these key features of data, and following that we will examine a number of formal properties of summary measures that will make it easier to make choices between alternatives.

Summary measures of location

The obvious starting point for summarizing a large set of data is with an index that locates the data as a whole on its measurement scale: in general *high*, *middling* or *low*. For example, if there is a risk to consumers due to contamination of a batch of chocolate during manufacture (as in the case of Cadbury's chocolate early in 2006), then how big is the risk? Is it

location a characteristic of a set of data that summarizes where the data are located on the measurement scale; measured by the mode, median, mid-mean or mean

spread a characteristic of a set of data that summarizes how much the data vary around a measure of location; measured by the range, mid-range or standard deviation

symmetry a balanced distribution of data points around a central value

Central tendency

so minute that any impact on community health would be hard to detect, as the company argued when challenged by the UK Health and Safety Executive? Whatever the researcher is interested in measuring, and however large or small the dataset, most people would be interested in where on its measurement scale the data as a whole are located. Four summary measures of location are commonly used – the mode, the median, the mean and the mid-mean – and we now consider each one in turn, using data on the pay for chief executives of US companies. Overall compensation data for the 200 highest paid CEOs in the USA in 2009 are reported in www.Forbes.com, and summarized in Figure 10.4. The lowest total compensation is $6.86 million, and the highest compensation is a scarcely believable $556.98 million.

CEO
compensation

```
$million Stem and Leaf

Frequency   Stem and Leaf

  63.00         0 . 666677777777777777777777777788888888888888889999
                    9999999999999999
  49.00         1 . 000000000000011111111111111112222222222222333333444
  28.00         1 . 5555555666667778888888899999
  12.00         2 . 001223333444
  13.00         2 . 5555666788899
   9.00         3 . 000123334
   8.00         3 . 56668899
   3.00         4 . 224
  15.00 Extremes    (>=48)

Stem width:    10.00
Each leaf:      1 case(s)
```

FIGURE 10.4   Stem and leaf display for CEO compensation data

Mode

mode
a summary
measure of
location; the
most frequently
occurring value
in a dataset

The mode is a simple form of summary measure of location: it is the commonest value among a set of scores. For some purposes, the mode as a measure of location can be informative (i.e. the music charts focus on who sells the most copies of their work), but the mode does have some quite severe drawbacks. The original CEO compensation data are reported in $million rounded to two decimal places; and almost all values are unique – there is no single modal value. However, the stem and leaf plot (Figure 10.4) shows the scores as whole numbers, and the modal compensation value is $7m. Grouping the scores together in different ways would create a different modal value depending on how the grouping is done. Thus, a problem with the mode as a summary of location for data on a continuous scale is that it depends upon how scores are grouped. A second problem is that it ignores the rest of the data and conveys nothing at all about what other values there might be in the data. Finally, there may be more than one mode, so that this measure of location need not have a unique value. All in all then, the mode is rarely a serious tool for summarizing location of data in business and management research.

median
a summary
measure of
location that
uses the ranks
of all the values
in a dataset in
its calculation;
the middle value
in an ordered
set of data
points

Median

The median is the middle value once scores have been placed in rank order, either from largest to smallest or from smallest to largest. It is the value that divides a set of data in half.

Where there is an even number of data points, the median is halfway between the middle two, in this case $12.86m. For an odd number of data points, the median is simply the middle one, counting in from either end. The median has some important properties, which are easy to grasp intuitively:

- Every observation in the data contributes something to determining the value of the median, unlike the mode. That makes the median more meaningful as a summary measure of location because it uses more of the information in the data in estimating location.

- Most of the data points do not contribute much – it is the rank position of a data point that matters rather than its precise value. That makes the median less efficient than it might be (it throws away the values of each observation and replaces them with rank-order information), but it has the great advantage that the median is insensitive to odd things happening to extreme scores. Adding a million to the largest data point (perhaps by forgetting to put in the decimal point when entering the data) does nothing to the median because it does not change the fact that this is still the largest data point. It also makes the median useful where the measurement scale is not particularly precise, and the researcher cannot be certain of the accuracy of the numbers.

- The median works better for data where the category at the top of a grouped continuous scale is open-ended. Examples include:

  - Family size may be judged on the basis of the number of children, and it often happens that the largest category is recorded as more than three (or four or five) children. These data will underestimate the actual number of children in a sample of families.

  - Data on survival rates following exposure to toxic hazards in the workplace will typically be over-estimates if they include people who were exposed to the hazard but are still alive at the time that data are collected.

- This kind of grouping of data at one end of the scale is called *censoring*. It gives no trouble at all for calculating the median, whether the censoring is at the bottom of the scale (left censoring) or at the top of the scale (right censoring).

Mean

The mean is the average value formed by adding all the scores and dividing by how many data points there are. The formula for the mean is:

$$M = \Sigma(X) / n$$

where M stands for the mean, X represents each data value, n indicates how many data points there are, and the Σ symbol is a summation sign. The mean CEO compensation level for top US CEOs is $23.4m. Just like the median, every score contributes to forming the mean, but the mean differs because it takes into account how big each score is. This can be both a benefit and a disadvantage. By using the mean as a summary measure of location, the researcher can be confident of making the most of the information in the data about where the data are centred. However, using the mean assumes that each data point is accurately recorded.

mean
a summary measure of location that uses all the values in a dataset in its calculation; the sum of all data points divided by the sample size

Mid-mean

The mid-mean is an average formed by first removing scores equally from both extremes of a dataset and then working out the mean of the remainder. It is part of a family of summary measures called trimmed means, which differ in how much is trimmed from each end of the distribution of data points. The mean is a zero per cent trimmed mean (with nothing trimmed), while the median is a 50 per cent trimmed mean. The mid-mean is a 25 per cent trimmed mean, the mean of the middle half of the data. It uses rank-order information (like the median) to select data points to ignore, but then uses the data values themselves (like the mean) to calculate the summary index.

Comparing summary measures of location

The different summary measures of location for the CEO compensation data in Figure 10.4 are:

Mode: $7m (data rounded to nearest whole number of millions)

Median: $12.86m

5 per cent trimmed mean: $17.37m

Mean: $23.44m

There are substantial differences between these estimates of where the centre of the data lies. The modal (or commonest) value is around $7m, while the median shows that half of the top 200 CEOs earn $12.86m or more (of course, the other half of the sample earn less than $12.86m). The mean gives the highest value of all, $23.44m, which is more than three times as much as the modal value.

Why do the summary measures of location differ so much? Figure 10.5, which shows that the data for the top CEOs are highly skewed, gives a clue. Three-quarters of the top 200 CEOs earn less than $30m, while those at the very top of the ranking list earn substantially more than that, with the highest paid CEO alone earning $556.98m (the same total compensation package as the bottom 65 CEOs in the sample combined). The median is based on the ranks of the scores, while the mean takes the size of each data point into account. Thus, the highest paid individual's salary influences the mean but not the median.

Which of these summary measures is most useful? The answer is that all of them are useful but for different purposes, while none of them is universally useful. Each summary measure captures different aspects of the data, which contain information about the feature of locatedness. When researchers calculate one of these summary measures to report where a dataset as a whole is located on its measurement scale, they are implicitly making a judgement about what matters in the data. If they want to emphasize what is typical (in the sense of commonest), they might prefer the mode. However, attention on inequalities in income in an organization, for instance, might lead someone to choose the median, which will show that half of the organization earns less than £x, while another group might prefer the mean because it takes into account the much higher pay of the most senior officials in the organization, which makes the pay levels look generally higher.

The most widely used summaries of location are the mean and the median. Less common, but useful, are the mid-mean and other forms of the trimmed mean. An important point to note is that even something as simple as working out an average is a choice. The consequences of making different choices about summary measures of location depend very much on the characteristics of a specific dataset, and which features of the data the researcher wishes to emphasize.

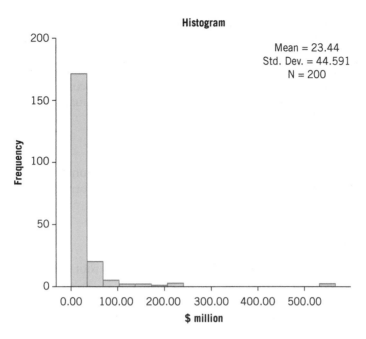

FIGURE 10.5   Histogram for CEO compensation data from Figure 10.4

Summary measures of spread

Most samples of data will contain variability around a central value, with some people scoring higher than others. How much spread there is around a measure of location is a valuable way of capturing something extra about a dataset as a whole. Three common measures of spread are: the range, the mid-range and the standard deviation. Like the measures of location considered in the previous section, each one captures different aspects of data.

Range

The range is the distance between the largest and the smallest scores. For the temperature data in Table 10.2, the lowest recorded midday temperature was −15°C and the highest was 33°C, so the range is 33 − −15 = 48°C. On a single day then, the spread of temperatures across a sample of locations in the world was enormous. The range of CEO compensation scores in Figure 10.4 is also large ($556.98m − $6.86m = $550.12m). While the range is easy to calculate, it is also potentially very misleading. Most people have seen the banner headlines in shop windows 'Up to 50 per cent off'. This means that at least one item is discounted by this much, but says nothing about how many other items are treated in the same way. Any summary index based on an extreme statistic (either largest or smallest) can be dangerously misleading.

Mid-range (interquartile range)

The mid-range is the range of the middle half of the data, calculated by dividing the data into quarters. The values in the data that mark the boundaries between four equal-sized segments are called 'quartiles', and the mid-range is the difference between the first quartile and the third quartile. It is often given the name interquartile range. Calculating the

range
a summary measure of spread; the difference between the largest and smallest data values

mid-range
a summary measure of spread; the range of the middle half of the data

interquartile range
see mid-range

mid-range starts in the same way as calculating the mid-mean: trim off the top and bottom quarter of the data values. Then, the mid-range is the difference between the largest and the smallest values in the middle half of the data: for the CEO compensation data in Figure 10.4, the mid-range is $14.98m. The mid-range gives a better indication of how diverse the data are, especially where the data are skewed by a few extreme scores at either end. Note that the compensation package for the highest paid CEO has a dramatic effect on the range, but none at all on the mid-range.

Standard deviation

standard deviation (SD)
a summary measure of spread; based on the average deviation of scores around the mean

The standard deviation (SD) measures the average spread around the mean; it is the most typical distance (or deviation) of scores from the mean. The formula for the standard deviation is:

$$SD = \sqrt{(\Sigma(X-M)^2 / n-1)}$$

where SD stands for the standard deviation, $\sqrt{}$ is the square root symbol and the other symbols are the same as in the formula for the mean.

variance
a summary measure of spread used in calculating the standard deviation; the average deviation of scores around the mean

The SD is calculated by working out the average squared deviation around the mean (this is called the variance) and then taking the square root. For each data point in turn, first work out how far it is above or below the mean (these are called 'deviations'). The mean of the scores in Figure 10.4 is 23.44, so the deviations around the mean are calculated like this:

$$556.98 - 23.44 = 533.54$$

$$222.64 - 23.44 = 199.20$$

$$\ldots$$

$$6.87 - 23.44 = -16.57$$

$$6.86 - 23.44 = -16.58$$

Next, each of the deviations is squared to remove the ± sign, and the average squared deviation is calculated by dividing by the number of items minus one. This gives the variance. The reasoning behind subtracting one before calculating the mean deviation is technical – dividing by $n-1$ rather than n makes the sample SD an unbiased estimate of the population SD. Finally, take the square root of the variance to give the standard deviation. For these data, the variance (based on $200 - 1 = 199$ as the sample size) is 1988.38, and the standard deviation is 44.59.

Comparing summary measures of spread

Just as we argued for summary measures of location, there is no single answer to the question of which measure of spread is most useful. The range is a measure of how much of the measurement scale is covered by sample data, from largest to smallest. This is sometimes useful to know, but is heavily influenced by a few extreme scores, while the mid-range is more informative, especially for data that are distributed symmetrically and follow roughly a bell-shaped curve.

The most widely used summaries of spread are the standard deviation and the mid-range, and measures of location and spread tend to be paired together. Thus, the mean and the standard deviation are the basis for many parametric significance tests, while the median and the mid-range are the basis for many non-parametric significance tests. Both types of test are described in the next section of this chapter.

The importance of symmetry

A third characteristic of the shape of a set of data is the extent to which scores are distributed evenly around a central value; that is, whether the data are symmetrical. *Positively* skewed data, such as the CEO compensation data in Figure 10.4, have many small values concentrated together and few large values. Most of the data are located at the low end of the distribution, while only 15 CEOs out of 200 receive extremely high pay packages. By contrast, *negatively* skewed data have many large values concentrated together at the top of the distribution and few small ones strung out at the bottom.

Why pay attention to symmetry in data? This feature is important for two reasons. Extreme values at either end of a distribution (but most likely at the high end of the range) may indicate gross errors, for which reason they should be sought out (perhaps by looking to a completed questionnaire in order to correct transcription errors, or by returning to the source of derived data) and correct values inserted instead. Data that are strongly asymmetrical are less naturally described in terms of summary measures of location. When data are symmetrical the mean and median will tend to coincide, while a symmetrical and unimodal distribution will tend to have the modal value (the most frequently occurring one) at the same point as the mean and median. When data are skewed, the different summary measures will not coincide. The mean will be influenced by the relatively small number of extreme scores, while the median will not be because it simply records the value below which 50 per cent of the scores lie.

We can summarize both location and spread for one or more variables in graphical form using the boxplot (also called the box-and-whisker plot). The plot shows a bar at the median value (the fiftieth percentile), and the box around it shows the spread of data between the first quartile (the 25th percentile) and the third quartile (the 75th percentile). The whiskers vary between forms of display, but most will also include the highest and lowest values excluding extreme outliers.

EXERCISE 10.2

Boxplot for grouped temperature data

Individual: Repeat the analysis of exercise 10.1 but this time show the results for each of the two groups (the northern hemisphere group of cities and the combined southern hemisphere and tropical groups of cities) in the form of boxplots. What are the main features of each group as shown by the boxplot, and what are the main differences?

> robustness
> the extent to which a summary measure is sensitive to disturbances in data quality

Formal features of summary measures

This section looks at two characteristics of summary measures, robustness and efficiency, which give a stronger conceptual basis for the choices that a researcher makes between alternative summary measures of location or spread.

Robustness

The extent to which a summary measure is sensitive to disturbances in data quality is known as robustness. There has been a lot of work by statisticians examining the consequences of

Robustness defined

robustness (or the lack of it) for commonly used summary indices and analyses that are based on them (see Jackson, 1986). Disturbances in data quality can arise either from small changes to many data values (e.g. by grouping of values on a measurement scale into a few categories) or by large errors in a few data values (e.g. by transcription errors). A summary measure is robust if disturbances like these do not greatly alter its value, while summary measures that are very sensitive to such disturbances are not robust.

We now examine three of the summary measures of location: the mean, the median and the mid-mean. Since the *mean* is the total of all the data points divided by the sample size, changing even a single data point through a transcription error would alter the mean. The more extreme the value introduced in error, the bigger the influence on the value of the mean. Similarly, small changes to all of the data values through, for example, grouping adjacent scores together on the measurement scale, would also alter the mean. It is obvious, therefore, that the mean is not very robust.

Since the *median* is based on the ranked scores, the effect of a single transcription error would be small, and if the error were made with either the largest or the smallest data value the median would not change at all. Changes such as coarse grouping of adjacent scores on the measurement scale would also have little effect on the value of the median. The *mid-mean* uses rank-order information to define the middle half of the data, and so extreme scores introduced in error will not have a major impact on its value, and in this respect it is robust like the median. Both the mid-mean and the median are thus more robust than the mean, and using either in preference to the mean would protect the researcher against disturbances in measurement quality.

Robust methods

Efficiency

Think of getting the juice out of a lemon. First, you have to cut the lemon in half. After that there are options. British celebrity chef Jamie Oliver squeezes each half in his hand; this has high screen appeal but does not extract all the juice – its efficiency is quite low. Another way is to use a juicer to macerate the flesh of the lemon and then filter out the juice. The juicer does not look as appealing on TV, but it is more efficient because it yields more juice. Applying this principle to statistical analysis, efficiency refers to how much a summary measure captures all the information within the data that is relevant to what is summarized. For summary measures of location, the mean is the most efficient index we know because it uses everything about the data that is relevant to summarizing where the data are located on their measurement scale. Of course, that is the very reason why we sometimes do not use it, because some scores are suspiciously large or because we do not trust the fine detail. The median is much less efficient than the mean, since it replaces scores with their ranks, while the mid-mean (as well as other varieties of trimmed mean) is almost as efficient as the mean.

efficiency the extent to which a summary measure captures all the information within the data that is relevant to what is summarized

Summary of formal features of summary measures

The two characteristics of summary measures tend to work in opposite directions: the mean is generally preferable to the median because it is more efficient, but the median is more robust. A lot then depends on the quality of data that the researcher has available and on how well variables are measured. Researchers who have confidence in the quality of their data will tend to prefer using summary measures, which are high in efficiency, such as the mean for location and the standard deviation for spread. These will work particularly well for data that are broadly symmetrical and do not have rogue values that are more extreme than the bulk of the data. However, where data are more rough and ready, and the researcher is less confident about measurement quality, summary measures based on ranks (the median for location and the mid-range for spread) may be used with more confidence.

RESEARCH IN ACTION

Working in data science

Eva-Marie Muller-Stuler

Eva-Marie Muller-Stuler is a Chief Data Scientist with a Doctorate from Philipps-University Marburg. For more than a decade she has developed solutions for customer growth and acquisition, risk and fraud detection, among many other areas.

How has 'big data' research changed the work of data analysts?

When I started out, there were only a few companies that harvested and analysed their data on a large scale. Business decisions were often based on gut feeling and previous experience. Today, the importance of data-driven decision-making has become recognized. Big data – if analysed well – supports decision-making in ever more sophisticated ways. Whereas in the past, clients asked us 'How can I push my product?', they now seek to ensure that they understand their markets well enough to deliver what people actually want in the first place. As data analysts, we help businesses to come to such understanding. For example, a food retailer might wonder how many salads, sandwiches or coffees they will be selling at a certain time of day. Through understanding the influence of weather, time of day, location, events and many other drivers, it is possible to reduce waste or to plan the staff and delivery times far more efficiently. For companies the question is no longer if they want to do data science but rather if they want to be the leader or the follower in the field.

Descriptive statistics and data visualizations open up a range of possibilities for examining data and identifying patterns. Quantitative analysis of big data can reveal complex patterns that are difficult to detect in smaller samples. Data visualizations can help to better interpret underlying distributions, structures and patterns. A good data visualization can also challenge assumptions and inspire new questions and ideas.

What are the challenges associated with big data research in business and management?

One of the biggest challenges is getting the input data right. This means collecting, cleaning and connecting data that are often spread over many departments and that may be available in various formats. For example, you may find that the data you are after are hidden in large files of scanned documents or in Excel sheets with inconsistent formatting and labelling. Depending on the size of the project, data preparation may take weeks!

TOP TIP

In business, never forget what kind of question you are trying to answer. Is your research about reasons for customer churn, product placement, or something else entirely? Sometimes, a seemingly more interesting question will present itself but it may not help you to answer your initial question.

Going beyond a sample

Relationships versus differences

Most introductory statistical texts organize their presentation of significance tests into two categories, according to whether the focus of attention is on differences between groups or on relationships between variables. This book is no different, and so we explain the basic idea behind each of them and then explain why the difference is actually an artificial one.

The idea of *group differences* is a simple one. It addresses questions such as:

1. Are small start-up businesses more innovative than large bureaucratic ones?

2. Are there more men than women on the boards of companies?

Each of these can be translated into a question about whether groups differ on a summary measure of a dependent variable (for question 1 the dependent variable is the level of innovation, while for question 2 the dependent variable is the percentage of women at board level). Tests have been developed to deal with variations in the number of groups and also in the kind of dependent variable (see later in this chapter).

The idea of *relationships between variables* is also quite a simple one. It addresses questions such as:

1. Is there a link between sunny weather and how people feel at work?

2. Does greater company use of social media (such as Facebook and Twitter) increase their reputation with customers?

Each of these questions is concerned with a pattern of association between two variables: are high levels of one variable (e.g. the number of hours of sunshine per day) associated with high levels of another variable (e.g. the morale of employees in an office)? There are specialist tests that have been developed for dealing with different kinds of relationship for a variety of types of variable.

Relationships and differences: what's the difference?

generalized linear models
a class of multivariate statistical models within which the relationships between DVs and PVs are linear, and DVs can be expressed through a transformation called a link function; it includes multiple regression analysis, ANOVA and logistic regression

While the distinction we just described is pretty straightforward, it can actually be quite misleading. Consider the question above about whether there are more men than women on the boards of companies. We just stated this in terms of a difference between two groups, but we could just as easily have expressed it in the language of relationships: is there a relationship between gender and board membership? Those are just two ways of talking about the same thing.

There was a time when work was done using a calculator or even pen and paper, which led researchers to develop shorthand techniques custom-made for each specific configuration of data. So, we have separate procedures in packages, such as SPSS, for looking at either group differences or relationships. However, statisticians have realized over the last 40 years or so that there are deep similarities between methods that were up to then regarded as quite different. Thus, we now have methods called generalized linear models, which use a common language (albeit a rather inaccessible algebraic one) to express research hypotheses, whether they be relationships or group differences. We won't spend much time in this book on these general models, but it is useful to remember that any hypothesis about differences between groups can also be expressed as a relationship involving the concept that underlies the group distinction.

The rationale of hypothesis testing

Every piece of empirical management research involves analysis of data from a sample of some kind at two levels: first, to identify patterns in that sample data; and second, to use the conclusions drawn from those patterns to make claims that go beyond the sample itself. The greatest part of the craft of quantitative data analysis lies in defining the limits to which it is appropriate to generalize beyond a specific sample. The studies listed in Table 10.1 at the start of this chapter each used quantitative data to address important research questions. The authors of those studies presented their data, but their conclusions relate not just to the specific sample but also to claims about theory based on the data. In general, scholars do not theorize on the basis of specific datasets alone; instead, theories are statements about relationships between concepts, about boundary conditions for when those relationships occur, and about causes and consequences. Hypothesis testing is about making inferences about populations based upon data drawn from samples. Because we want to go beyond a sample, there is always an element of judgement or guesswork involved, and mistakes can be made. Hypothesis testing allows the researcher to define how safe it is to go beyond a specific sample of data.

hypothesis testing
the process of making inferences about populations based upon data drawn from samples

EXAMPLE 10.1

Specifying a hypothesis

Bloom and van Reenen (2006) claim that family-owned firms are better run (and perform better) when the CEO is a professional manager and not chosen because he or she is a family member. Their claim is based on comparisons of management practice between groups of firms that differ in ownership and the status of the CEO. Having made statistical comparisons within their data, they go on to make broad statements about such things as the reasons for the rise of the USA in the early part of the twentieth century compared to the UK (something their data do not address directly).

As part of a long-lasting collaboration between one of the authors of this book and a large pharmaceutical company, data from company bi-annual employee opinion surveys were made available for research. One of the regular questions in the surveys was about the speed of decision-making within the company (it isn't really surprising to find that snail-like bureaucracy is a concern in a big company). Here we take a look at what two groups of employees think: those who have been in the company less than two years; and those with longer organizational tenure (more than two years).

In the survey questionnaire, respondents were offered three response alternatives: 1 = too fast; 2 = about right; and 3 = too slow. The mean scores for the two groups are:

Short tenure (< 2 years; n = 802):   mean = 2.40

Long tenure (2 or more years; n = 6993):   mean = 2.59

We can see that there is a higher mean score for longer-tenure employees, and this indicates that they are more likely to feel that decision-making is too slow. Taking another perspective, 44 per cent of short-tenure employees reported that decision-making is *too slow*, compared

univariate test
a test of a study
hypothesis,
which involves
consideration
of a single
dependent
variable

multivariate test
a test of a study
hypothesis
that involves
consideration
of several
dependent
variables
simultaneously

to a much higher proportion (64 per cent) of longer-tenure employees. It would appear that opinions about the speed of organizational decision-making differ according to how long employees have been within the company. But how confident can we be about that claim? The purpose of hypothesis testing is to enable the researcher to draw conclusions like that.

Formal steps in hypothesis testing

Whatever the statistical procedure that is applied, the underlying logic is the same. This chapter concentrates on the univariate test (taking one dependent variable at a time) while the next chapter looks at the multivariate test (where many variables are considered at once). However complex the dataset, the steps are the same. We spell out the five steps using the decision-making data as an example, and then set out in more general form the researcher's choices in setting out to test hypotheses with data.

Step 1: defining a research hypothesis to be tested

Null
hypothesis

The initial research question reflects the purpose of the study: to explore sample differences in speed of organizational decision-making as reported by company employees. The researchers had reason to believe that the two samples of employees might see decision-making speed differently, but observation of the data alone does not allow any firm conclusion to be drawn. In general, we are interested in two states of affairs: what the data would look like if there is a real difference between the two samples, and if there really is no difference between the samples. The research hypothesis, called H_1, is that there is a real difference between the two samples in decision-making speed. Note that making a decision about whether or not to accept this hypothesis does nothing to explain *why* such a difference might occur.

Step 2: defining a null hypothesis

null hypothesis (H_0)
the initial position adopted during hypothesis testing, which may be modified on the basis of evidence from data; for tests involving comparing groups, the null hypothesis is that the groups are nothing but random samples from a single population (see also alternative hypothesis)

In the absence of any evidence to the contrary, the simplest starting point is to assume that it makes no difference how the data were collected. This defines a null hypothesis (called H_0) that the responses for short-tenure employees are generated by the same process as the responses from long-tenure employees. If the evidence in favour of the alternative hypothesis (H_1) is inconclusive, then the reasonable conclusion to draw is the starting position (H_0). On the other hand, strong evidence of a difference in decision-making speed scores between the two samples would allow the researcher to modify this initial position. It is important to note the logic here. The null hypothesis has nothing to do with what the researcher *wants* to be true, and neither is it anything to do with a specific theory. Instead, it reflects a simple agnostic position that the data from the two samples were generated by the same process unless there is strong evidence otherwise.

Step 3: deriving a summary measure of a characteristic of interest

alternative hypothesis (H_1)
a position adopted during hypothesis testing if the evidence from data is strong enough to reject the null hypothesis (see also null hypothesis)

Having defined a null hypothesis, the third step is to calculate a summary index based on the characteristic of interest. In this case, the natural way to express the hypotheses is in terms of summary measures of the location of the data on the decision-making speed measurement scale. Earlier in this chapter we described three summary measures of location that could be used to test the research hypothesis: the median, the mean and the mid-mean. Whichever summary measure is chosen, the null hypothesis is that the difference between the location measures for the two samples is zero, while the alternative research hypothesis is that the difference is not zero. Thus, the hypothesis test is expressed in terms of the group difference in a measure of location. The previous section showed that the mean decision-making speed scores for the two groups are 2.40 and 2.59, with a group difference of 0.29. Of course, it is unrealistic to expect a difference of precisely zero in a specific study even if it can be guaranteed that the method of collecting data makes no difference. Repeated studies with the same structure would be expected to show differences in means (or medians or mid-means) between samples, but the differences would be expected to be small most of the time and very different only infrequently. The problem that the researcher faces is: what does similar mean? How different is very different? For these data, is a mean difference of 0.29 a large or a small difference? Addressing this problem is the job of the reference distribution in the next step.

Step 4: choosing a reference distribution and calculating a test statistic

The logic of hypothesis testing is that convincing evidence is needed from the study data before the researcher is prepared to move away from the null hypothesis in favour of an alternative. If the null hypothesis were true, how likely is the outcome observed in the study data? Quantifying the answer to this question requires the use of a reference distribution, which summarizes the alternatives available if the null hypothesis were true. Textbooks often refer to this as a sampling distribution, but we prefer the more general term to reflect the process of calibrating a result from one study against a reference standard. The reference distribution is not the distribution of the observations in a dataset, but rather it is the distribution of the hypothesis summary index for all possible outcomes, of which the one from a specific study is just one.

Sources of reference distributions

Selecting a reference distribution involves either using extra data (over and above that from a sample) or making assumptions about the data and the process that generated it. We consider three different sources of reference distributions:

1. *Standard reference distributions* are drawn from statistical theory, and choosing them is the commonest way of testing hypotheses. There are many families of reference distributions derived from theorizing about different kinds of idealized situations. For example, the normal distribution is the distribution of the sum of independent measures where the standard deviation of the reference distribution is known. The *t*-distribution is the same as the normal distribution, but differs only in that the standard deviation of the reference distribution is estimated from sample data. The binomial distribution is the distribution of entities that are binary (present/ absent, success/failure). These distributions are used for testing hypotheses about differences in location. The chi-square distribution is the distribution not of means but of variances, and is used for testing hypotheses about spread. The *F*-distribution is the distribution of ratios of variances, and is used for testing hypotheses about group differences in the spread of mean scores. All standard reference distributions share a number of characteristics:

   - *They are mathematically well defined* – their shape reflects a few features called parameters (this is the reason why tests using standard reference distributions are called parametric tests). For example, the precise form of the normal distribution depends only upon just two quantities: the mean and standard deviation.
   - *Their theoretical properties are well worked out* – for example, the normal distribution is symmetrical and bell-shaped. For a normal distribution with a mean of zero and a standard deviation of one, two-thirds (68 per cent) of the area under

reference distribution the distribution of all alternative values of a test statistic based on the assumption that the null hypothesis is true; used in hypothesis testing

sampling distribution a form of reference distribution derived from probability theory based on repeated sampling from a theoretical population; used in hypothesis testing

t-distribution a form of standard reference distribution; a form of the normal distribution where the standard deviation of the reference distribution is estimated from sample data

binomial distribution a form of reference distribution; the distribution of entities that are binary (present/ absent, success/ failure)

chi-square distribution a form of reference distribution; the distribution of variances used for testing hypotheses about spread

the curve lies in the range between –1 and +1 on the measurement scale: 34 per cent on either side of the mean. A further 13 per cent of the area under the curve lies either side of the mean in the range between –1 and –2 and between +1 and +2 on the measurement scale.

- *They are theoretical entities* – which do not exist in the real world, but researchers can use them as approximations to their own data. Thus, many of the tests described below (see Tables 10.4 and 10.7) are said to assume normally distributed data. Since real data never follow precisely any of the standard reference distributions, this assumption is almost never valid. However, the practical issue is whether the approximation to normality is close enough to allow reliable inference. Statisticians agree that most statistical tests that use standard reference distributions are robust in the face of departures from the ideal assumptions, provided that sample sizes are more than about 50 and that the distribution of sample data is approximately symmetrical. Small samples and 'wild' distributions should lead the researcher to consider one of the options below.

2. *Permutation distributions* are reference distributions formed by finding all possible permutations of ranked data. For example, consider tossing two dice. Overall, there are six different outcomes for each die, making 36 outcomes in all, and the distribution of all of these 36 alternatives is the permutation distribution. There is only one way of achieving a total score of 12, by throwing two sixes; similarly, there is only one way of achieving a score of 2, by throwing two ones. However, there are six ways of achieving a score of 7 (1 + 6, 2 + 5, 3 + 4, 4 + 3, 5 + 2, 6 + 1), and this is the commonest total score from throwing two dice. As the dice example shows, permutation distributions are derived by taking all possible alternative outcomes for a specific setting, and they do not rely on assuming anything about an underlying theoretical parametric distribution for data. As a result, tests using them are called non-parametric tests. Examples include the Mann-Whitney U test and the Kruskal-Wallis test for differences between groups, and Kendall's rank-order correlation test of association (see Tables 10.4 and 10.7).

3. *Bootstrap distributions* are reference distributions formed by treating the available data as all there is, and drawing repeated samples from it. The bootstrap procedure has been around for more than 40 years, but has only recently become easy to use (it is included as a standard option within SPSS version 20 onwards). For well-behaved data, the bootstrap will usually lead to the same conclusions as standard methods, but there are circumstances where bootstrapping is the only option (significance tests involving medians and tests for indirect effects in mediation analysis are two of them). Examples of how it works are given by Jackson (1986) and Wood (2005).

The next step in the hypothesis testing process is to calculate the difference between the two summary measures – either medians or means – for the two samples.

Step 5: drawing a conclusion

What is the probability of getting a difference as big as this if the null hypothesis were true? If the probability is small enough (the conventional criterion that is used is 1 in 20, equivalent to 5 in 100 or 5 per cent), then the researcher can conclude that the observed outcome is too surprising for the null hypothesis to be true, or stated another way, that the evidence from the data is convincing enough to modify the starting position. This is usually stated as: reject the null hypothesis at the 5 per cent level, or the difference between the groups is significant at the 0.05 level.

When someone makes a claim about how the world is on the basis of data, there are two kinds of mistakes that can be made, which are shown in Table 10.3. In the case of the example of the two sets of data collected for short- and long-tenure employees, there are two conclusions that could be drawn: either that there is a difference between the two groups in how employees see the speed of organizational decision-making, or that there is no difference. If there really is no difference between the groups but the researcher uses sample data to make the false claim that there is a difference, this is called a type I error. A type I error is made when someone claims a difference where none exists. However, if there really is a difference between the groups but the researcher falsely concludes that there is none, then this is called a type II error.

The convention is that type I errors are more serious than type II errors, since the type II error is the same as retaining the initial starting point before the data were collected. The type I error amounts to changing the initial state of affairs in falsely claiming something new about the world based on data. After all, it is possible to correct an error of omission by gathering more data, while making false positive claims on the basis of a single sample is altogether different. From time to time there are dramatic examples of such type I errors reported in the press. These include claims of finding so-called 'cold fusion' (offering potential for unlimited free energy for the world), emissions from PC screens as harmful to unborn babies, the triple MMR vaccine as a cause of autism. All of these claims were subsequently found to be false, but each one was a source of confusion for researchers and sometimes alarm for members of the public.

Bootstrapping explained

type I error
a false conclusion from a hypothesis test involving a claim that an effect exists (an association between variables or a group difference) when there is no such effect in the population

type II error
a false conclusion from a hypothesis test involving a claim that no effect exists (an association between variables or a group difference) when there is an effect in the population

TABLE 10.3   Options in drawing conclusions from data

Conclusion from data	True State of Affairs	
	Groups do not differ	Groups are different
Data show no difference between groups	Correct conclusion from sample data	Type II error
Data show a difference between groups	Type I error	Correct conclusion from sample data

Big data and hypothesis testing

With big data come big sample sizes, and in big samples everything is statistically significant. One approach to thinking statistically in a big data world is to look at effect sizes rather than significance levels. For an effect of a particular size (a small difference in means between two groups, a large impact of a particular risk factor in predicting health at work), the significance level is a function of the sample size, so that relying on statistical significance alone will lead the big data researcher to pay too much attention to results that are trivial. Hunting out significant results is thus more to do with how big your sample is than it is about the importance of the relationships that you identify.

With big data comes a different issue. Traditional teaching of quantitative methods makes much of the difference between sample and population. The sample is where your data are, while the population is what you would like to be able to talk about using your data to help you. With many applications of data mining, the researcher is concerned not with a sample but with the population, so what does traditional statistical inference have to say? Actually,

parametric test
a form of
hypothesis
test that uses
a standard
reference
distribution
derived from
probability theory
whose form is
defined by a
small number of
parameters (cf.
non-parametric
test)

normal distribution
a form of
standard
reference
distribution;
the distribution
of the sum of
independent
measures where
the standard
deviation of
the reference
distribution is
known (its shape
is sometimes
called the bell-
curve)

non-parametric
test
a form of
hypothesis
test that uses
a reference
distribution
derived from
all possible
permutations of
study outcomes
using the ranking
of data (cf.
parametric test)

statistical model fitting still has immense value even where the researcher is interested in the available data and not in a hypothetical population.

Selecting the right kind of statistical test

So far, we have set out the general principles of hypothesis testing, using the case of comparing the means of two samples of data. We next turn our attention to deciding how to choose the right significance test for a given situation.

For each type of test, two versions are listed: a parametric test, which assumes that the variables are measured on continuous scales, and also that the data are at least approximately bell-shaped, like the normal distribution; and a non-parametric test, which makes the simpler assumption that the variables are measured on ordinal category scales. The choice between tests depends on what the researcher is prepared to assume about the measurement scale for the variables involved (see Chapter 9). Sometimes the answer is very straightforward. When a study asks whether there are more men than women employed at the top level in a company, gender cannot be anything but measured on a category scale: male versus female. At other times, the issue is more a matter of judgement about the quality of measurement. When measurement quality is high, the researcher will probably be confident to think of the measurement scale as *continuous* and use the mean as a measure of location (choosing the mean because it is very efficient). This leads to choosing a parametric test such as the *t*-test or ANOVA for testing group differences. When there is more uncertainty about measurement quality, it is probably wiser to treat the scores as no more than ranked (an *ordinal* scale) and then rely on the median as a measure of location. This then leads to choosing non-parametric tests, which are more robust (because the summary measures they use are less influenced by extreme scores) but less efficient (because they throw away information that is in the data).

Testing for group differences: comparing groups

Table 10.4 lists procedures that can be used to test hypotheses about group differences in location. We distinguish between tests for comparing two groups, and tests for more complex datasets involving three or more groups. Table 10.5 picks out research questions that involve comparing groups from some of the studies listed in Table 10.1. Where there are

TABLE 10.4 Selecting the right kind of test for group differences

Purpose	Measurement scale	Characteristic of data	Test	Null hypothesis	Test statistic	Reference distribution
Compare 2 groups	Continuous	Location: means	*t*-test	Groups are from a single population	*t*-value	t
	Ordered category	Location: medians	Mann-Whitney U test	Groups are from a single population	U statistic	All combinations of ranks
Compare 3 or more groups	Continuous	Location: means	Analysis of variance (ANOVA)	Groups are from a single population	*F*-ratio	F
	Ordered category	Location: medians	Kruskal-Wallis test	Groups are from a single population	W statistic	All combinations of ranks

only two groups to compare, the choice is between the *t*-test for comparing means and the Mann-Whitney U test for ranked data. For each, the table sets out how the groups were defined and what variable was involved in the group comparison. The second two examples concern hypotheses about differences between three groups, and the appropriate choice here is between the analysis of variance (ANOVA) for comparing means and the Kruskal-Wallis test based on ranked data. We illustrate the process of using the *t*-test for testing for differences between two groups; though the general principles apply to analysis of variance too.

t-test
a form of
hypothesis test
for comparing
mean scores of
two groups

TABLE 10.5   Examples of research questions that involve comparing groups

Study	Groups to compare	Dependent variable
a) Testing for group differences – comparing two groups		
B2B relationships (Dyer and Hatch, 2006)	Two car companies – Toyota versus US	quality of supplier products
Locating your HQ (Birkinshaw et al., 2006)	Two types of HQ – business unit versus corporate	satisfaction of stakeholders
b) Testing for group differences – comparing three or more groups		
SOEs in China (Ralston et al., 2006)	Three categories – privately-owned versus foreign-owned versus state-owned	culture
MNEs' marketing strategies (Katsikeas et al., 2006)	Three groups of MNEs – US versus German versus Japanese	marketing strategies

Worked example of two-group comparison tests for the CEO compensation data

The data for this example come from the CEO compensation data summarized in Figures 10.4 and 10.5. Here we examine the relationship between pay level and the age of the CEO. We have created two groups: the larger group ($n = 164$) consists of those under 63 years of age, and a smaller group ($n = 36$) are 63+ years old. We use different forms of significance test to make a more precise inference about whether the two groups of employees differ in their level of pay. The null hypothesis is that there is no difference, such that two groups could have been defined by splitting the sample randomly into two groups. The null hypothesis is accepted unless there is sufficient evidence from the data to discard it in favour of the alternative that the two sets of observations are drawn from different populations. Figure 10.5 shows that pay is highly positively skewed, with one individual receiving over $500m. One question that we will explore is whether the shape of the data will have an influence on the conclusions drawn from the different ways of testing the same hypothesis.

The appropriate summary index that captures the relevant feature of the data depends on the type of test: the difference between the group means is used for the *t*-test and for the bootstrap test, while the ranked scores are used for the Mann-Whitney test (and so medians are reported in Table 10.6).

First, we explain the logic of the *t*-test, and then we show what happens when different forms of significance test are used. Table 10.6 shows that the mean (M_1) for the younger group is 19.55 ($n = 164$) and the mean (M_2) for the older group is 41.17 ($n = 36$). The difference in group means is $41.17 - 19.55 = 21.62$ and the null hypothesis is that this group difference is zero. The formula for the *t*-test is a ratio:

$$t = M_1 - M_2 / \text{SE (diff)}$$

Mann-Whitney
U test
a form of
hypothesis test
for comparing
two groups that
uses rank-order
data

analysis of
variance
(ANOVA)
a form of
hypothesis
test for
comparing
the means
of two or
more groups,
which may be
classified on
the basis of
other variables

Kruskal-Wallis
test a form of
hypothesis
test for
comparing
two or more
groups that
uses rank-
order data

TABLE 10.6 Summary statistics of CEO pay level (in millions of dollars) for two samples defined by age of the CEO, and results of significance tests

	Age under 63 years (n = 164)	Age 63+ years (n = 36)	Significance tests
Mean	19.55 (SD = 18.93)	41.17 (SD = 96.14)	t-test: t = 2.68, df = 198, p <.01 Conclusion: groups do differ Bootstrap test: p = 0.273 Conclusion: groups do not differ
Median	12.56 (IQR = 14.37)	13.90 (IQR = 19.89)	Mann-Whitney test: U = 2551.50, p = 0.203 Conclusion: groups do not differ

standard error (SE)
the standard deviation of a sampling distribution used in hypothesis testing; estimated from the standard deviations and the sample size within groups in a sample

2-tailed test refers to a non-directional alternative hypothesis relative to the null hypothesis; association between variables may be either positive or negative, or the means of two groups will differ in either direction

1-tailed test refers to a directional alternative hypothesis relative to the null hypothesis; a prediction of a positive association between variables, or the one group mean will be bigger than another

The top line is the difference between the group means (21.62), and the bottom line (which makes it possible to judge how big a difference this is) is the standard error of the difference (8.08). The standard error (SE) is calculated from the standard deviation and the sample size in each group. The smaller the spread of scores around the group mean and the larger the sample size, the smaller is the standard error. Applying this formula gives a t-value of 21.62 / 8.08 = 2.68.

If the null hypothesis (H$_0$) is true, the difference in means will be close to zero most of the time, and far from zero seldom. If the alternative hypothesis (H$_1$) is true, the difference in means will be far from zero most of the time and close to zero seldom. Where there is prior expectation about the direction of difference between the groups, the test is called a 2-tailed test; and where one group is expected to have a higher mean than the other (but there is no prior expectation as to which), the test is called a 1-tailed test.

In order to get an idea of how big the observed difference actually is, it is necessary to locate it on the t-distribution. The shape of the t-distribution is defined by two parameters: the mean as an estimate of location and the standard deviation as an estimate of spread. The mean of the reference distribution is estimated from the difference between the group means under the null hypothesis. The standard deviation of the reference distribution, also called the standard error of the difference in group means, forms the bottom line of the t-test formula. It is a scaling factor that allows us to say whether a given difference is large or small. The size of the standard error depends on the sample sizes in the groups and on the spread of scores around the mean in each of the groups. The standard error is inversely related to the total number of observations in the study, and this makes sense because most people would have more confidence in means based on large samples. It also depends on the spread around the group means in the observed data (as measured by the standard deviations of the two groups), and this too makes sense. If data points are widely dispersed around their respective group means, then the mean is a less precise indicator of where the data in each group lie on the measurement scale. Overall then, the size of the t-value obtained depends upon three things:

1. The difference in group means.

2. The spread around group means.

3. The sample size in each group.

In general, convincing evidence about whether groups differ comes from big differences between means, small spread around those means (thus increasing their precision) and large sample sizes.

The bigger the *t*-value obtained, the more convincing is the evidence from the data that the initial starting position of two samples from a single population is incorrect, and needs to be modified in the light of evidence from the data. The final step is to select a significance level (conventionally $p < .05$), and find in the test tables the value of *t* that would be necessary to achieve the desired significance level. If the researcher finds that the actual *t*-value is greater than the tabulated value, then he or she will reject the null hypothesis that the groups are random samples from a single population at that level of significance, in favour of the alternative hypothesis that they are sampled from different populations.

The shape of the reference distribution depends on a quantity called degrees of freedom (or *df*). For the two-sample *t*-test, this is calculated as the total sample size (200) minus the number of groups (2), giving the value of 198 shown in Table 10.6. The probability of achieving a *t*-value as big as 2.68 if the null hypothesis were really true is 1 in 1,000, shown in the table as $p < .01$. This is a small probability, and the conclusion is that the null hypothesis is very unlikely to be true and is rejected in favour of the alternative that the groups really do differ. Based on the *t*-test result, we would conclude that the younger group receive a lower level of pay than the older group. So far, so good, but remember that the CEO pay data are highly skewed, and so the means for the groups may not represent the data very well.

The *t*-test compares group means (which are reported in the first row of Table 10.6), and it appears that the very high mean score for the older group is influenced by the single extreme outlier of \$557m. Note that the difference in median scores for the two groups is much smaller than the difference in the means (we saw earlier that the median is not influenced by a few extreme scores). Next, we consider two different types of significance test that do not rely on the implausible assumption of normality.

The Mann-Whitney U test is a non-parametric test that works with the ranked scores, just as the median does. With the pay scores ranked from smallest to largest, the null hypothesis is that the two age groups are distributed evenly throughout the ranked scores. The most extreme version of the alternative hypothesis is that all of the members of one age group are distributed at one end of the ranked data, and the other group are distributed at the other end. For this data, the test statistic, U, is 2551.50, with an associated z score of −1.27, and a probability level that is higher than the conventional 0.05 level. The conclusion from this test is that the ranked pay levels for the younger group are not different from those for the older group. The bootstrap test follows a different logic, drawing repeated samples from the data itself, but the conclusion is the same as for the non-parametric test.

What do we conclude from these three forms of significance test? The parametric test indicated that the groups do differ, but the other two tests did not. The safest conclusion is that pay level for CEOs (at least in this data) does not relate to the age of the CEO. The *t*-test seems to have been highly influenced by a single atypical data point, and so the result using this method is not representative of the dataset as a whole. This shows the wisdom of looking at the shape of data and being prepared to look at the same data in different ways.

Testing association between variables

Table 10.7 lists procedures that can be used to test hypotheses about association between variables. If there is an association between two variables, then knowing how someone responds on one variable carries information that can be used to predict their response on the other. This definition applies regardless of the measurement scale of the variables being considered. Where the scale is at least ordered (either ordinal or continuous), we can be more precise and talk about the direction of the relationship in terms of a correlation. There is a *positive* correlation between two variables when high scores on one tend to occur with

degrees of freedom (*df*) the value that defines the shape of a standard reference distribution in hypothesis testing; for example, in testing association, *df* = sample size minus one

association two variables are associated where knowing a value on one variable carries information about the corresponding value on the other; can be measured by a correlation coefficient

high scores on the other, and similarly for low scores. A *negative* correlation is shown by people responding with high scores on one variable but low scores on the other. A *zero* correlation indicates that knowing about one variable does not help in telling us anything about the other. Table 10.8 shows examples of association between variables from the studies in Table 10.1.

anxiety & depression data

Different kinds of association between variables can be illustrated using data from a study of the impact of social support networks among unemployed adults. The study involved repeated interviews, and the figures below show data from measures of clinical anxiety and depression taken at the first and second interviews for 208 adults.

Figure 10.6 shows a *positive* association between two variables. The horizontal axis shows anxiety scores at the first interview, with low scores to the left and high scores to the right. The vertical axis shows the anxiety scores at the second interview, with low scores at the bottom and high scores at the top. In this plot there are more data points than there are circles, and the darker circles show multiple data points with the same combination of values. The drift of the data is from bottom-left to top-right: for the most part, people who reported being anxious at the first interview tended also to report high scores at the second interview (and vice versa). The correlation is 0.63, n = 208, p <.01. The high correlation is not surprising: levels of anxiety tend to be quite stable over time, reflecting either individual personality or stability in circumstances.

Figure 10.7 shows a *negative* association between two variables. The horizontal axis shows depression scores at the first interview, with low scores to the left and high scores to the right. The vertical axis shows the change in depression between the first interview and the second (calculated as $time_2$ score minus the $time_1$ score). A positive change score towards the top of the plot indicates someone reporting an increase in depression at the second interview, and a score towards the bottom of the plot indicates someone reporting a reduction in depression. Each data point is shown by a circle in the plot (with multiple overlapping points shown in darker circles), and the drift of the data is top-left to bottom-right. The top-left quadrant consists of people who reported low depression initially but an increase in depression at the second interview. The bottom-right quadrant consists of people with high depression at the first interview but whose depression score dropped at the second interview. This pattern is reflected in a negative correlation of –0.40, n = 208, p <.01. The negative correlation is not surprising: people with extreme scores at the first interview will tend to report scores that are closer to the mean second time around (this is called 'regression to the mean').

The specific test for association between two variables depends on the measurement scale. For variables measured on nominal category scales, the chi-square test (χ^2) is appropriate. Where the measurement scale is either ordinal or continuous, association between variables is assessed by a *correlation coefficient*. The correlation coefficient for continuous scales is the Pearson product-moment correlation. For data measured in the form of ranks, the Kendall rank-order correlation is used.

Testing association for nominal category measurement scales: the chi-square test

While it is possible to draw a scatterplot for looking at the association between variables measured on category scales, it is generally more convenient and informative to use a contingency table to show how a sample is divided up according to each person's score on the two variables we are interested in. Contingency tables do not have to be two-way, but they get much harder to read when we use more than two variables to divide up the sample. The chi-square test is used to test association between two category variables measured on nominal scales.

chi-square test
a form of hypothesis test for testing the association between two variables measured on nominal category scales

product-moment correlation
a test of association between two variables measured on continuous scales

rank-order correlation
a test of association between two variables measured on ordered category scales

Chi-square test

TABLE 10.7 Selecting the right kind of test for association

Purpose	Measurement scale	Characteristic of data	Test	Null hypothesis	Test statistic	Reference distribution
Association in a contingency table	Two nominal category scales	Co-variation of scores on two variables	Chi-square test	Independence – overall distribution applies to all groups	χ^2 (chi-square)	χ^2 distribution
	Two binary category scales (0 / 1)	Co-variation of scores on two variables	Phi coefficient	Independence – overall distribution applies to all groups	Φ (phi)	R distribution
Correlation between variables	Two continuous scales	Co-variation of scores on two variables	Pearson product-moment correlation	Independence	r	R distribution
	One continuous scale and one binary category scale	Co-variation of scores on two variables	Point bi-serial correlation	Independence	r	R distribution
	Two ordered category scales	Consistency of ranking on two variables	Rank-order correlation (Kendall); Rank-order correlation (Spearman)	Independence Independence	τ (tau) ρ (rho)	R distribution R distribution

TABLE 10.8 Examples of research questions that involve testing association between variables

Study	Association between:	
Influencing companies on environmental issues (Eesley and Lenox, 2006)	Different stakeholder actions	Positive corporate responses
MNEs' marketing strategies (Katsikeas et al., 2006)	Standardization of marketing strategy	Market environment
Locating your HQ (Birkinshaw et al., 2006)	HQ – business unit/corporate	Satisfying stakeholders
Is CSR smart as well as good? (Luo and Bhattacharya, 2006)	CSR activities of companies – cash donations/employee volunteering	Market value of company/customer satisfaction

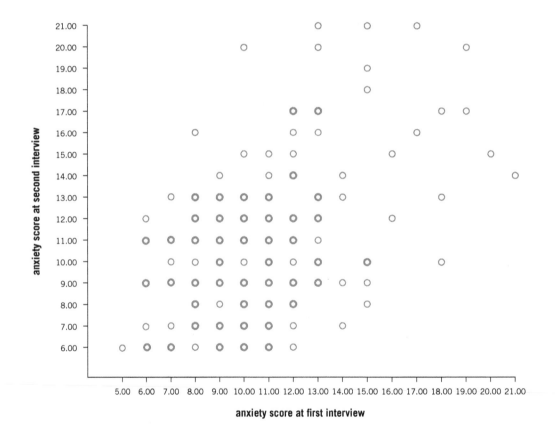

FIGURE 10.6 A positive association between two variables

An example of a contingency table is shown in Table 10.9, which is taken from a study by Anya Johnson, a doctoral student. She carried out a worldwide survey (18 countries) of over 3,000 professional managers (both men and women) who had been made redundant by their company and then enrolled in a career transition programme to help them get another job. One of the things that the student looked at was the effect of job loss on family relationships, and she asked the following question: *What is the effect of job loss on your relationship with your partner/spouse?* Participants could select from three responses: *bringing you closer together, having no effect at all* and *causing relationship difficulties.* She wondered whether unemployed men and women would answer this question differently, and the contingency table below shows the two variables together. The table shows the counts, and also the row percentages: each count as a percentage of the row total. The first row shows how men answered the question, and the second row shows responses for women.

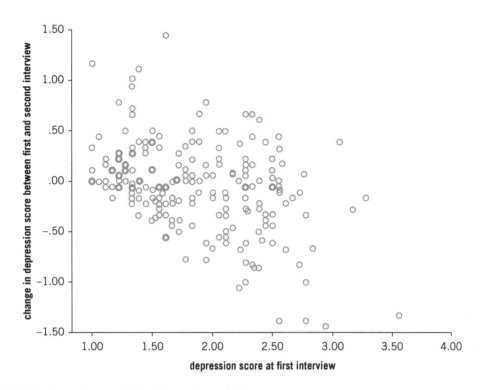

FIGURE 10.7   A negative association between two variables

TABLE 10.9   Contingency table showing frequencies of men and women according to the reported effect of job loss on the relationship with their partner

| | **Effect of Job Loss on Relationship with Partner** | | | |
	Brings them closer together	**No difference to the relationship**	**Causes difficulties in the relationship**	**Total**
Men	952 (43%)	874 (39%)	406 (18%)	2232 100%
Women	223 (35%)	276 (44%)	130 (21%)	629 100%
Total	1175 (41%)	1150 (40%)	536 (19%)	2861 100%

Note: Percentages are based on the row totals.

The bottom right-hand corner of the table shows that 2,861 people answered the relationship question and also reported their gender. The right-hand column with the row totals shows that there are 2,232 men in the analysis, and 629 women. The bottom row of the table shows how people answered the question about the effect of job loss on their relationship, and the effect seems to be mostly either positive or neutral. About four out of ten people (1,175 out of 2,861: 41 per cent) say that the experience has brought them closer together, and about the same number (1,150 out of 2,861: 40 per cent) say it has not affected their relationship. Only a minority (536 out of 2,861: 19 per cent) say that job loss has caused relationship difficulties.

One of the key questions that Johnson asked was whether the effect of the experience was different for men and women. In other words, is there an association between gender and the effect of job loss on the quality of the relationship with a partner? An initial step in addressing this question is to look at the pattern of responses for men and women separately, using the row percentages. For men, 43 per cent say that job loss has brought them closer together, compared to 35 per cent for women – so men tend to be more positive about how job loss has affected the relationship with their partner. Corresponding to this, 18 per cent of men say that job loss has caused relationship difficulties, compared to 21 per cent of women – men are less negative than women. Overall then, there does seem to be an association between gender and impact of job loss on partner relationship.

Interpreting this result is quite complicated. It could be that losing a job is really more damaging to the family relationships of women than it is for men; it could also be that harm is equally strong for both sexes, but that women are more aware of it than men. From the semi-structured interviews that Johnson carried out, she suspected that the second interpretation was more likely. These tended to show that men are less aware of their own feelings and those of their partner than are women, and so do not notice when relationship problems exist.

Having looked at the data, it would appear that there is an association between gender and the effect of job loss on the relationship, but this can be tested formally using the chi-square (χ^2) test of association. The null hypothesis for the chi-square test of association is that there is no relationship between the two variables. For a contingency table this means that the distribution of responses for the total sample (shown by the percentages in the bottom row of the table) applies equally to both men and women. The alternative hypothesis is that the distribution of responses is different for men and women, and that seems to be the case for these data. Exercise 10.3 invites you to calculate the chi-square test statistic for Table 10.9.

EXERCISE 10.3

Chi-square test

Individual: Just as with any significance test, the purpose is to estimate how likely would be the pattern observed in the data if the null hypothesis were true. Calculate the χ^2 statistic for Table 10.9. The degrees of freedom for the test with these data are 2: for χ^2 this is calculated as (number of rows – 1) times (number of columns – 1) = 2. What is the p-value associated with this test statistic, and what do you conclude about the relationship between gender and how people see the effect of job loss on the relationship with their partner?

EXERCISE 10.4

Contingency table analysis

Below is a contingency table presenting data from a large pharmaceutical company showing the number of men and women employed by the company divided into five regions where they operate.

gender by region data

TABLE 10.10   Contingency table showing the number of men and women employed by a large pharmaceutical company divided into five regions

		Gender		
		Female	Male	Total
Region	Middle East and Africa	315	401	716
	Asia Pacific	4304	5923	10227
	Europe	13618	12138	25756
	North America	2072	1771	3843
	Latin/Central America/Caribbean	1576	2085	3661
Total		21885	22318	44203

Individual: Explore the table to decide whether there are gender differences between the regions (hint: work out the row percentages, which will show you the proportion of women employed in each region). Then carry out a chi-square analysis in order to test whether there are significant gender differences between regions. Answer the following questions:

- What is your conclusion?

- What further information would you need in order to help you interpret the reasons behind your finding?

Testing association for continuous and ordered category scales: correlation between variables

For variables measured on scales that are at least ordered, association can be tested using a correlation coefficient. For continuous scales (whether interval or ratio), the test of choice is the Pearson product-moment correlation (r), while the test of choice for ordinal category scales is a rank-order correlation coefficient developed by Kendall (Kendall's tau), though there is another one developed by Spearman (Spearman's rho) which is less commonly used. Pearson's r is the extension of the variance to cover the co-variance between two variables: the extent to which variation in one variable is associated with variation in the other. Spearman's *rho* is the product-moment correlation of the ranked scores for two variables. Kendall's *tau* is an index of consistency of the two sets of ranked scores – how many swaps of scores are necessary to bring the two into consistency.

Kendall's tau
a test of association between two variables based on the ranks of the scores for each variable

Spearman's rho
a test of association between two variables: the product-moment correlation of the ranked scores for the two variables

Conclusion

The material we have covered in this chapter includes:

- Methods of looking at data and the key features that the researcher should pay attention to before summarizing those features using summary statistics.

- Measures of location and spread, and we have argued that choosing one form of summary measure rather than another has the effect of emphasizing some features of data and neglecting others.

- Making inferences about population characteristics based on data from samples. We described the common steps involved in testing hypotheses about group differences and about association between variables, using tests for variables taken one at a time.

The next chapter builds on the principles of hypothesis testing, applying them to the multivariate case where variables are considered together.

Further reading

An introduction to quantitative research methods, tailored to the needs of business and management researchers, this textbook is well-written and includes chapters on presenting, summarizing and investigating quantitative data:

Buglear, J. (2012) *Quantitative Methods for Business and Management Students*. Harlow: Pearson.

The focus of this book is getting the statistical work done rather than the dry statistical theory itself. It is accessible (provided you can tune into the author's sense of humour and his liking for selfies), and covers much of the material in this chapter and the next, plus a lot more:

Field, A. (2017) *Discovering Statistics Using IBM SPSS Statistics: And Sex and Drugs and Rock 'n' Roll*, 5th edn. Thousand Oaks, CA: Sage.

A different version of the book introduces statistics using the increasingly popular software tool R:

Field, A.P., Miles, J. and Field, Z. (2012) *Discovering Statistics Using R*. London: Sage.

Both the following books go into more detail on the logic of hypothesis testing and describe a much more extensive set of statistical tests for comparing groups or testing association between variables. The strengths of the author's approach are that he emphasizes the importance of looking at data intelligently before making decisions about forms of analysis, and he also explains clearly the conceptual underpinnings of the methods that are covered:

Howell, D. (2013) *Statistical Methods for Psychology*, 8th edn. Belmont, CA: Wadsworth.

Howell, D. (2013) *Fundamental Statistics for the Behavioral Sciences*, 8th edn. Nashville, TN: Broadman and Holman.

This is an accessible, non-technical introduction to telling stories about data using graphical methods:

Kirk, A. (2016) *Data Visualisation: A Handbook for Data Driven Design*. London: Sage

Data mining is the art and science of intelligent data analysis. This book introduces the concept and applications of data mining, using open source software:

Williams, G. (2011) *Data Mining with Rattle and R: The Art of Excavating Data for Knowledge Discovery*. New York: Springer.

Check your understanding online

Visit the website **https://edge.sagepub.com/easterbysmith6e** for useful resources that will help reinforce what you've read in this chapter:

 Take an interactive quiz to test your understanding of the key topics

 Review suggested answers to Exercises 10.1 to 10.4 above

 Use interactive flashcards to check your knowledge of essential concepts

Learning objectives

To identify what the variables are in a narrative statement of a research question.

To frame research questions according to alternative forms of multivariate statistical models.

To turn a research question into a form that can be analysed statistically.

MULTIVARIATE ANALYSIS

11

Chapter contents

The domain of multivariate analysis

Cause and effect

multivariate methods
a class of statistical methods that analyses the covariances among a number of variables simultaneously

The social world that we all live in is a complex system, and cannot really be understood just by looking at one thing at a time: causes interact with each other in complex ways; effects are not always simple to measure. Table 11.1 lists studies from the management literature that use multivariate methods to test theoretical propositions.

The complication arises because most of the interesting things researchers want to look at correlate with each other. The tools and methods that we considered in the previous chapter are basic ones for working with quantitative data two variables at a time, but they are not enough to deal with the complexities of the world of work. Aguinis and Edwards (2014) offer a wise analysis of many of these complexities. This chapter on multivariate analysis builds on the previous two, but it is more advanced because it deals with analytical methods for looking at complex data, which are intrinsically more difficult than the univariate methods considered in the previous chapter.

The purpose of multivariate analysis is to find a way of summarizing the relationship between variables, which is simpler than the original data but also captures the essence of that relationship. In that respect, working with quantitative data is no different from working with research evidence in any other form: research seeks out a conceptual model that is both simpler and richer. Simplicity is desirable so that the model is understandable; richness is desirable so that the model can stimulate new ways of thinking about the world. The models used in multivariate analysis are mathematical models, and a full understanding of multivariate statistics requires a fair amount of facility with matrix algebra. In this chapter we give a conceptual introduction to some of the methods, which can then be built on in a more advanced way.

Forms of interdependence in management research

interaction effects
where the effect on a variable depends on the context defined by another variable

synergy
a form of interaction between variables, where their joint effect is different from the sum of their individual effects

There are many kinds of interdependency among concepts within the domain of management research. The first kind of interdependence is interaction effects where variables have different effects depending on the context – these have been examined in a management context in the form of contingency theories. Examples of contingency theories can be found in cross-cultural management (e.g. what works well in a US business negotiation may cause offence among Arabs), in organizational design (different forms of organizing are needed to deal with rapidly changing markets compared to the stable bureaucracies that most people work in (Brown and Eisenhardt, 1998)), and in guidance on how organizations can effectively manage worker stress (Jackson and Parker, 2001).

The second kind of interdependency is that of synergy, one of the favourite buzzwords of the management change consultant. The idea is a simple one: plant a seed, give it both warmth and water and it will grow. Water alone will make it rot, warmth alone may lead the seed to become dormant; but both together can achieve the miracle of a new plant. This is the logic behind many organizational mergers where the capabilities of different partners are brought together with the intent of making a step change in performance.

The third kind of interdependency is that *influences on performance tend to occur together*, either because they affect each other or because they have common causes. Several of the studies in Table 11.1 share the same feature; that is, they control for organizational size in their analysis. Looking at the Brouthers and Brouthers study (2003), for example, their logic was simple – they were not directly interested in differences between large and small firms but they know that size makes a difference to lots of things, so ignoring it would probably bias answers to questions they were interested in. They wanted to study how service and manufacturing firms went about their internationalization through entering new foreign markets. If the service firms in their sample were smaller (or larger) on average than the manufacturing ones, then conclusions based on a comparison between the two sectors would be confounded by differences in size. As a result, including the size of the firm in statistical analysis makes sense.

TABLE 11.1   Examples of studies using multivariate statistical methods

---

Brouthers and Brouthers (2003): Mode of entry into foreign markets (DV) by service and manufacturing organizations (PV).

Coyle-Shapiro and Kessler (2000): Commitment of employees to the organization (DV) as a function of fulfilment of the psychological contract (PV).

Engelen, Gupta, Strenger and Brettel (2015): The relationship between firm performance (DV) and entrepreneurial orientation (PV), moderated by transformational leadership behaviours of top management.

Filatotchev (2006): The entry of firms into public ownership (DV) according to the characteristics of executives and involvement of venture capital (PV).

Gangloff, Connelly and Shook (2016): Investor reactions to CEO turnover (DV) following financial misrepresentation as a function of firm strategies to repair relationships with stakeholders (PV).

Murnieks, Mosakowski and Cardon (2014): This study looked at entrepreneurs and examined the origins of passion and ways in which passion energizes action.

Thompson (2004): Decline in national competitiveness (DV) as a function of cost factors or institutional arrangements (PV).

Wu, Parker and de Jong (2014): Individual innovation behaviour at work (DV) as a function of need for cognition, individuals' tendency to engage in and enjoy thinking (PV).

EXERCISE 11.1

Dealing with interdependence

Group discussion: Each person in the group takes an example study from Table 11.1 and considers possible factors that could affect the relationship between the Dependent Variable (DV) and the Predictor Variables (PVs). What options are there for dealing with them? Share your thoughts with the rest of the group, and discuss why options for dealing with external factors might differ from one study to another.

Ways of dealing with interdependence within quantitative analysis

In this section, we consider four ways of dealing with interrelated influences (see Table 11.2). Three involve simplification: through design, through selecting sub-samples and through statistical control. The final method is multivariate analysis, and this forms the main focus of this chapter. While all four methods are useful, most people develop a preference to suit their own style or the options open to them in their research area.

TABLE 11.2 How to deal with interrelated factors

Method	Action
1 Simplification through design	Sampling – select equal numbers within sub-groups
2 Simplification through selecting sub-samples	Restrict sample to one level of a key variable
3 Simplification through statistical control	Take variables two at a time, and use partial correlations to achieve statistical control
4 Multivariate analysis	Use multiple predictors and consider their joint influence

Simplification through design

The first way of dealing with interrelated influences is to design the study so that relevant causal factors are made independent of each other through the design itself (see also Chapter 4). Consider the case of age and salary level: as people get older, their experience grows and their salary level tends to go up. Thus, there is an association between age and salary, which can be summarized by a positive correlation (see Chapter 10). If a researcher picks employees at random, then the sample will be likely to reflect this association. However, another approach would be to divide the potential sample into groups based on age, and then select equal numbers of people at a number of salary levels within each age range. Even though age and salary may be correlated within the organization as a whole, the effect of this sampling strategy would be to create a sample of respondents where the two are independent of each other. The linkage between the two variables would not then be present in the sample.

The craft of research design (Shadish et al., 2002) is about developing imaginative ways of achieving simplicity of inference through creating a study design within which factors are orthogonal, where they are not independent of each other in the world at large. Such study designs are linked to statistical methods called *analysis of variance*, and designs with multiple factors are called factorial designs. Because they make analysis and inference simple even in research areas with many interrelated complicating factors, they have developed a strong appeal for some kinds of people. Experimental approaches based on structured research designs are widely used, particularly in work psychology, marketing and information systems research (Grant and Wall, 2009).

factorial designs a form of experimental design that includes combinations of more than one predictor variable

Simplification through selecting a sub-sample

The second way of dealing with interrelated influences is through selecting samples to be equal on potentially confounding factors. It is common to find that women are paid less than men, and one of the reasons is that men and women tend to do different jobs, which in turn command different pay levels. In random samples of men and women at work then, there will be different mixes of jobs for the two groups as well as differences in pay levels, and it is difficult to disentangle the relative influence of gender and job type. However, restricting a study sample to people doing the same job would mean that any gender difference cannot be attributed to job type but must be due to something else. The same logic was used by Hofstede (1991) in his research on national culture, where he gathered data only from IBM employees working in many countries across the world rather than by drawing random samples in each country. The differences he found led him to conclude that there were four basic dimensions of national culture: power distance, masculine-feminine, individual-collective and uncertainty avoidance (he later added long-term orientation). Relying on samples drawn from only one company means that he is controlling for differences in labour markets across the world.

Simplification through statistical control

The third way to deal with interrelated influences is through a form of statistical control called partial correlation. We saw in Chapter 10 that a correlation is a way of summarizing the extent to which people respond to two variables in consistent ways. A partial correlation is a correlation between two variables (we call them A and B) where the value of a third variable (we call this S) is adjusted statistically as if it were equal to the sample mean for everybody (this is usually referred to as *holding constant* a third variable). The correlation between A and B is written as r_{AB}. The symbol for the partial correlation is $r_{AB|S}$. The method of partial correlation allows the researcher to see how much of an observed correlation, say between A and B, can be accounted for by the relationship that both variables have with a third variable, S.

Partial correlation

statistical control a way of simplifying inference about the relationships among variables by adjusting for their covariance with another variable

Table 11.3 presents three possible patterns for r_{AB} and $r_{AB|S}$. We will use an example to explain the three patterns. Social media technologies such as blogs have become very popular, and it would not be surprising to find correlations between willingness to use blogs for external marketing (B) and both age (A) and salary level (S). A correlation between age and blogging (r_{AB}) could be interpreted in terms of the conservatism of older people when it comes to embracing new technologies. A correlation between blogging and salary (r_{BS}) could be interpreted in terms of more senior people in the organization having fewer direct links with customers. We have already suggested that a correlation between age and salary is plausible (r_{AS}), and so all three variables are likely to be correlated. The partial correlation of age and blogging with salary held constant identifies that part of the total correlation which is independent of salary. Pattern 1 shows a high AB correlation and also a high AB|S partial correlation, and here the S variable has not altered the correlation between A and B. Pattern 2 shows a high AB correlation but a zero AB|S partial correlation, and in this case the researcher would conclude that A and B are not really correlated at all. The relationship suggested by the AB correlation is spurious. Finally, pattern 3 shows an unusual but interesting case, where the AB correlation is zero, suggesting that A and B are not related at all. However, a high partial correlation implies that there really is a relationship between the two, but one that has been masked by the third variable, S.

partial correlation a correlation between two variables that is adjusted to remove the influence of a third variable

TABLE 11.3   Example of possible relationships between correlation and partial correlation

Pattern	Interpretation
1 r_{AB} is high; $r_{AB|S}$ is high	A and B are related; and S is irrelevant to both
2 r_{AB} is high; $r_{AB|S}$ is zero	A and B are not really related at all; but S has contributed to the appearance of a relationship between A and B
3 r_{AB} is zero; $r_{AB|S}$ is high	S is masking the 'real' relationship between A and B

Multivariate analysis

The final way of dealing with many interrelated factors builds on this logic of statistical control but extends it to many variables, and also to predictive relationships rather than simple associations as measured by correlations. Multivariate statistical methods are designed to allow researchers to include many variables in a single analysis and to assess the separate contribution of each variable within an overall model. These methods are the focus of the rest of this chapter. Their main feature is the specification of a conceptual model that expresses the researcher's hypotheses about the relationships among variables. The variables to be included in a model will be defined by the focus of the research. For example, in some of the studies considered already in this chapter, the size of the firm is treated as a 'nuisance' factor, which gets in the way of finding clear answers to interesting questions. However, there are other scholars for whom understanding the factors that make firms grow is the very focus of their work, and the size of the firm is not a nuisance factor at all.

Once a decision is made about which variables to include in a model, the next step is to specify what role each variable has in the model, usually as a cause (a predictor variable) or as an effect (a dependent variable). Making a decision about whether something is a dependent variable or a predictor variable is really a decision about how a variable is treated in the researcher's thinking. It is not an intrinsic characteristic of a variable, but instead a function of how it is used in a particular circumstance. This will depend to a large extent on the focus of a specific research project. Note that the role that a variable plays in statistical analysis reflects its position in the researcher's thinking, not something about the variable itself.

Latent
variable

Multivariate models can be specified using matrix algebra, for those with a strong mathematical training, and also represented graphically for those without such a background. We will use the graphical representation in this chapter for the sake of simplicity (see Figure 11.1). Variables are shown by boxes, which may be either rectangular or elliptical, and relationships among variables are shown by either single-headed or double-headed arrows. The variables used in multivariate models may be of two kinds: those that are measured directly by the researcher, called observed variables; and latent variables, which are not measured directly but are inferred from observed variables. Observed variables are shown by rectangular boxes, and latent variables are shown by elliptical boxes.

Figure 11.1(a) shows a model for observed variables, with a single dependent variable to the right (DV1) and two predictor variables (PV1 and PV2). The assumed causal relationship

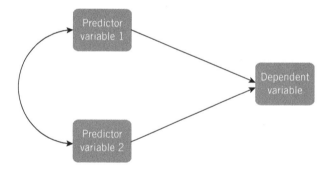

(a) Three observed variables (one DV and two PVs)

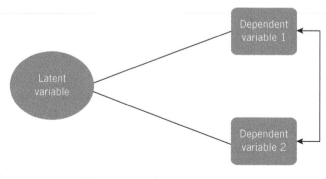

(b) Two observed DVs and one latent PV

FIGURE 11.1 Graphical representation of multivariate models

between the PVs and the DV is indicated by the single-headed arrows. The double-headed arrow connecting the two PVs indicates an association between them, which may or may not reflect a causal relationship (this relationship is called exogenous, because the specified model does not concern itself with its origins: it is taken as a given). Figure 11.1(b) shows a model with two observed variables (DV1 and DV2) and one latent predictor variable (LV). The LV is assumed to be a cause of both DV1 and DV2.

exogenous variables those variables that are part of a multivariate model, but whose causal influences are taken as given and do not form part of the model itself

RESEARCH IN ACTION

Multivariate analysis on 'real-world' datasets

Conor McDonald completed a PhD in Business and Economics at the University of Leeds in 2014. He now works as a Senior Data Scientist with Amazon. His interests include machine learning, natural language processing, applied statistics and data visualization, as well as programming in open source software languages, such as R and Python.

Conor McDonald

You have experience of analysing quantitative datasets for both academic and industry-related purposes. Are there any differences in terms of methods or approach?

Differences do arise because of the intended outcomes of quantitative analysis in academia and industry. For example, when analysing quantitative data as an academic, the objective is often to form a more nuanced understanding of a particular phenomenon or to test theory. To this end, the researcher needs to design their study and analysis to maximize the interpretability of their statistical model. For example, in an academic study it will often be important to employ a model that provides standardized coefficients (e.g. a linear or logistic regression) so that the analysis can reveal how changes in predictor variables change the dependent variable.

In contrast, in industry, the end goal is often increased value, decreased costs, a more optimized process or a highly accurate predictive model. To this end, the interpretability of the model is often secondary to its performance on the particular task. For example, in machine learning tasks (e.g. building a model to predict whether or not an incoming email is legitimate or spam), the analyst will focus more on improving the model's performance metric (e.g. predictive accuracy) than understanding the impact of different predictor variables. This means that the analyst is less confined in their choice of model or algorithm and, indeed, may combine multiple models in an ensemble in order to maximize predictive accuracy. This is not to say that interpretability is unimportant in industry, only that in many instances, it is secondary to the model performance.

As a Data Scientist, what are the main challenges you face when conducting multivariate analyses?

A common type of multivariate analysis that I perform as a Data Scientist is building predictive models that take as input multiple predictors (i.e. model features), which

(Continued)

are used to predict a target variable. This often requires decisions to be made about which variables to include in the model. For example, when predicting the price of a house (the target variable) you may have at your disposal hundreds of features (such as the number of rooms, square feet, local crime rates, etc.), but part of the 'art' of Data Science (and quantitative research more generally) is finding the 'signal' in the 'noise'. In a multivariate context, this often translates to identifying those variables that improve your model's ability to make predictions (the signals) versus those that do not (the noise). This is important, as in many instances the inclusion of noisy variables can confuse a model and lead to a significant reduction in its performance. In an industry context, this carries additional importance as a model with fewer features is less computationally intensive and, therefore, will run faster. This can often be beneficial when models are being run in real-time 'production' environments.

Therefore, a key consideration in multivariate analysis is whether or not greater model complexity actually improves performance. Sometimes the model with a few well-considered features is more interesting and performs better than one with hundreds!

causal model
a class of multivariate models of the causal relationships among a set of variables that can be fitted to data

The next sections give an introduction to multivariate analysis methods for analysing causal models. Measurement models explore the relationship between observed variables and latent variables. Causal models are of two kinds: those that involve only observed variables, and those that involve both observed and latent variables.

Multivariate analysis of causal models

Rationale for causal models

Causality cannot be proved

Using multivariate statistical methods to test causal models is a powerful technique that is widely used within management research. Its major value is that it forces the researcher to define very precisely both the variables to be included and the way in which they relate to each other. In return, the statistical methods offer specific tests of hypotheses that can allow the researcher to judge how good those models are. However, what causal modelling methods cannot do is prove a causal relationship. Instead, they allow decisions to be made about whether a given model is consistent with observed data. The plausibility of a particular model needs first to be established conceptually from theory, and then quantitative evidence can be used to assess whether the model is consistent with data. In their paper, Coyle-Shapiro and Kessler (2000) (see Table 11.1) developed a theoretical rationale for treating employee commitment as a dependent variable and psychological contract fulfilment as a predictor variable. Yet unless they have longitudinal data, with variables measured on more than one occasion, it is impossible for them to prove that this assumption is correct. Instead, all they can do is assess whether the conceptual model that they formulated is consistent with their data.

Defining what variables to include in the model

This step is important because any causal model will estimate the best values that it can for the contribution of each variable that is included. However, the estimation procedure can only take into account the information it has available to it. If the researcher leaves out (by accident or by design) a factor that is critically important, then the modelling procedure cannot find it, and the results obtained can be misleading. Studies that leave out important variables are very likely to produce misleading conclusions. Almost every week, some survey is reported in the newspapers showing that red wine is good/bad for health, or that chocolate/chips help you diet. Such studies almost always suffer from small and idiosyncratic samples, and their big failing is that the true causal factors behind good health or weight loss were not even included in the study. For the most part, the findings are either chance results that cannot be replicated, or are the spurious consequence of some other more important variable.

EXERCISE 11.2

Designing your own multivariate causal analysis project

Individual: Identify your research hypothesis and write it down in the same way as the summaries in Table 11.1. What is your dependent variable (DV), and how would you measure it? What are your predictor variables (PV), and how will you measure them?

Specifying causal models

Research propositions should be translated into formal causal models that can be tested statistically, either as a single model or as a sequence of models of increasing complexity. Comparing a simple model with a more complex one is a powerful way of testing research hypotheses, but it is important to remember that a more complex model, one that includes more variables or has more complex relationships among them, will always give a better fit to a given dataset. So, goodness of fit alone is not the most important criterion in selecting the best model. Instead, the researcher needs to take into account what the gain in the quality of the model is relative to the added complexity needed to achieve it. An example of the development of a series of causal models is shown in Example 11.1.

goodness of fit
a summary
measure of the
discrepancy
between
observed
values and the
fitted values
derived from a
hypothesized
model

EXAMPLE 11.1

Stakeholder relationship management and corporate financial performance: formulating alternative causal models

This example considers different accounts of how stakeholder relationship management links to corporate strategy and to the performance of the organization. Berman et al. (1999) propose two kinds of model, the normative model and the instrumental model, and show how they can be tested empirically. The normative model states that looking

(Continued)

after the interests of stakeholders is the right thing to do, and that the strategic goals set by senior management will be determined by a need to protect and promote the interests of their stakeholders. So principles of stakeholder relationship management guide how the organization formulates its corporate strategy, and strategy in turn has some influence on financial performance. Figure 11.2 expresses the normative model using blocks for the key variables and arrows to show the hypothesized causal relationships among them.

FIGURE 11.2   The normative model of stakeholder relationship management and corporate financial performance

Source: adapted from Berman et al., 1999. © Academy of Management Publishing Limited, all rights reserved.

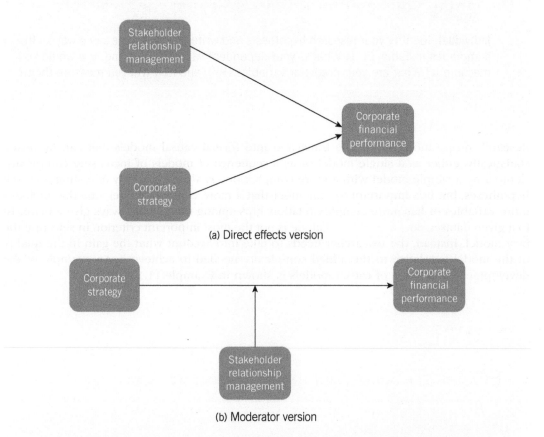

(a) Direct effects version

(b) Moderator version

FIGURE 11.3   The instrumental model of stakeholder relationship management and corporate financial performance

The instrumental model (Figure 11.3) states that organizations should pay attention to their stakeholders because they will benefit financially; thus the model proposes that both stakeholder relationship management and corporate strategy influence corporate financial performance. Berman et al. propose two variants of the instrumental model: the direct effects model shown in Figure 11.3(a) and the moderation model shown in Figure 11.3(b). The direct effects model differs from the normative model in that there is no path between corporate strategy and stakeholder relationship management, but there is a direct path from stakeholder relationships to financial performance. The moderation model is a more sophisticated version of the direct effects model, which proposes a different mechanism for the role of stakeholder relationship management, as modifying the link between strategy and performance. The logic behind this form of the model is that companies will find it easier to put their strategic goals into practice and benefit from them if they foster good relationships with their stakeholders.

Sample size

The trustworthiness of a model depends on how stable it is, and that means the sample size needs to be large enough to give confidence that the results could be replicated in new samples. Analyses based on small samples tend to give quirky results that may not be repeatable. The adequacy of a sample depends on the complexity of the model that is fitted to the data: complex models need larger samples. As a useful rule of thumb, multiplying the number of observed predictor variables by ten gives a minimum sample size (though this really is a minimum, and other factors such as the reliability of measurement would lead us to recommend larger samples than this).

Assessing the appropriate form of a causal model

Once the researcher has defined the conceptual model in a form that can be tested statistically, the next step is to check that the data available are expressed in a form that is appropriate for the assumptions required by the statistical method. This involves assessing both measurement quality and that the form of the statistical model is appropriate. The input for all multivariate analysis methods is a matrix containing the variances of each variable (indicating the spread of scores: see Chapter 10) and the covariances among them (these reflect the associations among each pair of variables and are used to calculate correlations). It is important therefore that there are no extreme scores on any of the study variables (outliers) that can distort the value of the variance as a measure of spread. It is also important to check the form of the association among each pair of variables to ensure that relationships are linear.

Assessing the quality of fitted causal models

All multivariate methods for analysing causal models share common characteristics. They give a summary measure of how good the prediction is for the model as a whole, generally expressed in terms of the proportion of variance in the dependent variable(s) accounted for by a set of predictors. They also report specific measures for components of the model, indicating the separate contribution of each predictor variable.

logistic regression a form of multivariate analysis of causal relationships among observed variables where the dependent variable is measured on a binary category scale

Generalized linear models

The multivariate methods considered in this chapter – multiple regression analysis, MANCOVA, MANOVA and logistic regression – have the same formal structure and they are all referred to as 'generalized linear models'. The technical details are beyond the scope of this book, but the management researcher benefits from these theoretical developments in statistics because they provide both a theoretical 'cleanness' to the models and also the basis for the computational algorithms used by statistical packages such as SPSS.

EXERCISE 11.3

Your multivariate causal analysis project

1   **Individual exercise**: Consider your DV – what kind of measurement scale would you use for it (category/continual scale)? What choices are there for statistical tests of your research hypothesis?

2   **Individual exercise**: Consider your PVs – what kind of measurement scale would you use for it (category/continual scale)? What choices are there for statistical tests of your research hypothesis?

multiple regression model
a multivariate method that includes a single dependent variable measured on a continuous scale and a set of predictor variables that may be measured on continuous or category scales

regression weight
the value of the independent contribution of a predictor variable to predicting a dependent variable in multiple regression analysis; also called a path coefficient

squared multiple correlation
an overall measure of the quality of a multiple regression model; the proportion of variance in a dependent variable accounted for by a set of predictor variables

Analysis of causal models for observed variables

This section describes three general classes of multivariate model for observed variables to illustrate how researchers can approach the analysis of causal relationships. Our purpose is to demonstrate what the methods have in common rather than their differences, and to show part of the craft of multivariate modelling. The main features of each class of model are summarized in Table 11.4. The table is in four parts for each method in turn. Part (a) shows what kinds of variables are appropriate for the method, according to the number of dependent variables used and the measurement scale for both DVs and PVs. Part (b) describes how the quality of the model as a whole is assessed in that method. Part (c) lists how the individual elements of the model are represented in the model. Part (d) outlines alternative options that are available within each method. First, we consider the multiple regression and analysis of covariance models whose characteristics are shown in column 1.

Multiple regression analysis (MRA)

The basic multiple regression model consists of a single dependent variable measured on a continuous scale and a set of predictor variables, which may be measured on continuous or category scales (see Table 11.4(a)). The model for two predictor variables can be expressed algebraically like this:

$$Y = a + b_1 X_1 + b_2 X_2 + e$$

where the symbol Y is used for the dependent variable, while the symbol X is used for each predictor variable, a is called the intercept or the constant (it is the value of Y when each X is zero), b is called a regression weight, and e is a residual (or error) term. On the predictor side of the model above, there are two kinds of variables. The PVs (shown here by X_1 and X_2) are the systematic part of the model chosen by the researcher. All other factors that influence the spread of scores on the DV are combined together into the residual term, e. The graphical form of this regression model is shown in Figure 11.4.

The quality of the regression model as a whole (Table 11.4(b)) is summarized by the squared multiple correlation, R^2, whose value varies between 0 and 1 and shows how much of the spread in DV scores can be accounted for by the predictors in the model. In MRA, the

TABLE 11.4 Multivariate methods for analysis of causal models for observed variables

	MRA/ANCOVA	MANOVA/MANCOVA	Logistic regression analysis
(a) Variables	DV – a single continuous variable PVs – one or more continuous and/or category variables MRA – one or more continuous variables ANCOVA – one or more category variables and one or more continuous variables	DVs – two or more continuous variables PVs – one or more continuous and/or category variables MANOVA – one or more category variables (factors) MANCOVA – one or more category variables and one or more continuous variables (covariates)	DV – a single dichotomous category variable PVs – one or more continuous and/or category variables
(b) Assessing quality of the model as a whole	Multiple R shows the validity of the model as a whole; multiple R^2 shows the proportion of variance in the DV accounted for. An F-ratio tests whether the multiple R is significantly different from zero.	Wilks' Lambda – multivariate test for each effect (category and continuous variable) shows the significance level for all DVs jointly An F-ratio tests the significance of Lambda	Model χ^2
(c) Contribution of individual elements of the model	Regression weights show the independent contribution of each PV; beta weights are regression weights standardized onto the same measurement scale for all variables. A t-test assesses whether a regression weight is significantly different from zero.	Separate tests for each dependent variable: • Univariate tests (which ignore correlations among the dependent variables). • Stepdown tests (which partial out the effects of dependent variables entered according to a pre-determined sequence).	Regression weights and odds ratios for each predictor variable
(d) Options available	• Simultaneous entry of all predictors. • Hierarchical regression – entry of variables in a sequence determined by the researcher. • Stepwise regression – sequential entry of variables determined by the predictive value of variables.	• Stepdown tests require a pre-determined sequence for the dependent variables. • Tests could be performed with and without covariates in the model.	• Simultaneous entry of all predictors. • Hierarchical logistic regression – entry of variables in a sequence determined by theory. • Stepwise logistic regression – sequential entry of variables according to their predictive value.

measure of spread that is used is the variance (see Chapter 10), and the R^2 measure is the proportion of variance in the DV accounted for by the PVs collectively. It is often multiplied by 100 to give a percentage of variance accounted for, from 0 per cent to 100 per cent. R^2 indicates the relative importance of the PVs and the residual term, which is shown to the right in Figure 11.4. Thus, where a set of predictors account for 20 per cent of the variance in a DV, this means that 80 per cent of the variance is accounted for by all other causal factors combined into the residual term. An F-test is used to test the null hypothesis that the proportion of variance accounted for by the PVs is zero against the alternative hypothesis that it is greater than zero. The individual components of the model are summarized in Table 11.4(c). The regression weights indicate the size of the independent contribution that each PV makes to predicting the spread in scores on the DV. When predictor variables are measured on different scales, the relative size of regression weights for different variables cannot be compared. So it is usual to transform each of the variables in MRA to a common measurement scale (this is called 'standardizing'), and then the regression weights are referred to as either standardized regression weights or β (beta) weights. The significance test for regression weights gives a t-value, and the null hypothesis tested is that the regression weight is zero against the alternative that it is different from zero.

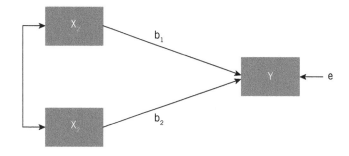

FIGURE 11.4   Graphical representation of a multiple regression model

EXAMPLE 11.2

Multiple regression analysis of predictors of quality commitment

Jackson (2004) reported a study of one aspect of employees' commitment to the values of their organization: their commitment to quality. There were three stages to the research: defining the concept of quality commitment itself; formulating a way of measuring it; and developing and testing a conceptual model of how quality commitment relates to both personal and organizational variables. Here, we focus on the third stage where a sequence of regression analyses were used to test the conceptual model.

Table 11.5 shows a matrix of correlations for quality commitment, demographic variables (age, company tenure and gender) and a number of measures of work design. Row 10 of the table shows the correlation between quality commitment and each of the other variables in the study. There is a strong relationship with age ($r = 0.30$, p < 0.001), indicating that older workers show higher quality commitment; and the relationship with company tenure is much lower but also significant ($r = 0.14$, p < 0.001). Gender differences are significant but small in size ($r = 0.09$, p < 0.05), with women showing higher quality commitment. Table 11.5 also shows, not surprisingly, that age and company tenure are correlated: those who have been employed longer with their company tend to be older. There are also consistently strong correlations between quality commitment and work design characteristics. Workers with more control over the timing and methods aspects of their jobs report higher quality commitment ($r = 0.21$, p < 0.001 and $r = 0.24$, p < 0.001 for timing and method control respectively); workers whose jobs are more mentally demanding in terms of problem solving ($r = 0.11$, p < 0.001) and system monitoring ($r = 0.23$, p < 0.001) also report higher quality commitment; and quality commitment is correlated with production responsibility ($r = 0.16$, p < 0.001): workers reporting more expensive consequences if they make a mistake have higher quality commitment.

However, interpreting these relationships is not simple, because the table shows that there are strong correlations among many of the study variables. For example, people who have been employed in the company for longer tend to report higher levels of the work design variables, presumably because they have jobs with more responsibility. We have also seen that age and company tenure are correlated. Testing the conceptual model means that it is necessary to tease out these relationships, and that is the purpose of multiple regression analysis.

In the analyses reported in Table 11.6, the DV is quality commitment, and the predictors are the demographic and work design variables. Two steps in hierarchical regression analysis

TABLE 11.5 Correlations among study variables

		1	2	3	4	5	6	7	8	9	10
1	Organization	–									
2	Age	.13	–								
3	Gender	–.43	–.09	–							
4	Company tenure	.02	.48	–.11	–						
5	Individual timing control	.28	.26	–.23	.23	–					
6	Individual method control	.29	.19	–.28	.24	.67	–				
7	Monitoring demands	–.08	.11	–.03	.17	.16	.28	–			
8	Problem-solving demands	.09	.00	–.22	.21	.20	.34	.52	–		
9	Production responsibility	.00	.02	–.11	.05	.02	.15	.42	.34	–	
10	Quality commitment	.02	.30	.09	.14	.21	.24	.23	.11	.16	–
Mean		.22	30.78	.78	5.74	2.83	3.09	3.85	3.00	3.19	3.97
Standard deviation		.62	11.12	.41	6.16	1.21	.93	.84	.88	1.06	.51

(Continued)

are shown in the table. In the first step, column 1, the demographic variables are used as PVs and the results show that both age and gender are significant predictors of quality commitment, while company tenure is not. This suggests that the correlation between company tenure and quality commitment arises because both variables are correlated with age: it would appear that quality commitment reflects a person's age rather than the length of employment with the employer. The second step (column 2) adds the work design predictors in order to test how much each one adds independently to predicting quality commitment, but also how important work design factors are relative to demographic factors. The regression weights shown here give a different picture from the correlations. Although all five work design variables were significantly correlated with quality commitment (Table 11.5), only three of the five regression weights are significant. Interpreting how important each individual work design variable is on the basis of how strongly it correlates with quality commitment is clouded by the correlations among the work design variables themselves. The difference in interpretation between pairwise correlation analysis and multiple regression analysis in this example shows how important it is to consider variables together.

TABLE 11.6　Hierarchical regression analysis for predicting quality commitment from demographic and work design variables

	Step 1	Step 2
Organization	.04	.02
Demographics		
Age	.30 **	.27 **
Gender	.14 **	.19 **
Company tenure	.01	−.05
Work design		
Individual timing control		.07
Individual method control		.15 **
Monitoring demands		.12 **
Problem-solving demands		.00
Production responsibility		.10 **
Multiple R^2	.10	.18
Change in Multiple R^2	.10	.08
F-ratio for test of change in R^2	36.03 **	18.47 **

Note: ** $p < 0.01$

hierarchical regression
a form of multiple regression analysis, which involves entering predictor variables sequentially in blocks

An example application of multiple regression analysis is shown in Example 11.2. It illustrates the basic elements of MRA, but also shows the value of a variant of MRA called hierarchical regression (see Table 11.4d) where predictors are entered sequentially in more than one block. Hierarchical regression allows the researcher to test hypotheses not just about the importance of individual predictors but also about variables entered into a model as groups. Table 11.6 (bottom row) shows that it is possible to compare the overall fit of one model to another with one or more predictor variables added. Each model has an R^2 value and the same F-test that was used to assess each individual R^2 can be used to test the change in R^2 between models.

Figure 11.5 shows two versions of a hypothetical regression model for three observed variables. In both models, the variable PV1 is assumed to be a cause of PV2, shown by the single-headed arrow between them, and PV2 in turn is assumed to be a cause of DV. The difference between the models lies in how PV1 relates to DV: in (a) there is a direct path between the two, while in (b) there is no path and any causal influence of PV1 on DV would have to work through PV2. Such a causal influence would make PV2 a mediator between PV1 and DV, and the model is called a mediational model. Hierarchical regression analysis could be used to test the mediational model as follows. First, model (a) is tested using both PV1 and PV2 as predictors of DV. The multiple R^2 shows what proportion of the variance in DV is accounted for by both predictors. Second, model (b) is tested by dropping PV1 from the set of predictors of DV, and again multiple R^2 is calculated. The only difference between model (a) and model (b) is the removal of PV1, so the difference between the two values of R^2 shows whether PV1 is a significant predictor of DV and therefore the path between them in Figure 11.5(a) is necessary.

mediational model
a form of causal model in which the causal influence of a predictor variable on a dependent variable is indirect, operating through an intermediary variable (called a mediator)

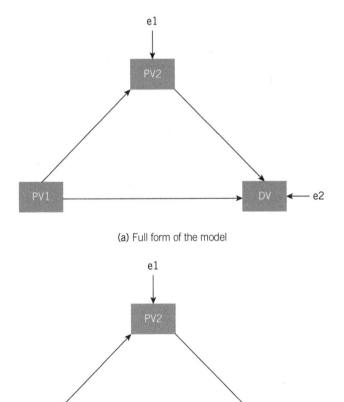

(a) Full form of the model

(b) Reduced form of the model with one path removed

FIGURE 11.5   Hierarchical regression analysis for testing mediational effects

There are other forms of regression analysis, called stepwise regression, which involve an automatic process of adding or subtracting variables according to how well they contribute to predicting the dependent variable. However, they rely on a blind search among predictors in order to identify those that make the greatest contribution to predicting the dependent variable, and such methods rarely have a place in management research.

Analysis of covariance (ANCOVA)

covariates
variables measured on continuous scales, which are included as predictors in analysis of group differences

ANCOVA is the name given to a form of multiple regression analysis where some of the predictors are continuous variables and others are category variables. It is a generalization of the methods for assessing differences between groups that were considered in Chapter 10, which allows the researcher to include predictors measured on continuous scales (these are called the covariates). Conclusions based on hypothesis tests about group differences can be seriously misleading if groups differ on variables other than the dependent variable. Analysis of covariance (ANCOVA) adjusts the dependent variable scores to what they would have been had the treatment groups been equal on the covariate. ANCOVA achieves a statistical matching between treatment groups by adjusting groups' means on the DV to what they would have been had the groups scored the same on the covariates. The next class of methods that we consider are multivariate analysis of variance (MANOVA) and multivariate analysis of covariance (MANCOVA), and their characteristics are listed in column 2 of Table 11.4.

analysis of covariance (ANCOVA)
a form of test of group differences on a continuous dependent variable, which also includes continuous variables as predictors (covariates)

MANOVA/MANCOVA

These methods bring together a number of methods that we have already considered, generalized to the situation where the researcher is interested in assessing the predictability of more than one dependent variable. MANOVA is used for comparing groups that are classified on the basis of one or more category variables. MANCOVA is the multivariate generalization of ANCOVA, which includes one or more continuous variables as covariates as well as at least one category variable.

multivariate analysis of variance (MANOVA)
a class of statistical methods for testing group differences for two or more dependent variables simultaneously

The practical problem addressed by this class of methods is that of interpreting the causal influences of predictors on dependent variables that are correlated among themselves. Taking correlated dependent variables singly can be misleading because each one carries not just information about the thing it measures but also something of what it shares with other dependent variables.

The quality of the model as a whole is shown by a multivariate test for the whole set of DVs taken together. There are several test statistics available, but the one most frequently used is called Wilks' Lambda (this varies between 0 and 1 and a small value is better), and an F-ratio tests the significance of Lambda. Having looked at each of the effects for the set of DVs taken together, the next step is to explore individual components of the model, and there are two options here. The first option is the univariate F-test and this is the same test as if the analysis had been performed for each DV separately, but with an adjustment in significance level made to take account of the number of dependent variables in the model. The univariate F-test thus ignores correlations among the DVs, and so its usefulness depends on how high those correlations are. Another option is a stepdown F-test, where the DVs are tested in a sequence decided upon by the researcher. In effect it is a form of analysis of covariance, which holds constant previous DVs. The first test is carried out ignoring the other DVs, the second test adjusts for the first DV, and so on. Stepdown tests are preferable to univariate tests because they take into account the correlations among the DVs, but their value is dependent on whether the researcher can give a justifiable ordering of the dependent variables. While the results from the univariate tests will be the same regardless

multivariate analysis of covariance (MANCOVA)
a class of statistical methods for testing group differences for two or more dependent variables simultaneously, which also includes one or more continuous variables as predictors

of which order the DVs are listed in, this is not true of stepdown tests. Univariate tests and stepdown tests will only give the same answers when the DVs are completely uncorrelated with each other.

univariate *F*-test
the test statistic in multivariate analysis of variance for group differences in a single dependent variable ignoring others

stepdown *F*-test
the test statistic in a multivariate analysis of variance of group differences, where the DVs are tested singly in turn in a sequence decided upon by the researcher holding constant DVs earlier in the sequence

EXAMPLE 11.3

Worked example of MANOVA

This example uses the same data as Example 11.2 from a developmental study of employees' commitment to quality (Jackson, 2004). Earlier, we used gender and a number of work design characteristics as predictors of individuals' quality commitment, and this example tests the hypothesis that there are gender differences in work design. Table 11.5 shows that there are correlations among the work design variables, so it may be misleading to ignore these relationships by taking each variable alone. Table 11.7 gives the main results from MANOVA with gender as a category variable predictor and five work design characteristics as dependent variables.

TABLE 11.7   Results of multivariate analysis of variance: gender differences in five work design characteristics (*n* = 967)

	Male (n = 209)	Female (n = 758)	*t*-test
(a) Univariate tests for each variable separately			
Individual timing control	3.37	2.69	7.24 **
Individual method control	3.60	2.96	9.25 **
Monitoring demands	3.89	3.84	0.76
Problem-solving demands	3.37	2.89	7.16 **
Production responsibility	3.41	3.12	3.51 **
(b) Multivariate test for all variables together			
Wilks' Lambda = 0.87, F = 27.73 **			

Note: ** indicates significant at 0.01 level

The mean scores for males and females on each work design variable are shown in Table 11.7(a), together with the results of univariate *t*-tests (ignoring the correlations among the DVs). This shows that women report significantly lower scores on four out of the five work design characteristics: they have less control over work timing and methods; the problem-solving demands on them are lower; and their responsibility for production mistakes is lower. These results would suggest that women's jobs in this sample are more routine and undemanding than those of the men in the sample.

However, the individual tests ignore the fact that there are correlations among the work design variables, and the multivariate test of the gender effect is shown in Table 11.7(b). This shows the Wilks' Lambda coefficient and its associated significance test, an

wilks' Lambda
the test statistic in multivariate analysis of variance for group differences in a set of two or more dependent variables

(Continued)

F-ratio. The null hypothesis being tested is that there is no gender difference in the set of DVs taken together, and this is rejected with a high level of confidence. There is clear evidence for a gender difference in work design in general, confirming what was observed for the analysis of the individual DVs.

Follow-up analyses could go in a number of directions, depending on the interests of the researcher. One direction would be to examine in more detail what job titles the men and women in this sample actually hold in order to determine whether men have higher-grade jobs in this sample or whether the observed effects reflect gender differences among people doing the same jobs. A different avenue to explore is whether there is a common factor underlying the work design variables (see the earlier section on measurement models), which might give a greater conceptual clarity to this analysis. Finally, we focused here on gender, but there may be other influential demographic differences between men and women, such as age or organizational tenure, which have been ignored. If so, any interpretation that focuses purely on gender would be misguided.

The final class of multivariate methods that we consider for causal analysis of observed variables is logistic regression analysis.

Logistic regression analysis

odds ratio
the relative likelihood of the two possible outcomes for a binary category variable; used to form the dependent variable in logistic regression analysis

This addresses the same questions as multiple regression analysis, except that the DV is a dichotomous category variable rather than a continuous variable (Table 11.4, column 3). Like MRA, predictor variables may be continuous or category variables or any mix of the two. Examples of dependent variables that might be used in logistic regression analysis include: the presence or absence of a risk factor for stress; the success or failure of a merger; the survival or not of a joint venture partnership. The dependent variable in logistic regression analysis is based on an odds ratio, which expresses the relative likelihood of the two possible outcomes. For example, if 20 per cent of mergers in a dataset of companies succeed while 80 per cent do not, then the odds of success are 4:1 against (20 per cent/80 per cent). It is the log of these odds that is used as the DV in logistic regression:

likelihood ratio chi-square
an index of the overall quality of a model fitted by the maximum likelihood method; used in logistic regression analysis

$$\log p \,/\, (1 - p)$$

where p is the probability of succeeding and $1 - p$ is the probability of failing. The model is used to assess the independent contribution of several predictor variables to the prediction of these odds.

Wald test
the test statistic in logistic regression analysis expressing the independent contribution of a predictor variable

Because the DV in logistic regression is a complex function of the probability of being in one category rather than another, the method used to fit the model is different from that used in multiple regression. This method gives a different test statistic for the quality of the model as a whole, a likelihood ratio chi-square. Despite this difference from multiple regression, the significance test tells the same story: whether the set of predictors as a whole account for significant variation in the DV. The individual components of the model are also evaluated by their regression weights, and each is tested by comparing its size relative to the standard error. In logistic regression, the result is called a Wald test, but its meaning is the same as in multiple regression. A worked example of logistic regression analysis is shown in Example 11.4.

EXAMPLE 11.4

A worked example of logistic regression analysis

This example uses data from the study by Sprigg and Jackson (2006) of stress in call centre staff. The DV is whether or not the respondent had experienced musculoskeletal disorder (MSD) caused by his or her work in the previous seven days (this includes back pain, aches in the wrist or shoulders, etc.). Logistic regression is appropriate because the DV is a category variable with two levels. The two predictors that we focus on here are: workload, a continuous variable assessing aspects of the demands of the job; and scripting, a three-point ordered category variable assessing to what degree call handlers followed a strictly worded script when they answered calls. The sample size for this analysis was 836, and of these 520 (62 per cent) reported MSD in the previous seven days. MSDs are thus relatively common in this sample of call handlers. The odds in favour of MSD are 62 relative to 38, and the odds ratio is calculated as:

Odds ratio = p / (1 − p) = 0.622 / 0.378 = 1.65.

Logistic regression takes the log of this odds ratio as the DV, and the hypothesis being tested is whether the predictor variables either increase or decrease the risk of experiencing MSD while working as a call handler.

Table 11.8 shows the results of logistic regression. The quality of the model as a whole is shown by a chi-square test statistic, and its value is 5.46, with 2 degrees of freedom (because there are two predictors). This is statistically significant, so we conclude that the two predictors together do account for a difference in the relative risk of MSDs.

The separate contribution of each predictor variable is shown by the standardized regression weights (labelled as beta weights in Table 11.8), just as in multiple regression. The hypothesis that the beta weight is zero is tested by a Wald statistic rather than a *t*-value for testing significance, but otherwise the interpretation of the coefficients is the same as for multiple regression. Both beta weights are positive in sign and statistically significant, indicating that higher workload is associated with an increased risk of MSDs and more use of a set script is also associated with an increase in risk. These influences are independent, so that someone who has high workload *and* greater use of a set script will tend to experience greater risk of MSD than someone who is high on only one predictor.

beta weight
a standardized regression coefficient

TABLE 11.8 Results of logistic regression analysis for MSD as a function of workload and following a set script

Overall fit of the model: chi-square = 5.46 (df = 2), p < .01

Variable	Beta weight	Wald statistic
Workload	.50**	29.90
Script	.28*	5.31

The options available to the researcher within logistic regression are exactly the same as for multiple regression analysis (see Table 11.4(d)). Predictor variables may be entered in a single block, or the researcher may have theoretical reasons for defining a sequence of models to be fitted hierarchically. Finally, stepwise logistic regression can be used to enter predictor variables purely on the basis of how well they predict the dependent variable. Just as for stepwise options in multiple regression analysis, we see limited scope for this within management research.

Analysis of observed and latent variables: structural equation modelling

Structural equation modelling (SEM) (Blunch, 2008; Hair et al., 2010; Tabachnick and Fidell, 2014) brings together the two kinds of multivariate methods that we have considered so far: measurement models for assessing hypotheses about relationships between observed and latent variables (Chapter 9), and structural models of the causal relationships among both observed and latent variables. As such, they provide within the same framework a way of expressing and estimating many of the different kinds of model used by management researchers. There are several statistical packages available for fitting structural equation models. The best known are: LISREL (www.ssicentral.com), EQS (www.mvsoft.com), Mplus (www.statmodel.com) and AMOS (www-03.ibm.com/software/products/en/spss-amos). The open source software R also contains packages to fit structural equation models. While the detailed characteristics differ among them, they all share the same underlying models and the graphical interface used to develop the model. AMOS has a reputation for being easier to use than the others, but the craft of SEM involves the same five steps whatever software is used (see Table 11.9).

Example 11.5

Studies using structural equation modelling

Wu, Parker and de Jong (2014): Individual innovation behaviour at work (DV) as a function of need for cognition, individuals' tendency to engage in and enjoy thinking. This study identified indicators for each of their key constructs, and then used confirmatory factor analysis (via Mplus) to check the acceptability of their measurement model.

Murnieks, Mosakowski and Cardon (2014): This study looked at entrepreneurs and examined the origins of passion and ways in which passion energizes action. They used existing theory to develop a full structural equation model for the antecedents of entrepreneurial passion and its relationship to entrepreneurial behaviour. They first used CFA to check the validity of their measurement model, and then tested the study hypotheses within their structural model.

TABLE 11.9   Steps in structural equation modelling

1   Define model hypotheses
2   Specify the model
3   Estimate model parameters
4   Evaluate the quality of the model
5   Consider alternative models

The first step in SEM is to *define model hypotheses*, specifying what variables are included within the model (both measured and latent variables), and what the relationships are among them. Any model fitting procedure will use the relationships among the variables that are included to estimate the parameter in the hypothesized model. There is no substitute for careful consideration of which variables to include in a model: leave out something important and the model obtained can be seriously biased and misleading. Furthermore, the use of latent variable models places the responsibility on the researcher to think carefully about what indicators to use for each latent variable and to ensure that they are measured reliably. The most sophisticated of statistical treatment cannot overcome the deficiencies introduced by sloppy thinking or poor measurement practice.

The second step in SEM is to *specify the model*, including either fixed or free parameters. Free parameters are those elements of the model whose values are to be estimated from data, while fixed parameters have a predefined value allocated to them (usually, but not always, zero). Fixed parameters are usually necessary to make a model identifiable (see below), and they also give the basis for testing theoretical propositions by comparing different models where fixed parameters are set free. The full structural equation model has both measured variables and latent variables, and may also include causal relationships among the latent variables. The model in Figure 11.6 looks quite different from the ones considered so far in this chapter, but it is almost the same as the model in Figure 9.1. Both models have three kinds of variable: observed variables shown in rectangles, latent variables (we called these common factors earlier) and specific factors both shown in ellipses. Apart from a cosmetic change in layout, the only difference is that there is a causal arrow linking the two latent variables in the centre of the model in Figure 11.6.

The left-hand side shows the measurement model for the latent variable labelled as PV (see the earlier section of this chapter). This model hypothesizes that the PV is a common factor that accounts for the correlations among observed variables 1–3, while the specific factor associated with each of the observed variables captures all influences on observed variable scores which are specific to that variable. The right-hand side shows the equivalent measurement model for the DV. At the centre of the figure is the structural model showing the hypothesized causal link between the two latent variables.

Each of the arrows in the figure represents a path between two variables and also a parameter to be estimated from the data. For measurement models, these parameters are called factor loadings, while for causal models, they are called regression weights or path coefficients. Since (by definition) latent variables cannot be measured directly, the only information the researcher has about them comes from the observed variables. For a structural equation model, there are two kinds of parameter that need to be defined. The first is the covariance among the latent and observed variables. The second is the variance of each latent variable, so that its measurement scale is defined. The variance of an observed variable indicates the spread of scores around the mean on its measurement scale and thus defines the scale, and the same is true of the variance of a latent variable. However, the scale of a latent variable is unobservable and so it has to be defined in another way. One common option is to assume that the measurement scale of a latent variable is the same as that of one of its indicator variables (it does not matter which one), and another is to assume that the scale is a standardized one with a variance of one. For each parameter, the researcher can either define a fixed value for a parameter (as shown in the CFA example in Chapter 9) or estimate a value from data. The commonest fixed values are zero for paths between variables, and 1 for variances of latent variables.

path coefficients
see regression
weight

The input to a model-fitting procedure consists of:

- the variances of the observed variables, which define their measurement scale
- the covariances among the observed variables.

If there are p observed variables, then the number of items of information available for model fitting is p variances and $p*(p-1)/2$ covariances. The model in Figure 11.6 contains six observed variables, so the number of items of information available is $6 + 6*5/2 = 21$. There are three possibilities for the relationship between the number of parameters to be estimated and the information available to do it, and together they define the identifiability of a model:

1. *Just identified*: there are the same number of parameters to estimate and information available. A just-identified model will always fit the observed data perfectly. Unique values for the parameters of the model can be estimated and their significance tested, but the model is as complex as the original data.

2. *Under-identified*: there are more parameters to be estimated than information available to define unique values for them, and it is then impossible to fit a model.

3. *Over-identified*: there are fewer parameters to be estimated than items of information. Here, the fitted model is simpler than the original data, and it is possible to calculate a significance test for the model as a whole as well as unique values for the individual parameters.

identifiability
the characteristic of a hypothesized model defined by the relationship between the number of parameters in a model to be estimated and the information available to do it; a model is identified if there are fewer parameters to be estimated than there are items of information available

covariance
a measure of association between two continuous variables expressed in the units of the measurement scales of the variables; its square root is the correlation coefficient

residual
the value of that portion of the variance of a dependent variable that cannot be accounted for by a set of predictor variables

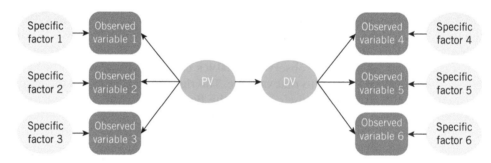

FIGURE 11.6   Full structural equation model

The third step in SEM is to *estimate model parameters*. All the programs work broadly in the same way. First, starting values for model parameters are formed, and these are used to calculate the initial estimate of the population covariance matrix (Σ). The difference between this and the sample covariance matrix (S) is called the residual matrix. The initial parameters are modified, and a new Σ matrix is formed. This procedure is repeated until no further improvements in goodness of fit can be achieved. The logic of SEM is to find estimates of the parameters in the statistical model in order to produce a population covariance matrix that is a close fit to the covariance matrix from the sample data. A close fit indicates that the hypothesized model is a plausible way of describing the relationships within the sample data. The goal of SEM therefore is to achieve a good fit between the hypothesized model and the data – shown by a small and non-significant index of goodness of fit.

A goodness of fit index is calculated based on the estimated population covariance matrix (Σ) and the sample covariance matrix (S). A common estimation method is called maximum likelihood, and the goodness of fit index that is minimized is called chi-square (χ^2).

The value of χ^2 depends on a function of the S and Σ matrices and on the sample size. This means that large values of χ^2 reflect either poor model fit or a large sample size, or both. Studies with large samples (e.g. over 1,000 participants) will almost always show significant χ^2 values, regardless of how good the fitted model is. As well as indices for the model as a whole, it is also important to look at the individual parameters within the model. A significance test for each parameter is reported by all of the programs, testing the null hypothesis that the population value of the parameter is zero.

The fourth step is to *assess the fit of a model*. The quality of the overall fit between a hypothesized model and the data can be assessed in a variety of ways; indeed, one version of AMOS has 24 different fit indices, and most published papers report three or four different indices (see Jaccard and Wan, 1996). They fall into three broad categories:

1. *Discrepancy-based indices.* The commonest index is the chi-square value, which is reported by every SEM program. It indicates the goodness of fit between the observed covariance matrix from the data and the predicted covariance matrix from the hypothesized model. A small value of chi-square indicates a close fit between the two, and suggests that the hypothesized model is a good one. However, there are problems with the chi-square index since a large value need not mean that the model is poor because chi-square varies with sample size.

2. *Relative fit compared to a null model.* As well as the hypothesized model, most of the SEM programs also fit a null model, which assumes that all the covariances among the observed variables are zero (this is often called the 'independence' model). A number of fit indices have been developed that adjust the chi-square value for a specific model according to how much better it is than the null model, and also take into account the complexity of the model (the number of parameters needed to achieve fit). One of these is the non-normed fit index (NNFI), whose values can vary between 0 and 1, and a value above 0.95 is regarded as acceptable (Bentler and Dudgeon, 1996).

3. *Relative fit adjusted for the complexity of the model.* Complex models will fit data better than simple models, and some indices assign a cost to this extra complexity; in other words, they reward parsimony. On these criteria a model that achieves a reasonable fit with few parameters is better than a model that gives a marginally better fit achieved at the cost of a large increase in complexity. One of these measures is RMSEA (the root mean squared error of approximation), which adjusts chi-square according to the degrees of freedom of the model and the sample size.

null model
a model within structural equation modelling which assumes that all the covariances among the observed variables are zero; used as the baseline for calculating incremental fit indices

parsimony
the extent to which a fitted model in SEM can account for observed data with fewer parameters

RMSEA
(root mean squared error of approximation) an index in SEM of the goodness of fit of a hypothesized causal model adjusted for the complexity of the fitted model

The fifth step in SEM after examining the fit of a particular model is to *consider alternative models*, and it is most unusual to fit only a single structural equation model to a set of data. Almost all SEM work involves modifying the model in some way, either to improve the fit of an initial model or to test hypotheses derived from theory. The logic of SEM is strictly confirmatory, since the method requires that the researcher define a set of observed and latent variables together with a hypothesized model for the relationships among them. However, many tests of theoretical propositions involve comparisons between models rather than fitting a single model. We have already considered two examples in this chapter. Example 11.1 presented three models of the impact of stakeholder relationship management on corporate financial performance. Testing these alternatives involves fitting a sequence of models. Similarly, mediational models (see page 355) can most effectively be tested by comparing a model including direct paths with a model that fixes the value of all these paths to zero. Model comparison tests like these are done by chi-square difference tests, the difference in goodness of fit between two models, in exactly the same way that we have seen already in hierarchical regression.

However, most researchers find that their *a priori* model does not fit the data to an acceptable degree and so they often undertake an exploration of alternatives using modification indices. The Lagrange multiplier (LM) test corresponds to forward stepwise regression, and tests what would happen if each one of the fixed parameters in the model were to be set free. The second type of index is called the Wald test and this corresponds to backwards stepwise regression. It tests which parameters currently included in the model have a value so small that they could be dropped from the model. The logic behind these procedures is similar to that used in the stepwise options available in the methods for multivariate analysis of causal models among observed variables (e.g. multiple regression and logistic regression). They involve a search through fixed parameters to see what the effect would be if fixed parameters were allowed to be free.

For example, the CFA model in Figure 11.7 has six free parameters representing the loading of each observed variable on a single latent common factor. However, there are also an additional seven fixed parameters, which are implied by the model in Figure 9.1. They are shown by dotted lines in Figure 11.7: six additional arrows linking observed and latent variables, and also a double-headed arrow between the two common factors indicating a correlation between them. There are even more implied fixed parameters, because the model also assumes that the specific factors to the left of the diagram are uncorrelated with each other. We have not drawn the double-headed arrows for those because it would complicate the diagram considerably.

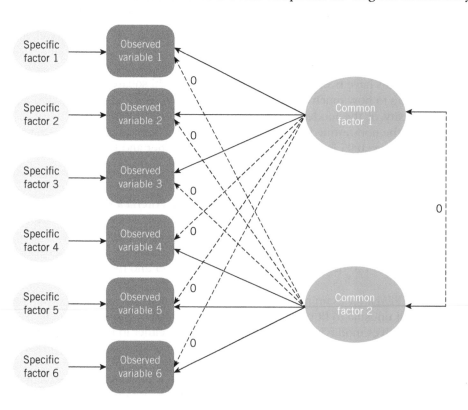

FIGURE 11.7   CFA model showing free parameters (solid lines) and fixed parameters (dotted lines)

If the hypothesized CFA model does not fit the data well, the researcher might decide that at least one of the items should load on both common factors, and thus relax the constraint of a fixed zero loading for that path. If this process is guided firmly by conceptual considerations, there could be a strong justification, but blind searching through multiple alternative models in the hope of finding one that is 'best' violates both the statistical requirements that underpin the SEM method and also the principles of sound research practice that we have described in this book. Theory development should be guided both by conceptual rigour and by the weight of evidence from data. Holding to theory regardless of what the data say is not good practice, but neither is blindly following data regardless of the theoretical justification.

Advanced features

The SEM area of statistics is developing rapidly, and each update of the programs adds features and options, such as:

- new goodness of fit indices for assessing the quality of models
- new estimation procedures for fitting the parameters in a hypothesized model
- additional methods for the preliminary assessment of data characteristics before fitting SEMs
- new models; for example for analysing multiple groups, for longitudinal designs, for testing differences in the means of latent variables, for complex sampling designs.

Researchers interested in keeping up with developments in SEM can go to the software distributors' websites listed at the start of this section. There is also the journal *Structural Equation Modeling* published by Taylor and Francis, but be aware that the articles tend to be very technical.

Conclusion

This chapter has introduced a number of methods for analysing the complexity of the world of business and management using quantitative data, including:

- Methods for working with complex concepts, which often cannot be measured directly but have to be inferred from observed variables.
- Conceptual introduction to ways of modelling causal relationships among both observed and latent variables, particularly using structural equation models.

The most important point is that the process of multivariate model fitting must be guided firmly by conceptual considerations. Fitting statistical models to quantitative data is not an automated process of blindly finding the 'best' model. Good-quality models are grounded both in rigorous conceptualization guided by existing literature as well as in an evidence base of data collected according to sound design and measurement principles.

Further reading

A helpful discussion on the use of control variables in management research:

Atinc, G., Simmering, M.J. and Kroll, M.J. (2011) 'Control variable use and reporting in macro and micro management research', *Organizational Research Methods*, 15: 57–74.

This is a readable book, which introduces both SEM and the key concepts underlying measurement models (such as reliability). The examples are based on the AMOS package, which is now an add-on to SPSS, but could easily be adapted for use with other software:

Blunch, N.J. (2013) *Introduction to Structural Equation Modelling Using SPSS and AMOS*, 2nd edn. London: Sage.

This is an excellent book on the use of multivariate methods in social science. The strength of the book is the applications it uses as illustration of the methods covered, and the focus on preparatory work to examine the properties of the data first before embarking on complex multivariate analysis. Again, see also Field (2017) listed at the end of the previous chapter.

Hair, J.F., Black, B., Babin, B., Anderson, R.E. and Tatham, R.L. (2010) *Multivariate Data Analysis*, 7th edn. Upper Saddle River, NJ: Prentice Hall.

A collection of chapters covering a wide range of quantitative methods for an advanced readership:

Kaplan, D. (2004) *The SAGE Handbook of Quantitative Methodology for the Social Sciences*. Thousand Oaks, CA: Sage.

An examination of a range of event studies in management research:

McWilliams, A. and Siegel, D. (1997) 'Event studies in management research: theoretical and empirical issues', *Academy of Management Journal*, 40: 626–57.

Two useful resources for getting started in data science:

Silver, N. (2012) *The Signal and the Noise: Why So Many Predictions Fail – But Some Don't*. New York: Penguin.

Sweigart, A. (2015) *Automate the Boring Stuff with Python: Practical Programming for Total Beginners*. San Francisco, CA: No Starch Press. Available at: https://automatetheboringstuff.com (accessed 22 December 2017).

This too is an excellent and thorough text on multivariate statistical methods for social science researchers. Its approach is practical rather than theoretical, and the authors cover all of the methods described in this chapter as well as others not covered here. For each method, they give its rationale, practical guidelines about how to use it, worked examples using a variety of statistical packages, and show how to present the results of analysis:

Tabachnick, B.G. and Fidell, L.S. (2014) *Using Multivariate Statistics*, 6th edn. Boston, MA: Pearson Education.

A good text for how the R package can be used for data science:

Wickham, H. and Grolemund, G. (2016) *R for Data Science*. Sebastopol, CA: O'Reilly. Available at: http://r4ds.had.co.nz (accessed 22 December 2017).

Check your understanding online

Visit the website **https://edge.sagepub.com/easterbysmith6e** for useful resources that will help reinforce what you've read in this chapter:

 Take an interactive quiz to test your understanding of the key topics

 Review suggested answers to Exercises 11.1 to 11.3 above

 Use interactive flashcards to check your knowledge of essential concepts

Learning objectives

To develop personal strategies for writing.

To appreciate different structures for writing.

To recognize the needs and interests of different audiences.

To develop awareness of the requirements of different forms of output.

To develop skills in publishing and disseminating research.

WRITING MANAGEMENT AND BUSINESS RESEARCH

12

Introduction

This book has examined the various ways of designing and conducting research: it has looked at how to choose and use the methods that will provide the relevant data; it has considered how to analyse, interpret and use data; and it has offered insights into the political and ethical aspects of doing research. This last chapter focuses on how to write up research findings, and how and where to disseminate research.

There are many potential audiences, including tutors, clients, academics, policy-makers and the general public, and these audiences correspond roughly to the stakeholders that we discussed in Chapter 5. As there are many ways of widening impact, we think it is important to consider communication early in the research process, preferably at the design stage. Although the written word dominates in the form of reports, articles and books, there are other important ways of getting the message across, including presentations, videos and media interviews. A dissemination strategy, therefore, may include the use of different media at different points of time during the research, and after it has been completed.

We start the chapter with writing, focusing on the generic skills that apply to any context. Second, we look at different forms of output, concentrating on how evaluative criteria vary, and discuss the stylistic differences between, for example, positivist and constructionist forms of research. Third, we provide guidance on the main elements of a report or dissertation, including literature reviews. Fourth, we consider different audiences and the media available for communication. Fifth, we look at the thorny subject of plagiarism, explaining the different forms that it can take, and providing advice on how to ensure that you won't be accused of plagiarism. Finally, we draw the threads together by looking at dissemination strategies.

The skills of writing

The main aim in writing about research is to communicate with an audience, and to persuade them that the research is serious, important and believable. It is therefore important to be clear about the potential *readership*. One technique that can help with this is to identify two or three 'typical' readers and bear them in mind while writing something.

Second, readers will be more interested in the document if it relates to their ongoing concerns. This is where Huff (1999) stresses the importance of trying to link into an existing 'conversation'. So it is important to start a journal article with a summary of the main debate that has appeared up to that point, and upon which the current article intends to build. Here the researcher needs to be aware of the main contributors in the field. Similarly, when writing a client report it is important to start with a brief statement of how the client has articulated the problem.

Dr Zina O'Leary's advice for writing up dissertation projects

Third, in order to increase the credibility of the research there are a number of rhetorical strategies that may be used in written accounts. Positivist authors often write in the third person so that the researcher seems distanced from the research, and this gives an impression of greater objectivity; they may cite articles by famous authors in order to give credibility to the present research; and present the research as a linear process designed in advance and executed precisely to plan. Constructionist authors often go to great lengths to be reflexive, indicating their engagement with the research setting and their influence on the research material; they often write up the research as it actually happened, indicating the problems that they encountered along the way, and how they tackled (sometimes heroically) these problems.

Writing as a habit

Woody Allen, the American comedian, director and author, has remarked that 90 per cent of the success in writing lies in getting started and finished on time, and the bit in the middle is easy. There is a key implication: don't wait until the end before starting to write. Get into the writing habit from the beginning, and sustain it throughout the research. Normally, reviews of the literature and research designs should be written up in the early stages of the research and 'banked' for later use. Of course they will have to be edited and rewritten later on, but they provide critical foundations upon which other parts can build.

Most people experience writing blocks at some stage or another: the blank page can be exhilarating or intimidating. There are many different strategies to overcome writing blocks. The American author John Steinbeck (1970) adopted an interesting strategy when writing *East of Eden*. He always began his daily sessions by writing a letter to his editor about what he planned to say that day. The letters were written on the left-hand pages of a large notebook (and not sent); on the right-hand pages he wrote the text of the book. He found this a useful way of starting his thought processes, and overcoming writing block.

Various academic authors offer advice on how to get into the flow of writing, including creating sufficient time and space for writing, setting modest goals on a daily basis and providing rewards for oneself, such as coffee breaks or Liquorice Allsorts after the next paragraph or section is completed. Murray and Moore (2006) emphasize the need to take time out from writing for exercise or social activities: it is fine if the writing is flowing, but if not, take a break and do something completely different for an hour or so.

Piled Higher and Deeper (also known as *PhD Comics*) is a webcomic by Jorge Cham that addresses some of the difficulties of scientific research and writing up, and the perils of procrastination, with a sense of humour.

PhD Comics: Not write

Developing structures

It is also important to develop an appropriate structure for the report or thesis, which can be done in a number of ways. First, an *emergent* structure comes from writing anything in order to get started, and once you have worked out what you are trying to say, deleting the initial paragraphs that may be a lot of rubbish. A *patchwork* structure comes from writing self-contained chunks of text and then starting to stitch them together into a coherent narrative. A *planned* structure involves trying to work out all the main sections and paragraphs in advance.

A good way of starting the planning process is to develop a 'mind-map'. This has the advantage that no commitments to linearity are required – one can simply type in ideas and then experiment to see how they group together. Mind-maps can help groups of researchers share their sense-making of research data, and they are also useful for authors when planning books and reports. But there is a limit to the amount of information that can be displayed on one page, and so it is generally best to move to a spreadsheet or slide pack in order to work out the details of a report and to order topics and ideas in a way that they develop into a coherent argument.

Generic structures for writing papers and research reports

Although research papers and reports conducted under different traditions may look quite different, there is much consistency in the basic issues and topics that they need to cover. The main differences come in the style and language used. In Table 12.1, we have summarized the main questions that need to be answered in academic research in the first column.

In the other two columns we summarize the way each of these questions gets operational-
ized, respectively in positivist or constructionist research reports.

As can be seen, there is much similarity in the earlier and later parts; the main differences
come in the articulation of the central research questions and in the handling of data. Although
most positivist studies follow the list of subheadings in the second column, there is often more
flexibility in how qualitative reports and client reports are presented, especially in the presentation of qualitative data. In this case there is an opportunity for the researcher to exercise some
creativity, depending on the needs of the situation, the actual research and the audience.

Where the research makes deliberate use of mixed methods, the normal solution is to structure the outer parts of the report according to whichever method is dominant, and then to
present the data in two separate sections. Alternatively, where qualitative data is used to explain
why various quantitative results are obtained, then it may be appropriate to present some qualitative data in relation to each of the quantitative hypotheses. However, as we said in Chapter
4, it is important to articulate in the research design/methodology section how the qualitative
and quantitative data are intended to support each other. It is important to note that the generic
structure presented below also translates into the basic structure of a dissertation or thesis, which
usually consist of an introduction (about 10 per cent of the word count), a literature review (20
per cent), a methods chapter (20 per cent), a findings section (20 per cent), a discussion (20 per
cent) and a conclusion (20 per cent). These presentations should be seen as a rule of thumb, as
there are variations depending on the discipline, research style and audience. For example, some
dissertations at undergraduate level put more of an emphasis on the literature review.

TABLE 12.1   Generic structure

Principle	Positivist research	Constructionist research	Chapter title
What is the research about?	Abstract	Abstract	Abstract and Introduction
What is already known?	Review of literature and previous studies	Review of literature and relevant theories	Introduction and Literature Review
What is new about this study?	Statement of aims and hypotheses	Identify the gap or research question(s)	Introduction and (end of) Literature Review
How was the research done?	Conceptual framework Description of procedures, samples and methods used	Conceptual framework Research setting, research design and methods	Introduction and Methods section
What did it find out?	Data tables and summary of results	Descriptions of data and interpretations	Findings
What are the implications?	How far the hypotheses are supported	How the data extend existing theory	Discussion and Conclusion
Next steps?	Limitations and suggestions for future research	Limitations and suggestions for future research	Discussion and Conclusion
Addenda	References, questionnaires, etc.	References, sample transcripts and analytic process	Appendix

Starting and finishing

Most experienced writers and editors agree that the start and end of any piece of writing
are crucial. Reviewers, examiners and editors often form provisional judgements by reading

the first and last pages, on the assumption that if the authors are able to communicate their message clearly in the first page, the rest of the document will be of similar quality; but if the initial page is unclear or confusing, this bodes badly for the rest of the document. Good titles are short and memorable. In academic work it is very common to write a title in two parts, separated by a colon. The first part summarizes the topic of the research, and the second part indicates the argument that the paper is taking, or the question that it is addressing. Once you have a good title the rest should be easy! Conversely, lengthy and convoluted titles usually indicate that the author is unclear about the central topic and main message of his or her document. Given the importance of the title we would recommend developing a provisional title very early in the writing process. This should evolve as the work develops, but at any point in time it provides a point of reference against which to check the coherence of what has already been written.

The introduction then sets the stage for what is to come. It should make for an engaging read so that the reader is drawn in and wants to read the full paper, report or dissertation. An introduction also needs to 'manage' the expectations of the reader. It provides a frame of reference and foreshadows some contributions (Tracy, 2013). A confusing introduction can raise false expectations, which can then become a problem when the reviewer or examiner evaluates the piece.

It is possible to summarize the four key elements that need to be in the introduction of an academic paper as follows:

1. Establish the *theoretical field* and why this particular topic is important.

2. Summarize previous research.

3. Identify the *niche*. What is the problem or question that is to be addressed?

4. State what the present study will *contribute* to this problem or question, and how it is tackled in this paper.

EXAMPLE 12.1

Structuring introductory paragraphs

Locke and Golden-Biddle (1997) provide a very interesting analysis of the way successful academic authors structure their introductory paragraphs. They conducted an analysis of 82 papers that had appeared in two leading journals (*Academy of Management* and *Administrative Science Quarterly*) over the 20 preceding years and identified two factors that were always present. First, the authors provided a coherent overview of the previous literature using one of three strategies: they either produced *progressive coherence*, showing how concepts and literature developed cumulatively over time; or *synthesized coherence*, where they identify links between streams of research or theory that have not been spotted before; or *non-coherence*, where the field is characterized by arguments, debates and general fragmentation. Second, authors try to identify a new niche that demonstrates how they can add to previous research. Three methods appeared to be most commonly used, either introducing new data, new theory or new research methods.

(Continued)

Table 12.2 shows the frequency with which different strategies were adopted in the 82 papers. As can be seen, the most common way of developing a new niche was to claim that new theory was being introduced, and the least common way was through introducing new methods. Progressive coherence was the most common way of characterizing past research, and this was most likely to be linked to the introduction of new theory.

TABLE 12.2   Academic introductions

		Finding the new niche		
		New data	New theory	New methods
Past research	Progressive coherence	13	18	3
	Synthesized coherence	11	11	3
	Non-coherence	6	13	2

Source: after Locke and Golden-Biddle, 1997

EXERCISE 12.1

Writing academic introductions

1   **Individual**: Select an academic article you have read – or would like to read. Download and read the whole article. Then examine its introduction more carefully.

   - How has the topic been introduced?

   - What strategy was adopted by the author(s)? New data? New theory? New methods?

   - Can you identify the research question?

   - Are there any findings that are outlined in the introduction? Are these the key findings?

2   **Individual**: Think about other ways in which the research presented in the article could be introduced.

3   **Group discussion**: Discuss what alternative (or better) titles the author(s) could have chosen.

4   **Group**: In groups of two to three students, plan and write a new introduction of 200–300 words. Who has come up with the best introduction?

Then we have the conclusions. As Table 12.1 indicates, the precise form of the conclusions may vary with different kinds of work: essentially they need to summarize the nature of the research, the main findings or contributions, provide an indication of the limitations of the work, and make suggestions for future research directions. They need to be clear and reasonably succinct (three or four paragraphs is enough for an academic paper, and 10 to 12 pages is enough for a doctoral thesis). Writing a conclusion can be challenging as it may feel like everything important has already been said. However, we have to bear in mind that many readers (and examiners) look at the introduction and conclusion first. When they come to the conclusion, they expect to see a very neat summary of the contribution of the research and why it matters. It may be tempting to copy and paste the main findings or elements of the abstract – but this does not make for a good read. Writing a conclusion is a great opportunity to think about one's research as a whole, and it can give the writer a great sense of closure – and a job done well.

Writing up the literature review

Literature reviews have many features in common with other forms of writing, plus some features that are distinct, hence there is some justification for considering the writing of literature reviews as a distinct art. In this section we cover five features of literature reviews that are often regarded as problematic: selection of material; different ways of structuring literature reviews; styles of presenting literature; the issue of criticality; and the conclusion of a literature review. In doing this we build on Chapter 2 on conducting literature reviews.

Selection of source material

In most topics the quantity of existing literature is almost limitless, and the problem for the researcher is to decide which bits to include and which bits to leave out. We have two main criteria that can determine the selection of literature for the review: importance and relevance. By *importance*, we mean the extent to which a particular book or article is regarded as central to the particular field on which you are working. By *relevance*, we mean the extent to which a particular book or article is linked to the line of argument that you are trying to develop in your work.

There is always a dilemma in deciding how many sources to quote in a literature review, and it is important to strike a balance between depth versus breadth of coverage. In general, dissertations and theses need to contain a wide coverage of literature. This helps you to demonstrate to tutors and examiners that you are fully aware of the breadth and range of the field, and the more focused coverage comes towards the latter end of the review. If you are seeking to publish an article in a journal, then it is less important to demonstrate that you know everything about the field, because a general level of familiarity will normally be assumed by the reader, and unless you have anything especially new to say about the traditional literature it is likely that it will be seen as boring to have to wade through material that is familiar to everybody.

Structures and styles

Structures refer to the way that you decide to marshal your literature, and the logic behind different ways of grouping the material. Structures of literature reviews are covered extensively in Chapter 2.

With regard to style, there is a reasonable amount of agreement between authors and experts regarding what is desirable or less desirable in the writing of a literature review (see Table 12.3).

First, the references cited in the text need to be selected on the grounds of relevance – first and foremost with a view to the topic of the literature review but also with a view to relevance of a source to the wider academic discourse. Sometimes it can be helpful to have a look at how often and where key references have been cited before, as this provides some indication of how well-known a paper is and how much impact it has had on a given debate or discourse. Each reference included in a literature review needs to make a distinct contribution to the general argument – or it should not be there. It is generally best for authors/ references to be mentioned close to the actual statement (even if this means including them in the middle of a sentence), rather than being added at the end to provide 'decoration' and an air of authority over what has just been said. In particular, when trying to develop an argument, it adds precision if you indicate the page numbers of the book or article where the particular elements of the argument are being made.

Second, and especially with constructionist research, it is important that the voice of the *author of the literature review* should be heard. In general, it is better to summarize what you think other writers are saying, rather than simply dropping quotations from these writers into your text. There is no problem with the occasional quote, if it is central to your argument, but there is a danger if there are lots of short quotes from other authors that the review will seem like a patchwork quilt. Again, there is also a dilemma here between depth and breadth. A good literature review will contain some of both. It will pay considerable attention to the more important and relevant works, but it will also demonstrate a reasonable awareness of related literature. Thus in a journal article one might expect to see five or six major pieces of work discussed in some depth, but with brief reference made perhaps to 50 other pieces of work. Of course, in longer documents such as dissertations or theses these numbers could be doubled or tripled.

Being critical

The literature review needs to demonstrate *criticality*. This does not mean being negative about everything that has previously been written. Far from it. It means demonstrating discernment about what is good and bad about the previous literature, and explaining why you have reached these judgements. Argument analysis, as discussed in Chapters 2 and 8, can assist with the development of a critical stance. This is where your voice, as author, is particularly important. One dilemma with regard to critical literature reviews is where the critique should be placed within the overall structure. For example, if you have divided your topic into five major themes, it might make sense to summarize the views and contributions of the main contributors to each theme, and then provide a critique at the end. But if there are major works contained within that overall theme, it may be better to interleave summaries of each work, with the main critiques produced by other people of that work, and then give your own view.

TABLE 12.3 Stylistic features in literature reviews

Stylistic features	Incorporate	Avoid
Framework for literature review	Thematic structure; progressive coherence	Annotated bibliography; no links between paragraphs
Selection of references	Clear relevance; functional; focused on argument development	Decorative use; long strings that are vaguely linked
Voice	Focus on key works; paraphrase others' arguments	Patchwork of quotes from other authors
Criticality	Explain strengths and limitations or weaknesses of previous studies; build on others' critiques	Sweeping dismissal of others' work

Conclusions of literature reviews

In our experience, literature reviews always take longer to write than one thinks. They are a key element of any academic study and, if done well, can assist the researcher a great deal in really understanding and framing the research problem they are investigating. However, they are also hard work. Sometimes, when a student or author gets to the end of the literature, they are so exhausted, or short of time, that they simply present material and then move on to the next chapter. But the whole point of the literature review, other than demonstrating that you have in-depth knowledge of the field you are investigating, is to provide a platform for the work that is yet to come within the research project. It is this analytical bit that is essential – and that readers and examiners look out for. This normally requires two elements. First, there needs to be a summary of the main features and arguments covered in the literature review, which may take the form of a diagram, a model, a table, a set of propositions or hypotheses. Second, it is essential to identify some sort of gap, contradiction, weakness or limitation in the previous work, which provides a justification for the work that you will be describing in the following chapters. Many authors therefore conclude the literature review by (re-)stating the main research problem, question(s) and hypotheses of their research, which, following the literature review, should appear more contextualized, meaningful and relevant.

The middle bits

The 'middle bits' are the most important sections of an academic manuscript because they comprise the methods section along with its findings, and a discussion of said findings. Depending on the type of manuscript (e.g. whether it is a paper, report or thesis), and the kind of research, the middle bits will be laid out in different ways: a report of a positivist study based on an experiment will be presented in a different way than, let's say, an ethnography. Bearing this in mind, in the following sections we provide some general guidance on how to approach the methods section, findings section and discussion.

The methodology section

Unfortunately, the methods section is often the weakest part of an academic manuscript. This is not just disappointing for those who enjoy writing about research methods, it is a great missed opportunity to impress reviewers and examiners. A methods section should provide a comprehensive account of the philosophical background, and the research design and methods used to conduct a given study. It should both articulate and justify the research design with a view to its appropriateness: is it the right methodology to answer a particular research question (or test a particular hypothesis) in a given setting?

Methods chapters of quantitative studies tend to involve the following sub-sections:

- Overview of the design
- Population and sample
- Research setting
- Limitations
- Sampling
- Data collection and data

- Variables

- Data analysis: statistical models/treatments.

The structure of a constructivist qualitative methods chapter may include similar headings but some of them mean different things and there is more flexibility. A common structure might be:

- Aims of the research

- Overview of the research design

- Research setting

- Data collection

- Data analysis

- Ethical considerations

- Quality criteria and limitations.

Most qualitative research requires a more detailed explanation of the setting or research context. We also agree with our colleague David Silverman (2013: 352) that when writing about qualitative methods it is essential to address the:

- (contested) theoretical underpinnings of methodologies

- the (often) contingent nature of the data chosen

- the (likely) non-random character of cases studied

- the reasons why the research took the path it did (both analytic and chance factors).

Findings

The structure of findings sections varies across studies. However, all findings sections should start with a cursory overview of the results and how they will be presented. Depending on the research design, topic and the findings themselves, subsections may be structured according to hypotheses, questions or themes. It is important to maintain a consistent approach. No matter the order in which the findings or results are presented, it remains the responsibility of the author to highlight in clear terms what findings are derived from the study.

One recurrent dilemma with constructionist studies is how to achieve a balance between qualitative data in the form of quotations, and discussions of the theoretical implications. Although some authors might be tempted to show large amounts of data, there is a limit to how far it will hold the attention of the reader without being contextualized within the wider narrative. Another way of grabbing the imagination of readers is to provide a sneak preview of the data right at the start of the paper – which can work a bit like a teaser trailer for a film – followed by setting the theoretical context, and then adding more sections of quotations and discussions (show-tell-show-tell). Tables that present sets of quotations can be a useful feature, but only when they are analysed and discussed. The same applies to figures and tables more generally: never include a table or figure without describing in the text what it is meant to illustrate!

Discussion

In the discussion section, the author interprets and discusses the findings in the light of previous research and theorizing. The discussion section can be one the most difficult to write. Many students and researchers struggle with its discursive nature. When planning the findings section, it can be really helpful to read the literature review and findings sections and create a mind-map, which connects new insights to pre-existing knowledge. During this process, it is essential not to lose sight of the research questions or hypotheses of the study when constructing an argument. It is not possible for us to provide a template for the development of an argument, but it is helpful to remember the basic principles of argument analysis introduced in Chapters 2 and 8. The following elements may form part of a discussion:

- restatement of the aim of the study
- summary of its findings
- discussion of the findings in relation to the literature
- discussion of the relevance of the findings
- explanation of conflicting findings or those that do not support the initial hypotheses
- limitations and generalisability of the results
- implications of the findings (theory and practical applications)
- recommendations for future research.

EXERCISE 12.2

One of the challenges of writing a good discussion can relate to language. Particularly for novices, the language used in academic writing can be difficult to master. The University of Manchester has compiled lists of common academic phrases according to the main sections of a research paper or dissertation. While we believe the phrasebank to be a useful resource, in particular for those whose first language is not English, we would also warn against making too much use of it. Academic writing is always a creative act – and putting together phrases that sound academic does not make for an academic contribution.

Academic phrasebank

1 **Individual**: Read two academic articles of interest to you and your research. Identify at least three useful phrases that could be added to the phrasebank and indicate which section(s) they should be added to.

2 **Group**: Compile the suggestions in class. What phrases are particularly useful?

Writing and editing

As researchers gain experience in writing, the ways in which they write a report or paper change. At school, most writing is about producing a decent first draft. Students write an essay, they receive feedback, and then they try to write a better essay for their next assignment.

This pattern begins to change when students write their first dissertation. An undergraduate dissertation is not so much about the first draft – but about the second or third. Most PhD students rewrite at least parts of their chapters three times or more. When you read an article published in an academic journal, chances are that it has been edited and rewritten at least ten times or more! What this tells us is that the initial draft, while important, is just a first attempt. It is there to be reviewed, edited, rewritten and improved upon. If you try to write a perfect first draft, you will fail. There is no perfect first draft – but there are good and bad foundations to start out with. A good structure will always help but be mindful that carefully plotted outlines have their limits. Writing tends to be messier than we first anticipate and the subsequent process of reading, rethinking, reorganizing, asking for comments, incorporating changes and more feedback is rarely of a linear nature. It requires a wide range of skills including (but by no means limited to) editing and the ability to engage constructively with criticism. Very few academics, if any, write effortlessly – and the students who do are not always the ones who achieve the best results.

Outputs and evaluation

What, then, are the different forms of output that can be generated by research, and how may they be evaluated? To some extent, the answer builds upon the discussion of political issues in Chapter 5. We can distinguish two main types of output: *unpublished outputs*, such as reports and dissertations, which are generally targeted at a very small number of people such as clients and examiners; and *published outputs*, such as articles and books, which are intended to be widely disseminated.

Unpublished outputs: reports, dissertations and theses

Reports and dissertations are initially aimed at a small number of people, and although some may eventually get published, this is the exception rather than the rule. The immediate audience is often involved in the evaluation of the work (possibly supplemented by a presentation), and this will result in the award of grades and educational qualifications. We will start with research reports, and then discuss dissertations and theses.

Client reports

Reports of projects conducted for clients usually have a different structure from the more academic reports and dissertations. Essentially, these need to be shorter, with more emphasis on the identification of the problem and the practical courses of action to be taken. There needs to be some explanation of methodology because this has a bearing on the quality of evidence underpinning the recommendations, but there is much less need for a literature review, which might be restricted to half a dozen references that have informed both the focus and methods of the study. Projects are increasingly being incorporated into undergraduate and postgraduate degree schemes where small groups of students tackle a real problem located in a company or other organization. Since the client project is being conducted as part of an educational qualification, those working on the project will face two different kinds of evaluation: first, they must come up with results or recommendations that satisfy the client; and second, they must produce a written document that satisfies the academic tutors and examiners.

RESEARCH IN ACTION

Writing up research

Charlotte Coleman

Charlotte Coleman is Insights Director at Big Sofa, an insight-led video tech company. Before pursuing her career in consumer insight, she was a Lecturer in Management and Organization at Alliance Manchester Business School where she enjoyed teaching academic and research skills. Charlotte holds a PhD from Leeds University Business School, where her love of qualitative research methods began.

The methods we use for conducting research in academia and industry can be quite similar but what about the ways in which we present our results?

A major difference between academic research and industry is speed. Whereas in academia, researchers often work on projects for years, most research projects I conduct take about six weeks from brief to debrief. 'Writing up' involves three steps. First, there are fieldwork notes. Then there are 'topline reports'. The team uses these to track and make sense of findings. Like memos, they provide initial analysis and highlight emerging themes and interesting quotes. The team reads the reports and holds analysis sessions. Finally, we present the findings usually in face-to-face meetings. Sometimes these presentations resemble a lecture (using slides with text and diagrams) and sometimes they are more like a seminar/workshop. So there are many similarities between formats and structure (see Table 12.4 below) but in industry the findings are presented rather than 'written up' in a detailed final report.

TABLE 12.4   Structure of an academic paper compared with a qualitative agency debrief

Academic paper	Qualitative insight agency debrief
Abstract	Key insights
Introduction	Background
Literature review	Defining the problem
Methodology	Research approach and plan
Findings	Findings
Discussion	Recommendations
Conclusions	Conclusions

Writing a research report or dissertation can be a daunting task. What advice do you have for students?

In the research process, we write for three main reasons. First, we write to help us remember what happened in the field. Second, we write to hone our ideas and to theorize. Putting ideas

(Continued)

down on the page helps to clarify our thinking. Third, we write because we want to share our ideas with other people, so our writing needs to be easy to understand. We tend to think about all writing as this third type, which is what we are doing during the 'write-up'. However, if you start writing earlier (in the first and second stage) it will make the third stage easier.

Start writing as soon as possible; write about what you think about papers when you are reading literature. Write when you are doing your data collection; write about your doubts and the gaps in your research. Remember that you are not writing chapters at this point, so just write. Save with file names and dates so that you can find, edit and recycle this text in the future. If you do this, you never have that scary moment when you have to 'begin the write-up'. This moment can become so scary for people that they procrastinate for months or make themselves unwell.

Writing is not like knitting, it's like collage. In knitting you must create row after row of perfect stitches or the final item will look poor. You cannot go back and redo a row in the middle without un-doing everything that went after it. Writing isn't like this. Writing is like collage, layering, moving pieces around and drafting as you go. While it is useful to have a structure, template or storyline before you start writing, you will never write perfect sentences without editing. If you write consistently during the research process, you will have plenty of text to weave together. You can begin to stick each section together, to work on the flow of the text and to redraft each sentence. Editing is an inevitable and lengthy process. This doesn't mean that you should tinker with each sentence as you write it. It is important to have both writing time and editing time.

In your view, what makes for a good style?

I think good style is about being clear and concise, no matter who the audience is. Sometimes academic papers can be very hard to read. Sentences are long. Each sentence contains multiple ideas. Complicated words are used. Often, plainer language would make contributions clearer.

How useful are visualizations and illustrations?

Pictures really do speak a thousand words. In non-academic research, photographs are often used to illustrate findings, either by showing the research setting or participants, or to demonstrate ideas or metaphors that enrich the insights. Diagrams are very useful. I find that drawing diagrams and illustrations helps in theorizing and expressing ideas. I love using a whiteboard or blackboard when you are beginning to analyse; you can easily play around with how concepts relate; rub things off; redo the diagram to see 'Is it more like this? Or perhaps this?' Sketching out your ideas can really help your thinking. Diagrams can also express complex ideas in a very immediate way for your audience. So include them in the final write-up.

TOP TIPS FOR WRITING BETTER

- Aim to keep sentences under 20 words.
- Aim to have one idea per sentence.
- Start sentences with the subject-verb near the start.

- Use the active tense.

- Learn how to correctly use a semi-colon.

- Spend some time reading about how to write well so that your writing appears effortless (see Strunk and White, 2000; Fish, 2011).

Dissertations

For Bachelor of Business Administration (BBA) and Masters' courses, the required dissertations are often longer than project reports (perhaps 10,000 to 20,000 words), and are the product of individual rather than group efforts. In most cases, they are written solely for academic evaluation. In general, it is worth following the suggested report structure in Table 12.1, although there is less of a requirement to demonstrate theoretical contribution than in the case of a doctoral thesis (see below). It is important that a dissertation is well-balanced in its structure, by which we mean the relative length of the sections should be in proportion. Usually, findings, discussion and conclusion should add up to about 50 per cent of the overall word count (excluding appendices and references).

Evaluative criteria will depend both on the nature of the dissertation and on the formal expectations of tutors and examiners. A general guide to criteria is given in Table 12.5, which summarizes seven features that should normally be present in a good dissertation, taken from Bloom's *Taxonomy of Educational Objectives* (Bloom and Krathwohl, 1956), and is organized hierarchically in terms of the increasing complexity of each feature. Thus, demonstrating knowledge of the field and comprehension of the problem to be addressed are relatively basic elements; the evaluation of literature and ideas and clear argumentation are regarded as more complex processes, which will therefore gather more brownie points when the dissertation is being evaluated. In most universities, guidelines on how dissertations are evaluated are available to all students and staff; and we always advise our students to read their course handbook. While these documents may not make for an engaging read, they do set out quite clearly what a student needs to do in order to achieve a high mark. We include a weblink to a generic marking matrix used to evaluate MSc dissertations at the University of Warwick. Again, remember the importance of a transparent structure and good signposting. While most examiners try their utmost to do justice to the dissertations they evaluate, most of them read quite a few in a day. Excellent signposting makes it easier for them to complete assessment sheets and this can have a positive impact on the overall outcome for everyone.

Dissertation marking criteria

There is some uncertainty at the moment about whether it is more important for management dissertations to demonstrate evidence of application or analysis. As we noted in Chapter 1, there is a long-standing debate in the UK about whether management education should emphasize practical or academic training (Whitley et al., 1981), and this has translated into the debate between mode 1 and mode 2 forms of research (Tranfield and Starkey, 1998; Huff, 2000). The rise of the MBA puts greater emphasis on practical relevance and application, while academics are likely to value the analytic and evaluative elements of the dissertation. Since most degrees are awarded by academics, it is prudent to include some elements of analysis and synthesis in the work submitted.

Doctoral theses

Doctoral theses are similar to Masters' dissertations in that they require a synthesis of ideas and data. In addition, they must provide critical evaluation of relevant work, and demonstrate some kind of original *contribution* to the field. This contribution can be provided in three main forms: as new knowledge about the world of management (substantive contribution), as new theories and ideas (theoretical contribution), or as new methods of investigation (methodological contribution). In each case the contribution needs to be stated explicitly in the conclusions, and there also needs to be a clear link back to the early part of the thesis where the existing theories and methods were reviewed and evaluated. The theoretical contribution is most important, although it may be supplemented by each of the others.

The final award of a doctorate depends on the judgement of independent examiners (though practice in this respect varies surprisingly widely across Europe and North America), and it is very important that the right choices are made. Not only do the examiners need to be conversant with the field of study, but they should also be sympathetic to the worldview and methodology of the researcher. In this context it is worth developing a provisional list of examiners early on in the period of study, which gets refined and updated as the theoretical and empirical work develops. If the candidate has done sufficient networking through conferences and learned societies (such as the British Academy of Management or the US-based Academy of Management), he or she should be clear about who the best examiners would be.

Whereas in the past most dissertations were based on the traditional structure of a report outlined in Table 12.1, many universities have introduced the so-called paper-based dissertation format. A paper-based PhD thesis, which is already well-established in economics, consists of at least three separate, publishable papers. The papers are free-standing (in the sense that they can be read and understood independently) but they all relate to one topic or theme. Together they are expected to present a coherent account of a unified research project. The papers are usually sandwiched between an extended introduction, which may be seen as combining elements of an introduction, a more concise literature review and a methods chapter, and an overarching discussion and conclusion chapter. The paper-based dissertation is particularly useful for students who conduct interdisciplinary research, as the distinct papers make it easier to communicate with distinct audiences, and for those who are keen to publish during their doctoral studies. However, not every topic and methodology lend themselves equally well to a paper-based approach. For example, students conducting ethnographic research may be well-advised to stick to the conventional format. PhD students considering a paper-based format should discuss this with their advisers early on, as the format implies a strategy for writing up that differs from that used for a monograph. Whatever the format, the general expectations, evaluative elements and overall assessment process remain the same.

substantive contribution
this is achieved when the research throws new light on the subject of study, whether it is a particular kind of organization or aspects of employee or managerial behaviour

theoretical contribution
this is achieved when new concepts are developed, or existing concepts are extended, in order to understand or explain behaviour and organizational phenomena

methodological contribution
this is achieved where an academic report or paper develops new methods of inquiry, or extends existing methods into new contexts

TABLE 12.5 Hierarchy of evaluative elements

7 Quality of argumentation
6 Evaluation of concepts
5 Synthesis of ideas and concepts
4 Analysis of data and evidence
3 Application of theories/ideas to practise
2 Comprehension of the problem addressed
1 Knowledge of the field

EXERCISE 12.3

Have a look at the two Guardian articles 'All nighters and self-doubt: learn from our dissertation disasters' and 'Ten things I wish I'd known before starting my dissertation' offering some advice on writing dissertations.

1   **Individual**: Read the articles and make a list of the challenges you think you are most likely to encounter (you know yourself best) and how you will meet them.

2   **Group discussion**: Discuss in groups of two to four students which of the many challenges discussed in the two articles are the most familiar to you. Why? When you encountered such problems how did you respond? What would you do differently now?

All-nighters and self-doubt: learn from our dissertation disasters

Ten things I wish I'd known before starting my dissertation

Published outputs: conferences, journals and books

Nowadays it is essential for aspiring academics to get their research into the public domain early in their career. It is advisable to attempt publication from doctoral research while the work is being conducted, and occasionally it is possible to publish results from Masters' dissertations. In each of these cases the evaluation takes place before the final copy of the work is produced, and this acts as a filter on the quality of work that appears in public. In general, it is easier to get a paper accepted for a conference than for a journal, although significant hierarchies exist within both categories. Hence many researchers will take an incremental approach, submitting the results of their work to a conference, and then on the basis of feedback rewriting the paper and submitting it to a journal.

With some conferences it is possible to submit extended abstracts, which are evaluated by two or three referees, and the feedback from the referees can be incorporated into the paper before the conference takes place. Other conferences, such as the Academy of Management, will only accept submission of full papers, but in these cases the feedback from referees can be more focused, and this can be combined with discussion and feedback at the conference itself in helping the authors revise the paper for submission to a journal. As we have mentioned earlier, participation at conferences is very important for publishing contacts and building up research networks. However, conference papers per se have limited value for academics wishing to build up their careers or to gain tenure. The 'gold standard' is acceptance of papers in academic journals, and preferably the more highly rated ones.

Sometimes edited books and special issues of journals are initiated at conferences, and the conference organizers often take on the editorial roles for these publications. Although peer review is normally used to support decisions, one of the easiest ways of getting included in such publications is to offer to co-edit the proceedings. You too can become a gatekeeper! But this is by no means the end of the road, because conference proceedings and book chapters only achieve modest ratings in the increasingly hierarchical world of academic publishing. As mentioned, the gold standard is the academic journal, and this is where some of the strictest hierarchies operate.

There are very clear hierarchies in the reputation of different journals. Most countries have their own journal ranking systems,[1] and internationally the International Scientific Indexing ISI impact factor and the *Financial Times* (FT) list are the most widely recognized indicators of quality. There are a number of factors that help to sustain the position of the top journals: they get large numbers of submissions and are therefore able to be very selective; people will usually only submit their very best work to the top journals; and the reviewing process is conducted with such rigour that the finally published paper is often significantly better than the initial submission. There are two simple ways of judging in advance the standing of an academic journal. First, submission and rejection rates indicate how much demand there is to get into the journal. Top journals will have rejection rates of over 95 per cent, while lesser journals may be around 50 per cent. Journals that take almost everything will not be considered as serious journals (but then they are unlikely to publish their rejection rates). Second, the citation index ISI Web of Knowledge produces annual rankings of journals based on the frequency with which papers from a given journal are cited by papers published in other respectable journals (see http://wok.mimas.ac.uk). These rankings use 'impact factor' as the key criterion. This is calculated as the number of citations appearing in ISI journals during the target year that refer to papers published in the focal journal during the two previous years, divided by the total number of papers published in the focal journal during the two previous years.

Web of Knowledge
a database that provides a single route to journals in the Social Sciences Citation Index

EXAMPLE 12.2

Table 12.6 calculates the 2013 impact factor for *Journal of Management Studies*.

TABLE 12.6   Impact factor for *Journal of Management Studies*

Number of citations			Number of articles		
to articles published in:	2012	122	published in:	2012	63
	2011	327		2011	74
	Sum:	449		Sum:	137
Calculation: Divide citations to recent articles by number of recent articles					
	449 ÷ 137 = 3.3				

Journals with impact factors over 3.00 are generally considered 'world class'; those between 1.5 and 3.0 are seen as very good international journals; those between 0.5 and 1.5 are respectable international journals; and those below 0.5 are in danger of relegation. Of course, interpretation of these ratings depends greatly on where your favourite journals fall, and it is also important to look at trends over several years since these ratings can be quite volatile!

---

[1]The dominant system in the UK is provided by the Association of Business Schools (the ABS List). It rates over 2,000 journals from 1 up to 4*, and the list is updated biennially in April.

Beyond that, you must make up your own mind, by reading past papers in the journal or by submitting something to it. If you want to get something published quickly or easily, then start with one of the more lowly journals. Top journals have much greater lead times, often running into several years. This is not because they are slow or inefficient, more that they will be dealing with a very large volume of material and they will be very exacting in their standards. For example, a paper that Mark Easterby-Smith published in the *Academy of Management Journal* (Easterby-Smith and Malina, 1999) was initially submitted in March 1996 (and that was based on earlier conference papers given in 1993 and 1995). The initial rewrite offer from the *Academy of Management Journal* arrived 11 weeks after submission and contained eight single-spaced pages of comments and advice from the editor and referees. Over the next two years the paper went through four rewrites, and on each occasion the guidance from the editorial office ran to four or five pages. Thus, by the time the paper was accepted in July 1998, the length of comments from the editorial office was greater than the eventual length of the paper. On occasions such as this, as Golden-Biddle and Locke (2007) comment, one starts to wonder whether the referees should be included as co-authors of the paper!

Our general advice regarding publication strategies is to aim for good journals wherever possible, and perhaps seek to submit papers with others (supervisors, examiners, people met at conferences) who have already been successful in getting published in the target journal.

It is important for people carrying out academic management research to understand some of the hidden rules and procedures, because these may determine whether they are eventually successful. Despite efforts to be fair and transparent, these hidden rules and procedures are inevitable. In general, it is easier for North Americans to get accepted in North American journals, and for Europeans to get accepted in European journals, because of the institutional and human networks that support these journals. American journals tend to prefer quantitative papers based on survey data; European journals often prefer qualitative papers based on in-depth case studies. But there are always exceptions to these rules, and therefore it is important to be alert and not to accept stereotypes too easily.

In order to get published in a peer-reviewed academic journal it is essential to understand the decision-making process for most journals, especially the role of referees. In Figure 12.1 we summarize the decision-making process of a typical journal. In this figure the numbers indicate the percentage of the original submissions that move to each of the successive stages. A number of papers (perhaps 60 per cent) will be rejected by the editors without being sent to the referees, a further number will be rejected after receipt of referees' reports, and most of the remainder will be sent an offer to revise and resubmit (R&R). It is extremely rare for a paper to be accepted outright by a good journal. For those lucky enough to have been sent an R&R, they then move on to the critical stage of responding to the criticisms/recommendations of reviewers and the editors. Frequently the reviewers will provide conflicting advice, and a good editor will notice the conflicts and provide guidance on which lines to follow.

The resubmitted paper needs to be accompanied by a letter to the editor (and referees) explaining how the recommendations have been implemented and providing a rationale where the authors feel that the recommendations are not appropriate. Sometimes these letters can get very lengthy, perhaps 10 to 20 pages, but long letters can irritate editors and make it difficult for referees to see how their suggestions have been implemented, so the advice is to deal with every point the editors and reviewers have made, but only discuss the critical issues at any length.

Finally, there is the possibility of publishing a book. Although in some subjects, such as history, it is quite normal to turn theses into books, this is relatively rare in the management field. Publishers have a preference for textbooks and handbooks because they have more general and sustained appeal. In order to develop a book proposal with broad appeal, it is generally necessary to collaborate with other scholars who can provide complementary perspectives, and this may not be a sensible option until several years after the PhD is completed. In the short term there are few academic credits for publishing books in the management field. Nevertheless, in the longer term they can contribute substantially to personal reputation and visibility, and this can also be measured in terms of 'hits' on Google Scholar. For most people, the direct financial rewards of publishing books are not great. Fortune is most likely to follow the fame of being a published author, and academic careers depend on both the reputation of the publisher and the quality of the reviews that ensue. The nice thing about books is that it is usually possible to develop ideas over a period of time with the help of the publisher. Once again, contacts with publishers are most easily established at conferences, where more of the relevant firms are represented.

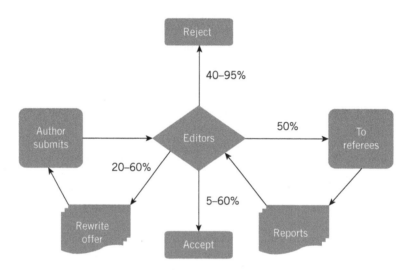

FIGURE 12.1   Flowchart of journal decision-making

Edited by Dr Inger Mewburn (ANU), the Thesis Whisperer is a blog newspaper dedicated to the topic of doing a thesis. An entire section of the blog focuses on academic writing – in particular (but not only) for doctoral students.

The Thesis
Whisperer
on Writing

Plagiarism

It is important to be aware of plagiarism, because over the years there has been a steady growth in cases of, and discussions about, plagiarism among students, which often reveal uncertainty and doubt about its significance. Acknowledging work and referencing sources mean that the student or researcher knows his or her topic, has read and searched for sources, and knows how to acknowledge the work of others. Plagiarism generally involves presenting the work and ideas of other people and passing them off as your own, without acknowledging the original source of the ideas used.

Although plagiarism is not a new issue, it is only through the advent of information technology and packages such as Turnitin (www.turnitin.com) that plagiarism can now be detected relatively easily (a screenshot of how Turnitin works is given in Figure 12.2). While Internet search engines may make information easier to acquire, they also serve to provide students with endless sources of material from which to 'cut and paste'. What were once cases of minor infringements have become a problem of epidemic proportions (Duggan, 2006).

The recurring themes as to what constitutes plagiarism include: copying another person's material without proper acknowledgement or reference; paraphrasing others without acknowledgement, thereby giving others the impression that the work represents your own original formulation; and, of course, buying ready-made material from professional writers. There is an increasing number of websites that offer such services and some of those being offered are extremely sophisticated. Of course, for those who have to undergo oral defence of their work, the fact they are not attached to the literature soon means they are caught out, while references that are not in the university libraries also raise suspicion.

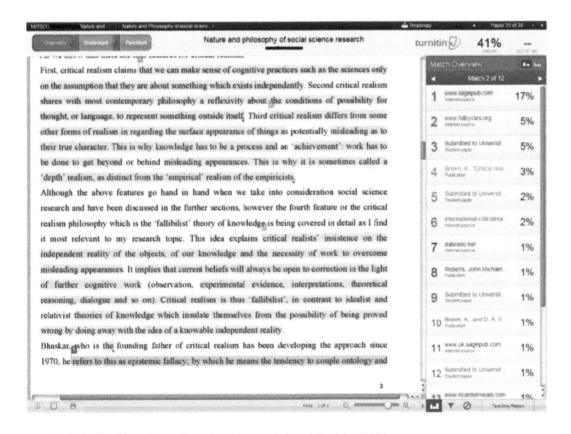

FIGURE 12.2   Turnitin software. Reproduced by permission of Turnitin UK Ltd.

In order to avoid plagiarism, students should ensure that they have clearly referenced where others' words and concepts have been used but also where others' ideas have influenced their thought process. This involves keeping up-to-date and precise references about where you have accessed material from, as even accidental plagiarism is considered a serious issue. Given the increase in plagiarism, universities are employing a zero-tolerance policy and students are increasingly being penalized over this issue. In an attempt to combat this problem, institutions are beginning to run courses that aim to educate students to ensure that they are aware of what constitutes plagiarism. Given that plagiarism is a difficult and confusing area, it may be worthwhile checking if any such courses are available at your institution, where you will most likely be given clear examples of both deliberate and accidental plagiarism to ensure that you are aware of the potential perils of careless referencing.

Dissemination strategies

In the previous section we concentrated on dissemination mainly to academic audiences, and here we focus on other audiences, especially policy-makers and practitioners. We start with some general comments on making public presentations (although this applies equally to client and conference presentations), then discuss publishing in practitioner journals and making the best use of the public media.

We hesitate to provide much advice on the technicality of presentations since most of our students nowadays are very expert and professional at structuring and presenting data. However, a common mistake is to provide too much material, especially in the form of slides, which puts the presenters under considerable time pressure and makes it extremely difficult for them to introduce any kind of interaction into the presentation. It is preferable to use a minimal number of slides (four or five for a ten-minute presentation) to provide a basic structure, and then provide stories and vignettes to illustrate the points that are being made. If it is a team presentation, then people can take different roles according to their strengths: providing introductions, telling stories, making jokes, encouraging interaction and dealing with questions. If the presentation is being made by an individual, it is often worth recording the session because you may be so focused on providing answers to questions that you do not listen to what people are really saying!

Publications in practitioner journals are also important because they reach much wider audiences and demonstrate that you are engaging with potential 'users'. However, it can be very difficult to get into the famous practitioner journals, such as *Harvard Business Review*, *Sloan Management Review* or *California Management Review*, because the majority of papers are written by established academics, who may have been invited by the editors to submit because they have recently published some interesting material in a top academic journal. So, there is a virtual cycle operating, and it may be quite difficult to break in.

Another way to increase the exposure of one's research results is to approach the media. This can most easily be done through a press release, which is circulated to relevant newspapers and radio stations. Most universities and learned societies have considerable experience in dealing with the media and should be able to provide advice on whom to contact. In Example 12.3 we provide some general guidance on writing press releases.

EXAMPLE 12.3

Guidance on writing press releases

Press releases should be quite short, with a maximum of 600 words printed on two sides of a single sheet of paper. From the outset, you have to convince the reader that you have something interesting to say, perhaps a new fact about the world or a new way of looking at an important issue that has topical relevance. The press release should start with the conclusions, and then provide the supporting evidence – which is opposite to the normal way of writing academic papers, which end with the conclusions. In summary:

- Begin with a catchy headline.
- Provide a general statement that sums up the main finding.
- Distil into three or four points the essence of the research.
- Back up these points with facts and figures.
- Finish with the main policy implications or the 'way forward'.
- Add your contact details, including email address and phone numbers.
- Above all, keep the language intelligible and jargon-free.

Source: personal communication from Romesh Vaitilingam

Naturally, there is much competition over access to the media, and those academics who excel in this respect generally build up excellent relationships over time with journalists and make themselves available 24/7. There are also wider political implications of building up reputations: credit for research should not be taken for granted; it depends very much on how much the researcher is able to exploit his or her work through contacts, publications and other forms of dissemination, as we discussed in Chapter 5.

Finally, one can also use events such as panel discussions or workshops with different stakeholders for dissemination purposes (again, see Chapter 5). Social media have also become a major route to impact, with Twitter, Facebook and other platforms providing plenty of opportunities for showcasing and disseminating research.

It is important to develop a dissemination strategy at the outset of any funded research projects, and perhaps halfway through doing a doctoral thesis. This should normally include two or three conferences with a brief synopsis of the possible paper in each case, and potential target journals for the next phase of each paper. It is also worth thinking about potential media strategies, including developing press releases towards the end of the research period. As with all forms of publishing, it is important to believe that you have something worth saying, and you have to consider what audience you wish to address.

EXERCISE 12.4

Putting Dissemination into Practice

1   **Individual**: Prepare a table of contents for your dissertation or thesis.

2   **Group**: Develop a short press release for the research project you are currently engaged upon. Share the results with colleagues for critique and suggestions.

3   **Group discussion**: Debate the proposition that: 'The public dissemination of social science results is harmful to the integrity and progress of research'. This can be done with different groups taking the *pro* or *anti* line.

Conclusion

We see the publication and dissemination of ideas not merely as a means to the researcher's own ends, but as an obligation that each researcher has to the wider community. That being said, it is important to understand how appropriate forms of writing and dissemination vary with the audience, the type of research and the form of output that is envisaged. In this chapter we have tried to provide advice on:

- Core skills in writing academic reports.

- Strategies and templates for developing appropriate structures.

- How to structure literature reviews.

- Criteria for evaluating different forms of output.

- The complex political processes involved in publishing and dissemination.

Overall, we hope that this book will have provided some of the armoury both to complete worthwhile research and to capitalize on it.

Further reading

A delightful book that looks at strategies for presenting qualitative research. It also provides good examples from the authors' own experiences of how to handle the complex politics of the review process when submitting papers to journals:

Golden-Biddle, K. and Locke, K. (2007) *Composing Qualitative Research*, 2nd edn. London: Sage.

The final chapter provides guidance on writing up literature reviews, with an emphasis on how to develop arguments and guidance on the elements that need to be included:

Hart, C. (1998) *Doing a Literature Review: Releasing the Social Science Research Imagination*. London: Sage.

This book provides lots of advice and guidance on the technicalities of writing, including grammar, style and structure. It is also very helpful for the more strategic and emotional aspects of academic research and writing:

Murray, R. (2002) *How to Write a Thesis*. Milton Keynes: Open University Press.

This is a thoughtful and practical book with lots of advice on how to manage and complete research work, especially at the doctoral level, with lots of examples and good humour from the authors:

Phillips, E.M. and Pugh, D.S. (2005) *How to Get a PhD: A Handbook for Students and their Supervisors*, 4th edn. Maidenhead: Open University Press.

An accessible and well-written book on how to develop a reflective and critical approach to academic reading and writing, which can be helpful for both practitioners and more experienced academics:

Wallace, M. and Wray, A. (2011) *Critical Reading and Writing for Postgraduates*, 2nd edn. London: Sage.

An overview of 50 diagrams used by consultants, managers and academics:

Duncan, K. (2014) *The Diagrams Book: 50 Ways to Solve Any Problem Visually*. London: LID Editorial.

We agree with Charlotte Coleman that the following style guides are invaluable for anyone who wants to write better:

Fish, S.E. (2011) *How to Write a Sentence*. New York: HarperCollins.

Strunk, W. (2007) *The Elements of Style*. London: Penguin.

Check your understanding online

Visit the website **https://edge.sagepub.com/easterbysmith6e** for useful resources that will help reinforce what you've read in this chapter:

 Take an interactive quiz to test your understanding of the key topics

 Review suggested answers to Exercises 12.1 to 12.4 above

 Use interactive flashcards to check your knowledge of essential concepts

GLOSSARY

1-tailed test refers to a directional alternative hypothesis relative to the null hypothesis; a prediction of a positive association between variables, or that one group mean will be bigger than another

2-tailed test refers to a non-directional alternative hypothesis relative to the null hypothesis; association between variables may be either positive or negative, or the means of two groups will differ in either direction

academic theory explicit ideas developed through exchanges between researchers to explain and interpret scientific and social phenomena

action research an approach to research that seeks understanding through attempting to change the situation under investigation

alternative hypothesis (H_1) position adopted during hypothesis testing if the evidence from data is strong enough to reject the null hypothesis (see also null hypothesis)

analysis of covariance (ANCOVA) a form of test of group differences on a continuous dependent variable, which also includes continuous variables as predictors (covariates)

analysis of variance (ANOVA) a form of hypothesis test for comparing the means of two or more groups, which may be classified on the basis of other variables

applied research studies that focus on tackling practical problems in organizations where the desired outcome will be knowledge about how to solve the problem

archival research collection and analysis of public documents relating mainly to organizational or governmental strategies

argument analysis an approach to the analysis of natural language data that identifies the data used in making claims, the premises made and the conclusions drawn by individuals about issues of relevance

association two variables are associated where knowing a value on one variable carries information about the corresponding value on the other; can be measured by a correlation coefficient

ATLAS.ti a software package that assists in the building and testing of theories through the creative assembly of qualitative analysis of textual, graphical and audio/visual data; available from www.atlasti.com

auto-ethnography a form of insider research often conducted by those studying in the organization in which they work

bar chart a form of graphical summary for category scales, with bars whose length indicates the frequency of responses for each category

basic research sometimes also referred to as fundamental research; its aim is to develop theory and greater understanding of an issue or phenomenon without there necessarily being any direct impact on a current problem

beta weight a standardized regression coefficient

bias in sampling design, a biased sample is one that does not represent the features of the population from which it is drawn (see representativeness)

big data extremely large datasets arising from the everyday processes of businesses, which may be structured or unstructured

binomial distribution a form of reference distribution; the distribution of entities that are binary (present/absent, success/failure)

bootstrap a way of forming a reference distribution by repeated sampling from a specific dataset; used in hypothesis testing

CAQDAS computer-assisted qualitative data analysis software

case method a research design that focuses in depth on one, or a small number of, organizations, events or individuals, generally over time

category scale a form of measurement scale where responses are recorded in a small number of discrete units, for example makes of car purchased (cf. continuous scale)

causal model a class of multivariate models of the causal relationships among a set of variables that can be fitted to data

chi-square distribution a form of reference distribution; the distribution of variances used for testing hypotheses about spread

chi-square test a form of hypothesis test for testing the association between two variables measured on nominal category scales

cluster sampling a modification of random sampling where the population is first divided into convenient units, called clusters, and then all entities within a cluster are selected

code a word or a short phrase that summarizes the meaning of a chunk of data, such as a statement, a sentence or an element in a picture

cognitive mapping a method of spatially displaying data in order to detect patterns and by so doing better understand their relationship and significance

common factors a class of latent variables in a measurement model, which are assumed to account for the covariances among a set of observed variables (see also specific factors)

confirmatory factor analysis (CFA) a multivariate method for testing measurement models of the relationship between a set of observed variables and a hypothesized set of latent variables (see also exploratory factor analysis)

content analysis a relatively deductive method of analysis where codes (or constructs) are almost all predetermined and where they are systematically searched for within the data collected

continuous scale a form of measurement scale where responses are recorded in a large number of discrete units, for example age recorded in months (cf. category scale)

convenience sampling a form of non-probability sampling design where entities are included in a sample on the basis of their ease of access

conversation analysis an analysis of natural language data used with naturally occurring conversations to establish linguistic patterns through the detailed examination of utterances

cooperative inquiry a form of action research where the research 'subjects' not only play a part in sense-making, but also are encouraged to determine the main questions to be researched

covariance a measure of association between two continuous variables expressed in the units of the measurement scales of the variables; its square root is the correlation coefficient

covariates variables measured on continuous scales, which are included as predictors in analysis of group differences

critical action learning a group-based inquiry that takes account of the viewpoint and feelings of members within a social and political context. The agenda and process are determined largely by members, rather than by academics

critical discourse analysis the analysis of natural language data, which emphasizes the power relations and ideologies that are both created and conveyed

critical incident technique a method of teasing out information often employed within interviews, which goes to the heart of an issue about which information is sought

critical realism an approach to social research with an explicit ontological position, which combines features of both positivism and constructionism

critical theory a philosophy that critiques the structures and outcomes of capitalist society, and examines how powerful members of society maintain their dominance over the less powerful members

Cronbach's alpha coefficient an index of the internal consistency of a composite variable formed by combining a set of items; a common measure of reliability

cross-sectional surveys these usually involve selecting different organizations, or units, in different contexts, and investigating the relationships between a number of variables across these units

Decision Explorer a software program for collecting, conveying and managing ideas and other kinds of qualitative information that surround complex and uncertain situations; available from Banxia software (www.banxia.com)

degrees of freedom (*df*) the value that defines the shape of a standard reference distribution in hypothesis testing; for example, in testing association, *df* = sample size minus one

dependent variables the factors that research is trying to predict (see independent variables)

discourse analysis covers a range of analysis approaches that focus on data in the form of language. This could be the language used or the context in which the form of language is used. Researchers focus on the development of and contribution to aspects of social theory and social action

dominance in the context of mixed methods research this refers to whether, or not, one method uses significantly more time and resource than the other

efficiency the extent to which a summary measure captures all the information within the data that is relevant to what is summarized

eigenvalues the term used in exploratory factor analysis for the summary measure of the amount of variance in the observed variables accounted for by a factor

embedded case a case within a larger case, for example, the A&E department within a hospital that was the primary case

emic insights into communities, societies or organizations as seen from the perspective of insiders

engaged research involves close collaboration between academics and practitioners in determining the research aims, its implementation, and the practical implications

epistemology views about the most appropriate ways of enquiring into the nature of the world

ethnography approaches to research and data collection that emphasize gaining access to the perspectives and experiences of organizational members

etic insights into communities, societies or organizations as seen from the perspective of outsiders

evaluation research research that has, as its focus, the systemic and rigorous assessment of an activity or object such that the information and insights gleaned can provide useful feedback

everyday theory the ideas and assumptions we carry round in our heads in order to make sense of everyday observations

exogenous variables those variables that are part of a multivariate model, but whose causal influences are taken as given and do not form part of the model itself

experimenter effect the idea that the act of observing or measuring any social process actually changes that process

exploratory factor analysis (EFA) a multivariate method for fitting measurement models, which describes the covariances among a set of observed variables in terms of a set of latent variables (see also confirmatory factor analysis)

exploratory surveys these are similar to cross-sectional surveys, but tend to focus on identifying patterns within the data through the use of factor analysis or principal components analysis

external validity whether the results of the research can be generalized to other settings or contexts

factorial designs a form of experimental design that includes combinations of more than one independent variable

factor loading the weight allocated to the path between a latent variable and an observed variable in a measurement model

factual surveys involve collecting and collating relatively 'factual' data from different groups of people

falsification a research design that seeks evidence to demonstrate that the current assumptions or hypotheses are incorrect

F-distribution a form of reference distribution; the distribution of ratios of variances used for testing hypotheses about group differences in means

feminism a philosophy that argues that women's experiences and contributions are undervalued by society and by science; also an emancipatory movement to rectify these inequalities

financial databases archives of records about companies or other entities, which contain financial data, such as income data, cash flow, profit and loss, share prices

focused codes codes that are directed, conceptual and analytical

focused or second-cycle coding techniques that build on the previous coding cycle and aim at developing a sense of the categorical and conceptual order arising from the open codes; based on a thorough examination of all codes created in the first cycle, researchers organize and synthesize them into more analytic secondary codes

framing the theoretical lens or device that guides and shapes the way research is conducted; framing can apply equally well to research design, data collection and analysis

frequency distribution a summary representation of a sample of data containing the number of responses obtained for each alternative on the measurement scale

generalizability the extent to which observations or theories derived in one context can be applicable to other contexts

generalized linear models a class of multivariate statistical models within which the relationships between DVs and PVs are linear, and DVs can be expressed through a transformation called a link function; it includes multiple regression analysis, ANOVA and logistic regression

goodness of fit a summary measure of the discrepancy between observed values and the fitted values derived from a hypothesized model

grand theory a coherent set of assumptions intended to explain social or physical phenomena; may or may not be empirically testable

grey literature literature that is not formally published in journals. As a consequence it is usually considered to be not widely accessible or available, e.g. reports or working papers; however, with the Internet, this is increasingly less the case

grounded analysis the linking of key variables (theoretical codes) into a more holistic theory that makes a contribution to knowledge in a particular field or domain

grounded theory an open (and inductive) approach to analysis where there are no a priori definitional codes but where the structure is derived from the data and the constructs and categories derived emerge from the respondents under study

hermeneutics a philosophy and methodology about the interpretation of texts; stresses that textual materials should be understood in the context within which they are written

hierarchical regression a form of multiple regression analysis, which involves entering predictor variables sequentially in blocks

histogram a form of bar chart for continuous scales, where scale points are first grouped together and the length of bars indicates the frequency of responses for each category

human relations theory assumes that performance of both individuals and organizations is dependent on the commitment and involvement of all employees, and hence managers need to foster positive relationships with, and between, employees

hypothesis testing the process of making inferences about populations based upon data drawn from samples

identifiability the characteristic of a hypothesized model defined by the relationship between the number of parameters in a model to be estimated and the information available to do it; a model is identified if there are fewer parameters to be estimated than there are items of information available

independent variables the factors that are believed to cause the effects that are to be observed; also called predictor variables (see dependent variables)

in-depth interview an opportunity, usually within an interview, to probe deeply and open up new dimensions and insights

inference drawing conclusions about a population based on evidence from a sample

inferential surveys surveys that are aimed at establishing relationships between variables and concepts

interaction effects where the effect on a variable depends on the context defined by another variable

internal realism a philosophical position which assumes that reality is independent of the observer, but that scientists can only access that reality indirectly

internal validity assurance that results are true and conclusions are correct through elimination of systematic sources of potential bias

interquartile range see mid-range

interval scale a form of continuous scale that has no true zero point, so that ratio calculations are not meaningful, for example temperature (cf. ratio scale)

interview bias occurs when the process of questioning influences the interviewee's response

Kendall's tau a test of association between two variables based on the ranks of the scores for each variable

Kruskal-Wallis test a form of hypothesis test for comparing two or more groups that uses rank-order data

laddering down a method of questioning that can be employed within interviewing, which can elicit examples that evidence general statements, views or values expressed in interview responses

laddering up a method of questioning that can be employed within interviewing, which can elicit the values that underpin statements or actions made by respondents

Lagrange multiplier test a form of modification index in SEM that indicates the value of a fixed parameter if it were to be set free

latent variables a class of variables within a multivariate model, which are not measured directly but are inferred from observed variables

leading question a form of wording of a question that leads the respondent to give the answer preferred by the questioner

likelihood ratio chi-square an index of the overall quality of a model fitted by the maximum likelihood method; used in logistic regression analysis

Likert scale a form of ordinal category scale for measuring attitudes from very positive to very negative

local knowledge ideas and principles that are relevant to the setting of a particular organization or social setting, but which may not apply in other contexts

location a characteristic of a set of data that summarizes where the data are located on the measurement scale; measured by the mode, median, mid-mean or mean

logistic regression a form of multivariate analysis of causal relationships among observed variables where the dependent variable is measured on a binary category scale

Mann-Whitney U test a form of hypothesis test for comparing two groups that uses rank-order data

mean a summary measure of location that uses all the values in a dataset in its calculation; the sum of all data points divided by the sample size

measurement model a multivariate model for the relationship between observed variables and latent variables

median a summary measure of location that uses the ranks of all the values in a dataset in its calculation; the middle value in an ordered set of data points

mediational model a form of causal model in which the causal influence of a predictor variable on a dependent variable is indirect, operating through an intermediary variable (called a mediator)

memo-writing written notes that allow researchers to document and reflect on codes, categories and concepts, as well as research questions and emerging ideas; a method of crucial importance for grounded analysis

methodological contribution this is achieved where an academic report or paper develops new methods of inquiry, or extends existing methods into new contexts

methodology a combination of methods used to enquire into a specific situation

methods and techniques the instruments and processes for gathering research data, analysing it and drawing conclusions from it

middle-range theory a set of ideas and concepts relevant to explaining social or physical phenomena within relatively specific contexts, normally empirically testable

mid-mean a summary measure of location; the mean of the middle half of the data

mid-range a summary measure of spread; the range of the middle half of the data (also called the interquartile range)

mixed methods research involves utilizing and integrating methods from different research traditions

mode a summary measure of location; the most frequently occurring value in a dataset

mode 1 research the generation of theoretical knowledge through detached scientific research

mode 1½ research the generation of useful knowledge through combining scientific research methods with practical engagement

mode 2 research the generation of practical knowledge through direct engagement with practice

modification index an estimate in SEM of the change in goodness of fit of a fitted model if a fixed parameter were allowed to become free

multiple regression model a multivariate method that includes a single dependent variable measured on a continuous scale and a set of predictor variables that may be measured on continuous or category scales

multi-stage sampling a process of dividing up a population into hierarchical units, such as countries, regions, organizations, work groups, and applying random sampling at each level

multivariate analysis of covariance (MANCOVA) a class of statistical methods for testing group differences for two or more dependent variables simultaneously, which also includes one or more continuous variables as predictors

multivariate analysis of variance (MANOVA) a class of statistical methods for testing group differences for two or more dependent variables simultaneously multivariate methods a class of statistical methods that analyses the covariances among a number of variables simultaneously

multivariate test a test of a study hypothesis that involves consideration of several dependent variables simultaneously

narrative analysis focuses on stories or accounts of individuals (or groups) in order to capture within social science research and management the accounts of individuals

narrative methods ways of conducting research that concentrate on collecting the stories told among organizational members

natural language data the term is used in this book to signify data that are presented in the form of words (spoken) or text (written). These data can be analysed and interpreted in a variety of different ways in order to make inferences in relation to such things as content, meaning and practice

nominalism an ontological view that objects in the world are 'formed' by the language we use and the names we attach to phenomena

nominal scale a form of category scale where the scale units have no natural ordering, for example makes of car purchased (cf. ordinal scale)

non-experimental designs positivist research conducted through comparing groups for which the members have not been assigned at random; similar to quasi-experimental designs

non-parametric test a form of hypothesis test that uses a reference distribution derived from all possible permutations of study outcomes using the ranking of data (cf. parametric test)

non-probability sampling designs sampling designs where the likelihood of each population entity being included in the sample cannot be known

non-proportional stratified random sampling a form of sampling where the population is divided into subsets (called strata) and different sampling proportions are used for each stratum for selecting a sample

normal distribution a form of standard reference distribution; the distribution of the sum of independent measures where the standard deviation of the reference distribution is known (its shape is sometimes called the bell-curve)

normative theory describes how organizations should be structured and managed

null hypothesis (H_0) the initial position adopted during hypothesis testing, which may be modified on the basis of evidence from data; for tests involving comparing groups, the null hypothesis is that the groups are nothing but random samples from a single population (see also alternative hypothesis)

null model a model within structural equation modelling which assumes that all the covariances among the observed variables are zero; used as the baseline for calculating incremental fit indices

NVivo a software package that assists in the building and testing of theories by classifying, sorting and arranging information; available from QSR International (www.qsrinternational.com)

observational methods ways of collecting data that involve direct sampling of aspects of behaviour

observed variables a class of variables in a multivariate model that are directly measured; they can be used to estimate latent variables

observer effects influences on behaviour that result from study participants knowing that they are being observed

odds ratio the relative likelihood of the two possible outcomes for a binary category variable; used to form the dependent variable in logistic regression analysis

ontology views about the nature of reality

open or first-cycle coding techniques used by researchers as a first analytical step; such codes are often *descriptive* or aid the *organization of the data* (e.g. coding of actors and attributes)

ordinal scale a form of category scale where the scale units have a natural ordering, for example social class (cf. nominal scale)

paradigm a consensual pattern in the way scientists understand, and inquire into, the world

parametric test a form of hypothesis test that uses a standard reference distribution derived from probability theory whose form is defined by a small number of parameters (cf. non-parametric test)

parsimony the extent to which a fitted model in SEM can account for observed data with fewer parameters

partial correlation a correlation between two variables that is adjusted to remove the influence of a third variable

participant observation a form of ethnography where there is close involvement in the organization in order to gain a detailed understanding of other people's realities

path coefficients see regression weight

permutations all possible ways of rearranging a set of entities; used in forms of non-parametric testing of hypotheses

population the set of entities about which a researcher wishes to draw conclusions

positivism the key idea of positivism is that the social world exists externally, and that its properties should be measured through objective methods

postal questionnaire survey a form of survey distribution that involves postal distribution, and relies on respondents to complete a survey themselves and return it to the researcher

postmodernism a collection of philosophies that are opposed to realism, and are generally critical of scientific progress

pragmatism a philosophical position that argues that knowledge and understanding should be derived from direct experience

precision the level of confidence that the researcher has in estimating characteristics of the population from evidence drawn from a sample; it depends on sample size but not on the sampling proportion

predictor variables the factors that are believed to cause the effects that are to be observed; also called independent variables (see dependent variables)

primary data new information that is collected directly by the researcher

principal components analysis a mathematical procedure that assists in reducing data and by so doing indicates possible relationships between a number of uncorrelated variables: the first principal component accounts for as much of the variability in the data as possible, successive components (of which there may be two, three or four) account for as much of the remaining variability as possible

probability sampling designs sampling designs where the likelihood of each population entity being included in the sample is known

probe a device used as an intervention technique to improve and sharpen the interviewees' response

product-moment correlation a test of association between two variables measured on continuous scales

proportional stratified random sampling a form of sampling where the population is divided into subsets (called strata) and within strata the same sampling proportion is used for selecting a sample

pure research research for which the primary objective/output is the development of theory

purposive sampling a form of non-probability sampling design where the criteria for inclusion in a sample are defined, and entities are first screened to see whether they meet the criteria for inclusion; those entities that meet the criteria are included in the sample

qualitative data the authors of this book see the logic or framing that defines the research questions of social scientists as little different, whether structural equation models are used or methods of discourse analysis. Qualitative data requires relevance to be identified, categories and concepts defined, and theories developed as well as particular truths. In addition, data is usually (but not always) gathered through the engagement of the researcher

qualitative interviews offer ways by which rich and detailed information can be gathered from respondents to reveal aspects of their lives, understandings or experience.

quasi-experimental design the use of multiple measures over time in order to reduce the effects of control and experimental groups not being fully matched

quota sampling a form of non-probability sampling design where the population is divided into units and a target sample size (quota) is defined for each unit; entities that meet the criteria for a specific unit are added to the sample until the target sample size for the unit is achieved

random assignment where the objects of the experiment (e.g. people) are assigned at random to either the experimental treatment or to the control (non-treatment) groups

range a summary measure of spread; the difference between the largest and smallest data values

rank-order correlation a test of association between two variables measured on ordered category scales

ratio scale a form of continuous scale that has a true zero point, so that ratio calculations are meaningful, for example height (cf. interval scale)

realism an ontological position which assumes that the physical and social worlds exist independently of any observations made about them

reference distribution the distribution of all alternative values of a test statistic based on the assumption that the null hypothesis is true; used in hypothesis testing

reflexivity where researchers think about the effects they have had or may have on the outcome and process of research

regression weight the value of the independent contribution of a predictor variable to predicting a dependent variable in multiple regression analysis; also called a path coefficient

relativism an ontological view that phenomena depend on the perspectives from which we observe them; also an epistemological position that observations will be more accurate/credible if made from several different perspectives

reliability the consistency of measurement in a composite variable formed by combining scores on a set of items; can be measured by Cronbach's alpha coefficient

repertory grid a tool for uncovering an individual's (or group's) view of the world based on the constructs they develop and hold

representativeness in sampling design, this refers to how much the characteristics of a sample are the same as the characteristics of the population from which the sample is drawn

research design a research design may be defined as a strategy that lays out the principles of the research methodology for a given study. It articulates methods and techniques for all stages of the research process and justifies their appropriateness in relation to both the research question or hypothesis and the research context

residual the value of that portion of the variance of a dependent variable that cannot be accounted for by a set of predictor variables

RMSEA (root mean squared error of approximation) an index in SEM of the goodness of fit of a hypothesized causal model adjusted for the complexity of the fitted model

robustness the extent to which a summary measure is sensitive to disturbances in data quality

sample a subset of the population from which inferences are drawn based on evidence

sample size the number of entities included in a sample

sampling distribution a form of reference distribution derived from probability theory based on repeated sampling from a theoretical population; used in hypothesis testing

sampling frame the list of all of those eligible to be included in a sample

sampling proportion the size of a sample relative to the size of a population

sampling strategy sets out the criteria to be adopted by a researcher when selecting a subset (or sample) from a wider population of individuals, organizations, industries (or whatever unit of analysis that is being investigated)

scholarship this is a term given to the development of high levels of knowledge about a particular issue or topic, largely on the basis of secondary data

search engine a program that will find text relating to the keyword(s) entered

secondary data research information that already exists in the form of publications or other electronic media, which is collected by the researcher

secondary visual data relates to the analysis of verbal accounts that respondents give in response to visual images

semi-concealed research a form of ethnography where there is negotiated access with research agendas that the researchers are not always willing to reveal to all those they meet

semi-detached design a mixed methods design where there are no direct linkages between the two parts of the study

sequencing in the context of mixed methods research this refers to whether or not the methods are used in a discernible order

simple random sampling a form of sampling where every entity in the population has an equal chance of being included in the sample

snowball sampling a form of non-probability sampling design where the criteria for inclusion in a sample are defined; entities that meet the criteria are included in the sample and then asked whether they know others who also meet the criteria

social constructionism the idea that 'reality' is determined by people rather than by objective and external factors, and hence it is most important to appreciate the way people make sense of their experience

social desirability where people adjust their answers to a survey in order to project a positive image of themselves to the interviewer

Spearman's rho a test of association between two variables: the product-moment correlation of the ranked scores for the two variables

specific factors a class of latent variables in a measurement model, which is assumed to account for idiosyncratic aspects of an observed variable (see also common factors)

spread a characteristic of a set of data that summarizes how much the data vary around a measure of location; measured by the range, mid-range or standard deviation

squared multiple correlation an overall measure of the quality of a multiple regression model; the proportion of variance in a dependent variable accounted for by a set of predictor variables

standard deviation (SD) a summary measure of spread; based on the average deviation of scores around the mean

standard error (SE) the standard deviation of a sampling distribution used in hypothesis testing; estimated from the standard deviations and the sample size within groups in a sample

standardization the process of transforming a variable in order to express it on a scale with a mean of zero and a standard deviation of one; often carried out for variables measured on interval scales (with no true zero point) so that regression weights can be compared between predictor variables

statistical control a way of simplifying inference about the relationships among variables by adjusting for their covariance with another variable

stepdown F-test the test statistic in a multivariate analysis or variance of group differences, where the DVs are tested singly in turn in a sequence decided upon by the researcher holding constant DVs earlier in the sequence

stepwise regression a form of multiple regression analysis where predictor variables are automatically entered or dropped sequentially on the basis of the extent of their independent contribution to predicting the dependent variable

stratified random sampling a form of sampling where the population is divided into subsets (called strata) and within strata every entity in the population has an equal chance of being included in the sample

structural equation model a multivariate model of the hypothesized causal relationships among a set of variables, which may include both observed and latent variables

structural models a multivariate model of the hypothesized relationships among a set of variables, which may include both observed and latent variables

structuration theory an epistemology that assumes that social structure and individual behaviour are interlinked, and that each is produced and reproduced by the other

structured interview where the interviewer follows a prescribed list of questions each of which may have predetermined response categories

structured interview survey a form of survey where an interviewer locates each participant, and completes the survey face-to-face by asking structured questions

substantive contribution this is achieved when the research throws new light on the subject of study, whether it is a particular kind of organization or aspects of employee or managerial behaviour

summarizing describing a characteristic of a dataset such as location or spread based on aggregating data from all respondents

survey feedback the collection of opinions about the management of an organization, which is then fed back to all employees to stimulate change and improvements

symmetry a balanced distribution of data points around a central value

synergy a form of interaction between variables, where their joint effect is different from the sum of their individual effects

systematic random sampling a process of random sampling where every nth entity from the population is selected

systematic review a means of synthesizing research on a topic or within a field in such a way that is both transparent and reproducible

t-distribution a form of standard reference distribution; a form of the normal distribution where the standard deviation of the reference distribution is estimated from sample data

telephone interview survey a form of survey where an interviewer locates each participant, and completes the survey by telephone by asking structured questions

template analysis a method of qualitative data analysis that enables a systematic, thematic analysis of text

testing effect where changes observed in individual behaviour or attitudes over time are caused by the measures having been made in the first place

theoretical contribution this is achieved when new concepts are developed, or existing concepts are extended, in order to understand or explain behaviour and organizational phenomena

topic guide a prepared list of areas (rather than specific questions) that need to be covered during the course of an interview

triangulation using different kinds of measures or perspectives in order to increase confidence in the accuracy of observations

trimmed mean a family of summary measures of location where a proportion of the largest and smallest values are ignored in calculating a mean; the mid-mean is a 25 per cent trimmed mean, and the median is a 50 per cent trimmed mean

t-test a form of hypothesis test for comparing mean scores of two groups

type I error a false conclusion from a hypothesis test involving a claim that an effect exists (an association between variables or a group difference) when there is no such effect in the population

type II error a false conclusion from a hypothesis test involving a claim that no effect exists (an association between variables or a group difference) when there is an effect in the population

unit of analysis the main level at which data is aggregated: can be individuals, groups, events, organizations, etc.; within relativist studies researchers look for relationships between attributes that vary across different units of analysis

univariate F-test the test statistic in multivariate analysis of variance for group differences in a single dependent variable ignoring others

univariate test a test of a study hypothesis, which involves consideration of a single dependent variable universal theories theories that may be derived in one social organizational setting, and which are applicable in any other setting or context

validity the extent to which measures and research findings provide accurate representation of the things they are supposed to be describing

variance a summary measure of spread used in calculating the standard deviation; the average deviation of scores around the mean

verification a research design that seeks evidence to demonstrate that the current assumptions or hypotheses are correct

visual analysis a combination of research traditions that come together to analyse various forms of visual data, typically characterized by its volume, homogeneity and dynamic nature

visual metaphors an approach to eliciting the views of individuals or groups with the notion of metaphors in order to get individuals (or groups) to draw and describe issues or events as they currently see them or would like to see them in the future

Wald test the test statistic in logistic regression analysis expressing the independent contribution of a predictor variable

Web of Knowledge a database that provides a single route to journals in the Social Sciences Citation Index

web-based survey a form of survey where a website link is sent to each potential participant, and respondents complete the survey by recording their answers online; answers may be checked for consistency and then stored on a database for analysis

Wilks' Lambda the test statistic in multivariate analysis of variance for group differences in a set of two or more dependent variables

Zetoc a current awareness service for higher education institutions in the UK; the service gives access to the British Library's table of contents database and a Zetoc alert can provide users with information on the contents of new journals as soon as they are issued

BIBLIOGRAPHY

AACSB (2013) *The Promise of Doctoral Education: Setting the Pace for Innovation, Sustainability, Relevance and Quality*. Tampa, FL: AACSB International.

Abrahamson, M. (1983) *Social Research Methods*. Englewood Cliffs, NJ: Prentice Hall.

Ackermann, F. and Eden, C. (2011) *Making Strategy: Mapping Out Strategic Success*, 2nd edn. London: Sage.

Ackroyd, S. and Fleetwood, S. (2000) 'Realism in contemporary organizational and management studies', in S. Ackroyd and S. Fleetwood (eds), *Realist Perspectives on Management and Organizations*. London: Routledge, pp. 3–25.

Agar, M.H. (1986) *Speaking of Ethnography*. Beverly Hills, CA: Sage.

Aguiar, M., Bils, M., Charles, K.K. and Hurst, E. (2017) *Leisure Luxuries and the Labor Supply of Young Men*. Cambridge, MA: National Bureau of Economic Research.

Aguinis, H. and Edwards, J.R. (2014) 'Methodological wishes for the next decade and how to make wishes come true', *Journal of Management Studies*, 51: 143–74.

Ahmed, S. (1998) *Differences that Matter: Feminist Theory and Postmodernism*. Cambridge: Cambridge University Press.

Ahuja, G. (2000) 'Collaboration networks, structural holes, and innovation: a longitudinal study', *Administrative Science Quarterly*, 45: 425–55.

Aiken, H.D. (1956) *The Age of Ideology*. New York: Mentor.

Allcott, H. and Gentzkow, M. (2017) 'Social media and fake news in the 2016 election', *Journal of Economic Perspectives*, 31 (2): 211–36.

Alvesson, M. (1990) 'Organization: from substance to image', *Organisation Studies*, 11: 373–94.

Alvesson, M. (1998) 'Gender relations and identity at work: a case study of an advertising agency', *Human Relations*, 51 (8): 969–1005.

Alvesson, M. (2003) 'Beyond neopositivists, romantics, and localists: a reflexive approach to interviews in organisation research', *Academy of Management Review*, 28 (1): 13–33.

Alvesson, M. and Deetz, S. (2000) *Doing Critical Management Research*. London: Sage.

Alvesson, M. and Kärreman, D. (2011) 'Decolonializing discourse: critical reflections on organizational discourse analysis', *Human Relations*, 64 (9): 1121–46.

Alvesson, M. and Sköldberg, K. (2000) *Reflexive Methodology: New Vistas for Qualitative Research*. London: Sage.

Alvesson, M. and Willmott, H. (eds) (2003) *Studying Management Critically*. London: Sage.

Amis, J. and Silk, M.L. (2008) 'The philosophy and politics of quality in qualitative organizational research', *Organizational Research Methods*, 11: 456–80.

Anderson, L. (2008a) 'Participant observation', in R. Thorpe and R. Holt (eds), *The SAGE Dictionary of Qualitative Management Research*. London: Sage, pp. 150–2.

Anderson, L. (2008b) 'Reflexivity', in R. Thorpe and R. Holt (eds), *The SAGE Dictionary of Qualitative Management Research*. London: Sage, pp. 183–5.

Anderson, L., Gold, J., Stewart, J. and Thorpe, R. (2015) *Professional Doctorates in Business and Management*. London: Sage.

Anderson, L.M. (2008) 'Critical action learning: an examination of the social nature of management learning and development', unpublished PhD thesis, University of Leeds, Leeds University Business School, April.

Anderson, M.L. (1993) 'Studying across difference: race, class and gender in qualitative research', in J.H. Stanfield and R.M. Dennis (eds), *Race and Ethnicity in Research Methods*. London: Sage, pp. 39–52.

Andersson, R. (2014) *Illegality, Inc.: Clandestine Migration and the Business of Bordering Europe*. Oakland, CA: University of California Press.

Aristotle, with Brown, L. (ed.) and Ross, D. (trans.) (2009) *The Nicomachean Ethics*. Oxford: Oxford University Press.

Ashton, D.J.L. and Easterby-Smith, M. (1979) *Management Development in the Organisation*. London: Macmillan.

Astley, W.G. and Zammuto, R.F. (1992) 'Organisation science, managers, and language games', *Organization Science*, 3: 443–60.

Atinc, G., Simmering, M.J. and Kroll, M.J. (2011) 'Control variable use and reporting in macro and micro management research', *Organizational Research Methods*, 15: 57–74.

Atkinson, P. (2010) *Handbook of Ethnography*. Thousand Oaks, CA: Sage.

Austin, J.H. (1978) *Chase, Chance and Creativity*. New York: Columbia University Press.

Ayer, A.J. ([1936] 1971) *Language, Truth and Logic*. Harmondsworth: Pelican.

Back, L. (2006) *ESRC Research Development Initiative Conference*. London: Royal College of Physicians.

Bailey, J. (2008) 'First steps in qualitative data analysis: transcribing', *Family Practice*, 25 (2): 127–31.

Baker, C.D., Emmison, M. and Firth, A. (2005) *Calling for Help*. Amsterdam: John Benjamins.

Baker, S. (1996) 'Consumer cognitions: mapping personal benefits relating to perfume purchase in the UK and Germany', 207th ESOMAR Seminar, Capturing the Elusive Appeal of Fragrance: Techniques, Experiences, Challenges. Amsterdam.

Baker, S. and Knox, S. (1995) 'Mapping consumer cognitions in Europe', in M. Bergadaa (ed.), *Marketing Today for the 21st Century*. Proceedings of the 24th EMAC Conference, Cergy-Pontoisse, France, 1: 81–100.

Bales, R.F. (1950) *Interaction Process Analysis*. Cambridge, MA: Addison-Wesley.

Bales, R.F. (1970) *Personality and Interpersonal Behavior*. New York: Holt, Rinehart & Winston.

Bales, R.F. (1988) 'A new overview of the SYMLOG system: measuring and changing behavior in groups', in R.B. Polley, A.P. Hare and P.J. Stone (eds), *The SYMLOG Practitioner*. New York: Praeger, pp. 319–44.

Bales, R.F., Cohen, S.P. and Williamson, S.A. (1979) *SYMLOG: A System for the Multiple Level Observation of Groups*. New York: The Free Press.

Bancroft Library Oral Histories (2014) *Venture Capitalists Oral History Project*. Edited by Project Director and Interviewer: Sally Smith Hughe. Regional Oral History Office (ROHO), The Bancroft Library, University of California, Berkeley. Available at: http://bancroft.berkeley.edu/ROHO/projects/vc/transcripts.html (last accessed 14 August 2014).

Banks, M. (1995) 'Visual research methods', *Social Research Update*, 11: 1–6.

Banks, M. (2008) *Using Visual Data in Qualitative Research*. London: Sage.

Bannister, D. and Fransella, F. (1971) *Inquiring Man: The Theory of Personal Constructs*. Harmondsworth: Penguin.

Barbour, R.S. (2014) 'Quality of data analysis', in U. Flick (ed.), *SAGE Handbook of Qualitative Data Analysis*. London: Sage, pp. 496–509.

Barley, S.R. (1986) *The Innocent Anthropologist: Notes from a Mud Hut*. Harmondsworth: Penguin.

Barry, C.A. (1998) 'Choosing qualitative data analysis software: Atlas/ti and Nudist compared', *Sociological Research Online*, 3 (3). Available at: www.socresonline.org.uk/3/3/4.html (last accessed 27 October 2008).

Barry, L.R. (2004) 'NVivo 2.0 and ATLAS.ti 5.0: a comparative review of two popular qualitative data-analysis programs', *Field Methods*, 16: 439–64.

Bartunek, J.M. and Louis, M.R. (1996) *Insider/Outsider Team Research*. Thousand Oaks, CA: Sage.

Bartunek, J.M., Rynes, S.L. and Daft, R.L. (2001) 'Across the Great Divide: knowledge creation and transfer between practitioners and academics', *Academy of Management Journal*, 44: 340–55.

Barwise, P., Marsh, P., Thomas, K. and Wensley, R. (1989) 'Intelligent elephants and part-time researchers', *Graduate Management Research*, Winter: 12–33.

Bazeley, P. (2013) *Qualitative Data Analysis with NVivo*, 2nd edn. London: Sage.

Belk, R. (2014) 'Alternative conceptualizations of the extended self', *Advances in Consumer Research*, 42: 251–54.

Bell, E. and Bryman, A. (2007) 'The ethics of management research: an exploratory content analysis', *British Journal of Management*, 18 (1): 63–77.

Bell, J. and Waters, S. (2014) *Doing your Research Project: A Guide for First-time Researchers*, 6th edn. Maidenhead: Open University Press.

Bennis, W.G. and O'Toole, J. (2005) 'How business schools lost their way', *Harvard Business Review*, 83 (5): 1–9.

Bentler, P.M. and Dudgeon, P. (1996) 'Covariance structure analysis: statistical practice, theory and direction', *Annual Review of Psychology*, 47: 563–92.

Berger, P.L. and Luckman, T. (1966) *The Social Construction of Reality*. London: Penguin.

Berger, R. and Rosenberg, E. (2008) 'The experience of abused women with their children's law guardians', *Violence Against Women*, 14: 71–92.

Berghman, L., Matthyssens, P. and Vandenbempt, K. (2006) 'Building competences for new customer value creation: an exploratory study', *Industrial Marketing Management*, 35 (8): 961–73.

Bergmann, J.R. (2004) 'Conversation analysis', in U. Flick, E. Kardorff and I. Steinke (eds), *A Companion to Qualitative Research*. London: Sage, pp. 296–302.

Berman, S.L., Wicks, A.C., Kotha, S. and Jones, T.M. (1999) 'Does stakeholder orientation matter? The relationship between stakeholder management models and firm financial performance', *Academy of Management Journal*, 42 (5): 488–506.

Bernard, H.R. (2011) *Research Methods in Anthropology: Qualitative and Quantitative Approaches*, 5th edn. Lanham, MD: AltaMira.

Berrone, P., Fosfuri, A., Gelabert, L. and Gomez-Mejia, L.R. (2013) 'Necessity as the mother of "green" inventions: institutional pressures and environmental innovations', *Strategic Management Journal*, 34: 891–909.

Bessant, J., Binley, S., Cooper, C., Dawson, S., Gernard, J., Gardiner, M., Gray, A., Jones, P., Mayer, C., Magee, J., Pidd, M., Rowley, G., Saunders, J. and Stark, A. (2003) 'The state of the field in UK management research: reflections of the Research Assessment Exercise (RAE) Panel', *British Journal of Management*, 14: 51–68.

Bettis, R.A. and Prahalad, C.K. (1995) 'The dominant logic: retrospective and extensions', *Strategic Management Journal*, 16 (1): 5–14.

Beynon, H. (1973) *Working for Ford*. Harmondsworth: Penguin.

Beynon, H. (1988) 'Regulating research: politics and decision making in industrial organisations', in A. Bryman (ed.), *Doing Research in Organisations*. London: Routledge, pp. 21–33.

Bhaskar, R. (1978) *A Realist Theory of Science*. New York: Harvester Press.

Bhaskar, R. (1989) *Reclaiming Reality: A Critical Introduction to Contemporary Philosophy*. London: Verso.

Billig, M. (1988) 'Review of: Murderous Science: Elimination by Scientific Selection of Jews, Gypsies and Others in Germany, 1933–1945 [B. Muller-Hill, Oxford: OUP]', *The Psychologist*, December: 475–6.

Billig, M. (1991) *Ideology and Opinions: Studies of Rhetorical Psychology*. London: Sage.

Billig, M. (1999) 'Whose terms? Whose ordinariness? Rhetoric and ideology in conversation analysis', *Discourse & Society*, 10 (4): 543–82.

Birkinshaw, J., Braunerhjelm, P., Holm, U. and Terjesen, S. (2006) 'Why do some multinational corporations relocate their headquarters overseas?', *Strategic Management Journal*, 27 (7): 681–700.

Blaikie, N. (2007) *Approaches to Social Enquiry*, 2nd edn. Cambridge: Polity Press.

Bloom, B.S. and Krathwohl, D.R. (1956) *Taxonomy of Educational Objectives*. London: Longman.

Bloom, N. and van Reenen, J. (2006) 'Measuring and explaining management practices across firms and countries', CEP Discussion Paper No. 716. London: London School of Economics.

Blunch, N.J. (2008) *Introduction to Structural Equation Modelling Using SPSS and AMOS*. London: Sage.

Boissevain, J. (1974) *Friends of Friends*. Oxford: Blackwell.

Boje, D.M. (1991) 'The storytelling organization: a study of storytelling performance in an office supply firm', *Administrative Science Quarterly*, 36: 106–26.

Boje, D.M. (1995) 'Stories of the story-telling organization: a postmodern analysis of Disney as "Tamara-land"', *Academy of Management Journal*, 38 (4): 997–1035.

Boje, D.M. (2001) *Narrative Methods for Organizational and Communication Research*. London: Sage.

Boje, D.M. (2003) 'Using narratives and telling stories', in D. Holman and R. Thorpe (eds), *Management and Language: The Manager as Practical Author*. London: Sage, pp. 41–53.

Boje, D.M. (2008) 'Storytelling in management research', in R. Thorpe and R. Holt (eds), *The SAGE Dictionary of Qualitative Management Research*. London: Sage, pp. 213–15.

Borgatti, S.P. (2006) 'Identifying sets of key players in social network', *Computational and Mathematical Organisation*, 12 (1): 21–34.

Borgatti, S.P., Everett, M.G. and Freeman, L.C. (2002) *Ucinet for Windows: Software for Social Network Analysis*. Harvard, MA: Analytic Technologies. Available at: www.analytictech.com (last accessed 24 November 2011).

Borgatti, S.P., Mehra, A., Brass, D.J. and Labianca, G. (2009) 'Network analysis in the social sciences', *Science*, 323: 892–5.

Boudreau, K. (2012) 'Let a thousand flowers bloom? An early look at large numbers of software "apps" developers and patterns of innovation', *Organization Science*, 23 (5): 1409–27.

Bourne, H. and Jenkins, M. (2005) 'Eliciting managers' personal values: an adaptation of the laddering interview method', *Organizational Research Method*, 8 (4): 410–28.

Bouty, I. (2000) 'Interpersonal and interaction influences on informal resource exchanges between R&D researchers across organizational boundaries', *Academy of Management Journal*, 43: 50–65.

Bowey, A.M., Thorpe, R. and Hellier, P. (1986) *Payment Systems and Productivity*. London: Macmillan.

Bowey, A.M., Thorpe, R. Michell, H.M., Nichols, G., Gosnold, D., Lawson, S. and Hellier, P. (1982) *Effects of Incentive Payment Systems, United Kingdom 1977–1980*, Research Paper No. 36. London: Department of Employment.

Box, G.E.P., Hunter, S.J. and Hunter, W.G. (2005) *Statistics for Experimenters: Design, Innovation, and Discovery*, 2nd edn. Chichester: Wiley.

Boyacigiller, N.A. and Adler, N.J. (1991) 'The parochial dinosaur: organizational science in a global context', *Academy of Management Review*, 16: 262–90.

Boyatzis, R.E. (1982) *The Competent Manager: A Model for Effective Performance*. New York: Wiley.

Brandi, U. and Elkjaer, B. (2008) 'Pragmatism', in R. Thorpe and R. Holt (eds), *The Sage Dictionary of Qualitative Management Research*. London: Sage, pp. 169–71.

Brass, J.B., Galaskiewicz, J., Greve, H.R. and Tsai, W. (2004) 'Taking stock of social networks and organizations: a multi-level perspective', *Academy of Management Journal*, 47 (6): 795–817.

Brewer, J.D. (2000) *Ethnography*. Buckingham: Open University Press.

Brouthers, K.D. and Brouthers, L.E. (2003) 'Why services and manufacturing entry mode choices differ: the influence of transaction cost factors, risk and trust', *Journal of Management Studies*, 40 (3): 1179–204.

Brown, S.L. and Eisenhardt, K.M. (1998) *Competing on the Edge: Strategy as Structured Chaos*. Boston, MA: Harvard University Press.

Bryman, A. and Bell, E. (2003) *Business Research Methods*. Oxford: Oxford University Press.

Bryman, A. and Bell, E. (2007) *Business Research Methods*, 2nd edn. Oxford: Oxford University Press.

Bryman, A. and Cramer, D. (2004) *Quantitative Data Analysis with SPSS 12 and 13: A Guide for Social Scientists*. London: Routledge.

Buchanan, D.A. (1980) 'Gaining management skills through academic research work', *Personnel Management*, 12 (4): 45–8.

Buchanan, D.A. (1999) 'The role of photography in organisation research: a re-engineering case illustration', *Journal of Management Inquiry*, 10: 151–64.

Buchanan, D.A. and Badham, R. (2008) *Power, Politics and Organizational Change: Winning the Turf Game*, 2nd edn. London: Sage.

Buchanan, D.A. and Bryman, A. (2007) 'Contextualizing methods choice in organizational research', *Organizational Research Methods*, 10 (3): 483–501.

Buchanan, D.A., Boddy, D. and McCalman, J. (1988) 'Getting in, getting on, getting out, getting back: the art of the possible', in A. Bryman (ed.), *Doing Research in Organisations*. London: Routledge, pp. 53–67.

Buglear, J. (2012) *Quantitative Methods for Business and Management Students*. Harlow: Pearson.

Bulmer, M. (1988) 'Some reflections upon research in organization', in A. Bryman (ed.), *Doing Research in Organizations*. London: Routledge, pp. 151–61.

Burawoy, M. (2009) *The Extended Case Method: Four Countries, Four Decades, Four Great Transformations, and One Theoretical Tradition*. Berkeley, CA: University of California Press.

Burgess, R.G. (1982) *Field Research: A Source Book and Field Manual*. London: Allen and Unwin.

Burgoyne, J. and James, K.T. (2006) 'Towards best or better practice in corporate leadership development: operational issues in Mode 2 and design science research', *British Journal of Management*, 17: 303–16.

Burgoyne, J. and Stuart, R. (1976) 'The nature, use and acquisition of managerial skills and other attributes', *Personnel Review*, 15 (4): 19–29.

Burkhardt, M.E. (1994) 'Social interaction effects following a technological change: a longitudinal investigation', *Academy of Management Journal*, 37: 869–98.

Burrell, G. (1993) 'Eco and the Bunnymen', in J. Hassard and M. Parker (eds), *Postmodernism and Organizations*. London: Sage, pp. 71–82.

Burrell, G. and Morgan, G. (1979) *Sociological Paradigms and Organisational Analysis*. London: Heinemann.

Butterfield, L.D., Borgen, W.A., Amundson, N.E. and Maglio, A.T. (2005) 'Fifty years of the critical incident technique: 1954–2004 and beyond', *Qualitative Research*, 5 (4): 475–97.

Buzan, T. (2004) *Mind Maps: How to Be the Best at Your Job and Still Have Time to Play*. New York: Plume.

Calder, A. and Sheridan, D. (1984) *Speak for Yourself: A Mass-Observation Anthology 1937–49*. London: Cape.

Calhoun, M.A., Starbuck, W.H. and Abrahamson, E. (2011) 'Fads, fashions and the fluidity of knowledge: Peter Senge's The Learning Organization', in M. Easterby-Smith and M. Lyles (eds), *The Handbook of Organizational Learning and Knowledge Management*, 2nd edn. Chichester: Wiley, pp. 225–48.

Callegaro, M., Manfreda, K.L. and Vehovar, V. (2015) *Web Survey Methodology*. Thousand Oaks, CA: Sage.

Calori, R., Johnson, G. and Sarnin, P. (1994) 'CEOs' cognitive maps and the scope of the organization', *Strategic Management Journal*, 15 (6): 437–57.

Cassell, C. (2015) *Conducting Research Interviews for Business and Management Students* (Mastering Business Research Methods). Thousand Oaks, CA: Sage.

Cassell, C. and Symon, G. (2004) *Essential Guide to Qualitative Methods in Organizational Research*. London: Sage.

Castells, M. (2000) *The Rise of the Network Society*, 2nd edn. Oxford: Blackwell.

Chambers, R. and Loubere, N. (2017) 'Liberating development inquiry: freedom, openness and participation in fieldwork', in G. Crawford, L.J. Kruckenberg, N. Loubere and R. Morgan (eds), *Understanding Global Development Research: Fieldwork Issues, Experiences and Reflections*. London: Sage, pp. 27–46.

Charmaz, K. (2000) 'Grounded theory: objectivist and constructivist methods', in N.K. Denzin and Y.S. Lincoln (eds), *SAGE Handbook of Qualitative Research*, 2nd edn. Thousand Oaks, CA: Sage, pp. 509–35.

Charmaz, K. (2014) *Constructing Grounded Theory: A Practical Guide Through Qualitative Analysis*, 2nd edn. London: Sage.

Checkland, P.B. (1989) 'Soft systems methodology', *Human Systems Methodology*, 8 (4): 273–89.

Chen, C.-Y. (2008) 'How virtual teams use media to manage conflict', unpublished PhD thesis, University of Manchester.

Chia, R. (2008) 'Postmodernism', in R. Thorpe and R. Holt (eds), *The Sage Dictionary of Qualitative Management Research*. London: Sage, pp. 162–3.

Chouliaraki, L. and Fairclough, N. (2010) 'Critical discourse analysis in organisational studies: towards an integrationist methodology', *Journal of Management Studies*, 47 (6): 1213–18.

Chunyan Peng, A. and Tjosvold, D. (2011) 'Social face concerns and conflict avoidance of Chinese employees with their Western or Chinese managers', *Human Relations*, 64 (8): 1031–50.

Churchill, J. (1990) 'Complexity and strategic decision making', in C. Eden and J. Radford (eds), *Tackling Strategic Problems: The Role of Group Decision Support*. London: Sage, pp. 11–17.

Clarke, J. (2007) 'Seeing entrepreneurship: visual ethnographies of embodied entrepreneurs', unpublished PhD thesis, University of Leeds, Leeds University Business School.

Clarke, J. (2011) 'Revitalizing entrepreneurship: how visual symbols are used in entrepreneurial performances', *Journal of Management Studies*, 48 (6): 1365–91.

Coch, L. and French, J.R.P. (1948) 'Overcoming resistance to change', *Human Relations*, 1: 512–33.

Coffey, A. and Atkinson, P. (1996) *Making Sense of Qualitative Data*. London: Sage.

Coghlan, D. and Brannick, T. (2014) *Doing Action Research in Your Own Organization*, 4th edn. London: Sage.

Cohen, W.M. and Levinthal, D.A. (1990) 'Absorptive capacity: a new perspective on learning and innovation', *Administrative Science Quarterly*, 35: 128–52.

Coleman, J.S. (1988) 'Social capital in the creation of human capital', *American Journal of Sociology*, 94: S95–S120.

Collier, J. and Collier, J. (1986) *Visual Anthropology: Photography as a Research Method*. Albuquerque, NM: University of New Mexico.

Collins, H.M. (1983) 'An empirical relativist programme in the sociology of scientific knowledge', in K.D. Knorr-Cetina and M. Mulkay (eds), *Science Observed: Perspectives on the Social Study of Science*. London: Sage, pp. 3–10.

Collinson, D.L. (1992) *Managing the Shop Floor: Subjectivity, Masculinity, and Workplace Culture*. New York: de Gruyter.

Collinson, D.L. (2002) 'Managing humour', *Journal of Management Studies*, 39: 269–88.

Comte, A. (1853) *The Positive Philosophy of Auguste Comte* (trans. H. Martineau). London: Trubner.

Conan Doyle, A. (1891) 'The Adventures of Sherlock Holmes: Adventure I – A Scandal in Bohemia', *The Strand Magazine*, 2 (7): 61–75.

Cook, S.D.N. and Brown, J.S. (1999) 'Bridging epistemologies: the generative dance between organizational knowledge and organizational knowing', *Organization Science*, 10 (4): 381–400.

Cooper, R. (1992) 'Formal organization as representation: remote control, displacement and abbreviation', in M. Reed and M. Hughes (eds), *Rethinking Organization*. London: Sage, pp. 254–72.

Cooper, R. and Burrell, G. (1988) 'Modernism, postmodernism and organizational analysis: an introduction', *Organization Studies*, 9 (1): 91–112.

Corbin, J.M. and Strauss, A. (2008) *Basics of Qualitative Research: Techniques and Procedures for Developing Grounded Theory*. London: Sage.

Corbin, J.M. and Strauss, A. (2015) *Basics of Qualitative Research: Techniques and Procedures for Developing Grounded Theory*. London: Sage.

Cornelissen, J.P. (2006) 'Metaphor in organization theory: progress and the past', *Academy of Management Review*, 31 (2): 485–8.

Cornelissen, J.P. (2011) *Corporate Communications: A Guide to Theory and Practice*, 3rd edn. London: Sage.

Cotterill, P. (1992) 'Interviewing women: issues of friendship, vulnerability and power', *Women's Studies International Forum*, 15 (5/6): 593–606.

Cotterill, S. and King, S. (2007) 'Public sector partnerships to deliver local e-government: a social network study', paper presented at the Sixth International EGOV Conference, Regensburg (Germany), 3–7 September. Available at: www.springerlink.com/content/a646737037n18g70 (last accessed 24 November 2011).

Couper, M.P. (2008) *Designing Effective Web Surveys*. Cambridge: Cambridge University Press.

Couper, M.P., Traugott, M.W. and Lamias, M.J. (2001) 'Web survey design and administration', *Public Opinion Quarterly*, 65 (2): 230–53.

Coyle-Shapiro, J. and Kessler, I. (2000) 'Consequences of the psychological contract for the employment relationship: a large scale survey', *Journal of Management Studies*, 37 (7): 903–30.

Crawford, G., Kruckenberg, L.J., Loubere, N. and Morgan, R. (2017) 'Global development fieldwork: a relational perspective', in G. Crawford, L.J. Kruckenberg, N. Loubere and R. Morgan (eds), *Understanding Research in Global Development: Fieldwork Issues, Experiences and Reflections.* London: Sage, pp. 3–24.

Crawford, S.D., Couper, M.P. and Lamias, M.J. (2001) 'Web surveys: perceptions of burden', *Social Science Computer Review*, 19 (2): 146–62.

Creswell, J.W. (2003) *Research Design: Qualitative, Quantitative and Mixed Methods Approaches*, 2nd edn. Thousand Oaks, CA: Sage.

Creswell, J.W. (2013) *Qualitative Inquiry and Research Design: Choosing Among Five Approaches*, 3rd edn. Thousand Oaks, CA: Sage.

Creswell, J.W. (2014) *A Concise Introduction to Mixed Methods Research*. London: Sage.

Creswell, J.W. and Plano Clark, V.L. (2011) *Designing and Conducting Mixed Methods Research*, 2nd edn. Thousand Oaks, CA Sage.

Crotty, M. (1998) *The Foundations of Social Research: Meaning and Perspective in the Research Process.* London: Sage.

Cryer, P. (2000) *The Research Student's Guide to Success*. Buckingham: Open University Press.

Cukier, W., Trenholm, S., Carl, D. and Gekas, G. (2011) 'Social entrepreneurship: a content analysis', *Journal of Strategic Innovation and Sustainability*, 7 (1): 99–119. Available at: www.na-business press.com/jsis/cukierweb.pdf (last accessed 14 August 2014).

Cunliffe, A.L. (2001) 'Managers as practical authors: reconstructing our understanding of management practice', *Journal of Management Studies*, 38: 351–71.

Cunliffe, A.L. (2002a) 'Reflexive dialogical practice in management learning', *Management Learning*, 33 (1): 35–61.

Cunliffe, A.L. (2002b) 'Social poetics as management inquiry: a dialogical approach', *Journal of Management Inquiry*, 11 (2): 128–46.

Cunliffe, A.L. (2003) 'Reflexive inquiry in organizational research: questions and possibilities', *Human Relations*, 56 (8): 983–1003.

Cunliffe, A.L. (2008) 'Discourse analysis', in R. Thorpe and R. Holt (eds), *The SAGE Dictionary of Qualitative Management Research*. London: Sage, pp. 81–2.

Cunliffe, A.L. (2010) 'Retelling tales of the field: in search of organizational ethnography 20 years on', *Organizational Research Methods*, 13 (2): 224–39.

Cunliffe, A.L. (2011) 'Crafting qualitative research: Morgan and Smircich 30 years on', *Organizational Research Methods*, 14 (4): 647–73.

Curran, J. and Downing, S. (1989) 'The state and small business owners: an empirical assessment of consultation strategies', paper presented at the 12th National Small Firms Policy and Research Conference, Barbican, London.

Cyert, R.H. and March, J.G. (1963) *A Behavioral History of the Firm*. Englewood Cliffs, NJ: Prentice Hall.

Czarniawska, B. (1998) *A Narrative Approach to Organization Studies*. London: Sage.

Daft, R.L. and Lengel, R.H. (1986) 'Organisational information requirements, media richness and structural design', *Management Science*, 32: 554–71.

Daiute, C. and Lightfoot, C. (2004) *Narrative Analysis: Studying the Development of Individuals in Society*. Thousand Oaks, CA: Sage.

Dalton, M. (1959) *Men Who Manage: Fusion of Feeling and Theory in Administration*. New York: Wiley.

Dalton, M. (1964) 'Preconceptions and methods in *Men Who Manage*', in P. Hammond (ed.), *Sociologists at Work*. New York: Basic Books, pp. 50–95.

Davies, G., Chun, R., Da Silva, R. and Roper, S. (2002) *Corporate Reputation and Competitiveness.* London: Routledge.

Davies, J. and Easterby-Smith, M. (1984) 'Learning and developing from managerial work experiences', *Journal of Management Studies*, 21: 169–82.

Davila, C. (1989) 'Grounding management education in local research: a Latin American experience', in J. Davies, M. Easterby-Smith, S. Mann and M. Tanton (eds), *The Challenge to Western Management Development: International Alternatives*. London: Routledge, pp. 40–56.

Dawson, A. and Hjorth, D. (2012) 'Advancing family business research through narrative analysis', *Family Business Review*, 25 (3): 339–55.

Dawson, C. (2016) *100 Activities for Teaching Research Methods*. Thousand Oaks, CA: Sage.

DeCuir-Gunby, J.T., Marshall, P.L. and McCulloch, A.W. (2011) 'Developing and using a codebook for the analysis of interview data: an example from a professional development research project', *Field Methods*, 23 (2): 136–55.

Deem, R. and Brehony, K. (1997) 'Research students' access to research cultures: an unequal benefit?', paper presented at Society for Research in Higher Education Conference, University of Warwick.

Denzin, N.K. (1994) 'The art and politics of interpretation', in N.K. Denzin and Y.S. Lincoln (eds), *Handbook of Qualitative Research*. Thousand Oaks, CA: Sage, pp. 500–15.

Denzin, N.K. and Lincoln, Y.S. (eds) (2006) *SAGE Handbook of Qualitative Research*, 3rd edn. Thousand Oaks, CA: Sage.

Derrida, J. (1978) *Writing and Difference*. London: Routledge and Kegan Paul.

Detert, J.R. and Edmondson, A.C. (2011) 'Implicit voice theories: taken-for-granted rules of self-censorship at work', *Academy of Management Journal*, 54 (3): 461–88.

DeVellis, R.F. (2012) *Scale Development: Theory and Applications*, 3rd edn. Thousand Oaks, CA: Sage.

Dewey, J. (1916) *Democracy and Education*. London: Collier Macmillan.

Dhanaraj, C., Lyles, M.A., Steensma, H.K. and Tihanyi, L. (2004) 'Managing tacit and explicit knowledge transfer in IJVs: the role of relational embeddedness and the impact on performance', *Journal of International Business Studies*, 35 (5): 428–43.

Dillman, D.A., Smyth, J.D. and Christian, L.M. (2014) *Internet, Mail, and Mixed-Mode Surveys: The Tailored Design Method*, 4th edn. New York: John Wiley.

Dimitratos, P., Johnson, J.E., Plakoyiannaki, E. and Young, S. (2016) 'SME internationalization: How does the opportunity-based international entrepreneurial culture matter?' *International Business Review*, 25 (6): 1211–22.

Ditton, J. (1977) *Part-time Crime*. London: Macmillan.

Dobson, A.J. (2001) *Introduction to Generalized Linear Models*, 2nd edn. London: Chapman and Hall.

Douglas, J.D. (ed.) (1976) *Investigative Social Research*. Beverly Hills, CA: Sage.

Drisko, J.W. (2004) 'Qualitative data analysis software: a user's appraisal', in D. Padgett (ed.), *The Qualitative Research Experience*. Belmont, CA: Wadsworth, pp. 193–209.

Dubois, A. and Gadde, L.-E. (2002) 'Systematic combining: an abductive approach to case research', *Journal of Business Research*, 55 (7): 553–60.

Duggan, F. (2006) 'Plagiarism: prevention, practice and policy', *Assessment & Evaluation in Higher Education*, 31 (2): 151–4.

Duncan, K. (2014) *The Diagrams Book: 50 Ways to Solve Any Problem Visually*. London: LID Publishing.

Duriau, V.J., Reger, R.K. and Pfarrer, M.D. (2007) 'A content analysis of the content analysis literature in organization studies: research themes, data sources, and methodological refinements', *Organizational Research Methods*, 10 (1): 5–34.

Dyer, J.H. and Hatch, N.W. (2006) 'Relation-specific capabilities and barriers to knowledge transfers: creating advantage through network relationships', *Strategic Management Journal*, 27 (8): 701–19.

Easterby-Smith, M. ([1986] 1994) *Evaluation of Management Education, Training and Development*. Aldershot: Gower.

Easterby-Smith, M. (1997) 'Disciplines of organizational learning: contributions and critiques', *Human Relations*, 51 (9): 1085–116.

Easterby-Smith, M. and Ashton, D. (1975) 'Using repertory grid technique to evaluate management training', *Personnel Review*, 4 (4): 15–21.

Easterby-Smith, M. and Lyles, M. (2011) *The Handbook of Organizational Learning and Knowledge Management*. Oxford: Blackwell.

Easterby-Smith, M. and Malina, D. (1999) 'Cross-cultural collaborative research: toward reflexivity', *Academy of Management Journal*, 42 (1): 76–86.

Easterby-Smith, M., Li, S. and Bartunek, J. (2009) 'Research methods for organizational learning: the transatlantic gap', *Management Learning*, 40 (4): 439–47.

Easterby-Smith, M., Thorpe, R. and Holman, D. (1996) 'The use of repertory grids in management', *Journal of European Industrial Training*, 20 (3): 1–30.

Easterby-Smith, M., Thorpe, R. and Holman, D. (2010) 'Using repertory grids in management', in F.B. Birks and T. Macer (eds), *Marketing Research*, Vol. 2. London: Routledge, pp. 448–90.

Easterby-Smith, M., Graca, M., Antonacopoulou, A. and Ferdinand, J. (2008) 'Absorptive capacity: a process perspective', *Management Learning*, 39 (5): 483–501.

Eden, C. (1990) 'Strategic thinking with computers', *Long Range Planning*, 23 (6): 35–43.

Eden, C. (1992) 'On the nature of cognitive maps', *Journal of Management Studies*, 29 (3): 261–5.

Eden, C. and Ackermann, F. (1998) *Making Strategy: The Journey of Strategic Management*. London: Sage.

Eden, C. and Huxham, C. (1995) 'Action research for the study of organisations', in S. Clegg, C. Hardy and W. Nord (eds), *Handbook of Organisation Studies*. Beverly Hills, CA: Sage, pp. 526–42.

Eden, C. and Huxham, C. (1996) 'Action research for management research', *British Journal of Management*, 7 (1): 75–86.

Eden, C. and Huxham, C. (2002) 'Action research', in D. Partington (ed.), *Essential Skills for Management Research*. London: Sage, pp. 254–72.

Eden, C. and Huxham, C. (2007) 'Action research and the study of organisations', in S. Clegg, C. Hardy and W. Nord (eds), *Handbook of Organisation Studies*. London: Sage, pp. 526–42.

Eden, C., Jones, S. and Sims, D. (1983) *Messing About in Problems: An Informal Structured Approach to their Identification and Management*. Oxford: Pergamon.

Edwards, J. (2008) 'To prosper, organizational psychology should … overcome methodological barriers to progress', *Journal of Organizational Behavior*, 29: 469–91.

Eesley, C. and Lenox, M.J. (2006) 'Firm responses to secondary stakeholder action', *Strategic Management Journal*, 27 (8): 765–81.

Eisenhardt, K.M. (1989) 'Building theories from case study research', *Academy of Management Review*, 14 (4): 532–50.

Eisenhardt, K.M. and Graebner, M.E. (2007) 'Theory building from cases: opportunities and challenges', *Academy of Management Journal*, 50 (1): 25–32.

Eisenhardt, K.M., Graebner, M.E. and Sonenshein, S. (2016) 'From the editors – Grand challenges and inductive methods: rigor without rigor mortis', *Academy of Management Journal*, 59 (4): 1113–23.

Ellwood, P., Thorpe, R. and Coleman, C. (2013) 'A model for knowledge mobilisation and implications for the education of social researchers', *Contemporary Social Science*, 8 (3): 191–206.

Emerson, R.M., Fretz, R. and Shaw, L.L. (2011) *Writing Ethnographic Fieldnotes*, 2nd edn. Chicago, IL: University of Chicago Press.

Engelen, A., Gupta, V., Strenger, L. and Brettel, M. (2015) 'Entrepreneurial orientation, firm performance, and the moderating role of transformational leadership behaviors', *Journal of Management*, 41: 1069–97.

Engeström, Y. (1999) 'Activity theory as a framework for analysis and redesigning work', *Ergonomics*, 43 (7): 960–74.

Engeström, Y. (2000) 'Activity theory and the social construction of knowledge: a story of four imports', *Organisation*, 7 (2): 302–10.

Ernst, P. (1996) 'The nature of mathematics and teaching', *Philosophy of Mathematics Education Journal*, 9. Available at: http://people.exeter.ac.uk/PErnest/pome/pompart7.htm (last accessed 25 February 2015).

ESRC (2009) *Postgraduate Training and Development Guidelines*. Swindon: Economic and Social Research Council.

Evers, F.T. and Rush, J.C. (1996) 'The bases of competence: skill development during the transition from university to work', *Management Learning*, 27 (3): 275–300.

Fahy, K.M., Easterby-Smith, M. and Lervik, J.E. (2014) 'The power of spatial and temporal orderings in organizational learning', *Management Learning*, 45 (2): 123–44.

Fairclough, N. (1992) *Discourse and Social Change*. Cambridge: Polity Press.

Fairclough, N. and Hardy, G. (1997) 'Management learning as discourse', in J. Burgoyne and M. Reynolds (eds), *Management Learning: Integrating Perspectives in Theory and Practice*. London: Sage, pp. 144–60.

Fairhurst, E. (1983) 'Organisational rules and the accomplishment of nursing work on geriatric wards', *Journal of Management Studies*, Special Issue, 20 (3): 315–32.

Farquhar, J. (2012) *Case Study Research for Business*. London: Sage.

Fayol, H. ([1916] 1950) *Administration Industrielle et Generale*. Paris: Dunod.

Fendt, J. and Sachs, W. (2007) 'Grounded theory method in management research: users' perspectives', *Organizational Research Methods*, 11 (3): 430–55.

Fetters, M. and Freshwater, D. (2015) 'The 1+1=3 integration challenge', *Journal of Mixed Methods Research*, 9: 115–17.

Field, A. (2017) *Discovering Statistics Using IBM SPSS Statistics: And Sex and Drugs and Rock 'n' Roll*, 5th edn. Thousand Oaks, CA: Sage.

Field, A.P., Miles, J. and Field, Z. (2012) *Discovering Statistics Using R*. London: Sage.

Fielding, N.G. and Fielding, J.L. (1986) *Linking Data*. Newbury Park, CA: Sage.

Fielding, N.G., Lee, R.M. and Blank, G. (2017) *The SAGE Handbook of Online Research Methods*, 2nd edn. London: Sage.

Filatotchev, I. (2006) 'Effects of executive characteristics and venture capital involvement on board composition and share ownership in IPO firms', *British Journal of Management*, 17: 75–92.

Finch, J. (1986) *Research and Policy: The Uses of Qualitative Methods in Social and Educational Research*. London: Falmer Press.

Fink, A. (2005) *Conducting Research Literature Reviews: From the Internet to Paper*. Thousand Oaks, CA: Sage.

Firth, J.R. (1957) *Papers in Linguistics, 1934–1951*. London and New York: Oxford University Press.

Fish, S.E. (2011) *How to Write a Sentence: And How to Read One*. New York: HarperCollins.

Flanagan, J.C. (1954) 'The critical incident technique', *Psychological Bulletin*, 1: 327–58.

Fleetwood, S. (2005) 'The ontology of organisation and management studies: a critical realist approach', *Organization*, 12 (2): 197–222.

Flick, U. (2007) *Managing Quality in Qualitative Research*. London: Sage.

Flick, U. (2009) *An Introduction to Qualitative Research*, 4th edn. London: Sage.

Flick, U. (2014) *SAGE Handbook of Qualitative Data Analysis*. London: Sage.

Flick, U., Kardorff, E. and Steinke, I. (2004) *A Companion to Qualitative Research*. London: Sage.

Foucault, M. (1979) *Discipline and Punish*. Harmondsworth: Penguin.

Fournier, V. and Grey, C. (2000) 'At the critical moment: conditions and prospects for critical management studies', *Human Relations*, 52 (1): 7–32.

Freeman, R.E. (1984) *Strategic Management: A Stakeholder Approach*. London: Pitman.

Freeman, R.E, Harrison, J.S., Wicks, A., Parmar, B.L. and de Colle, S. (2010) *Stakeholder Theory: The State of the Art*. Cambridge: Cambridge University Press.

Friese, S. (2012) *Qualitative Data Analysis with ATLAS.ti*. London: Sage.

Gabriel, Y. and Griffiths, D. (2004) 'Stories in organizational research', in C. Cassell and G. Symon (eds), *Essential Guide to Qualitative Methods in Organizational Research*. London: Sage, pp. 114–26.

Gadalla, E., Abosag, I. and Keeling, K. (2016) 'Second Life as a research environment: avatar-based focus groups (AFG)', *Qualitative Market Research: An International Journal*, 19 (1): 101–14.

Gadamer, H.-G. (1989) *Truth and Method*, 2nd rev. edn (trans. J. Weinsheimer and D.G. Marshall). New York: Crossroad.

Galman, S.C. (2007) *Shane, the Lone Ethnographer: A Beginner's Guide to Ethnography*. Lanham, MD: AltaMira.

Galman, S.C. (2013) *The Good, the Bad, and the Data: Shane the Lone Ethnographer's Basic Guide to Qualitative Data Analysis*. Walnut Creek, CA: Left Coast Press.

Gangloff, K.A., Connelly, B.L. and Shook, C.L. (2016) 'Of scapegoats and signals: investor reactions to CEO succession in the aftermath of wrongdoing', *Journal of Management*, 42: 1614–34.

Gash, S. (2000) *Effective Literature Searching for Research*. Aldershot: Gower.

Gatewood, J.B. (1983) 'Deciding where to fish: the skipper's dilemma in Southeast Alaskan salmon seining', *Coastal Zone Management Journal*, 10 (4): 347–67.

Geary, L., Marriott, L. and Rowlinson, M. (2004) 'Journal rankings in business and management and the 2001 Research Assessment Exercise in the UK', *British Journal of Management*, 15: 95–141.

George, G., Haas, M.R. and Pentland, A. (2014) 'Big data and management', *Academy of Management Journal*, 57: 321–6.

Gergen, K.J. (1995) 'Relational theory and discourses of power', in D-M. Hosking, H.P. Dachler and K.J. Gergen (eds), *Management and Organization: Relational Alternatives to Individualism*. Aldershot: Avebury, pp. 29–49.

Gergen, K.J. (1999) *An Invitation to Social Construction*. London: Sage.

Ghauri, P. and Grønhaug, K. (2010) *Research Methods in Business Studies*. Harlow: Prentice Hall.

Gibbons, M.L., Limoges, C., Nowotny, H., Schwartman, S., Scott, P. and Trow, M. (1994) *The New Production of Knowledge: The Dynamics of Science and Research in Contemporary Societies*. London: Sage.

Gibbs, G.R. (2014) 'Using software in qualitative analysis', in U. Flick (ed.), *SAGE Handbook of Qualitative Data Analysis*. London: Sage, pp. 277–94.

Gibbs, G.R., Friese, S. and Mangabeira, W.C. (2002) 'The use of new technology in qualitative research', *Introduction to Forum Qualitative Sozialforschung/Forum: Qualitative Social Research*, 3 (2), Art. 8. Available at: http://nbn-resolving.de/urn:nbn:de:0114-fqs020287 (last accessed 29 October 2008).

Giddens, A. (1984) *The Constitution of Society: Outline of the Theory of Structuration*. Cambridge: Polity Press.

Glaser, B.G. (1978) *Theoretical Sensitivity*. Mill Valley, CA: Sociological Press.

Glaser, B.G. (1992) *Basics of Grounded Theory Analysis: Emergence versus Forcing*. Mill Valley, CA: Sociology Press.

Glaser, B.G. (1998) *Doing Grounded Theory: Issues and Discussions*. Mill Valley, CA: Sociology Press.

Glaser, B.G. and Strauss, A.L. (1967) *The Discovery of Grounded Theory: Strategies for Qualitative Research*. New York: Aldine.

Glenn, P. and LeBaron, C. (2011) 'Epistemic authority in employment interviews: glancing, pointing, touching', *Discourse & Communication*, 5 (1): 3–22.

Gold, J. (2008) 'Postcards', in R. Thorpe and R. Holt (eds), *The SAGE Dictionary of Qualitative Management Research*. London: Sage, pp. 157–60.

Gold, J., Hamblett, J. and Rix, M. (2000) 'Telling stories for managing change: a business/academic partnership', *Education through Partnership*, 4 (1): 36–46.

Gold, J., Holman, D. and Thorpe, R. (2002) 'The role of argument analysis and storytelling in facilitating critical thinking', *Management Learning*, 33 (3): 371–88.

Gold, J., Thorpe, R. and Holt, R. (2007) 'Writing, reading and reason: the "three Rs" of manager learning', in R. Hill and J. Stewart (eds), *Management Development: Perspectives from Research and Practice*. Abingdon: Routledge, pp. 271–84.

Goldacre, M.J., Davidson, J.M. and Lambert, T.W. (2004) 'Country of training and ethnic origin of UK doctors: database and survey studies', *British Medical Journal*, 329 (11): 597–600.

Golden-Biddle, K. and Locke, K. (1993) 'Appealing work: an investigation of how ethnographic texts convince', *Organisation Science*, 4 (2): 595–616.

Golden-Biddle, K. and Locke, K. (2007) *Composing Qualitative Research*, 2nd edn. London: Sage.

Goodall, H.L. (1989) *Casing a Promised Land: The Autobiography of an Organizational Detective as Cultural Ethnographer*. Carbondale, IL: Southern Illinois University Press.

Goodall, H.L. (2007) *A Need to Know: The Clandestine History of a CIA Family*. Walnut Creek, CA: Left Coast Press.

Goodwin, C. and Goodwin, M.H. (1996) 'Seeing as a situated activity: formulating planes', in Y. Engeström and D. Middleton (eds), *Cognition and Communication at Work*. Cambridge: Cambridge University Press, pp. 61–95.

Goodwin, M.H. (1995) 'Assembling a response: setting and collaboratively constructed work talk', in P. Have and G. Psathas (eds), *Situated Order: Studies in the Social Organization of Talk and Embodied Activities*. Lanham, MD: University Press of America (Studies in ethnomethodology and conversation analysis, No. 3), pp. 173–86.

Goulding, C. (2002) *Grounded Theory: A Practical Guide for Management, Business and Market Researchers*. Thousand Oaks, CA: Sage.

Granovetter, M. (1973) 'The strength of weak ties', *American Journal of Sociology*, 78: 1360–80.

Grant, A.M. and Wall, T.D. (2009) 'The neglected science and art of quasi-experimentation: why-to, when-to, and how-to advice for organizational researchers', *Organizational Research Methods*, 12 (4): 653–86.

Green, S. and Li, Y. (2011) 'Rhetorical institutionalism: language, agency and structure in institutional theory since Alvesson 1993', *Journal of Management Studies*, 48 (7): 1662–97.

Gremler, D.D. (2004) 'The critical incident technique in service research', *Journal of Service Research*, 7 (1): 65–89.

Grey, C. (2016) *A Very Short, Fairly Interesting and Reasonably Cheap Book about Studying Organizations*, 4th edn. London: Sage.

Grugel, J. and Morgan, R. (2017) 'Encounters with the powerful: researching elites', in G. Crawford, L.J. Kruckenberg, N. Loubere and R. Morgan (eds), *Understanding Global Development: Reflections on Fieldwork Experiences*. Thousand Oaks, CA: Sage, pp. 123–39.

Guba, E.G. and Lincoln, Y.S. (1989) *Fourth Generation Evaluation*. London: Sage.

Gubrium, J.F. and Silverman, D. (eds) (1989) *The Politics of Field Research*. London: Sage.

Gubrium, J.F., Holstein, J., Marvasti, A.B. and McKinney, K.D. (2012) *The SAGE Handbook of Interview Research: The Complexity of the Craft*, 2nd edn. Thousand Oaks, CA: Sage.

Gummesson, E. ([1988] 1991) *Qualitative Research in Management*. Bromley: Chartwell-Bratt.

Gummesson, E. (1992) *Case Study Research in Management: Methods for Generating Qualitative Data*. Stockholm: Stockholm University Press.

Gunn, H. (2002) 'Web-based surveys: changing the survey process', *First Monday*, 7 (12). Available at: www.firstmonday.dk/issues/issue7_12/gunn/#note3 (last accessed 24 November 2011).

Habermas, J. (1970) 'Knowledge and interest', in D. Emmett and A. Macintyre (eds), *Sociological Theory and Philosophical Analysis*. London: Macmillan, pp. 36–54.

Habermas, J. (1971) *Towards a Rational Society*. London: Heinemann.

Hair, J.F., Black, B., Babin, B., Anderson, R.E. and Tatham, R.L. (2010) *Multivariate Data Analysis*, 7th edn. Upper Saddle River, NJ: Prentice Hall.

Hales, C.P. (1986) 'What do managers do? A critical review of the evidence', *Journal of Management Studies*, 23 (1): 88–115.

Hamer, B. (Director) (2003) *Kitchen Stories* (Salmer fra kjøkken) [Motion picture]. Norway: IFC Films.

Handy, C. (1996) *Beyond Certainty: The Changing Worlds of Organizations*. London: Arrow Books.

Hanneman, R.A. and Riddle, M. (2005) *Introduction to Social Network Methods*. Riverside, CA: University of California Press. Available at: http://faculty.ucr.edu/~hanneman (last accessed 24 November 2011).

Hansen, M.T. (1999) 'The search-transfer problem: the role of weak ties in sharing knowledge across organization subunits', *Administrative Science Quarterly*, 44: 82–111.

Hardy, C. (1996) 'Understanding power: bringing about strategic change', *British Journal of Management*, 7 (Special Issue): S3–S16.

Harper, D. (1989) 'Visual sociology: expanding sociological vision', in G. Blank, J.L. McCartney and E. Brent (eds), *New Technology in Sociology: Practical Applications in Research and Work*. New Brunswick, NJ: Transaction Books, pp. 81–97.

Harper, D. (1994) 'On the authority of the image: visual methods at the crossroads', in N.K. Denzin and Y.S. Lincoln (eds), *Handbook of Qualitative Research*. Thousand Oaks, CA: Sage, pp. 403–12.

Harris, K.J., Wheeler, A.R. and Kacmar, K.M. (2009) 'Leader-member exchange and empowerment: direct and interactive effects on job satisfaction, turnover intentions, and performance', *Leadership Quarterly*, 20: 371–82.

Hart, C. (2018) *Doing a Literature Review: Releasing the Social Science Research Imagination*. London: Sage.

Harvey, C., Morris, H. and Kelly, A. (eds) (2007) *Association of Business Schools Academic Journal Quality Guide*. London: Association of Business Schools.

Harzing, A.-W. (ed.) (2007) *Journal Quality List*, 27th edn. Available at: www.harzing.com (last accessed 24 November 2011).

Hassard, J. and Parker, M. (eds) (1993) *Postmodernism and Organizations*. London: Sage.

Hatch, M.J. (1996) 'Irony and the social construction of contradiction in the humor of a management team', *Organization Science*, 8 (3): 275–388.

Hayano, D.M. (1979) 'Auto-ethnography paradigms, problems and prospects', *Human Organisation*, 38: 99–104.

Hayes, R.H. and Abernethy, W.J. (1980) 'Managing our way to economic decline', *Harvard Business Review*, 58: 67–77.

Heath, C. and Hindmarsh, J. (2002) 'Analyzing interaction: video, ethnography and situated conduct', in T. May (ed.), *Qualitative Research in Action*. London: Sage, pp. 99–122.

Heisenberg, W. (1927) 'Über den anschaulichen Inhalt der quantentheoretischen Kinematik und Mechanik', *Zeitschrift für Physik*, 43: 172–98. (English translation: J.A. Wheeler and H. Zurek (1983) *Quantum Theory and Measurement*. Princeton, NJ: Princeton University Press, pp. 62–84.)

Heritage, J. and Maynard, D.W. (2006) *Communication in Medical Care: Interaction between Primary Care Physicians and Patients*. Cambridge: Cambridge University Press.

Heritage, J., Robinson, J.D., Elliott, M.N., Beckett, M. and Wilkes, M. (2007) 'Reducing patients' unmet concerns in primary care: the difference one word can make', *Journal of General Internal Medicine*, 22 (10): 1429–33.

Hernes, T. (2009) *Understanding Organization as Process: Theory for a Tangled World*. London: Routledge.

Heron, J. (1996) *Co-operative Inquiry: Research into the Human Condition*. London: Sage.

Herzberg, F., Mausner, B. and Snyderman, B.B. (1959) *The Motivation to Work*. New York: Wiley.

Hickson, D.J. (1988) 'Ruminations on munificence and scarcity in research', in A. Bryman (ed.), *Doing Research in Organizations*. London: Routledge, pp. 136–50.

Hine, C. (2017) 'Ethnographies of online communities and social media: modes, varieties, affordances', in N. Fielding, R.M. Lee and G. Blank (eds), *The SAGE Handbook of Online Research Methods*. Los Angeles: Sage, pp. 401–13.

Hobday, M. and Rush, H. (2007) 'Upgrading the technological capabilities of foreign transnational subsidiaries in developing countries: the case of Thailand', *Research Policy*, 36: 1335–55.

Hofstede, G. (1980) *Culture's Consequences: International Differences in Work-Related Values*. Beverly Hills, CA: Sage.

Hofstede, G. (1991) *Cultures and Organizations: Software of the Mind*. Maidenhead: McGraw-Hill.

Holman, D. (1996) 'The experience of skill development in undergraduates', PhD thesis, Manchester Metropolitan University.

Hong, J., Easterby-Smith, M. and Snell, R. (2006) 'Transferring organizational learning systems to Japanese subsidiaries in China', *Journal of Management Studies*, 43 (5): 1027–58.

Howell, D. (2013a) *Fundamental Statistics for the Behavioral Sciences*, 8th edn. Nashville, TN: Broadman and Holman.

Howell, D. (2013b) *Statistical Methods for Psychology*, 8th edn. Belmont, CA: Wadsworth.

Hsieh, H.F. and Shannon, S.E. (2005) 'Three approaches to qualitative content analysis', *Qualitative Health Research*, 15 (9): 1277–88.

Huczynski, A.A. (1996) *Management Gurus: What Makes Them and How to Become One*. London: International Thomson Business Press.

Huff, A.S. (1999) *Writing for Scholarly Publication*. Thousand Oaks, CA: Sage.

Huff, A.S. (2000) 'Changes in organizational knowledge production', *Academy of Management Review*, 25 (2): 288–93.

Huff, A.S. (2009) *Designing Research for Publications*. London: Sage.

Huff, A.S. and Jenkins, M. (2002) *Mapping Strategic Knowledge*. London: Sage.

Humphreys, M. and Brown, A.D. (2002) 'Dress and identity: a Turkish case study', *Journal of Management Studies*, 39 (7): 927–52.

Humphreys, M. and Brown, A.D. (2008) 'An analysis of corporate social responsibility: a narrative approach', *Journal of Business Ethics*, 80 (3): 403–18.

Hurmerinta-Peltomaki, L. and Nummela, N. (2006) 'Mixed methods in international business research: a value-added perspective', *Management International Review*, 46: 439–54.

Hurston, Z.N. (1942) *Dust Tracks on a Road*. New York: Harper Collins.

Hutchby, I. and Wooffitt, R. (2008) *Conversation Analysis*, 2nd edn. Cambridge: Polity Press.

Huxham, C. (2003) 'Action research as a methodology for theory development', *Policy and Politics*, 31 (2): 239–48.

Hyder, S. and Sims, D. (1979) 'Hypothesis, analysis and paralysis: issues in the organisation of contract research', *Management Education Development*, 10: 100–11.

Ibarra, H. (1992) 'Homophily and differential returns: sex differences in network structure and access in an advertising firm', *Administrative Science Quarterly*, 37: 422–47.

Irwin, A. (1994) 'Science's social standing', *The Times Higher Educational Supplement*, 30 September: 17–19.

Jaccard, J. and Wan, C.K. (1996) *LISREL Approaches to Interaction Effects in Multiple Regression*. Thousand Oaks, CA: Sage.

Jackson, M.C. (2000) *Systems Approaches to Management*. New York: Klewer Academic/Plenum.

Jackson, P.R. (1986) 'Robust methods in statistics', in A.D. Lovie (ed.), *New Developments in Statistics for Psychology and the Social Sciences*. London: British Psychological Society and Methuen, pp. 22–43.

Jackson, P.R. (1989) 'Analysing data', in G. Parry and F.N. Watts (eds), *Behavioural and Mental Health Research: A Handbook of Skills and Methods*. London: Lawrence Erlbaum, pp. 55–79.

Jackson, P.R. (2004) 'Employee commitment to quality: its conceptualisation and measurement', *International Journal of Quality & Reliability Management*, 21 (7): 714–30.

Jackson, P.R. and Parker, S.K. (2001) *Change in Manufacturing: Managing Stress in Manufacturing*. London: HSE Publications.

James, W. ([1907] 1979) *Pragmatism*. Cambridge, MA: Harvard University Press.

Janesick, V.J. (2003) 'The choreography of qualitative research design: minuets, improvisations, and crystallization', in N.K. Denzin and Y.S. Lincoln (eds), *Strategies of Qualitative Inquiry*. Thousand Oaks, CA: Sage, pp. 46–79.

Jansen, J.P., Van den Bosch, F.A.J. and Volberda, H.W. (2005) 'Managing potential and realised absorptive capacity: how do organizational antecedents matter?', *Academy of Management Journal*, 48 (6): 999–1015.

Jarzabkowski, P., Balogun, J. and Seidl, D. (2007) 'Strategizing: the challenges of a practice perspective', *Human Relations*, 60 (1): 5–27.

Jefferson, G. (2004) 'Glossary of transcript symbols with an introduction', in G.H. Lerner (ed.), *Conversation Analysis: Studies from the First Generation*. Amsterdam: John Benjamins, pp. 13–31.

Jesson, J., Matheson, L. and Lacey, F.M. (2011) *Doing Your Literature Review: Traditional and Systematic Techniques*. London: Sage.

Jick, T.D. (1979) 'Mixing qualitative and quantitative methodologies: triangulation in action', *Administrative Science Quarterly*, 24 (4): 602–11.

Jobber, D. and Horgan, I. (1987) 'Market research and education: perspectives from practitioners', *Journal of Marketing Management*, 3 (1): 39–49.

Johnson, G., Scholes, K. and Whittington, R. (2008) *Exploring Corporate Strategy*, 7th edn. London: Prentice Hall.

Johnson, P. and Duberley, J. (2000) *Understanding Management Research: An Introduction to Epistemology*. London: Sage.

Johnson, S., Cooper, C.L., Cartwright, S., Donald, I., Taylor, P. and Millet, C. (2005) 'The experience of work-related stress across occupations', *Journal of Managerial Psychology*, 20 (2): 178–87.

Jones, O. (2006) 'Developing absorptive capacity in mature organizations: the change agent's role', *Management Learning*, 37 (3): 355–76.

Jones, S. (1985) 'The analysis of depth interviews', in R. Walker (ed.), *Applied Qualitative Research*. Aldershot: Gower, pp. 56–70.

Kalaitzidakis, P., Mamuneas, T.P. and Stengos, T. (2001) *Ranking of Academic Journals and Institutions in Economics*. Available at: www.le.ac.uk/economics/research/rankings/econ-rankings.html (last accessed 24 November 2011).

Kandola, B. (2012) 'Focus groups', in G. Symon and C. Cassell (eds), *Qualitative Organisational Research: Core Methods and Current Challenges*. London: Sage, pp. 258–74.

Kaplan, D. (2004) *The SAGE Handbook of Quantitative Methodology for the Social Sciences*. Thousand Oaks, CA: Sage.

Karra, N. and Phillips, N. (2007) 'Researching "back home": international management research as autoethnography', *Organizational Research Methods*, 11 (3): 541–61.

Katsikeas, C.S., Samiee, S. and Theodosiou, M. (2006) 'Strategy fit and performance consequences of international marketing standardization', *Strategic Management Journal*, 27 (9): 867–90.

Kelly, G.A. (1955) *The Psychology of Personal Constructs*. New York: Norton.

Kendall, G. (2007) 'What is critical discourse analysis? Ruth Wodak in conversation with Gavin Kendall', *Forum: Qualitative Social Research*, 8 (2). Available at: www.qualitative-research.net/index.php/fqs/article/view/255/561 (last accessed 14 August 2014).

Kilduff, M. and Brass, D.J. (2010) 'Organizational social network research: core ideas and key debates', *The Academy of Management Annals*, 4 (1): 317–57.

King, N. (1998) 'Template analysis in qualitative methods and analysis', in G. Symon and C. Cassell (eds), *Organizational Research: A Practical Guide*. London: Sage.

King, N. (2004) 'Using templates in the thematic analysis of text', in C. Cassell and G. Symon (eds), *Essential Guide to Qualitative Methods*, 2nd edn. London: Sage, pp. 118–34.

King, N. (2014) Template analysis website, University of Huddersfield. Available at: www.hud.ac.uk/hhs/research/template-analysis (last accessed 14 August 2014).

King, N. and Brooks, J.M. (2017) *Template Analysis for Business and Management Students* (Mastering Business Research Methods). Thousand Oaks, CA: Sage.

King, N. and Horrocks, C. (2010) *Interviews in Qualitative Research*. Thousand Oaks, CA: Sage.

Kirk, A. (2016) *Data Visualisation: A Handbook for Data Driven Design*. London: Sage.

Knoblauch, H., Baer, A., Laurier, E., Petschke, S. and Schnettler, B. (2008) 'Visual analysis: new developments in the interpretative analysis of video and photography', *Forum: Qualitative Social Research*, 9 (3): Visual Methods. Available at: www.qualitative-research.net/index.php/fqs/article/view/1170 (last accessed 14 August 2014).

Knoblauch, H., Tuma, R. and Schnettler, B. (2014) 'Visual analysis and videography', in U. Flick (ed.), *SAGE Handbook of Qualitative Data Analysis*. London: Sage, pp. 435–49.

Knorr-Cetina, K.D. (1983) 'The ethnographic study of scientific work: towards a constructivist interpretation of science', in K.D. Knorr-Cetina and M. Mulkay (eds), *Science Observed: Perspectives on the Social Study of Science*. London: Sage, pp. 115–40.

Knox, H., O'Doherty, D., Vurdubakis, T. and Westrup, C. (2008) 'Enacting airports: space, movement and modes of ordering', *Organization*, 15 (6): 869–88.

Koenig, T. (2008) 'CAQDAS comparison'. Available at: www.lboro.ac.uk/research/mmethods/research/software/caqdas_comparison.html (last accessed 29 October 2008).

Kolb, D.A. (1984) *Organisational Psychology: An Experimental Approach to Organisational Behaviour*. Englewood Cliffs, NJ: Prentice Hall.

Kolb, D.A. (1986) *Experiential Learning*. Englewood Cliffs, NJ: Prentice Hall.

Kolk, A., Rivera-Santos, M. and Rufín, C. (2014) 'Reviewing a decade of research on the "Base/Bottom of the Pyramid" (BOP) concept', *Business & Society*, 53 (3): 338–77.

Konopásek, Z. (2008) 'Making thinking visible with ATLAS.ti: computer assisted qualitative analysis as textual practices', *Forum Qualitative Sozialforschung/Forum: Qualitative Social Research*, 9 (2), Art. 12. Available at: http://nbn-resolving.de/urn:nbn:de:0114-fqs0802124 (last accessed 29 October 2008).

Kotter, J. (1982) *The General Managers*. Glencoe, IL: Free Press.

Krech, D., Crutchfield, R.S. and Ballachey, E.L. (1962) *Individual in Society*. London: McGraw-Hill.

Krueger, R.A. and Casey, M.A. (2009) *Focus Groups: A Practical Guide for Applied Research*, 4th edn. Thousand Oaks, CA: Sage.

Kuhn, T.S. (1962) *The Structure of Scientific Revolution*. Chicago, IL: University of Chicago Press.

Kunda, G. (1993) *Engineering Culture: Control and Commitment in a High-tech Corporation*. Philadelphia, PA: Temple University Press.

Kvale, S. (1996) *InterViews*. London: Sage.

Kvale, S. and Brinkmann, S. (2009) *InterViews: Learning the Craft of Qualitative Research Interviewing*, 2nd edn. Thousand Oaks, CA: Sage.

Kwon, W., Clarke, I. and Wodak, R. (2009) 'Organizational decision-making, discourse, and power: integrating across contexts and scales', *Discourse and Communication*, 3 (3): 273–302.

Labov, W. (1972) *Language in the Inner City*. Oxford: Blackwell.

Latour, B. (1988) 'The politics of explanation: an alternative', in S. Woolgar (ed.), *Knowledge and Reflexivity: New Frontiers in the Sociology of Knowledge*. London: Sage, pp. 155–77.

Latour, B. and Woolgar, S. (1979) *Laboratory Life: The Social Construction of Scientific Facts*. Beverly Hills, CA: Sage.

Law, J. (1994) *Organizing Modernity*. Oxford: Blackwell.

Lawler, S. (2002) 'Narrative in social research', in T. May (ed.), *Qualitative Research in Action*. London: Sage, pp. 242–58.

Lawrence, P.R. (1986) *Invitation to Management*. Oxford: Blackwell.

Lawrence, P.R. and Lorsch, J.W. (1967) *Organisational Environment: Managing Differentiation and Integration*. Boston, MA: Division of Research, Graduate School of Business Administration, Harvard University.

Lawrence, T.B., Dyck, B., Maitlis, S. and Mauws, M.K. (2006) 'The underlying structure of continuous change', *MIT Sloan Management Review*, 47 (4): 59–66.

Lawrence, T.B., Mauws, M.K., Dyck, B. and Kleysen, R.F. (2005) 'The politics of organizational learning: integrating power into the 4I framework', *Academy of Management Review*, 30 (1): 180–91.

Leask, B. (2006) 'Plagiarism, cultural diversity and metaphor: implications for academic staff development', *Assessment & Evaluation in Higher Education*, 31 (2): 183–99.

Lee, F.S. (2007) 'The Research Assessment Exercise, the state and dominance of mainstream economics in British universities', *Cambridge Journal of Economics*, 31: 309–25.

Lee, R.M. (2000) *Unobtrusive Methods in Social Research*. Buckingham: Open University Press.

Legge, K. (1984) *Evaluating Planned Organisational Change*. London: Academic Press.

Leitch, S. and Palmer, I. (2010) 'Analysing texts in context: current practices and new protocols for critical discourse analysis in organisational studies', *Journal of Management Studies*, 47 (6): 1194–212.

Lervik, J.E., Fahy, K.M. and Easterby-Smith, M. (2010) 'Temporal dynamics of situated learning in organizations', *Management Learning*, 41 (3): 285–301.

Lewin, K. (1948) 'Frontiers in group dynamics', *Human Relations*, 1: 5–41.

Lewins, A. (2008) 'CAQDAS: computer assisted qualitative data analysis', in N. Gilbert (ed.), *Researching Social Life*, 3rd edn. London: Sage, pp. 394–419.

Lewins, A. and Silver, C. (2009a) *QSR NVivo 8 Distinguishing Features and Functions*, Working Paper No. 004, 1–5, CAQDAS. Guildford: University of Surrey.

Lewins, A. and Silver, C. (2009b) *ATLAS.ti 6 Distinguishing Features and Functions*, NCRM Working Paper. Guildford: University of Surrey.

Lewins, A. and Silver, C. (2009c) *Choosing a CAQDAS Package*, NCRM Working Paper. Guildford: University of Surrey.

Liebow, E. (1993) *Tell Them Who I Am: The Lives of Homeless Women*. New York: Penguin.

Locke, K. (1997) 'Re-writing the discovery of grounded theory after 25 years?', *Journal of Management Inquiry*, 5: 239–45.

Locke, K. (2001) *Grounded Theory in Management Research*. London: Sage.

Locke, K. and Golden-Biddle, K. (1997) 'Constructing opportunities for contribution: structuring intertextual coherence and "problematizing" in organization studies', *Academy of Management Journal*, 40 (5): 1023–62.

Locke, T. (2004) *Critical Discourse Analysis*. London: Continuum.

Löfgren, K. (2013) 'Qualitative analysis of interview data: a step-by-step guide'. YouTube tutorial, 19 May. Available at: www.youtube.com/watch?v=DRL4PF2u9XA (last accessed 14 August 2014).

Lofland, J. and Lofland, L.H. (1984) *Analyzing Social Settings: A Guide to Qualitative Observation and Analysis*, 2nd edn. Belmont, CA: Wadsworth.

Lok, J. and Rond, M. de (2013) 'On the plasticity of institutions: containing and restoring practice breakdowns at the Cambridge University Boat Club', *Academy of Management Journal*, 56 (1): 185–207.

Loubere, N. (2017) 'Questioning transcription: the case for the Systematic and Reflexive Interviewing and Reporting (SRIR) Method', in *Forum Qualitative Sozialforschung / Forum: Qualitative Social Research*, 18 (2). Available at: www.qualitative-research.net/index.php/fqs/article/view/2739 (last accessed 19 May 2017).

Lowe, A. (1998) 'Managing the post merger aftermath by default remodelling', *Management Decision*, 36 (2): 102–10.

Lu, Y. and Heard, R. (1995) 'Socialised economic action: a comparison of strategic investment decision-making in China and Britain', *Organization Studies*, 16: 395–424.

Luff, P., Hindmarsh, J. and Heath, C. (eds) (2000) *Workplace Studies: Recovering Work Practice and Informing System Design*. Cambridge: Cambridge University Press.

Luker, K. (2008) *Salsa Dancing into the Social Sciences: Research in an Age of Info-glut*. Cambridge, MA: Harvard University Press.

Luo, X. and Bhattacharya, C.B. (2006) 'Corporate social responsibility, customer satisfaction, and market value', *Journal of Marketing*, 70 (4): 1–18.

Lupton, T. (1963) *On the Shop Floor: Two Studies of Workshop Organization and Output*. New York: Macmillan.

Lyles, M.A. and Salk, J.E. (1996) 'Knowledge acquisition from foreign parents in international joint ventures: an empirical examination in the Hungarian context', *Journal of International Business Studies*, Special Issue, 27: 877–903.

Lyotard, J.-F. (1984) *The Postmodern Condition: A Report on Knowledge*. Manchester: Manchester University Press.

Macbeth, D. (2001) 'On "reflexivity" in qualitative research: two readings, and a third', *Qualitative Inquiry*, 7 (1): 35–68.

Macbeth, D. (2004) 'The relevance of repair for classroom correction', *Language in Society*, 33: 703–36.

Macdonald, S. (2010) 'British social anthropology', in P. Atkinson (ed.), *Handbook of Ethnography*. Thousand Oaks, CA: Sage, pp. 60–79.

Macfarlane, G. (1985) *Alexander Fleming: The Man and the Myth*. Oxford: Oxford University Press.

MacInnes, J. (2017) *An Introduction to Secondary Data Analysis with IBM SPSS Statistics*. Thousand Oaks, CA: Sage.

Mackinlay, T. (1986) 'The development of a personal strategy of management', unpublished MSc dissertation, Manchester Polytechnic, Department of Management.

MacLean, D., Macintosh, R. and Grant, S. (2002) 'Mode 2 management research', *British Journal of Management*, 13: 189–207.

Maclean, T.L. (2001) 'Thick as thieves: a social embeddedness model of rule breaking in organizations', *Business & Society*, 40 (2): 167–96.

Macmillan, K. (2005) 'More than just coding? Evaluating CAQDAS in a discourse analysis of news texts' (57 paragraphs), *Forum Qualitative Sozialforschung/Forum: Qualitative Social Research*, 6 (3): Art. 25. Available at: http://nbn-resolving.de/urn:nbn:de:0114-fqs0503257 (last accessed 29 October 2008).

Macpherson, A. (2006) 'Learning to grow: the evolution of business knowledge in small manufacturing firms', PhD thesis, Manchester Metropolitan University.

Macpherson, A., Kofinas, A., Jones, O. and Thorpe, R. (2010) 'Making sense of mediated learning: cases from small firms', *Management Learning*, 41 (3): 303–23.

Madden, R. (2010) *Being Ethnographic: A Guide to the Theory and Practice of Ethnography*. London: Sage.

Mangham, I.L. (1986) 'In search of competence', *Journal of General Management*, 12 (2): 5–12.

Margolis, E. and Pauwels, L. (2011) *The SAGE Handbook of Visual Research Methods*. Thousand Oaks, CA: Sage.

Marshall, C. (2000) 'Policy discourse analysis: negotiating gender equity', *Journal of Education Policy*, 15 (2): 125–56.

Marshall, S. and Green, N. (2007) *Your PhD Companion: A Handy Mix of Practical Tips, Sound Advice and Helpful Commentary to See You Through Your PhD*, 2nd edn. Oxford: Cromwell Press.

Mason, J. (1996) *Qualitative Researching*. London: Sage.

Mauch, J.E. and Birch, J.W. (1983) *Guide to the Successful Thesis and Dissertations: A Handbook for Students and Faculty*. New York: Marcel Dekker.

Maxwell, J.A. and Chmiel, M. (2014) 'Generalization in and from qualitative analysis', in U. Flick (ed.), *SAGE Handbook of Qualitative Data Analysis*. London: Sage, pp. 541–53.

Mayo, E. (1949) *The Social Problems of an Industrial Civilisation*. London: Routledge and Kegan Paul.

McCann, L., Granter, E., Hyde, P. and Hassard, J. (2013) 'Still blue-collar after all these years? An ethnography of the professionalization of emergency ambulance work', *Journal of Management Studies*, 50 (5): 750–76.

McClelland, D.A. (1965) 'Achievement and enterprise', *Journal of Personal Social Psychology*, 1: 389–92.

McClelland, D.A. (1967) *The Achieving Society*. Princeton, NJ: Van Nostrand.

McCullagh, P. and Nelder, J. (1989) *Generalized Linear Models*. London: Chapman and Hall.

McLaughlin, H. and Thorpe, R. (1993) 'Action learning – a paradigm in emergence: the problems facing a challenge to traditional management education and development', *British Journal of Management*, 4: 19–27.

McWilliams, A. and Siegel, D. (1997) 'Event studies in management research: theoretical and empirical issues', *Academy of Management Journal*, 40: 626–57.

Mehra, A., Kilduff, M. and Brass, D.J. (1998) 'At the margins: a distinctiveness approach to the social iden-tity and social networks of underrepresented groups', *Academy of Management Journal*, 41: 441–52.

Mehrabian, A. (1981) *Silent Messages: Implicit Communication of Emotions and Attitudes*, 2nd edn. Belmont, CA: Wadsworth.

Miles, M.B. and Huberman, A.M. (1984) *Qualitative Data Analysis: A Sourcebook of New Methods*. London: Sage.

Miles, M.B. and Huberman, A.M. (1994) *An Expanded Sourcebook: Qualitative Data Analysis*, 2nd edn. London: Sage.

Miles, M.B., Huberman, A.M. and Saldaña, J. (2014) *Qualitative Data Analysis*, 3rd edn. Thousand Oaks, CA: Sage.

Miller, D. (1993) 'The architecture of simplicity', *Academy of Management Review*, 18 (1): 116–38.

Miller, D.C. and Salkind, N.J. (2002) *Handbook of Research Design & Social Measurement*, 6th edn. Thousand Oaks, CA: Sage.

Mintzberg, H. (1973) *The Nature of Managerial Work*. London: Harper and Row.

Mintzberg, H. (2005) *Managers not MBAs: A Hard Look at the Soft Practice of Managing and Management Development*. San Francisco, CA: Berrett-Koehler.

Moeran, B. (2005) 'Tricks of the trade: the performance and interpretation of authenticity', *Journal of Management Studies*, 42: 901–22.

Moingeon, B. and Edmondson, A. (1997) *Organizational Learning and Competitive Advantage*. London: Sage.

Molina-Azorin, J.F. (2012) 'Mixed methods research in strategic management: impact and applications', *Organizational Research Methods*, 15: 33–56.

Molina-Azorin, J.F. and Cameron, R. (2015) 'History and emergent practices of mixed and multiple methods in business research', in Johnson, R.B. and Hesse-Biber, S. (eds), *The Oxford Handbook of Multimethod and Mixed Methods Research Inquiry*. New York: Oxford University Press, pp. 466–85.

Molina-Azorin, J.F., Bergh, D.D., Corley, K.G. and Ketchen, Jr., D.J. (2017) 'Mixed methods in the organizational sciences: taking stock and moving forward', *Organizational Research Methods*, 20 (2): 179–92.

Molina-Azorin, J.F., Lopez-Gamero, M.D., Pereira-Moliner, J. and Pertusa-Ortega, E. (2012) 'Mixed methods studies in entrepreneurship research: applications and contributions', *Entrepreneurship & Regional Development*, 24: 425–56.

Molina-Azorín, J.F., Tarí, J., Pereira-Moliner, J., López-Gamero, M.D. and Pertusa-Ortega, E. (2015) 'The effects of quality and environmental management on competitive advantage: a mixed methods study', *Tourism Management*, 50: 41–54.

Moreno, J.L. (1934) *Who Shall Survive?* Washington, DC: Nervous and Mental Disease Publishing.

Morgan, D.L. (1997) *Focus Groups as Qualitative Research*, 2nd edn. Thousand Oaks, CA: Sage.

Morgan, G. and Smircich, L. (1980) 'The case for qualitative research', *Academy of Management Review*, 5: 491–500.

Moser, C.A. and Kalton, G. (1971) *Survey Methods in Social Investigation*, 2nd edn. London: Heinemann.

Mosse, D. (2004) *Cultivating Development: An Ethnography of Aid Policy and Practice*. London: Pluto.

Mosse, D. and Kruckenberg, L.J. (2017) 'Beyond the ivory tower: researching development practice', in G. Crawford, L.J. Kruckenberg, N. Loubere and R. Morgan (eds), *Understanding Research in Global Development: Fieldwork Issues, Experiences and Reflections*. London: Sage, pp. 193–211.

Murnieks, C.Y., Mosakowski, E. and Cardon, M.S. (2014) 'Pathways of passion', *Journal of Management*, 40 (6): 1583–606.

Munir, K.A. and Phillips, N. (2005) 'The birth of the "Kodak moment": institutional entrepreneurship and the adoption of new technologies', *Organization Studies*, 26 (11): 1665–87.

Murray, R. (2002) *How to Write a Thesis*. Milton Keynes: Open University Press.

Murray, R. and Moore, S. (2006) *The Handbook of Academic Writing: A Fresh Approach*. Maidenhead: McGraw-Hill.

Nadin, S. and Cassell, C. (2006) 'The use of a research diary as a tool for reflexive practice: some reflec-tions from management research', *Qualitative Research in Accounting & Management*, 3 (3): 208–17.

Nguyen, P. (2005) 'Public opinion polls, chicken soup and sample size', *Teaching Statistics*, 27 (3): 89–91.

Nonaka, I. (1988) 'Toward middle-up-down management: accelerating information creation', *Sloan Management Review*, Spring: 9–18.

Nonaka, I. and Takeuchi, H. (1995) *The Knowledge-Creating Company: How Japanese Companies Create the Dynamics of Innovation*. Oxford: Oxford University Press.

Nor, S.M. (2000) 'Privatisation and changes in organization: a case study of a Malaysian privatised utility', PhD thesis, Lancaster University.

Norman, M. (2006) 'Student teachers' perceptions of becoming teachers and their experiences of confidence during their transition to teaching', PhD thesis, University of Manchester.

O'Connor, H., Madge, C., Shaw, R. and Wellens, J. (2008) 'Internet-based interviewing', in N. Fielding, R.M. Lee and G. Blank (eds), *The SAGE Handbook of Online Research Methods*. London: Sage, pp. 271–89.

O'Reilly, D. and Reed, M. (2010) '"Leaderism": an evolution of managerialism in UK public service reform', *Public Administration*, 88 (4): 960–78.

Obstfeld, D. (2005) 'Social networks, the tertius iungens orientation, and involvement in innovation', *Administrative Science Quarterly*, 50: 100–30.

Oliver, P. (2012) *Succeeding with your Literature Review: A Handbook for Students*. Maidenhead: Open University Press.

Padgett, D.K. (2008) *Qualitative Methods in Social Work Research*. Thousand Oaks, CA: Sage.

Park, C. (2003) 'In other (people's) words: plagiarism by university students – literature and lessons', *Assessment & Evaluation in Higher Education*, 28 (5): 471–88.

Parry, O. and Mauthner, N.S. (2004) 'Whose data are they anyway? Practical, legal and ethical issues in archiving qualitative research data', *Sociology*, 38 (1): 139–52.

Patriotta, G. (2003) *Organizational Knowledge in the Making*. Oxford: Oxford University Press.

Pears, D. (1971) *Wittgenstein*. London: Fontana.

Peters, T.J. and Waterman, R.H. (1982) *In Search of Excellence: Lessons from America's Best Run Companies*. New York: Harper and Row.

Petticrew, M. and Roberts, H. (2006) *Systematic Reviews in the Social Sciences: A Practical Guide*. Malden, MA: Blackwell.

Pettigrew, A.M. (1985) *The Awakening Giant: Continuity and Change in Imperial Chemical Industries*. Oxford: Blackwell.

Pettigrew, A.M. (1990) 'Longitudinal field research on change: theory and practice', *Organization Science*, 1 (3): 267–92.

Phillips, E.M. (1984) 'Learning to do research', *Graduate Management Research*, 2 (1): 6–18.

Phillips, E.M. and Pugh, D.S. (2005) *How to Get a PhD: A Handbook for Students and their Supervisors*, 4th edn. Maidenhead: Open University Press.

Phillips, N., Sewell, G. and Jaynes, S. (2008) 'Applying critical discourse analysis in strategic management research', *Organizational Research Methods*, 11 (4): 770–89.

Pike, K.L. (1954) *Language in Relation to a Unified Theory of the Structure of Human Behavior*. Glendale, CA: Summer Institute of Linguistics.

Pink, S. (2001) *Doing Visual Ethnography: Images, Media and Representation in Research*. London: Sage.

Plano Clark, V. and Ivankova, N. (2016) *Mixed Methods Research: A Guide to the Field*. Thousand Oaks, CA: Sage.

Platt, J. (1976) *Realities of Social Research: An Empirical Study of British Sociologists*. Brighton: Sussex University Press.

Popper, K. (1959) *The Logic of Scientific Discovery*. London: Hutchinson.

Porter, L.W. and McKibbin, L.E. (1988) *Management Education and Development: Drift or Thrust into the 21st Century?* New York: McGraw-Hill.

Potter, J. and Wetherell, M. (1987) *Discourse and Social Psychology Beyond Attitudes and Behaviour*. London: Sage.

Potter, J. and Wetherell, M. (1988) *Social Psychology and Discourse*. London: Routledge.

Potter, S. (2006) *Doing Postgraduate Research*. London: Sage.

Prasad, P. and Elmes, M. (2005) 'In the name of the practical: unearthing the hegemony of pragmatics in the discourse of environmental management', *Journal of Management Studies*, 42 (4): 845–67.

Prieto, I.M. and Easterby-Smith, M. (2006) 'Dynamic capabilities and the role of organizational knowledge: an exploration', *European Journal of Information Management*, 15: 500–10.

Pritchard, K. (2011) 'From "being there" to "being […] where?": relocating ethnography', *Qualitative Research in Organizations and Management: An International Journal*, 6 (3): 230–45.

Psathas, G. (1995) *Conversation Analysis: The Study of Talk-in-Interaction*. Thousand Oaks, CA: Sage.

Pugh, D.S. (1983) 'Studying organisational structure and process', in G. Morgan (ed.), *Beyond Method*. Beverly Hills, CA: Sage, pp. 45–55.

Pugh, D.S. (1988) 'The Aston research programme', in A. Bryman (ed.), *Doing Research in Organisations*. London: Routledge, pp. 123–35.

Pugh, D.S. and Hickson, D.J. (1976) *Organisation Structure in its Context: The Aston Programme*. Farnborough: Saxon House.

Punch, K.F. (1998) *Introduction to Social Research: Qualitative Approaches*. London: Sage.

Punch, K.F. (2016) *Developing Effective Research Proposals*, 3rd edn. Thousand Oaks,CA: Sage.

Punch, M. (1986) *The Politics and Ethics of Fieldwork*. Beverly Hills, CA: Sage.

Putnam, H. (1987) *The Many Faces of Realism*. La Salle, IL: Open Court.

Ralston, D.A., Terpstra-Tong, J., Terpstra, R.H., Wang, X.L. and Egri, C. (2006) 'Today's state-owned enterprises of China: are they dying dinosaurs or dynamic dynamos?', *Strategic Management Journal*, 27 (9): 825–43.

Ram, M. and Trehan, K. (2010) 'Critical action learning, policy learning in small firms: an inquiry', *Management Learning*, 41 (4): 414–28.

Rappoport, R.N. (1970) 'Three dilemmas in action research', *Human Relations*, 23 (4): 499–513.

Reason, P. (1988) *Human Inquiry in Action*. London: Sage.

Reason, P. and Bradbury, H. (2001) *Handbook of Action Research: Participative Inquiry and Practice*. London: Sage.

Reason, P. and Bradbury, H. (2006) *Handbook of Action Research: The Concise Paperback Edition*. Thousand Oaks, CA: Sage.

Reason, P. and Bradbury, H. (2013) *The SAGE Handbook of Action Research: Participative Inquiry and Practice*, 2nd edn. Thousand Oaks, CA: Sage.

Rerup, C. and Feldman, M. (2011) 'Routines as a source of change in organizational schemata: the role of trial-and-error learning', *Academy of Management Journal*, 54 (3): 577–610.

Richards, L. and Morse, J.M. (2013) *Read Me First for a User's Guide to Qualitative Methods*, 3rd edn. Thousand Oaks, CA: Sage.

Ricoeur, P. (1981) 'What is a text? Explanation and understanding', in J.B. Thompson (ed.), *Paul Ricoeur, Hermeneutics and the Human Sciences*. Cambridge: Cambridge University Press, pp. 145–64.

Ridley, D. (2012) *The Literature Review: A Step-by-Step Guide for Students*. London: Sage.

Riessman, C.K. (1996) *Narrative Analysis*. Newbury Park, CA: Sage.

Riessman, C.K. (2003) 'Narrative analysis', in M.S. Lewis-Beck, A. Bryman and T. Futing Liao (eds), *The SAGE Encyclopedia of Social Science Research Methods*. Thousand Oaks, CA: Sage, pp. 705–9.

Roberts, K.A. and Wilson, R.W. (2002) 'ICT and the research process: issues around the compatibility of technology with qualitative data analysis' (52 paragraphs), *Forum Qualitative Sozialforschung/ Forum: Qualitative Social Research*, 3 (2), Art. 23. Available at: http://nbn-resolving.de/urn:nbn: de:0114-fqs0202234 (last accessed 29 October 2008).

Roethlisberger, F.J. and Dickson, W.J. (1939) *Management and the Worker*. Cambridge, MA: Harvard University Press.

Rogers, B. and Ryals, L. (2007) 'Using the repertory grid to access the underlying realities in key account relationships', *International Journal of Market Research*, 49 (5): 595–612.

Rose, G. (2001) *Visual Methodology: An Introduction to the Interpretation of Visual Materials*. London: Sage.

Rouleau, L. (2005) 'Micro-practices of strategic sensemaking and sensegiving: how middle managers interpret and sell change every day', *Journal of Management Studies*, 42 (7): 1413–41.

Roulston, K. (2010) *Reflective Interviewing: A Guide to Theory and Practice*. London: Sage.

Roy, D. (1952) 'Quota restriction and goldbricking in a machine shop', *American Journal of Sociology*, 57: 427–42.

Roy, D. (1954) 'Efficiency and "the fix": informal intergroup relations in a piecework machine shop', *American Journal of Sociology*, 60 (3): 255–66.

Roy, D. (1970) 'The study of southern labour union organising campaigns', in R. Haberstein (ed.), *Pathway to Data*. New York: Aldine, pp. 216–44.

Rubin, H.J. and Rubin, I. (2012) *Qualitative Interviewing: The Art of Hearing Data*, 3rd edn. Thousand Oaks, CA: Sage.

Rugg, G. and Petre, M. (2004) *The Unwritten Rules of PhD Research*. Maidenhead: Open University Press.

Runco, M.A. (2004) 'Creativity', *Annual Review of Psychology*, 55: 657–87.

Ryan, G.W. and Bernard, H.R. (2003) 'Data management and analysis methods', in N.K. Denzin and Y.S. Lincoln (eds), *Collecting and Interpreting Qualitative Materials*. Thousand Oaks, CA: Sage, pp. 259–309.

Ryan, G.W. and Bernard, H.R. (2006) 'Testing an ethnographic decision tree model on a national sample: recycling beverage cans', *Human Organization*, 65 (1): 103–14.

Ryave, A.L. and Schenkein, J.N. (1974) 'Notes on the art of walking', in R. Turner (ed.), *Ethnomethodology: Selected Readings*. Harmondsworth: Penguin, pp. 265–74.

Said, E. (1978) *Orientalism*. London: Routledge and Kegan Paul.

Saldaña, J. (2015) *The Coding Manual for Qualitative Researchers*, 3rd edn. Thousand Oaks, CA: Sage.

Sapsford, R. (2006) *Survey Research*, 2nd edn. London: Sage.

Saunders, M., Lewis, P. and Thornhill, A. (2012) *Research Methods for Business Students*, 6th edn. Harlow: Pearson Education.

Sayer, A. (2000) *Realism and Social Science*. London: Sage.

Scarbrough, H. (ed.) (2008) *The Evolution of Business Knowledge*. Oxford: Oxford University Press.

Scarbrough, H. and Swan, J. (1999) 'Knowledge management and the management fashion perspective', *Proceedings of British Academy of Management Conference*, Manchester, Vol. II: 920–37.

Schegloff, E.A. and Sacks, H. (1973) 'Opening up closings', *Semiotica*, 8 (4): 289–327.

Schmitt, N. and Stults, D.M. (1985) 'Factors defined by negatively keyed items: the results of careless respondents?', *Applied Psychological Measurement*, 9 (4): 367–73.

Schon, D.A. (1983) *The Reflective Practitioner: How Professionals Think in Action*. London: Maurice Temple Smith.

Schyns, B., Kiefer, T., Kerschreiter, R. and Tymon, A. (2011) 'Teaching implicit leadership theories to develop leaders and leadership – how and why it can make a difference', *Academy of Management Learning and Education*, 10 (3): 397–408.

Scoble, R. and Israel, S. (2006) *Naked Conversations: How Blogs are Changing the Way Businesses are Talking to Customers*. Hoboken, NJ: Wiley.

Scott, M. (1997) 'PC analysis of key words – and key key words', *System*, 25 (1): 1–13.

Scott, M. (2001) 'Comparing corpora and identifying key words, collocations, and frequency distributions through the WordSmith Tools suite of computer programs', in M. Ghadessy, A. Henry and R.L. Roseberry (eds), *Small Corpus Studies and ELT: Theory and Practice*. Amsterdam: John Benjamins, pp. 47–67.

Scott, M. (2002) 'Picturing the key words of a very large corpus and their lexical upshots – or getting at the Guardian's view of the world', in B. Kettemann and G. Marko (eds), *Teaching and Learning by Doing Corpus Analysis*. Amsterdam: Rodopi, pp. 43–50.

Scott, M. (2010) 'What can corpus software do?', in A. O'Keeffe and M.J. McCarthy (eds), *Routledge Handbook of Corpus Linguistics*. London: Routledge, pp. 136–51.

Seale, C. (2000a) 'Resurrective practice and narrative', in M. Andrews, S.D. Sclater, C. Squire and A. Treacher (eds), *Lines of Narrative*. London: Routledge, pp. 36–47.

Seale, C. (2000b) 'Using computers to analyse qualitative data', in D. Silverman (ed.), *Doing Qualitative Research: A Practical Handbook*. London: Sage, pp. 154–74.

Secrist, C., Koeyer I., de Bell, H. and Fogel, A. (2002) 'Combining digital video technology and narrative methods for understanding infant development', *Forum: Qualitative Social Research*, 3 (2). Available at: www.qualitative-research.net/fqs-texte/2-02/2-02secristetal-e.htm (last accessed 14 August 2014).

Selvin, H.C. and Stuart, A. (1966) 'Data-dredging procedures in survey analysis', *American Statistician*, 20: 20–3.

Senge, P. (1990) *The Fifth Discipline: The Art and Practice of the Learning Organization*. London: Century.

Shadish, W.R., Cook, T.D. and Campbell, D.T. (2002) *Experimental and Quasi-Experimental Designs for Generalized Causal Inference*. Boston, MA: Houghton Mifflin.

Shalley, C.E. and Gilson, L.L. (2004) 'What leaders need to know: a review of social and contextual factors that can foster or hinder creativity', *The Leadership Quarterly*, 15 (1): 33–53.

Shotter, J. (1993) *Conversational Realities*. London: Sage.

Shotter, J. (1995) 'The manager as a practical author: a rhetorical-responsive, social constructionist approach to social-organizational problems', in D. Hosking, H.P. Dachler and K.J. Gergen (eds), *Management and Organization: Relational Alternatives to Individualism*. Aldershot: Avebury, pp. 125–47.

Shrader, C.B., Lincoln, J.R. and Hoffman, A.N. (1989) 'The network structures of organizations: effects of task contingencies and distributional form', *Human Relations*, 42: 43–66.

Sidnell, J. (2011) *Conversation Analysis: An Introduction*. Malden, MA: Wiley-Blackwell.

Siggelkow, N. (2007) 'Persuasion with case studies', *Academy of Management Journal*, 50 (1): 20–4.

Silver, C. and Lewins, A. (2014) *Using Software in Qualitative Research: A Step-by-Step Guide*, 2nd edn. Thousand Oaks, CA: Sage.

Silver, M. (1991) *Competent to Manage*. London: Routledge.

Silver, N. (2012) *The Signal and the Noise: Why So Many Predictions Fail – But Some Don't*. New York: Penguin.

Silverman, D. (1993) *Interpreting Qualitative Data: Methods for Analysing Talk, Text and Interaction*. London: Sage.

Silverman, D. (2003) 'Analyzing talk and text', in N.K. Denzin and Y.S. Lincoln (eds), *Collecting and Interpreting Qualitative Materials*. Thousand Oaks, CA: Sage, pp. 340–62.

Silverman, D. (2013) *Doing Qualitative Research: A Practical Handbook*, 4th edn. London: Sage.

Simon, H.A. (1959) *Administrative Behaviour*, 2nd edn. London: Macmillan.

Simpson, B. (1995) 'A university: an organisation for learning … but a learning organisation?', unpublished MSc dissertation, Manchester Metropolitan University.

Sims, D. (1993) 'Coping with misinformation', *Management Decision*, 3: 18–21.

Sims, D. (2003) 'Between the millstones: a narrative account of the vulnerability of middle managers' storying', *Human Relations*, 56: 1195–211.

Slater, D. (1989) 'Corridors of power', in J.F. Gubrium and D. Silverman (eds), *The Politics of Field Research*. London: Sage, pp. 113–31.

Smeyers, P. and Verhessen, P. (2001) 'Narrative analysis as philosophical research: bridging the gap between the empirical and the conceptual', *International Journal of Qualitative Studies in Education*, 14 (1): 71–84.

Snell, R.S. (1993) *Developing Skills for Ethical Management*. London: Chapman and Hall.

Spector, P.E. (1992) *Summated Rating Scale Construction: An Introduction*. Newbury Park, CA: Sage.

Sprigg, C.A. and Jackson, P.R. (2006) 'Call centers as lean service environments: well-being and the mediating role of work design', *Journal of Occupational Health Psychology*, 11 (2): 197–212.

Stake, R.E. (2006) 'Qualitative case studies', in N.K. Denzin and Y.S. Lincoln (eds), *SAGE Handbook of Qualitative Research*, 3rd edn. Thousand Oaks, CA: Sage, pp. 443–66.

Starbuck, B. (2004) *Journals Ranked by Citations per Article*. Available at: http://pages.stern.nyu.edu/~wstarbuc (last accessed 24 November 2011).

Starkey, K. and Tiratsoo, N. (2007) *Business Schools and the Bottom Line*. Cambridge: Cambridge University Press.

Stavraki, G. (2016) 'Understanding consumers' relationships with contemporary artworks through identity narratives', *Journal of Service Theory and Practice*, 26 (6): 811–36.

Steedman, P. (1991) 'On the relations between seeing, interpreting and knowing', in F. Steier (ed.), *Research and Reflexivity*. London: Sage, pp. 193–209.

Steenkamp, J.-B.E.M. and Geyskens, I. (2006) 'What drives the perceived value of web sites? A cross-national investigation', *Journal of Marketing*, 70 (3): 136–50.

Steers, R.M., Bischoff, S.J. and Higgins, L.H. (1992) 'Crosscultural management research: the fish and the fisherman', *Journal of Management Inquiry*, 1 (4): 321–30.

Steinbeck, J. (1970) *Journal of a Novel: The East of Eden Letters*. London: Pan.

Stewart, R. (1967) *Managers and their Jobs*. Maidenhead: McGraw-Hill.

Stewart, R. (1982) *Choices for the Manager: A Guide to Managerial Work and Behaviour*. London: McGraw-Hill.

Stewart, V., Stewart, A. and Fonda, N. (1981) *Business Applications of Repertory Grid*. Maidenhead: McGraw-Hill.

Steyaert, C. and Bouwen, R. (2004) 'Group methods of organizational analysis', in C. Cassell and G. Symon (eds), *Essential Guide to Qualitative Methods in Organizational Research*. London: Sage, pp. 140–53.

Stokes, D. and Bergin, R. (2006) 'Methodology or "methodolatry"? An evaluation of focus groups and depth interviews', *Qualitative Market Research: An International Journal*, 9 (11): 26–37.

Strauss, A.L. (1987) *Qualitative Analysis for Social Scientists*. Cambridge: Cambridge University Press.

Strauss, A.L. and Corbin, J. (1990) *Basics of Qualitative Research: Grounded Theory Procedures and Techniques*. Thousand Oaks, CA: Sage.

Strauss, A.L. and Corbin, J. (1998) *Basics of Qualitative Research: Techniques and Procedures for Developing Grounded Theory*, 2nd edn. Thousand Oaks, CA: Sage.

Strunk, W. and White, E.B. (2000) *The Elements of Style*. London: Allyn and Bacon.

Suddaby, R. (2006) 'From the Editors: what grounded theory is not', *Academy of Management Journal*, 49 (4): 633–42.

Sweigart, A. (2015) *Automate the Boring Stuff with Python: Practical Programming for Total Beginners*. San Francisco, CA: No Starch Press. Available at: https://automatetheboringstuff.com (accessed 22 December 2017).

Symon, G. and Cassell, C. (eds) (2012) *Qualitative Organizational Research: Core Methods and Current Challenges*. London: Sage.

Tabachnick, B.G. and Fidell, L.S. (2014) *Using Multivariate Statistics*, 6th edn. Boston, MA: Pearson Education.

Tashakkori, A. and Teddlie, C. (1998) *Mixed Methodology: Combining Qualitative and Quantitative Approaches*. Thousand Oaks, CA: Sage.

Tashakkori, A. and Teddlie, C. (eds) (2010) *Handbook of Mixed Methods in Social and Behavioral Research*. Thousand Oaks, CA: Sage.

Taylor, B. (1999) 'Patterns of control within Japanese manufacturing plants in China: doubts about Japanisation in Asia', *Journal of Management Studies*, 36 (6): 853–73.

Taylor, F.W. (1947) *Scientific Management*. London: Harper and Row.

Taylor, S.J. and Bogdan, R. (1984) *Introduction to Qualitative Research Methods*. New York: Wiley-Interscience.

Teagarden, M.B., von Glinow, M.A., Bowen, D.E., Frayne, C.A., Nason, S., Huo, Y.P., Milliman, J., Arias, M.E., Butler, M.C., Geringer, J.M., Kim, N.M., Scullion, H., Lowe, K.B. and Drost, E.A. (1995) 'Toward a theory of comparative management research: an ideographic case study of the best international human resources management project', *Academy of Management Journal*, 38: 1261–87.

Teddlie, C. and Tashakkori, A. (2009) *Foundations of Mixed Methods Research: Integrating Quantitative and Qualitative Approaches in the Social and Behavioral Sciences*. London: Sage.

Tesch, R. (1990) *Qualitative Research, Analysis Types & Software Tools*. New York: Falmer.

Thomas, A. (2004) *Research Skills for Management Studies*. New York: Routledge.

Thomas, W.I. and Thomas, D.S. (1928) *The Child in America: Behavioural Problems and Progress*. New York: Knopf.

Thompson, E.E. (2004) 'National competitiveness: a question of cost conditions or institutional circumstances?', *British Journal of Management*, 15: 197–218.

Thorpe, R. (1980) 'The relationship between payment systems, productivity and the organisation of work', MSc thesis, Strathclyde Business School.

Thorpe, R. (2000) 'Reward strategy', in R.R. Thorpe and G. Homan, *Strategic Reward Systems*. London: Pearson, pp. 30–45.

Thorpe, R. and Cornelissen, J. (2003) 'Visual media and the construction of meaning', in G. Holman and R. Thorpe (eds), *Management and Language: The Manager as Practical Author*. London: Sage, pp. 67–81.

Thorpe, R. and Danielli, A. (1996) 'Oldham Town Park', unpublished study conducted for Oldham Borough Council.

Thorpe, R., Eden, C., Bessant, J. and Ellwood, P. (2011) 'Rigour, relevance and reward: introducing the knowledge translation value-chain', *British Journal of Management*, 22: 420–31.

Thorpe, R. and Holloway, J. (2008) *Performance Management: Multidisciplinary Perspectives*. Houndsmill: Palgrave Macmillan.

Thorpe, R. and Holt, R. (2008) *The SAGE Dictionary of Qualitative Management Research*. London: Sage.

Thorpe, R., Holt, R., Macpherson, A. and Pittaway, L. (2005) 'Knowledge within small and medium-sized firms: a review of the evidence', *International Journal of Management Reviews*, 7 (4): 257–81.

Tilly, C. (2006) *Why?* Princeton, NJ: Princeton University Press.

Tjosvold, D., Dann, V. and Wong, C. (1992) 'Managing conflict between departments to serve customers', *Human Relations*, 45 (10): 1035–54.

Todd, D.J. (1979) 'Mixing qualitative and quantitative methods: triangulation in action', *Administrative Science Quarterly*, 24: 602–11.

Todorova, G. and Durisin, B. (2007) 'Absorptive capacity: valuing a reconceptualization', *Academy of Management Review*, 32 (3): 774–86.

Toulmin, S. (1979) *Introduction to Reasoning*. New York: Macmillan.

Toulmin, S. (2001) *The Uses of Argument*. Cambridge: Cambridge University Press.

Tracy, S.J. (2010) 'Qualitative quality: eight "big-tent" criteria for excellent qualitative research', *Qualitative Inquiry*, 16 (10): 837–51.

Tracy, S.J. (2013) *Qualitative Research Methods: Collecting Evidence, Crafting Analysis, Communicating Impact*. Chichester: Wiley-Blackwell.

Tranfield, D. (2002) 'Formulating the nature of management research', *European Management Journal*, 20 (4): 378–82.

Tranfield, D. and Starkey, K. (1998) 'The nature, social organization and promotion of management research: towards policy', *British Journal of Management*, 9: 341–53.

Tranfield, D., Denyer, D. and Marcos, J. (2004) 'Co-producing management knowledge', *Management Decision*, 42 (3/4): 375–86.

Tranfield, D., Denyer, D. and Smart, P. (2003) 'Towards a methodology for developing evidence-informed management knowledge by means of systematic review', *British Journal of Management*, 14 (3): 207–22.

Tsai, W. and Ghoshal, S. (1998) 'Social capital and value creation: the role of intrafirm networks', *Academy of Management Journal*, 41 (4): 464–76.

Tsang, E.W.K. (1997) 'Learning from joint venturing experience: the case of foreign direct investment by Singapore companies in China', PhD thesis, University of Cambridge.

Tsang, E.W.K. (1999) 'Internationalisation as a learning process: Singapore MNCs in China', *Academy of Management Executive*, 13 (1): 91–101.

Tsang, E.W.K. (2002) 'Acquiring knowledge by foreign partners from international joint ventures in a transition economy: learning-by-doing and learning myopia', *Strategic Management Journal*, 23: 835–54.

Tsoukas, H. and Hatch, M.J. (1997) 'Complex thinking, complex practice: the case for a narrative approach to organisational complexity', paper presented to the American Academy of Management.

Turner, B.A. (1988) 'Connoisseurship in the study of organisational cultures', in A. Bryman (ed.), *Doing Research in Organisations*. London: Sage, pp. 108–21.

Ullman, J.B. (2006) 'Structural equation modeling: reviewing the basics and moving forward', *Journal of Personality Assessment*, 87 (1): 35–50.

Uzzi, B. (1997) 'Social structure and competition in interfirm networks: the paradox of embeddedness', *Administrative Science Quarterly*, 42: 35–67.

Vanderplas, J. (2016) *Python Data Science Handbook*. Sebastopol, CA: O'Reilly.

Van de Ven, A.H. and Johnson, P.E. (2006) 'Knowledge for theory and practice', *Academy of Management Review*, 31 (4): 802–21.

van Maanen, J. (1991) 'The smile factory: work at Disneyland', in P.J. Frost, L.F. Moore, M.R. Louis, C.C. Lundberg and J. Martin (eds), *Reframing Organizational Culture*. Newbury Park, CA: Sage, pp. 58–76.

van Maanen, J. (2011) 'Ethnography as work: some rules of engagement', *Journal of Management Studies*, 48 (1): 218–34.

Veeck, G. (2001) 'Talk is cheap: cultural and linguistic fluency during field research', *Geographical Review*, 91 (1–2): 34–40.

Venkatraman, M. and Nelson, T. (2008) 'From servicescape to consumptionscape: a photo-elicitation study of Starbucks in the New China', *Journal of International Business Studies*, 39 (6): 1010–26.

Von Bertalanffy, L. (1962) 'General systems theory – a critical review', *General Systems*, 7: 1–20.

Walker, G.B. and Sillars, M.O. (1990) 'Where is argument? Perelman's theory of values', in R. Trapp and J. Schuetz (eds), *Perspectives on Argumentation*. Long Grove, IL: Waveland Press, pp. 121–33.

Walker, R. (1985) *Applied Qualitative Research*. Aldershot: Gower.

Wall, T.D., Jackson, P.R. and Davids, K. (1992) 'Operator work design and robotics system performance: a serendipitous field experiment', *Journal of Applied Psychology*, 77: 353–62.

Wall, T.D., Kemp, N.J., Jackson, P.J. and Clegg, C.W. (1986) 'Outcomes of autonomous workgroups: a long-term field experiment', *Academy of Management Journal*, 29 (2): 282–304.

Wallace, M. and Wray, A. (2011) *Critical Reading and Writing for Postgraduates*, 2nd edn. London: Sage.

Walsh, G. and Beatty, S.E. (2007) 'Customer-based corporate reputation of a service firm: scale development and validation', *Journal of the Academy of Marketing Science*, 35 (1): 127–43.

Walsh, G., Mitchell, V.-W., Jackson, P.R. and Beatty, S.E. (2009) 'Examining the antecedents and consequences of corporate reputation: a customer perspective', *British Journal of Management*, 20 (2): 187–203.

Wansink, B. (2003) 'Using laddering to understand and leverage a brand's equity', *Qualitative Market Research: An International Journal*, 6 (2): 111–18.

Warr, P.B., Cook, J.D. and Wall, T.D. (1979) 'Scales for the measurement of some work attitudes and aspects of psychological well-being', *Journal of Occupational Psychology*, 52: 129–48.

Waters, C.D.J. (2011) *Quantitative Methods for Business*, 5th edn. Harlow: Financial Times/Prentice Hall.

Watford, A.J. (1980–87) *Watson's Guide to Reference Material: Vol. 2 – Social and Historical Sciences, Philosophy and Religion*. London: Library Association.

Watson, T.J. (1994) *In Search of Management: Culture, Chaos and Control in Managerial Work*. London: Routledge.

Watson, T.J. (2011) 'Ethnography, reality, and truth: the vital need for studies of "how things work" in organizations and management', *Journal of Management Studies*, 48 (1): 202–17.

Watzlawick, P. (ed.) (1984) *The Invented Reality*. London: Norton.

Weick, K.E. (1989) 'Theory construction as disciplined imagination', *Academy of Management Review*, 14 (4): 516–31.

Weick, K.E. (1995) *Sense-making in Organisations*. London: Sage.

Weick, K.E. (2003) 'Theory and practice in the real world', in H. Tsoukas and C. Knudsen (eds), *The Oxford Handbook of Organization Theory*. Oxford: Oxford University Press, pp. 453–75.

Weitzman, E.A. (1999) 'Analyzing qualitative data with computer software', *Health Services Research*, 34 (5/2): 1241–63.

Wertsch, J.V. (1991) *Voices of the Mind: A Socio Cultural Approach to Mediated Action*. Cambridge, MA: Harvard University Press.

Welch, C., Piekkari, R., Plakoyiannaki, E. and Paavilainen-Mäntymäki, E. (2011) 'Theorising from case studies: towards a pluralist future for international business research', *Journal of International Business Studies*, 42 (5): 740–62.

Whitley, R., Thomas, A. and Marceau, J. (1981) *Masters of Business?* London: Tavistock.

Williams, G. (2011) *Data Mining with Rattle and R: The Art of Excavating Data for Knowledge Discovery*. New York: Springer.

Whyte, W.F. (1997) *Creative Problem Solving in the Field: Reflections on a Career*. Walnut Creek, CA: AltaMira Press.

Wickham, H. and Grolemund, G. (2016) *R for Data Science*. Sebastopol, CA: O'Reilly. Available at: http://r4ds.had.co.nz (accessed 22 December 2017).

Winter, S.G. (2003) 'Understanding dynamic capabilities', *Strategic Management Journal*, 24: 991–5.

Wittgenstein, L. (1953) *Philosophical Investigations*. Oxford: Blackwell.

Woo, Y., Kim, S. and Cooper, M.P. (2015) 'Comparing a cell phone survey and a web survey of university students', *Social Science Computer Review*, 33: 377–410.

Wood, M. (2005) 'Bootstrapped confidence intervals as an approach to statistical inference', *Organizational Research Methods*, 8: 454–70.

Wright, R.P. (2006) 'Rigor and relevance using repertory grid technique in strategy research', *Research Methodology in Strategy and Management*, 3: 295–348.

Wu, C.-H., Parker, S.K. and Jong, J.P.J. de (2014) 'Feedback seeking from peers: a positive strategy for insecurely attached team-workers', *Human Relations*, 67 (4): 441–64.

Ybema, S., Yanow, D., Kamsteeg, F.H. and Wels, H. (eds) (2009) *Organizational Ethnography: Studying the Complexity of Everyday Life*. London: Sage.

Yin, R.K. (2013) *Case Study Research: Design and Methods*, 5th edn. Thousand Oaks, CA: Sage.

Zahra, S.A. and George, G. (2002) 'Absorptive capacity: a review, reconcepualisation, and extension', *Academy of Management Review*, 27 (2): 185–203.

Zimmerman, D. (1992) 'The interactional organization of calls for emergency assistance', in P. Drew and J. Heritage (eds), *Talk at Work: Interaction in Institutional Settings*. Cambridge: Cambridge University Press, pp. 418–69.

INDEX